HOMELESSNESS

GARLAND REFERENCE LIBRARY
OF SOCIAL SCIENCE
(VOL. 534)

HOMELESSNESS
An Annotated Bibliography

Volume I

James M. Henslin

GARLAND PUBLISHING, INC. • NEW YORK & LONDON
1993

Library of Congress Cataloging-in-Publication Data

Henslin, James M.
    Homelessness : an annotated bibliography / by James M. Henslin.
        p.   cm. — (Garland reference library of social science ; v. 534)
    ISBN 0-8240-4115-1 (alk. paper)
    1. Homelessness—Bibliography. 2. Homeless persons—Bibliography. I. Title.
II. Series.
Z7164.H72H46   1993
[HV4493]
016.3625—dc20   92-41254
                                                                      CIP

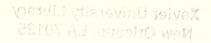

Printed on acid-free, 250-year-life paper
Manufactured in the United States of America

This bibliography is dedicated to the many homeless people who discussed their situation with me during my research across the United States and to the several hundred thousand other homeless persons who live in conditions that no one should face. To them, my sincere wish is a more enlightened society and a brighter future.

CONTENTS

The Main Bibliography...3
     All items are annotated. Following this bibliography proper
are the following 41 sections or subbibliographies, each devoted to
a subtopic of homelessness. In these sections, the full citation
is given, but no annotations are repeated. The 41 divisions are:

JOURNEY TO NOWHERE:

An Annotated Bibliography of Homelessness, 1528 to 1992

James M. Henslin

The literature on homelessness is immense and demonstrates broad historical sweep. Martin Luther's preface
to _Liber Vagatorum_, a treatise which for generations was
widely circulated in Europe, goes back to 1528. A few
other sources originate in still earlier periods. By the
1870s the American literature on the homeless, reflecting
the dominant ethos of its time, was fairly well developed. Recent years have witnessed a deluge of studies
and analyses of the homeless.

Whether considering homelessness a phenomenon of
past or contemporary eras, scholars cannot adequately
apprehend their subject unless they examine this vast
literature. For example, if an historian were to desire
to ascertain attitudes toward the homeless at a given
point in time or changes in attitudes between two
periods, or a philosopher to examine the philosophical
underpinnings of dominant attitudes, he or she must
consult this literature. Similarly, sociologists and
other empirical social researchers of the present must
compare their findings with what has already been written
on the topic. Because this literature crosses interdisciplinary lines, however, and is widely scattered, it
remains essentially unfamiliar to researchers. Up to
now, no central source has existed which scholars could
consult to determine which writings apply to their
particular interests.

Having done research on homelessness for several
years, I experienced the frustration that comes from this
scattering of the literature. Indeed, this problem is
what drew me to this present project. Had such a
bibliography already existed when I began my own research
on the homeless, it would have greatly simplified the
research process, saving much time and effort. It was
out of the frustration at not having such a source that
I began the arduous process of producing this bibliography.

The scattering of this extensive literature has been detrimental to social research. Scholars from various fields who are writing on the homeless have been forced to duplicate one another's efforts. Each researcher, obliged to begin anew to discover relevant sources, has been able to gain familiarity with only a small segment of the appropriate literature. Typically, researchers have given up that frustrating search to concentrate instead on the more intellectually rewarding analytical process.

In order to provide such a guide for scholars, then, I have produced this annotated bibliography on the homeless. The purpose is to help make this vast literature accessible by pulling disparate sources together and providing annotations that guide researchers to references applicable to their topics. It is for them that this guide to the abundant literature on the homeless is dedicated.

The sources for this bibliography have been located in several ways. The first was my wide-ranging reading in the social sciences, where references to the homeless would unexpectedly show up. The second was "snowball" sampling: that is, as I came across articles and books on homelessness, I sent for each item on the homeless that was referenced therein; I then searched the references in each of those new sources, identifying those relevant to the topic, and sent for the newly identified ones, a process repeated almost <u>ad infinitum</u>. The third was my own subscription to the <u>Wall Street Journal</u> and clippings from the <u>New York Times</u> graciously provided by Bill Feeney--which is why these two sources are so heavily referenced. The fourth was the kindness of friends and colleagues who sent clippings from many sources, some of them esoteric. The fifth was a technological change while this bibliography was in preparation: Libraries added computers that made it possible to search through huge data bases, such as O.C.L.C. At this point in time, these data bases are of limited value as they consist mostly of recent sources. As they expand in time and add the capacity to provide a printout of textual sources-- unavailable at the library I utilized--such searches will become increasingly easier and more efficient, assuming, of course, the adequacy of the data input.

To make this volume useful to researchers, I have annotated all items. The annotating has been done with a dual purpose: first, to provide a succinct overview of each item's theme, main points, or topics, and second, to stress those aspects likely to interest researchers.

Four aspects of the form of this bibliography may be somewhat unconventional. First, the items are not numbered. Second, there is no subject index. Numbering and subject index seemed unnecessary as the entries are divided into 41 sections. Listed below, these categories make for ease of reference. Third, rather than inserted throughout the entries, all anonymously written or unattributed sources are listed at the end of the main bibliography and each section. Two reasons underlie this decision. First, there are so many anonymous writers on this topic that it seemed worthwhile to give them their own place, and second, in my estimation such items tend to get "lost" as they are intermixed with attributed items, and this form provides them more visibility. The lines, then, that precede items at the end of the bibliography proper and the sections represent anonymity, not the last named author. Fourth, I have not used lines to indicate multiple works by the same author, but instead have repeated the author's name. I would hope that my ignoring of this convention does not provide too great an offense to anyone.

Although homelessness is generally viewed as an extraneous appendage of modern society, this bibliography reveals its historical depths--how, although it ebbs and flows, homelessness extends into the very roots of Western civilization. Homelessness, which preceded industrialization, has remained an essential part of society since then. Consequently, as an essential part of Western life, as well as a cross-cultural phenomenon, many well-known historical figures have addressed this topic--including Martin Luther, Charles Dickens, and Theodore Roosevelt.

This bibliography also reveals that the literature on homelessness contains numerous themes. Among these themes are the continuing controversy over the causes of homelessness, especially whether the essential cause is structural or personal; what to do about homelessness, which depends much upon assumptions made in the first theme; the issue of worthy versus unworthy homeless people; the appropriate philosophy to guide reactions to the homeless; conditional and unconditional charity; institutionalization, deinstitutionalization, and reinstitutionalization; the lack of community mental health support facilities for the homeless mentally ill; forced treatment and the civil rights of the homeless; a backlash against the homeless, including efforts to make it difficult for homeless people to live in a city or area of a city; the country's financial crises and the amount spent on the homeless; the types of shelters that should be offered; rehabilitation; advocacy; controversy over how many homeless people live in the United States and methodological issues in counting them, with advocates maximizing the number and the government minimizing it--except municipal governments for which a larger census nets more money from the federal government; special concerns about homeless families and children; crimes by and crimes against the homeless; whether or not people have a constitutional right to housing; continuing dissatisfaction with definitions of homelessness; the race to the bottom and the fear that treating the homeless well will attract homeless people from other areas and swell the rolls of homeless people from the "still housed but near homeless"; volunteer efforts by the religious and not-so-religious; a mixture of shame, guilt, embarrassment, and disgust about the problem; and, of course, an annual outpouring of sentiment by the media at Thanksgiving and Christmas.

Occasionally researchers report inane findings. One of my favorites is that homeless people have a higher rate of poverty than do other people. I have tried not to reproduce such findings in the annotations--although perhaps I should have emphasized them as a lesson in the foolishness that sometimes marks social research.

Following the main bibliography, where the items are annotated, are 41 topical classifications presented alphabetically (by topical words other than homeless or homelessness): Advocacy, AIDS, Alcoholism Among the Homeless, Backlash, Bibliographies, Homeless Children, Homelessness in Countries Other than the United States, Crimes Against the Homeless, Crimes by the Homeless, the Criminal Justice System, the Culture of the Homeless, Deinstitutionalization, Early Publications, Homeless Families, First-Person Accounts of Homelessness, Health Issues, Hobos, Housing Issues, Hunger, Intentional Homelessness, Legal Aspects of Homelessness, Mental Illness, Militancy, Methodological Issues, Prostitution by the Homeless, Reinstitutionalization, Runaways, Rural Homelessness, Issues in Shelters and Sheltering, Skid Row, Social Work, Soup Kitchens, SROs, Suburban Homelessness, Subways, Taxonomies of the Homeless, Homeless Veterans, Volunteer Workers, Voting Issues, Welfare Hotels, and Homeless Women. A careful reading of the annotations can produce further classifications.

As each author knows so well, no book is the product of a single mind or effort. Each is built upon what has come before and incorporates the contributions of many others. In a bibliography, this is especially apparent, more so than in most scholarly endeavors.   Yet the contributions of many who are involved in the process remain invisible.   To remedy this, I wish to publicly acknowledge my appreciation to David Gonzalez for the title proper; to Larry Rice, who first interested me in this topic, prodding my sociological conscience with his insistence that the homeless are not epiphenomenal but an essential phenomenon of our times; to Bob Fortado, Director of the U.S. Government Documents Library of Lovejoy Library at Southern Illinois University Edwardsville, who patiently searched arcane sources; to Linda Carlisle, who directs the Social Science Library at Lovejoy Library, who tirelessly retrieved publications; to Gary Denue, Director of Lovejoy Library, for awarding extra amounts of interlibrary loan resources; to Lovejoy's interlibrary loan staff for the many hundreds of requests they processed; to the staff of Hayner Library in Alton, Illinois, for patience with my many requests for verification of publishing information; to the many graduate research assistants who worked on various aspects of this seemingly endless project; to the Graduate School of Southern Illinois University Edwardsville, the School of Social Sciences, and the Department of Sociology for assigning research assistants to me; to the Graduate School of Southern Illinois University Edwardsville for a summer research fellowship; to Phyllis Korper, editor at Garland Press, who signed this project and remained patient as the preparation process extended years beyond its scheduled completion date; to Samuel Pearson, Dean of the School of Social Sciences of Southern Illinois University Edwardsville, for providing a computer for me to work on this project; and, finally, to the American Library Association for awarding me a Whitney Carnegie Fund grant.

As usual, my wife deserves special commendation, this time for her patience and understanding while I went into a marathon schedule to complete the project, which interrupted our long-laid travel plans.

Finally, this volume is a sort of love offering for my fellow researchers. When I began the task, I had no idea that it would require such diligence--or so many years. I intended it to be but a byproduct of my own literature search.   Instead, it became consuming, exorbitantly demanding of energy and time, an entity of its own that multiplied in the process of becoming. It is my sincere desire that researchers find this product useful. Only then will it have merited the many resourc-

es and countless hours expended in the exacting research
process of producing it.

Homelessness

Aarts, Han. "1987: UN Shelter for the Homeless." Counterpart, 3 (2), 1986:2-5.

The Netherlands Habitat Committee is attempting to draw the Dutch public's attention to what is called the "habitat issue." This organization stresses that the industrialized nations do not address the problems of the homeless in the developing countries because their primary interest is not people but seeing that their investments "pay off." For example, by promoting agriculture the industrialized nations see outcomes such as an increase in production or jobs. The primary growth of jobs in the developing nations, however, is in their cities, to which vast numbers of people are moving. Here is where the serious problems of homelessness occur. If the industrialized nations provide funds to build homes for the homeless, they will find a "pay off," for much economic activity in the developing nations is home-based. To construct homes is not enough, however, for the developing nations also need more infrastructure, cheap credit, more schools, and better health care.

Abbot, Elizabeth. "Sheltering the Homeless." New York Times, September 18, 1988:35.

A former YMCA in New York City is being converted to a "combination of emergency, transitional and permanent shelter for the homeless and office space for social service agencies."

Abbott, Ann A. "A Volunteer's Guide to Working with the Homeless." Journal of Voluntary Action Research, 17 (1), January-March 1988:60-65.

Designed to help volunteers work with the homeless, this manual includes guidelines for assessing the homeless and techniques for self-protection.

Abbott, Edith. "Abolish the Pauper Laws." The Social Science Review, 8 (1), March 1934:1-16.

After providing a history of poor laws as they apply to the United States, the author lists reasons that current relief arrangements are inadequate and makes the case that the federal government needs to take the leadership role.

Abbott, Edith. "Poor Law Provision for Family Responsibility." The Social Service Review, 12 (4), December 1938:598-618.
    The author reviews the history of the laws that require relatives (adult children, parents, grandparents, grandchildren, brothers and sisters) to furnish support to a needy relative if one is of "sufficient ability" and takes the position that such laws should be abolished.

Abbott, Martin L., and Gerald R. Blake. "An Intervention Model for Homeless Youth." Clinical Sociology Review, 6, 1988:148-158.
    The Street Youth Employment Program, located in a major west coast city, focuses on stabilizing living conditions of homeless youths and providing them part-time employment, education, and on-the-job training. The youths also participate in developing program policy and its implementation. For a program with street youths to be successful, it must provide for their medical and mental health needs and link meaningful employment with stable living arrangements. The author reviews the results of 16 program participants, aged 16-20, most of whom left the streets and went to work or school.

Abell, Troy, and Larry Lyon. "Do the Differences Make a Difference?: An Empirical Evaluation of the Culture of Poverty in the United States." American Ethnologist, 6 (3), 1979:602-620.
    To test Oscar Lewis's thesis that the poor pass to their children social characteristics that perpetuate poverty from one generation to the next, the authors utilize a national random sample spanning two generations. Supporting the thesis is the finding that cultural values that differentiate the poor from the middle class are transmitted across generations. Two-thirds of the income gap between descendants of the poor and those of the middle class, however, are determined by structural variables.

Abramson, Marc F. "The Criminalization of Mentally Disordered Behavior: Possible Side-Effect of a New Mental Health Law." Hospital and Community Psychiatry, 23 (4), April 1972:101-105.

   This overview of California's 1969 Lanterman-Petris-Short Act suggests that an unanticipated consequence of this legislation is the criminalization of large numbers of the mentally ill. Although a background on deinstitutionalization is provided, including attitudes of the psychiatric profession, it does not mention the homeless directly.

Achs, Nicole. "1991 Municipal Leader of the Year." *American City and County*, 106 (13), December 1991:22-28.
   This profile of Joseph Riley, mayor of Charleston, South Carolina, mentions his work in providing shelters for the homeless.

Ackley, Sheldon. "A Right to Subsistence." *Social Policy*, 8 (5), March-April, 1978:3-11.
   Basing his position on the contract theory of the state, the author argues that in spite of its lack of explicit constitutional basis the government should guarantee all citizens the "fundamentals" (basic necessities) of life. These include food, housing, clothing, and minimal health care. Because the government creates the conditions of poverty, it is its obligation to develop public policy that provides the fundamentals of life.

Adair, James R. *The Old Lighthouse: The Story of the Pacific Garden Mission*. Chicago: Moody Press, 1966.
   This overview of the founding, philosophy, purposes, and approach of Chicago's "old lighthouse," Pacific Garden Mission, recounts numerous case stories.

Adams, Charles Ely. "The Real Hobo: What He Is and How He Lives." *Forum*, 33, March-June 1902:438-449.
   The author's thesis is that unlike the ways that theorists see them, hobos are not the victims of a materialistic social system, moral degenerates, parasites, or refugees from work. Rather, hobos are an industrial factor on which large business enterprises such as railway construction and wheat harvesting depend. The author reviews their working conditions and discipline and includes a description of hobo camps. He makes the point that hobos are often literate and clean. Basically, hobos are itinerant laborers, losers who are caught in a web of ignorance, who squander their earnings and beg while traveling to new, temporary jobs. The solution is universal compulsory education that will

enable one to learn the essential moralities and to gain proficiency in foresight and moral regeneration.

Adams, Gerald R.   "Runaway Youth Projects: Comments on Care Programs for Runaways and Throwaways." Journal of Adolescence, 3 (4), 1980:321-334.
Homelessness due to running away is caused by psychological factors, family relationships, school problems, and deviant peer pressures.   The author develops a two-fold typology of runaway and throwaway youth.   Class I are young, temporary escapists; they are middle-class loners who are unrestrained and highly peer oriented.   Class II consist of those who are rejected and constrained; they are pushouts (socially rejected) who are rebellious, normless, and unrestrained.   The solution is to develop intervention strategies based on the type of runaway.

Adams, Gerald R., and Gordon Munro.   "Portrait of the North American Runaway: A Critical Review." Journal of Youth and Adolescence, 8 (3), 1979:359-373.
The usual psychological profiles of the runaway (insecure, unhappy, impulsive individuals who have low self-esteem--which could be either antecedent to or the consequence of running away) are compared with a counter literature which suggests that "runaways have equivalent psychosocial aptitudes and abilities as those of non-runaway peers." Most literature suggests that the major reasons for running away are "loss of authority and structure in American institutions, parental rejection, alcoholism, diminishing value of work, peer groups, and social change." The research problem is to determine why some youth choose to run away instead of alternative behaviors.   The author suggests two models (alternative values and deindividuation) as frameworks that "can be used to synthesize and integrate the growing literature."

Adams, Gerald R., Thomas Gullotta, and Mary Anne Clancy. "Homeless Adolescents: A Descriptive Study of Similari-ties and Differences Between Runaways and Throwaways." Adolescence, 20 (79), Fall 1985:715-724.
Control and psychopathology perspectives hold promise for understanding three categories of homeless adolescents: runaways, throwaways, and societal rejects.

Addams, Jane. Twenty Years at Hull House. New York: New American Library, 1981. Originally published in 1910.

The author reviews her childhood background as it relates to the spiritual and social convictions that motivated her to work with the poor and homeless. She recounts the founding and operation of Hull House, a social settlement for the poor of Chicago. She describes this work as "an experimental effort to aid in the solution of the social and industrial problems which are engendered by the modern conditions of life in a great city."

Agnew, Lea. "Three for the Money." Foundation News, 33 (1), January-February 1992:30-33.
This recounting of funding problems in grantmaking, which uses the Robert Wood Johnson foundation as a model of success, mentions grants for programs with the homeless.

Alexander, Suzanne. "Colleges Reorient Freshman Orientation To Focus Attention on Society's Problems." Wall Street Journal, September 17, 1992:B11.
A new curriculum goal of universities such as Brandeis University, Columbia College, Massachusetts Institute of Technology, and the University of Michigan is to acquaint their students with urban poverty. Requiring freshmen to paint homeless shelters is listed as an example.

Alger, I., ed. "Depicting the Plight of Our American Homeless." Hospital and Community Psychiatry, 36 (7), July 1985:709-710.
The author reviews three video tapes that focus on the homeless: Asylum in the Streets, Shelter, and Shopping Bag Ladies.

Allardyce, Archie. "Wandering Minds and Wandering Feet." Occupations, November 1934:153-155.
Interviews with 230 boys passing through Cincinnati show that they lack vocational instruction. The author's main conclusion is that the schools have failed.

Allen, Anne. "Who Killed Rebecca Smith?" Foundation News, 23 (3), May-June 1982:13-16.
Although well-intended, deinstitutionalization has led to problems because it confronted the twin obstacles of civil liberties and budget cutting. The author provides results of participant observation at Luther Place in Washington, D.C., contrasts the individual's civil right to refuse help versus the community's right

to force treatment, and examines the comparative abilities and responsibilities of the community to provide
help.

Allen, William H.   "The Vagrant: Social Parasite or
Social Product." In Proceedings of the National Conference of Charities and Correction, Isabel C. Carrows, ed.
May 6-12, 1903:379-386.
    The public must be taught that the real reason they
give to vagrants (which the author calls superficial
samaritanism) is not to help others but to purchase for
themselves self-complacency, relief from annoyance, and
a reputation for generosity. Also needed are a vagrancy
census, a clearinghouse of information on vagrants, the
understanding that individual giving only harms vagrants,
political centralization for dealing with vagrants, and
removing the stigma from receiving public charity.

Allsop, Kenneth.   Hard Travellin': The Hobo and His
History. New York: New American Library, 1967.
    This overview of hobos and migrant workers, which is
partially based on participant observation and also
focuses on social upheavals in the United States,
contains many quotations from hobos, as wells as from
songs and literature about them. The author also
provides information on the American labor movement and
the I.W.W.

Alperstein, G., C. Rappaport, and J. M. Flanigan.
"Health Problems of Homeless Children in New York City."
American Journal of Public Health, 78 (9), September
1988:1232-1233.
    The medical records of 265 homeless children under
5 years of age were compared with a control group of
housed children of similar socioeconomic status. Both
groups were treated in the same pediatric clinic. The
main finding is that the homeless children have more
health problems, such as delayed immunization, elevated
blood lead levels, rate of hospital admission, neglect,
and child abuse.

Alstrom, C. H., Rolf Lindelius, and Inna Salum. "Mortality Among Homeless Men." British Journal of Addiction,
70, 1975:245-252.
    Over a three-year period 6,032 homeless men in
Stockholm had 327 deaths versus 87 expected deaths, an
excess mortality ratio of 4. The homeless men showed
excess mortality for all causes of death, but were

especially high in accidents and diseases of the digestive and respiratory systems.

Alter, Jonathan, Alexander Stille, Shawn Doherty, Nikki Finke Greenberg, Susan Agrest, Vern E. Smith, George Raine, and Darby Junkin. "Homeless in America." Newsweek, January 2, 1984:20-29.

The authors review the increase in homelessness and changes in the types of homeless Americans, whom they identify as drifters, dropouts, winos, and bag ladies. They also examine public and private shelters. The primary causes of homelessness are demolition of cheap lodging as a result of urban renewal, federal housing policy, and deinstitutionalization. The proposed solutions are counseling and permanent housing. The authors also stress the need of the community to act and not to rely on the federal government. Presents a case study of street girls and compares the extreme approaches of Arizona and Massachusetts.

Alter, Jonathan, Nikki Finke Greenberg, and Shawn Doherty. "The Homeless: Out in the Cold." Newsweek, 106, December 16, 1985:22-23.

Homelessness is a political issue and the federal government's response is inadequate.

Altman, Drew, Ellen L. Bassuk, William R. Breakey, et al. "Health Care for the Homeless." Society, 26 (4), May-June 1989:4-5.

This brief overview concludes with this statement: "As we witnessed the suffering of America's poorest citizens, we came to understand that the individual health problems of homeless people combine to form a major public health crisis. We can no longer sit as spectators to the elderly homeless dying of hypothermia, to the children with blighted features poisoned by lead in rat-infested dilapidated welfare hotels, to women raped, to old men beaten and robbed of their few possessions, and to people dying on the streets with catastrophic illnesses such as AIDS. Without eliminating homelessness, the health risks and concomitant health problems, the desperate plight of homeless children, the suffering, and the needless deaths of homeless Americans will continue."

Ambrosino, Lillian. "Runaways." Today's Education (NEA Journal), 60, December 1971:26-28.

After estimating the number of runaways in the United States, the author looks at the attempt of runaways to seek "action" in the city. She also examines approaches used by groups to help runaways, stresses the runaways' distrust of authority, and provides advice to teachers who wish to help potential runaways.

Ambrosino, Lillian. <u>Runaways</u>. Boston: Beacon Press, 1971.
    In her overview of runaways in the United States, the author examines their composition and motivation, the problems they face, their methods of survival, and legal and medical issues. Included is a list of places where runaways can find help.

Ames, Lynne. "Social Skills for Homeless Children." <u>New York Times</u>, February 24, 1991:WC2.
    St. Bernard's Church in White Plains, New York, operates a day care program for homeless children in which they teach preschoolers basic skills in order to better equip them for success in school, and, hopefully, life.

Ames, Lynne. "Students Meet Homeless on Outing." <u>New York Times</u>, February 2, 1991:WC8.
    Teaching young people to help the homeless is a goal of the Quaker work camp in Purchase, New York.

Amidei, Nancy. "The Caretakers." <u>Commonweal</u>, <u>112</u>, December 20, 1985:694-695.
    The author disagrees with the common conception that "the country has become a bastion of self-centered, egomaniacal yuppies." Among the evidence she presents for her contention are medical students from the University of Pennsylvania and Temple University who are "working with the city's homeless, many of whom live on the streets near their classrooms."

Anderson, Chris. "NORC Study Describes Homeless." <u>Chronicle</u> (University of Chicago), 1986:5, 9.
    Using a weighted sample of city blocks, NORC researchers found that 2,000 to 3,000 people were homeless in Chicago on any given night and that 5,000 to 7,000 were homeless at some point during the year. These numbers are much less than previous estimates of 10,000 to 25,000. Among the findings are: the average cash income from all sources of a homeless person in Chicago is less than $6 a day; one in four is a former mental

patient; one in five is a former prisoner; two in five had been sentenced to prison but were put on probation; three of four are men; the median age is 40; and 60 percent are black. The solutions proposed are: public aid agencies need to aggressively reach these people with the benefits for which they are eligible; hospitals and mental health agencies should do a better job of monitoring discharged patients; the mentally and physically ill need places for recuperation and ongoing treatment; and families could be given incentives to keep poor relatives from drifting onto the streets. The author also provides a detailed overview of the methodology used to estimate the numbers of homeless.

Anderson, David C. "He Thought Football Was Forever." New York Times, March 5, 1991:B9.
    This article profiles Travis Williams, former running back for the Green Bay Packers, who died homeless at the age of 45.

Anderson, David C. "Poor Home, Great Track." November 10, 1991:Section 4:18.
    The author takes the position that conditions at the Fort Washington Armory, a city-run homeless shelter, are so sordid that it should be shut down and returned to its earlier use, hosting high school track and field events.

Anderson, David C. "The Recreation Director." New York Times, May 7, 1991:B13.
    The author profiles Nate Archibald, former National Basketball Association star, who works with the homeless in New York City.

Anderson, David C. "Reinstitutionalize the Homeless?" New York Times, November 28, 1991:A26.
    After considering legal and ethical issues concerning reinstitutionalizing the mentally ill homeless, the author suggests that the better solution is more single room occupancy residences.

Anderson, Harriet E. "Centralized Care of the Homeless." The Family, 11 (10), February 1931:318-319.
    The author's thesis is that individualized (personal) treatment by social workers can be effective in dealing with homeless men and transient families.

Anderson, Harriet E. "Travelers and Non-Residents." The Family, 9 (3), May 1928:75-79.

The author provides an overview of national and local efforts to deal with the homeless and transient.

Anderson, Kurt. "Left Out in the Cold." Time, December 19, 1983:14-15.

In examining what is called the "winter crisis" of homelessness, the author looks at conditions in Chicago, Phoenix, Milwaukee, New York, and Washington, D.C. He also suggests that mental illness is the basic cause of homelessness.

Anderson, Margo. "Planning the Future in the Context of the Past." Society, 25 (3), March-April 1988:39-47.

Included in this analysis of problems and controversies facing the 1990 U.S. census are suggestions for counting the homeless.

Anderson, Nels. The American Hobo: An Autobiography. Leiden: E. J. Brill, 1975.

In detailing his experiences in wandering and working, the author looks at his early family background and his sociological training at the University of Chicago.

Anderson, Nels. "Highlights of the Migrant Problem Today." Proceedings of the National Conference of Social Work, 67, New York: Columbia University Press, 1940:109-117.

In contrasting present migration with the recent past, the author emphasizes current economic (or labor) factors. In presenting his solution, which is to provide jobs, he stresses that if private jobs are not available then the men should be given three to four months of public work a year.

Anderson, Nels. The Hobo: The Sociology of the Homeless Man. Chicago: University of Chicago Press, 1923.

The author, a hobo who became a sociologist, describes the various types of hobos he encountered during his wanderings, their sex life, health, work, intellectual life, and political and social organization. He also analyzes lodging houses, hobo jungles, and missions.

Anderson, Nels. "The Juvenile and the Tramp." Journal of the American Institute of Criminal Law and Criminology, 14, August 1, 1923:290-312.

The author reports on findings from interviews with 400 tramps during the summer of 1921. The approximately two million homeless in the United States are almost all young men. There are both internal and external causes of homelessness. The internal causes are inadequate personalities, defective mentalities, and physical defects. The external causes are impelling forces (unemployment and personal crises) and attracting forces (pioneering, work, climate, and transportation). There are five types of boy tramps: wanderlust, egocentric, mentally defective, home trouble, and work. The author also covers relationships of boy and adult tramps, perversion (homosexuality), recruitment, and attachment. His solutions for prevention are: educational campaigns, cooperation of organizations, requirement to show a birth certificate to enter the armed services, cooperation of hotels, keeping boys away from tramp areas, assignment of plainclothes men, and supervised recreation.

Anderson, Nels. <u>Men on the Move</u>. Chicago: University of Chicago Press, 1940.
    In examining migrants as marginal people, the author provides a history of vagrancy laws, the frontier, westward migration, and Coxey's army (homeless men who marched on Washington in the 1890s). He also focuses on current migrant workers and homeless who are unattached and in families. As causes, he identifies labor reloca-tion, agricultural and industrial change, depression, and seasonal work. The solutions he proposes are to get jobs and workers together through efficient employment information services, to offer public works programs (especially conservation work to preserve the public resources and tide migrants over while they find more permanent work), and to provide relief when there is no work.

Anderson, Nels. <u>The Milk and Honey Route</u>: <u>A Handbook for Hobos</u>. New York: The Vanguard Press, 1931. (Written under the pseudonym Dean Stiff.)
    This overview of hobohemia as seen by hobos emphasizes missions, social workers, panhandling, clothing, sexual sublimation, avoiding work, cooking, famous hobos, and hobo poems. In his introduction to <u>Men on the Move</u>, the author says he wrote this book as a parody of hobos.

Anderson, Nels. "Sociology Has Many Faces: Part II." Journal of the History of Sociology, 3 (2), Spring-Summer 1981:1-19
    The author recounts his professional journey as a sociologist, in which his first book, The Hobo, played a critical role. After publishing this book in 1923, Anderson felt stigmatized by the topic and unable to secure an academic job.

Anderson, Paul Ernest. "Tramping with Yeggs." Atlantic Monthly, 36, December 1925:747-755.
    Basing his conclusions on three month's participant observation, the author distinguishes between tramps, hobos, and bums, and focuses on their crimes, especially safe cracking, "weeding a dump," and other "yegging." Emphasis is placed on socialization into tramp culture and secrecy.

Anderson, Ralph, and Kyra Jones Osmus. "Cold Nights and Long Days--A Comparison of Male and Female Volunteers in a Night Shelter." Journal of Voluntary Action Research, 17 (1), January-March 1988:54-59.
    The authors explore gender differences among volunteers at a night shelter for men in Chattanooga, Tennessee. They conclude that men are more likely to have an instrumental approach to their work (the shelter serves to keep men off the streets), while women take a more personal approach to their work (more individualistic). These differences are outcomes of differential socialization.

Anderson, Sandra C. "Alcoholic Women on Skid Row." Social Work, 32 (4), July-August 1987:362-365.
    Comparing women who received treatment for alcoholism in Portland's skid row with similar groups studied in the 1970s shows that today's homeless women are younger, have more formal education, and began to drink earlier. The author argues that the disaffiliation hypothesis must be questioned as these women maintain contact with their children, relatives, and friends.

Anello, Rose, and Tillie Shuster. A Guide for Non-Profit Shelter Operators in New York City: Negotiating the Public Assistance System on Behalf of Homeless Adults. New York: Community Service Society, May 1984.
    This manual to help operators of facilities for the homeless in New York City obtain public assistance for homeless adults contains copies of interview schedules,

stresses the problems that homeless people encounter, and emphasizes the need to develop a liaison approach in order to be effective.

Angela, Sister. "Rootless and Homeless Men in Aberdeen." Health Bulletin, 38 (2), March 1980:75-76.
There are four types of lodging house residents: pensioners, workers, unemployed, and unemployable. The author reports that a general practitioner consults in the lodging house in Aberdeen and that the experience is generally positive.

Annis, H. M., and C. B. Liban. "A Follow-up Study of Male Halfway House Residents and Matched Non-Resident Controls." Journal of Studies on Alcohol, 40 (1), 1979:63-69.
The authors matched 35 male alcoholics in a halfway house program with controls. Although there was no difference in the amount of drunkenness, more men in the experimental group readmitted themselves to detoxification programs. From this, the authors conclude that the halfway house program integrated the men into the health care network and enabled them to seek services on their own.

Ansberry, Clare. "Over at the Rainbow: Hunger's Persistence Is a Growth Industry." The Wall Street Journal, June 14, 1988:2-3.
The plight of the poor has been getting worse. "[T]hough the number of Americans living in poverty has climbed by three million since 1980, roughly one million fewer people are getting food stamps today...cutbacks in the federal food-surplus program, which distributes free cheese, rice and powdered milk, are likely to exacerbate the situation." Consequently, not only has the number of soup kitchens grown but their services have also expanded. As a result, some soup kitchens are taking on the character of social service agencies.

Anthes, Gary H. "Computers Play a Part in Addicts' Recovery." Computerworld, 25 (37), September 16, 1991:45.
The author profiles a program to provide computer training for recovering alcohol and drug addicts run by New Way Recovery at a Washington, D.C., shelter. After a six-week detoxification program, the homeless addicts study computer repair, spreadsheets, MS-DOS, word processing, or database programs.

Appelbaum, Richard P. "The Affordability Gap." Society, 26 (4), May-June 1989:6-8.

"There are a number of reasons homelessness is a rapidly worsening problem today, but the basic cause is simple enough: current shifts in the economy are producing a growing number of poor people who cannot pay enough in rents or mortgages to make low-income housing investment profitable. The result is a supply-and-affordability crisis that is pushing those least able to cope onto the streets....Past approaches--which were predicated on making the market profitable--are doomed to failure. The affordability gap will continue to widen, as rising housing costs confront eroding incomes. Public subsidies are too costly, too inefficient, and ultimately too ineffective. The solution lies with federally funded, nonprofit housing of various forms, an approach reflected in several bills currently before Congress."

Appelbaum, Richard P. "A Report on the Homeless and Emergency Shelters." In HUD Report on Homelessness: Joint Hearing before the Subcommittee on Housing and Community Development of the Committee on Banking, Finance and Urban Affairs and the Subcommittee on Manpower and Housing of the Committee on Government Operations, House of Representatives. Washington, D.C.: U.S. Government Printing Office, May 24, 1984:166-179.

The author focuses on methodological problems of measuring the homeless and criticizes published estimates, especially methodological inadequacies that "converge to bias estimates in a downward direction" and "the failure to provide information which might permit an independent evaluation of its findings."

Appelbaum, Richard P. "Testimony." In HUD Report on Homelessness: Joint Hearing before the Subcommittee on Housing and Community Development of the Committee on Banking, Finance and Urban Affairs and the Subcommittee on Manpower and Housing of the Committee on Government Operations House of Representatives. Washington, D.C.: U.S. Government Printing Office, May 24, 1984.

The author discusses the methodological problems of each of four methods for estimating the numbers of homeless: (1) published estimates, (2) interviews with experts, (3) extrapolation from estimates made by shelter operators, and (4) street and shelter counts. Each estimate provides considerably different numbers.

Appelbaum, Richard P., Michael Dolney, Peter Dreier, and John I. Gilderbloom. "Scapegoating Rent Control: Masking the Causes of Homelessness." <u>Journal of the American Planning Association</u>, <u>57</u> (2), Spring 1991:153-164.

The authors argue that William Tucker's conclusion that rent control is a primary cause of housing shortages and homelessness is fatally flawed. They claim that his measure of homelessness, selection of a sample, and choice of causal variable are inadequate.

Applebome, Peter. "The Homeless Become A Presence in Texas." <u>New York Times</u>, August 10, 1986:E5.

At the Star of Hope Women's Shelter in Houston, Texas, about a quarter of the residents are children. Homelessness in Texas is increasing because of the bust in oil.

Applebome, Peter. "Homeless Shelters Jammed in Southwest." <u>New York Times</u>, November 15, 1986:Y6.

Because an increasing number of people are using their services, homeless shelters and foundations are finding it difficult to meet their expenses. Includes the example of Kenneth and Jean Vanderdoes and their family who had formerly contributed to the homeless but who now have become homeless themselves. Concludes that corporations, churches, and private organizations cannot solve the problem independently, that "it has to be a combination of all of them."

Appleby, Lawrence, Nancy Slagg, and Prakash N. Desai. "The Urban Nomad: A Psychiatric Problem?" <u>Current Psychiatric Therapies</u>, <u>21</u>, 1982:253-262.

Not only has deinstitutionalization led to a decline in the resident psychiatric population, but it has also created a rapidly increasing readmission rate. This "new type" of patient, usually referred to as a chronic recidivist or a revolving-door patient, is termed by these authors an urban nomad. Urban nomads are younger, more mobile, more socially isolated, reactive, volatile "floaters." Using short periods of hospitalization as a refuge from the streets, they usually refuse aftercare services. Often viewed as public nuisances and vulnerable to exploitation, these "psychiatric hoboes" are in need of psychiatric services. The authors suggest that more "inviting," appropriate, and effective interventions be developed. They propose a 24-hour drop-in center (lodge), located in a neighborhood residence close to or in a marginal area, that offers "access to basic elements of survival" (food, clothing, shelter, and medicine) and "simple means to cope with problems of daily living" (advocacy, case management, and skill training).

Aptekar, Lewis. "Family Structure in Colombia: Its Impact on Understanding Street Children." Journal of Ethnic Studies, 17 (1), Spring 1989:97-108.
    After giving psychological tests (Block Design, Bener Gestalt, and Human Figure Drawing) to 56 street children aged 7-12 in Colombia, the authors conclude that the children are functioning fine. The close friendships of these children with one another are a key to their adequate functioning. Rather than being abandoned, the children were reared by their mothers to achieve early independence. Consequently, childhood cannot be under-stood apart from its cultural definition.

Aptekar, Lewis. "The Street Children of Colombia: How Families Define the Nature of Childhood." International Journal of Sociology of the Family, 18 (2), Autumn 1988:283-295.
    After giving psychological tests (Block Design, Bener Gestalt, and Human Figure Drawing) to 56 street children aged 7-12 in Colombia, the authors conclude that the children are functioning fine. The close friendships of these children with one another are a key to their adequate functioning. Rather than being abandoned, the children were reared by their mothers to achieve early independence. Consequently, childhood cannot be under-stood apart from its cultural definition.

Arce, A. Anthony, Marilyn Tadlock, Michael J. Vergare, and Stuart H. Shapiro. "A Psychiatric Profile of Street People Admitted to an Emergency Shelter." Hospital and Community Psychiatry, 34 (9), September 1983:812-817.
    Based on a 1981-1982 study of a Philadelphia emergency shelter, the authors identify three types of shelter users: habitual street people, episodic homeless, and people not usually on the street but who now are because they are undergoing an acute crisis. The proposed solutions are psychiatric expertise in treating the homeless, psychiatric intervention, treating physical medical problems, screening out those who are not truly needy, relocation and housing, and coordinated efforts among the city's government departments. Mentions the schizophrenic fear of Joe No Name to enter a shelter. The causes of the homeless problem are much more than deinstitutionalization.

Archard, Peter. "Sad, Bad or Mad: Society's Confused Response to the Skid Row Alcoholic." In <u>Contemporary Social Problems in Britain</u>, Roy Bailey and Jock Young, eds. Westmead: Saxon House, 1973:127-143.

The articles contrast ideological, historical, and theoretical bases of understanding skid row alcoholics. They also compare professional views of skid row alcoholics and contrast attitudes in the United States and Great Britain.

Archard, Peter. "Vagrancy: A Literature Review." In <u>Vagrancy: Some New Perspectives</u>, Tim Cook, ed. London: Academic Press, 1979:11-28.

In this overview of the history of vagrancy, the editor presents both empirical and naturalistic accounts, with the goal to go beyond the literature and develop a full social theory of vagrancy.

Archard, Peter. <u>Vagrancy, Alcoholism and Social Control</u>. London: Macmillan, 1979.

Through participant observation, the author provides "a symbolic interactionist account of skid row, and skid row alcoholism and its intersection with social control agents, their institutions and ideological premises." In focusing on the life style of homeless alcoholics and society's reaction to "the skid row man," he stresses how "heavy drinking in the context of skid row social relationships simultaneously divorces alcoholics from the normal community and consolidates their identification with the skid row world." He concludes that "homeless alcoholics are not socially isolated, as is commonly supposed, but have constructed a web of relationships that are socially meaningful to them."

Argeriou, Milton, and Dennis McCarty, eds. <u>Treating Alcoholism and Drug Abuse Among Homeless Men and Women: Nine Community Demonstration Grants</u>. Special issue of the <u>Alcoholism Treatment Quarterly</u>, <u>7</u> (1). New York: Haworth Press, 1990.

The articles in this special issue summarize nine community demonstration projects designed to develop and expand alcohol and drug abuse treatment services for homeless men and women. Funded under the 1987 Stewart B. McKinney Homeless Assistance Act, these projects are located in Anchorage, Boston, Los Angeles, Louisville, Minneapolis, New York City, Oakland, and Philadelphia.

Argersinger, Jo Ann E.   "Assisting the 'Loafers':
Transient Relief in Baltimore, 1933-1937."   Labor
History, 23, Spring 1982:226-245.
     Following an overview of latter 19th century
legislation directed against the transient unemployed
homeless, the author reviews how the Federal Emergency
Relief Act of 1933 was applied in Baltimore.

Armstrong, Clairette, P. "A Psychoneurotic Reaction of
Delinquent Boys and Girls."   Journal of Abnormal and
Social Psychology, 32, 1937:329-342.
     The author compares statistics on 660 runaway boys
with those of 122 runaway girls in New York City.   In
general, the runaways are immigrants, below average in
intelligence, below their grade level in school, and come
from broken homes.   The author concludes that running
away is a psychoneurotic reaction to "a more or less
continuous state of fear, distress, and insecurity."

Armstrong, Clairette P.   660 Runaway Boys: Why Boys
Desert Their Homes. Boston: Richard G. Badger, 1932.
     Six hundred sixty boys who were arraigned in the
Children's Court in New York City on charges of desertion
are compared with control groups of 60 delinquent and 152
non-delinquent boys.   The author compares their age,
intellect, nationality, education, economics, family,
nervous habits, physical defects, overcrowding at home,
court experience and offenses, companions, and specifics
on the desertions.   She identifies the causes of running
away as the failure of the family to function satisfacto-
rily as a unit coupled with specific factors that
stimulate the running away.   Her proposed solutions are
the better exercise of parental responsibility, court
intervention, removal of children from problem families,
helping immigrants adjust to their new lives, birth
control, and the utilization of church and schools in
"preventive mental hygiene."

Arnold, Martin. "West Side Asks Aid with Misfits." New
York Times, March 16, 1965:41.
     Upper West Side businessmen complain about the
deterioration of their area due to the congregating of
welfare recipients, drug users, and prostitutes.   The
suggested solutions are to change city policies that
encourage welfare recipients to cluster in one area, for
the police to be more vigilant, and to speed up urban
renewal in order to provide more middle-income housing

and to keep buildings from converting to single-room occupancy.

Aronow, Ina. "Homeless Students Get Chance to Stay Put." New York Times, October 6, 1991:WC10.
     Instability of residence is a major problem for the education of homeless youngsters, as the resulting transfer from one school to another disrupts their education. A pilot program to solve this problem has begun. Ten school districts have agreed to guarantee homeless children a permanent place even though their parents move about.

Asander, Harje. "A Field Investigation of Homeless Men in Stockholm: A Socio-Psychiatric and Clinical Follow-up Study." Acta Psychiatrica Scandinavica, 61, Supplementum 281, 1980:1-125.
     The author examines the background (age, place of birth, childhood, education, military, marital status, criminality, etc.) of 6,032 homeless Swedish males in 1970 and reports on their work history, alcohol and drug abuse, and mortality.

Asher, Julie. "Shelter Serves 'New Poor' Who Don't Know How to Beg." Our Sunday Visitor, January 16, 1983:3.
     This look at the "new poor" of Denver stresses that the churches have an obligation to help. Focuses on shelters, shelter rules, families, lack of jobs, and the shock of being on the streets for the first time.

Augustin, Joseph. The Human Vagabond. London: Hutchinson, 1933.
     The author recounts his experiences in tramping around England.

Auletta, Ken. The Underclass. New York: Vintage Books, 1982.
     The foci are the size, causes, and effects of the underclass, the feminization of poverty, broken families, crimes of the underclass, the welfare mentality, whether causes are systemic or individualistic, rural and racial aspects of the underclass, possible solutions, and available options.

Aulette, Judy, and Albert Aulette. "Police Harassment of the Homeless: The Political Purpose of the Criminalization of Homelessness." Humanity and Society, 11 (2), May 1987:244-256.

The authors argue that the homeless are victims of both the economic and criminal justice systems. Due to poverty and unemployment, they have no homes; due to not having homes, they are harassed by the police. For example, they may be arrested for carrying a concealed weapon--a cardboard cutter to make a shelter.

Austin, Blair. "The Plight of the Homeless." Kiwanis Magazine, October 1985:37-40.
This brief, wide-ranging overview of the homeless includes the addresses of five homeless organizations.

Austin, Charles. "Churches See Charity's Limits." New York Times, July 31, 1983:E20
The author reviews how churches have responded to President Reagan's cutbacks in antipoverty programs and his call for the private sector to fill the gap. An unanticipated consequence of greater citizen involvement in dealing with homelessness may be to cause volunteers to question why there should be a problem in the first place. Perhaps getting the private sector more actively involved may be laying the groundwork for greater social activism, with today's volunteers being tommorow's reformers.

Austin, Shirley Plumer. "Coxey's Commonweal Army." Chatauquan, 19, June 1894:332-336.
Jacob Sechler Coxey and Carl Browne, along with "General" Coxey, organized a march of the unemployed from the West onto Washington, D.C. This "army" of the unemployed consisted of about 250 men, with "desertions evenly balancing the enlistment". The author reveals that Coxey and Browne slept in good hotels during the march and that much food contributed to the army never reached the men. She concludes that this march "led by a hypnotized dreamer and a scheming demagogue, may be the pebble of revolution which, thrown into the lake of national peace, will cause commotion to the farthest corner."

Austin, Shirley Plumer. "The Downfall of Coxeyism." Chatauquan, 19, July 1894.
The author claims that Coxey's boast that the Commonweal (the "army of the unemployed") represented 66,000,000 people is fraudulent, that only ten or 15 of the several hundred men who reached Washington were actually unemployed workingmen, the rest being beggars and idlers. Most were "negroes of very low order."

Concludes that "these armies are simply organized bands of wandering mendicants, with little regard for law or rights of property." They are composed of "the country's worthless, restless elements and cranks." In short, these men are "human parasites" who should be dispersed.

Averbach, Alvin. "San Francisco's South of Market District, 1850-1950: The Emergence of a Skid Row." *California Historical Quarterly*, 52, 1973:197-223.
     In this detailed history of San Francisco's South of Market district, the author stresses that this area has been inhabited by homeless men "since the earliest days of the city." This traditional habitation of the homeless is now threatened by the Yerba Buena project, an urban renewal effort that follows "a dubious long tradition of land-grabbing...in which stores, a sports arena, a convention center, a parking garage, and other facilities will replace the dwellings and diversions of the old, largely single, male residents."

Awdeley, John. *The Fraternitye of Vacabondes*. London: N. Trubner & Co., 1561.
     According to D. B. Thomas's introduction to *Liber Vaga-torum*, this is the earliest English work on the subject. A version also appears in *Queene Elizabethes Academy, A Booke of Precedence, &c.* Boston: Dutton & Co., 1869, which includes a lengthy account of the history of the work and its relationship to other works on the subject. Lists 19 types of vagabonds, the terms for them, and a short description of each. An additional three are explicated in greater detail (curtesy man, cheatour or fingerer, and a ring faller). Also contains 25 Orders of Knaves.

Axelson, Leland J., and Paula W. Dail. "The Changing Character of Homelessness in the United States." *Family Relations*, 37 (4), October 1988:463-469.
     The authors present a broad historical sketch of the changing character of the homeless in the United States. The homeless today are made up of single mothers, runaway youths, the working poor, the mentally and chemically disabled, and others who have experienced economic, social, or personal crises. An underlying cause is the shrinkage of low-income housing. Contains recommendations for social policy.

Ayers, Michael, and H. Brent De Land, Jr. "Economic Development and the Poor: What Are Their Chances?" Illinois Issues, June 1985:22-28.

This wide-ranging coverage includes economic growth and development, poverty programs, problems in defining poverty, race, ethnicity and poverty, families in poverty, policy changes, history of poverty programs, changes in attitudes toward the poor, current directions, unemployment, AFDC, defederalization, welfare and the desire to work, the culture of poverty, unemployment, minimum wage, and hospital care.

B

Baasher, T., D. Elhakim, K. El Fawal, R. Giel, T. W. Harding, and V. B. Wankiiri. "On Vagrancy and Psychosis." Community Mental Health Journal, 19 (1), Spring 1983:27-41.

The authors compare the situation of the mentally ill in Egypt and Lesotho with the United States. They conclude that changes in mental health legislation have forced the mentally handicapped of the developed world to be in the same situation as those in the developing world who never had contact with a mental health service. Focusing on the vagrant psychotic, the authors detail the mentally handicapped's physical health and relationship to the community and skid row. They also wrestle with the problem of defining the terms psychotic and vagrant.

Bachrach, Leona L. "Ambiguities in Treating the Homeless Mentally Ill." Newsletter of the American Association of General Hospital Psychiatrists, 7 (2), Fall 1985:2-3.

Ambiguities about the homeless plague their psychiatric treatment: an inadequate definition of homelessness; where the homeless belong in the psychiatric service system; the diversity of the homeless; problems of "catchmenting" versus no fixed address; rapport; and problems of the proper use of resources. The solution is to establish a pluralistic services system (networks of interrelated agencies with specific responsibilities—a rational division of labor) so the homeless can receive comprehensive and longitudinal care.

Bachrach, Leona L. "Asylum and Chronically Ill Psychiatric Patients." <u>American Journal of Psychiatry</u>, <u>141</u> (8),
August 1984:975-978.
    Deinstitutionalization has destroyed the sanctuary
(a place offering safety and security) that some patients
need. Our current community-oriented service system
often overlooks the needs of the chronically psychiatrically ill. The solution is to use three guiding
principles in making plans for treating the non-institu-
tionalized mentally ill: functional equivalence, cultural
relevance, and potential trade-offs.

Bachrach, Leona L. "A Conceptual Approach to Deinstitutionalization." <u>Hospital and Community Psychiatry</u>, <u>29</u>
(9), September 1978:573-578.
    Although the author does not deal with homelessness
directly, she reviews the ideals and philosophy that
underlie deinstitutionalization, obstacles to its
implementation, and difficulties in its evaluation.

Bachrach, Leona L. "Continuity of Care for Chronic
Mental Patients: A Conceptual Analysis." <u>American
Journal of Psychiatry</u>, <u>138</u>, 1981:1449-1456.
    "Continuity of care" is a central issue in treating
the deinstitutionalized mentally ill. The author lists
what she calls "dimensions of continuity," stressing that
these dimensions must be implemented if we are to meet
the needs of the deinstitutionalized.

Bachrach, Leona L. "The Homeless Mentally Ill and Mental
Health Services: An Analytical Review of the Literature."
In <u>The Homeless Mentally Ill</u>, H. Richard Lamb, ed.
Washington, D.C.: American Psychiatric Association,
1984:11-53.
    The topics of this article are the growth of the
homeless mentally ill population; problems in defining
and counting the homeless; the context of care; diversi-
fication, continuity, and comprehensiveness in care;
barriers to care; admission policies; inadequate services; geographical responsibility; inappropriate expectations; and social distance between professionals and the
homeless mentally ill. The author also presents nine
principles for planning mental health services for the
homeless.

Bachrach, Leona L. <u>The Homeless Mentally Ill and Mental
Health Services: An Analytical Review of the Literature</u>.

Washington, D.C.: Department of Health and Human Services, 1984.

The author summarizes the precipitating factors in the homelessness of the mentally ill, methodological barriers to studying the chronically mentally ill homeless, problems resulting from deinstitutionalization, and difficulties in meeting the needs of this population. She also outlines nine principles for improving services to the mentally ill homeless, stressing that "the needs of the homeless mentally ill must be based on the understanding of the unique interaction of chronicity and homelessness."

Bachrach, Leona L. "Homeless Women: A Context for Health Planning." The Milbank Quarterly, 65 (3), 1987:371-397.

After examining the differences between "houselessness" and "homelessness," differences in time of people's homelessness ("street people" and "episodically homeless"), mobility of the homeless, and the question of mental illness of the homeless, the author focuses on homeless women. She examines correlates of their homelessness, the effects of deinstitutionalization, disaffiliation, life on the streets, disability and barriers to care, service needs, and continuity of care. She concludes that to solve this problem we must (1) make progress in defining homelessness, (2) appreciate the health problems of homeless women, (3) be concerned that homelessness is a political issue involving "rhetoric and gamesmanship," which is used for self-interests, and (4) understand that the multiple disabilities of homeless women are complicated by gender discrimination.

Bachrach, Leona L. "Interpreting Research on the Homeless Mentally Ill: Some Caveats." Hospital and Community Psychiatry, 35 (9), September 1984:914-917.

Findings from the studies on the homeless mentally ill entail problems with the definitions of both homelessness and chronic mental illness, as well as complexities of the population subsumed under this single concept. Consequently, we must use restraint in adopting those findings.

Bachrach, Leona L. "Is the Least Restrictive Environment Always the Best?: Sociological and Semantic Implications." Hospital and Community Psychiatry, 31 (2), February 1980:97-103.

The concept of "least restrictive environment" plays a significant role in deinstitutionalization. This concept, however, is imprecise, leading to errors in logic and faulty generalizations. More adequate conceptualizations of restrictions and environment are suggested.

Bachrach, Leona L. "Overview: Model Programs for Chronic Mental Patients." American Journal of Psychiatry, 137, 1980:1023-1031.
    The author evaluates model programs for delivering mental health services to the deinstitutionalized chronically mentally ill, concluding that model programs are only of limited value. They are "experimental efforts, not solutions." Because knowledge can be gained from them, however, it is possible that they can be translated into "systems-related action."

Bachrach, Leona L. Psychiatric Bed Needs: An Analytical Review. Rockville, Maryland.: U.S. Department of Health, Education, and Welfare, 1975.
    The author presents a brief assessment of the need for psychiatric beds in the United States in light of deinstitutionalization.

Bachrach, Leona L. "Research on Services for the Homeless Mentally Ill." Hospital and Community Psychiatry, 35 (9), September 1984:910-913.
    After briefly reviewing general findings and suggesting areas that need to be researched, the author stresses that the barriers to research are the lack of precise definitions, the diversity of the homeless, cultural disparity, lack of rapport, and the mobility of the homeless.

Bacquet, Dean. "Drifter Sought Bellevue Help Before Murder." New York Times, June 21, 1991:B1.
    Kevin McKiever, who is identified as a drifter charged with stabbing a woman to death near New York City's Central Park, reportedly sought help at Bellevue Hospital before the attack. Instead of treatment, he was given the number of a cocaine hot line and sent away.

Baer, W. C. "Housing in an Internationalizing Region: Housing Stock Dynamics in Southern California and the Dilemmas of Fair Share." Environment and Planning D: Society and Space, 4, 1986:337-349.
    The author reports that housing in Southern California has become extremely expensive, that it is 55 percent above the national median. Although "the region has a

disproportionately high percentage of homeless...Yet at
the same time it has about as many people living in units
valued in excess of $1,000,000 as our homeless." Due to
changing migration patterns "a number of Third World
characteristics are being introduced into the region."
These include "extremes of housing, wealth, over-crowding, reghettoization of its urban cores." He concludes
that we need to reconsider the land-use and housing
regulations of local governments.

Bahr, Howard M.   "Birth Order and Failure: The Evidence
from Skid Row." Quarterly Journal of Studies on Alcohol,
32, September 1971:669-686.
    Testing the hypothesis that first-borns will be
under-represented on skid row, the author found "no
consistent relationship of birth-order and residence on
skid row...except that only-borns were over-represented."

Bahr, Howard M., ed.   Disaffiliated Man: Essays and
Bibliography on Skid Row, Vagrancy, and Outsiders.
Toronto: University of Toronto Press, 1970.
    In addition to an annotated bibliography of 831
items divided into 12 sections, this book contains
articles on disaffiliation entitled: The Sociologist and
The Homeless Man; Societal Forces and the Unattached
Male; Homelessness, Disaffiliation, and Retreatism;
Survivorship and Social Isolation: The Case of the Aged
Widower; and Dimensions of Religious Defection.

Bahr, Howard M.   "Family Size and Stability as Antecedents of Homelessness and Excessive Drinking." Journal of
Marriage and the Family, August 1969:477-483.
    Using a control sample, the author tests assumptions
that broken homes and large family size are background
factors of skid row residence. Those assumptions are not
supported.

Bahr, Howard M.   "The Gradual Disappearance of Skid Row."
Social Problems, 15, 1967:41-45.
    The decline in the skid row population is not due to
a decline in homelessness, but to the dispersal of the
homeless.

Bahr, Howard M.   Homelessness and Disaffiliation.   New
York: Columbia University Press, 1968.
    Comparing men who are living on New York City's
Bowery with lower-class men who are institutionalized and
others who are living in a low-income residential

neighborhood, the author concludes that skid row is not the beginning of disaffiliation but the terminal stage of a disaffiliative career.   He suggests that we focus rehabilitative efforts on the partially disaffiliated who have not yet moved to skid row.

Bahr, Howard M.   "Homelessness, Disaffiliation, and Retreatism." In Disaffiliated Man: Essays and Bibliography on Skid Row, Vagrancy, and Outsiders.   Howard M. Bahr, ed. Toronto: University of Toronto Press, 1970:39-50.
     The author considers definitions of homelessness, disaffiliation, and retreatism.

Bahr, Howard M.   "Institutional Life, Drinking, and Disaffiliation."   Social Problems, 16 (1), Summer 1968:365-375.
     Life histories from two samples of skid-row men are compared with a control sample of lower-class metropolitan males. The author concludes that institutional life is usually only a phase in a history of work, but also finds that skid-row men have more institutionalization and heavier drinking. Those with greater histories of institutional life are not more disaffiliated.

Bahr, Howard M. "Lifetime Affiliation Patterns of Early- and Late-Onset Heavy Drinkers on Skid Row." Quarterly Journal of Studies on Alcohol, 30, September 1969:645-656.
     "Life history interviews" were obtained from samples of men living in New York City's Bowery and in Camp LaGuardia, "a rehabilitation center for aged and infirm Skid Row men." Focus was placed on the age at which heavy drinking began and the men's "subsequent affiliative histories." The author concludes that compared with "late-onset heavy drinkers" (those who began heavy drinking after age 30) the "early-onset heavy drinkers" were more disaffiliated and had lower occupational status.

Bahr, Howard M. Skid Row: An Introduction to Disaffiliation. New York: Oxford University Press, 1973.
     This review of the popular and professional literature focuses on alcoholism, power, affiliation, attitudes about the homeless, characteristics of skid row men, types of homeless, the social organization of skid row, encounters with the police and courts, the sense of

hopelessness and the binding to skid row. Contains a separate chapter on homeless women.

Bahr, Howard M., and Gerald R. Garrett. Women Alone: Disaffiliation among Urban Women. Lexington, Massachusetts: Lexington Books, 1976.
   The authors compare a random sample of women in three census tracts with women living in a hotel in Manhattan. They also make a brief comparison with homeless men. Major topics are disaffiliation, characteristics of homeless women, broken homes, possible solutions, and social policy.

Bahr, Howard M., and Kathleen C. Houts. "Can You Trust a Homeless Man?: A Comparison of Official Records and Interview Responses by Bowery Men." Public Opinion Quarterly, 35 (3), 1971:374-382.
   The authors examine the validity and reliability of survey data by comparing data obtained from interviews with 203 Bowery men and 199 clients at Camp LaGuardia with their shelter records. They conclude that homeless men are no more untruthful than are most other disadvantaged populations. The accuracy of the men's reports varies with the recency and complexity of the information being sought.

Bahr, Howard M., and Stephen J. Langfur. "Social Attachment and Drinking in Skid-Row Life Histories." Social Problems, 14 (4), Spring 1967:464-472.
   Using interviews with a random sample of persons registered at six hotels and lodging houses in the Bowery, the authors test the disaffiliation (undersocialization) thesis. They found that most respondents have low degrees of social attachment. The heavy drinkers have more ties to family, church, and recreational organizations than do abstainers and moderate drinkers, while the order is reversed for the economic sector.

Bahr, Howard M., and Theodore Caplow. Old Men Drunk and Sober. New York: New York University Press, 1973.
   In the Columbia Bowery Project of 1963-1969, homeless men in New York City were compared with a control sample of settled men. Data were gathered through a survey, life histories, and interviews. Background data were gathered on the men's families, education, occupation, aspiration, anomie, achievement, and religion. Major foci are socialization into skid row, drinking patterns, and happiness. The authors deal with

the issues of validity and reliability. The interview schedule is included.

Bailey, E. Lamar. "Tramps and Hoboes." Forum, 26, October 1898:217-221.
The author, who had been a tramp, concludes that there are four types of homeless men. The genuine tramp has chosen tramping as a pursuit in life, is harmless, and has the goal of having fun and avoiding responsibility and mental concentration. Hobos are tramps in the first stage. They are unemployed men who move about to seek work. Vagrants have been driven from the city. A fourth type is criminals in flight. The causes for each differ. Hobos suffer from industrial conditions (unemployment). For solutions to be effective, they must differ with the type. Hobos should be offered a chance, for they can still be saved; but genuine tramps should be given up as hopeless.

Bailey, Marjorie, and Henry Brodaty. "Life After Hospital: Trials of a Boarding House 'Mother.'" Australian and New Zealand Journal of Psychiatry, 16 (4), December 1982:289-292.
This first-person account of a boarding house in which discharged psychiatric patients are cared for emphasizes the boarding house's culture and the adjustment of rules to their inhabitants' backgrounds.

Bailey, Ron. The Squatters. Baltimore, Maryland: Penguin Books, 1973.
The author recounts a campaign to occupy unused housing, an illegal but occasionally effective strategy to provide homes for the homeless.

Bailey, Willard. "Charity Care: A Matter of Mission, Fund Raising, and Survival." Fund Raising Management, 20 (1), March 1989:66-67.
This analysis of the threat to hospitals' tax-exempt status due to their failure to care for the poor exalts the fund-raising efforts of Peter Ghiorse of St. Vincent's Hospital and Medical Center in New York City. The charitable activities of this hospital include health programs for the homeless.

Bailey, William A. Bill Bailey Came Home: As a Farm Boy, as a Stowaway at the Age of Nine, a Trapper at the Age of Fifteen, and a Hobo at the Age of Sixteen. Logan, Utah: Utah State University Press, 1973.

The author, born in 1895, focuses primarily on his early life in Colorado at the turn of the century. Contains materials on his experiences as a runaway and hobo from ages 14 to 17.

Baker, Deborah M.   "Flood without Relief: The Story of the Tug Valley Disaster."   Southern Exposure, 6 (1), Spring 1978:20-27.

Thousands of people were left homeless when the Tug River (on the Kentucky-West Virginia border) flooded. The authors contrast the official response, mostly unsatisfactory and uncaring, with the more satisfactory approach of a voluntary group, the Tug Valley Recovery Center.

Baker, James N., Patricia King, Lynda Wright, and Jo Beth McDaniel.   "The Homeless Turn Militant."   Newsweek, 111, January 18, 1988:28.

Focusing on the "new militancy" among homeless groups and their advocates, breaking into empty houses, boarded-up apartments, and abandoned hotels, and the demand for permanent housing, the authors state that increasingly the homeless are single black parents with children, the families of out-of-work unskilled laborers, and the "new poor"--college-educated people whose jobs were phased out or whose businesses folded.

Baker, Patricia, and Barbara Ferrer.   Down and Out: A Manual on Basic Rights and Benefits for the Homeless in Massachusetts.   Boston: Massachusetts Law Reform Institute and the Coalition for the Homeless, 1984.

This resource manual for the homeless reviews emergency programs, public benefit programs, legal problems, AFDC, general relief, FEMA housing, relocation, and fire insurance, with an emphasis on the resources available to the homeless.

Baker, Ray Stannard.   "Lift Men from the Gutter?   Or Remove the Gutter? Which?"   American Magazine, 68, July 1909:227-239.

The author provides an account of the McAuley Mission in New York City.   For the individual, the proposed solution is a new life following conversion to Jesus.   For the church, the proposed solutions are extending true brotherhood and working on the problems of unemployment, degradation, and exploitation.

Balanon, Lourdes G. "Street Children: Strategies for Action." Child Welfare, March-April 1989:159-166.
Large numbers of Filipino children live on city streets because of "an alarming growth of urban population, aggravated by severe economic crisis, inadequate distribution of resources, and inadequate social services." The recommendations to "address the activities and needs of street children" include legislation (a greater budget for programs to protect these children), interagency collaboration (concerted action by governmental and non-governmental agencies), and research (to determine the effectiveness of programs and the physical and psychological effects of street life on these children).

Ball, F. L. Jessica, and Barbara E. Havassy. "A Survey of the Problems and Needs of Homeless Consumers of Acute Psychiatric Services." Hospital and Community Psychiatry, 35 (9), September 1984:917-921.
To explore why homeless adults repeatedly use hospital-based psychiatric services and under-use community mental health services, the authors used snowball sampling. They interviewed 112 homeless recidivists in San Francisco. The respondents gave low priority to community mental health services, tending to blame their hospital readmissions on lack of basic resources for survival (housing, money, job, food, and counseling). Based on the perspective of the homeless in their natural settings, the authors suggest that meeting the basic survival needs of the homeless mentally ill would increase the feasibility of their continuing care in the community.

Balser, B. H. "A Behavior Problem--Runaways." Psychiatric Quarterly, 13, 1939:539-557.
The author interviewed 300 runaways at the psychiatric clinic of the New York Travelers Aid Society. Not only children, but also young wives and mothers were interviewed. The author concludes that running away can be a positive step in problem solving. The peak year for running away is 17. The reasons these youths ran away include emotional factors in the home, broken homes, economic insecurity, physical and mental disorders, and the desire for adventure.

Barak, Gregg, and Robert M. Bohm. "The Crimes of the Homeless or the Crime of Homelessness? On the Dialectics of Criminalization, Decriminalization, and Victimization." <u>Contemporary Crises</u>, <u>13</u> (3), September 1989:275-288.

Using the homeless as a focus, the authors, who describe themselves as radical criminologists, "attempt to synthesize the older and newer trends in radical criminology--to integrate the issues of criminalization, decriminalization, and victimization." They view homelessness within the general framework of "trends in the developing political economy of welfare capitalism," especially the increased marginality and impoverishment of workers. They argue that "criminologists should...focus on efforts to 'criminalize' the condition of homelessness...." By this, they mean that we should establish "structural forces and government policies" that will eliminate homelessness for all who want a home. In contrast, we should "decriminalize most of the acts of survival of the homeless;" that is we should be tolerant, offer help, and avoid repression. Homelessness is attributed to four factors: (1) individual characteristics (alcoholism, mental illness, lack of marketable skills, (2) family disruption and lack of family support, (3) deinstitutionalization, and (4) market forces related to housing affordability.

Barbanel, Josh. "Alternatives to Despair: Private Shelters Hearten New York's Homeless." <u>New York Times</u>, March 13, 1988:17.

Detailing the approach used at B-nai Jeshurun, in which the homeless are treated with care and dignity, the authors point out that city shelters cost $30 a person a night to operate, while the volunteer labor at private shelters cuts direct costs to $2.60.

Barbanel, Josh. "Credibility of Homeless Woman Is Debated in Court." <u>New York Times</u>, November 28, 1987:10.

Court appointed attorneys for Joyce Brown, "the first person picked up on a new city program for the mentally ill homeless," argued that in spite of Miss Brown's living "in front of a hot air vent in Manhattan for nearly a year...and her use of the streets as a bathroom and her shouting at passers-by...the city had failed to prove she was either mentally ill or a danger to herself or anybody else."

Barbanel, Josh. "Homeless in New York Shelters Dip." <u>New York Times</u>, January 26, 1988:16.

The author reports that "each winter for the last decade the number of single people in shelters has surged ever higher. The city had forecast a peak of 11,700 this winter, a 10 percent increase over last year's total, in 25 shelters and six Bowery hotels. But, instead, an average of 250 fewer men turned up in the system in December than during the previous December." This decline could be caused by an "expansion of the present system or even the deaths and hospitalizations of shelter residents with AIDS."

Barbanel, Josh. "Homeless Lawyer on Drugs Finds a Safety Net in New York City Shelters." New York Times, July 5, 1988:Y14.
   A Scarsdale lawyer who was making $200,000 a year became homeless after drug abuse destroyed his professional and personal lives.

Barbanel, Josh. "Homeless Response." New York Times, December 17, 1988:11.
   The author examines why shelters fail the homeless. They are so bad that many homeless prefer to sleep in the city streets. The shelters are "part of the problem, not the solution...(for) huge shelters with mixtures of criminals, the mentally ill, addicts and other troubled people, are inherently unmanageable." The Mayor of New York City, Edward I. Koch, said that "many homeless people prefer the street to the shelters. Because their lack of motivation comes from drug addiction, alcoholism, mental disease of one form or another, we are dealing with the most difficult people, who have no support system." Due to pressure from the state government and from homeless advocates, the city has begun to reduce the size of its largest shelters, breaking them into smaller units.

Barbanel, Josh. "Homeless to Get Cash Grants." New York Times, January 20, 1988:1, 18.
   New York City is putting into effect a plan that will provide payments of $50 a month to single homeless people living in shelters. To quality for the money, single homeless people will have to identify themselves and "participate in employment or education programs, or, in some cases, in drug and alcohol rehabilitation." It is estimated that 10,000 single men and women are living in New York City's homeless shelters.

Barbanel, Josh. "Homeless Woman to Be Released After Being Forcibly Hospitalized." New York Times, January 19, 1988:15.

Joyce Brown, the first homeless person taken to a psychiatric hospital after being given a psychiatric evaluation on the streets, will be released from the mental hospital in which she has been incarcerated for 12 weeks. The treating physician made the decision because "a state judge had barred them from treating her with anti-psychotic drugs against her will."

Barbanel, Josh. "Hospitalizing Homeless Lags in New York City." New York Times, April 11, 1988:16.
    The author reviews the results of the first five months of a program initiated by Mayor Edward I. Koch to forcibly hospitalize mentally ill homeless people. Contrary to projections of 40 persons per month staying an average of 21 days at Bellevue, an average of 27 persons has been hospitalized each month with an average stay of 47 days. Arguments both for and against the program are summarized.

Barbanel, Josh. "Koch Orders Forced Sheltering of Homeless on Frigid Nights." New York Times, November 14, 1985:21.
    Briefly mentioned are deinstitutionalization, causes of homelessness, extent of the problem in New York City, civil rights, and the issues of choice and force.

Barbanel, Josh. "Koch Says Some Homeless Refused Shelter Offers." New York Times, November 20, 1984:B3.
    Briefly covered are people sleeping in welfare offices and emergency rooms, shelters, homeless families, and welfare hotels.

Barbanel, Josh. "New Psychiatric Ward To Aid Homeless Plan." New York Times, September 14, 1987:Y18.
    Mayor Koch of New York City has a plan to "remove severely mentally ill homeless people from the streets of Manhattan" to "a new psychiatric ward at Bellevue Hospital Center" for treatment in a single ward specializing in the homeless mentally ill. A diagram illustrates the steps to be taken following the apprehension of a mentally ill person on the street--their contact with community agencies, the police, outreach teams, and city shelters; the determination by a team of psychiatrists, nurses, and social workers evaluating the homeless person; their stay in Bellevue Hospital; and their exit from Bellevue into other forms of treatment or some type of discharge.

Barbanel, Josh. "New Shelter Set to Open for Homeless Veterans." <u>New York Times</u>, October 25, 1987:18.

A 275-bed shelter will open in Long Island City. It will probably be "the only emergency shelter in the country for homeless veterans....the shelter, to be run by the Salvation Army under contract to the city, will provide, for the most part, the same beds, meals, social work, health and medical care available in other city shelters, with additional counselling on veterans' benefits." The goal will be to "create a concept of the family," so that homeless veterans "will begin to look out for each other, to have a support group."

Barbanel, Josh. "New York Center Offers Homeless an Alternative." <u>New York Times</u>, May 10, 1988:15.

In order to discourage the homeless from loitering in the bus terminal, which makes many commuters uncomfortable, the Port Authority of New York and New Jersey has established a "drop-in center for the homeless" at Ninth Avenue and 41st street.

Barbanel, Josh. "New York City Proposes Using Ships as Shelters." <u>New York Times</u>, October 10, 1987:Y17.

The Koch administration is "seeking proposals for floating shelters for homeless adults to be built on surplus troop ships, ocean liners, oil rigs or barges and moored at waterfront piers. Each shelter would house 200 to 400 people in large dormitories or private cabins...If the idea is feasible, as many as six floating shelters will be commissioned next year." Although some thought this idea novel, Kim Hopper, an advocate for the homeless, points out that "the first municipal shelter known as Municipal Lodging House, was established in 1898 on a barge moored in the East River. Until that time, people with no place else to go had stayed at police station houses. During the 1930s, the two largest shelters were on piers at South Ferry and East 25th Street."

Barbanel, Josh. "New York Court Frees a Woman Taken Off Street." <u>New York Times</u>, November 13, 1987:1, 14.

A New York State judge ordered the release of Joyce Brown, the first person forcibly removed from the streets of New York under a plan instituted by the Koch Administration to incarcerate mentally ill homeless persons against their will. The author recounts the conflicting testimony of officials and psychiatrists who wanted to keep her incarcerated and those who wanted her freed.

Barbanel, Josh. "New York Homeless: Who They Are." <u>New York Times</u>, January 30, 1988:11.

Because the homeless are a diverse lot, it is deceptive to think of them as "disheveled, middle-aged alcoholics sprawled on the floor in Grand Central Terminal," for "beyond this world of doorways, benches and trash can fires in the night are thousands of homeless people who have never lived on the streets of New York." Perhaps the "only unifying elements" of the homeless are "drifting downward to a huge shelter system--from the homes of friends and relatives, from the hospitals, jails, foster homes and eviction proceedings." The author reports that "roughly one-third of the shelter population suffered from a mental illness, one-third had drug, alcohol or behavior problems that made them unable to work, and one-third were able-bodied and capable of holding a job....9 percent of single women in the shelters and 22 percent of the men had spent time in jail." Perhaps 7 to 10 percent of shelter residents are active users of crack. "The typical homeless family entering the system has two children, is headed by a mother in her late 20s and comes from a neighborhood where the poor are concentrated....Before becoming homeless, one-third of families typically had their own apartments, while others had moved frequently and were doubled up and had paid no rent." "For families who stay more than six months, the typical length of stay is a year, for those who stay less than six months, the typical stay is two months."

Barbanel, Josh. "New York Homeless Woman Rising Up From Anonymity." <u>New York Times</u>, February 15, 1988:15.

Joyce Brown, a former secretary from New Jersey, was the first homeless person forcibly hospitalized under the policy of the Koch Administration to hospitalize mentally ill homeless people against their will. This article reports on Miss Brown's life following her release from the hospital. She has become something of a media celebrity and has been "wined and dined" at some of New York's finest restaurants. She has also spoken about the life of the homeless to some of the area's law schools.

Barbanel, Josh. "New York Shifts Debate on Homeless Problem." <u>New York Times</u>, November 23, 1987:Y16.

Both the Koch Administration and advocates for the homeless want the city to "move from a situation where we are providing the basic necessities to a situation where we are providing an opportunity to get out of homelessness....The city's Human Resources Administration runs a shelter system that has an annual budget of more than $500 million....Under the city's plans, the unruly hotels that house families would be bought or leased by the city and turned into service centers in which the families would get intensive help to get organized and out on their own or into city renovated apartments. Specialized shelters would be set up for the elderly, young people, veterans, or mentally ill so each group can get the services it needs. Others would be assigned permanent places in adult homes or community residences....The city hopes to duplicate model transitional residences for homeless people operated by the Red Cross and the Henry Street Settlement House that provide a calm environment, intensive social work support, day care and other services." Critics reply that "the city's new plan does not go far enough towards creating permanent housing to end the problem."

Barbanel, Josh. "New York's Dilemma In Sheltering Homeless." New York Times, December 14, 1988:Y18.
    New York City will not use "the criminal laws, the courts and the police to deal with the homeless except in extreme situations." This stance is in line with court decisions that have struck down loitering laws and vagrancy ordinances that have been used to discriminate against the homeless. The author also reports on discriminatory laws and practices in Jacksonville, Florida, Atlanta, Georgia, and Phoenix, Arizona.

Barbanel, Josh. "Officials Oppose Federal Cuts In Aid for Homeless Families." New York Times, March 29, 1988:49.
    Government officials have severely criticized the rules proposed by the Reagan Administration to "cut emergency Federal Aid for homeless families."

Barbanel, Josh. "On Streets, Test for Homeless Policy." New York Times, November 15, 1985:15.
    Topics reviewed in this article include mental illness, hospitalization, individual rights versus community concerns, civil liberties, and the Mafia control of shelters.

Barbanel, Josh. "Societies And Their Homeless." New York Times, November 29, 1987:E1, E8.
    Controversy surrounds Joyce Brown, the first home-less person to be forcibly removed from the streets of

New York for treatment in a mental hospital. Miss Brown sued for the right to live on the streets and won that suit. Includes a summation of official reactions to the homeless in New York City from the early 1900s to 1920s. The author includes a summary of official reaction to the homeless in Tokyo, Paris, and West Germany. He also mentions "Greyhound therapy," getting rid of the homeless by giving them bus tickets to other cities.

Barbanel, Josh. "Terminal: Home for Hundreds." New York Times, January 9, 1988:1, 11.
　　The author reports that "across the country, bus terminals and train stations have become refuges for the homeless." Some homeless have settled permanently into Port Authority Bus Terminal. Some have televisions, while others "have public services delivered to their blanket." The Salvation Army delivers "soup, stew, coffee, cake, and fruit" to homeless people outside the terminal, while "the Coalition for the Homeless moves through the terminal handing out box lunches from large canvas rucksacks."

Barbanel, Josh. "Trying to Reach Francois: New York Seeks the Homeless." New York Times, October 31, 1987:10.
　　The controversy between those who advocate the forcible hospitalization of the mentally ill homeless and those who support the rights of these people to live when and how they wish is pinpointed by the detention of Francois, a male of indeterminate age who was taken from the streets of New York to a psychiatric ward at Bellevue.

Barbour, John. "Razing of Nation's Skid Rows Scatters Winos and Drifters." The Associated Press, February 7, 1987.
　　The author reports on the demise of skid rows across the country due to "commercial development and gentrification." Many skid row inhabitants, who chose to live in skid row as a sort of "low rent district," have now been dispersed "into that other shadowy community, called vaguely the homeless, the displaced, the under-educated, the out-of-but-seeking work, and those people released from mental institutions but still somewhere on the other side of reality."

Barden, J. C. "After Release from Foster Care, Many Turn to Lives on the Streets." <u>New York Times</u>, January 6, 1991:1.

Many of the homeless are young people who have been released from foster care without money or a supportive social network, and without having been taught skills to support themselves.

Barnes, Kerron R. "Sheltering the Homeless: Creating Permanent Housing." <u>Journal of Housing</u>, <u>46</u> (5), September-October 1989: 229-232.

A program in Orange County, New York, "involved private, county, state, and federal funding; utilized the resources of banks, non-profit agencies, and several county departments." Under this program, expected to produce 48 housing units within the next year, non-profit sponsors purchase scattered-site rental buildings containing two to four units. These units are then rented to clients of the department of social services at the rate paid for emergency (motel) housing for a period of eighteen months. The down payment and closing costs are provided through HUD community development funds. The mortgage principle is significantly reduced in the first eighteen months, at the end of which the apartment is rented at the Section 8 Fair Market Rent and still finances all expenses.

Barr, Peter B., Dinesh S. Dave, and Sammy Amin. "Perceptual Attitudes of a Charitable Organization: An Investigative Approach." <u>Health Marketing Quarterly</u>, <u>8</u> (3, 4), 1991:81-95.

The United Way reports that it needs to raise people's level of awareness of some of its activities. Among those activities is its outreach to the homeless.

Barringer, Felicity. "U.S. Homeless Count Is Far Below Estimates." <u>New York Times</u>, April 12, 1991:A11.

A count of the homeless by the U.S. Census Bureau tallied 230,000 homeless people nationwide.

Barron, James. "Bulldozers Leave Some Bereft, Some Relieved." <u>New York Times</u>, October 16, 1991:B2.

A tent city inhabited by about 200 homeless people was bulldozed in Alphabet City in Manhattan, New York. The author contrasts the difficulties the bulldozing creates for the homeless and the relief it brings other area residents.

Barron, James. "Cold Forces Reluctant Homeless Into Sometimes Dangerous Shelters." New York Times, December 13, 1988:1, 16.
   Boston and New York City officials are trying to protect the homeless from freezing weather by rounding them up on the streets and forcing them into city-run shelters.

Barron, James. "Convention Details Plans for Security." New York Times, May 24, 1992:35.
   This analysis of the security plan for the Democratic National Convention to be held in New York City's Madison Square Garden mentions that the homeless people living on nearby sidewalks are considered a security problem.

Barron, James. "Law on Rooms for Poor Is Voided in New York." New York Times, November 24, 1987:12.
   The author reviews reactions to the New York State Supreme Court decision ruling that "a New York City law that order the owners of vacant-single-room-occupancy hotels to rehabilitate them and rent the rooms to low-income tenants to be unconstitutional."

Barry, M., C. Wall, L. Shirley, et al. "Tuberculosis Screening in Boston's Homeless Shelters." Public Health Reports, 101 (5), September 1986:487-493.
   A screening of homeless people between February 1984 and March 1985 identified 26 people in Boston's homeless shelters as having tuberculosis. Because the homeless are at high risk of tuberculosis, intensive intervention and outreach efforts should be instituted.

Barsky, Neil. "In the New York Race, Front-Runner Dinkins Remains an Enigma." Wall Street Journal, October 27, 1989:A1, A6.
   This article on the 1989 mayoral race in New York City mentions that 50,000 residents of New York City have no homes.

Bartle, Ronald. "The Problem of the Vagrant Alcoholic." Justice of the Peace, 140, August 7, 1976:426-427.
   The author, a judge in London Municipal Court, reports that two unsatisfactory options are available for dealing with the vagrant alcoholic: imprisonment or release to a voluntary body. The government's plan to create detoxification centers will cost too much and they ought not to be voluntary. The solutions are compulsory

detention and treatment for a third conviction within six months.

Basler, Barbara. "Addicts and Vandals Troubling City Libraries." New York Times, July 11, 1981:1, 16.
    Patrons and librarians complain that former mental patients who have been dumped in the community now use the library as a place to stay during the day.

Basler, Barbara. "City Proposes 20 Emergency Shelters." New York Times, November 2, 1986:E7.
    Officials of New York City have come under attack for providing inadequate facilities for the growing numbers of homeless. Mayor Koch has proposed building 20 new shelters, which would increase the City's capacity to shelter the homeless from 4,500 to 6,000 families and from 9,000 to 10,000 single adults. Contains a table showing the numbers of families and individuals housed in New York City shelters and welfare hotels from 1981 to 1986.

Basler, Barbara. "11 Hotels for Homeless Face Foreclosure Move." New York Times, December 27, 1985:12.
    Hotels in Brooklyn and Queens that are used by the homeless, whose bills are paid by the city, are being foreclosed because of back taxes, water, and sewage bills.

Basler, Barbara. "Group Announces A Major Program for Homeless." New York Times, July 3, 1986:15.
    Temporary housing has been planned that will accommodate about one-fourth of the 4,100 homeless families in New York City. Private investors will be reimbursed in seven to nine years by the city and state for their purchase costs of buildings for the homeless.

Basler, Barbara. "The Homeless Found Haven on New York's Edge." New York Times, June 19, 1986:16.
    A 15-year-old boy was found dead at the site of an abandoned section of the elevated West Side Highway, where a few homeless individuals were living. A 46 year old man is the suspect.

Basler, Barbara. "Homelessness as a Ballot Box Issue." New York Times, May 11, 1986:E6.
    A drive is underway to put on the ballot a proposition that would require the city to provide shelter for

any homeless family. This would create a right that does not now exist, the right to adequate housing provided by the government. Although the courts have ruled that single men and women have the right to shelter, the city has refused to extend that right to families. Because 40,000 to 80,000 families in New York City now "double up," the city is concerned about costs.

Basler, Barbara. "Innovative Red Cross-Leased Hotel is a Haven for Homeless in New York." New York Times, February 3, 1986:14.
    The Red Cross has leased a tourist hotel, the Travel Inn, to show that the homeless can be given better shelter, with much better services, at less cost than the city pays at welfare hotels. For $64 a night, the Red Cross can provide a family of five not only shelter but also social workers, relocation assistance, a day care center, and after-school tutoring. The solution to the problem is to provide good quality emergency shelter with quality services, to stabilize families and get them out of the system.

Basler, Barbara. "Koch Seeks to Build 20 Shelters for Homeless." New York Times, October 30, 1986:17.
    The Mayor of New York City announced that the city would build 20 new shelters for the homeless, distributing them equitably among all five boroughs. Fifteen are to be family shelters, each with private rooms, and five adult shelters, each with 200 beds. The cost will run about $100 million.

Basler, Barbara. "Lead and Asbestos Hazards Cited in Shelter for Homeless." New York Times, March 11, 1986:19.
    The Legal Aid Society threatened to sue the city if it does not remove 300 people from a shelter that they say poses immediate health hazards due to lead and asbestos. The city denies the accusation.

Basler, Barbara. "Midtown Groups Seek to Bar More Homeless." New York Times, October 31, 1986:49.
    The administration of New York City faces "organized, well-financed and politically savvy opposition" to its policy of housing more than 1,000 homeless families in a handful of midtown hotels. Financed by real-estate interests, the opposition is coming from neighborhood residents, business interests, and the clergy. The opposition is focusing its argument on the increase in

crime since the homeless have been housed in this area, such as a greater number of robberies, assaults, and burglaries at the Prince George Hotel.

Basler, Barbara. "The Numbers Keep Growing As the City Struggles To Cope." New York Times, November 17, 1986:13.
    Twenty-five percent of the 27,000 homeless people sheltered by New York City are "chronically mentally ill," half are children in families headed by single women, "almost all of the 4,500 families in the shelter system are black or Hispanic, and nearly all are on welfare." The average age of the 9,500 single homeless men and women sheltered by the city is 35.

Basler, Barbara. "Offices Used as Shelter, Officials Say." New York Times, February 22, 1986:11.
    The Harlem Block Association, which was paid thousands of dollars a month to house homeless families, has been accused of putting the homeless up in office cubicles.

Basler, Barbara. "Owner Refuses to Convert Hotel to a Homeless Shelter." New York Times, September 18, 1986:19.
    The owner of the Collingwood Hotel in Manhattan, with whom New York officials had been negotiating, decided to keep his hotel open to tourists rather than to house 200 homeless families. The hotel is located in an area where merchants and residents are organizing to oppose the placement of more homeless.

Basler, Barbara. "Two City Shelters Set for Homeless." New York Times, February 15, 1986:12.
    New York City plans on transforming two armories into group shelters, where homeless men, women, and children will be housed in one large communal room, a plan opposed by the Coalition for the Homeless. A new city policy requires that families housed in welfare hotels either accept any permanent available apartment or move into a group shelter.

Basler, Barbara. "Two Shelters in New York Present Stark Contrasts." New York Times, November 16, 1985:11.
    The author compares the Fort Washington Men's Shelter in Manhattan with the Harlem Men's Shelter, supposedly a model shelter. She juxtaposes problems

faced by the homeless who stay in the shelters with problems they confront if they stay on the streets.

Bass, Paul. "Homeless: No Longer a Stereotype." <u>New York Times</u>, August 5, 1984:Section 23:1.
    This report on the Governor's Task Force on the Homeless poses shelters and low-income housing as solutions to the problem.

Bassuk, Ellen L. "Addressing the Needs of the Homeless." <u>Boston Globe Magazine</u>, November 6, 1983:12-13, 60, 62, 64, 66, 68, 70, 72, 74, 76, 78, 80.
    The causes of homelessness are unemployment, cuts in the federal budget, lack of low-cost housing, and deinstitutionalization. Although emergency shelters are a start to solving this problem, they neither address systemic ills nor provide long-range plans. About 40 percent of the homeless are psychotic who need protection, but who have been abandoned through deinstitutionalization to face tragic circumstances. The solution is an adequately managed and funded effective system of care and protection.

Bassuk, Ellen L. "Dr. Bassuk Replies." <u>American Journal of Psychiatry</u>, <u>142</u> (8), August 1985:997-998.
    The author defends the position she took in her article, "Is Homelessness a Mental Health Problem?" (with Lenore Rubin and Alison Lauriat, <u>141</u> (12), December 1984:1546-1550), against an attack by John F. Tanquary.

Bassuk, Ellen L. "The Feminization of Homelessness: Homeless Families in Boston Shelters." Speech given at Harvard Science Center, Cambridge, Massachusetts, June 11, 1985. Mimeo.
    Findings from interviews with 51 mothers and 78 children in six family shelters and two battered women's shelters in Boston show that the causes of the feminization of homelessness are a breakdown in family structure, poverty, the housing crisis, and reduced welfare benefits. The author summarizes characteristics of these families and emphasizes their emotional problems. Family shelters are only a stop-gap measure. The solutions are to connect families to appropriate available services; to offer effective parenting models, a childcare worker in each family shelter, group programs for mothers, a health care team, a child staffer who coordinates programs and links children to services, parent aides, day care, and transitional shelters; and to encourage coalitions,

advocacy for homeless families, and long-term planning. Emergency services combined with primary prevention are necessary to break the emergent cycle of intergenerational homelessness.

Bassuk, Ellen L. "Homeless Families: Single Mothers and Their Children in Boston Shelters." In The Mental Health Needs of Homeless Persons, Ellen L. Bassuk, ed. San Francisco: Jossey-Bass, 1986:45-53.
     After presenting background data on the characteristics of homeless families, the author reports on families in a Boston shelter. She stresses disorganization, abuse, and emotional problems; expresses concern about the development of emotional problems of the children in these families; and presents a case example.

Bassuk, Ellen L. "The Homelessness Problem." Scientific American 25 (1), 1984:40-45.
     This wide-ranging discussion of homelessness includes an estimate of their numbers, mental illness, meeting the needs of the mentally ill homeless, and causes of homelessness (unemployment, recession, low-cost housing, changes in benefits programs, changes in national policy for the mentally ill, and deinstitutionalization), as well as charts on housing, deinstitutionalization, and the median rent paid by low-income people.

Bassuk, Ellen L., ed. The Mental Health Needs of Homeless Persons. San Francisco: Jossey-Bass, 1986.
     This anthology of nine chapters focuses on the homeless who are deinstitutionalized, their shelter network and community support systems, homeless families, homeless battered women, homeless adolescents, and housing and sheltering the homeless.

Bassuk, Ellen L. "Research Perspectives on Homelessness: A Response to the APA Recommendations on the Homeless Mentally Ill." Psychosocial Rehabilitation Journal, 4, 1985:31-34.
     Although the American Psychiatric Association called for more research on the mental illness of the homeless, response is limited by a lack of knowledge about homeless persons and the methodological problems of current research findings. The solution is to utilize a comprehensive research strategy. Currently, we have only stop-gap measures, partly because we really do not wish to know about these people.

Bassuk, Ellen L. "Who Are the Homeless Families? Characteristics of Sheltered Mothers and Children." Community Mental Health Journal, 26 (5), October 1990:425-434.
     Descriptive data on 80 families with 155 children who were staying at 14 family shelters in Massachusetts show that the mothers have high rates of relocation, welfare, psychiatric symptoms, infant mortality, isolation, interpersonal conflict, substance abuse, illness, and divorce. Their children suffer from high rates of school failure and psychiatric symptoms.

Bassuk, Ellen L., and Ellen M. Gallagher. "The Impact of Homelessness on Children." Child and Youth Services, 14 (1), 1990:19-33.
     Based on interviews with 80 families living in shelters in Massachusetts, the authors explore how children are affected by growing up in shelters and welfare hotels. They also examine the coping devices these youngsters use.

Bassuk, Ellen L., et al. "Supplementary Statement on Health Care for Homeless People." Humanity and Society, 12 (4), November 1988:313-317.
     The nine authors, who served on the Committee on Health Care for Homeless Persons of the Institute of Medicine, wrote this supplemental statement because they felt that the original statement captured neither their shame and outrage nor the systemic nature of homelessness. Systemic solutions such as income maintenance, access to health care and supporting services, and housing, are needed if we are to solve the problem.

Bassuk, Ellen L., and H. Richard Lamb. "Homelessness and the Implementation of Deinstitutionalization." In The Mental Health Needs of Homeless Persons, Ellen L. Bassuk, ed. San Francisco: Jossey-Bass, 1986:7-14.
     The editor's introduction to the book stresses that negative attitudes about chronically mentally ill persons have led to their homelessness and underlie the resistance of communities and caregivers toward accepting the chronically mentally ill.

Bassuk, Ellen L., and Lenore Rubin. "Homeless Children: A Neglected Population." American Journal of Orthopsychiatry, 57 (2), April 1987:279-286.
     Interviews with 156 children living in 14 homeless shelters in Massachusetts uncovered developmental delays,

depression, anxiety, and learning difficulties.   About
half the children need psychiatric treatment.

Bassuk, Ellen L., Lenore Rubin, and Alison Lauriat.
"Characteristics of Sheltered Homeless Families."
American Journal of Public Health, 76 (9), September
1986:1097-1101.
     Interviews with 80 homeless mothers and 151 children
living in 14 family shelters in Massachusetts reveal that
these women had long histories of residential instability. Compared with the state average, twice as many had
been on AFDC for two years.   About two-thirds either
lacked or had minimal supportive relationships. About 15
percent of the children showed mental lags and anxiety,
depression, and learning difficulties.   The authors
recommend that the cycle of instability of family
breakdown be interrupted by comprehensive psychosocial
and economic interventions.

Bassuk, Ellen L., Lenore Rubin, and Alison Lauriat. "Is
Homelessness a Mental Health Problem?" American Journal
of Psychiatry, 141 (12), December 1984:1546-1550.
     The authors discuss changes in the population of
skid row and the characteristics of the homeless. A one-
day census of 27 skid-row facilities found that 91
percent of the homeless had serious mental illnesses.
The "hallmark" of the homeless mentally ill is social
isolation--a virtually total loss of connections to
family, friends, and social service agencies.

Bassuk, Ellen L., and Lynn Rosenberg. "Why Does Family
Homelessness Occur? A Case-Control Study." The American
Journal of Public Health, 78, July 1988:783-788.
     The authors compared 49 homeless female-headed
families with 81 housed female-headed families in Boston.
They found that "homeless mothers had more frequently
been abused as children and battered as adults and the
support networks were fragmented; the housed mothers had
female relatives and extended family living nearby whom
they saw often." They also found that "the frequency of
drug, alcohol, and serious psychiatric problems was
greater among the homeless mothers." They suggest that
the homeless mothers were "more vulnerable to the current
housing shortage because they lack support in time of
need." The solutions are "an increase in the supply of
decent affordable housing, income maintenance, and
assistance from social welfare agencies focused on
rebuilding supported relationships."

Bassuk, Ellen L., Rebecca W. Carman, Linda F. Weinreib, and Margaret M. Herzig. <u>Community Care for Homeless Families: A Program Design Manual</u>. Washington, D.C.: Interagency Council on the Homeless, 1990.
    This manual has five sections: (1) a description of the problem of family homelessness, (2) a discussion of community-based program development and family empowerment, (3) a summary of programs to meet basic needs (housing, job training and placement, supports to community and family, and health care), (4) an examination of the needs of children (educational and socio-emotional), and (5) an analysis of special needs (family violence, substance abuse, and psychiatric disorders).

Bassuk, Ellen L., and Samuel Gerson. "Deinstitutionalization and Mental Health Services." <u>Scientific American</u>, <u>238</u> (3), February 1978:46-53.
    The authors review the numbers of patients in mental hospitals from 1900 to 1975, the rates of hospitalization and admission from 1940 to 1975, the shift to outpatient services from 1955 to 1973, and the role of nursing homes in absorbing some of the deinstitutionalized patients. Proposed as solutions are national health insurance, an integrated system of direct services, providing places of asylum, and caution with new approaches to treatment.

Bassuk, Ellen L., William R. Breakey, Alan A. Fischer, Charles R. Halpern, Gloria Smith, Louisa Stark, Nathan Stark, Bruce Vladeck, and Phyllis Wolfe. "Supplementary Statement on Health Care for Homeless People." <u>Humanity and Society</u>, <u>12</u> (4), November 1988:313-317.
    The nine authors of this statement are members of the Committee on Health Care for Homeless Persons of the Institute of Medicine. With this supplementary statement, they intend to address what they feel are inadequacies in the committee's report, namely, a lack of emphasis on their heartfelt indignation about the problem, the systemic nature of homelessness, and the need of long-term strategies to address the systemic context with housing, income maintenance, support services, and access to health care.

Batchelor, Bronson. "The Hotel de Gink." <u>The Independent</u>, <u>81</u>, January 25, 1915:127-128.
    With New York suffering from the worst unemployment in its history, hobos are opening up a shelter for themselves.

Battle, Stanley F. "Homeless Women and Children: The Question of Poverty." Child and Youth Services, 14 (1), 1990:111-127.

 In reviewing the effects of poverty on homeless women and children, the author makes the case that we must address the problems of low birth weight, malnutrition, and inadequate housing. Neither political party is addressing these problems with any degree of competence.

Baumohl, Jim. "Alcohol, Homelessness, and Public Policy." Contemporary Drug Problems, 16 (3), Fall 1989:281-300.

 After providing a brief history of homelessness in the United States, with a focus on the public's reaction to the homeless, the author argues that "homelessness should not be reduced to a housing problem. While it is likely that living-wage jobs, adequate income supports, adequate child care, and affordable housing would shrink dramatically the size of the homeless population and prevent its further growth, which under current circumstances seems inevitable, for some among the homeless, material resources alone are not the answer. Homelessness is created in some part by a process of rejection and stigmatization rooted in reaction to behavior that is intolerable by the basic standards of our culture. In turn, this behavior often derives from alcoholism, drug addiction, major mental disorder, and the ways we manage such afflictions." He concludes, "given what seems to be the public's growing crankiness about homeless substance abusers and the remarkable propensity of American governments to build one prison after another, we must promote alternatives to massive institutionalization."

Baumohl, Jim, ed. Alcohol, Homelessness, and Public Policy. Special issue of Contemporary Drug Problems, 16 (3), Fall 1989.

 This special issue includes articles on the historical connection between alcoholism and homelessness, estimating the prevalence of drug problems among the homeless, the resettlement of homeless persons with drug problems, alcohol abuse by homeless adolescents, homelessness among participants in residential alcohol programs, housing models for recovery programs, and treatment and research with homeless alcoholics.

Baumohl, Jim. <u>Research Agenda: The Homeless Population with Alcohol Problems</u>. Rockville, Maryland: National Institute on Alcohol Abuse and Alcoholism, March 1987.
These six papers, presented at a conference sponsored by the National Institute on Alcohol Abuse and Alcoholism, report on the epidemiology of homelessness and alcohol abuse, review methodological issues, and stress that service implementation needs to take into account the diversity of the homeless population.

Baumohl, Jim, and Henry Miller. <u>Down and Out in Berkeley</u>. Berkeley: University of California, Community Affairs Committee, 1974.
The authors present a systematic descriptive portrait of street people in Berkeley, California, their demographic, familial, and individual backgrounds and lifestyles. Findings from self-administered questionnaires and interviews with 239 males and 56 females show that these street people tend to be white, ill educated, drawn from all over the United States (with some from Canada and Europe), unemployed, in poverty, drug experienced, veterans, and having arrest records. Most are willing to work, but are unskilled. The causes are family problems, limited psychological and intellectual equipage, and the realities of the labor market. Their survival techniques are scrounging, hustling, begging, and stealing. They are disabled both psycho-socially and occupationally. The long-term solution requires an alteration of the economic and occupational possibilities available to youth; the short-term solutions are to feed, house, and counsel them, and to provide for their medical needs.

Baxter, Ellen, and Kim Hopper. "The New Mendicancy: Homeless in New York City." <u>American Journal of Orthopsychiatry</u> <u>52</u> (3), July 1982:393-408.
The authors review changes in the size and composition of the homeless population of New York City. Any solutions, such as deinstitutionalization, that attempt to provide rehabilitation without safe and accessible shelter will fail. Clinicians should take an advocacy role because the therapeutic and social needs of the homeless are intimately linked.

Baxter, Ellen, and Kim Hopper. "Pathologies of Place and Disorders of Mind." <u>Health/PAC Bulletin</u>, <u>11</u> (4), March-April 1980:1-2, 6-12, 21-22.

The authors focus on the deinstitutionalized homeless, including their experiences in SROs, proprietary homes for adults, and the men's shelter in the Bowery. The background causes of homelessness include increased rents, reduced availability of low-income housing, and an increase in single-person households. The solutions proposed by state officials of increasing group shelters is inadequate. The homeless are experiencing a backlash by liberals. The authors take the position that shelter is a fundamental need, not a mental health service to be given or withheld on the basis of one's mental status.

Baxter, Ellen, and Kim Hopper. <u>Private Lives/Public Spaces: Homeless Adults on the Streets of New York City</u>. New York: Community Service Society, February 1981.

Stressing the magnitude of the homeless problem and the need for advocacy research and public and private shelters, the authors examine what life on the streets is like. The causes of homelessness are deinstitutionalization, the reduced availability of low-cost housing, unemployment, eviction, the withdrawal of family support, and failure of aftercare services. They recommend a series of immediate, short-term, long-term, and preventive measures.

Baxter, Ellen, and Kim Hopper. "Troubled on the Streets: The Mentally Disabled Homeless Poor." In <u>The Chronic Mental Patient: Five Years Later</u>, John A. Talbott, ed. Orlando: Grune and Stratton, 1984:49-62.

The authors present an overview of deinstitutionalization and attempts to estimate the proportion of the homeless who are in need of mental health services.

Bean, Gerald J., Mary E. Stefl, and Steven R. Howe. "Mental Health and Homelessness: Issues and Findings." <u>Social Work</u>, <u>32</u> (5), September-October 1987:411-416.

To test the idea that deinstitutionalization of mental patients and restrictive admission policies to psychiatric hospitals have contributed to the rising number of homeless Americans, the authors report findings from an epidemiological study of 979 homeless people in Ohio. They found that just under one-third of the sample was "in need of mental health services." They mention the interactive effects of mental illness and homelessness, how each contributes to the other.

Beard, John H., Rudyard N. Propst, and Thomas J. Malamud. "The Fountain House Model of Psychiatric Rehabilitation." Psychosocial Rehabilitation Journal, <u>5</u> (1), January 1982:47-53.
  The authors examine what is considered one of the most successful efforts to "create a restorative environment within which individuals who have been socially and vocationally disabled by mental illness can be helped to achieve or regain the confidence and skills necessary to lead vocationally productive and socially satisfying lives." The major components of this program are identified as: (1) the prevocational day program, (2) the transitional employment program, (3) the evening and weekend program (seven days a week), (4) the apartment program, (5) reach-out programs, (6) the thrift shop program, (7) clubhouse newspapers, (8) medication, psychiatric consultation, and health, and (9) evaluation and clubhouse accountability.

Beck, Frank O. <u>Hobohemia</u>. Rindge, New Hampshire: Richard R. Smith, 1956.
  This account of "the wonders, the beauties, and degradations of human nature" which the author discovered in his experiences of "low road" society includes many anecdotes about homeless people.

Becker, Alvin, and Herbert C. Schulberg. "Phasing Out State Hospitals--A Psychiatric Dilemma." <u>New England Journal of Medicine</u>, <u>294</u> (5), January 29, 1976:255-261.
  Phasing out state mental hospitals is feasible, but only if a network of community services is made available to the discharged patients. Without these, as is presently the case, the program is discredited and unlikely to succeed.

Beggs, L. <u>Huckleberry's for Runaways</u>. New York: Ballantine Books, 1969.
  The author, founder of this refuge for runaways, details procedures followed by Huckleberry's and San Francisco juvenile institutions, as well as the procedures Huckleberry uses for contacting and negotiating with families of runaways. He also includes descriptions of runaways and interviews with runaways and their families and stresses that running away is an S.O.S. signal--actually an attempt to change the situation, not simply to desert it. Accordingly, running away should be considered a family problem, not a police problem. To

adequately deal with this problem, we need to provide around the clock services.

Belcher, John R. "Adult Foster Care: An Alternative to Homelessness for Some Chronically Mentally Ill Persons." Adult Foster Care Journal, 1 (4), Winter 1987:212-225.
     A study of 132 seriously ill mental patients who were released into the community shows that many became homeless and illustrates the need for systematic after-care.

Belcher, John R. "Are Jails Replacing the Mental Health System for the Homeless Mentally Ill?" Community Mental Health Journal, 24 (3), Fall 1988:185-195.
     The author tracked 132 mental patients who were being released from acute care in a midwest state hospital. During the next six months, 47 became home-less. Twenty-three of the homeless were arrested and placed in jail. The author concludes that street life leads to impairment of cognitive and social functioning, as well as extreme difficulties in maintaining family relationships, a process that "contributes to further distancing from normative reality," to a "high level of frustration and confusion." This, in turn, leads to deviant activities, bringing individuals to the attention of the police. The author concludes that "homeless mentally ill persons are struggling to reintegrate themselves into the community, but they are also in need of structured supports as they seek to resolve that struggle."

Belcher, John R. "Exploring the Struggles of Homeless Mentally Ill Persons: A Holistic Approach to Research." Case Analysis, 2 (3), Fall 1988:220-240.
     Based on a study of 132 patients discharged from a mental hospital in Ohio in 1985, the author illustrates how field research can lead to in-depth understanding of the homeless mentally ill.

Belcher, John R. "Rights versus Needs: In Search of an Advocacy-Based Model of Intervention with Seriously Mentally Ill Homeless People." Arete, 13, 1, Summer 1988:7-15.
     Regarding the dilemma of individual rights versus intervention, the author argues for advocacy-based social work, meaning that social workers should try to commit the seriously mentally ill homeless to mental hospitals in order to restore their dignity. After treatment, they

can then exercise their individual rights. The author's conclusions are based on a field study of 132 patients discharged from a mental hospital in Ohio in 1985.

Belcher, John R. "Rights versus Needs of Homeless Mentally Ill Persons." Social Work, 37, September-October 1988:398-402.
　　Rights in conflict is the author's focus: the rights of the clients of social workers to their own self-determination versus the right of society to attempt to provide "potential mental restoration" for the homeless mentally ill. The ethical and moral dilemmas this conflict poses for social workers are discussed.

Belcher, John R., and Frederick A. DiBlasio. "The Needs of Depressed Homeless Persons: Designing Appropriate Services." Community Mental Health Journal, 26 (3), June 1990:255-266.
　　A sample of 61 homeless persons in an urban area in Maryland shows that depression is correlated with low self-esteem, food deprivation, family relations, goal orientation, health, drug abuse, previous mental hospitalizations, disabilities, and race. Social casework services for the homeless are inadequate if they do not meet the basic needs of the homeless and help them in goal attainment.

Belcher, John R., and Jeff Singer. "Homelessness: A Cost of Capitalism." Social Policy, 18, 4, Winter-Spring 1988:44-48.
　　The authors' thesis is that welfare state activities serve the "business interests of America by controlling the poor and providing them with such a minimal level of support that they may be forced to work for low wages and in hazardous conditions. Policies such as deinstitutionalization and programs such as Medical Assistance offer aid, but also act as a means to limit cost to an acceptable level of expenditure by the welfare state. For those who 'fall through the safety net,' and are thus of little value to business interests in America, the process of homelessness is a method of reducing government costs while providing an object lesson to other working persons." Maintaining unemployed workers represents huge costs that are shifted from businesses to the states. To solve this problem requires a holistic view of government policies, legislation to inhibit corporate mergers and businesses fleeing to overseas locations, central planning on economic matters, more

taxes on businesses to pay the unemployed, tax penalties
for businesses that refuse to provide information to
public agencies, steps designed to "increase the cost to
American businesses that conduct their affairs without
regard to the human cost of their decisions." In short,
the cost of making business decisions that increase
homelessness should be made "prohibitively expensive."

Belcher, John R., and Paul H. Ephross. "Toward an
Effective Practice Model For the Homeless Mentally Ill."
Social Casework, 70 (7), September 1989:421-427.
     The authors argue that social workers must be
flexible when dealing with the homeless mentally ill,
that they cannot simply link clients with existing
services but need to assume the role of advocate.
Social workers also need to recognize that the homeless
mentally ill are not "competent and rational citizens."
A model to meet the needs and realities of both the
deinstitutionalized mentally ill and the organizations
that treat them is proposed.

Belcher, John R., and Richard J. First. "The Homeless
Mentally Ill: Barriers to Effective Service Delivery."
Journal of Applied Social Sciences, 12 (1), Fall-Winter
1987-88:62-78.
     Within six months, 36 percent of 132 patients
discharged from a mental hospital in Ohio were homeless.
A system of community support services is needed.

Bell, Clark W. "The Homeless Need More Help." Modern
Health Care, January 6, 1989:21.
     The federal government needs to provide more money
for the health care of the homeless. Such action not
only will alleviate human suffering but, ultimately, will
also cut the cost of indigent care.

Beller, Janet. Street People. New York: Macmillan,
1980.
     This book of pictures and short prose, intended to
let street people tell why they are doing what they are
doing, reveals that only some of the people who spend
their time on the streets of New York City are homeless.

Bence, Evelyn. "Two Kinds of Thanks." Christianity
Today, 31, January 16, 1987:34.
     The author reports on her feelings after spending an
evening in a shelter for homeless women.

Benda, Brent B. "Crime, Drug Abuse and Mental Illness: A Comparison of Homeless Men and Women." Journal of Social Service Research, 13 (3), 1990:39-59.
    In 1985 and 1986, 444 homeless persons were interviewed in Richmond, Virginia. During the past year, homeless men drank more often and were arrested for crime more frequently, while homeless women attempted suicide more often and suffered more anxiety attacks. No gender differences, however, were noted in psychiatric hospitalizations, current hallucinations, or drug use. The author suggests that a "drift down" theoretical approach has utility because the findings show that homelessness is often "a recent stage in a long evolving series of afflictions that date back to childhood (psychiatric ills, substance abuse, and crime), and not the result of unique crises."

Benda, Brent B. "Crime, Drug Abuse, Mental Illness, and Homelessness." Deviant Behavior, 8 (4), 1987:361-375.
    Interviews with 345 homeless men in Richmond, Virginia, support the "drift down" hypothesis of homelessness. Personal experiences such as drug use, for example, preceded hospitalization for mental problems.

Benda, Brent B., and Patrick Dattalo. "Homeless Women and Men: Their Problems and Use of Services." Affilia, 5 (3), Fall 1990:50-82.
    Interviews with a sample of 444 homeless persons in Richmond, Virginia, indicate that the roads to homelessness differ according to gender. Women are more likely to become homeless after years of abuse of nonprescription drugs, while the path for men is likely to be crime and alcohol abuse. The authors propose social policies based on the feminist perspective.

Bendiner, Elmer. The Bowery Man. New York: Thomas Nelson, 1961.
    Based on on-site informal interviewing and making liberal use of colorful characters and situations, the author attempts to recount the history and offer a "flavor" of the Bowery.

Benedict, Annette, Jeffrey S. Shaw, and Leanne G. Rivlin. "Attitudes toward the Homeless in Two New York City Metropolitan Samples." Journal of Voluntary Action Research, 17 (3-4), July-December 1988:90-98.
    Questionnaires from 224 urban and suburban residents of New York City reveal little difference in attitudes

toward the homeless. Although most felt the problem had worsened in recent years, respondents did not favor locating a shelter for the homeless in their own neighborhoods. Those who had given money to the homeless expressed more favorable attitudes.

Bennet, James. "Arson at Manhattan Bridge Shanties Leaves One Dead." New York Times, May 31, 1992:31.
    An elderly homeless man died in a fire in a lower Manhattan shantytown. The cause of the fire was arson.

Bennet, James. "Homeless Man Set Afire on Bronx Subway Train." New York Times, March 27, 1992:B3.
    In New York City's Bronx, a 39-year old homeless man was severely burned as he slept on a subway train. Four teenagers, not yet apprehended, are suspected of setting him on fire.

Bennet, James. "Trial Will Test Limits of Culpability in a Slaying." New York Times, May 3, 1992:41.
    The author reviews the legal theory that underlies the charges against fifteen New York City youths who are accused of beating homeless people on Wards Island. One homeless man was beaten to death.

Bennett, Amanda. "Lori Schiller Emerges From the Torments of Schizophrenia." Wall Street Journal, October 14, 1992:A1, A8.
    This overview of one person's journey "to hell and back," mentions that many schizophrenics who are released from institutions join the ranks of the homeless.

Benson, Ben (Hobo). Hoboes of America: Sensational Life Story and Epic of Life on the Road. New York: Hobo News, 1942.
    Written by the man elected King of the Hobos at the 1941 hobo convention in Britt, Iowa, this account provides an insider's view of hobo life.

Benton, Sarah. "Shut up, Nobody's Listening." New Statesman, 115, January 8, 1988:21-23.
    In reviewing the political lobbies that were behind the changes in the Social Security Act of Great Britain, the author analyzes the role of the "voluntary sector" as a "poverty lobby."

Berger, Joseph. "Friars Give Refuge to Homeless Men." New York Times, December 28, 1985:11.

The author discusses the "Waldorf" of shelters, St. Christopher's Inn of Garrison, New York.

Berger, Joseph. "Many Homeless at P.S. 194: Happily, It's Hard to Notice." New York Times, February 23, 1991:A29.
On the positive side, the homeless children who attend Public School 194 in Harlem, New York, get along well with their classmates. On the negative side, their homelessness prevents them from taking part in extracurricular activities, and they receive little or no medical care.

Berk, Richard L. "Conservatives Urge Bush to Act on Homeless." New York Times, December 12, 1988:8.
Politicians are increasingly coming to recognize that homelessness is a serious problem. One consequence is pressure on the Reagan Administration to initiate action to solve the problem. Political conservatives dislike Mitch Snyder, a "nationally known spokesman for the homeless."

Berk, Richard L. "Girding for Bid to Count Homeless." New York Times, December 16, 1988:Y14.
The author summarizes the plans of the U.S. Census Bureau to conduct a national census of the homeless in the United States, along with criticisms leveled against those plans.

Berk, Richard L. "Kemp Vows Effort on 'Appalling' Homelessness." New York Times, January 28, 1989:7.
Jack F. Kemp, testifying at the congressional hearing for his confirmation as head of H.U.D., said that "homelessness is a national tragedy of appalling proportions," and he promised to make homelessness his "top priority." Kemp's testimony was interrupted by six demonstrators from an advocacy group for the homeless, who shouted that his policies as a Congressman "have hurt the homeless."

Berkow, Ira. "Ray Felix Is Not Forgotten." New York Times, August 1, 1991:B9.
This article profiles Ray Felix, former basketball star with the New York Knickerbockers, who at his death was the director of Harlem One, a shelter for the homeless.

Berman-Rossi, Toby, and Marcia B. Cohen. "Group Development and Shared Decision Making: Working with Homeless
Mentally Ill Women." <u>Social Work with Groups</u>, <u>11</u> (4),
1988:63-78.
The author reviews a five-year program in which
mentally ill women in a single room occupancy hotel were
motivated toward rehabilitation through personal empowerment.

Berreby, David. "Shelter From the Storm." <u>The National
Law Journal</u>, <u>4</u> (40), June 14, 1982:1, 35-36.
Robert Hayes, a former wealthy Wall Street lawyer
who became a full time advocate for the homeless, is
profiled.

Besser, James David. "The Skid Row Explosion." <u>The
Progressive</u>, <u>39</u>, October 1975:51-53.
The recession has forced a massive wave of newcomers
onto skid row. There are four types of newcomers: the
elderly poor, the youths with no prospects, those for
whom hard times have transformed ordinary problems into
emotional monsters (such as an unemployed father deserting his family so they can get welfare), and the deinstitutionalized. The author mentions tension between old
timers and newcomers, and adaptation to skid row subculture (getting used to dependence) that closes off
alternatives.

Bibby, Reginald W., and Armand L. Mauss. "Skidders and
Their Servants: Variable Goals and Functions of the Skid
Road Rescue Mission." <u>Journal for the Scientific Study
of Religion</u>, <u>13</u>, 1974:421-436.
This analysis of a Seattle mission concludes that
although official objectives remain unrealized, the
mission continues because it meets the leaders' personal
goals.

Bigart, Homer. "Grim Problems of the Bowery Complicate
Clean-Up Drive." <u>New York Times</u>, November 20, 1961:1,
36.
Because housing developments are impinging on the
Bowery and the city plans to eliminate skid row, real
estate prices have risen. The Mayor of New York City
says that 12,000 homeless people who live on the Bowery
must be resettled. To do so will require housing for the
aged, work for the employable, and physical and mental
services. The author recounts citizen reactions to
derelicts and describes street scenes.

Bijlani, H. U. "Strategies for Urban Shelter: The Improvement of Slums, Squatter Settlements, and Sites-and-Services." Habitat International, 12 (4), 1988:45-53.

The author describes a "sites-and-services" strategy for developing urban land to meet shelter needs of the homeless and near-homeless in India.

Billig, N., and C. Levinson. "Homelessness and Case Management in Montgomery County, Maryland: A Focus on Chronic Mental Illness." Psychosocial Rehabilitation Journal, 11 (1), July 1987:59-66.

Case managers who serve the mentally ill of Montgomery County, Maryland, visit shelters in order to develop trusting relationships with homeless clients. Five case management tools are used: assessment, goal setting, linkage, monitoring, and advocacy.

Binder, Rudolph M. "The Treatment of Beggars and Vagabonds in Belgium." Journal of Criminal Law and Criminology, 6, March 1916:835-848.

In this analysis of legislation and penal colonies designed to suppress begging and vagabondage, the author summarizes the conditions and regulations of poorhouses and workhouses. The proposed solutions are to prevent the propagation of the unfit, to teach people the value of work, to provide the opportunity to learn a trade and get an education, and to improve economic conditions so men can work.

Bingham, Richard D., Roy E. Green, and Sammis B. White, eds. The Homeless in Contemporary Society. Newbury Park: Sage Publications, 1987.

This book contains 15 articles by 20 authors whose backgrounds range from university professors to politicians and policy planners. The seven articles in the first part, intended to provide a background understanding of homelessness, examine the history of homelessness in the United States, problems with counting the homeless, the need to develop a national perspective, homeless veterans, homeless women and children, the deprivations faced by the homeless, and the relationship of housing to homelessness. The second part focuses on policy and program options. Its eight articles deal with religious and nonprofit organizations, a national health care program, approaches taken in Los Angeles, Portland, and the state of New York, the federal role in the United States, and third world solutions. By comparing homelessness in the United States with that in other parts of the world, the book closes with a broad perspective.

Birch, Eugenie Ladner, ed. <u>The Unsheltered Woman: Women and Housing in the 80's</u>. New Brunswick: Center for Urban Policy Research, 1985.

The 20 selections in this anthology on gender-related housing are intended to trace the effects on housing policy and practice of what the authors call "the demographic revolution." The articles are organized into three parts: identifying the unsheltered woman and her needs, planning for the unsheltered woman, and implementing plans for housing the unsheltered woman. The book also contains an introduction, an epilogue, a bibliography, an index, two appendices on gender-related housing problems, and 129 "exhibits" (tables, photos, and diagrams). The following topics are featured: female-headed families, the elderly, living arrangements, housing preferences, aspirations, housing designs, single parents, single rooms, shared housing, rehabilitation projects, architectural innovations, and financing. Not all the articles focus on unsheltered women: For example, there is a selection on executive women.

Bird, David. "Franciscans Who House the Homeless Find Spending \$2 Million Is a Challenge." <u>New York Times</u>, July 6, 1985:10.

Money from New York City's legal settlement with Harry Macklowe, a real estate developer who illegally demolished a Times Square welfare hotel, has been given to a society of St. Francis of Assisi. The author examines how the Franciscans run their shelters, especially their attempts to establish a family-like atmosphere, few rules (no drinking, no fighting), and a tenant's council.

Birnbaum, Jeffrey H. "Some Lawmakers Go Homeless for a Night, Don't Like It Much." <u>Wall Street Journal</u>, March 5, 1987:1, 16.

This report on "The Grate American Sleep-Out" organized by "Mitch Snyder, a homeless-aid advocate," focuses on the experiences of Congressmen who participated in this event.

Bishop, Katherine. "After 41 Years, a Deserter Is in U.S. Custody." <u>New York Times</u>, April 20, 1991:A7.

Big Brother never forgets. A 68-year old homeless man was arrested in San Francisco, California, for deserting from the military--forty-one years ago during the Korean War.

Bishop, Katherine. "Homeless Are Greeted With Food for Psyche." New York Times, July 9, 1989:8.
        The author profiles Sarah Howard, a psychological counselor hired by the Downtown Merchants Association of San Rafael, California, "as a roving dispenser of self-esteem to the approximately 150 homeless people who appear to be living there."

Bishop, Katherine. "In Death He Finds a Home in Hearts." New York Times, December 7, 1988:10.
        The author reports on the death and memorial service of a homeless man in San Francisco, Joseph Emerson Eaton, Jr., "the 38-year-old son of prominent Massachusetts family."

Bishop, Katherine. "Plan Aims to Insure That Beggars Don't Put Cash in Wrong Pockets." New York Times, July 26, 1991:A10.
        To prevent homeless beggars in Berkeley, California, from using their donations to buy drugs and alcohol, a program has been set up that allows people to give them vouchers that can be used only for food and service.

Bishop, Katherine. "The Tenderloin Times Finds a Voice." New York Times, May 7, 1987:Y14.
        A newspaper, "The Tenderloin Times," reports on matters of interest to those living in the Tenderloin district of San Francisco. Because this paper includes items such as the lack of heat in some residential hotels for the homeless, it is read enthusiastically by many homeless.

Bishop, Katherine. "Tent Cities Becoming the Front Lines." New York Times, 138, September 11, 1989:A14.
        This examination of "the new militancy of the homeless and their growing tendency to form communities" looks at various tent camps that have sprung up around the nation. Because these camps are "an eyesore," political pressure has grown to remove them.

Bishop, Kathryn Porter. Soup Lines and Food Baskets: A Survey of Increased Participation in Emergency Food Programs. Washington, D.C.: The Center on Budget and Policy Priorities, May 1983.

"This first nationwide survey of private non-profit agencies that operate emergency food programs," which presents findings from a sample of 16 food banks, including 425 agencies and 160 organizations, focuses on the increase in programs and costs.

Bittner, Egon. "The Police on Skid-Row: A Study of Peace Keeping." American Sociological Review, 32 (5), October 1967:699-715.
    The patrolman's conception of the social order of skid-row life helps to determine their procedures of control. To manage their peace-keeping, they utilize an aggressively personalized approach, attenuated regard for questions of culpability, and coercion.

Bjorkman, Frances Maule. "The New Anti-Vagrancy Campaign." Review of Reviews, 37, February 1908:206-211.
    Americans do not realize the extent of the tramp problem. The solution is to conduct a national anti-tramp crusade that will make it more uncomfortable to be a loafer than to be a worker. The Massachusetts program of jail confinement with hard labor and requiring work in return for staying in municipal lodging-houses is exemplary. Tramps need to be saved for their own sake, while society needs to be protected from the evil of tramps.

Black, Jack. You Can't Win. New York: Macmillan, 1927.
    This autobiography of a reformed thief and burglar contains graphic descriptions of tramp life in the 1890s.

Blackburn, Madeleine C. "A Health Profile of Homeless vs Non-Homeless Families in Central London." Health Visitor, 54 (9), September 1981:364-365.
    After conducting a year of intensive health visits with homeless families in the Camden District of London, the author concluded that the health profiles of these families were not different from a control group. Although this could mean that the homeless have no particular need of intensive health visits, the author suggests that the findings were due to concentrated health visits with the control group during the previous year.

Blacker, Edward, and David Kantor. "Half-Way Houses for Problem Drinkers." Federal Probation, 24, June 1960:18-23.

Based on a survey of 30 halfway houses in the United States and Canada, the author details the ideal halfway house: small numbers, sobriety required, employment that allows each to pay his own way, and a therapeutic environment (group therapy, religious and vocational counseling, and meetings of Alcoholics Anonymous). The current success rate appears to be about 35 percent.

Blair, Gwenda. "Saint Mitch." Esquire, 106, December 1986:222-231.
This summary of the background and activities of Mitch Snyder, the foremost member of the Community for Creative Non-Violence focuses on his 33-day fast that culminated in the Washington, D.C., city government providing $5 million for repairs to rehabilitate the shelter for the homeless run by Snyder.

Blakeman, Eleanor Greenleaf. "The Sailors' Snug Harbor." The Altruist Interchange, 4 (3), 1896:12-14.
Robert Richard Randall, in a will drawn by Alexander Hamilton, provided the bulk of his estate for homeless sailors. Built in 1831, this home provides a library, a reading room, private lockers, and dignity in a religious atmosphere. All residents are required to work.

Blankertz, Laura E., Ram A. Cnaan, Kalma White, Jim Fox, and Karlyn Messinger. "Outreach Efforts with Dually Diagnosed Homeless Persons." Families in Society, September 1990:387-395.
"Dually diagnosed" homeless persons are homeless people with "severe mental health problems and drug and alcohol abuse." Such persons "often fall between the cracks of the mental health and substance-abuse service systems." The authors provide an outreach model for dually diagnosed homeless persons. They base their model upon a framework of symbolic interactionism in order to attempt to understand the world of homeless persons and the meanings the homeless attach to themselves, the physical space around them, others with whom they interact, and service system providers. The authors suggest that symbolic interactionism provides the key to establishing good outreach efforts to the homeless, and is especially valuable in the critical engagement phase.

Blasi, Gary L. "Rights of the Homeless: Litigation Concerning Homeless People." Public Law Forum, 4 (433), Spring 1985:433-443.

The author, a lawyer, reviews his experiences in litigation that affects the rights of homeless people to shelter. He concludes that communities go through five stages in addressing problems of the homeless: (1) denial, (2) rejection, (3) studying the problem, (4) taking action, and (5) reevaluation.

Blasi, Gary L. "Social Policy and Social Science Research on Homelessness." Journal of Social Issues, 46 (4), 1990:207-219.
In this introductory article to this journal's special issue on homelessness, the author concludes that social scientists should spend less time studying the characteristics of the homeless and, instead, "turn the instruments of their science around, to look at the wider society and the elites who make social policy in this country."

Blatchly, Charles K. "A State Farm for Tramps and Vagrants." Survey, 24, April 9, 1910:87-89.
A New York bill would establish a compulsory labor colony for tramps.

Blau, Joel S. "The Limits of the Welfare State: New York City's Response to Homelessness." Journal of Sociology and Social Welfare, 16 (1), March 1989:79-91.
As illustrated by the policies in New York City, the welfare state is limited by the need to attract and maintain business. Yet business interests do not dominate, for the welfare state also retains relative autonomy. From the perspective of conflict theory, social policy for the homeless can be viewed as a reproduction of the labor force.

Blau, Joel S. "On the Uses of Homelessness: A Literature Review." Catalyst, 6 (2), 1988:5-25.
The author's review of the literature on the homeless over the past century identifies six chronological categories that, reflecting changing economic and political conditions, reveal shifting ideologies about the causes and cures of homelessness.

Blau, Raphael David. "Magnificent Hobo." Holiday, 18, December 1955:178, 180-183, 185.
The author provides a humorous account of General Daniel Pratt, G.A.T. (Great American Traveler), a well-traveled hobo who would lecture to Dartmouth and Yale students utilizing large words in non-sequiturs.

Bliss, Robert R. "Providing for the Needy." New York Times, September 11, 1988:30.
     The Worcester Committee on Homelessness and Housing has been successful in its efforts to construct apartments for the homeless.

Block, Marvin A. "A Program for the Homeless Alcoholic." Quarterly Journal of Studies on Alcohol, 23, December 1962:644-649.
     The author's thesis is that the solution to the rehabilitation of homeless alcoholics is to use agencies. By agencies, the author means in-hospital services, outpatient clinics, foster homes, half-way houses, rehabilitation centers, permanent supervision, and state hospitals, all of which need to utilize a core of trained professionals.

Blood, L., and R. D'Angelo. "A Progress Research Report on Values Issues in Conflict Between Runaways and Their Parents." Journal of Marriage and the Family, 36, 1974:486-491.
     Based on a pilot study in Ohio in which 60 runaways were compared with 50 non-runaways, the authors found that the major factors that differentiated the runaways from the non-runaways were: on the part of the parents--not expressing love and affection and lack of respect for the children's ideas; on the part of the children--unhappiness and low self-esteem and a feeling that their parents do not listen to them.

Bloom, Marc. "The Homeless Drive Teen Age Athletes Into the Cold." New York Times, January 16, 1988:15.
     The 102d Engineers Armory in Washington Heights, owned by New York State and used by the National Guard, has been turned into a city-operated shelter for the homeless, housing up to a thousand men during the winter. This has caused resentment because high school track teams that used to use the Armory for practice must now practice outside.

Blum, Howard. "Creedmoor Homeless Plan Disputed." New York Times, December 6, 1983:B4.
     A dispute about relative responsibility has arisen between the New York state and city governments because homeless people are turned away from hospitals and shelters.

Blum, Jeffrey D., and Judith E. Smith. <u>Nothing Left to Lose: Studies of Street People</u>. Boston: Beacon Press, 1972.
    The authors present case studies, with analytical commentary, of 33 homeless persons who stayed at The Sanctuary in Boston.

Blumberg, Leonard U., Irving Shandler, and Thomas E. Shipley, Jr. "The Philadelphia Skid Row Project: An Action-Research Program." In <u>Sociology in Action: Case Studies in Social Problems and Directed Social Change</u>, Arthur B. Shostak, ed. Homewood, Illinois: The Dorsey Press, 1966:158-165.
    The authors review a pilot project in Philadelphia that is designed to relocate men from skid row. They discuss the program's ideology, development of an image, role-related relationships, social power, and the significance of power phenomena.

Blumberg, Leonard U., and Thomas E. Shipley, Jr. "Follow-up of the Philadelphia Skid-Row Project." In <u>Putting Sociology to Work: Case Studies in the Application of Sociology to Modern Social Problems</u>, Arthur B. Shostak, ed. New York: David McKay, 1974:83-93.
    The authors report on their follow up interviews with skid row men. To do "action research" (today called applied sociology) is difficult and time consuming: One must especially be wary of fudged data provided by organizations. Although individuals who have life experiences similar to clients make desirable personnel, to get competent workers may require undesirable trade-offs. The authors raise questions of the significance of applied sociology and its relationship to traditional university positions.

Blumberg, Leonard U., Thomas E. Shipley, Jr., and Irving W. Shandler. "The Homeless Man and Law Enforcement Agencies." <u>Prison Journal</u>, <u>45</u> (1), 1965:29-35.
    Based on 2,249 interviews with homeless men in Philadelphia, the authors report on the men's history of conflict with the law. They hypothesize that the criminal involvement of homeless men is higher than that of the general population, but have no control data to support their assumption.

Blumberg, Leonard U., Thomas E. Shipley, Jr., and Irving W. Shandler. "Seven Years on Skid Row: Diagnostic and Rehabilitation Center/Philadelphia." In <u>Creating Social</u>

Change, Gerald Zaltman, Philip Kotler, and Ira Kaufman, eds. New York: Holt, Rinehart, and Winston, 1972:429-437.

The authors discuss topics related to the men of skid row: ideology, image, role-related relationships, power structure, and institutional-organizational trends. To be successful in helping skid row men, program participants need to focus on program problems, not the ideology of their own disciplines. Action without research is a treadmill, and research without action neglects important human values.

Blumberg, Leonard U., Thomas E. Shipley, Jr., and Irving W. Shandler. Skid Row and Its Alternatives: Research and Recommendations from Philadelphia. Philadelphia: Temple University Press, 1973.

Discussed here are conditions of skid row, drinking, alcoholism, police and courts, exploitation employment, death, and the men's self identification. The proposed solutions are halfway houses, rehabilitation, counseling, and programs.

Blumberg, Leonard, Thomas E. Shipley, Jr., Irving W. Shandler, and Herman Niebuhr. "The Development, Major Goals and Strategies of a Skid Row Program: Philadelphia." Quarterly Journal of Studies on Alcohol, 27 (2), June 1966:242-258.

The authors report on a program designed to relocate and rehabilitate residents of skid row and at the same time avoid creating a new skid row. Their conclusions are based on interviews with 2,249 men on skid row. The solutions they suggest are to teach skid row men how to use the opportunities available in the wider community and "limited optimal discrepancy," a basic orientation of how to approach skid row problems. They argue that it is possible to eliminate skid-rows and alcoholism through a political process.

Blumberg, Leonard U., Thomas E. Shipley, Jr., and Joseph O. Moor, Jr. "The Skid Row Man and the Skid Row Status Community: With Perspectives on their Future." Quarterly Journal of Studies on Alcohol, 32, 1971:909-941.

In this analysis of skid row as a community, these characteristics of skid row men are examined: powerlessness, employment, victimization, status, reciprocity, jargon, community identification, and relationship to the larger community. Several policy recommendations are suggested.

Blumberg, Leonard U., Thomas E. Shipley, Jr., and Stephen F. Barsky. <u>Liquor and Poverty: Skid Row as a Human Condition</u>. New Brunswick, New Jersey: Rutgers Center of Alcohol Studies, 1978.

This overview of skid rows in the United States, with a focus on San Francisco, Philadelphia, and Detroit, discusses the origins of skid row, attempts at redevelopment, blacks and women, and wanderers. The author emphasizes that skid row is a social institution that interacts with the larger society, that there are skid row-like people throughout our metropolitan areas, and suggests solutions for bringing the residents of skid row back into the "normal political and social mainstream."

Blumstock, Robert. "Going Home: Arthur Koestler's Thirteenth Tribe." <u>Jewish Social Studies</u>, <u>48</u> (2), Spring 1986:93-104.

The author discusses how Arthur Koestler uses homeless in the sense of an intellectual who does not feel rooted, but is intellectually wandering" in search of self-identity.

Boffey, Phillip M. "Homeless Plight Angers Scientists." <u>New York Times</u>, September 20, 1988:1, 12.

Ten of the 13 members of a panel, the Committee on Health Care for Homeless People, which was "convened by the National Academy of Sciences to study health needs of the homeless," have protested that the bland form of reporting that they were required to follow "made it impossible to voice our sense of shame and anger over the plight of the homeless."

Bogner, Jacque. "Kiwanians Turn Lodge Into Temporary Home." <u>Kiwanis Magazine</u>, October 1985:41.

The cause of homelessness is the economic system: high rents, underemployment, and unemployment. Kiwanian work with the homeless is highlighted by focusing on Bob Hughes, who runs a shelter.

Bogue, Donald J. <u>Skid Row in American Cities</u>. Chicago: Community and Family Study Center, 1963.

This summary of the results of a 1957-58 survey conducted by the National Opinion Research Center contains maps of skid rows in 41 cities. Skid row has seven types of inhabitants: the elderly, physically disabled, resident workingmen, migratory workers, bums, criminals, and alcoholics. The author reports on their typical day, their work, drinking, illness, migration, recreation, religion, and family background, and makes 12 suggestions on how to eliminate skid row.

Boorstin, Robert O. "Guest of Soviet Back With Plea For More Homes." New York Times, September 1, 1986:L27.
    Joseph Mauri, who played a homeless person in "The Man from Fifth Avenue," a Soviet television documentary focusing on economic inequality in the United States, returns from a visit to the Soviet Union.

Borg, Stefan. "Homeless Men: A Clinical and Social Study with Special Reference to Alcohol Abuse." Acta Psychiatrica Scandinavica, Supplementum 276, 1978:11-90.
    This study of 158 men who visited the Bureau for Homeless Men in Stockholm in 1969 and 1970 reports their age, results of chemical tests, housing condition, marital status, occupational histories, economic condition, social histories (education, family, drunkenness offenses, criminality) and mortality. It also contains a history of the homeless in Sweden, as well as individual life histories.

Borus, Jonathan F. "Deinstitutionalization of the Chronically Mentally Ill." New England Journal of Medicine, 305 (6), August 6, 1981:339-342.
    These myths surround deinstitutionalization: mental hospitals are harmful and are not needed, the public wants deinstitutionalization, outpatient treatment is needed, the costs of treating the mentally ill will be reduced, and someone else is responsible for these patients. Deinstitutionalization is actually a political solution to a problem, not a medical solution: It may well be followed by another remedy--reinstitutionalization.

Botkin, B. A., ed. The American People: In Their Stories, Legends, Tall Tales, Traditions, Ballads and Songs. London: Pilot Press, 1946:322-325.
    This account of American folk culture contains two hobo songs, "The Big Rock Candy Mountain" and "Pie in the Sky."

Botkin, B. A., and Alvin F. Harlow, eds. A Treasury of Railroad Folklore: The Stories, Tall Tales, Traditions, Ballads and Songs of the American Railroad Man. New York: Crown, 1953.
    This collection of 263 items contains 11 pieces on hobos.

Bottorff, Sara. "City Council Triples Shelters for Homeless Over Protest." The Los Angeles Daily Journal, January 26, 1987:B1.
The week after Mayor Tom Bradley decided that Los Angeles could not allow the homeless in city buildings due to "massive liability problems," four street people died of cold-related ailments. The city council then announced that it was expanding its facilities to shelter the homeless.

Bottorff, Sara. "L.A. City Council Opens Its Doors To the Homeless." The Los Angeles Daily Journal, January 21, 1987:1.
After four homeless people died of cold-related deaths on the city streets within a week, members of the city council "tossed aside liability warnings, along with cautions that they may be violating state building laws, to open City Hall doors to the homeless,... making temporary, 72-hour homeless shelters out of their own council chambers and out of City Hall stairs and hall-ways."

Boulter, Bryan F. "The Homeless Persons Act and Inten-tional Homelessness." Solicitor's Journal, 124, October 17, 1980:715-717.
A dilemma is posed by British law that requires local councils to provide housing for involuntarily homeless persons but does not obligate them to house people who become homeless voluntarily. Many councils withhold housing from people by determining that home-lessness is voluntary.

Bowler, Alida C. "The Problems of the Transient Boy--In Relation to a Community's Social Hygiene Program." Journal of Social Hygiene, April 1933:188-193.
Deploring the existence of runaway lads, the author presents two case stories, calls for a study of what is being done to help transient boys, and warns against the "unhealthy influences of intimacies of box-car and jungle life."

Boxill, Nancy A., and Anita L. Beaty. "Mother-Child Interaction among Homeless Women and Their Children in a Public Night Shelter in Atlanta, Georgia." Child and Youth Services, 14 (1), 1990:49-64.
Based on their participant observation in a night shelter for homeless women in Atlanta, Georgia, the

authors analyze the impact of homelessness on the interaction between mothers and children.

Boyd, Gerald M. "Kemp, Picked as Chief of H.U.D., Pledges to Combat Homelessness." New York Times, December 20, 1988:1, 13.
    After President Bush named Jack F. Kemp as Secretary of Housing and Urban Development, Mr. Kemp said that "he would aggressively pursue joint public and private initiatives to combat the appalling tragedy of homelessness and joblessness." President Bush praised Mr. Kemp for his "innovative approach to homelessness."

Boyle, Alix. "Law Students Extend Help to the Homeless." New York Times, December 15, 1991:CN14.
    Students from Yale Law School offer free legal advice to the homeless at the Community Soup Kitchen in New Haven, Connecticut.

Bracakey, William R., and Pamela J. Fischer. "Letter to the Editor." Wall Street Journal, November 2, 1989:A23.
    The authors take issue with an editorial in the Wall Street Journal that quoted their research. They stress that the interactions between health and homelessness are complex, as are other causes of homelessness, and more careful study and research are necessary.

Brace, Charles Loring. The Dangerous Classes of New York, and Twenty Years' Work Among Them. Third Edition. New York: Wynkoop and Hallenbeck, 1880.
    In this overview of the urban poor, the author makes the case that the children must be saved before they are perverted by the evil influences of their homes and neighborhoods. This can be done by providing them religion, education, and a changed environment.

Brace, Charles Loring. "Letter from Mr. Brace." Proceedings of the Conference of Boards of Public Charities, 1877:126-128.
    To control tramps, we need a pass-system, accompanied by a labor test for anyone who is to receive charity.

Brackett, Jeffrey R. The Transportation Problem in American Social Work. New York: Russell Sage Foundation, 1936.
    This brief overview of how the homeless problem has been accentuated by the policy of providing free trans-

portation in order to remove the homeless from a locality includes a history and summary of the transportation agreements of the National Conference of Charities and Correction.

Bradford, Michael. "Ice Cream Maven Urges Business Aid for Disadvantaged." Business Insurance, 25 (19), May 13, 1991:23-24.
   The article features Ben Cohen, chairman of Ben & Jerry's Homemade, Inc., and commends the company's lead in charitable activities. Among those activities is designating a portion of its profits for the homeless.

Bradshaw, J. W. "Treatment of Tramps in Small Cities." Proceedings of the National Conference of Charities and Correction, 1896:227-232.
   There are two kinds of tramps: those who avoid work and those who want work. The practice of arresting and imprisoning vagrants does not discriminate between these two types. A proper solution is to provide work, which will attract the latter and repel the former. How tramps are dealt with in Ann Arbor, Michigan, illustrates the value of this policy. When the policy of making tramps saw wood in return for meals and lodging went into effect, the number of tramps decreased.

Bradshaw, J. W. "The Treatment of Tramps in Small Cities. " The Charities Review, 5 (7), May 1896.
   The tramp evil consists of two classes of men who "call for wholly different treatment." The genuine tramp is a man who will not work, while among the vagrant beggars are men who truly desire employment and will "gladly and faithfully do any work which is provided for them." To provide board and lodging for tramps at public expense only attracts tramps. The proper way of dealing with the tramp evil is to require that tramps work in order to receive public board and lodging. The genuine tramp will flee such an area, while those who truly desire work will be provided temporary relief which they deserve.

Brahams, Diana, and Malcolm Weller. "Crime and Homelessness Among the Mentally Ill--I." New Law Journal, June 28, 1985:626-627.
   "Closure of long-stay hospital beds and savage financial cut-backs of funding" have made many people homeless. "For some patients a long-stay hospital is a community and home, and for whom 'release' amounts to

eviction with nowhere to go except a bus shelter or park bench, with appalling hardship and homelessness as a consequence--and even crime and prison."

Brandon, David. "Homeless Single Persons." British Journal of Psychiatric Social Work, 10 (2), 1969:80-84.
    Focusing on social isolation and mental illness, the author suggests that casework and treatment facilities be moved into the community. Treating the homeless involves a civil rights issue: voluntary versus compulsory treatment, including the right of individuals to reject society.

Braun, Peter, Gerald Kochansky, Robert Shapiro, Susan Greenberg, Jon E. Gudeman, Sylvia Johnson, and Miles F. Shore. "Overview: Deinstitutionalization of Psychiatric Patients, A Critical Review of Outcome Studies." American Journal of Psychiatry, 138 (6), June 1981:736-749.
    Experimental alternatives to hospitalization of patients have led to psychiatric outcomes not different from those of patients in control groups. Satisfactory deinstitutionalization appears to depend on the availability of appropriate programs for care in the community.

Breakey, William R. "Treating the Homeless." Alcohol Health and Research World, 11 (3), Spring 1987:42-47, 90.
    The four main types of homeless people are street people, homeless alcoholics, the situationally homeless, and the chronically mentally ill. This diverse target population brings different receptiveness to helping services and differences in needs. Consequently, clinicians need to join forces with advocates for the homeless, other political activists, and rehabilitation experts to form coalitions that will bring pressure on policy makers to develop adequate service systems.

Breakey, William R., and Pamela J. Fischer. "Down and Out." Johns Hopkins Magazine, June 1985:16-24.
    Homelessness is not unidimensional, but consists of four types of people: the chronic alcoholic, the situational homeless, the mentally ill, and street people. Street people are the most difficult to reach and the "least likely to be reassimilated" because they have opted out of regular society and are committed to their way of life. All four populations share the central characteristic of lacking a loving support network, so

much so they do not even band together themselves. This "disturbed and disturbing underclass" needs extended service and support."

Breakey, William R., and Pamela J. Fischer. "Homelessness: The Extent of the Problem." <u>Journal of Social Issues</u>, <u>46</u> (4), 1990:31-47.
    "The homeless are not a homogeneous category of people, but include a wide variety of types. The first problem in establishing the parameters of the homeless population is one of definitions." Each of the various methods of attempting to count the homeless has some validity, but each also has disadvantages. Consequently, any national estimate of the numbers of the homeless must be regarded with caution. The numbers of people in the various subgroups of the homeless is of central importance for establishing sound public policy. The general needs of the homeless are adequate housing and income, but specific subgroups such as the mentally ill, alcoholics and drug abusers, AIDS victims, and families with small children, need special services. Consequently, in order to do adequate planning, we must establish the extent of these subgroups.

Bremner, Robert H. <u>From the Depths: The Discovery of Poverty in the United States</u>. New York: New York University Press, 1956.
    This overview of poverty and social reform movements from 1830 to 1925 examines poverty in literature, the rise of social work, child labor, and the contrasting images of poverty as good and bad, as both the producer and destroyer of character and virtue.

Bremner, Robert H. "'Scientific Philanthropy,' 1873-93." <u>The Social Service Review</u>, <u>30</u>, 1956:168-173.
    Efforts to establish scientific philanthropy were based on the assumption that much of the money given for the poor was wasted on impostors while that which reached the poor degraded them. Giving money, to be discouraged, was to be substituted by giving help, which, separated from religion, would provide self-respect, hope, ambition, courage, and character by removing the underlying cause. The author analyzes changes in the emphases of the movement, especially the contrasting emphases of reforming the individual and removing economic and environmental causes of distress.

Brennan, Tim, David Huizinga, and Delbert S. Elliott. The Social Psychology of Runaways. Lexington: Lexington Books, 1978.

This overview of runaways in American society examines motivations for running away and the family background of runaways. Focusing on the testing of theories based on two cross-sectional surveys of over 7,000 youths, the authors conclude that the data support the social psychological theory of weak bonds (attenuated or initially inadequately developed) combined with high levels of stress and strain. The suggested solutions are to strengthen weak social integration bonds, strengthen internal commitment bonds, reduce attenuating-strained conditions, and minimize exposure to delinquent peers.

Brenner, Elsa. "Down and Out: When There's Nowhere Else to Go." New York Times, December 15, 1991:WC1.

The author recounts how some of the homeless in Yonkers, New York, became homeless. She also estimates the cost of providing them social services.

Brent, Ruth Stumpe. "Usage of Public Restroom Lounges as Support Systems by Elderly Females." Qualitative Sociology, 4 (1), Spring 1981:56-71.

Based on observations of eight ladies' restroom lounges in a midwest city, the author concludes that these lounges provide a support system that anchors their identity.

Brentlinger, W. H. "The Emotional Stability of the Transient." The Journal of Applied Psychology, 20 (2), April 1936:193-207.

In the winter of 1934-35, 741 transients were tested with the Woodworth P.D. Sheet. These results were compared with those of college freshmen and neurasthenics and psychoneurotics.

Brenton, Myron. The Runaways: Children, Husbands, Wives, and Parents. Harmondsworth: Penguin, 1978.

This history of nomadism in the United States includes runaways and left-behinds, suggests causes of running away, and proposes ways to help deal with this problem.

Breton, Margot. "A Drop-In Program for Transient Women: Promoting Competence through the Environment." Social Work, 29 (6), 1984:542-546.

To help homeless women, the author proposes "sistering," providing transient women a home base in order to build and maintain competence. What competence is depends on the type of transience: It may be to teach them to be streetwise and self-protective, to sustain the decision to leave a spouse, or to teach them how to face non-institutional life. The author discusses social contact, symbolic identification, task instrumentality, and growth in problem solving, and analyzes sistering in terms of old and new approaches in social work.

Breton, Margot. "The Need for Mutual-Aid Groups in a Drop-In for Homeless Women: The Sistering Case." Social Work with Groups, 11 (4), 1988:47-61.
The author discusses a sistering program designed to meet the needs of homeless women in Toronto, Ontario.

Brewer, W. H. "What Shall We Do With Our Tramps?" New Englander and Yale Review, 37, July 1878:521-532.
Beggars are like a hostile class, a cruel and atrocious tribe of savages. They have their own instincts, tastes, traditions, and codes. The Jews are a good example of a group that has eliminated pauperism. The poorer classes have been immigrating into the United States, and if paupers grow in numbers they can threaten not only our political system but also civilization. Beggars must be throttled or they will throttle us.

Brickner, Philip W., and Arthur Kaufman. "Case Finding of Heart Disease in Homeless Men." Bulletin of the New York Academy of Medicine, 49 (6), June 1973:475-484.
Because homeless men are largely removed from contact with the medical care system, St. Vincent's Hospital and the Visiting Nurse Service of New York City have established three clinics in welfare hotels. Of 434 men seen in these clinics, 54 had either arteriosclerotic or hypertensive problems. The cooperation of these men was poor, but 25 percent remained in long-term treatment. The authors conclude: "We believe that by going outside the hospital to sustain consistent, sympathetic contact with these men, some of them will trust us and be motivated to enter the health care mainstream."

Brickner, Philip W., Brian C. Scanlan, Barbara A. Conanan, Alexander Elvy, John McAdam, Linda Keen Scharer, and William J. Vicic. "Homeless Persons and Health Care." Annals of Internal Medicine, 104 (3), March 1986:405-409.

Although the homeless suffer from a broad range of acute and chronic diseases due to their unsuitable living conditions, their chronic stress they face, and their sociopathic behavior, health care is generally unavailable to them. Their most common problems are trauma, tuberculosis, infestations, and vascular disease, exacerbated by incomplete and fragmentary medical care. To re-establish and maintain health service to the homeless, we must imaginatively construct teams of physicians, nurses, and social workers.

Brickner, Philip W., Linda Keen Scharer, Barbara A. Conanan, Alexander Elvy, and Marianne Savarese, eds. Health Care of Homeless People. New York: Springer, 1985.

This overview of health issues in providing care for the homeless reviews their physical and mental disorders: infestations, trauma, infections, nutritional and vitamin deficiencies, hypertension, vascular disease, alcoholism, and tuberculosis. The authors also discuss deinstitutionalization, organization of health care services, team work, access to benefits, and interservice cooperation, and summarize viable programs in Boston, New York City, Springfield, Massachusetts, and Washington, D.C.

Brickner, Philip W., Linda Keen Scharer, Barbara A. Conanan, Marianne Savarese, and Brian C. Scanlan, eds. Under the Safety Net: The Health and Social Welfare of the Homeless in the United States. New York: W. W. Norton, 1990.

Focusing on the health needs and health care of the homeless, the authors of these twenty-six articles examine the special situations of runaways, homeless families, homeless women, the homeless elderly, homeless alcoholics, homeless AIDS patients, and the homeless mentally ill. They also review programs that are available to meet these needs.

Brieland, Donald. "O Give Me a Home." Foundation News, December 1986:61-62.

The author reviews Hardship in the Heartlands (Dan Salerno, Kim Hopper, and Ellen Baxter), Housing the Poor of Paris, 1850-1902 (Ann-Louise Shapiro), and The Making of America's Homeless (Kim Hopper and Jill Hamberg).

Brintnall, Michael. "Future Directions for Federal Urban Policy." Journal of Urban Affairs, 11 (1), 1989:1-19.

This analysis of how city governments are responding to cutbacks in federal support as the federal government focuses attention on the national deficit and economy mentions that nonprofit agencies have stepped in to fill part of the gap.

Broadhead, Robert S., and Kathryn J. Fox. "Takin' It to the Streets: AIDS Outreach as Ethnography." Journal of Contemporary Ethnography, 19 (3), October 1990:322-348.
The authors examine similarities between doing ethnography by social researchers and trying to stop the spread of AIDS by community health outreach workers. Listed as a target group of the latter are homeless youths.

Brody, Hugh. Indians on Skid Row: The Role of Alcohol and Community in the Adaptive Process of Indian Urban Migrants. Ottowa: Department of Indian Affairs and Northern Development, 1971.
This participant observation study of the skid row of "Prairie City," Canada, focuses on Indians who have migrated to the city: displacement, culture shock, bars, street corners, alcohol, community, sources of income, socioeconomic status, drunkenness, fighting, and relationships to whites and social workers. Short-term solutions are to provide a native center, information, and social and legal advisory services for urban migrants, while long-term solutions are to improve their socioeconomic status and education.

Brower, Bonnie. "Profits Add Unnecessary Costs." New York Times, October 2, 1988:E6.
Removing the profit motive is necessary to provide housing for low-income and homeless families. To do so will require the use of non-profit options in financing, production, and management.

Brown, Carl, Steve McFarlane, Ron Paredes, and Louisa Stark. The Homeless in Phoenix: Who are They? and What Should Be Done? Phoenix, Arizona: Phoenix South Community Mental Health Center, 1983.
The authors interviewed 345 homeless persons, about a third of Phoenix's estimated homeless population of 1,189. They present demographic background information on the homeless, analyze reasons for homelessness, and suggest that a three-tiered plan for service delivery be implemented, which should consist of emergency shelter

care, transitional services, and affordable, long-term, independent housing.

Brown, Edward A. "Tramp Art Mechanical Bank." Antiques & Collecting Hobbies, 93, September 1988:37.
    This short review of "tramp art," a "craft initially practiced by hobos and tramps as they wandered around the countryside working at odd jobs" contains a photo of a mechanical bank made by a tramp or hobo.

Brown, Edwin A. "Broke": The Man Without the Dime. Chicago: Browne and Howell, 1913.
    Between 1908 and 1912, the author did participant observation of the homeless in Denver, New York City, Chicago, Washington, D.C., Pueblo, Salt Lake City, Kansas City, Boston, Philadelphia, Pittsburgh, Omaha, San Francisco, Los Angeles, Portland, Tacoma, Seattle, Spokane, Minneapolis, Albany, Cleveland, Cincinnati, Louisville, Memphis, Houston, San Antonio, Milwaukee, and Toledo. The suggested solutions are to create labor and to open municipal emergency homes. He offers detailed suggestions for operating these homes.

Brown, Frank Dexter. "Where's the Help for the Homeless?" Black Enterprise, August 1987:27.
    The author makes the point that the homeless are a diverse group, that 80 to 90 percent of those seeking shelter assistance are black, that homelessness is a major concern of black elected officials, that the black community must deal with this issue, and that the future will bring more homelessness.

Brown, James M. "How the City of Toledo Provided for Her Unemployed." The Arena, October 1894:715-820.
    The author is impressed with how volunteers in the city of Toledo raised money and financed public works for the unemployed. He concludes that the spirit of cooperation between the various religious groups and the spirit in which the poor did their assigned work indicates that "the time has come when the spirit of a better and broader brotherhood is possessing the race."

Brown, John. I was a Tramp. London: Selwyn and Blount, 1934.
    This first-person account of tramping in England was written by a man who left school at 16 to support his family, went to sea, later became a socialist political

organizer, and eventually graduated from Oxford University.

Brown, Kaaren Strauch, and Marjorie Ziefert. "A Feminist Approach to Working with Homeless Women." Affilia, 5 (1), Spring 1990:6-20.
Based on their interviews with homeless women in two shelters, the authors describe how a developmental model can be applied to working with homeless women. The goal, to develop affiliation, attachment, and relationships, requires that the individual move away from an emphasis on the self so she can develop reconnections with the community. Because there are three types of homeless women--the chronically, episodically, and situationally homeless--the stage of development a woman is in must be considered in working with her.

Brown, Phil. "Psychiatric Dirty Work Revisited: Conflicts in Servicing Nonpsychiatric Agencies." Journal of Contemporary Ethnography, 18 (2), July 1989:182-201.
Based on interviews and participant observation in a walk-in clinic, the author focuses on "dirty work," tasks that the staff does not consider public service, that anger them because they are expected to perform them, and that they try to avoid. Performing social control functions, rather than providing psychiatric services, is high on the list of dirty work. Dealing with homeless persons (as well as prison prereleases and welfare and disability eligibilities) is also considered dirty work.

Brown, Sara A. "Neglected Children of Migrant Workers." Missionary Review of the World, 46 (7), July 1923:515-520.
This report on the living conditions of migrant families includes an example of a family living in their auto.

Bruce, Robert V. 1877: Year of Violence. Indianapolis: Bobbs-Merrill, 1959.
This account of the strikes and riots of 1877 includes scattered material on the role of tramps in these events.

Bruck, Peter A., and Stuart Allan. "The Commodification of Social Relations: Television News and Social Intervention." Journal of Communication Inquiry, 11 (2), Summer 1987:79-86.

The authors argue that the current presentation of statistical information on television news broadcasts in Canada supports the capitalist order and should be replaced by statistics of greater value to the average citizen. Among those statistics would be a measure of homelessness.

Bruere, Robert W. "The Industrial Workers of the World." Harper's Monthly Magazine, 127, July 1918:250-257.
    Deleterious labor conditions have given rise to the I.W.W., whose membership includes many homeless men.

Bruno, C. C. "Why I Am Homeless: Hard lessons in Supply and Demand." The Humanist, May-June 1989;10-11, 36.
    The author reports that the farm jobs he has been working at in the Imperial Valley of California since the 1950s have been taken by legal aliens who are working in the fields on ninety-day permits under the Group I and Group II of the Immigration Reform Act. Consequently, he finds himself on the streets.

Bruno, Frank J. "Principles of Case Work Involved in the Treatment of Non-Resident and Transient Families." The Family, 10 (5), July 1929:150-156.
    The author suggests how social workers should work with transient families.

Bruno, Frank J. Trends in Social Work, 1874-1956: A History Based on the Proceedings of the National Conference of Social Work. New York: Columbia University Press, 1957.
    This work, which contains isolated reference to tramps, who are "obviously feeble-minded," also suggests a work-test for vagrants.

Bruns, Roger A. Knights of the Road: A Hobo History. New York: Methuen, 1980.
    This well-documented, analytical overview of hobo life reviews their basic culture, famous hobos, relationship of hobos to economic conditions, and reasons for the demise of hobos.

Bryan, J. Y. "The Mental Ability of Literate Transients." Journal of Abnormal Social Psychology, 31, 1936:276-284.
    Five hundred transients at Durham, North Carolina, and Cincinnati, Ohio, were given I.Q. tests (Henmon-Nelson Test of Mental Ability and Bregman Revision of the

Army Alpha). The author concludes that it is not a low mental ability that prevents the employability of transients, but, rather, alcoholism, defective health, physical handicaps, wanderlust, indolence, and psychopathologies.

Bryan, Michael. "Domestic Violence: A Question of Housing?" _Journal of Social Welfare Law_, July 1984:195-207.
The application of rules concerning intentional homelessness by housing authorities discriminates against people made homeless by domestic violence.

Bryan, Michael. "Housing (Homeless Persons) Act 1977--Domestic Violence--Relevance of Applicant's Housing Rights to Decision Whether to Grant Ouster Order." _Journal of Social Welfare Law_, November 1985:372-375.
British courts face a dilemma when they are requested to evict a husband or boyfriend who has battered his partner in cases where that eviction will cause the man to be homeless.

Buff, Daniel D., James F. Kenny, and Donald Light, Jr. "Health Problems of Residents in Single-Room Occupancy Hotels." _New York State Journal of Medicine_, 80 (13), December 1980:2000-2005.
The topics of this analysis are deinstitutionalization, the nature and origin of SRO hotels, and the health problems, health care, and use of health services of their residents.

Buffington, Adaline A. "Automobile Migrants." _The Family_, 6 (5) July 1925:149-153.
Some "flivver hobos" (auto migrants) who request public aid are suspected of picking up children "in some unexplainable manner" and using them to "provide meal tickets." The causes of this problem are wanderlust, the search for wealth, new homes, and work. The solutions are to establish State Employment Bureaus that will move labor about the country as needed and educating communities not to give to auto migrants.

Bull, William L. "Trampery: Its Causes, Present Aspects, and Some Suggested Remedies." _Proceedings of the National Conference of Charities and Correction_, July 15-22, 1886, Isabel C. Barrows, ed. Boston: George H. Ellis, 1886:188-206.

In what is one of the earliest empirical studies, the author summarizes 130 questionnaires from around the country. Respondents report 47 different causes of trampery ranging from drink and laziness to "pure cussedness" and type of civilization. The author divides these reported causes into subjective and objective causes or primary and secondary causes. The solutions submitted by respondents are similarly varied, ranging from Christianity and ideals to lodging houses and the whipping post. The author suggests imposing a head tax on immigrants to prevent the entrance of paupers into the United States, legislation for compulsory education and manual training in the schools, and a work test in order to receive public aid, with the work to be directed toward the maintenance of public roads.

Bunce, Frank. "I've Got to Take a Chance." The Forum, 89, February 1933:108-112.
This first-person account by a 27-year-old man who has been unemployed and homeless for two years deals with the question of social versus personal causation. The author concludes that he is ready to commit crime in order to survive.

Burnham, Linda Frye. "Hands Across Skid Row: John Malpede's Performance Workshop for the Homeless of L.A." The Drama Review, 31, Summer 1987:126-149.
This review of the background of the performers of L.A.P.D., the Los Angeles poverty department, contains monologues presented in these street people's performances, as well as 17 pictures.

Burnham, M. Audrey, and Paul Koegel. "Methodology for Obtaining a Representative Sample of Homeless Persons: The Los Angeles Skid Row Study." Evaluation Review, 12 (2), April 1988:117-152.
The research strategy presented for obtaining a representative sample of homeless persons uses samples proportionate to the use of facilities and services.

Burns, Leland S. "Hope for the Homeless in the U.S.: Lessons from the Third World." Cities, 5 (1), February 1988:33-40.
The author proposes that the United States and the First World can learn from the self-help approaches to housing the homeless practiced by the Third World.

Burns, Leland S.   "Third-World Models for Helping U.S. Homeless." <u>Wall Street Journal</u>, January 2, 1986:10.
Conventional wisdom about the homeless is wrong. Our problem is parallel with the phenomenon of squatters in the Third World. A cost-effective approach would be to allow squatter settlements. The author also discusses deinstitutionalization, and, concerning mental illness among the homeless, asks which is the cause and which the effect.

Burritt, Bailey B.   "Unemployed Crowd Lodging House." <u>The Survey</u>, <u>25</u>, February 11, 1911:806-807.
Reports that increasing numbers of men are staying at The Municipal Lodging House of New York and suggests three changes: more temporary employment, penal institutions for those who don't want to work, and colonies for inebriants and vagrants.

Burt, Martha R., and Barbara E. Cohen.   "Differences among Homeless Single Women, Women with Children, and Single Men." <u>Social Problems</u>, <u>36</u> (5), December 1989:508-524.
Interviews with 1,704 people in March 1987 using a "three-stage random sample of homeless adult users of soup kitchens and shelters in U.S. cities with populations of 100,000 or more" showed that 73 percent were single men, 9 percent single women, 9 percent women accompanied by at least one child, 7 percent men accompanied by a spouse or partner but without children, 2 percent women accompanied by a spouse or partner but without children, and 1 percent men with children. The authors delineate differences between homeless single women, homeless women with children, and homeless men and argue that the assumption of policy makers that the personal problems of the homeless must be "fixed" before a homeless person can maintain a stable housing situation be replaced with an approach that moves people into permanent housing while providing flexible supports to help them maintain it.

Burt, Martha R., and Barbara E. Cohen.   "Who Is Helping the Homeless?   Local, State, and Federal Responses." <u>Publius</u>, <u>19</u> (3), Summer 1989:111-128.
The authors contrast the role of the private and government sectors in providing services to the homeless and make policy recommendations for improving these efforts.

Butler, Rosalie. "Separation of Charities and Correction." The Charities Review, 2, June 1893:164-170.
    The author of this overview of the organization of
the Department of Charities and Correction of the city of
New York argues that charities should be separated from
correction.

Byfield, Natalie P.   "Help for L.A.'s Homeless."
American Lawyer, 8, July-August 1986:102-105.
    Prestigious law firms in Los Angeles do pro bono
work on behalf of the homeless. They have made "motions
barring the county from sending homeless to substandard
skid row hotels."

Byrne, J. K. "The Vagrant Adolescent." The Kiwanis
Magazine, February 1933:53, 90.
    Because 250,000 American youth are wandering around
the country and are subject to evil forces such as paid
communists, the Kiwanians should become actively
involved in solving the problem. They can do this by
publicizing the problem and helping coordinate the social
agencies in their communities to adopt some agreed-upon
program.

Byrnes, Thomas. "The Menace of 'Coxeyism': Character and
Methods of the Men." The North American Review, 158,
June 1894:696-701.
    Reports on the type of homeless men who are marching
on Washington, with an emphasis on the threat they pose
to the social order.

                              C

Cadwalder, Chace, Dall, and Tousey (last names not
given). "Debate on Tramps." Proceedings of Conference
of Boards of Public Charities, 1877:130-133.
    The debate (actually a discussion) between these
four individuals shows disgust with tramps. They agree
that a get-tough policy is desirable.

Cain, Mead. "The Consequences of Reproductive Failure:
Dependence, Mobility, and Mortality among the Elderly of
Rural South Asia." Population Studies, 40 (3), November
1986:375-388.

Field work in several rural South Asian communities shows that the failure to rear a surviving son increases income problems in old age, including the risk of homelessness.

Caldwell, Erskine, and Margaret Bourke-White. Say, Is This the U.S.A. New York: Duell, Sloan and Pearce, 1941.
This photographic essay of people and places contains a few paragraphs ("smoke artists and rail-benders") on riding freight trains and the good company they offer.

Caldwell, Erskine, and Margaret Bourke-White. You Have Seen Their Faces. New York: Modern Age Books, 1937.
Based on the photos in this pictorial overview of southern tenant farmers, one might ask: When is a home not a home?

Calkins, Clinch. Some Folks Won't Work. New York: Harcourt, Brace, 1930.
The title of this volume, which overviews the plight of the unemployed in the Great Depression, some of whom have become homeless, is sarcastic.

Callison, J. William. "Low-Income Housing Credit Now Even More Complex." Journal of Taxation, 72 (3), March 1990:148-155.
This analysis of the low-income housing credit of Internal Revenue Code Section 42 mentions that it can be applied to housing for the homeless.

Campbell, Richard, and Jimmie L. Reeves. "Covering the Homeless: The Joyce Brown Story." Critical Studies in Mass Communication, 6 (1), March 1989:21-42.
This examination of the approach of television news concerning socioeconomic problems focuses on television's coverage of Joyce Brown, a homeless woman whom New York authorities institutionalized against her will.

Caplow, Theodore. "The Sociologist and the Homeless Man." In Disaffiliated Man: Essays and Bibliography on Skid Row, Vagrancy, and Outsiders, Howard M. Bahr, ed. Toronto: University of Toronto Press, 1970:3-12.
This overview of sociological research on the homeless and attitudes toward them discusses the themes of what skid row is; alcohol, discouragement, and dissolution of social relations; no invariant etiology;

lack of consistent findings; proposed solutions; middle-
class attitudes inherent in conclusions about skid row
people; and the right to be disaffiliated.

Caplow, Theodore. "Transiency as a Cultural Pattern."
American Sociological Review, 5 (5), October 1940:731-
739.
    Based on contact with 1,200 hobos through partici-
pant observation in the summer and autumn of 1939, the
author analyzes the culture of hobos. The article also
contains historical materials.

Caplow, Theodore, Howard M. Bahr, and David Sternberg.
"Homelessness." In International Encyclopedia of the
Social Sciences, 6, David Sills, ed. New York: Macmillan, 1968:494-499.
    The authors argue that there is a homelessness syn-
drome, contrast modern homelessness with homelessness as
an ideal in earlier ages, and focus on contemporary forms
of homelessness: refugees, migrants, the skid row man.

Carling, Paul J. Developing Family Foster Care Programs
in Mental Health: A Resource Guide. Washington, D.C.:
U.S. Government Printing Office, October 1984.
    The intent of this guide is to delineate key factors
to be taken into consideration in planning family foster
care programs and in accessing area resources. It is
based on the Proceedings of the National Institute of
Mental Health Workshop on Family Foster Care for "Chronically Mentally Ill" Persons sponsored by the U.S. Department of Health and Human Services. One of the specified
target populations is "the large number of homeless
persons who are psychiatrically disabled." Looking at
programs in West Brentwood, New York, Trenton, New
Jersey, Fulton County, Georgia, Little Rock, Arkansas,
Washington, D.C., and two more general programs in New
York and Indiana, the author reviews program models,
recruiting, screening, and matching clients with providers, recruiting and training providers, licensing,
regulating, monitoring, and financing family foster care.

Carlinsky, Dan. "America on $0 a Day: The Private World
of a Compulsive Hobo." New York Times, October 22,
1972:1, 15.
    The author profiles Steamtrain, a hobo who owns his
own home, is married and has two daughters and five
grandchildren, and hobos for fun. The article reviews
the culture of the professional, "gentleman" hobo.

Carlson, Eric. "Perspectives and Prospects for Global Housing Action." <u>Ekistics, 307</u>, July-August, 1984:288-302.
This overview of global housing shortage due to global urbanization compares the problems of developing and developed nations. The United Nation's International Year of Shelter for the Homeless (IYSH) is 1987.

Carlyle, E. "Day Nurseries." <u>Charities Review</u> <u>1</u>, June 1892:365-376.
This history of asylums for children--from ancient Rome to contemporary Paris and London--places emphasis on Sunny Side Day Nursery in New York City. The author also covers the prevention of delinquency, criminality, and homelessness among the poor.

Carmody, Deirdre. "Brooklyn Church Helps Homeless Help Themselves." <u>New York Times</u>, February 16, 1985:A25.
This profile of St. Vincent de Paul in New York City, a shelter for the homeless, focuses on its rules and discipline.

Carmody, Deirdre. "The City Sees No Solutions for Homeless." <u>New York Times</u>, October 10, 1984:A1, B4.
This article is a wide-ranging coverage of interrelated topics: hard-core homeless, the visibility of street people, mental illness of the homeless, the numbers of homeless in New York City, shelters, emergency help, Project HELP, hospitals, deinstitutionalization, costs, SRO hotels, new housing, shelter users in the 1960s contrasted with the present, legal advocacy, and causes.

Carmody, Deirdre. "Study Blames Poverty for Most Homelessness." <u>New York Times</u>, November 2, 1984:B5.
The causes of homelessness are family disruption, an inadequate supply of low-income housing, an increase in poverty and unemployment, and the inadequacy of public assistance. The author stresses the need for housing programs in New York City.

Carmody, Deirdre. "The Tangled Life and Mind of Judy, Whose Home Is the Street." <u>New York Times</u>, December 17, 1984:81.
Judy, a 41-year-old woman who occupies the corner of 64th Street and Lexington Avenue in New York City, is a college graduate with a major in political science and enough credit for a master's degree. She is a schizo-

phrenic, however, and after divorcing three husbands, she now lives on the streets of New York City. Judy is such a regular inhabitant of this corner that United Parcel Service "pulls up to the corner and picks up Judy's boxes which she sends home to the Middle West." She keeps herself clean, and often is rational. However, she also shouts obscenities into the night. Attempts to incarcerate her have not been successful, and neighbors are worried about her.

Carroll, Vincent. "Origin of a Housing Squeeze." Wall Street Journal, October 13, 1986:10.
Contrary to almost all the housing literature, the author argues that we do not have a housing crisis. We have no shortage of housing (only pocket problems in fast-growing areas and markets tightened by political decisions to institute rent control and zoning), national vacancy rates for rental and home owner units rose between 1980 and 1984, the rate of housing production runs higher than the rate of household formation, and the quality of dwellings has improved (the number of rooms per unit rising and the number of people per room declining). The one negative trend in housing is a rising price, and this is due to increased quality and political decisions (project development fees for parks, streets, schools, and environmental impact reviews). Consequently, current government programs and subsidies are misdirected.

Carter, Robert. "Notes from the Diary of an American 'Wild Boy.'" The New Republic, March 8, 1933:92-95.
The author, a young man, reports on his travels through the South while vainly seeking work. He covers his experiences with missions, begging, police, and racism.

Carty, Patrick J. "Preventing Homelessness: Rent Control or Rent Assistance?" Notre Dame Journal of Law, Ethics, and Public Policy, 4 (2), Summer 1989:365-383.
In this analysis of rent control versus rent subsidies for reducing homelessness, the author argues that, in the long run, rent control curtails the availability of low-rent housing while rent subsidies enhance poor people's buying power in the housing rental market. Consequently, the federal government should concentrate on rental assistance and lower the requirements for such subsidies.

Casey, Jim, and Leon Pitt. "Vigilante Victim, Pal Charged in Slaying of Girl." Chicago Sun-Times, June 26, 1986:1, 2.
    One of the two individuals charged with the rape and murder of a 14-year-old girl was identified as "a drifter who police said lived in an abandoned car."

Cates, Ellan. "New York Case Argues Voting Rights of People Who Live on the Streets." The Los Angeles Daily Journal, October 5, 1984:3.
    Although New York State and City officials have agreed to allow voting by persons who list their addresses as homeless shelters and welfare hotels, they refuse to register street people who list their addresses as a public place, such as a park bench or sidewalk grate. Attorneys for the homeless argue that these persons' constitutional rights are being violated.

Caton, Carol L. M. "The Homeless Experience in Adolescent Years." In The Mental Health Needs of Homeless Persons, Ellen L. Bassuk, ed. San Francisco: Jossey-Bass, 1986:63-70.
    This overview of the psychological and social needs of adolescent (runaway) homeless, including their school problems, antisocial behavior, depression, and suicide attempts contains case examples.

Caton, Carol L. M., Richard Jed Wyatt, Jeffrey Grunberg, and Alan Felix. "An Evaluation of a Mental Health Program for Homeless Men." American Journal of Psychiatry, 147 (3), March 1990:286-289.
    To evaluate an on-site mental health program for homeless men staying in a crisis shelter in New York City, the authors interviewed 32 men before they entered the program and after they left it. The results were both positive and negative. On the positive side, living in the streets was eliminated, use of shelters decreased, and contacts with the criminal justice system were cut in half. On the negative side, psychiatric hospitalization and unemployment increased after exit from the program.

Cecil, William A. "A Plea for the Tramp." National and English Review, 43, August 1904:964-971.
    The author argues against harsh treatment for wandering, homeless men. He makes the point that many of these men are simply itinerant laborers, homeless poor, who are driven to wandering because of lack of work, while others are physically sick, mentally disabled, or

elderly. He suggests that harsh treatment of these people be replaced with "kindness blended with firmness," nourishing the sick, kindly supervision for those "weak in mind," the return of the elderly to their native homes, and allowing those who want to keep wandering to wander.

Celis, William, III. "Homeless Census in March Raises Fears Method May Cut Tally, Hurting Funding." Wall Street Journal, February 12, 1990:A9B.
On March 20-21, the U.S. Census Bureau, in a project dubbed "Shelter and Street Night," will count the nation's homeless population. The Census Bureau plans "to only count homeless people in shelters and those in pre-identified street locations. Eliminated from the count will be cars, rooftops, and dumpsters, popular havens for the homeless." City officials and advocates for the homeless are concerned that the tally will not adequately reflect the homelessness problem, that "a low tally will hurt funding for homeless programs." It is expected that the count will produce a tally of 500,000 to 650,000.

Celis, William, III. "Public-Housing Units Are Rapidly Decaying, Causing Many to Close." Wall Street Journal, December 15, 1986:1, 14.
The problems of low-cost, government-subsidized housing include inadequate repairs, maintenance, and financing. Cutbacks in financing and HUD policies have exacerbated the problem. Without illegal doubling up in public housing, the nation's homeless problem would be even worse.

Chackes, K. M. "Sheltering the Homeless: Judicial Enforcement of Governmental Duties to the Poor." Journal of Urban and Contemporary Law, 31, Winter 1987:155-199.
The homeless are the poorest of America's poor. They lack the basic necessities of life, including health and safety. The author examines state and local laws that make the provision of assistance for the homeless a duty of the government.

Chamberlin, C. R., Jr. "Running Away During Psychothera-py." Bulletin of the Menninger Clinic, 24, 1960:288-294.
Studying the history of a 14-year-old boy who ran away from a state hospital, the author concludes that the boy fled in order to meet four needs: to show indepen-

dence, to be loved, to raise his self-esteem, and to express aggression toward authority.

Chamberlin, J.   "An Ex-Patient's View of the Homeless Mentally Ill."   Psychosocial Rehabilitation Journal, 8 (4), April 1985:11-15.
    The author, a former mental patient, takes issue with the report of the task force of the American Psychiatric Association. He argues that to categorize a group of people as homeless mentally ill will segregate that group and lead to unwanted services being forced upon them. She states that the basic causes of homeless must be addressed, which are social and economic and asserts that homeless people can solve their own problems through organizing, self-help, and political action.

Chambers, Marcia.   "Santa Barbara's Moves Against the Homeless Draw Protest."   New York Times, March 31, 1986:8.
    The homeless hold a candlelight vigil and Easter service to protest Santa Barbara's policies.   Mitch Snyder has threatened to ship thousands of homeless people to Santa Barbara.   The mayor, defending those policies, claims that Santa Barbara is poorer than the average city in California. He adds that Santa Barbara is opening a 40-bed shelter, while a 100-bed shelter is already in operation.

Chambers, Marcia.   "Tolerant Policy on Homeless Divides Santa Monica."   New York Times, March 23, 1986:14.
    From just a handful six years ago, Santa Monica, a city of 90,000 in Los Angeles County, now has 1,000 homeless.   The city installed "bum bars," dividers on park benches to prevent the homeless from sleeping on them.   Due to negative reactions, the city has removed them.

Chambliss, William J.   "A Sociological Analysis of the Law on Vagrancy."   Social Problems, 2, 1964:67-77.
    The author presents an overview of vagrancy laws in England from the 1300s to the 1700s, with a note on their application to the United States. Vagrancy laws arose to help supply cheap labor when serfdom was breaking down. After going into dormancy, they were reasserted when commerce and industry arose, with a change in focus from the idle to rogues and vagabonds.   The thesis is that changing social needs create a perceived need for legal changes.

Chaplin, Ralph. Wobbly: The Rough-and-Tumble Story of an American Radical. Chicago: University of Chicago Press, 1948.
   This autobiographical account by a leader of the radical labor movement in the United States includes a brief section on his travels in freight cars and meetings with hobos.

Chapman, Christine. America's Runaways. New York: William Morrow, 1976.
   This overview of running away in America, with an emphasis on the problems from which children run and the problems they encounter after running away, covers such topics as the runaway culture of sex, dope, and hustling, and the dangers and exploitation of runaways. It contains separate sections on runaways and police, the law, psychiatry, and youth advocacy.

Chappell, Helen. "The Rent Boy Scene." New Society, 78 (1244), October 31, 1986:8-9.
   This analysis of "rent boys," teenage male prostitutes in the Piccadilly area of London, points out that many are homeless boys driven to prostitution.

Chartrand, Sabra. "Made homeless by Missiles, 1,000 Israelis Fight for Aid." New York Times, January 25, 1991:A10.
   The approximately 1,000 Israelis who were left homeless from Iraqi SCUD missile attacks seek financial help from the Israeli government to rebuild their homes.

Chase, Marilyn, and Carrie Dolan. "California's Beacon to Newcomers Dims as Services Face Cuts." Wall Street Journal, September 1, 1992:A1, A6.
   This overview of a bleaker economy in California estimates that the state has 66,000 homeless people and that as a result of welfare cuts some welfare recipients who are not now homeless may be forced into homeless shelters.

Chase, Morris. "The Homeless Woman Alcoholic." In Proceedings of the Annual Conference of the National Committee on Alcoholism, the Institute on the Skid Row Alcoholic of the Committee on the Homeless Alcoholic. New York: Department of Welfare, 1956:1-8. Very little help is available to the female alcoholic. They need "differential handling."

Chaves, Lydia. "10,000 Children in New York on Welfare."
New York Times, July 16, 1987:24.
    City officials are concerned about the future of the
children of the homeless. More than 1,300 such children
live in just one hotel, the Prince George Hotel on East
28th Street. About 9,000 children live in various hotels
throughout the city. By the turn of the century, there
may be an additional 20,000 such children. Officials
express concern about the deprivation of these children,
from discontinuity in their education to their nurturing
and emotional deprivation. The prediction is that these
children will become alienated adults, unable to establish relationships and "tending toward anger, criminality
and poor educational achievement."

Chaze, William L. "Behind Swelling Ranks of America's
Street People." U.S. News & World Report, 96, January
30, 1984:57-58.
    In reviewing the growing problem of homelessness,
the author focuses on deinstitutionalization.

Chaze, William L. "Helping the Homeless: A Fight Against
Despair." U.S. News and World Report, January 14,
1985:54-55.
    The causes of homelessness are deinstitutionaliza-
tion, the lack of low-income housing, and a tightened
federal budget. The solutions are help from churches,
charities, private groups (such as Harvard students), and
foundations. A backlash has developed in Chicago due to
fears of the homeless. This has resulted in new building
codes, making it more difficult to start a shelter.

Chaze, William L. "Street People: Adrift and Alone in
America." U.S. News and World Report, 92, March 8,
1982:60-61.
    The emphases are deinstitutionalization, alcoholics,
and difficulties of life on the streets. The author
mentions the difficulties that homeless shelters are
having due to a cutback in federal funds, and the refusal
to accept help by some of homeless. Rebecca Smith, who
froze to death in Manhattan, is also mentioned.

Chessare, John B., John M. Pascoe, and Evelyn F. Baugh.
"Smoking During Pregnancy and Child Maltreatment: Is
There an Association?" International Journal for
Biosocial Research, 8 (1), 1986:37-42.
    Of 201 babies whose homeless mothers had come to an
obstetrics clinic for prenatal care, 23 percent whose

mothers smoked were referred to social services for maltreatment, compared with 8 percent whose mothers did not smoke.

Chesterton, Mrs. Cecil.   In Darkest London.   London: Stanley Paul, 1926.
    This book is a first-person account of a middle-class woman's purposeful excursion into homelessness in London "to see what would happen if I started from zero with nothing but my personality to stand on." Sexual discrimination favors the treatment of homeless men. There are four types of homeless women: tramps, prostitutes, those temporarily down on their luck, and rovers (women born with a migratory instinct). The solutions are to open free shelters and employment bureaus.

Chipkin, Harvey. "Hotel Rooms for Homeless: Koch Ready to Sue Reluctant Properties." Hotel and Motel Management, December 15, 1986:1, 33.
    The mayor of New York threatens to sue hotels that he contends have empty rooms but refuse to rent them to homeless families.

Christ, Winifred R., and Sharon L. Hayden. "Discharge Planning Strategies for Acutely Homeless Inpatients." Social Work in Health Care, 14 (1), 1989:33-45.
    This paper reviews characteristics of people who become homeless while admitted to a hospital and suggests approaches which may be used to identify and prevent this syndrome. Potentially homeless persons can be identified at admission to a hospital through screening mechanisms that identify combinations of six factors: the patient has (1) an admitting residence that appears unstable, (2) multiple recent hospital admissions, (3) a history of prolonged impairment in performing the activities of daily life, (4) inadequate funds, (5) a dual diagnosis, and (6) no involved family or significant other. Suggests that social workers build alliances with agencies and groups that are concerned with the prevention of homelessness so they can establish contacts and referral sources and inform community providers of the stringent regulations under which hospitals must operate.

Christner, Anne M., and Harry Sterling. "Emergency Food Provision by Nonprofit and Religious Organizations: A Call to Study Users and Nonusers of Food Pantry Services." Paper presented at the Society for the Study of Social Problems, New York City, August 1986. Mimeo.

Because of a lack of adequate data on hunger and malnutrition in the United States, the authors surveyed providers and users of emergency food and shelter services in Rhode Island. Most of the paper is an argument that the demand for these services is growing and action should be taken. Researchers should not use the term emergency as it allows us to blame victims, nor use hunger as it cannot be measured or defined.

Cibulskis, Ann M., and Charles Hoch. "Homelessness: An Annotated Bibliography." Chicago: CPL Bibliographies, December 1985.

This bibliography contains 138 references, 71 of which are annotated. The entries are divided into 11 categories.

Cimons, Marlene. "A Refuge for Homeless Women." Los Angeles Times, May 23, 1976:1-4.

The author profiles the House of Ruth in Washington, D.C., run by Veronica Maz, a sociologist. She reviews their approach to homeless women and suggests that special shelters be opened for women.

Clandinen, Dudley. "Atlanta Homeless Find Place in Public Eye." New York Times, December 9, 1986:11

A proposal has been made to clear the downtown area of Atlanta of the homeless "by strict enforcement of the laws against panhandling, public drunkenness and vagrancy." The rights of the homeless to use public space are being defended by advocates for the homeless, who help make their case by using art and skits produced by the homeless.

Clandinen, Dudley. Homeless in America. New York: Acropolis Books, 1988.

This book is the result of a joint photographic project of the National Mental Health Association and Families for the Homeless. The purpose of the project is "to raise the level of public awareness and concern over the plight of America's homeless population."

Clark, Michael E., and Margaret Rafferty. "The Sickness That Won't Heal: Health Care for the Nation's Homeless." Health/PAC Bulletin, 16 (4), 20-28.

This overview of the health problems of the homeless, which focuses on the inability of current institutional arrangement to meet these health needs, reports on the high incidence of such diseases as TB, lung disease, pneumonia, skin ulcers, lacerations, contusions, and liver and heart disease. The high incidence of these diseases is related to the lack of a home. Consequently, permanent housing is a necessary part of the treatment of the diseases of the homeless. Henry Street Settlement House in New York City is suggested as a successful model.

Clarke, E. Dillon. "The Experiences of a Tramp." The Economic Journal, 16, June 1906:284-291.
    The author did participant observation for a few days to discover what tramps are like. In reporting his experiences at a boarding house, doss-houses, and work houses, he comments on the unfairness he has seen. He concludes that not many tramps want to work.

Clarke, R. V. G. "Absconding and Adjustment to the Training School." British Journal of Criminology, 1968:285-295.
    Based on a sample of 822 boys who ran away from Kingswood Classifying and Training School in Bristol, England, the author concludes that boys who run away from one institution will generally run away from another and that persistent absconders from training school are likely to be sent to another school or detention center rather than to receive a release under supervision.

Clarke, R. V. G. "Seasonal and Other Environmental Aspects of Absconding by Approved School Boys." British Journal of Criminology, 7, 1967:195-202.
    Based on 476 boys who ran away from the Kingswood Classifying and Training School in Bristol, England, the author concludes that running away increases in winter, is not related to rainfall, and is slightly affected by the distance of the boy's home area.

Clay, Phillip L., and Bernard J. Frieden. "A Plea for Less Regulation." Society, 21 (3), March-April 1984:48-53.
    This positive evaluation of the 1982 Report of the President's Commission on Housing contrasts liberal and conservative approaches to housing and evaluates implications of each for more or less regulation in the housing market. The solution is regulatory reform of housing, with the burden on communities to justify regulations that restrict housing.

Clayton, Joseph. "Tramps, Vagrants, and Beggars." Albany Review, 2, February 1908:568-574.
On the basis of five tramps he has met, the author makes distinctions between tramps, vagrants, and professional mendicants.

Clement, Priscilla Ferguson. "The Transformation of the Wandering Poor in Nineteenth-Century Philadelphia." In Walking to Work: Tramps in America, 1790-1935, Eric H. Monkkonen, ed. Lincoln: University of Nebraska Press, 1984:56-84.
Based on city records of Philadelphia, the author analyzes changes in the numbers of tramps or vagrants, making comparisons by sex, race, and American and foreign born. He relates the variations to structural conditions, especially those of relative prosperity and job opportunities.

Closson, Carlos C., Jr. "The Unemployed in American Cities." Quarterly Journal of Economics, 8, January 1894:168-217.
This state-by-state overview of unemployment and relief during the depression of the 1890s occasionally mentions tramps.

Closson, Carlos C., Jr. "The Unemployed in American Cities." Quarterly Journal of Economics, 8, April 1894:453-477.
This outline of the methods used by agencies for the relief of the unemployed during the winter of 1893-94 includes wayfarer's lodges, wood-yards, and work-tests.

Clouston, Harry. The Happy Hobo. London: Stanley Paul, 1937.
A New Zealander writes a first-person account of his hoboing around the world. His travels began as the result of a bet with friends.

Cluff, Leightone E. "Letter to the Editor." Wall Street Journal, November 2, 1989:A23.
The article quotes a study by James Wright indicating that homelessness is due to multi-faceted causes.

Cohen, Carl I., and Frances Briggs. "A Storefront Clinic on the Bowery." Journal of Studies on Alcohol, 37, September 1976:1336-1340.
The patient population of a small storefront clinic on the bowery reveals the emergence of a new category of

bowery residents--young, white, schizophrenic men with
little history of alcoholism.

Cohen, Carl I., and Jay Sokolovsky. "Toward a Concept of
Homelessness Among Aged Men." Journal of Gerontology, 38
(1), 1983:81-89.
    Based on a sample of 48 men living on New York's
Bowery and in SRO hotels, the authors conclude that
homelessness is not a uniform category and that homeless
men cannot always be easily distinguished from the
general populace. They apply Bogue's model of skid row
social formation and examines the men's networks of
association and modes of adaptation.

Cohen, Carl I., Jeanne Teresi, and Douglas Holmer. "The
Mental Health of Old Homeless Men." Journal of the
American Geriatrics Society, 36 (6), June 1988:492-501.
    The authors interviewed 86 street-dwelling and 195
non-street-dwelling males aged 50 and over on New York
City's Bowery. Those who had been previously hospitalized for mental illness did not differ substantially from
homeless males who had not been hospitalized for mental
problems. Concludes that homelessness should be considered the primary problem, mental illness a secondary
handicap.

Cohen, Carl I., Jeanne Teresi, Douglas Holmer, and Eric
Roth. "Survival Strategies of Older Homeless Men." The
Gerontologist, 128, February 1988:58-65.
    During 1982-1983, the authors interviewed 281
homeless men (Bowery residents) who were fifty year old
and over. The study included information on need fulfill-
ment, alcoholism, psychoses, depression, mental symptoms,
stress, structural network, interactional network,
institutional and agency contacts, network proclivity,
and physical health. The authors focus on survival
techniques of these older homeless men, especially money,
food, and shelter. Health care and social supports are
also foci of this coverage of the "daily struggles the
men faced."

Cohen, Erik. "Nomads from Affluence: Notes on the
Phenomenon of Drifter-Tourism." International Journal of
Comparative Sociology, 14, January-February 1973:89-103.
    A recent phenomenon of travelers are drifter
tourists, international tourists who go on their own and
venture from the beaten track, have no connection with
the tourist establishment, have no fixed itinerary or

timetable, become immersed in the host culture, and often take odd-jobs to keep themselves going. Historical antecedents are discussed. The author classifies them as full timers (adventurers and itinerant hippies) and part timers (mass drifters and fellow travelers).

Cohen, Marcia B. "Social Work Practice with Homeless Mentally Ill People: Engaging the Client." Social Work, 34 (6), November 1989:505-508.
    Critical for social work practice with the homeless mentally ill is the engagement phase--the process of establishing mutual respect and trust in the helping relationship in order to reduce fear and enable the "real work" to begin. The author suggests an empowerment-oriented approach that encourages homeless clients to maximize their control over the helping process--"to participate fully in identifying needs, determining goals, and setting the terms of the helping processs. "

Cohen, Neal L. "Stigma Is in the Eye of the Beholder: A Hospital Outreach Program for Treating Homeless Mentally Ill People." Bulletin of the Menninger Clinic, 54 (2), Spring 1990:255-258.
    The author reviews efforts to help reduce stigmatization of the homeless mentally ill by medical personnel in New York City.

Cohen, Neal L., J. F. Putnam, and A. M. Sullivan. "The Mentally Ill Homeless: Isolation and Adaptation." Hospital and Community Psychiatry, 35 (9), 1984:922-924.
    Project Help is a mobile outreach unit established in New York City in 1982 to provide crisis medical and psychiatric services to impaired homeless persons. Providing services to these people is made difficult because they distrust authority and are unwilling to provide information about themselves. The "more disaf-filiated" homeless need more extensive services than those who use sheltered care.

Cohen, Neal L., and L. R. Marcos. "Psychiatric Care of the Homeless Mentally Ill." Psychiatric Annals, 16 (2), 1986:729-732.
    The author discusses the legal barriers to involun-tary treatment of the mentally ill, the "revolving door" of inpatient care, and the shift to providing involuntary care to the homeless.

Cole, Tony. "Moving Houses." <u>New Statesman & Society</u>, June 30, 1989:27.
    The article focuses on the trends and quality of owner-occupied housing, privately rented housing, and council housing.

Coleman, John R. "Diary of a Homeless Man." <u>New York Magazine</u>, February 21, 1983:27-35. (This article is reprinted in the 5th (1988), 6th (1991), and 7th (1993) editions of <u>Down to Earth Sociology: Introductory Readings</u>, James M. Henslin, ed. New York: The Free Press.)
    The author, a former president of Haverford College, dressed as a homeless man and spent 10 days as a participant observer on the streets of New York City. He presents an insider view of the degradation of the homeless, even by those whose job it is to help them. He also provides understanding of why violence among the homeless is triggered so easily.

Coleman, Richard. "Racial Differences in Runaways." <u>Psychological Reports</u>, <u>22</u> (1), 1968:321-322.
    Using a sample of 458 white and 58 black boys who ran away from Lyman School, a training institution for delinquents, the author found that the mean age for both black and white runaways was 14.8 years, blacks were less likely to run away, and blacks who did run away were more likely to have been in the institution longer.

Collins, Thomas G. "Low-Income Taxpayer Problems." <u>Tax Lawyer</u>, <u>43</u> (4), Summer 1990:1311-1314.
    This overview of Section 7108 of the Omnibus Budget Reconciliation Act of 1989 mentions that the low-income housing credit applies to transitional housing for the homeless.

Conant, Jennet, and Nikki Finke Greenberg. "`Holiday Inn' for the Homeless." <u>Newsweek</u>, <u>106</u> (2), 44.
    The authors focus on protest activities on behalf of the homeless, especially those by Mitch Snyder and the Community for Creative Nonviolence in Washington, D.C..

Conason, Joe. "Body Count: How The Reagan Administration Hides the Homeless." <u>Village Voice</u>, December 1985:25-28, 30.
    The author highlights criticisms of HUD's <u>A Report to the Secretary on the Homeless and Emergency Shelters</u>.

Conklin, John J. "Homelessness and Deinstitutionalization." <u>Journal of Sociology and Social Welfare</u>, <u>12</u> (1),
March 1985:41-61.
    Solutions to the problem of the deinstitutionalized
mentally ill becoming homeless are proposed.

Conlin, Joseph. "The House That G.E. Built." <u>Successful
Meetings</u>, <u>38</u> (9), August 1989:50-58.
    The author recounts how salespeople from G.E.
Plastics renovated San Diego's Vincent de Paul Joan Kroc
urban center for the homeless in a single day. An
underlying motivation for the renovation was to teach the
salespeople team work, communication, planning, and
trust. Not only was the center renovated, but bed space
was increased from 400 to 600.

Connerly, Charles E. "Housing Trust Funds: New Resources
for Low-Income Housing." <u>Journal of Housing</u>, <u>47</u> (2),
March-April 1990:96-99.
    This overview of housing trust funds, government
funds earmarked for low-income and moderate-income
housing, mentions that such funds can be designated for
special groups such as the homeless.

Connolly, Mark. "Adrift in the City: A Comparative Study
of Street Children in Bogota, Colombia, and Guatemala
City." <u>Child and Youth Services</u>, <u>14</u> (1), 1990:129-149.
    The author, who did participant observation of
street children in Bogota and Guatemala City, describes
their lifestyle, including their mores, sanctions, and
values, and recommends a review of national policy in
order for the United States to avoid developing a similar
situation.

Cook, Blanche Wiesen. "The Impact of Anti-Communism in
American Life." <u>Science and Society</u>, <u>53</u> (4), Winter
1989-90:470-475.
    After reviewing effects of anti-communism on
American life, the author provides examples, including
homelessness, to illustrate that conservative (and right-
wing) policies have not led to a better world.

Cook, Tim, and Guy Braithwaite. "A Problem for Whom?"
In <u>Vagrancy: Some New Perspectives</u>, Tim Cook, ed.
London: Academic Press, 1979:1-10.
    The authors seek an answer to why a proposal to
relocate a day care center for the homeless in a working-
class section of London provoked such harsh reactions.

They conclude that the homeless are seen as undeserving because they do not reflect ordinary values: do not work, are irregular, unpunctual, dirty, unkempt, irrational, unpredictable, uncooperative, and take a chance-oriented approach to life. Such characteristics can also be seen, not as values, but as consequences of inadequate services; that is, the homeless are a human residue. Because they are a waste product of the socio-economic machine, they receive inferior status and "conceptual liquidation."

Cooke, J. "Vagrants, Beggars, and Tramps." Quarterly Review, 209, October 1908:388-408.
The author presents a history of vagrancy and laws from Saxon and Norman times. The problem today consists of beggars not seeking work, children being sold, and the public wasting money in misguided philanthropy. For beggars, the solutions are compulsory labor colonies that are self-supporting and possibly self-supplying; for their children, the solution is to provide compulsory industrial schools.

Cooper, Arthur Neville. "A Tramp's Lesson-Book." Chamber's Journal, 83, June 1906:470-473.
Based on his travel experiences, the author recommends a walking tour of Europe.

Cooper, Patricia A. "The 'Traveling Fraternity': Union Cigar Makers and Geographic Mobility, 1900-1919." In Walking to Work: Tramps in America, 1790-1935, Eric H. Monkkonen, ed. Lincoln: University of Nebraska Press, 1984:118-138.
The author analyzes the mobility of union cigar makers, a mobility encouraged by business downturns, strikes, and the workers' culture.

Cordes, Colleen. "The Plight of Homeless Mentally Ill." APA Monitor, 15 (2), February 1984:1, 13.
The deinstitutionalized mentally ill, many of whom are now homeless, have multiple needs. The solution is not to reinstitutionalize them, but to make available to them an expanded and coordinated array of community services that include "basic life supports such as housing, income and food, mental health treatment, including but not limited to outreach, crisis intervention, medication and supportive therapy, and, when necessary, some degree of protection, supervision and advocacy." Innovative approaches are summarized, with an

emphasis on mental health professionals who work on-site in city shelters and missions.

Cordtz, Dan. "On the Street." Financial World, 157, November 29, 1988:26-31.
After reviewing the background conditions behind the demolishment, abandonment, or conversion of low-rent housing units, the author analyzes factors that led a "coalition of state and local governments, charitable foundations, community organization, and major profit-making corporations" to rehabilitate low-income housing. Includes a report on successful rehabilitation efforts in various cities.

Corrigan, Eileen M., and Sandra C. Anderson. "Homeless Alcoholic Women on Skid Row." American Journal of Drug and Alcohol Abuse, 10 (4), 1984:535-549.
The authors, who interviewed 31 homeless alcoholic women on New York City's skid row, found heterogeneity and the lack of a life-long pattern of marginality. Many of the women had lived with their family, husband, or male partner before coming to the shelter, about a third had lived alone, homelessness was sometimes preceded by the death of someone close to them, and for many the two years prior to their move to the shelter were a period of instability and transient living. More resources are needed for shelter care.

Cosgrove, John G. "Towards a Working Definition of Street Children." International Social Work, 33 (2), April 1990:185-192.
The author's definition of street children results in a nine-cell matrix based on the extent of family involvement and conformity to accepted norms of social behavior. Each cell identifies a different category of street children and degree of risk of joining their ranks.

Coston, Charisse Tia Maria. "The Original Designer Label: Prototypes of New York City's Shopping-Bag Ladies." Deviant Behavior, 10 (2), 1989:157-172.
The author reports on her interviews with 35 homeless women in the "main bag lady territory" of Manhattan, between 30th and 52nd Streets in New York City. She summarizes the "forces that lead to a life-style of living on the streets," the women's modes of survival, the reactions of the police, their victimization, and their communication networks. The author

presents a typology of homeless women: (1) the full-time shopping-bag lady, (2) the part-time shopping-bag lady, (3) the situational shopping-bag lady, and (4) the mentally-troubled shopping-bag lady. The author con-cludes with suggestions for meeting the needs of shopping bag ladies.

Coughlin, Ellen K. "Studying Homelessness: The Difficul-ty of Tracking a Transient Population." The Chronicle of Higher Education, October 19, 1988:A6-A12.

It is very difficult to accurately determine how many homeless there are. Sociologist Peter H. Rossi used scientific techniques to estimate the number of homeless in the city of Chicago. The Chicago count cost about $600,000, and a national survey might run about $6 million. Rossi reports that even without precise measurements we know there are at least a quarter of a million homeless, and that's enough for us to know that we should do something about homelessness. Rossi's suggested solution to the problem is "increased spending on the federal program Aid to Families with Dependent Children, up to abut $45-billion a year.... and income support for poor families who subsidize destitute adult relatives, a program he estimates could cost as much as $15-billion a year."

Coulson, Crocker. "The $37,000 Slum." The New Republic, 169, January 19, 1987:15-16.

The author denounces the political conditions that have led to paying exorbitant prices for accommodations for homeless families in miserable conditions, New York City's welfare hotels. He makes the point that "to some degree, the City depends by miserable accommodations to keep the number of the homeless down," that providing decent accommodations could initiate a "bottomless demand," by which "any impoverished family could immedi-ately boost its income simply by becoming homeless." The two solutions are to move families out of welfare hotels and into apartments and to make permanent apartments available.

Cousins, Anne. "Profile of Homeless Men and Women Using an Urban Shelter." Journal of Emergency Nursing, 9 (3), May-June 1983:133-137.

The author's profiles of homeless men and women are drawn from interviews with 25 shelter users. She covers age, occupation, the streets not as a choice but due to lack of alternatives, social isolation, alienation, illness, alcoholism, and thoughts of suicide.

Cowdrey, Robert H. <u>A Tramp in Society</u>. Chicago: Francis J. Schulte, 1891.
    This novel presents a contrast between social classes by telling the story of a tramp who finds a patron and then makes an adjustment to upper class society.

Cox, Gail Diane. "Gramm-Rudman Cuts Hit County Homeless." <u>Los Angeles Daily Journal</u>, September 16, 1988:1.
    Gramm-Rudman cuts of 4.2 percent will require agencies and shelters that are serving the homeless to cut down on the number of meals they serve the homeless and the purchase of disposable diapers for babies unless Los Angeles County makes up the lost money.

Cox, Gail Diane. "Homeless Children Rule Puts State in Contempt of Court." <u>Los Angeles Daily Journal</u>, <u>99</u>, August 4, 1986:B1.
    Confusion has resulted from a judge's ruling that the State of California must stop its policy of denying emergency shelter to needy children unless their families are split up. The confusion is uncertainty whether this means that the state must provide shelter for the entire family, which was the goal of the advocates for the homeless who brought the case to court.

Cox, Gail Diane. "S. M. City Attorney Set to Testify For Defense in 'Justiceville II' Trial." <u>Los Angeles Daily Journal</u>, <u>98</u>, October 15, 1985:B1.
    The city attorney of Santa Monica, California, who has stopped prosecuting homeless people for trespass, will testify in the trial of three homeless persons who "entered a fenced piece of vacated property on Bixel Street (in downtown Los Angeles) with plans to set up a tent city." The defense "will argue that the county has failed its legal responsibility to be a provider of last resort for the indigent and force the three to try to create a safe haven for themselves."

Cox, Gail Diane. "Suit Asserts Policy of Welfare Dept. Breaks Up Families." <u>Los Angeles Daily Journal</u>, April 18, 1986:1.
    Advocates for the homeless are trying to get the courts to rule that it is a violation of state welfare laws to "provide emergency shelter to children only if

they are put in foster care (for this) has the effect of either denying aid or necessarily breaking up the families." The author makes the point that because they fear that their children will be removed from them homeless parents often keep their children invisible.

Cox, Gail Diane. "U.S. Funds for Homeless Seen 'Inappropriate'." Los Angeles Daily Journal, October 28, 1985:1.
Los Angeles County officials are attempting to locate money to help the homeless, which has become more difficult since the chief administrative officer of Los Angeles County has ruled that "federal funding earmarked to keep the elderly poor in their homes should not be used to help the homeless."

Cox, Gail Diane. "Welfare Rule Hit for Causing Rise in Homelessness." Los Angeles Daily Journal, January 3, 1985:1.
Poverty lawyers argue against "the legality of the county's withholding welfare benefits for two months from those deemed to be able-bodied but not cooperating with instructions to look for employment, or join on work project or job training." They claim that this rule is inappropriately applied for "minor workplace infractions, like turning in a form a half-hour late." As a result, "people are sentenced to two months of homelessness." County officials reply that the rules are appropriately applied and estimate that eliminating these rules "would add $4 million a year to the county's current $12 million expenditure for general relief."

Cox, John E. "Objectives of the UN International Year of Shelter for the Homeless (IYSH)--1987." Ekistics, 307, July-August 1984:284-288.
Industrialization has created a word wide movement to cities, housing problems, and unemployment, all of which are affecting human welfare. The author proposes a shelter strategy for developing countries and enumerates technical and structural problems in working on this problem.

Cox, Meg. "Rap Music Is Taking a Positive Turn and Winning Fans." Wall Street Journal, October 8, 1992:A1, A4.
This profile of Arrested Development, a "positive" rap group, mentions that homelessness is one of the group's subjects.

Cravatts, Richard L.   "Loosen Codes and House the Homeless." Wall Street Journal, February 6, 1992:A14.
   By reducing low-cost rental units, the government's efforts to eliminate Single Room Occupancy units as dangerous to tenants and undesirable for neighborhoods had the unintended effect of increasing homelessness. SROs should be brought back in.

Crawford, J. H.   The Autobiography of a Tramp.   London: Longmans and Green, 1900.
   The author, who was born of tramping parents, recounts his socialization as a child into tramping as a way of life. He also tells about later experiences. The focus is tramping as a subculture, its values, norms, pleasures, and ways of coping.

Crist, Raymond E. "Export Agriculture and the Expansion of Urban Slum Areas." American Journal of Economics and Sociology, 48 (2), April 1989:143-149.
   Focusing on Brazil, the author analyzes how the emphasis on exporting agricultural products has led to deforestation and an increase in the "new barbarians within the gate"--the hungry, homeless, and alienated. The production of soybeans for export, for example, decreased the production of black beans, on which many of the poor depend, and bean riots ensued. Comparisons are made with agricultural exports and homelessness in the United States.

Cross, William T.   "The Poor Migrant in California." Social Forces, 15, March 1937:423-427.
   This overview of the continued migration of the poor to California even after the closing of the frontier discusses seasonal workers, riots and government intervention, funds for the "unsettled poor" (those without legal residence in a state), and the closing of California's borders to the indigent. The proposed solution is to direct public policy to the assimilation of interstate immigrants in order to establish a stable existence for the outcast fringe of a mobile population. This will require public health, medical services, education, and employment--all of which will help the unsettled poor develop community ties.

Cross, William T., and Dorothy E. Cross. Newcomers and Nomads in California. Stanford: Stanford University Press, 1937.

Large numbers of migrants, who are unwelcome, are coming to California. The proposed solutions are federal emergency legislation, rehabilitation work, and organized assistance designed to meet the needs of three differentiated populations: local homeless, state homeless, and transients.

Crossette, Barbara. "Price of Success for Bombay: Homelessness and Squatters." New York Times, April 25, 1991.

The author reviews homelessness in Bombay where "hundreds of thousands of migrants, drawn to Bombay by streets of gold, end up living on the sidewalks, defying most attempts to move them in the interests of beautification, sanitation or the free flow of pedestrians."

Crossley, B., and J. C. Denmark. "Community Care: A Study of the Psychiatric Morbidity of a Salvation Army Hostel." British Journal of Sociology, 20 (4), 1969:443-449.

According to the Salvation Army, 10 percent of the homeless are tramps, 40 percent come from broken homes, running away, or ex-prisoners, 25 percent suffer from physical or mental ill health, and 25 percent are old-age pensioners. Interviews with 51 men in a hostel indicate that many of the deinstitutionalized still need asylum.

Crouse, Joan M. "Homeless." Contemporary Sociology, May 1988:371.

The author traces negative attitudes toward the homeless to Europe, from where they were brought to the United States, and summarizes government programs for the homeless during the Great Depression. She also analyzes the reactions of local residents and the homeless to social policies regarding the homeless and suggests that the failures and successes of past policies can help inform current policy making.

Crouse, Joan M. The Homeless Transient in the Great Depression: New York State, 1929-1941. Albany, New York: SUNY Press, 1986.

This summary of programs of private agencies and federal, state, and local governments for dealing with the homeless during the Great Depression includes reactions of the homeless to those policies. The author argues that negative attitudes toward the homeless were transmitted from Europe to the United States.

Crowther, M. A.   The Workhouse System, 1834-1929: The
History of an English Social Institution.   Athens,
Georgia: University of Georgia Press, 1982.
     The author examines background influences and
conceptualizations that led to the formation of the
modern welfare state.   Residential institutions were seen
as the solution for many social ills, including unemployment, friendless children, and the helpless.   The
purposes of residential institutions were to improve the
moral standards of the poor, discóurage crime, and raise
wages.   Some of these workhouses developed into hospitals, others into homes for the aged and handicapped
children.

Crystal, Stephen.   "Homeless Men and Homeless Women: The
Gender Gap."   The Urban and Social Change Review, 17 (2),
Summer 1984:2-6.
     This critical review of how the concepts of disaf-
filiation and impaired functioning are applied to the
homeless compares homeless men and women in New York
shelters by examining their marital status, psychiatric,
employment, and correctional histories, and their
relationship to their children.

Crystal, Stephen, Merv Goldstein, and Rosanne Levitt.
Chronic and Situational Dependency: Long-Term Residents
in a Shelter for Men.   New York: Human Resources Administration of the City of New York, May 1982.
     Characteristics of the 128 men who stayed more than
two months at the Keener Building Shelter in New York
City are presented in tabular form.   Most of the men are
minority with long-term attachment to New York City and
much alcohol and drug abuse.   Many have been psychiatrically hospitalized.   Unlike the stereotypes, more than a
fifth of the men had at least some college, half are high
school graduates, and more than 40 percent had some
contact with family during the past six months.   The
proposed solutions are to develop independent living
arrangements, specialized residences for the mentally ill
homeless, and a long range plan for New York City's
shelter system.

Crystal, Stephen, Susan Ladner, and Richard Towber.
"Multiple Impairment Patterns in the Mentally Ill
Homeless."   International Journal of Mental Health, 14
(4), 1986:61-73.
     Based on interviews with 8,061 men and women in the
public shelters of New York City, the authors report on

the age, gender, ethnicity, psychiatric and physical problems, substance abuse, residence, barriers to employment, financial benefits, and length of time these persons have stayed in the shelters. Mental disorders were reported by 24.9 percent. Compared with those who did not report such problems, this psychiatric group stayed in shelters more, was more likely to be receiving entitlements, have more physical problems and more barriers to employment. The modal public shelter client is "a young (mid-30s), black male who lived in an apartment of his own or with family or friends during the three to six months before entering the shelter. His inability to find a job has been the major barrier to employment." In contrast, the modal person in the psychiatric group is "a white woman (also in her mid-30s)."

Culhane, Dennis P. "Poorhouse Revisited." New York Times, November 18, 1991:A15.
    Social policies that promote shelters for the homeless are no better than policies from the unenlightened past that promoted poorhouses. We should help prevent homelessness by social policies that help people keep their homes.

Culver, Benjamin F. "Transient Unemployed Men." Sociology and Social Research, 17, July-August 1933:519-535.
    The author presents background information on 136 men who stayed at the Shelter for Transient Men at Palo Alto, California, in the fall of 1932. About two-thirds of the men were American-born citizens. Their median age was 31. Only one half had attended school beyond the 8th grade. Seventy-nine percent were unmarried, 13 percent married, and 8 percent divorced or widowed. Seventy-five percent had been unemployed for 6 months or more. Almost half had been employed in the manufacturing and mechanical industries. Their median annual income was $1,593, with 9 percent ranging above $3,000. Eighty percent were physically capable of employment, and 43 percent admitted that personal reasons such as sickness or carelessness with earnings or excessive use of alcohol had contributed to their unemployment. The others would not reply to the question or insisted that the depression was the only cause of their unemployment.

Cumming, Elaine. "Prisons, Shelters, and Homeless Men." Psychiatric Quarterly, 48 (4), 1974:496-504.

The author examines the role of police, prisons, missions, and shelters in dealing with the homeless. With deinstitutionalization, we need to offer care, not cure, to those who choose nonconforming life styles. The solutions are providing medical care for hangovers, food, and tolerance. The definition of homelessness is the lack of any social home.

Cummings, Judith. "A Division on Shelter in the West." New York Times, October 13, 1987:14.
     In compliance with a California law that requires communities to identify potential shelters for the homeless, Irvine officials have proposed that their new city animal shelter that has never yet housed animals be renovated to house the homeless. This has created a controversy, especially from nearby residents who fear that an influx of the homeless will bring an increase in crime.

Cummings, Judith. "Fast Food, Migration, Homeless." New York Times, October 20, 1986:10.
     Skid Row Park, established as a benefit for the homeless, has been invaded by drug dealers. To stop their activities at night, Los Angeles is planning a $300,000 renovation, which will include sprinklers that will go on intermittently from 8 P.M. to 8 A.M.

Cummings, Judith. "'Hands Across America' Makes Grants Amid Controversy Over Time Lag." New York Times, November 21, 1986:Y13.
     The first grants from "last spring's nationwide hand-holding campaign against homelessness" will be dispersed. Controversy has arisen concerning the amount of money that was spent in raising $32 million, as well as "the long-term value of such a project."

Cummings, Judith. "The Homeless of Los Angeles Make Their Numbers Felt." New York Times, December 15, 1985:E5.
     Southern California is attracting large numbers of homeless because of its generous public assistance. Perhaps it could be declared a disaster area for purposes of receiving federal aid. Greyhound therapy is discussed, as well as the conflict that has arisen with businesses and developers. Homelessness is a moral issue.

Cummings, Judith. "Increase in Homeless People Tests U.S. Cities' Will to Cope." New York Times, May 3, 1982:1, 16.

This discussion of an increase in urban homelessness mentions New York City, Balboa Park, San Diego, Detroit, Washington, Columbus, Houston, Los Angeles, East St. Louis. Its causes are deinstitutionalization, mental illness, a national tax revolt, and urban renewal. The author discusses the "bed of nails" theory to reduce the number of applicants to shelters.

Cummings, Judith. "Los Angeles Homeless Adapt Lives for Theater." New York Times, July 18, 1986:6.

City Stage is a skid-row theater where homeless men dramatize their street experiences. The author discusses people who are homeless by choice, being free to pursue thoughts and talents without having to punch a time clock.

Cummings, Judith. "Sympathy and Ire As the Homeless Take to the Beach." New York Times, September 25, 1987:8.

Three hundred fifty-six homeless people have moved to Venice Beach where they have erected pup tents and various types of windbreaks. Neighboring residents are upset because of "small-time criminals who sell drugs and snatch purses, winos who aggressively panhandle, and the mentally ill whose behaviors can be unpredictable and threatening." Some residents, however, are quick to defend what they describe as "the truly homeless," those who "mind their own business and seem to want mainly to be left alone."

Cunningham, J. "Municipal Lodging Houses." St. Louis Public Library Monthly Bulletin, New Series 10, 1912:327-348.

This overview of reports on the homeless from across the nation, with a focus from 1910-1912, includes Boston, Buffalo, Chicago, Cincinnati, Cleveland, Denver, Detroit, Kalamazoo, Kansas City, Louisville, Milwaukee, Minneapolis, New Bedford, New York City, Philadelphia, Providence, Salem, San Francisco, Seattle, Syracuse, Toledo, and Worcester, with more detailed information provided for St. Louis.

Cuomo, Mario M. 1933/1983--Never Again. A Report to the National Governor's Association Task Force on the Homeless. Portland, Maine: July 1983. Lithograph, 88 pages.

This overview and history of homelessness also examines the definition of homelessness and the self-concept of homeless people. The causes of homelessness are unemployment, scarcity of affordable housing, deinstitutionalization, cutbacks in social service and disability, and domestic violence. The short-term solutions are emergency food and shelter programs, while the long-term solutions are improvements in psychiatric care, public assistance, general relief, and better housing policies.

Curry, Chuck. "Say, Brother: 'I Robbed Peter to Pay Paul, but in the Process I Became One of the Homeless.'" *Essence*, 17, November 1986:8.
This first-person account is written by an individual who used to work in television news broadcasting. He became homeless after his independent television network was taken over by a major media conglomerate.

Cutler, Robin. "After Civil Rights Victories, Homeless Man Finds Two Sides to Fame." New York Times, September 1, 1991:NJ1.
The author profiles Richard Kreimer, a homeless man who gained fame for initiating successful lawsuits against the city of Morristown, New Jersey.

D

Dahl, Jonathan. "A Lost Brother Sends One Man on a Search with Few Guideposts." Wall Street Journal, March 18, 1991:A1.
The author recounts his search for his homeless brother, and his frustrations upon finding him.

Dahl, Jonathan. "More Homeless People Take Shelter at Airports." Wall Street Journal, November 9, 1989:B1.
Many homeless peope use airport waiting areas as shelters. In New York City and Chicago, the police do not eject the homeless, but in places such as Atlanta and Los Angeles the police give them tickets or arrest them. In Newark, authorities removed seats from one terminal to "discourage the homeless."

Dahl, Jonathan. "Ripping Out Asbestos Endangers More Lives as Laws Are Ignored." <u>Wall Street Journal</u>, March 5, 1986:1, 26.

This account of asbestos removal around the United States mentions that homeless men were hired to remove asbestos from the St. Anthony Hotel in San Antonio. They did so without protection.

Dahl, Jonathan. "Street Triage: A San Diego Shelter Feeds the Homeless with an Uneven Hand." <u>Wall Street Journal</u>, February 18, 1992:A1.

The author features Joe Carroll and the St. Vincent de Paul Village program for the homeless in San Diego, California. There, those who are seen as having little chance of getting out of homelessness, such as winos and addicts, are given basic care, while those who are seen as having a good chance of moving back into regular life, such as persons who held down jobs but are now newly homeless, are provided first-class care, including gourmet meals and opportunities to make job and professional contacts.

Dahl, Jonathan. "Up to 20% of Homeless People Carry AIDS Virus, Says New Report by CDC." <u>Wall Street Journal</u>, November 12, 1991:B4.

The Centers for Disease Control in Atlanta, Georgia, reports that nationally the rate of AIDS infection is less than 0.5 percent, but among the homeless it runs from 1 percent to 20 percent, depending on the city, two to forty times higher than the national rate. "Experts said the extraordinarily high figures reflect use of intravenous drugs and risky sex, practices of many homeless people. In addition, as people infected with the virus exhaust their finances paying for treatment, an increasing number fall into the ranks of homelessness."

Dail, Paula W. "The Psychosocial Context of Homeless Mothers with Young Children: Program and Policy Implications." <u>Child Welfare</u>, <u>69</u> (4), July-August 1990:291-308.

Using interview and questionnaire data from 124 homeless women with children staying at 18 shelters, the author details their family history, health, parenting concerns, use of public assistance, and history of homelessness. The women had difficulties in setting goals, self control and social adjustment. Their ability to cope is correlated with their sense of control and social adjustment, while psychopathology and impulsiveness correlate with the age of the oldest child. The author includes suggestions for public policy and social intervention.

Daley, Suzanne. "Children on the Street: AIDS Begins Scourge." <u>New York Times</u>, May 30, 1988:12.
     Robert, a 19-year-old street male, is the first reported case of a runaway dying of AIDS. Robert is more properly a case of a "throwaway," because no one was really looking for him. As is evident in this case, such street children "do not even have a place to die." Many homeless people have abandoned their usual "haunts" because they are afraid of a new law that has gone into effect that allows them to be taken off the streets to mental hospitals against their will.

Daley, Suzanne. "City Shelters Won't Split Up Childless Homeless Couples." <u>New York Times</u>, August 13, 1986:45.
     In a policy switch, New York City will allow an estimated 50 to 200 childless homeless couples to stay together in dormitory-type quarters if they provide evidence that they are married. The Legal Action Center for the Homeless claims this change is a result of a lawsuit they filed.

Daley, Suzanne. "Hard Times at Covenant a Year After Ritter's Ouster." <u>New York Times</u>, February 20, 1991:B1.
     A year ago, following allegations of child molesta- tion, Father Bruce Ritter resigned from Covenant House, an organization he had founded to work with street children. Donations have plummeted.

Daley, Suzanne. "Homeless Fear Forced Removal in Koch Policy." <u>New York Times</u>, October 12, 1987:16.
     Since a program initiated by Mayor Koch to involun- tarily hospitalize the mentally ill homeless has gone into effect, many homeless people are no longer in their usual "haunts."

Daley, Suzanne. "Homeless New Yorkers Seek Harbor at Airport." <u>New York Times</u>, July 6, 1987:13.
     About 120 homeless people sleep at the Kennedy International Airport. They are better dressed than most homeless, and appear to be "more organized." Most of them blend in with passengers and persons waiting for travelers. Some of them collect pensions. "Officials are uneasy about what might happen if the numbers of homeless swell."

Daley, Suzanne. "Illness and Despair Live Alongside Hope." <u>New York Times</u>, December 21, 1988:1, 10.
In describing the program of Access House, which specializes in helping the homeless mentally ill, the author details the histories of several residents.

Daley, Suzanne. "In New York, Cautious Help for the Helpless." <u>New York Times</u>, September 5, 1987:1, 8.
Project Help, a program of the Health and Hospitals Corporation, has an annual budget of $750,000 to keep track of homeless people living on the streets of New York City, establishing contact with them, and developing a relationship in order to "keep an eye on their physical as well as mental condition." When the team notes deterioration in individuals, it is authorized to remove them to mental hospitals. In 1986 Project Help picked up 125 men and women. On any given day, the teams check about 15 people.

Daley, Suzanne. "In New York, the Hidden Homeless Increase." <u>New York Times</u>, June 17, 1987:1, 14.
The "hidden homeless" are persons who "drift from place to place, doubling or tripling up with friends or relatives." They are also known as "couch people." These are people who "have not yet resorted to shelter system, but are likely to end up there." Perhaps up to 100,000 families are "couch people," a number that includes up to 200,000 children. The author details the case of Jackie and her son.

Daley, Suzanne. "Keeping Faith: Feeding the Homeless in Harlem." <u>New York Times</u>, September 1, 1987:11.
Emma Blake, a woman of meager means, operates a soup kitchen at Faithful Workers of Christ of God Church in Harlem, New York.

Daley, Suzanne. "New York City Hospitalizes Some Homeless Involuntarily." <u>New York Times</u>, August 29, 1987:Y9.
A new program allows New York City homeless to be involuntarily hospitalized after they have been inter-viewed on the street by a team of experts, including a psychiatrist. Physicians at Bellevue must concur with the need for hospitalization, and "people taken from the street will be informed that they are entitled to a lawyer upon admission to Bellevue."

Daley, Suzanne. "New York City, The Landlord: A Decade of Housing Decay." New York Times, February 8, 1988:1, 35.
    New York City has accumulated 4,000 buildings from tax-delinquent landlords. These buildings house 37,000 families, and are in bad condition. The city has no master plan for running these buildings, nor has it taken an overall survey of needed repairs or general conditions inside the buildings. Reporters who have investigated this matter report that the city is operating buildings in violation of its own code, a code that it enforces on private owners.

Daley, Suzanne. "New York's Homeless Children: Struggling to Survive in a System's Grasp." New York Times, February 3, 1987:11.
    Severe problems exist in educating "hotel kids," the children of homeless parents who are sheltered in New York City's hotels for the homeless. About 7,000 school-age children live in New York City's hotels and shelters for the homeless. Their problems include sleepiness, vice, attendance, and hunger.

Daley, Suzanne. "Robert M. Hayes: Anatomy of a Crusader for the Homeless." New York Times, October 2, 1987:14.
    The author summarizes the background and activities of Robert M. Hayes, a legal advocate for the homeless in New York.

Daley, Suzanne. "Study Finds Families Stay Too Long in Shelters for Homeless." New York Times, November 17, 1988:12Y.
    Problems plague the "large congregate shelters" of New York City. About 500 families stay in these shelters, including about 400 children. Their average stay is 11 weeks. Specific problems are lack of privacy, no place for the children to do homework, children missing school, contagious illnesses, and huge expense for little return, as it costs about $95 to $170 a night to house an average family.

Daley, Suzanne. "U.S. Is Seeking to Reduce Aid to the Homeless." New York Times, August 15, 1987:10.
    New York City officials are angry about the new regulations to be published in the Federal Register that will limit to 30 days the amount that the federal government will reimburse New York City for housing homeless people. City officials point out that the

average stay in hotels is 13 months, that "the problems
these families face don't always go away in a mere 30
days." About half of the $156 million spent for housing
and service for homeless families comes from the federal
government.

Daley, Suzanne. "Working Homeless Get Own Shelter." New
York Times, January 1, 1987:9.
     A shelter for the working homeless has been opened
in New York City. "To get into the program the man must
sign a contract agreeing among other things to work at
least 35 hours a week, put half their salaries into a
savings account and attend workshops on personal hygiene,
how to keep a job, how to look for an apartment and how
to budget money....If the men lose their jobs or do not
find a place (within 90 days), they must return to other
shelters."

Daly, Gerald. "Health Implications of Homelessness:
Reports from Three Countries." Journal of Sociology and
Social Welfare, 17 (1), March 1990:111-125.
     The author offers "a glimpse at the range of
projects which have evolved" in Britain, Canada, and the
United States during the 1890s. Mentioned as health
implications of homelessness are sleep deprivation,
nutritional problems, skin diseases, respiratory ailments, physical illnesses, mental illnesses, and AIDS.
States that information and advocacy centers, outreach
projects, education programs, programs for youth,
programs for women, and programs for AIDS patients have
evolved. Needed is "a comprehensive range of programs,
including permanent housing and long-term commitments to
health care" and a "focus on certain populations which
have been hidden or neglected," such as battered women
and runaway youth.

Daly, Gerald. "Homelessness and Health: A Comparison of
British, Canadian, and U.S. Cities." Cities, 6 (1),
February 1989:22-38.
     After comparing American, British, and Canadian
social policies concerning the poor, the author concludes
that poverty and homelessness cannot be treated in a
vacuum, as though specific problems were unrelated to one
another. Instead, comprehensive programs for the
homeless and other poor are required. Also examines the
incidence of tuberculosis and other infectious diseases
among the homeless.

Daly, Gerald. "Homelessness and Health: Views and Responses in Canada, the United Kingdom, and the United States." <u>Health Promotion</u>, <u>4</u> (2), 1989:115-128.

After comparing American, British, and Canadian social policies concerning the poor, the author concludes that poverty and homelessness cannot be treated in a vacuum, as though specific problems were unrelated to one another. Instead, comprehensive programs for the homeless and other poor are required. Also examines the incidence of tuberculosis and other infections diseases among the homeless.

Daniel, Leon. "The Street People." <u>The Los Angeles Daily Journal</u>, <u>22</u>, 1984:4.

This profile of the life and activities of Mitch Snyder, an outspoken advocate for the homeless and a major leader of the Community for Creative Non-Violence (CCNV) focuses on his leadership style, reactions of politicians, and controversies centering around his advocacy for the homeless.

Darcy, L., and D. L. Jones. "The Size of the Homeless Men Population of Sydney." <u>Australian Journal of Social Issues</u>, <u>10</u> (3), 1975:208-215.

The author reviews possible ways to measure homeless populations, applies one method, and concludes that Sydney has 3,200 homeless men.

Darden, Edwin. "Educators Seek Answers to Dilemma Created by Homeless Students." <u>Education Daily</u>, <u>21</u> (247), December 28, 1988:1-2.

In order to comply with the Stewart B. McKinney Homeless Assistance Act, states must determine how they will provide education for homeless children. Some states want to "place financial responsibilities on the district in which the student resided before losing his or her permanent home," while others take the position that these children "have a right to be educated in whichever communities they are located." The difficulties in providing education for these children are compounded by problems of transportation, residency requirements, the children staying home to baby-sit younger brothers and sisters, and teasing by classmates.

Darlin, Damon. "America's New Poor Swallow Their Pride, Go to Soup Kitchens." <u>Wall Street Journal</u>, January 11, 1983:1, 20.

The author reports that homelessness is growing, and uses examples from Tulsa, Detroit, Cleveland, and Elyria, Ohio. The problem of dealing with pride and facing up to their situation is especially difficult for those undergoing downward social mobility.

Darling, Drew. "Keys Are a Dead Giveaway." University of Minnesota Update, 13 (4), April 1986:4-5.
Laura Sue Epstein, who wrote a play about the homeless, Home at Seven, and is now attending law school, says that to have keys means that one belongs somewhere; the homeless don't carry keys.

Daswani, Mona. "Shelter and Women: A Perspective." Indian Journal of Social Work, 48 (3), October 1987:273-285.
A new perspective on housing is needed, one in which women participate in designing housing and planning urban settlements.

Dattalo, Patrick, and Brent B. Benda. "Providers of Services to the Homeless: Problems and Prospects." Administration in Social Work, 15 (3), 1991:105-119.
A survey of 137 workers and 23 organizations that serve the homeless in Richmond, Virginia, found that only five were established during the past seven years. Consequently, the authors conclude that there is no new service system and indicate support for the advocates for the homeless who claim that the current system is inadequate.

Davidson, Barbara Parmer, and Pamela J. Jenkins. "Class Diversity in Shelter Life." Social Work, 34 (6), November 1989:491-495.
The class diversity between shelter providers (likely to be middle class) and those using shelter facilities (likely to be lower class) creates a class conflict (a gap in life experiences and values) that "can create obstacles to effective working relationships between shelter residents and staff members." Specific areas in which class bias shows up are "staff expectations of residents, the value and practice of counseling, child discipline methods, and resident's planning for the future." To bridge this gap requires "a more comprehensive understanding of economic realities and a social context of resident's lives."

Davidson, Joe. "How a 24-Year-Old Reigned as Local Hero
Until His Drug Arrest." Wall Street Journal, November
13, 1989:A1, A5.
   This article on Rayful Edmond III, identified as a
drug kingpin in Washington, D.C., mentions that Edmond
bought beans for the homeless.

Davies, Gaye. "Managing Organizational Change: Strategies for the Female Health Care Supervisor." Health Care
Supervisor, 8 (4), July 1990:9-14.
   The author recommends that women enter health care
because the field is growing and women are nurturing. If
they do, one beneficiary will be the homeless.

Davies, William H. The Autobiography of A Super-Tramp.
London: Jonathan Cape, 1942. (First published in 1908.)
   This first-person account of choosing and living the
life of a tramp in England in the late 1800s examines the
subculture of tramps, especially their attitudes and
coping mechanisms. The preface was written by George
Bernard Shaw.

Davis, David. "The Homeless Elect an Ambassador."
Progressive, 49, December 1985:16.
   Chris Sprowal, a homeless man, organizes the
homeless in Philadelphia and uses dramatic demonstrations
to protest their treatment.

Davis, Michael. "Forced to Tramp: The Perspective of
the Labor Press, 1870-1900." In Walking to Work: Tramps
in America, 1790-1935, Eric H. Monkkonen, ed. Lincoln:
University of Nebraska Press, 1984:141-170.
   Based on a study of the four most influential labor
newspapers of the 1800s, the author summarizes attitudes
toward tramp legislation and the distinctions made
between honest and dishonest tramps. He traces the
causes of these armies of the unemployed to economic
conditions, discrimination by marital status, job
insecurity, and the weakness of trade unions. The
article contains a section on women tramps, various
species of tramps, and the struggle against tramp laws.

Davis, Mike. "Homeowners and Homeboys: Urban Restructuring in LA." Enclitic, 11 (3), 1989:9-16.
   This analysis of the LA (Los Angeles) School of
urban theory mentions that this blend of political and
sociological Marxist theory has illuminated the connec-

tion between the homeless and the decline of inner-city labor markets.

Davis, Philip. "Child Labor and Vagrancy." <u>Chautauquan</u>, <u>50</u>, May 1908:416-424.
    The author uses case stories to illustrate another evil of child labor--that it underlies much adult vagrancy.

Dawson, William Harbutt. "Society's Duty to the Tramp." <u>Fortnightly Review</u>, O.S. <u>74</u>, N.S. <u>68</u>, December 1900:953-966.
    Loafers and idlers come in four types: nomads of the highway (the begging, blackmailing, and pillaging vagabond); the settled, residential loafer; the intermittent loafer (usually an inebriate); and the promiscuous women of the lowest class of society (illegitimate and irresponsible maternity). The solution is rigorous laws to stamp out tramps. Loafing should be made a legal offense, with detention at hard labor (working on sewage systems) the punishment; police permission should be required to travel in search of work; severe laws should be passed against begging; and free lodging-houses should be abolished. Germany and Switzerland provide excellent examples of the right way to deal with this problem.

Dawson, William Harbutt. <u>The Vagrancy Problem: The Case for Measures of Residence for Tramps, Loafers, and Unemployables; With a Study of Continental Detention Colonies and Labour Houses</u>. London: P. S. King and Son, 1910.
    The parasitic class has four types: the nomad or unmitigated vagabond, the settled resident loafer, the intermittent loafer, and the promiscuous woman with her illegitimate and irresponsible maternity. Charity and indulgence only encourage idleness. The solutions are to transfer all loafers from the Poor Laws to the Penal Laws and to send them to prisons and labour houses. Reports on how the labour colonies operate in Belgium, Germany, and Switzerland.

Day, Beth. <u>No Hiding Place</u>. New York: Henry Holt, 1957.
    Vincent Tracy was raised in the upper-middle class but ended up homeless on the Bowery because of alcoholism. After being rehabilitated, he founded Tracy Farms in upstate New York. Alcoholism is not a disease, but a moral problem. The solution is to clearly see one's

problems and to overcome them through a strengthened
will.

Dear, Michael, and Jennifer Wolch.   Landscapes of
Despair: From Deinstitutionalization to Homelessness.
Princeton, New Jersey: Princeton University Press, 1987.
     The authors attempt to explain why homelessness has
exploded at this particular historical moment, who the
homeless are, and what can be done to alleviate their
plight.   Social welfare policies are poorly implemented
and inadequately funded. In the 1950s, deinstitutionalization led to the development of "service-dependent
population ghettos" in cities across the United States
and Canada. They argue that reducing social services and
targeting traditional zones in the central city for urban
renewal and housing rehabilitation displaces people from
low-income housing and makes them homeless.   This
increase in homelessness has led to the "invasion" of the
homeless into areas whose inhabitants resent their
presence, creating pressure to "reinstitutionalize" them.
Steps should be taken to prevent large numbers of people
from being involuntarily committed to large institutions.
The authors argue that the homeless have a right to a
"fair share" of services in the community, residents of
the community must be educated about the problems of the
homeless, and necessary resources must be committed to
develop the community-based service system upon which
deinstitutionalization was predicated. The goal should
be to create a "landscape of caring."

Decker, Gilbert S.   "Footloose Families."   Survey
Graphic, 21, May 1932.
     In reaction to an article by Kimble (Survey Graphic,
21, May 1, 1932), Decker argues that the tramp, not the
hobo "is at the bottom of the transient scale." He says
that "the true hobo is essentially a working-man." He
supports this point through a discussion of the hobo's
argot.

De Cordoba, Jose. "Posner Is Sentenced to Set Up Program
for the Homeless." New York Times, February 16, 1986:8.
     Victor Posner, who pleaded no contest to tax
evasion, was sentenced to set up a $3 million program for
the homeless and to work on this homeless project an
average of 20 hours a week for five years.

Dees, Jesse Walter, Jr. Flophouse: An Authentic Undercover Study of "Flophouses," "Cage Hotels," Including

<u>Missions, Shelters and Institutions Serving Unattached</u>
<u>(Homeless) Men</u>. Francestown, N.H.: Marshall Jones, 1948.
    This overview of public and private relief efforts
in Bloomington, Oklahoma City, St. Louis, Kansas City,
Seattle, Decatur, Minneapolis, Philadelphia, New York
City, and Cleveland. Focus on Chicago, 1930-1938
contains a section based on participant observation. The
solutions are a better attitude toward the homeless,
better qualified case workers who don't simply process
them but try to meet their needs, various institutional
care on the basis of different needs, medical care,
separating minors from adults, and providing the men cash
so they can rent their own rooms and escape the evils of
the shelters.

Deisher, Robert, Greg Robinson, and Debra Boyer. "The
Adolescent Female and Male Prostitute." <u>Pediatrics</u>
<u>Annals</u>, <u>11</u> (10), October 1982:819-820, 822-825.
    This article gives a general overview of young
prostitutes, with suggestions for how physicians should
change their background expectancies.

Delaney, Joan. "Making a Difference." <u>Venture</u>, <u>10</u> (12),
December 1988:67-70.
    This profile of several corporate heads who give
generously to philanthropic causes mentions the homeless
as a recipient of furniture from Seaman Furniture
Company.

Delia-Loyle, Donna. "Port Profile: The Earth Moved."
<u>Global Trade</u>, <u>110</u> (9), September 1990:44, 46.
    This report on consequences of the October 17, 1989,
earthquake in northern California on the Regional
Automated Cargo Expediting and Release System of the
Golden Gates Ports mentions that the earthquake left
thousands homeless.

DeMaria, Alfred, Jr., Kathleen Browne, Steven L. Berk,
Edward J. Sherwood, and William R. McCabe. "An Outbreak
of Type 1 Pneumococcal Pneumonia in a Men's Shelter."
<u>Journal of the American Medical Association</u>, <u>244</u> (13),
September 26, 1980:1446-1449.
    The author suggests that an increase of type 1
pneumococcal bacteremia at Boston City Hospital in 1978
was due in part to an outbreak of this disease among
alcoholic male clients of Boston's largest shelter.

Demone, Harold W., Jr., and Edward Blacker. <u>The Unattached and Socially Isolated Residents of Skid Row</u>.
Boston: Boston Community Development Program, July 1961.
    The types of skid rowers identified in this Boston
study are the elderly, physically disabled, resident
working men, migratory workers, bums (beggars and
panhandlers: transient and resident), criminals, alcoholics, adventurers, vacationers, mentally unsound, sex
perverts, and normal residents. The solutions are a
network of community agencies and services, temporary aid
stations, half-way houses, a screening and processing
center staffed by medical, psychiatric, and social
service specialists, and continued research.

Dennis, D. L. <u>Research Methodologies Concerning Homeless
Persons with Serious Mental Illness and/or Substance
Abuse Disorders</u>. Rockville, Maryland: Alcohol, Drug
Abuse, and Mental Health Administration, 1987.
    These proceedings of a two-day conference sponsored
by the Alcohol, Drug Abuse, and Mental Health Administration in July of 1987 focus on five concerns in researching homeless persons who have mental illness and/or
substance abuse problems: (1) unique methodologies, (2)
improving methodologies and expanding research, (3)
stimulating quality applications for funding, (4)
developing research strategies, and (5) improving
communication between researchers and treatment providers.

Dennis, Elaine A. "Mobile Outreach Program Provides
Health Services to Sheltered Homeless Children in New
York City." <u>Public Health Report</u>, <u>104</u> (4), July-August
1989:405.
    Reports on the first year of operation of the New
York Children's Health Project, "a special program
designed to provide comprehensive health services to
children of homeless families sheltered in New York
City."

Dennis, Richard. "'Hard to Let' in Edwardian London."
<u>Urban Studies</u>, <u>26</u> (1), February 1989:77-89.
    The housing problem in London, in which there are
simultaneously many homeless and many vacant buildings,
must be seen in the broader context of land values and
ownership, wages and employment.

Denny, C. S. "The Whipping-Post for Tramps." <u>Century
Magazine</u>, <u>27</u>, April 1895:794.

The mayor of Indianapolis proposes that a return to flogging would eliminate tramps.

DePalma, Anthony. "About New Jersey." <u>New York Times</u>, November 24, 1991:NJ25.
The author profiles Rev. John P. Hourihan and St. John's Roman Catholic Church in Newark, New Jersey, commending their work on behalf of the homeless.

DePalma, Anthony. "Florida Rejects Miami Plan to Temporarily Put Homeless in Stadium." <u>New York Times</u>, July 15, 1991:B7.
State officials rejected a plan proposed by officials of Miami, Florida, to move several hundred homeless men who are living under a highway to a baseball stadium.

DePalma, Anthony. "New York Plays Reluctant Landlord." <u>New York Times</u>, December 24, 1986:RY1, RY4.
Due to tax foreclosures, New York City now owns and manages 4,180 buildings with 38,356 apartments and between 140,000 and 150,000 tenants. The original plan was to make repairs on the buildings and to sell them to private owners. This became impossible because the buildings cost more to run than the rents that are collected. Many of the buildings are in extremely poor condition, and there is a long wait for repairs. In order to prevent homelessness, when the city closes a building it relocates the tenants to other city-owned tenements. Although the city entered this activity reluctantly, it appears that it has become a permanent landlord.

DeParle, Jason. "Aid for Homeless Focuses on Veterans." <u>New York Times</u>, November 11, 1991:A8.
The author profiles several support groups for veterans that are trying to meet the needs of homeless veterans. He sees this change in focus as a national trend.

DeVere, William. <u>Tramp Poems of the West</u>. Tacoma: Cromwell, 1891.
Although most of these 20 poems focus on the author's experiences in mining camps, some deal with tramping.

Devers, Katherine C., and J. Gardner West. "Exclusionary Zoning and Its Effect on Housing Opportunities for the

Homeless." <u>Notre Dame Journal of Law, Ethics, and Public Policy</u>, <u>4</u> (2), Summer 1989:349-363.
Free market competition can increase the supply of housing and hold down prices. Exclusionary zoning (prohibition of the construction of apartments and the conversion of single-family to multifamily dwellings in designated segments of a city) restrict housing opportunities and contribute to homelessness. Other factors are inflation and rising standards of acceptable housing.

Devine, Edward T. "The Shiftless and Floating City Population." <u>Annals of the American Academy of Political and Social Science</u>, <u>10</u>, September 1897:149-164.
The large number of beggars in the cities has become a problem. The solutions are anti-begging societies, centralized control of national shelters, labor colonies, and imprisonment both for beggars and those who encourage them by giving them help. Such a program operated in Germany under Bismarck.

Devine, Edward T. "Social Forces." <u>Charities and The Commons</u>, <u>20</u>, April 4, 1908:1-3.
This review of opinions about unemployment and its proposed solutions stresses that artificial employment should not be considered until all savings are exhausted and life is threatened. New York city has about 35,000 homeless men.

Dexheimer, Lynda. "Look Who's Helping the Homeless." <u>Association Management</u>, <u>40</u> (12), December 1988:28-38.
The author's summary of activities of organizations that are trying to help the homeless includes the American Bar Association, the Apartment Association of Tarrant County, Texas, the American Institute of Architects, the Columbus (Ohio) Board of Realtors, and the National Association of Home Builders.

Dexter, Walter. <u>Some Rogues and Vagabonds of Dickens</u>. London: Cecil Palmer, 1927.
Chapter 8, "Kings of the Road," contains several accounts by Dickens of tramps.

Dick, Raymond G. "HUD Report Proves Point, More Aid Needed for Homeless." <u>Nation's Cities Weekly</u>, <u>7</u>, May 7, 1984:1, 5.
The author reviews criticisms leveled against HUD's estimate of the number of homeless in the United States.

Dickens, Charles. <u>American Notes</u>. Gloucester: Peter Smith, 1968. (Previously published in Boston by Ticknor and Fields in 1867.)

The author's recount of his travels to America contains observations on the poor and public institutions for the poor.

Diesenhouse, Susan. "A Judge in Boston, From His Bench, Fights for and Assists the Homeless." <u>New York Times</u>, July 26, 1988:10.

Mark E. Lawton, a judge in Boston Municipal Court, has used private charities and state agencies in order to find homes for the homeless. He is specially concerned that children not be separated from their parents, and takes the view that actions taken now will prevent severe problems later.

Diesenhouse, Susan. "A Partnership of Affordability." <u>New York Times</u>, July 20, 1986:RY1.

An innovative solution to make housing affordable to the poor is being tried by a coalition of banks, businesses, community-development corporations, state and city officials, and social leaders. They have arranged a package of financing and subsidies to rehabilitate housing which is rented for as low as $75 a month.

Dietsch, Deborah. "Mission Accomplished." <u>Architectural Record</u>, <u>176</u>, November 1988:94-97.

Accompanying five photos is a detailed description of the St. Vincent De Paul/Joan Kroc Center in San Diego for the "motivated homeless." This facility is designed "not for down-and-out drifters, drug addicts, or chronic alcoholics" but primarily "families who have run into a crisis, lost jobs, or suffered illness." The center accommodates up to 350 residents, its dinning hall serves those 350 plus 1,500 more. The facilities include a drug and medical clinic, reception lobby, an interdenominational chapel, a children's playroom, TV rooms, a library, and a laundromat. The center also has an employment counseling office, private conference rooms, offices, and a parking garage.

Digby, Peter Wingfield. <u>Hostels and Lodgings for Single People</u>. London: Her Majesty's Stationery Office, Office of Population Censuses and Surveys, 1976.

The author reports on a national survey of 674 hostels and lodging houses in Great Britain, summarizing changes between 1965 and 1972, accommodations available in 1972, and details on the specific facilities they provide. The volume contains a survey of residents: demographics on male residents, use of and attitudes toward accommodations, employment, medical, and prison background, and benefits received. It also presents some background information on female residents.

Digit. The Confessions of a Twentieth Century Hobo. London: Herbert Jenkins, 1924.
    In this first-person account, the author talks about his travels in the early 1920s from Surrey, England, to San Francisco, California, which he made for a total outlay of seventy-five cents. He recounts his jobs and experiences in the United States.

Dinkins, David N., and Nancy Wackstein. "Addressing Homelessness." Social Policy, 17 (2), Fall 1986.
    The city of New York has made severe mistakes in its approach to the homeless. City officials have concentrated the homeless in just a few neighborhoods, created huge facilities, failed to provide increased municipal services, and not consulted and negotiated with community leaders prior to placing shelters in their neighborhoods. The authors suggest a "fair share" policy of distributing the homeless around the city, the development of a comprehensive plan, and using shelters only on a temporary basis while permanent housing is created.

Doan, Michael. "Washington's Hero of the Homeless." U.S. News & World Reports, 100, June 16, 1986:11.
    The author profiles Mitch Snyder, a head of Washington's Community for Creative Non-Violence (CCNV).

Doctor, Richard F. "Drinking Practices of Skid Row Alcoholics." Quarterly Journal of Studies on Alcohol, 28, December 1967:700-708.
    Based on interviews with 172 males in southern California, the author summarizes the drinking patterns of skid row alcoholics.

Doeringer, Peter B., and Michael J. Piore. "Unemployment and the 'Dual Labor Market.'" The Public Interest, 38, Winter 1975:67-79.
    The structuralist, Keynesian, and dual labor market theories of unemployment are compared. The author raises the question of whether unemployment is chronic and involuntary or temporary and voluntary and examines youth

and minority unemployment. Each theory indicates a different social policy.

Dolan, Paul, and David Swaysland. "New Deal for the Homeless?" Social Work Today, 9 (14), November 29, 1977:11-12.
    This report on Great Britain's Housing (Homeless Persons) Act of 1977 assesses intentionality in homeless-ness and priority of need if help is to be provided. The solutions are social work--prevention through interven-tion, assistance, organization of emergency services, support and accommodation. Also includes deinstitu-tionalization.

Dolbeare, Cushing N. "The Low-Income Housing Crisis." In America's Housing Crisis: What Is To Be Done?, Chester Hartman, ed. Boston: Routledge and Kegan Paul, 1983:29-75.
    The causes of homelessness are a lack of organized consumer and public interest-based advocacy, the poor image of federal low-income housing programs, and a reluctance to face up to the cost of an adequate low-income housing program. The solution is a comprehensive housing policy (eight specific points) with entitlement (the right to housing assistance for all low-income people). To put this into practice will require an aroused constituency.

Doty, Alvah H. "The Danger to the Public Health." North American Review, 158, June 1898:701-705.
    The author claims that because of a lack of sanitary conditions Coxey's army of homeless men marching on Washington presents a threat to the public health.

Douglas, Robin. Sixteen to Twenty-One. London: A. M. Philpot, 1925.
    This first-person account is written by an individu-al who, after being falsely accused of theft in cadet school, refused a commission in the navy, and at the age of 16 began tramping.

Downs, Susan Whitelaw, and Michael W. Sherraden. "The Orphan Asylum in the Nineteenth Century." Social Service Review, 57 (2), June 1983:272-290.
    An examination of the records of the Protestant Orphan Asylum in St. Louis, Missouri, indicates that this institution developed to meet the needs of families in transition.

Drake, Madeline.   "Fifteen Years of Homelessness in the
UK."   Housing Studies, 4 (2), April 1989:119-127.
    The underlying cause of homelessness in Great Brit-
ain is not the legislation entitling homeless people to
help, as some posit, but market changes in the supply and
demand of housing.

Drake, Madeline.   "Who Are the Homeless?"   New Society,
42 (791), December 1, 1977:464-465.
    The author argues that "dispute" is an overlooked
cause of some homelessness. The overcrowding caused by
people moving in with friends or relatives leads to
dispute, or conflict, and thus to their eviction.

Drake, Madeline, Maureen O'Brien, and Tony Biebuyck.
Single and Homeless.   London: Her Majesty's Stationery
Office, 1982.
    Interviews with 521 single homeless people in seven
districts in England, a survey of 6,531 clients of a
national referral agency, and a survey of 308 users of an
East London Night Shelter, combined with participant
observation and group discussions, show that those more
likely to have problems are men, those over 50 (either
men or women), those who have been homeless the longest,
and those who are the least educated. The authors
develop four profiles of the single homeless: the young,
the middle-aged worker with obsolete skills, the middle-
aged "doser," and the old long-term hostel-dweller. They
also present demographics of sex, age, marital status,
education, skills, occupation, medical problems, drug use
and a list of nine recommendations to better meet the
needs of the single homeless.

Drake, R. E., M. A. Wallach, and J. S. Hoffman. "Housing
Instability and Homelessness Among Aftercare Patients of
an Urban State Hospital."   Hospital and Community
Psychiatry, 40 (1), 1989:46-51.
    Following their discharge from an urban state mental
hospital, 17 percent of 187 patients were "predominately
homeless," and "10 percent occasionally homeless." The
younger male patients were more likely to be homeless.
Apparently many homeless patients perceive the mental
hospital as a shelter from street life. The homeless
have a much higher rate of rehospitalization than do the
discharged non-homeless.

Dreier, Peter. "Community-based Housing: A Progressive Approach to a New Federal Policy." Social Policy, 18, Fall 1987:18-22.
    The growth of homelessness is spurring the federal government to move back into housing programs. The basic cause of homelessness is the shortage of affordable housing. The solution is for non-profit groups to "build the housing and rent or sell it at cost, rather than at what the market can bear. Once these costs exceed what the poor can afford, additional subsidies will be necessary--that go directly to those that need help, not developers and absentee landlords." Contains proposals for insulating this housing from speculation.

Dreier, Peter, and John Atlas. "Grassroots Strategies for the Housing Crisis: A National Agenda." Social Policy, Winter 1989:25-38.
    The national housing crisis, which is causing homelessness, is created by the affordability gap, declining home ownership, rising rents, and the "privatizing" of subsidized housing. What is necessary is a cooperative national effort built upon strong, stable grassroots organizations in order to influence future housing policy in local, state, national levels. The major issues are (1) preserving existing subsidized housing, (2) regulating lenders to provide capital for affordable housing, (3) constructing new affordable housing and increasing home ownership opportunities through community-based non-profit development groups, and (4) preventing homelessness and promoting tenants' rights.

Dreier, Peter, and Richard Appelbaum. "American Nightmare: Homelessness." Challenge, 34 (2), March-April 1991:46-52.
    That millions of Americans sleep in alleys, subways, and cars, and on park benches represents fundamental shifts in the American economy, primarily deindustrialization and gentrification. Home prices, which have escalated due to the high cost of mortgages and because housing is viewed as speculative investment, have also contributed to the problem. The author specifies the essentials of a new housing policy.

Dubin, William R., and Beatrice Ciavarelli. "A Positive Look at Boarding Homes." Hospital and Community Psychiatry, 29 (9), September 1978:593-595.

The authors give positive marks to a Philadelphia program to house former state hospital patients in boarding homes. There, the otherwise homeless enter a warm and therapeutic environment.

DuBuclet, Linda. "Seeking Out the Homeless." Washington Post, March 8, 1984:C3.
        Mitch Snyder, a leader of the Community for Creative Non-Violence, visits the homeless living on the heating vents in Washington, D.C.

Duffy, Bruce. "Catching A Westbound Freight: The Hard Freedom of the American Hobo." Harper's Magazine, June 1989:49-61.
        This first-person account of travels across the country with two hobos, Beargrease and Slim provides an insider's perspective on the function of hardships in the construction of self identity.

Dugger, Celia W. "Albany May Halt Funds to Build Group Homes for the Mentally Ill." New York Times, December 27, 1991:A1.
        If enacted, a proposal before the New York Senate to place a five-month moratorium on building shelters for the homeless mentally ill would have a direct impact on how New York City responds to its estimated 20,000 mentally ill homeless persons.

Dugger, Celia W. "At a Shelter, Lacking Blankets and a Crib." New York Times, May 3, 1991:B4.
        New York City is not complying with a court order that requires it to provide a bed or crib for each member of a homeless family.

Dugger, Celia W. "Big Shelters Hold Terrors for the Mentally Ill." New York Times, January 12, 1992:1.
        The mentally ill homeless fear sexual attacks, disease, and robbery in the large congregate shelters for the homeless operated by New York City.

Dugger, Celia W. "Crusader Amid Despair Says Farewell to Flock." New York Times, June 27, 1991:B3.
        Glenn Backes, who performed vital services as an outreach worker for the homeless and was paid only $22,000 a year, is a casualty of cutbacks in New York City's budget.

Dugger, Celia W. "Dinkins Seeking to Stem Dispute Over Proposals for the Homeless." New York Times, February 5, 1992:A1.
     Responding to proposals made by the commission he appointed to revamp the city's shelter system, New York City Mayor David Dinkins says that he especially favors the idea of using nonprofit groups to develop sites for shelters.

Dugger, Celia W. "Families Seek Out Shelters as Route to Better Homes." New York Times, September 4, 1991:A1.
     Critics point their finger at an abuse of New York City's shelter system--people who, although they could live elsewhere, sign up for the shelters in order to move to the top of the list of those eligible and waiting for permanent subsidized housing.

Dugger, Celia W. "Gambling on Honesty on the Homeless." New York Times, February 17, 1992:B1.
     The author discusses the controversy among New York City officials--whether it is better to deceive or be honest with citizens about the extent of crack use among the city's homeless.

Dugger, Celia W. "Here, Poorest Are Resented by the Poor." New York Times, November 6, 1991:B1.
     Long-time, poor residents of New York City's Bronx complain that city officials are dumping homeless families in their neighborhoods in spite of the area already being overcrowded. They also express resentment that the homeless families are given renovated apartments while they must put up with less.

Dugger, Celia W. "Judge Orders Relocation of Homeless Families." March 26, 1991:B3.
     Homeless families placed in welfare hotels lack stoves on which they can cook meals and sterilize baby bottles. Citing these conditions, along with the frequent illness of the children in such families, a Manhattan judge ordered New York City officials to move 460 homeless families out of welfare hotels.

Dugger, Celia W. "Longtime Poor Resent Homeless as Interlopers." New York Times, November 6, 1991:A1, A13.
     The author examines antagonisms between the homeless and the chronically poor. The chronically poor have many resentments about what they perceive as the special treatment given the homeless. They are especially

resentful that vacant apartments are renovated for homeless families when the city does not refurbish the apartments of its long-time poor residents. Typical is the view of a 53-year old tenant whose apartment is a shambles--her bathtub faucet runs perpetually, the pipes below her kitchen sink spew water, and her radiator smokes so badly she can barely breathe. She says, "[w]hy, when it comes to regular tenants' apartments, does the city say it doesn't have the materials or supplies to fix my apartment? But the empty apartments are fixed beautifully. It's too much. We're living like animals here."

Dugger, Celia W. "New York and Other Cities Diverge Over How to Help the Homeless." New York Times, March 1, 1992:31.
    The author compares New York City's policy concerning shelters for the homeless with the policies of other American cities.

Dugger, Celia W. "New York Losing Weapons Against Poverty." New York Times, July 10, 1991:A1.
    Although social programs were severely cut in New York City's austere budget, shelters for homeless women were spared.

Dugger, Celia W. "New York Report Finds Drug Abuse Rife in Shelters." New York Times, February 16, 1992:1.
    According to a survey by a mayoral commission, 80 percent of the men who use New York City's shelters and 30 percent of the adults in shelters for families abuse drugs or alcohol. The commission also found high rates of AIDS, mental illness, and violence among the homeless.

Dugger, Celia W. "Panel's Report on Homeless Is Criticized by Dinkins' Staff." New York Times, February 1, 1992:A1.
    Proposals made by the commission appointed by David Dinkins, the Mayor of New York City, to examine how to overhaul the city's shelter system conflict with administration policies.

Dugger, Celia W. "Report to Dinkins Urges Overhaul in Shelter System for the Homeless." New York Times, January 31, 1992:A1.
    Among the recommendations made by the commission appointed by David Dinkins, the Mayor of New York City, to examine how to overhaul the city's shelter system are

rent subsidies, drug treatment, psychotherapy, and job training for the homeless.

Dugger, Celia W. "Writing in Fear, Homeless Plead to Save Drop-In Centers." New York Times, April 27, 1991:A27.
    The homeless have written David Dinkins, Mayor of New York City, pleading for a change in the city's new budget which calls for the closing of eight drop-in centers for the homeless.

Dukakis, Michael. "States Take a Fresh Look at Housing." Journal of State Government, 60, May-June 1987:95-97.
    The Governor of Massachusetts writes that he is proud of the progress his state has made in providing affordable new housing and chides the federal government for leaving the housing field. He stresses that "we are the society that cannot tolerate homelessness for any of our people."

Duke, Donald. "The Railroad Tramp." American Railroad Journal, 2, 1967-68:32-45.
    After the Civil War thousands of young soldiers who had acquired a taste for adventure began traveling across the country. Between 1865 and 1900, many "teenagers possessed with wanderlust" joined them, and their numbers increased to between one and two million. There were six types of tramps: the professional tramp, who worked only when forced to; the hobo, a migratory worker; the bum, who moved from town to town and habituated saloons; women tramps; tramp-criminals, persons wanted by the police, many of whom would murder and rob their brother tramps; and the saloon bum, tramps too old or disabled to ride the trains. Each large city had a "tramp district which catered to saloon bums." The article contains illustrations of hobo signs and symbols.

Dullea, Georgia. "Welfare Hotel: Where the Displaced Live Grim Lives Amid Faded Glory." New York Times, November, 18, 1986:15.
    At the Prince George Hotel, 455 homeless families live at a cost to the government of $53 a day for family of four. The author focuses on the interaction of the residents, their attitudes, drug crimes, and physical and psychological deprivation.

Dumont, Matthew P. "Tavern Culture: The Sustenance of Homeless Men." American Journal of Orthopsychiatry, 37

(5), October 1967:938-945. (Reprinted in <u>Down to Earth</u>
<u>Sociology: Introductory Readings</u>, Third Edition, James M.
Henslin, ed. New York: The Free Press, 1981:103-111.)
    Based on participant observation of a skid row bar,
the author discusses urban renewal, plateau drinking,
alienation, the tavern as a support system and center for
socializing. He proposes that taverns be made into
outposts of the mental health profession.

Dunham, H. Warren. "A Closer Look at the Homeless
Alcoholic." In <u>The Homeless Alcoholic: Report of First</u>
<u>Annual International Institute on the Homeless Alcoholic</u>.
Detroit: Detroit Mayor's Rehabilitation Committee on
"Skid Row" Problems and the Michigan State Board of
Alcoholism, September 12-13, 1955:23-31.
    This informal account of the author's varied
experiences with the homeless and a brief history of
awareness and reform suggests that an understanding of
the homeless from "the inside," will lead to respect for
them. The author also discusses the quandary of civil
rights: the necessity to allow people to live in a way
that you don't approve.

Dunham, H. Warren. <u>Homeless Men and Their Habitats: A</u>
<u>Research Planning Report</u>. Detroit: Wayne University,
1953.
    The author develops a general sociological theory of
homeless men centering around ecological growth, incomplete socialization, subculture, and social change. The
solutions are more study, social control, coordination of
services and policies within and between cities. The
volume also contains a typology of homeless men.

Dunlap, David W. "Despite Protests, Panel Approves
Razing of Central Park Band Shell." <u>New York Times</u>,
January 19, 1992:30.
    Despite protests, the New York City Art Commission
approved the demolition of the Naumburg Bandshell in
Central Park.

Dunlap, David W. "For Homeless With AIDS, a Home." <u>New</u>
<u>York Times</u>, January 5, 1987:Y18.
    New York City opened Bailey House, its first
residence for homeless persons with AIDS. It is expected
that the average stay will be five months, ending in
death after a last trip to the hospital. The annual
budget of $1.3 million will eventually support a staff of
39.

Dunlap, David W. "A Homeless Shelter From the 1700's? Signs of Almshouse Are Unearthed." New York Times, April 7, 1989:Y23.

Archaeologists suggest that the remains of a structure behind City Hall, discovered while laying a new water pipe, was an almshouse, an institution for the poor that took in trespassers, rogues, unruly and ungovernable servants, and slaves.

Dunlap, David W. "New Park Rules Urged To Limit the Homeless." New York Times, April 16, 1989:Y23.

A new rule is proposed for New York City parks that would make it a violation to beg or panhandle, to leave belongings unattended for more than two hours, to spread out on a bench so that it interferes with other people, to reside or sleep in parks overnight or even to create the appearance of intending to do so by stockpiling belongings there. Critics claim that the proposed rule is discriminatory and unconstitutional.

Dunn, Martha Baker. "Philosophy and Tramps." Atlantic, 97, June 1906:776-783.

The author writes a romanticized account of conversations with and philosophic influences of an American tramp of Swedish ancestry. The causes of his homelessness are adventure-seeking and flight.

Durham, Mary L. "The Impact of Deinstitutionalization on the Current Treatment of the Mentally Ill." International al Journal of Law and Psychiatry, 12 (2-3), 1989:117-131.

The author reviews causes and unintended consequences of the deinstitutionalization of the mentally ill and claims that the causal link between criminalization of the mentally ill and deinstitutionalization has not been demonstrated. Mental health reform must be seen in historical perspective, and the "next wave of reform" will be the reinstitutionalization of the mentally ill.

Dutton, Jane E., and Janet M. Dukerich. "Keeping an Eye on the Mirror: Image and Identity in Organizational Adaptation." Academy of Management Journal, 34 (3), September 1991:517-554.

Based on their study of how the Port Authority of New York and New Jersey has reacted to the homeless people who stay at its facilities, the authors conclude that an organization's image and identity guide its actions and interpretations of issues.

E

Eberle, George, Jr. "Finding Shelter for the City's Homeless." <u>St. Louis Post-Dispatch</u>, September 11, 1986:E3.

There can be no one solution for homelessness because there is no single cause. Its multiple causes include domestic violence, mental illness, substance abuse, poverty, poor housing, traveling, unemployment, and choice (street people). Reports on the Homeless Services Network instituted in St. Louis, a coordinated system for providing shelter, transportation, places to stay during the day, counseling, training, and locating jobs and permanent homes. Still needed are more low-income rental units, as well as greater state support for the mentally ill homeless and families with dependent children.

Ebringer, Lorna, and J. R. W. Christie-Brown. "Social Deprivation Amongst Short Stay Psychiatric Patients." <u>British Journal of Psychiatry</u>, <u>136</u>, January 1980:46-52.

The author reports percentages of psychiatric patients in London who come from permanent and transitory accommodations and no fixed abode.

von Eckardt, W. "The Greening of Skid Row." <u>Time</u>, <u>120</u>, July 19, 1982:81.

Los Angeles has opened a Skid Row Park, a park designed for "skid row bums."

Edelman, Marian Wright, and Lisa Mihaly. "Homeless Families and the Housing Crisis in the United States." <u>Children and Youth Services Review</u>, <u>11</u> (1), 1989:91-108.

Families are the fastest growing group of homeless people in the United States. The primary reasons are inadequate family incomes and a shrinking supply of affordable housing. Several recommendations for solving this problem are provided.

Edge, William. <u>The Main Stem</u>. New York: Vanguard Press, 1927.

This first-person account by a runaway boy who recounts his varied work experiences mentions hobos and <u>Hobo News</u>.

Edwards, Griffith, Valerie Williamson, Ann Hawker, Celia Hensman, and Seta Postoyan. "Census of a Reception

Centre." <u>British Journal of Psychiatry</u>, <u>114</u> (513), 1968:1031-1039.
     The topics are the history of vagrancy in Great Britain, questionnaire research on demographics, social stability, physical and mental illness, drinking, drugs, and imprisonment. The author reports demographics associated with pathological drinking. The solution is a hostel service that operates small hostels directed at the special requirements of particular subgroups.

Egan, Timothy. "Homeless Addicts in Oregon Find Aid in Restoring Lives." <u>New York Times</u>, December 22, 1988:1, 11.
     Portland provides a model of a successful program for homeless alcoholics and drug abusers. Those who are willing to stay off drugs and alcohol are offered a room in a residential hotel for up to six months. Using that housing as an anchor, the individuals are given intensive counseling and therapy. About a third of the residents leave the program with a job, and 70 percent leave free of chemical dependence. The cost of the program is $165 a month for each resident, a cost that includes counseling.

Egan, Timothy. "School for Homeless Children: A Rare Experience." <u>New York Times</u>, November 17, 1988:8.
     The city of Tacoma, Washington, operates a school for children of the homeless. About 40 children attend this school each day. Unlike their treatment at other schools, these children are not laughed at by their classmates for they all wear similar clothing and share similar experiences, such as sleeping under bridges and in cars. Two other schools exclusively for children of the homeless are located in Santa Clara, California, and Salt Lake City, Utah.

Egan, Timothy. "A Shelter for Rural Homeless: Trees and Sky." <u>New York Times</u>, May 11, 1992:A1, A9.
     In the Cascade Mountains, just outside Cottage Grove, Oregon, the National Park Service has opened the first campground for homeless people. Although the park service was reluctant to get into social policy, offi-cials now say they are simply acknowledging what was already a fact, for many homeless people have taken up permanent residence deep within the national forests.

Ehlert, Bob. "Life in the Hole in the Wall." <u>Star Tribune Sunday Magazine</u>, January 17, 1988:3, 5-6, 13, 16-17, 19-21, 23-24.

In order to typify the life styles of tramps who choose to be homeless, the author details the background and activities of King Luther White.

Ehrenreich, Barbara, and Frances Piven. "The Feminization of Poverty." Dissent, Spring 1984:162-170.
    The reasons that poverty is being feminized are the family wage system, the prevailing low income for women in the labor market, and divorce. The authors give an overview of effects of federal social welfare programs. The solutions are an expansion of the welfare state through higher AFDC, income-maintenance programs, and child-care provisions. Feminists should lead the resistance against the conservatives' attempt to destroy the welfare state.

Eitzen, D. Stanley. "Conflict and Order: Implications for a Research Agenda." Mid American Review of Sociology, 14 (1-2), Winter 1990:89-92.
    The author's recounting of his research experiences, motivated by the conflict paradigm, include homelessness.

Ek, Carl A., and Lala Carr Steelman. "Becoming A Runaway: From the Accounts of Youthful Runners." Youth and Society, 19 (3), March 1988:334-358.
    Seventeen youths were located by means of a snowball sample. Running away is preceded by a problematic relationship at home--characterized by strange relationships, lack of love, verbal or physical turbulence, power struggles, and conflict with siblings. The flight itself is precipitated by a fight about the youths' transgression of parental orders. Running away was not done for adventure, and required the management of affairs and handling logistical problems of transportation, destination, and survival.

El Masri, Souheil. "Displacements and Reconstruction: The Case of West Beirut, Lebanon." Disasters, 13 (4), December 1989:334-344.
    Many have been left homeless because of 14 years of fighting between Christians and Moslems in Lebanon. The author proposes short- and long-term policies.

Elam, Samuel Milton. "Lady Hoboes." New Republic, 61, January 1, 1930:164-169.
    The use of conversational narrative to present the stories of several female hobos provides an insider's perspective into this phenomenon.

Ellickson, Robert C. "The Homelessness Muddle." The Public Interest, 99, Spring 1990:45-60.
    The central policy to solve homelessness proposed by advocates, more government-funded housing projects, is wrong. Instead, "policy makers should devise aid programs that better reflect the diversity of the homeless population and that do more to discourage dependency." To spend more on shelter programs is to increase the reported number of homeless people because "new beds in free shelters draw not only people from the streets, but also those who are housed." Few homeless families or homeless individuals were leading ordinary lives before they slipped into homelessness. A major cause of family homelessness is the relative inability of heads of homeless families to function independently, while most homeless individuals suffer from mental illness or substance abuse. "The great majority of homeless people are not random victims of a housing-market squeeze, but rather deeply troubled individuals and families who, when deserving of government aid, should be given tailored financial assistance and help in managing their lives more successfully." Suggested are vouchers, encouragement to enter the job market, limitations on length of stay in shelters, and letting state agencies pay rent directly to landlords.

Elliott, Marta, and Lauren J. Krivo. "Structural Determinants of Homelessness in the United States." Social Problems, 38 (1), February 1991:113-131.
    Multivariate analysis on data from the 1980 Census and the U.S. Department of Housing and Urban Development shows that the strongest predictors of an area's level of homelessness are the unavailability of low-income housing and mental health care. Consequently, to reduce homelessness, investments should be made in these areas.

Ellison, Jerome. "The Shame of Skid Row." Saturday Evening Post, 225 (25), December 20, 1952:13-15, 48, 51.
    This article's focus is Detroit's skid row. Its topics include policing on skid row, its culture and social ranking, panhandling, and attempts at rehabilitating its residents. Giving money to panhandlers perpetuates the horrors of skid row. The author also presents a case study.

Ellwood, Charles A. "Alms House Abuses and Their Correction." Proceedings of the National Conference of

<u>Charities and Correction</u>, Isabel C. Barrows, ed. May 6-12, 1903:386-391.

Alms houses have these problems: little or no separation of the sexes, no classification of types of inmates, no provision for the sick, no work-test for the able-bodied, and being run by the lowest bidder. These problems can be corrected by legislation and inspections by local boards and state officials. Contains documentation of abuse in Missouri.

Elman, Richard M. <u>The Poorhouse State: The American Way of Life on Public Assistance</u>. New York: Pantheon, 1966.

With a focus on New York City, the author examines the problems the homeless have in establishing their indigence so they can qualify for aid. City officials play a misinformation game that results in a frustrating circle of referrals. The book contains a case history of a man who refuses to follow the established channels of the welfare system.

Elsworth, Steve. "100 Homeless Families Face Mass Eviction." <u>New Statesman, 107</u> (6), February 24, 1984:6.

The Council of London pays the hotel rents for homeless families, but they are housed in unsuitable hotels. Finsbury Park of North London is used by several London boroughs as a dumping ground for the homeless. The author accuses the Council of following racist policies.

Engel, Margaret, and Edward D. Sargent. "Meese's Hunger Remarks Stir More Outrage Among Groups." <u>Washington Post</u>, December 11, 1983:A1, A10.

Presidential counselor Edwin Meese was severely criticized for his comment that "some people go to soup kitchens because the food is free and that's easier than paying for it."

English, Clifford. "Leaving Home: A Typology of Runaways." <u>Society</u>, <u>10</u> (5), July-August:22-24.

On the basis of participant observation at Ozone House, a drop-in center for runaways in Ann Arbor, Michigan, the author identifies four types of runaways: floaters, runaways, splitters, and hard road freaks.

English, Clifford, and Joyce Stephens. "On Being Excluded: An Analysis of Elderly and Adolescent Street Hustlers." <u>Urban Life</u>, <u>4</u> (2), July 1975:201-212.

Based on participant observation in a Midwestern city, the authors examine the fantasies of street hustlers (their unrealistic expectations of success), how the dynamics of exclusion affects their life styles, their disenfranchisement, how they survive by hustling and running cons, the significance of avoiding dependence, their fears, suspicions, violence, and marginal survival on the streets.

Erickson, Rosemary, and Kevin Eckert. "The Elderly Poor in Downtown San Diego Hotels." The Gerontologist, 17 (5), 1977:440-446.
Interviews with 82 residents in 12 skid-row, working-class, and middle-class hotels in downtown San Diego showed that an informal social support system plays a highly significant role in the residents' lives. Those in the middle-class hotels exhibited a more intact primary support system and had more contact with relatives, friends, and neighbors.

Erlanger, Steven. "For One Family: Struggle and Success." New York Times, October 12, 1987:17.
An illegal squatter now owns the building that he had illegally occupied. He was defended in court by the Association of Community Organization for Reform Now (ACORN).

Erlanger, Steven. "Squatters to Homesteaders: Signs of Success in New York." New York Times, October 12, 1987:1, 17.
Persons who had been illegal squatters now legally live in 58 buildings that they have been rehabilitating. This is a form of "mutual housing"--"a new form of social contract between the city and its poorer residents, who get buildings at a nominal fee while giving up their right to speculate and maximize profits." Neighborhood residents form a collective and contribute money and "sweat equity" to rehabilitate buildings for their own use in return for public support and limited ownership.

Estroff, Sue E. Making It Crazy: An Ethnography of Psychiatric Clients in an American Community. Berkeley: University of California Press, 1981.
Participant observation in Berkeley uncovers normal crazies, insiders, and outsiders. As the author examines the social construction of a crazy reality, subsistence strategies, deinstitutionalization, she always attempts to show the patient's perspective.

Estroff, Sue E.   "Medicalizing the Margins: On Being
Disgraced, Disordered, and Deserving."   Psychosocial
Rehabilitation Journal, 8 (4), April 1985:34-38.
    This essay on the causes of homelessness questions
the role of the mental health professionals and the
reemergence of the idea of deserving and undeserving
homeless.

Estroff, Sue E.   "...On Benevolent Anarchy, Malignant
Anarchy, and Benevolent Malpractice: What about the
Patients?"   Medical Anthropology Quarterly, 15 (1),
November 1983:4, 17-19.
    The debate represented in the literature--only
somatic psychiatric treatment for the homeless mentally
ill versus kindness toward and autonomy of patients--
represents the ideologies of the proponents, not the
realities of the world of patients and staff. Underlying
this debate are the professional and ideological concerns
that led to the neglect of the chronically mentally ill
in the first place.

Etulain, Richard W., ed.   Jack London on the Road: The
Tramp Diary and Other Hobo Writings.   Logan, Utah: Utah
State University Press, 1979.
    This edited collection of the 14 stories that Jack
London, based on his own experiences, wrote about tramps
addesses three main types of tramps: the profesh (the
aristocracy), the bindle stiffs (working tramps), and
stew bums (those who passively exist).   The tramp is a
by-product of capitalism, part of its surplus labor
force.   Some men are tramps because there is not enough
work (the able and involuntary), some don't want to work
(the able and voluntary), and some can't work (the unable
and involuntary). (The parenthetical classifications are
the annotator's.)

Evans, Gregory L. "Federal Emergency Shelter Assistance
to the Homeless: Mandating a Standard of Decency." Notre
Dame Journal of Law, Ethics, and Public Policy, 4 (2),
Summer 1989:325-347.
    Because users of homeless shelters are often
exploited, abused, and arbitrarily removed, the author
proposes a federal standard of care to cover housekeeping, physical facilities, and the administration of
shelters.   He also suggests that shelters be made more
accessible to the handicapped, offer more privacy, and
provide separate accommodations for families.

Evans, Olive. "The Aged Share Homes and Lives." <u>New York Times</u>, January 7, 1988:15.
     The author discusses "shared housing," unrelated individuals who share a home and have their own private rooms. Shared housing is also called group homes.

Eversley, David Edward Charles. "Population and Regional Planning." <u>New Society</u>, <u>29</u> (616), July 25, 1974:223-225.
     Although fertility is falling to such an extent that Great Britain may soon have a shortage of labor, the increase in two-wage earning families is likely to keep competition in the housing market high and thus increase problems of homelessness.

F

Fabricant, Michael. "Beyond Bed and Board: Teaching about Homelessness." <u>Journal of Teaching in Social Work</u>, <u>2</u> (2), 1988:113-130.
     With foci on empowerment, advocacy, dispelling myths, and problems that social workers experience in working with the homeless, the author outlines a graduate course on the homeless for social workers.

Fabricant, Michael. "Creating Survival Services." <u>Administration in Social Work</u>, <u>10</u> (3), Fall 1986:71-84.
     The author argues that budget cutbacks have led to new service populations, such as the homeless. Because social services are not organized or funded to meet the needs of such groups, however, we must create new and independent services.

Fabricant, Michael. "Empowering the Homeless." <u>Social Policy</u>, <u>18</u> (4), Spring 1988:49-55.
     The author argues that the mismatch between available social welfare services and the needs of the homeless can be remedied by empowering the homeless.

Fabricant, Michael. "The Political Economy of Homelessness." <u>Catalyst</u>, <u>6</u>, 1, 1987:11-28.
     The author compares contemporary shelters for the homeless with workhouses of the nineteenth century and argues that homelessness is a result of the crisis in capital accumulation. He suggests ways of combatting homelessness at its roots.

Fabricant, Michael, and Irwin Epstein. "Legal and Welfare Rights Advocacy: Complementary Approaches in Organizing on Behalf of the Homeless." Urban and Social Change Review, 17 (1), Winter 1984:15-19.

Legal advocacy, especially effective in New York City, has forced city officials to provide shelter and food for the homeless. The authors review their efforts at welfare advocacy in Elizabeth, New Jersey--documenting violations of welfare statutes to develop a class action lawsuit and organizing the homeless into a political force--which met with positive results, but lasted only a short time. The basic causes of homelessness are alcoholism, public policies that lead to deinstitutiona- lization and gentrification, eviction, the lack of low- cost housing, and unemployment due to the contraction of the economy. The best solution appears to be a combina- tion of legal advocacy and welfare case advocacy.

Fadiman, Anne. "A Week in the Life of a Homeless Family." Life, December 1987:31-38.

The author documents the coping strategies of the Damm family in Los Angeles County, as they attempt to stay together and survive within the welfare system.

Fagan, Ronald J. "A Glossary of Skid Road Jargon." Nursing Forum, 11 (1), 1963:110-112.

The author lists 50 terms used by skid rowers.

Faison, Seth, Jr. "Tougher Campaign Is Vowed Against Homeless in Subway." New York Times, October 19, 1991:A1.

Expecting an onslaught of homeless people when the weather gets cold, the head of the New York City Transit Police said that his officers will vigorously enforce laws against panhandling, fare evasion, and sleeping in the subways.

Fall, Merrick. "Streets Apart." UNESCO Courier, June 1985:25-27.

The massive transfer of population into the cities of the developing nations--"the final act in the process of industrialization"--is often disastrous for family life. One consequence is that many children end up living on city streets. Bogota, Colombia, alone has 5,000 youngsters roaming its streets. Bosconia-La Florida is a project established by the Salesian Congre- gation to wean abandoned children from the streets. Here they first learn to play in an open setting during the day, then to spend the night in a dormitory, then to attend classes, and, finally, to learn a trade.

Farmer, R. D. T., and P. G. Harvey. "Alienated Youth: Preliminary Study of a Group of Rootless Young People-- Social and Personality Characteristics." Social Science and Medicine, 8 (4), April 1974:191-195.

Three questionnaires (social history, Eysenck Personality Inventory, and the Hostility and Direction of Hostility) were administered to 57 rootless young people (persons under the age of 30 who have no permanent address) in Birmingham, England. They showed more hostility than the general population, as well as more neuroticism.

Farney, Dennis. "The Former President, A Bush Issue for 1988, Has New Champions." Wall Street Journal, June 24, 1988:1, 11.

Jimmy Carter, former President of the United States, works with Habitat for Humanity, a non-profit group that build homes for the homeless. "The former President saws boards and pounds nails."

Farnsworth, Steve. "Critics Dispute Census of Homeless." The Denver Post, August 11, 1984:13A.

A dispute exists over how many homeless there are in the United States.

Farr, R., P. Koegel, and A. Burnam. A Study of Homeless- ness and Mental Illness in the Skid Row Area of Los Angeles. Los Angeles County Department of Mental Health, Los Angeles, California, 1986.

After describing how they were able to develop a comprehensive probability sample of homeless individuals in Los Angeles, the authors report a predominately young, male, minority population. Administration of the NIMH's Diagnostic Interview Schedule indicates that about 28 percent are chronically mentally ill, 34 percent are chronic substance abusers, and 38 percent have no diagnosis. They make the point that although we need more conceptually and methodologically rigorous research in order to understand and better serve this population, we also need to act now in order to help the homeless mentally ill.

Farrant, Wendy, and Angela Taft. "Building Healthy Public Policy in an Unhealthy Political Climate: A Case

Study from Paddington and North Kensington." Health Promotion, 3 (3), 1988:287-292.
National policies in Great Britain, as well as those of local governments, undermine the health of the homeless. The authors suggest social policies that will be more responsive to the health needs of disadvantaged populations.

Farrington, Donald S., William Shelton, and James R. MacKay. "Observations on Runaway Children from a Residential Setting." Child Welfare, 42, June 1963:286-291.
This study of 22 boys and six girls who ran away from the Spaulding Youth Center in Tilton, New Hampshire, cites crisis situations, attention-getting, withdrawal, and impaired family relationships to be the underlying causes.

Feder, Leah H. Unemployment Relief in Periods of Depression: A Study of Measures Adopted in Certain American Cities, 1857 through 1922. New York: Russell Sage Foundation, 1936.
This volume contains extensive materials on private and public efforts directed towards the homeless during this period, as well as information on shelters.

Feeney, Frances E., Dorothee F. Mindlin, Verna H. Minear, and Eleanor E. Short. "The Challenge of the Skid Row Alcoholic: A Social, Psychological and Psychiatric Comparison of Chronically Jailed Alcoholics and Cooperative Alcoholic Clinic Patients." Quarterly Journal of Studies on Alcohol, 16, December 1955:645-667.
Fifty males sent to a clinic for alcoholics by the drunk court in Washington, D.C., were compared with 50 volunteer patients. The authors report differences in their intelligence, education, occupations, arrest record, social resources, motivation, prognosis, and work, family, medical, and marital histories. The program is more successful with those who have higher intelligence, motivation, and resources in the community.

Feigelman, William, and Arnold R. Silverman. "The Long-Term Effects of Transracial Adoption." Social Service Review, 58 (4), December 1984:588-602.
Based on questionnaire responses from 373 adoptive families that showed transracial adoptees to be as well adjusted as intra-racial adoptees, the authors propose

transracial adoption as a viable policy option for dealing with homeless minority children.

Fein, Esther B. "Soviet Quake Toll Rises to Over 100." New York Times, May 1, 1991:A3.
   An earthquake in Soviet Georgia left tens of thousands homeless.

Feinberg, Mark. "Japanese Companies Yen to Be Corporate Good Guys." Business and Society Review, 77, Spring 1991:9-15.
   The author suggests that the nation's homeless shelters be funded through the generosity of American-based Japanese corporations.

Feldman, Saul. "Out of the Hospital, Onto the Streets: The Overselling of Benevolence." The Hastings Center Report, 13, June 1983:5-7.
   The author discusses the overselling of community mental health, legislative Darwinism, ethics and dilemmas in the field of mental health, and the background and motivations of health officials in proposing deinstitutionalization as a social policy.

Fellin, Phillip, and Kaaren Strauch Brown. "Application of Homelessness to Teaching Social Work Foundation Content." Journal of Teaching in Social Work, 3 (1), 1989:17-33.
   For teaching generalist social work practice, the homeless are a rich source of examples and applications.

Felsman, J. Kirk. "Abandoned Children: A Reconsideration." Children Today, May-June 1984:13-18.
   A sample of 300 street children in Cali, Colombia, indicates that 7 percent were orphaned or abandoned, 61 percent maintain active family connections (often bringing home at night money or goods they obtained during the day), while 32 percent are abandoners (they have abandoned their families, 76 percent of whom left home before the age of 12). Why do some children abandon their families when their siblings remain home? The author suggests an interaction of factors: physiology, temperament, intelligence, and character. The distinctive personality of these children must be considered in developing social policy. The author stresses the strengths of the street culture: loyalty, support, and the sense of physical freedom.

Felsman, J. Kirk. "Street Urchins of Colombia." <u>Natural History</u>, <u>90</u>, April 1, 1981:41-49.
  Major cities of Colombia, especially the capital city of Bogota, are characterized by <u>gaminismo</u> (the problem of numerous street children). The basic cause of this urban phenomenon is the "tremendous rural-to-urban migration." Bogota has approximately 5,000 street children. The three types of <u>gamins</u> (street children) are: (1) those who have family connections and bring money and goods home after nightfall, (2) the orphaned or physically abandoned, and (3) the abandoning children (those who have left their family, opting for a life on the street). Although some children are loners, the mass majority of these children travel in groups of eight to fifteen in which membership and leadership are fairly rigid. Reports on the attitudes of Colombians toward the <u>gamins</u> and small programs designed to help them.

Ferguson, Anne. "Housing's Flawed Foundation." <u>Management Today</u>, April 1989:60-68.
  Among problems noted by the United Kingdom Audit Commission is that the number of homeless families has grown due to a shortage of housing.

Fergusson, Robert Menzies. <u>The Vagrant: What to Do with Him</u>. London: James Nisbet, 1911.
  The proposed solutions are police control and labor colonies. The labor colonies should be designed for rehabilitation, but even if they fail in this purpose they will succeed in keeping the vagrants off the streets. Specialized labor colonies are also necessary.

Ferlauto, Richard, and Daniel Hoffman. "Organizing for Housing Benefits." <u>Social Policy</u>, <u>19</u> (3), Winter 1989:39-43.
  The authors propose that, because housing has become less affordable for low- and moderate-income workers and an estimated 350,000 to three million people are homeless, unions use their political and economic clout to help provide homes for the disadvantaged.

Feron, James. "Jackson Outlines a Plan for Affordable Housing." <u>New York Times</u>, May 26, 1991:WC1.
  In a speech at an annual "Hope for the Homeless" dinner in Westchester County, New York, Jesse Jackson accused the Bush administration of creating nationwide homelessness and proposed that public and private pension funds be put to work to build low-cost housing.

Ferrer, Fernando, Howard Golden, and Claire Shulman. "No Way to Treat the Homeless." New York Times, October 8, 1987:27.
    The author argues that the proposal by the Koch Administration of New York City to build 11 transitional residences for homeless families and individuals "ranks as one of the largest boondoggles in the city's recent history." Implementation of this proposal will simply "relocate the homeless from the privately-owned welfare hotels in Manhattan to city-owned welfare hotels in Brooklyn, Queens and the Bronx." The result will be a "permanent underclass of public-assistance recipients who cannot obtain decent housing."

Fiddle, Seymour. "Catting: A Synoptic View of Addicts' Living Outside Conventional Shelters." The International Journal of the Addictions, 15 (1), January 1980:39-45.
    This article discusses catting, the practice of sleeping in public places by drug addicts in order to save rent.

Field, Frank. "What is Poverty?" New Society, 33 (677), September 25, 1975:688-691.
    The number of homeless families and persons is suggested as one of six measures of poverty designed to serve as the basis of an annual report to evaluate the relative success of government policy in combatting poverty.

Filer, Randall K. "What We Really Know About the Homeless." Wall Street Journal, April 10, 1990:A22.
    The author takes the position that social policy concerning the homeless is not based on an understanding of the issues. To demonstrate this thesis, he reviews research on the size of the problem, whether conditions are getting worse, who the homeless are, and causes of homelessness. He concludes by saying, "Although we should not wait for a full understanding of the causes of and cures for homelessness before we begin to act, it is imperative that we begin to ask the right questions before we waste resources on ineffectual solutions."

Finder, Alan. "11 Shelters Approved in New York City." New York Times, August 20, 1987:14.
    The Board of Estimates approved the construction of 11 of 15 new shelters for the homeless that had been sought by the Koch administration. The City's Human Resources Administration provides temporary housing for

about 5,060 families or about 8,650 people, who stay in 25 shelters and 63 hotels. The city plans to rehabili- tate buildings it owns so homeless families can live in them.

Finder, Alan. "Food Stamps for Homeless Ordered Cut." *New York Times*, October 23, 1986:17.
      Officials of the U.S. Department of Agriculture ruled that the city and state consider the money paid to hotel owners for rent as income to the homeless families, thus reducing the families' food-stamp benefits. As a result, the food stamps received by families living in hotels have been cut in half. The city says it will somehow make up for this policy change and not let these families go hungry.

Finder, Alan. "New Bill on Converting S.R.O. Hotels Is Sought." *New York Times*, December 14, 1986:25.
      New York City officials and housing advocates fear that if the city's ban on eliminating its S.R.O. rooms expires many of the occupants of those rooms will become homeless. They will have no place but the streets to live if the owners are allowed to renovate the units for upper-income housing.

Finder, Alan. "New Study Reports Thousands on Brink of Being Homeless." *New York Times*, September 21, 1986:21.
      Because two of every three families that come to New York City Shelters arrive after having lived doubled-up, the 103,000 families who are now doubling-up are in danger of becoming homeless. Twenty thousand New York City apartments are lost each year through abandonment. No coherent policy is designed to prevent homelessness. The suggested solutions for prevention include public assistance grants for increased rents, a faster take-over of buildings on which taxes are not paid, making it legally difficult to convert rental apartments to condominiums, preventing "warehousing" (keeping apart- ments vacant in anticipation of conversion), and provid- ing lawyers for low-income tenants threatened with eviction.

Finder, Alan. "S.R.O. Bill Has Room for Complaint." *New York Times*, January 25, 1987:9.
      The New York City Council passed a bill that will allow the conversion of single-room-occupancy hotels only if the owners pay $45,000, which will be applied to

building low-income housing. S.R.O.'s with fewer than 25 units are exempted.

Finder, Alan. "S.R.O.'s Displace Many Despite Conversion Ban." <u>New York Times</u>, January 22, 1987:49
In spite of a law designed to protect S.R.O. tenants by prohibiting the authorization of the demolition of the buildings, many tenants have become homeless because the S.R.O. owners have turned off the heat, the water, or locked them out in anticipation that the ban on conversion will be only temporary.

Finestone, Harold. "Cats, Kicks, and Colors." <u>Social Problems</u>, <u>5</u> (1), July 1957:3-13.
The author analyzes black, street-living drug users, whose driving force in life is getting kicks.

Finn, Peter. "Decriminalization of Public Drunkenness: Response of the Health Care System." <u>Quarterly Journal of Studies on Alcohol</u>, <u>46</u>, 1985:7-23.
In this broad coverage of decriminalization of public drunkenness, the author mentions the specific problem of skid row alcoholics, pointing out that the Uniform Alcoholism and Intoxication Treatment Act stipulates that "if a public inebriate has no home, the approved public treatment facility shall assist him in obtaining shelter." The author indicates that for this Act to be effective, "public inebriates should be provided with shelter for an indefinite period of time in protective living situations in which alcohol use is permitted and counseling and treatment are available."

Finn, Peter. "Street People." Rockville, Maryland: National Institute of Justice, 1988.
The street people who are problems for the police are not those who are homeless as a result of economic dislocation, but rather, single males with drinking or drug problems "who appear to prefer to live on the street and to survive by begging or petty theft." The author discusses collaboration between the police and social service workers in Boston, San Diego, Portland, and New York City.

Finn, Peter E., and Monique Sullivan. "Police Respond to Special Populations: Handling the Mentally Ill, Public Inebriate, and the Homeless." <u>NJR Reports</u> (National Institute of Justice), <u>209</u>, May-June 1988:2-8.

The homeless are one of several "special populations" that, due to deinstitutionalization, decriminalization of public intoxication laws, and jail crowding,
have led to more calls for police assistance. The
following statement summarizes the view expressed here:
"Police are often called on to remove the homeless from
streets and parks. The homeless have a dampening effect
on business, and they invite crime by creating an appearance of community neglect. The homeless are often a
danger to themselves, particularly in subfreezing
weather. Law enforcement officers dealing with the
homeless on the street have few options. Not only is
shelter space limited, but most shelters refuse to admit
the large percentage of homeless who are also mentally
ill or alcoholic." Networking with social service
agencies is the solution to this challenge to law
enforcement. The authors discuss the common features of
networks, the benefits of networking, how to establish a
network, effective communication, the role of civil
statutes, and funding. The networks in Los Angeles,
Boston, San Diego, and Washtenaw County, Michigan, are
highlighted.

Firebaugh, W. C. The Inns of the Middle Ages. Chicago:
Pascal Covici, 1924.
     By examining the inns, taverns, and alehouses of the
Middle Ages, the author analyzes the quality of life in
Europe during this period. The volume contains material
on vagabonds.

First, Richard J., and Beverly G. Toomey. "Homeless Men
and the Work Ethic." Social Service Review, 63 (1),
March 1989:113-126.
     Based on interviews with 979 homeless men in Ohio,
the authors conclude that because "homeless men are not
a single population," they require different levels of
intervention. The authors identify three groups of
homeless men: "about a quarter are severely disabled; a
third need a moderate range of services; and the remain-
der are displaced from the work force but capable of
independence." The men in the long-term needs group
"have serious personal limitations and also lack the
resources to establish an independent life-style to meet
their basic needs for food, clothing, and shelter." The
men in the moderate needs group are "moderately disabled"
but have "the potential for maintaining a semi-indepen-
dent life-style." Men in the short-term needs group "are
the least at risk of long-term homelessness." They are

homeless because they have had "an immediate crisis in their housing, family composition or employment." Different services need to be provided the men on the basis of their different needs.

First, Richard J., Dee Roth, and Bobbie Darden Arewa. "Homelessness: Understanding the Dimensions of the Problem for Minorities." Social Work, 33 (2), March-April, 1988:120-124.

A study of 13 American cities in 1985 shows that 52 percent of the homeless are black, 33 percent white, and 15 percent Hispanic, Native Americans and Asian Americans. To determine the specific characteristics of homelessness for blacks, 979 homeless people were interviewed in Ohio, of whom 292 were black. White and black homeless persons are compared regarding the reasons for their homelessness, income during the past month, primary source of income, arrest and job history, psychiatric hospitalization, psychiatric symptomatology, behavior disturbances, problem drinking, physical health problems, and social support from family and friends. The researchers found that blacks "are over represented in the homeless population, tend to be younger, have a somewhat higher educational level and represent a slightly greater proportion of Vietnam veterans than other homeless persons." Blacks used the social service system more than did whites, and had less psychiatric hospitalization, jail detention, alcohol problems, and physical health problems.

Fischer, Pamela J. Alcohol, Drug Abuse and Mental Health Problems Among Homeless Persons: A Review of the Literature, 1980-1990: Executive Summary. Rockville, Maryland: U.S. Department of Health and Human Services, March 1991.

The topics in this review of the literature are the historical context of homelessness; definitions, sampling, and measurement of prevalence; correlates of mental illness, alcohol, and other drug use; comorbidity of alcohol, drug, and mental disorders; and the application of prevalence estimates.

Fischer, Pamela J. "Estimating the Prevalence of Alcohol, Drug and Mental Health Problems in the Contemporary Homeless Population: A Review of the Literature." Contemporary Drug Problems, 16 (3), Fall 1989:333-389.

The author compares prevalence estimates in 239 studies of alcohol, drug, and mental health problems in the homeless population. The estimates of alcohol problems among the homeless vary remarkably, ranging from 2 percent to 86 percent, while the estimated prevalences of mental health problems range from 2 percent to 90 percent. The author suggests that underlying this wide variance is a lack of uniformity of definitions, which makes it difficult to contrast the findings of the various studies. "To date, there is little agreement on defining either the homeless population in general or specific subgroups within it. Researchers have frequently opted for specificity in defining their target populations, mainly to facilitate the logistics of field operations. It is easier to focus on users of shelters for homeless people than to attempt to identify the homeless among soup kitchen clients, street dwellers, inmates of various institutions, and the like, or to grapple with hard-to-classify groups such as SRO hotel residents, migrant laborers, doubled-up-housing occupants, and other marginal groups."

Fischer, Pamela J., Sam Shapiro, William R. Breakey, James C. Anthony, and Morton Kramer. "Mental Health and Social Characteristics of the Homeless: A Survey of Mission Users." *American Journal of Public Health*, 76 (5), May 1986:519-524.
A probability sample of 51 mission users is compared with 1,338 domiciled men in the same community. The homeless exhibited higher prevalence rates in every diagnostic category of mental illness, higher rates of hospitalization for both mental and physical problems, fewer social contacts, and higher arrest rates.

Fischer, Pamela J., and William R. Breakey. "Homelessness and Mental Health: An Overview." *International Journal of Mental Health*, 14 (4), 1986:6-41.
After reviewing definitions of homelessness, estimates of numbers, typology, health, mental disorders, deinstitutionalization, substance abuse, social supports, criminalization, transience, services for the homeless, this literature review specifies gaps in our knowledge.

Fischer, Pamela J., and William R. Breakey. "Profile of the Baltimore Homeless with Alcohol Problems." *Alcohol Health and Research World*, 11 (3), Spring 1987:36-37.
Based on interviews with 700 homeless persons randomly selected from missions, shelters, and the Baltimore jail, the authors report on the prevalence of mental disorders and alcoholism in this population. Administering the Short Michigan Alcoholism Screening

Test (SMAST) to 162 respondents, the authors specify differences in socio-economic, social support, drinking behavior, other substance abuse, physical health, mental health, and criminal activity between alcoholic homeless persons and non-alcoholic homeless persons.

Fischer, Pamela J., William R. Breakey, Sam Shapiro, and Morton Kramer. "Baltimore Mission Users: Social Networks, Morbidity, and Employment." Psychosocial Rehabilitation Journal, 9 (4), April 1986:51-63.

A probability sample of 51 mission users is compared with 1,338 domiciled men in the same community. The homeless had more psychiatric disorders, substance abuse, arrests, deficient networks of social support, and less employment. They are not homogenous and require a variety of approaches for rehabilitation, which should consist of alcoholism treatment, social skills training, psychiatric treatment, vocational training, housing, and income maintenance.

Fisher, Eileen. "Homeless Families: A Scheme of Notification to Ensure Effective Care." Nursing Times, 76 (27), July 3, 1980:77-80.

The author details a reporting system that she says would improve the health services of the homeless in London who are being sent to hotel bed and breakfast accommodations.

Fisher, Lawrence M. "Suddenly Homeless in California, the Prosperous and the Poor Both Suffer." New York Times, October 23, 1989:Y9.

The author writes about families that became homeless due to a 1989 earthquake in northern California. His focus is on the blow to their pride as they went from self-sufficient people to persons who must take handouts from others.

Fishman, Walda Katz. "The Struggle for Women's Equality in an Era of Economic Crisis: From the Morality of Reform to the Science of Revolution." Humanity and Society, 11 (4), November 1987:519-532.

The application of the theory of historical materialism (the revolution of the working class) is suggested as the solution to the economic crisis that has dismantled welfare reforms and led to homelessness, unemployment, poverty, and hunger.

Fitch, John A.   "Class Fighters and a Hobo Who Solved a
Problem."   Survey, 32, September 5, 1914:558-560.
    This report on the hearings before the Commission on
Industrial Relations probing the cause of labor unrest
focuses on Henry Pauley, business agent of Seattle's
Local 22 of the Itinerant Workers' Union, or "'Hoboes'
Union of America," who has tried to make an organized
group of hoboes self-supporting.

Fitchen, Janet M.   "Homelessness in Rural Places:
Perspectives from Upstate New York." Urban Anthropology,
20 (2), Summer 1991:177-210.
    Based on field research from upstate New York, the
author concludes that rural homelessness is increasing
due to reduced availability of low-cost housing, higher
unemployment, and an increase in single-parent households. In addition, home costs have escalated because of
rural gentrification and uncontrolled real estate
development.

Fleming, Anne Taylor.   "The Homeless."   Syndicated
Columnist, June 30, 1983.
    The author discusses falling through the safety net,
deinstitutionalization, and the invisibility of the
homeless (their taken-for-granted presence).   The
solutions she proposes are government spending, churches
turning their unused rooms into living quarters, and
providing emergency shelter for families--with dignity.

Flower, B. O.   "Plutocracy's Bastiles: Or Why the
Republic is Becoming an Armed Camp."   The Arena, 10,
October 1894:601-621.
    A hard-hitting analysis that today would be termed
radical.   The thesis is that the government has come
under control of the wealthy, who are manipulating
Congress into producing more wealth for themselves.
While Wall Street is robbing the public, armories are
being built throughout the country to protect the wealthy
from the people. As a consequence of this state of
affairs, common people cannot afford to own their own
homes.

Floyd, Andress.   My Monks of Vagabondia.   Union, New
Jersey: Self Master Press, 1913.
    In this collection of stories about "outcast men"
who have been changed by the Family of Self Masters, the
author develops the thesis that vagabonds can be helped
to live productive lives when they are freed from some

self-destructive habit and given hope to turn from the destructive to the constructive.

Flynt, Josiah. "The American Tramp." Contemporary Review, 60, August 1891:253-261.
   The author argues that men become tramps because of drinking, laziness, and discouragement. His topics include ethnicity and tramps, female and child tramps, jargon, noms de tramp, transportation, begging, stealing, and communication. Tramps are described as "a rotting sore on the body politic," with the solution being a thorough and universal enforcement of laws.

Flynt, Josiah. "How Men Become Tramps: Conclusions from Personal Experience as an Amateur Tramp." The Century, 28, October 1895:941-945.
   The causes of men becoming tramps are irresponsible parents, the failure of our system of correction and reformation to deal with the restless young, Wanderlust, and liquor. Tramp culture is transmitted in jails and around railroad watering tanks.

Flynt, Josiah. The Little Brother: A Story of Tramp Life. New York: Century, 1902.
   This prolific chronicler of tramps in the last decade of the nineteenth century has written a novel about a runaway boy.

Flynt, Josiah. "The Tramp and the Railroads." Century Magazine, 58 (2), June 1899:258-266. (pseudonym of J. F. Willard)
   The author was hired by a railroad to investigate the extent of the tramp problem. The railroads had taken no action because they thought it would be too expensive, there would be no legislative and police support, and tramps would retaliate. The author reports what he learned from participant observation. No other country in the world gives free train rides to its beggars, tramps became numerous only after the Civil War, and there are about 60,000 professional tramps in the United States today. Railroads lose money by providing free transportation, through the disappearance of goods, and through claims for personal injuries. The country loses because this free railroad transportation spreads the tramp nuisance over a wide territory, helps to concen-trate criminal elements in the cities, makes it difficult to locate dangerous people in flight, and encourages out-of-works to degenerate into vagabonds and children to run

away from home. The solution is concerted action by the railroads.

Flynt, Josiah. "The Tramp at Home." Century Magazine, 47 (4), February 1894:517-526.
    Because his conclusions about the American tramps' nationality, numbers, and unwillingness to work were challenged, the author spent ten days in 1891 with tramps. He reports here his experiences with 300 tramps on this journey, defending his original conclusions.

Flynt, Josiah. "Tramping with Tramps: The American Tramp Considered Geographically." Century Magazine, 47 (1), November 1893:99-108.
    The characteristics of tramp life are compared in the north, east, west, and south.

Flynt, Josiah. "What to Do with the Tramp." Century Illustrated Monthly Magazine, 48 (5), September 1894:794-796.
    Almost all tramps avoid work. The solutions are to stop people from giving to tramps, even if it means fining the giver; to offer work to penniless wanderers to determine which are honest; to severely punish professional beggars by sentencing them to work houses and penitentiaries; to guarantee two to three years imprisonment for any tramp caught in the company of a boy; and to establish specialized institutions for juvenile tramps.

Flynt, Josiah. My Life. New York: Outing, 1908.
    The author presents a first-person account about tramping in the late 1800s.

Flynt, Josiah. Tramping with Tramps: Studies and Sketches of Vagabond Life. College Park, Maryland: McGrath Publishing Company, 1969. (First published in 1893. Another edition was published in 1972 by Patterson Smith of Montclair, New Jersey.) (Josiah Flynt is a pseudonym of J. F. Willard.)
    The author of this first-person account of tramping in the late 1800s describes himself as "a fellow traveler with tramps and a casual observer." Topics include criminals, children, culture, types of tramps, and international tramping: Germany, England, Russia. Boys and girls become tramps for four basic reasons: 1) being born on the road, 2) being driven there by poverty and the parents' drunkenness and abuse, 3) being enticed to the road (the disillusioned, the worshippers of the

tough, and those with Wanderlust), and 4) becoming voluntary slaves (enticed by hobo stories, they become willing slaves of a hobo).

Foderaro, Lisa W.   "New York State Eases a Bar to Homeless Housing." New York Times, February 16, 1992:44.
    Because of a legal quirk, Westchester County, New York, was required to provide housing for the homeless but was barred from building permanent housing. A new interpretation of the State Constitution may allow counties to build housing for the poor.

Foderaro, Lisa W.   "Quirk of Geography Turns Town to Homeless Capital." New York Times, January 17, 1989:1, 24.
    Due to its concentration of hotels, a village of 3,300 permanent residents has 378 homeless people living in it. Only nine come from the village. The author reports on the strain the villagers feel due to this influx of the homeless, as well as the resentment felt by the homeless.

Foderaro, Lisa W.   "Westchester's Far-Flung Homeless." New York Times, January 11, 1989:12.
    A social service system that places homeless families two hours away from the schools their children attend, pays $143 a day for two rooms, and spends $220 taxi fare each day for a child to attend school is irrational.

Foley, Matthew. "Coping Strategies of Street Children." International Journal of Offender Therapy and Comparative Criminology, 27 (1), 1983:5-20.
    Street children have dropped out of school, are aggressive, live in a gang style, and lack adult role models. The author offers suggestions for implementing his proposed solution, personality development.

Foote, Caleb.   "Vagrancy-Type Law and Its Administration." University of Pennsylvania Law Review, 104, March 1956:603-650.
    The author reviews vagrancy laws from the feudal period to the present, with a focus on their current application in Philadelphia. Based on observations, interviews, and an examination of records, he discusses inadequate definitions of vagrancy and little concern about vagrants' physical and mental illnesses, the assumption of guilt, the use of laws to "clean up" areas

of the city, and discrimination on the basis of residence. The proposed solutions are to extend procedural safeguards to vagrancy cases, such as making voluntary defenders available, to centralize these cases by transferring them to municipal courts, to use jail only as a last resort, and to encourage cooperation between the court and social welfare agencies.

Fopp, Rodney. "A Report from the Senate Standing Committee on Social Welfare: A Review." <u>Australian Journal of Social Issues</u>, <u>18</u> (1), February 1983:70-74.
    The author criticizes the "Report on Youth Homelessness" issued by the Standing Committee of the Australian Senate on the basis that it was insensitive to social problems, its emphases on the privatization of and efficiency in welfare services were misplaced, and its attention to unemployment superficial.

Fopp, Rodney. "Unemployment, Youth Homelessness and the Allocation of Family Responsibility." <u>Australian Journal of Social Issues</u>, <u>17</u> (4), November 1982:304-315.
    The author discusses the relationship of unemployment to homelessness among Australian youths. After reviewing the burden on families and problems of obtaining accommodations, he suggests that a data base be established to determine the numbers of unemployed youths, unemployment benefits be increased, and more state and federal funds be appropriated for emergency accommodations.

Forbes, James. "Individual Vagrants." In <u>Proceedings of the National Conference of Charities and Correction</u>, Isabel C. Barrows, ed. May 6-12, 1903:416-417.
    Vagrants are of two types, local and migratory. Because employment is currently plentiful, tramps are criminals. The solutions to this problem are active cooperation of private organizations and police departments, a national plan of administration and rehabilitation, and efficient policing of the railroads.

Forbes, James. "The Jockers and the Schools They Keep." <u>Charities</u>, <u>11</u> (7), November 7, 1903:432-436.
    The term jockers refers to adult pederast tramps. This article focuses on the moral deterioration of boys who travel with adult tramps and argues that the solutions must be tailored to the individual.

Forbes, James.   "The Tramp; Or, Caste in the Jungle."
Outlook, 98, August 19, 1911:869-875.
    The Secretary of the National Association for the
Prevention of Mendicancy reports on life on the road.
The types of tramps are mush fakers, gay cats, transient
workmen, and good people (the aristocracy of the professional idlers).   The author exposes the recruitment of
naive youth by persuasion or force by jockers, who force
them into a kind of slavery.   He also discusses the
sexual and racial divisions among tramps.

Fors, Stuart W., and Dean G. Rojek.   "A Comparison of
Drug Involvement Between Runaways and School Youths."
Journal of Drug Education, 21 (1), 1991:13-25.
    Survey data from 253 runaway-homeless adolescents
show that runaway-homeless youths are two to three times
more likely to be involved in drug use and abuse than are
youths who remain in school.

Foster, Charles I. "The Urban Missionary Movement: 1814-
1837." Pennsylvania Magazine of History and Biography,
75 (1), January 1951:47-65.
    This account of religious work among the urban
American poor includes mention of the destitute, tramps,
and hobos.

Foster, Joan M.   "The Nurse in a Center for the Homeless." Nursing Management, 23 (4), April 1992:38-39.
    The author profiles the role of the nurse in
treating the homeless chronically mentally ill at the Day
Treatment Center run by the Department of Veterans
Affairs in New York City.

Foster, Randall M.   "Intrapsychic and Environmental
Factors in Running Away from Home." American Journal of
Orthopsychiatry, 32, 1962:486-491.
    Based on data from 175 delinquent children, the
author examines individual and intrafamilial factors in
running away.   Parent-child separation proved to be the
most specific factor because it intensifies the fear of
rejection and abandonment, making it more difficult to
cope with the resulting anger and frustration.

Foster, William Z.   Pages From a Worker's Life.   New
York: International Publishers, 1939.
    As the author recounts his lifetime experiences as
a communist labor organizer, he presents details on his
working as a casual laborer, strikes, and violence.   He

includes a chapter on hoboes, the basic cause of which is capitalism. The solution is for workers to take control of the social institutions.

Fox, Elaine R., Lisa Roth, David Stiveson, Ruth Leventhol, Marcelino Martinez, and Gerald Porter. "Homeless Children: Philadelphia as a Case Study." <u>Annals of the American Academy of Political and Social Science</u>, <u>506</u>, November 1989:141-150.
This overview of homelessness in Philadelphia, Pennsylvania, focuses on the health, development, and education of homeless children.

Fox, Martin. "Judge Bars Vote on Shelter for City's Homeless Families." <u>New York Law Journal</u>, <u>196</u>, August 22, 1986:1.
"The State Supreme Court Justice ruled that there is no legal basis for placing before New York City voters a referendum to force the City to provide separate sleeping areas for every homeless family."

Fox, Richard Michael. <u>Drifting Men</u>. London: Hogarth, 1930.
This first-person account of vagabonds in Europe, especially London, includes details on their attitudes.

Fox, Richard Michael. "Rolling Stones." <u>The Nineteenth Century</u>, <u>107</u>, June 1930:846-854.
This article is a novelistic treatment of several vagabonds supposedly known by the author. He notes racial distinctions among tramps.

Frame, Randall L. "The Two Faces of Christmas." <u>Christianity Today</u>, <u>29</u>, December 13, 1985:18-19.
The author contrasts idealized images of peaceful Christmas with the mean realities of human suffering, including that of the homeless.

Frances, A., and S. Goldfinger. "'Treating' A Homeless Mentally Ill Patient Who Cannot Be Managed in the Shelter System." <u>Hospital and Community Psychiatry</u>, <u>37</u> (6), 1986:577-579.
The first step in effectively reaching the homeless mentally ill is for mental health professionals to establish a positive relationship with clients. A key is to offer tangible benefits such as paying for a hotel room or bus pass. Establishing trust in such ways can be

the opening for providing comprehensive services, support, and treatment.

Frank, Henry. "The Crusade of the Unemployed." <u>Arena</u>, <u>10</u>, July 1894:239-244.
    The author defends the character and objectives of the industrial army of the unemployed and homeless, then marching on Washington.

Franklin, Ben A. "H.U.D. Is Sued Over Delays on Funds for the Homeless." <u>New York Times</u>, September 29, 1987:13.
    The National Coalition for the Homeless has sued the government for failing to meet a deadline in publishing the distribution rules that would allow city and county applicants to participate in the $1 billion program of aid to the homeless. This article contains reactions of Housing Urban Development officials to the lawsuit.

Franklin, Ben A. "Pentagon Lag on Homeless Assailed." <u>New York Times</u>, June 18, 1987:10.
    A Federal district judge has ruled that the Defense Department "abdicated its statutory responsibility by delaying for three years a program to open unused military structures to the homeless." In spite of Congress having appropriated $8 million to pay for the program, the Pentagon had not opened unused barracks and other military buildings as shelters for the homeless. Pentagon lawyers provided no excuse.

Franklin, Ben A. "Wright To Press For Homeless Aid." <u>New York Times</u>, January 11, 1987:8.
    After touring a dormitory for the homeless run by Mitch Snyder, a Washington advocate for the homeless, Jim Wright, the Speaker of the House, pledged to rush through Congress a $500 million program to build shelters for the homeless. Wright pointed out that it would cost each citizen only two dollars.

Frazier, Shervert H. "Responding to the Needs of the Homeless Mentally Ill." <u>Public Health Reports</u>, <u>100</u> (5), September-October 1985:462-469.
    The causes of homelessness are economic deprivations, lack of low-cost housing, discontinuities in social service systems, and changes in the composition of the family. Mental illness is intertwined in these causes as it impedes people's capacities to cope with these problems. The solutions are to define the target

population, to develop innovations in the mental health service system, to teach the homeless mentally ill how to cope, to design work projects, to create special worlds for coping on a limited scale, and to increase organization and cooperation among researchers, policy makers, and care providers.

Freedman, Alix M. "Art Being Her Bag, This Bag Lady Wins Acclaim in Chicago." Wall Street Journal, March 27, 1985:1, 25.

Lee Godie, a homeless woman in Chicago, paints and sells her wares. She keeps her paintings in lockers at the Trailways bus station. Although her paintings are in demand and she shops at expensive stores, she remains homeless.

Freedman, Samuel G. "The Homeless and Veterans: Time to Share." New York Times, December 25, 1986:1, 14.

The Vietnam Veterans Ensemble Theatre Company performed at New York City's shelters for the homeless. Camaraderie was expressed between the Vietnam veterans who make up this theatre company and the homeless Vietnam veterans who live in those shelters.

Freeman, Richard B., and Brian Hall. "Permanent Homelessness in America?" Population Research and Policy Review, 6 (1), 1987:3-27.

Interviews with 516 homeless persons in New York City support the Department of Housing and Urban Affairs' estimates of the numbers of homeless. Homelessness is a long-term state and is increasing, a decline in low-rent housing units accounts for much homelessness, few of the homeless receive general assistance or welfare, and many have been in jail. Economic recovery alone is inadequate to solve the problem, for what is needed is change in the housing market.

Freeman, Stanley J., Anton Formo, A. Gopala Alampur, and A. Frank Sommers. "Psychiatric Disorder in a Skid-Row Mission Population." Comprehensive Psychiatry, 20 (5), September-October, 1979:454-462.

The authors examine the prevalence of mental illness and demographic correlates (age, class, record of arrest, transience) of users of the services at Scott Mission in Toronto, Canada. They conceptualize the mission population as a "community back ward."

Freidmutter, Cindy Lynn. <u>From Country Asylums to City Streets: The Contradiction Between Deinstitutionalization and State Mental Health Funding Priorities</u>. New York: City of New York, 1979.

The number of patients in New York state mental hospitals has dropped from 85,000 in 1965 to 25,000 in 1979, but no hospitals have been closed and staffing has been constant since 1972. The discharged mental patients are being dumped into the community with little after-care. The solutions are to review all state mental hospitals, close some to save money, find new uses for the closed hospitals, retrain the displaced workers, increase the state's share of funding, and increase funding for on-site psychiatric services (at hotels and shelters) and at municipal hospitals.

Freitag, Michael. "Citizen Panel Warns of Failings In Battle to Halt Spread of AIDS." <u>New York Times</u>, November 27, 1989:12.

Homeless youths are listed among the "hidden groups" who have not been targeted for educational efforts to help people avoid AIDS. In reviewing the housing crisis, the author uses individual cases to illustrate how the income of many people has failed to keep up with spiraling rents.

Freitag, Michael. "For the Homeless, Public Spaces Are Growing Smaller." <u>New York Times</u>, October 1, 1989:E5.

Critics charge that the new rules of conduct adopted for New York City's bus and rail terminals, subway stations, and parks are directed against the homeless. City officials deny this charge, asserting that the codes of conduct are simply an effort to codify "quality of life" regulations. Critics reply, however, that these rules are "cruel efforts to force the homeless out of sight and into shelters that are dangerous." Officials claim that they simply "need to protect public safety and order." The result is a contraction of public places which the homeless are able to habitate. The article includes a map of "shelters and sanctuaries."

Freitag, Michael. "Grand Central Barriers to Homeless at Station." <u>New York Times</u>, September 17, 1989:25.

The closure of the main waiting room of Grand Central Terminal for a restoration project has made life more difficult for the homeless who used it as a shelter. Perhaps 1,000 homeless people frequent Grand Central during the winter, and 150 live there full-time. A proposed "rules of conduct," critics claim, is designed to discriminate against the homeless.

French, Howard W. "Hotels Dispute Charges in Suit." <u>New York Times</u>, November 2, 1986:E7.
    The Human Resources Administration has sued the Golden Gate Motor Inn of Brooklyn and the Richmond Avenue Holiday Inn in Staten Island for refusing to accept homeless guests even though the government is paying their bill.

French, Howard W. "In New York, an Oasis for Homeless." <u>New York Times</u>, March 30, 1988:13.
    The author discusses the routine of the homeless who live in New York City's Pennsylvania Station, focusing on the relationship of the homeless to the police.

French, Laurence. "Victimization of the Mentally Ill: An Unintended Consequence of Deinstitutionalization." <u>Social Work</u>, <u>32</u> (6), November-December 1987:502-505.
    The deinstitutionalization of the mentally ill was supposed to be accompanied by a network of community mental health center facilities. Because this network was not set up, many of the deinstitutionalized became homeless. A new wave of homeless consists of never-treated youth and the elderly. A legal and clinical network should be developed to deal with this problem.

Friedland, William H., and Robert A. Marotto. <u>Street-people and Straightpeople in Santa Cruz, California: A Report of the Downtown Study</u>, Santa Cruz: University of California Division of Social Sciences, May 1985. (mimeo)
    The four overlapping types of street people in Santa Cruz are professional drug merchants, the mentally disabled, the involuntary poor (those who are interested in getting off the street and in finding employment), and the voluntary poor (those who have developed adaptive ways of handling themselves and who seem to enjoy their lifestyle). The authors discuss conflict with straight-people and negative reactions by mall merchants. They also list policy options of push (increased police activity, park limitations and closures, civic education programs, expansion or park utilization) and pull (night shelter, day time shelters, and street people community development). They propose general community policies of expanded mental health services and encourage private initiative and a city task force on street people. A

copy of the interview schedules used for the survey is included.

Friedman, Emily. "On the Street: Hospitals Wrestle with the Problem of Homeless Patients." Hospitals, 57 (16), August 16, 1983:97-98, 102, 105.
    The author discusses how hospitals are becoming service providers to the homeless.

Friedman, I. K. The Autobiography of a Beggar. Boston: Small, Maynard and Company, 1903.
    This humorous account of a fictional beggar's club includes stories of simulated disabilities. Some of the stories first appeared in the Saturday Evening Post.

Friedman, Lucy N. "Cost-Effective Compassion." New York Times, December 28, 1991:A19.
    The author criticizes New York City's policy that homeless families move three times a year until they are given permanent housing.

Friedman, Sally. "Helping Homeless Pregnant Teenagers." New York Times, July 14, 1991:NJ8.
    The author profiles a shelter in Burlington County, New Jersey, that is set up to meet the needs of homeless pregnant teenagers.

Friedricks, Jurgen. Affordable Housing and the Homeless. Hawthorne, New York: Aldine de Gruyter, 1988.
    Focusing on affordable housing and the homeless as an international problem, the authors of these 13 selections examine the problem in Sweden, Czechoslovakia, West Germany, the Netherlands, Great Britain, France, and the United States. Divided into three sections that focus on (1) how structural economic changes have decreased the supply of low-income housing, (2) housing problems in West Germany, the Netherlands, Sweden, and Czechoslovakia, and (3) the new homelessness that is a consequence of the economic change that has reduced housing affordability, the book examines the crisis of affordable housing in capitalist societies and contains proposals for providing elementary forms of shelters to cope with the housing shortage.

Frum, David. "Why Would Anyone Live in Penn Station?" Wall Street Journal, May 30, 1990:A12.
    The author reports on two visits to Penn Station in April, 1990, noting the unsavory homeless who sleep

there. He profiles several of them, focusing on drunks and ex-cons. He notes that commuters to the Pennsylvania Station will no longer have to see such persons, for new regulations forbid the homeless from sleeping in the station.

Fry, L. J., and J. Miller. "Responding to Skid Row Alcoholism: Self-Defeating Arrangements in an Innovative Treatment Program." Social Problems, 22, June 1975:675-688.
The authors did participant observation of a comprehensive alcoholism treatment system in California. The program failed because of conflicts over goals, interests, and resources. The program made an unanticipated contribution to skid row alcoholism, however, as it introduced some men to the area who might otherwise not have found their way there.

Fuerbringer, Jonathan. "Homeless Aid Approved by House, But Money May Never Be Spent." New York Times, March 6, 1987:9.
The House of Representatives voted approval of a bill for aid to the homeless. Some congressmen expressed concerns that the cost could run up to $725 million.

Fuerbringer, Jonathan. "Homeless Are Not Duty of U.S., Top Aide Says." New York Times, February 19, 1986:9.
During Congressional hearings on the federal budget and deficit, James C. Miller, the budget director, said that the homeless were a problem of the state and local governments, not a federal responsibility. When Miller said the federal government was helping with this problem by providing Community Service Block Grants, he was informed that the administration had proposed eliminating these grants in its budget cutting for fiscal 1987, and that this cut had been prepared under Miller's supervision.

Fuerbringer, Jonathan. "Senate 77 to 6, Votes $50 Million To Provide Help for the Homeless." New York Times, January 31, 1987:8.
The Senate voted to transfer $50 million from the Federal Emergency Management Agency's disaster relief program to the agency's food and shelter program for the purpose of spending this money on the homeless.

Fuller, Arthur F. An Odd Soldiery. Forth Worth: Solar Music and Literary Bureau, 1910.

This first-person account is written by an individual, who due to ill health, undergoes a role change from musician to wandering peddlar.

Fuller, Ronald.   The Beggar's Brotherhood.   London: George Allen and Unwin, 1936.
The author describes tramps and beggars and social reactions to them in 16th century Britain.

Fustero, Steven.   "Home On the Street."   Psychology Today, 18, February 1984:56-63.
Homelessness has become a problem in the United States because of the deinstitutionalization of mental patients. The number of patients in mental hospitals has been reduced from 550,000 in 1955 to approximately 125,000 now. Private and community mental health systems, however, have failed to adequately treat the deinstitutionalized patients. Consequently, the homeless population on skid rows has changed from an alcoholic derelict population to a repository for chronically and seriously mentally ill people. The causes of homelessness include economic recession, high unemployment rates, cutbacks in federal programs, the conversion of single-room-occupancy hotels, and gentrification. Advocates for the homeless have emerged. A three-tiered model for the homeless has been proposed, "with each tier designed to provide a step toward complete independence and stabilization of the homeless person." Tier I is emergency shelter; tier II provides transitional shelter "where more demands are made on residents and more service provided; while in tier III, the goal is independence and normalization of lifestyle. Such a program will require increased federal funding. "If the problem is ever to be solved, if people are to stop living and dying on the street, there has to be a reduction in the public's willingness to tolerate the situation and concerted, coordinated efforts, involving the courts, lawmakers and public and private organizations."

G

Galbreath, Sam.   "Assisting the Homeless: Policies and Resources."   Journal of Housing, 43 (5), September-October 1986:211-216.

The author concludes that the cooperation of non-profit public and private organizations is the key to develop successful programs to help the homeless. Emphasis is placed on the coordination of resources from diverse sources. The author outlines ways in which cooperation can be fostered among the private sector (foundations, businesses, banking, hotel, and insurance), non-profit social service organizations, and governmental entities at the local, state and federal levels. He reports on the Emergency Housing Assistance and Emergency Housing Apartment Program in which a few apartments in selected buildings are leased at a per diem rate that is higher than the usual rent, with the landlord using the excess income to make repairs to the building.

Gallagher, Mary Lou. "Grand Central Partnership." <u>Planning</u>, <u>57</u> (3), March 1991:11-12.
This analysis of the Grand Central Partnership, a coalition of property owners, tenants, and city officials whose goal is to revitalize 53 blocks around New York City's Grand Central Station, mentions that it is the city's first improvement district to offer services for the homeless.

Gans, Herbert J. "Culture and Class in the Study of Poverty: An Approach to Anti-Poverty Research." In <u>On Understanding Poverty: Perspectives From the Social Sciences</u>, Daniel P. Moynihan, ed. New York: Basic Books, 1968:201-228.
The topics are the moral assumptions of poverty research, the role of culture in change, behavioral and aspirational culture, the culture of poverty and the culture of affluence, culture and social class, basic research and policy questions, structuring opportunities, and the need for social experiments (altering conditions and observing how people respond).

Gans, Herbert J. "The Failure of Urban Renewal: A Critique and Some Proposals." <u>Commentary</u>, <u>39</u> (4), 1965:29-37.
Urban renewal has made money for developers and failed the poor. The author offers a proposal for a rehousing program.

Gans, Herbert J. "The Uses of Poverty: The Poor Pay All." <u>Social Policy</u>, July-August 1971:20-24. (This article is reprinted in various editions of <u>Down to Earth</u>

Sociology: Introductory Readings, James M. Henslin, ed. New York: The Free Press.)

Applying functional analysis to the persistence of poverty, the author identifies 13 functions that poverty and the poor perform for American society. Functional alternatives, which would benefit the poor, would be dysfunctional for the affluent as they would require a redistribution of income and power.

Gape, W. A. <u>Half a Million Tramps</u>. London: George Routledge and Sons, 1936.

This first-person account was written by an individual who, after running away from a brutal home, spent 22 years tramping through England, Canada, South America, and the United States. He details the subculture of tramps and suggests that the solutions are public awareness and public funds.

Gapen, Phyllis. "Homeless Mentally Ill Create Legal, Medical Crisis." <u>American Medical News</u>, <u>27</u>, February 3, 1984:3, 15-16.

The Port Authority bus terminal and Grand Central Station have been described "as among the largest mental wards in the country." Bus stations and nursing homes (which house one million to two million chronically mentally ill people) are not the answer. What is needed is "a network of hospitals to respond to acute psychiatric illnesses and to treat relapses if necessary until local communities can establish mental health systems that effectively treat the chronically mentally ill." Laws need to be refocused in order to provide adequate medical treatment. To provide rights to patients that only end up giving them "freedom to live on the streets" is cruel.

Gapen, Phyllis. "One-Third of D.C.'s Homeless are Schizophrenic, Study Says." <u>American Medical News</u>, <u>28</u>, May 10, 1985:41.

Ralph Nader's Health Research Group has concluded that "more than one-third of the homeless people in Washington, D.C., suffer from schizophrenia and are on the city's streets because of a poorly administered system for deinstitutionalizing the chronically mentally ill." The suggested solutions include: each physician and psychiatrist in Washington spending two hours a week treating the poor, money being redirected from St. Elizabeth's to the treatment of the deinstitutionalized, changes in commitment laws, and policy changes for St. Elizabeth's.

Garard, G. A. "Boy Tramps and Reform Schools: A Reply to Mr. Flynt." The Century Illustrated Monthly Magazine, 51 (new series 29), April 1896:955.
   The author disputes Josiah Flynt's assertion that "the present reform-school system directly or indirectly forces boys into trampdom."

Garbarine, Rachelle. "Remaking Bronx Shells into Homes." New York Times, May 15, 1992:B10.
   The author reports on plans to rehabilitate two apartment buildings in New York City's Bronx. Ten percent of the apartments will be reserved for the homeless, the others for low-income tenants.

Gardner, Sandra. "Homeless: More Join the Rolls." New York Times, January 22, 1984:Section 11:1.
   The causes of homelessness are displacement, low welfare, and a lack of affordable housing.

Gargan, Edward A. "Ducking for Cover Over the Homeless." New York Times, November 27, 1983:E7.
   The governor of New York and the mayor of New York City trade accusations about cause and responsibility for the homeless. Listed as types of homeless are former mental patients, alcoholics, and the poor.

Garoogian, Andrew. The Homeless in America: A Select Bibliography. Monticello, Illinois: Vance Bibliographies, #P 1461, June 1984.
   Following three pages of introduction is a list of 22 books, 20 reports, studies, and pamphlets, 23 government publications, 75 periodical articles, and 169 newspaper articles.

Garraty, John A. Unemployment in History: Economic Thought and Public Policy. New York: Harper and Row, 1978.
   As the author overviews unemployment, he covers historical practices and attitudes toward the homeless, industrialization, the Great Depression, the Keynesian Revolution, economics, politics, and public police regarding employment.

Garrett, Gerald R. "Alcohol Problems and Homelessness: History and Research." Contemporary Drug Problems, 16 (3), Fall 1989:301-332.

After explaining why homeless alcoholics have been "tracked down" by social researchers in "all of their habitats" in spite of their constituting no more than 5 to 10 percent of Americans with alcohol problems, the author presents a thorough overview of the literature on these subjects. One of the author's major conclusions is that of all the attempts to work with homeless alcoholics over the decades, none has been successful. One of the major findings of the research on homelessness in the 1980s is that the "homeless are a more heterogenous group than the homeless in earlier decades: they are younger and better educated and are drawn from more diverse backgrounds; there is a higher proportion of minorities, women and children among them; they have more serious health problems, including a high prevalence of alcohol and drug abuse and mental illness." He then makes a plea for more ethnographic studies of the homeless which, he says, in contrast to the many done in earlier years, are being ignored by contemporary researchers. "Qualitative approaches permit understanding about the behavior of homeless people based on their beliefs, attitudes, and viewpoints."

Garrett, Gerald R., and Howard M. Bahr. "The Family Backgrounds of Skid Row Women." Signs: Journal of Women in Culture and Society, 2 (2), Winter 1976:369-381.

Comparing results from interviews with 52 women staying at the Women's Emergency Shelter in New York's Bowery with those from 184 low-income women and 199 men staying at Camp LaGuardia, the authors conclude that "women from broken homes are over represented among shelter women, in comparison with other women as well as with skid row men." Thus, "failure in marriage may very well be a key variable in explaining the 'skid careers' of women, while among homeless men it seems to play a relatively minor role."

Garrett, Gerald R., and Howard M. Bahr. "Women on Skid Row." Quarterly Journal of Studies on Alcohol, 34 (4A), December 1973:1228-1243.

The authors compare the drinking patterns of men and women in separate shelters in New York City. Women took their first drink later than men, are lighter drinkers, are not as likely to drink in bars or in public, and have

no bottle gang.   The authors suggest that women are the
most isolated and disaffiliated residents of skid row.

Garrett, Gerald R., and Russell K. Schutt.   "Social
Services for Homeless Alcoholics: Assessment and Response."   <u>Alcohol Health and Research World</u>, <u>11</u> (3),
Spring 1987:50-53.
     Case managers are critical in linking appropriate
services to the homeless who abuse alcohol or who have
psychiatric problems and want help.   The first step in
providing appropriate services and aftercare is an
accurate assessment of the homeless individual.   Commonly
used assessment techniques are self-classification,
objectively studying patterns of alcohol consumption,
probing the extent to which a client has had problems
associated with drinking, and using published operational
criteria such as the DSM-III.   The authors commend
procedures followed at the intake assessment done at
Boston's Long Island Shelter.

Gartner, Michael.   "Biggest Robbery in History: You're
the Victim."   <u>Wall Street Journal</u>, August 9, 1990:A9.
     Upset that his neighbor was killed by a homeless
man, the author says that some of the money directed for
the savings-and-loan bailout could have been used to help
the homeless, prevent crime, conquer disease, hire
police, and build parks.

Gartner, Michael.   "Subway Beggars Do Have a Message:
Desperation."   <u>Wall Street Journal</u>, May 17, 1990:A15.
     The author takes the position that recent court
rulings that forbid begging in New York subways is a
violation of the free speech of homeless people and a
legal fraud perpetrated on the public.

Gave, Keith.   "Tough Family Is Camping Out, Isn't On
Welfare."   Associated Press, April 19, 1984.
     This is an account of a husband, wife, and son in
Chicago who, in spite of the cold, are staying in a tent,
refusing welfare, and hoping for a job.   The author
emphasizes their pride and determination.

Geisler, Charles C., and Hisayoshi Mitsuda. "Mobile Home
Growth, Regulation, and Discrimination in Upstate New
York."   <u>Rural Sociology</u>, <u>52</u> (4), Winter 1987:532-543.
     This analysis of the relationship between mobile
home zoning and social class mentions that the regulation

of mobile homes in rural areas has practical implications for the rural homeless.

Geist, William E. "A Street Man Tangles With I.R.S." New York Times, August 12, 1987:15.

This article profiles John Ed Croft, a homeless painter, from whom the I.R.S. is seeking $11,486.72. Now living in an abandoned building, Croft is a former computer-program analyst who became homeless after his apartment house burned down. This former vice-president of the Greenwich Art Society is attempting to pay the I.R.S. bill bit by bit with empty aluminum cans, "the currency of the street."

Gelber, Seymour. "Developing An AIDS Program in a Juvenile Detention Center." Children Today, January-February, 1988.

The author argues that "an emergency shelter for detainees with AIDS as well as homeless, dependent adolescents must be established so that juveniles are provided temporary homes until medical attention and more permanent settings can be found."

Gelberg, Lillian, and Lawrence S. Linn. "Social and Physical Health of Homeless Adults Previously Treated for Mental Health Problems." Hospital and Community Psychiatry, 39 (5), May 1988:510-516.

Based on a study of 529 homeless adults in Los Angeles County, the authors conclude that those who previously had been admitted to a mental hospital were more likely to experience serious physical symptoms than those who had never used mental health services or had only been seen on an outpatient basis. They are more likely to seek food from garbage cans and to have the least adequate personal hygiene. The request of these homeless was for improved social relations, employment, shelter, and money.

Gelberg, Lillian, Lawrence S. Linn, and Barbara D. Leake. "Mental Health, Alcohol and Drug Use, and Criminal History among Homeless Adults." American Journal of Psychiatry, 145 (2), February 1988:191-196.

A survey of 529 homeless adults showed that those who had been previously hospitalized for psychiatric problems are more likely to have mental health problems, to use more drugs and alcohol, and to be more involved in criminal activities.

Gelfand, Donald E., and Rebeca Bialik-Gilad. "Immigration Reform and Social Work." <u>Social Work</u>, <u>34</u> (1), January 1989:23-27.
This overview of the implications of the 1986 Immigration Reform and Control Act mentions that social workers will have to confront the problem of homelessness.

Getschow, George. "The Day Laborer's Toil Is Hard, Pay Minimal, Security Nonexistent." <u>Wall Street Journal</u>, June 22, 1983:1, 6.
The focus is Houston, where the abuse of labor pools of powerless, homeless men is similar to the 19th century industrial revolution. The author details the hazardous conditions under which these men work and how liquidated damages and forced deductions eat up their wages and keep them in debt. He also discusses techniques of their exploitation and the use of force and threats.

Getschow, George. "Homeless Northerners Unable to Find Work Crowd Sun Belt Cities." <u>Wall Street Journal</u>, November 12, 1982:1, 14.
Displaced families living in Tramp City U.S.A., just outside Houston, who are being called tramps, are working-class people who have been dispossessed. The problem is worsening. Its causes are unemployment and urban renewal. No welfare is given to employables, and no food stamps to those without an address. Some of the new poor are angry at God. Reports survival techniques of scavenging and selling blood.

Getschow, George. "Houston's Tent City Gets Into a Big Flap Over Publicity Blitz." <u>Wall Street Journal</u>, January 14, 1983:1, 5.
As the mass media pour into Tent City (a new Hooverville, a group of homeless people living outside Houston), residents report that they feel like characters acting in their own soap opera. Confusion is reported on the part of Houstonians, and opposition to Tent City is growing.

Getschow, George. "Louisiana Labor Camps Supply 'Warm Bodies' the Oil Business Needs." <u>Wall Street Journal</u>, June 23, 1983:1, 20.
The jobless pour into the Louisiana oil patch. As a new industry rises, so do labor camps. Spartan buildings are turned into bunkhouses. Their residents, exploited and abused, acquire debt for lodging and

fictive charges. Sometimes these exploitative facilities operate under innocent-sounding names, such as St. Mary Council on Alcoholism and Drug Abuse, which is run by a hardened man with a criminal record. As the author details the abuses and economics of the labor camps, he compares them with slavery.

Gewirtzman, Rena, and Iris Fodor. "The Homeless Child at School: From Welfare Hotel to Classroom." Child Welfare, 66 (3), May-June 1987:237-247.
    As the authors focus on the psychological impact of multiple stresses (rootlessness, moving, economic hardships, and lack of community) experienced by the children of homeless families who live in welfare hotels, they stress that schools have three tasks to perform for homeless children in the classroom: to provide structured, stable, non-threatening environment, to help the children express their fear and frustrations, and to provide recreational outlets.

Geyelin, Milo. "Star of Legal Reform Kindles Controversy But Collects Critics." Wall Street Journal, October 16, 1992:A1, A4.
    The author of this review of the movement for legal reform in the United States mentions the problem of statistical knowledge. To illustrate this point, he uses the example of the controversy over the number of American homeless.

Geyelin, Milo, and Amy Stevens. "Thermography Is Valid Procedure, New Jersey Supreme Court Rules." Wall Street Journal, August 8, 1991:B4.
    Among the court cases mentioned in this roundup of judiciary decisions is a ruling that homeless New Yorkers cannot sue the city for failing to provide public restrooms.

Gibbs, Archie. U-Boat Prisoner: The Life Story of a Texas Sailor, Eugene Leuchtman, ed. Boston: Houghton Mifflin, 1943.
    This autobiography is of a vagrant who, after being taken prisoner on a German U-Boat, became a national hero.

Giesbrecht, Norman A., P. James Giffen, Sylvia Lambert, and Gus Oki. "Changes in the Social Control of Skid Row Inebriates in Toronto: Assessments by Skid Row Infor-

mants." <u>Canadian Journal of Public Health</u>, <u>72</u> (2),
March-April 1981:101-104.
   Based on interviews with 80 former or current skid
row inebriates, 11 administrators of services for skid
row men, 10 policemen, statistics on intervention and
admissions to detoxification centers, and observations
while accompanying policemen on patrol, the authors
conclude that there is greater leniency toward public
drunkenness on the part of the police and courts and an
improvement in the way the police deal with inebriates.
The majority of informants think that skid row inebriates
are drinking more, begging more, using other drugs more,
and suffering from a deterioration in health. Although
the skid row men expressed appreciation for the chance to
'dry out' in the detoxification centers, the police and
administrators felt that the detoxification centers were
not serving the public inebriate adequately.

Giffen, P. J. "The Revolving Door: A Functional Interpretation." <u>Canadian Review of Sociology and Anthropolo-
gy</u>, <u>3</u>, 1966:154-166.
   Public intoxication laws are used to control
homeless, unattached men, with the courts serving to
legitimize this control. Criminal stigmatization further
alienates homeless alcoholics from society. This article
also contains a section on "skid row drinking society."

Gilbert, Evelyn. "Shelby Insurance Group Helps the
Homeless." <u>National Underwriter</u>, <u>94</u> (36), September 3,
1990:13-14.
   The Shelby Insurance Group of Shelby, Ohio, has
begun a program whereby the company contributes two
dollars to aid the homeless for each application for a
homeowners' policy.

Gilbert, Jeanne G., and James C. Healey. "The Economic
and Social Background of the Unlicensed Personnel of the
American Merchant Marine." <u>Social Forces</u>, <u>21</u>, 1942:40-
43.
   In presenting the background (nativity, education,
age, years of service, and previous occupations) of 326
men who filled out questionnaires, the authors note that
"only 25.77 percent have any residence which might be
called a home." These men lack "the realization that
somewhere in the wide world he travels there is someone
who cares for him and thinks of him as he spends his
years on the lonely waste of waters."

Gilbert, Neil.   <u>Capitalism and the Welfare State:</u>
<u>Dilemmas of Social Benevolence</u>. New Haven: Yale University Press, 1983.
   Topics are the emergence of welfare capitalism (welfare for profit), the drift toward universalism, contradictions of universal entitlement, dilemmas of family policy, the resiliency of voluntary aid, and the future of welfare capitalism. The solution is a middle course of social responsibility in a mixed economy.

Gilderbloom, John I., James L. Spates, and John J. Macionis. "Is Urban Sociology Dying?" <u>Teaching Sociology</u>, <u>16</u> (4), October 1988:443-447.
   A criticism made during a review symposium on <u>The Sociology of Cities</u> (a book by the second two authors) is that it neglects homelessness.

Gilderbloom, John I.   "Housing Regulations: Help or Hindrance?"   <u>Journal of Housing</u>, <u>48</u> (6), November-December 1991:300-304.
   The author's thesis is that the causes of homelessness identified by the Bush-Kemp Commission on Housing (too much governmental interference by laws that govern urban growth, rents, environment, historic preservation, and building codes) is incorrect, that the real causes are tax policies, the scandals at the U.S. Department of Housing and Urban Development and in the savings and loan industry, high interest rates, and the reduction in low-income and moderate-income shelter programs.

Gilford, Barbara.   "Cartoon Hero's Message to Children: Let's Help Others." <u>New York Times</u>, April 7, 1991:NJ1.
   Gene Iossa, the creator of the cartoon character Lil' Gruesome, helps the homeless.

Gillin, J. L. "Vagrancy and Begging." <u>American Journal of Sociology</u>, <u>35</u>, November 1929:424-432.
   Beggars and vagrancy are analyzed as phenomena of civilized society, the result of economic change, social instability, and social disorganization. This account contains a history of begging and vagrancy, and their regulation.   The Belgian and Swiss labor colonies are proposed as models.

Gilmore, Harlan W.   <u>The Beggar</u>. Chapel Hill: University of North Carolina Press, 1940.
   The author presents a history of begging, delineates types of beggars and their techniques, analyzes motiva-

tions for giving, and suggests methods for the social control of beggars.

Gilmore, Harlan W. "Social Control of Begging." <u>The Family</u>, October 1929:179-181.
    The solutions to begging are for the public to give money to agencies not to beggars (as giving only encourages them) and for the police to rigorously follow the law and arrest beggars.

Gilvert, John J., III. "Should Any Low-Income Housing Be Left in Private Hands? A Need for Entrepreneurs." <u>New York Times</u>, October 2, 1988:E6.
    New York City's rent control is actually a subsidy for higher-income people. Rent subsidies should be given "to those people who truly need it," which can be done "simply by taking the subsidy away from the people who don't need it."

Ginsberg, Leon. "Shelter Issues in the 1980s: The Potential Roles of Adult Foster Care and Community Residential Facilities." <u>Adult Foster Care Journal</u>, 2 (4), Winter 1988:260-272.
    Adult foster care and community residential facilities are proposed as two ways to alleviate the problem of homelessness.

Ginsburg, Norman. "Racial Harassment Policy and Practice: The Denial of Citizenship." <u>Critical Social Policy</u>, 9 (2), Autumn 1989:66-81.
    This analysis of racial attacks in Great Britain mentions that housing improvement and investment for all tenants, including the homeless, is part of the solution.

Gittelman, Martin. "We Need a National Plan for the Homeless Mentally Ill Now." <u>New York Times</u>, September 28, 1987:26.
    The author argues that the deinstitutionalization of the mentally ill has saved the nation billions of dollars--all at a tragic cost. He suggests that we need an effective national plan for the chronically mentally ill.

Gittelman, Martin, and Peter P. Smith. "Sheltering the Homeless." Letters to the Editor, <u>Wall Street Journal</u>, March 20, 1985:29.
    The authors address deinstitutionalization versus reinstitutionalization and say that the solutions are

long-term psychiatric care for a few, and community support with psychiatric, psychological, and social services for most. They mention Project Domicile, churches, and adopting a homeless person or family.

Gitterman, Alex. "Building Mutual Support in Groups." Social Work With Groups, 12 (2), 1989:5-21.
    Homelessness is mentioned as among the "difficult life statuses" that people will share in successful support groups.

Glaberson, William. "Effort Renewed to Give Begging Legal Sanction." New York Times, March 1, 1991:B3.
    Claiming that begging is a constitutionally-protected form of speech, advocates for the homeless have filed a lawsuit to make begging legal.

Glaberson, William. "From Suburbs, New Aid for the Homeless." New York Times, October 21, 1991:B1.
    The author discusses how teenagers from the suburbs of New York City are helping to provide blankets and food to the homeless.

Gladden, Washington. "What to do With the Workless Man!" The Ohio Bulletin of Charities and Correction, 5, June 1899:10-17.
    The solutions are to provide charity for workless men who are not able-bodied (the sick, disabled, aged, and infirm) and who have no relatives on which they can depend and, for the able-bodied, a work test to separate those who are willing to work from those who are not. The able-bodied who are willing to work need to be provided training in work skills that will make them independent. Only when private agencies fail should state agencies step in.

Gladstein, Eva. "The Philadelphia Story: Building the Tenant Action Group." Shelterforce, 11 (3), October-November 1988:8-11.
    The Tenant Action Group, formed in Philadelphia in 1973 to support rent control and tenants' rights, has a subsidiary corporation that provides financial assistance to prevent homelessness.

Glascoe, Stephen. "Homes for Tuberculous Homeless Alcoholics." British Medical Journal, 2, 1978:1373.

In this letter to the editor, the author expresses appreciation that the <u>British Medical Journal</u> expressed interest in the homeless.

Glasser, Irene. <u>More Than Bread: Ethnography of a Soup Kitchen</u>. Alabama: University of Alabama Press, 1988.
For four years, the author did participant observation in a soup kitchen, supplemented with two surveys. She finds that the soup kitchen provides much more than food for the hungry, that it helps fulfil the social needs of the poor--to feel socially connected and part of a community. It accomplishes this although it is composed of a diverse group--single mothers, drug addicts, alcoholics, the mentally ill and chronically unemployed, different ethnicities, and a wide range of ages. In short, the soup kitchen functions beyond its obvious purpose to fulfill needs for the poor and disenfranchised to feel socially connected and part of a community.

Glastonbury, Bryan. <u>Homeless Near a Thousand Homes: A Study of Families without Homes in South Wales and the West of England</u>. London: George Allen and Unwin, 1971.
In Great Britain homeless families and homeless women are given temporary accommodations in state-run hostels, single homeless men are given accommodation by voluntary groups, and those who need help to adjust to permanent housing conditions are provided counseling in temporary and halfway housing. As an early warning system, the courts notify social service agencies when a family is in danger of being evicted. The causes of homelessness are handicaps in family structure (particularly women left unsupported to care for children), unemployment and poverty, poor housing, pathological behavior (mental illness), and domestic upsets (marriage breakdown). The author also details problems in defining and measuring homelessness.

Glazier, Daniel. "Legal Rights of Homeless in St. Louis." <u>Public Law Forum</u>, <u>4</u>, Spring 1985:461-462.
The Missouri Code provides that homeless individuals have a right to shelter.

Gleason, William F. <u>The Liquid Cross of Skid Row</u>. Milwaukee: Bruce, 1966.
The author details six days in the life of a priest, Ignatius McDermott, who works on skid row. The volume

contains life histories and an overview of the social institutions of skid row.

Glenn, John. "Co-operation Against Beggary." <u>Charities Review</u>, <u>1</u>, December 1891:67-72.
   Although it may appear to be an ordinary offense, begging is a crime against society because labor is the foundation of wealth, and the man who will not labor himself can only live through the labor of others. We promote pauperism and begging by indiscriminate giving. The solutions require the cooperation of government, police, church, and citizens in not giving to beggars and in requiring them to work.

Gmelch, George, and Sharon Bohn Gmelch. "Begging in Dublin: The Strategies of a Marginal Urban Occupation." <u>Urban Life</u>, <u>6</u> (4), January 1978:439-454.
   The author's focus is "the strategies used by beggars among one migrant group (the Tinkers) in the city of Dublin to manipulate individuals into giving alms." The strategies in this almost exclusively female activity include maximizing sympathy by faking physical disablement, a uniform of tattered clothing, carrying an infant, and making pleas for such small amounts ("a sup of milk") that to refuse seems miserly.

Gold, Allan R. "Thousands March on Washington In Protest Against Homelessness." <u>New York Times</u>, October 8, 1989:12.
   About 35,000 persons (or 140,000, depending upon the estimates) demonstrated in Washington, D.C. Their goal was to draw attention to the need for low-cost housing, especially the plight of homeless children.

Goldberg, Martin. "The Runaway Americans." <u>Mental Hygiene</u>, <u>56</u>, January 1972:13-21.
   Those in flight are likely to be characterized by high dependence masked by hostility, problems with interpersonal relationships, frustration, impulsiveness, self misrepresentation, and alienation. The author provides a psychiatric profile of these people who are in our society but not of it. The solutions are to recognize their marginality, decrease deinstitutionalization, decrease rejection and exclusion, provide a sense of community, and open half-way houses as centers for offering a family-like or community-like setting with a variety of social services.

Goldberg, Michael. "Hands Across America Reaches Out."
Rolling Stone, February 27, 1986:13.
     Plans for Hands Across America are proceeding well.
Nearly 600 celebrities have signed up for the event.

Goldberger, Paul. "Designing a Decent Alternative for
the Homeless." *New York Times*, March 27, 1988:H39.
     To support the thesis that architects are concerned
about turning their talent toward social concerns, the
author reports on building projects for the homeless
undertaken by Alexander Cooper & Partners and Skidmore,
Owings & Merrill. The purpose of the projects, unlike
welfare hotels, is to offer transitional housing in
buildings that "offer a testament to the possibility of
decent city living for people who have known mainly
frustration and denial."

Golden, Stephanie. "The Transforming Tree: Finding our
Roots in the Homeless Women." *Conditions*, 4, Winter
1979:82-95.
     Based on her experiences with homeless women, the
author confronts her own humanity, including rage,
despair, and feelings of persecution. This psychology of
homeless women contains case stories.

Goldfarb, Charles. "Patients Nobody Wants--Skid Row
Alcoholics." *Diseases of the Nervous System*, 31,
1970:274-281
     After an overview of the characteristics of skid
row, why people live there, the skid row personality, the
Bowery, the hazards of skid row, the law and the alcoholic, and chronic alcoholism, the author summarizes the
treatment of skid row alcoholics in the Manhattan Bowery
Project.

Goldfinger, Stephen M., John T. Hopkin, and Robert W.
Surber. "Treatment Resisters or System Resisters?
Toward a Better Service System for Acute Care Recidivists." In *Advances in Treating the Young Adult Chronic
Patient*, B. Pepper and H. Ryglewicz, eds. San Francisco:
Jossey-Bass, March 1984:17-27.
     To meet the needs of the chronic, uncooperative,
abusive users of psychiatric facilities would require an
effective system, one that is capable, comprehensive,
continuous, and individualized, with a willing and
tolerant staff that provides flexible and meaningful
treatment.

Goldman, Howard H., Antoinette A. Gattozzi, and Carl A. Taube. "Defining and Counting the Chronically Mentally Ill." Hospital and Community Psychiatry, 32 (1), January 1981:21-27.

Deinstitutionalization, which has led to homelessness, has also led to a lack of definitive information on the scope of the problem of chronic mental illness. The authors propose what they say is a better definition of the chronically mentally ill and a national estimate of their prevalence.

Goldman, Howard H., and Joseph P. Morrissey. "The Alchemy of Mental Health Policy: Homelessness and the Fourth Cycle of Reform." American Journal of Public Health, 75, 1985:727-731.

The authors analyze public mental health policy in terms of four cyclical reform movements: reform in the early 19th century, the hygiene movement in the early 20th century, the community mental health movement in the mid 20th century, and a current movement of community support systems in which the goal is to care for chronic patients through a network of community-based mental health, social welfare, and housing services. The causes of homelessness are deinstitutionalization without community support and adequate housing, a lack of jobs, and a lack of services. A central question that must be resolved is, who among the homeless are mentally ill, and who among the mentally ill are homeless?

Goldman, Howard H., Neal H. Adams, and Carl A. Taube. "Deinstitutionalization: The Data Demythologized." Hospital and Community Psychiatry, 34 (2), February 1983:129-134.

The authors present evidence to disprove that outpatient care has replaced inpatient care, community-based facilities have replaced state mental hospitals, and public resources to pay the cost of caring for the mentally ill have been replaced by private resources. They also discuss the problem of defining the structure and function of the public health service system.

Goldsborough, Ernest W., and Wilbur E. Hobbs. "The Petty Offender." The Prison Journal, 36, April 1956:3-26.

Some of the men who are released from the House of Corrections in Philadelphia become homeless. The causes are lack of assets, family difficulties, lack of trade or skills, physical or mental illness, and their criminal

record.   The solutions are more community resources,
half-way houses, and better record-keeping.

Goldthorpe, Harry.   <u>Room at the Bottom</u>.   Bradford,
England: Sunbeam Press, 1960.
     The author of this first-person account of experi-
ences as the secretary of an Unemployed Association
argues that the solution to homelessness is cooperation,
as there is no room at the top.

Goleman, Daniel.   "Experts Fault Koch's Homeless Plan."
<u>New York Times</u>, September 2, 1987:12.
     The author argues that Mayor Koch's program to
involuntarily reinstitutionalize the severely mentally
ill homeless needs to go beyond "dumping people back into
snake pits of an earlier age" and needs to have a second
step, a release program in supervised residences.

Gonzales, Diana Ettel.   "Homemaker Tells of Life in D.C.
Streets as 'Bag Lady'."   <u>Minneapolis Star and Tribune</u>,
November 11, 1987:M13.
     Beulah Lund, a 50-year-old homemaker, who posed as
a homeless woman and stayed in emergency shelters and on
the streets, urges the American public to "take an active
role in addressing the problem of the homeless."

Gonzalez, David.   "Charity Comes Too Close to Home." <u>New
York Times</u>, November 13, 1991:B1.
     The author summarizes the conflict felt by many New
Yorkers: sympathy for the homeless but fears that if a
shelter is built in their neighborhood it will bring with
it crime and violence.   A common attitude is that the
homeless are best seen and helped from afar.

Gonzalez, David.   "Journeys to Nowhere Fill the Nights of
the Homeless."   <u>New York Times</u>, February 15, 1992:A25.
     The author takes the reader into the night life of
New York City's homeless who struggle to survive the cold
winter.

Gonzalez, David.   "Street Patrol Gives Veterans Purpose
and a Home."   <u>New York Times</u>, August 4, 1991:42.
     The author features the Veterans Civilian Observa-
tion Patrol, a group of homeless veterans who patrol the
streets of Brooklyn.

Gonzalez, David.   "Undercount No Surprise in the Shacks."
<u>New York Times</u>, April 14, 1991:27.

Advocates for the homeless claim that the count of the homeless by the U.S. Census was an undercount.

Goode, Stephen. "Homeless Find Shelter in the Courts." Insight, <u>3</u> (7), February 16, 1987:56-57.
The author summarizes legal activism, and legal decisions and their controversies regarding the homeless from 1979 to 1986. In 1979 a New York court made a landmark ruling based on the state constitution that citizens have a "right to shelter," which is to be provided by the government if all else fails. In 1981 a court ruling extended that duty to include care for homeless women. Similar legal decisions have been made in West Virginia, New Jersey, Missouri, Massachusetts, and California. In 1983 Congress passed a homeless relief law, ordering "the military to make available unused space at military facilities nationwide for use by the homeless."

Goodman, Walter. "TV Journalists' Urge to Prettify the News." <u>New York Times</u>, February 19, 1992:C20.
The portrayal of the homeless in television news programs, in which they are consistently depicted as hard-working, straight-living people temporarily down on their luck, is a gross distortion of reality.

Goodwin, Michael. "Cheap Residential Hotels: Endangered Species in N.Y." <u>New York Times</u>, January 27, 1980:E7.
The number of low-priced hotels in New York City, those renting rooms for under $50 a week, is dropping because of the city's tight housing market and inflation. Flophouses on the Bowery are being converted into artists' lofts.

Goodwin, Michael. "New Program in Shelters Stresses Work Ethic." <u>New York Times</u>, September 7, 1983:B1.
Solving homelessness by rehabiliting people through work is being tried in New York City with a program called the Work Experience Program. The program is only for single adults, who work in exchange for shelter and a stipend.

Gordon, C. Wayne. "Socialization Characteristics and Life Career Patterns of the Skid Row Alcoholic." <u>Institute on the Skid Row Alcoholic, Annual Conference</u>. New York: National Committee on Alcoholism, 1956:6-13. Mimeo.

Using a sample of skid row alcoholics, the author examines the process of adaptation to chronic drunkenness. The alcoholic is socialized into alcoholism by drinking places and work groups. Institutionalized living (army, work camps, etc) also contributes to this process. Characteristically, these patterns are accompanied by withdrawal from job and family.

Gordon, James. "Running Away: Reaction or Revolution." Adolescent Psychiatry, 7 1979:54-70.

The author first presents an historical overview of running away from the colonial era to the 1970s. During the nineteenth century homeless young people came "to be regarded as a special and serious problem," a danger to property, morals, and political life. In the early twentieth century a theoretical view of adolescence developed that has persisted to the present: adolescence is "a stage of development characterized by continuous crisis." In the 1960s American youths came "to see their own powerlessness as a mirror of black people's, and began "to think about youth rights as well as civil rights." In a climate characterized by disputes about politics, sex, drugs, and grooming, large numbers of young people left their homes. The author then analyzes the context and meaning of running away, familial relations, and runaway houses.

Gore, M. S., J. S. Mathur, M. R. Laljani, and H. S. Takulia. The Beggar Problem in Metropolitan Delhi. Delhi: Delhi School of Social Work, 1959.

The authors present an overview of beggars in Delhi, India: their social characteristics (demographics and social background), work life, relation to society, and beggar communities, religious and secular. The solutions they suggest are prevention (medical and economic assistance) and rehabilitation (productive work at home and detention in institutions for reeducation and occupational training, with separate colonies for lepers, aged beggars, mentally sick and deficient beggars, and child beggars). The remaining are to be placed in a poor house.

Gothberg, Laura C. "A Comparison of the Personality of Runaway Girls with a Control Group as Expressed in the Themes of Murray's Thematic Apperception Test." American Journal of Mental Deficiency, 51, 1947:627-631.

The author compares a matched sample of ten females at the Mansfield State Training School in Connecticut with ten who had run away. For both groups, the two most recurring themes were "need for love and protection" and "self-aggression."

Gottlieb, Martin. "The Homeless Issue." New York Times, May 25, 1992:A23.
   The author summarizes conflicts between David Dinkins, Mayor of New York City, and Andrew M. Cuomo, whom Dinkins appointed head of the Commission on the Homeless.

Gottlieb, Martin. "Space Invaders: Land Grab on the Lower East Side." Village Voice, December 14, 1982:10-14, 16, 50.
   This article examines the invasion of the Lower East Side by newcomers to New York, skyrocketing property values, the attempts of landlords to evict old tenants, and the resistance to change by some of the traditional inhabitants of this area.

Gould, Martin, and Robert Ardinger. "Self Advocacy: A Community Solution to Access Discrimination and Service Problems Encountered by the 'Homeless Disabled.'" Journal of Voluntary Action Research, 17 (1), January-March 1988:46-53.
   Based on opportunities, needs, and approaches revealed from a survey of 120 service agencies, the authors advocate self advocacy service programs for the homeless disabled.

Gould, Robert, and Robert Levy. "Psychiatrists as Puppets of Koch's Roundup Policy." New York Times, November 27, 1987:Y27.
   The case of Joyce Brown, the first homeless person picked up on the streets by the "health squad," illustrates the potential for abuse in this program. The authors urge that an array of basic services be provided the homeless: public baths, a full range of housing opportunities, and an inventory of community mental health services.

Grabowski, Gene. "Homeless to Get Free Health Care from Charities." Associated Press, December 19, 1984.
   Pew Memorial Trust (of Philadelphia) and Robert Wood Johnson Foundation (of Princeton, New Jersey) gave a $25 million grant to 18 cities to establish free health clinics in shelters and soup kitchens. These projects are to include referrals to local public health agencies

and coordination with agencies to help secure welfare and housing assistance and jobs.

Graham, Ellen. "How Private Company Helps Welfare Clients Find and Keep Jobs." Wall Street Journal, April 17, 1990:A1, A6.
America Works is a program that trains welfare recipients and gets them jobs. The article mentions Wiletta Parker, who used to sleep in the subways but now works at a clerical job.

Graham, Ellen, and Roger Ricklets. "AIDS Has Been Cruel To Greenwich Village and Its Homosexuals." Wall Street Journal, March 13, 1987:1, 12.
Reporting on the extensive impact of AIDS on Greenwich Village, the author indicates that about 750 homeless people with AIDS live in New York City.

Grass, Jane. "The First Glimpse of the Homeless: Raw Sight for Tourists in New York." New York Times, November 9, 1987:Y21.
The author explores reactions and attitudes of out-of-towners to the homeless in Grand Central Terminal and the Port Authority bus station.

Graves, Theodore D. "The Personal Adjustment of Navajo Indian Migrants to Denver, Colorado." American Anthropologist, 72 (1), 1970:35-54.
To explain "excessive Indian drunkenness," the author focuses on such background factors as type of parental role models, pre-migration job training, and marital status. "After showing that better prepared Indians have far fewer drinking problems than less well prepared Indians, we can then understand their high drinking rates in comparison to other urban groups by virtue of the fact that their preparation for successful, unstressful urban living is far poorer." The "typical Navajo social drinking group" is "seen as an adaptive response to structural conditions." The implication of analyzing "drinking cliques" as due to "marginal economic position in the midst of affluence" that "generates strong feelings of relative deprivation" is that "the vast majority of Navajo drunkenness, at least in Denver, can be accounted for without recourse to the fact that our subjects are Indians."

Gray, Christopher. "Pioneer Home for the Homeless." New York Times, March 31, 1991:Section 10:7.

The author features the Tompkins Square Boys' Lodging house, the oldest surviving structure for the homeless in New York City. It was built in 1887.

Gray, Frank. <u>The Tramp: His Meaning and Being</u>. London: J. M. Dent and Sons, 1931.

Based on participant observation, the author concludes that there are ten types of tramps: genuine tramps (free and true), genuine workers (unemployed), quasi-genuine workers (work and quit), seafaring men, hoppers (seasonal workers), professional beggars (vagrant peddlers), habitual drunkards, habitual criminals, physical degenerates (deformed or undersized), and mental degenerates (lunatics). To solve this problem is a national obligation. Solutions should consist of medical examinations, treatment according to types, registration for work, better diet, reception centers, imprisonment for habitual vagrants, and the use of specialized officials.

Grayson, L. M., and Michael Bliss, eds. <u>The Wretched of Canada</u>. Toronto: University of Toronto Press, 1971.

This volume contains letters written between 1930 and 1935 to R. B. Bennett, the Prime Minister of Canada, by people pleading for relief from their poverty. It also contains an occasional letter of complaint that the government is feeding bums or that the people on relief are wasteful.

Green, Arnold W. "A Re-Examination of the Marginal Man Concept." <u>Social Forces</u>, <u>26</u> (1), October 1947:167-171.

After detaining the history of the concept, the author concludes that "marginal man" has been widely adopted in sociology but that the term is ambiguous, has not been rigorously used, and has little scientific value.

Green, Mark J. "Runaways on the Legal Leash." <u>Trial</u>, <u>7</u> (5), 1971:28-29.

The author provides a brief overview of laws regarding children and youth, especially runaways. He points out that our laws on runaways violate three basic principles of civil liberties granted adult Americans: the right of personal freedom (to live where one wants), the right to be left alone, and the right to travel.

Greenberg, Michael R., Frank J. Popper, and Bernadette M. West. "The TOADS: A New American Urban Epidemic." Urban Affairs Quarterly, 25 (3), March 1990:435-454.
  Among the problems associated with TOADS (Temporarily Obsolete Abandoned Derelict Sites) is that these deserted industrial and residential sites provide makeshift housing for the homeless.

Greenberger, Robert S. "Joblessness Can Mean Hunting for Your Food and Living in the Car." Wall Street Journal, March 7, 1983:1, 16.
  Using the case histories of Jerry Weaver and Thomas Harrington, who became homeless after losing their jobs, the author discusses the new poor, welfare cuts, and a new migration across America.

Greene, Nancy B., and T. C. Esselstyn. "The Beyond Control Girl." Juvenile Justice, 23 (3), 1972:13-19.
  The decision to call a juvenile "beyond control" is highly subjective, often a synonym for sexual precocity. The five main areas of beyond control behavior among females are school, unwed pregnancy, sex delinquency, running away, and incorrigibility. Their typology of runaways are the rootless, the anxious, and the terrified.

Greene, W. A. "Squatting and the Law." Solicitor's Journal, 125, June 5, 1981:384-386.
  This article provides a succinct review of the history of squatting and the rights of squatters in Great Britain.

Greenwood, Anthony. "Langley House Trust and the Problem of the Homeless Ex-Offender." Prison Service Journal, 20, 1975:5-8.
  Langley House Trust operates three types of homes for those released from prison: halfway, fully supportive communities, and homes for those with no further work expectancies. This article describes the program's attempt to provide family-like support, its goals, functions, and limitations.

Greider, William. "America's Desperate Housing Crisis." Rolling Stone, December 1, 1988:41-43.
  The "housing squeeze," the cost of housing rising faster than the incomes of poor persons, is forcing some individuals onto the streets. The single most important cause of the housing squeeze is "high interest rates

combined with stagnant or declining wages. As a result, millions of young families have simply been priced out of the market for new houses....The real cost of financing a home--the nominal mortgage-interest rate minus the rate of inflation--is many times higher than it was in the late 1970's....If the federal government cared, it could knock down the price and sell its bloated stock of housing to people who desperately need it....The solution to the housing crisis is obvious--America has to devote more energy and capital to building housing." This will require a renewal of "federal spending for low-income housing; reforms of local zoning laws to spur housing for people of modest means; lower interest rates; new tax incentives for low-income housing and tax breaks for low-income families." Without such programs, we are facing the "disintegration of the American dream of home ownership."

Greve, John, Dilys Page, and Stella Greve. <u>Homelessness in London</u>. Edinburgh: Scottish Academic Press, 1971.
     The primary cause of homelessness is a shortage of affordable housing. The common attitude is that there are two distinct types of homeless people: those who are homeless due to no fault of their own (victims of the housing shortage) and those whose housing problems are due to their own fault (personal failures or deficien- cies). The primary solution is to provide affordable housing: rent and tenancy legislation, housing associa- tions, early warning system (prevention), rehabilitation, and follow-up services.

Grigsby, Charles, Donald Baumann, Steven E. Gregorich, and Cynthia Roberts-Gray. "Disaffiliation to Entrench- ment: A Model for Understanding Homelessness." <u>Journal of Social Issues</u>, <u>46</u> (4), Winter 1990:141-156.
     The authors argue that disaffiliation and reaffili- ation processes are keys to understanding entrenchment in homelessness and developing remediation strategies. Survey data collected from 166 homeless persons in Austin, Texas, identified four clusters of homeless: (1) the Recently Dislocated have small social networks and mild mental health problems; (2) the Vulnerable have been homeless longer, have fewer people in their social networks, and border on severe dysfunction; (3) the Outsiders, who have been homeless about as long as the Vulnerable, have much larger social networks and function as well as the Recently Dislocated; (4) the Prolonged have been homeless for more than five years, have few

people in their networks, and appear moderately dysfunctional." The authors stress the significance of social
networks of support, concluding that "an individual who
has only a few people to call on for support probably
needs a very different kind of action plan than does one
who has an extensive network, including a large number of
other homeless people."

Grimaldi, Lennie. "Students Take Crash Course in City
Life." New York Times, January 20, 1991:CN1.
    Students from Fairfield University participate in a
program in which they work with homeless people in
Bridgeport, Connecticut.

Gross, Jane. "Cruel Odyssey of the Homeless Seeking a
Bed." New York Times, January 16, 1984:B1, B22.
    The author explores problems that the homeless
experience in getting assigned to a shelter in New York
City.

Gross, Jane. "The Deadly Specter of AIDS Brings Added
Turmoil for Gay Teen-Agers." New York Times, October 21,
1987:Y12.
    In examining behaviors and attitude of gay teenagers
in New York City, the author refers to hustling by
homeless teenagers.

Gross, Jane. "Group of New York AIDS Victims Denied U.S.
Benefits for Disabled." New York Times, February 23,
1987:12.
    The residents of Bailey House, a former hotel that
is now an innovative residence in Greenwich Village for
homeless victims of AIDS, fear that they will be denied
payment by the Social Security Administration.

Gross, Jane. "Lawyers Redirect Lives As They Help
Homeless." New York Times, December 18, 1988:16.
    The author details problems confronted by lawyers in
San Francisco who offer their skills to homeless street
people.

Gross, Thom. "Room for Improvement." St. Louis Post-
Dispatch, November 16, 1986:B4.
    Although the homeless express severe dissatisfaction
with homeless shelters in the City of St. Louis, city
officials point out that the city is providing a wide
range of services to the homeless. These services
include a reception center; transportation to medical

appointments, job placement, Operation Night Watch (a street ministry patrolling city streets after dark looking for homeless people who need help), counseling to break the cycle of homelessness, and a day center for the elderly and mothers with small children.

Grout, Pam. "Helping the Homeless." Fund Raising Management, 22 (6), August 1991:41-44.
The author reports on a fund-raising campaign of the Salvation Army called the Bed and Bread Club, which provides food and shelter to the homeless.

Gruenberg, Ernest M., and Janet Archer. "Abandonment of Responsibility for the Seriously Mentally Ill." Millbank Memorial Fund Quarterly, 57 (4), 1979:485-506.
This article reviews the history of state responsibility for the seriously mentally ill, from 18th century to the present, and gives the historical background of current abandonment or community neglect. The authors reply negatively to the questions of whether decreased hospital admissions indicates program success, increased hospital admissions indicates program failure, hospital care is always harmful to patients, state care is inherently restrictive, community psychiatric services provide good care for all patients, and reducing state hospital beds saves money. The solutions are to reappraise ways to organize mental health services in order to develop their most constructive use, with the focus of attention placed on chronic mental patients.

Gruson, Lindsey. "Philadelphia Forced to Face Homeless Issue." New York Times, February 8, 1987:Y34.
Although Philadelphia has a network of 136 boarding homes and shelters that can house 4,000 people a night, the author criticizes the city for not being active enough in getting people into its shelter system, suggesting that the city is responsible for the overtly psychotic who freeze to death in the streets.

Gude, John. "Accommodating the Single Homeless." Social Work Today, 8 (34), May 31, 1977:10-13.
Nottinghamshire probation service has licensed lodging houses in the community where homeless ex-prisoners can stay. This review of the program contains a description of how administrators locate landladies and place homeless felons according to their special needs. The author explains how probation is supervised and details costs of the program, the goal of which is to

provide supportive community-like homes for women with children.

Gudeman, Jon E., Barbara Dickey, Laura Rood, Sondra Hellman, and Lester Grinspoon. "Alternative to the Back Ward: The Quarterway House." <u>Hospital and Community Psychiatry</u>, <u>32</u> (5), May 1981:330-334.

The authors evaluate a quarterway house founded in Boston in 1978. Compared with a control group of inpatients, those who participated in the quarterway house showed an improvement in general functions and survival skills, a decrease in medication and seclusion, but no decline in psychotic symptoms, obstreperousness, or antisocial behavior. Nor did they learn to live independently.

Gudeman, Jon E., and Miles F. Shore. "Beyond Deinstitutionalization: A New Class of Facilities for the Mentally Ill." <u>The New England Journal of Medicine</u>, <u>311</u>, September 27, 1984:832-836.

The authors review deinstitutionalization from 1955 to 1980 and give an overview of the programs of the Massachusetts Mental Health Center. They argue that about 6 percent of the deinstitutionalized should be reinstitutionalized in specialized-care facilities: the elderly, mentally retarded, brain-damaged, and schizophrenics. These facilities need to have stringent pre-admission screening, programs targeted to their sub-populations, a multi-disciplinary staff, and be located on grounds of state hospitals and affiliated with an acute-care psychiatric hospital. It is necessary to avoid political problems (anxiety about the correctness of reinstitutionalization). The operating auspices could be public or privately contracted.

Guenther, Robert. "New York Entices Landlords, But Homeless Units are Few." <u>Wall Street Journal</u>, May 7, 1986:31.

New York City is paying $1,500 a month per homeless family in a welfare hotel. City officials are offering a $9,700 bonus to landlords who agree to rent an apartment to a homeless family of four for $270 a month for two years. Single Room Occupancy Housing Corporation in Los Angeles has bought and renovated seven transient hotels totaling 786 units at a per room cost of only $5,000 to $7,000 plus $12,000 to $15,000 in renovations. They rent them for $143 to $185 a month. Help I is building

transitional, modular housing in Brooklyn. The program
brings up the question of communal versus private dining.

Guild, Jane Purcell. "Transient in New Guise." Social
Forces, 17, March 1939:366-372.
    For dealing with transients, the usual case work
procedures are inadequate. The solution is to obtain
accurate background information on transients through
fingerprinting, centralization of facilities, and case
records.

Gunasekara, M. G. S. "The Problem of Absconding in Boys'
Approved Schools in England and Wales." British Journal
of Criminology, 4, 1963:145-151.
    Comparing 19 absconders with 25 non-absconders from
training schools in England and Wales, the author found
no striking differences. Both were rootless, confirmed
truants, educationally retarded, and had low IQs.

Gunn, John. "Prisons, Shelters, and Homeless Men."
Psychiatric Quarterly, 48 (4), 1974:505-512.
    Deinstitutionalization has increased homelessness in
Great Britain. The solutions are flexibility, collaboration, consent, and meeting the special needs of different
kinds of patients, including the inadequate and antisocial homeless.

Gupta, Udayan. "Enterprise: Groups Provide Bridge into
Ranks of Employed." Wall Street Journal, March 10,
1992:B1.
    The author profiles groups whose goal is to help
homeless people cross the bridge between the world of
unemployed homelessness and the working world.

Guthrie, Woody. Bound for Glory. New York: E. P.
Dutton, 1976.
    This autobiographical account contains much material
on the author's wandering travels, including hoboing by
freight train.

Gutierres, Sara, and John W. Reich. "A Developmental
Perspective on Runaway Behavior: Its Relationship to
Child Abuse." Child Welfare, 60 (2), February 1981:89-
94.
    Running away is due to many factors, including
physical and sexual abuse. Rather than becoming aggressive, the abused juvenile is likely to become withdrawn.
Those who become delinquent need special treatment.

Gutman, David. "The Sleep of Reason: How the Insane Were Turned into the Homeless." <u>American Scholar</u>, <u>60</u> (3), Summer 1991:446-452.
    The author reviews <u>Madness in the Streets: How Psychiatry and the Law Abandoned the Mentally Ill</u> by Rael Jean Isaac and Virginia C. Armat.

Guyon, Janet. "In Abundance of U.S. Hunger Is Often Sign of a Deeper Social Ill." <u>Wall Street Journal</u>, March 9, 1984:1, 19.
    The U.S. Conference of Mayors reports that different groups of people are hungry: the mentally ill, the elderly on fixed incomes, drifters, single mothers, and the new poor.

H

H., J. A. "Leaves from the Diary of a Tramp." <u>Living Age</u>, <u>262</u>, July 17, 1909:143-149.
    A young Englishman recounts the miseries of his forced tramping following the loss of his job at a mill.

Haardt, Sara. "Jim Tully." <u>American Mercury</u>, <u>14</u>, May 1928:82-90.
    At the time this biography was written, Tully had become a Hollywood writer.

Haas, J. Eugene. "The Philippine Earthquake and Tsunami Disaster: A Reexamination of Behavioral Propositions." <u>Disasters</u>, <u>2</u> (1), 1978:3-11.
    This analysis of the 1976 Philippine earthquake mentions that 55,000 people were left homeless.

Haddon, Alfred Cort. <u>The Wanderings of Peoples</u>. Cambridge: Cambridge University Press, 1912.
    Two main factors determine human migrations: the driving force and the control. The driving force is expulsion and attraction. Expulsion is usually due to over-population or a lack of food. Attraction, a much rarer cause, is a craving for more. Control is due mainly to geographical conditions. Based on evidences of the physical characters of peoples, their artifacts, customs, folk-tales, and languages, the author traces migrations in Asia and Oceania, Europe, Africa, North America, and South America.

Hagen, Jan L. "Gender and Homelessness." Social Work, 32 (4), July-August 1987:312-316.

To contrast the characteristics of homeless males and females, the author examined 227 records of persons who had requested services from a centralized in-take service in "a moderately-sized community." Compared with men, the female homeless were more likely to be local residents, to have an income from unemployment, and to be homeless due to eviction or domestic violence. They were less likely to report previous psychiatric hospitaliza-tions, incomes below the poverty line, being homeless because of running away, being thrown out, alcohol or drug abuse, or release from jail or a medical hospital. The author concludes that "the findings document the need for immediate, concrete services such as food and shelter as well as for intensive relational services such as crisis counseling, long-term counseling, alcohol treat-ment, transitional-supported living environments, and case management."

Hagen, Jan L. "Participants in a Day Program for the Homeless: A Survey of Characteristics and Service Needs." Psychosocial Rehabilitation Journal, 12 (4), April 1989:29-37.

Interviews with 47 homeless men and women in Albany, New York, indicate that because of low education, substance abuse, health problems, previous psychiatric hospitalizations, and probation or parole, independence through employment is not a likely route out of homeless-ness. The various subgroups within the homeless popula-tion must be targeted to meet their specific needs.

Hagen, Jan L. "The Heterogeneity of Homelessness." Social Casework, 68 (8), October 1987:451-457.

The author interviewed 227 homeless men and women who were helped by the Capital District Travelers Aid Society in Albany, New York, during December 1984. He summarizes demographic characteristics of the sample, reasons for their homelessness, client needs, service patterns, and differences in gender, race, and age. He concludes that homelessness is heterogenous--it has many causes, and many different kinds of people are homeless. Accordingly, multiple intervention strategies must be developed to meet the needs of the various subgroups.

Hagen, Jan L. "Whatever Happened to 43 Elizabeth I, c.2?" Social Service Review, 56 (1), March 1982:108-119.

A review of the evolution of the poor laws, with a delineation of their underlying principles. The author examines court cases and the current status of the poor laws, while assessing their influence on the development and implementation of our social welfare system.

Hagen, Jan L., and Andre M. Ivanoff. "Homeless Women: A High-Risk Population." *Affilia*, 3 (1), Spring 1988:19-33.

Interviews with 51 homeless women in Albany, New York, indicate heterogeneity. Different intervention strategies must be developed to meet the needs of specific subgroups of homeless women.

Hagen, Jan L., and Elizabeth Hutchison. "Who's Serving the Homeless?" *Social Casework*, 69 (8), October 1988:491-497.

Mailed questionnaires to service providers in Albany, New York, indicate that most service providers are inexperienced, work at entry level positions, and are not trained in social work.

Haggard, Loretta, and Anne D. Lezak. "Reports Available from the National Institute of Mental Health Concerning the Homeless Mentally Ill." Rockville, Maryland: National Institute of Mental Health, July 1986.

This bibliography contains 33 annotated sources, divided into the topics of policy, research, and services.

Hale, Edward E. "Reports on Tramps." *Proceedings of the Conference of Boards of Public Charities*, 1877:102-110.

Giving handouts to tramps should be avoided because handouts encourage tramping. The solutions to the problem of tramping are public provision in return for work, unannounced occasional enforcement of vagrancy laws in all parts of the state on the same day, and letters of membership provided by societies of workmen to authenticate an individual's search for work.

Hall, Judy A., and Penelope L. Maza. "The Effects of Homelessness on Families and Children." *Child and Youth Services*, 14 (1), 1990:35-47.

Based on data from 163 homeless families, including 340 children, the authors make suggestions for public policy, public education, and social work.

Hall, Trish. "Tackling Homelessness Near Home." New York Times, October 31, 1989:24.
    The author profiles the work of Midtown Life Link, a project funded by the 53rd Street Association of New York City to help the homeless. This private group has hired two social workers who walk the streets and offer help to homeless individuals.

Haller, Beth. "The Homeless of Southern Illinois." Southern Illinoisan, April 3, 1988:A1, A6; April 4, 1988:A5; April 5, 1988:A1, A5.
    Case studies are used to highlight the problems and coping mechanisms of the homeless. The articles include a discussion of the welfare cycle, the mentally ill, the down and out, the near homeless who live in substandard housing, and suggestions on how to increase the stock of low-income housing.

Hallwachs, G. M. "Decentralized Care of the Homeless in a Crisis." The Family, 11, February 1931:314-317.
    The relief agencies in New York City, such as the bread lines and soup kitchens run by charitable groups, are decentralized. This attracts vagrants into the city and demoralizes those who are trying to help. Centralization is needed in order to prevent this attraction and demoralization.

Halpern, Sue. "The Rise of the Homeless." The New York Review of Books, February 16, 1989:24-27.
    In this review of Jonathan Kozol's book, Rachel and Her Children: Homeless Families in America, the author recounts her own experiences in visiting the Martinique Hotel. She also covers the criticism by Ellen Bassuk that Kozol has naively assumed the only difference between homeless and housed families is the lack of home.

Halstead, Peter. "Vulnerability." New Law Journal, 133, July 1, 1983:589-591.
    The author reviews court decisions in Great Britain regarding the obligation of local councils to provide housing for the homeless.

Hamberg, Jill. Building and Zoning Regulations: A Guide for Sponsors of Shelters and Housing for the Homeless in New York City. New York: Community Service Society of New York, November 1984.
    The author focuses on how the building and zoning regulations of New York City apply to establishing

shelters for the homeless. She reviews types of facilities for the homeless, the basic laws relating to
building and zoning, and the relationship of building
codes and zoning issues to selecting and designing
facilities for the homeless.

Hampson, Rick. "New York City Finding Homes in Expensive
Hotels for the Homeless." Associated Press, August 24,
1983.
    New York City allows $32 a night for a homeless
family of three. Because all hotel space available at
this price has been used up, city officials have had to
pay more, being more willing, it seems, to do this for
the new poor. They pay $98 a night in the Hilton Hotel
at Kennedy International Airport. The causes of sudden
homelessness are displacement: fires, landlord abandonment, and eviction. The monthly rental allowance for
welfare recipients is $218, which has not been raised
since 1975. Alternatives to hotels for the suddenly
displaced are neighbors, relatives, friends, and private
agencies.

Hamsun, Knut. <u>Vagabonds</u>. New York: Grosset & Dunlap,
1930. (Translated from a Norwegian version by Eugene
Gay-Tifft.)
    This novel is about the experiences of Edivart, a
traveling man.

Handlin, Oscar. <u>Boston's Immigrants: A Study in Accul-
turation</u>. Cambridge: Belknap Press, 1959. (Originally
published in 1941.)
    Although the relevance of this book is highly
limited, it does contain some materials on pauperism in
Boston and charitable institutions that care for the
homeless and destitute.

Handberg, Roger, Charles M. Unkovic, and James Feuer-
stein. "Organizational and Ecological Explanations for
Violence against the Police: A Preliminary Analysis."
<u>International Review of History and Political Science</u>, <u>23</u>
(3), August 1986:1-14.
    Using Pearson product moment correlations, the
authors test two hypotheses--that police generate
violence against themselves through their own aggressive-
ness or that characteristics of the community (including
the number of social misfits and the extent of homelessness and poverty) create frustration that leads to
violence. The latter is supported.

Hanley, Robert. "Homeless Man Has Deal in Second Suit in Morristown." New York Times, March 3, 1992:B7.

Richard R. Kreimer is called the most litigious homeless man in Newark, New Jersey. Kreimer won $150,000 from the city of Morristown and just settled a suit with the city's public library for an undisclosed sum. Another suit regarding the library's eviction rules is pending.

Hanley, Robert. "Homeless Man Will Appeal Decision on Library Rules." New York Times, March 26, 1992:B8.

Courts rejected the suit of Richard B. Kreimer, a homeless man who had been evicted from the public library of Morristown, New Jersey. Kreimer says that he will appeal the decision.

Hanley, Robert. "Libraries Can't Ban the Homeless, U.S. Court in Newark Rules." New York Times, May 23, 1991:B1.

A federal judge ruled that the regulations used by the public library in Morristown, New Jersey, to ban the homeless are unconstitutional. Library rules cannot be aimed at the homeless, but must be neutral in their effects.

Hanley, Robert. "Library Edgy Over Order to Tolerate Homeless." Wall Street Journal, May 29, 1991:B1.

After numerous complaints from patrons about hygiene and staring, the public library in Morristown, New Jersey, passed rules to exclude the homeless. Because a federal court ruled the exclusionary regulations unconstitutional, library officials fear an influx of homeless who will come not to use the library but just to spend time.

Hanley, Robert. "Library Wins in Homeless-Man Case." New York Times, March 25, 1992:B8.

After his eviction from the public library in Morristown, New Jersey, because of his hygiene and personal habits, Richard R. Kreimer, a homeless man, sued. A lower court ruled in favor of Kreimer, but an appeals court overturned that ruling and found in favor of the library.

Hanley, Robert. "U.S. Approves $150,000 Deal for New Jersey Homeless Man." New York Times, November 9, 1991:A29.

Richard Kreimer, a homeless man in Morristown, New Jersey, was awarded $150,000 in his lawsuit against the city.

Hapgood, Hutchins. <u>Types from City Streets</u>. New York: Funk and Wagnalls, 1910.
This account of the "low lifes" and characters of the Bowery contains a section on hobos.

Harlow, Alvin F. <u>Old Bowery Days: The Chronicles of a Famous Street</u>. New York: D. Appleton, 1931.
The author presents a detailed history of the Bowery from 1626 to 1930.

Harman, Lesley D. "The Creation of the 'Bag Lady': Rethinking Home for Homeless Women." Mimeo, no date.
The author examines the common-sense creation of social reality, the definition of social problems and homelessness, the role of the mass media, typification, and gender differences in the experience of homelessness.

Harman, Lesley D. "Expressive Roles, Female Dependency, and the Downward Spiral of the Hostel Circuit." Paper presented at the annual meeting of the Society for the Study of Social Problems, Washington, D.C., August 1985.
This paper focuses on homeless women, especially how programs designed to meet their needs reinforce the female expressive role and dependency. The author examines role and status displacement and suggests that the correct solutions are feminism, independence, and a role-integrated society.

Harman, Thomas. <u>A Caveat or Warning for common cursetors vulgarly called Vagabonds</u>, 1567.
The author lists 24 different types of vagabonds, and includes a lengthy description of most of them. In his introduction to Martin Luther's <u>Liber Vagatorum</u>, D. B. Thomas says that this is probably the second oldest English publication on the subject. A version appears in <u>Queene Elizabethes Academy, A Booke of Precedence, & co.</u> (Boston: Dutton & Co., 1869) which also contains a lengthy account of the history of the work and its relationship to other works on the subject.

Harper, Douglas. <u>Good Company</u>. Chicago: University of Chicago Press, 1982.
As he rides the freights, the author, a sociologist, meets Carl, a long-time tramp, who shows him the ropes.

Based on participant observation, the author delineates essential elements of the world as seen by tramps. Topics include migrant work, socialization, coping, and fellowship among tramps. The types of tramps are airedale, apple knocker, bundle stiff, boxcar, bum, high-roller, hobo, homeguard, mission stiff, outside 'bo, rubber tramp, wino, and working stiff.

Harper, Douglas. "Images of Good Company." Society, 20, September-October 1983:69-74.
    This source consists of eight photographs of a tramp with accompanying captions.

Harring, Sidney L. "Class Conflict and the Suppression of Tramps in Buffalo, 1892-1894." Law and Society Review, 11 (5), Summer 1977:873-911.
    In the depression years of 1893-1894, several hundred thousand of the three to four million unemployed workers in the United States "took to the rails" in search of work. The Tramp Laws of the 1870s and 1880s, which outlawed travel without visible means of support and threatened a punishment of a prison sentence at hard labor, were used against these tramps. This article focuses on the origins, scope, and context of the Tramp Act in New York State, the relationship of tramps to the working class, and the enforcement of the Tramp Act. The author recounts how "tramp armies" bound for Washington, D.C. (one headed by "Count" Joseph Rybakowski, 175 strong, and another called Jeffries' Commonwealth, an army of 350) met violence at the hands of Buffalo police and citizens. These "armies" were part of a mass movement of unemployed workers, generally known as Coxey's Army. The article contains an account of Jack London being jailed for vagrancy in Buffalo. The author concludes that the data support "the Marxist contention that the police are not neutral in the class struggle, but rather are an instrument of ruling class domination."

Harrington, Michael. "Hiding the Other America." New Republic, 176, February 26, 1977:15-17.
    This article centers around the definition of the poverty line, the use and interpretation of statistics, and the role of in-kind transfers. The author illus-trates how definitions and political decisions increase and decrease the visibility of the poor.

Harrington, Michael. The New American Poverty. New York: Penguin Books, 1984.

In this overview of poverty in the United States, the author stresses that, unlike common ascriptions, the causes of poverty are not the characteristics of the poor, but, rather, the social and economic conditions imposed upon the poor. The proposed solution is full employment through the creation of jobs. In Chapter 5, Harrington proposes that the term "uprooted" is a more apt term than "homeless." After presenting a brief history of the homeless in England, he suggests a definition of homeless, overviews deinstitutionalization, discusses how people profit from the homeless (nursing homes), and touches on the finances of the homeless, gentrification and housing, SROs, and the political powerlessness of the homeless.

Harrington, Michael. "The New Gradgrinds." <u>Dissent</u>, Spring, 1984:171-181.
    The author examines the meanings of facts, the definition of poverty, where to draw the poverty line, the relationship of poverty to inequality, the value of in-kind benefits, the role of the underground economy, and the conflicting interpretations of economic factors by the right and the left.

Harrington, Michael. <u>The Other America: Poverty in the United States</u>. Baltimore: Penguin Books, 1963.
    The author presents an overview of poverty and the culture of poverty in the United States. The proposed solutions are to recognize the existence of the poor in our midst, provide opportunities to instill hope, campaign to develop a comprehensive program to break the culture of poverty, eliminate racism, and make housing, medical care, social security and minimum wage available for everyone.

Harrington, Michael. <u>The Vast Majority: A Journey to the World's Poor</u>. New York: Simon and Schuster, 1977.
    This book provides an overview of economic, social, and political realities of capitalism, developed nations, and the Third World, with an emphasis on structural interrelationships and exploitation.

Harris, Sara. <u>Skid Row: U.S.A.</u> Garden City: Doubleday, 1956.
    To gain an overview of American skid rows, the author presents a series of case histories. The causes of homelessness are undersocialization (lacking the nourishment of normal affection and understanding in

early life, lack of healthy relationships, and fear and insecurity that impede marital relationships). The solution is to help the homeless gain self-respect and a normal place in society. The types of people who inhabit skid row are madmen, feeble-minded, cripples, blind, alcoholics, hobos, syphilitic prostitutes, old rebels, pensioners, and the young able-bodied. All suffer from an inadequate self concept.

Hartman, Ann. "Homelessness: Public Issue and Private Trouble." Social Work, 34 (6), November 1989:483-484.
    This editorial is a plea for social workers to actively fight the problem of homelessness. "But bearing witness, attempting to ameliorate private troubles, and setting up innovative helping programs is not enough. We must be clear that homelessness cannot be reduced appreciably by treating individual troubles. The problem of homelessness is a public issue and can only be resolved through public action and major changes in public policy. Poverty must be reduced and low-cost housing must be made available. This effort, of course, requires a major reordering of our national agenda. It requires a major investment in the welfare of the nation's vulnerable citizens. It demands the rebuilding and expansion of social programs and the recognition that economic resources do not 'trickle down' but must be redistributed through public consensus....We must join with others to bring about a change in public policy. We must advocate on national, state, and local levels and demand from our legislatures a response to what perhaps should be reframed as 'the housing crisis.' We must resist the ever-present pressure to redefine this public issue and disgrace as a private trouble."

Hartman, Chester, ed. America's Housing Crisis: What Is to Be Done? Boston: Routledge and Kegan Paul, 1983.
    In the introduction, the editor summarizes 17 major points about the housing crisis in the United States.

Hartman, Chester. "The Housing Part of the Homelessness Problem." In The Mental Health Needs of Homeless Persons, Ellen L. Bassuk, ed. San Francisco: Jossey-Bass, 1986:71-85.
    Regardless of their specific characteristics, all homeless people lack a normal place to live. The basic cause of homelessness is a low-cost housing crisis, which is a manifestation of the structural defects in the country's housing system. The low-cost housing crisis

has these elements: (1) housing costs are consuming steadily larger proportions of household incomes, (2) two-and-a-half million people are displaced annually from their homes, (3) mortgage delinquency among homeowners has increased, (4) over-crowding is a serious problem, (5) substandard conditions exist that create health problems for their residents, and (6) the cost of utilities and property taxes have increased.

Hartman, Chester. "San Francisco's International Hotel: Case Study of a Turf Struggle." Radical America, 12 (3), 1978:47-58.
    The International Hotel in San Francisco, a three-story 155-room residential hotel, was slated for destruction and replacement with new buildings. The low-income residents of the hotel refused to move, and eventually, after much publicity, controversy, and tension, the police evicted the residents in spite of the physical resistance of a couple of thousand community supporters. The author was actively involved in this struggle.

Hartman, Chester. "Shelter and Community." Society, 21 (3), March-April 1984:18-27.
    The author discusses why the cost of quality housing has moved beyond the reach of increasing proportions of Americans. He examines housing expenditures and costs relative to income, costs of utilities and taxes, displacement of residents from their homes, health problems due to substandard housing, effects of federal budget decisions on affordable housing, and rental costs. The solution is to develop federal policies and budgets that reduce the basic cost of housing. Specific suggestions to reach this goal are offered.

Hartman, Chester, Dennis Keating, and Richard LeGates. Displacement: How to Fight It. Berkeley: National Housing Law Project, 1982.
    The authors examine housing control and housing needs. The basic causes of displacement are speculation, demolition, condo conversions, deinvestment, and abandonment. The basic solution is group resistance to each of these, while preserving rental housing, keeping and improving SROs, and developing programs of rent control, eviction control, and home ownership for the poor.

Harvey, Brian, and Mary Menton. "Ireland's Young Homeless." Children and Youth Services Review, 11 (1), 1989:31-43.

Although reports of homeless children in Ireland go back to the eighteenth century, a serious problem emerged in the 1970s. The government promised greater assistance for homeless youths, but, instead, reduced its funding of social services and earmarked more funds for the juvenile justice system.

Harvey, F. Barton. "A New Enterprise: Allying Business, Government, and Citizens in the Fight Against Homelessness." The Humanist, May-June 1989:14, 38.
    The author reviews the work of the Enterprise Foundation, a national effort that "works through nonprofit, grass-roots groups serving the very poor" by helping those groups "build their capacity to produce housing and provide other services."

Harvey, James W., and Kevin F. McCrohan. "Strategic Issues for Charities and Philanthropies." Long Range Planning (UK), 21, 6, December 1988:44-55.
    Among the reasons given for the diminished support for charity is the increase in the numbers of homeless. Techniques that philanthropies can use to increase giving are suggested.

Harvey, Nigel. "Concerning Casuals: Life on the Roads." The Spectator, 160, April 29, 1938:742-743.
    The author stresses that "life on the roads is hell" because of vermin, sleeping accommodations, effects on the mind, and isolation. Society has come up with no effective treatment for tramps (men "on the toby").

Haupt, Arthur. "Another Winter for the Homeless." Population Today, February 1989:3-4.
    The author reviews the methodology used by the Urban Institute to survey a nationally representative sample of 1,846 homeless people in twenty cities. The article contains a table that lists the percentages of homeless people by composition, single or household, sex, race, history of hospitalization and jail, and meals eaten per day.

Haupt, Donald N., and David R. Offord. "Runaways from a Residential Treatment Center: A Preliminary Report." Corrective Psychiatry and Journal of Social Therapy, 18 (3), 1972:14-21.
    Compared with males who did not run away, male runaways had a greater number of foster home placements and experimental hardships. The opposite was true for

females. Boys were more likely to run during the fall
and winter, girls in spring and summer. The author
contrasts "cries for help" versus "real runs."

Hay, Walter R. "Case of the Homeless in St. Louis."
The Family, October 9, 1928:209-219.
     Homelessness involves a problem with definitions.
Homelessness is not simply a lack of shelter, but also
includes not being a responsible part of a family group.
The solution is to not try to do everything for everybody
but to concentrate on those most likely to respond to
rehabilitation--young boys and men who have good work
records or who have been on the road only for a short
time.

Hayes, Arthur S. "Environmental Poverty Specialty Helps
the Poor Fight Pollution." *Wall Street Journal*, October
9, 1992:B5.
     A sub-item of this article reports that advocates
for the homeless filed suit against the U.S. Census
Bureau for allegedly undercounting homeless people. The
National Law Center on Homelessness and Poverty claims
that "the one-night count by the bureau missed the vast
majority of the people who have no homes." Advocates
claim a total of 700,000 homeless people, while the
bureau tallied 228,621.

Hayes, Robert M. "Homeless Children." *Proceedings of
the Academy of Political Science*, 37 (2), 1989:58-69.
     Taking the position that the underlying causes of
family homelessness are lack of housing and poverty and
that a "precipitating event" accounts for the homelessness of specific individuals, the author stresses the
miseries that children in poverty experience. He uses
case studies to illustrate the harm that homelessness
causes children and proposes three solutions: (1) to
balance the housing market (funding efficient state
housing programs), (2) to increase the income of dependent people, and (3) to intelligently administer publicly
funded initiatives, that is, housing, schools, and day
care.

Hayes, Robert M. "The Issue Is Housing." *New York
Times*, November 27, 1986:27.
     The author argues that homelessness has a three-word
solution: housing, housing, housing. He also argues for
the need to preserve S.R.O.'s.

Hayes, Robert M. "The Mayor and the Homeless Poor." City Limits, August-September, 1985:6-9.

As Ed Koch, the Mayor of New York City, has dealt with the problem of homelessness, he has had both positive and negative results. The author emphasizes that the homeless are those who have lost the competition for housing and criticizes the mayor for responding to homelessness as a political reaction to public sentiment rather than according to the moral nature of the issue. He also raises the question of why, after men had won the legal right to shelter, the mayor took the position that homeless women did not have that same right.

Hayes, Robert M. "Top Law Firms Enlist in Litigation for Decent Housing for the Homeless." New York Law Journal, March 12, 1986:31.

This summary of the history of litigation on behalf of the homeless in New York City focuses on the Coalition for the Homeless.

Hayner, Norman S. "Taming the Lumberjack." American Sociological Review, 10, April 1945:217-225.

Technological changes in logging have domesticated loggers, making them more socially respectable. A minority of loggers are homeless men.

Hays, Constance L. "Two Women Sexually Assaulted in Central Park." New York Times, August 12, 1989:27.

A homeless man was arrested after two woman joggers reported that a man had jumped onto the dirt path and fondled their breasts.

Hayter, Earl W. The Troubled Farmer, 1850-1900: Rural Adjustment to Industrialism. Dekalb, Illinois: Northern Illinois University Press, 1968.

This book contains a section on the "tramp nuisance" as experienced by farmers.

Hazleton, Lesley. "About the Homeless Men on My Door-step." New York Times, October 3, 1987:15.

The author explains why she is reacting fairly positively to the homeless who live in the park across from her condominium in a renovated landmark building in New York City. She stresses that they want recognition as individuals and also explores her biases against the homeless.

Healey, Anne. "Homeless Women Find 'Family' at House of
Ruth." Catholic Standard, July 1, 1976.
    The focus in this Washington, D.C., residence for
homeless women is to reestablish relationships.

Healy, Joseph F. "Boys on the Loose." The Commonweal,
17-18, March 22, 1933:574-576.
    Estimates of the numbers of youth under twenty-one
now roaming America vary from 200,000 to one million.
There is no unified plan for "handling the wandering
boy," but on February 13, 1933, the Senate passed the
Couzens Bill "appropriating $20,000,000 for the care of
88,000 unemployed youths from fifteen to twenty-one years
of age idle at least six months." Typical policies vary
from escorting a boy from a freight train to the local
relief station where he is put up overnight (and told to
move on the next morning) to arresting them. In many
Southern towns the boys are exploited by being "arrested
and put to work on farms and other private holdings"
while "someone collects the hire for their labor."
Potentially fruitful solutions include education (a more
diversified curricula, extended class hours, and more
trade courses), letting community groups use school
equipment, and opening gymnasiums, athletic parks and
fields. Especially promising are supervised clubs for
boys.

Healy, Thomas F. "The Hobo Hits the Highroad." American
Mercury, 8, July 1926:334-338.
    There are four types of hobos: the working stiff who
works for his living, the john who begs for his, the
highway yegg who robs for his, and the auto-tramp or
gasoline gypsy "who outwardly neither works, nor begs,
nor steals, but lives on society by ways and means
peculiar to himself." The author analyzes the yegg and
the auto-tramp.

Heath, Clark W., Jr., and Jack Zusman. "An Outbreak of
Diphtheria Among Skid-Row Men." New England Journal of
Medicine, 267, 1962:809-812.
    An outbreak of diphtheria (six cases, including one
death) in Omaha, Nebraska, between November 1961 and
March 1962 was "associated with a charity mission
providing food and shelter for migrant homeless
men....Crowded living conditions and low resistance to
disease appeared to be important factors in the outbreak,
although its exact source could not be traced."

Hechinger, Fred M. "Plight of the Homeless." New York Times, April 5, 1987:27.
     There are three million homeless children in the United States. This article focuses on the educational problems of these children, especially their right to obtain an education.

Hechinger, Fred M. "Toward Educating the Homeless." New York Times, February 2, 1988:24.
     Because many homeless children are not being educated, the author states that the provisions of the Stewart B. McKinney Homeless Assistance Act be vigorously implemented. The number of homeless children is given as between 500,000 and 700,000.

Heisterman, Carl A., and Paris F. Keener. "Further Poor Law Notes." The Social Service Review, 12, December 1938:43-49.
     The authors review laws of 14 states in which paupers may not vote or hold office.

Helou, Paul. "Adoption as Alternative to Homelessness." New York Times, October 13, 1991:LI20.
     Because many homeless persons were in foster care when they were children, social service agencies in New York City are encouraging the adoption of older children. They see this as a step in preventing homelessness.

Hely, Kathryn. "The Homeless Man in a Community Mental Health Service." Australian Occupational Therapy Journal, 18 (4), October 1971:30-33.
     Based on experiences in Sydney, Australia, the author suggests that the solution to the problem of the homeless mentally ill is the coordination of agencies in rehabilitation programs that provide psychiatric assessment, consultation, and occupational counseling for the homeless and training for agency personnel.

Henry, J. Marilyn. "NAHRO in the Twin Cities." Journal of Housing, 47 (5), September-October 1990:250-254.
     This review of steps taken by the Twin Cities (Minneapolis and St. Paul, Minnesota) to improve its housing mentions that the homeless are targeted for housing assistance.

Henry, Neil. "The Long, Hot Wait for Pickin' Work, Part I." Washington Post, October 9, 1983:A1, A16.

A reporter for the <u>Washington Post</u> profiles Washington's SOME House soup kitchen. He focuses on attitudes of its residents toward the bus drivers who take destitute men to work on southern farms. Their view is that the bus drivers are "nothing but a flim-flam artist, that the grueling work he offers will amount to little more than slavery, that the pay is meager and the beds much worse than those at the city's fetid public shelters."

Henslin, James M. "It's Not a Lovely Place to Visit, and I Wouldn't Want to Live There." <u>Studies in Qualitative Sociology: Reflections on Field Experience</u>, <u>2</u>, Robert Burgess, ed. New York: JAI Press, 1990:51-76.
The author reviews his participant observation experiences with the homeless in a dozen cities. He examines the significance of the researcher's front, reality shock, the immersion process, strategies for locating subjects, emotional and self-identity risks, and possible effects of the researcher's socio-biological characteristics (gender, race, and age).

Henslin, James M. "Program Trends in Serving the Homeless." Paper presented at the annual meetings of the Society for the Study of Social Problems, New York City, August 1986.
This paper traces, by decades, the major trends in programs and policies regarding the homeless from 1870 to 1986.

Henslin, James M. <u>Sociology: A Down-to-Earth Approach</u>. Boston: Allyn and Bacon, 1993.
Several of the vignettes that open the chapters of this introductory sociology textbook recount the author's field work experiences with the homeless.

Henslin, James M. "Today's Homeless." Paper presented at the annual meeting of the Society for the Study of Social Problems, August 1985.
Based on field research, the author presents a typology of America's homeless. Fifteen types are analyzed: pushouts, victims of environmental catastrophe, mentally ill, new poor, technologically unqualified, migrant workers, elderly, runaways, criminals, demoralized, drug addicts, alcohol addicts, ease addicts, road dogs, and excitement addicts.

Herbers, John. "Neighborhood Pressure Bringing More Lending in Inner Cities." <u>New York Times</u>, May 5, 1986:15.

Because of pressures from various coalitions for the poor, especially the threat to take legal action to stop bank mergers and acquisitions, major banks have begun a policy of "reinvestment," making home loans to people with low incomes. This demonstrates that the solution to the problem of homelessness is legal activism.

Herbers, John. "Poverty of Blacks Spreads in Cities." New York Times, January 26, 1987:1, 13.
This review of poverty in the larger cities mentions that although Toledo's Kitchen for the Poor was established in 1969 as a free food center on a temporary basis, it is still operating today. There, street people can receive a noon meal.

Herbers, John. "Why So Many Are Priced Out of the Market." New York Times, March 16, 1986:E5.
The proportion of potential first-time home buyers who can afford homes is now lower than it was during the three previous decades. Tables present data from the mid-1960s to the present on purchasing power, single-family housing starts, median home cost, mortgage interest rates, median mortgage payments, median family income, and shifting mean incomes by quintiles.

Herman, Robin. "City's Homeless: Story of Bobby Cruz." New York Times, January 16, 1982:27, 31.
An individual, Bobby Cruz, is used as an example to review the change in age and racial composition of New York's homeless.

Herman, Robin. "One of City's Homeless Goes Home—in Death." New York Times, January 31, 1982:34.
Rebecca Smith, a homeless woman, was found frozen to death in a cardboard box on New York City's 10th Avenue.

Herman, Robin. "Some Freed Mental Patients Make It, Some Do Not." New York Times, November 19, 1979:B1, B4.
The author presents case studies of two schizophrenics who were discharged from mental hospitals into the community: Edward M., who found no supportive world and is still a resident of men's shelters, and Sara J., who is making a good adjustment in a private rehabilitation program. Deinstitutionalization failed because the planned network of mental health centers were not established.

Hersch, Patricia. "Coming of Age on City Street." *Psychology Today*, 22, January 1988:28-37.
    The author recounts the sexual hustling of runaways, stressing the danger and prevalence of AIDS. Contrary to a lingering perception of runaways as adolescent adventurers, many are victims of dysfunctional families and are fleeing from a stressful environment. "Thirty-six percent run from physical and sexual abuse; 44 percent from other severe long-term crises such as drug-abusing, alcoholic parents or stepfamily crises; 20 percent from short-term crises such as divorce, sickness, death and school problems." The author mentions the possibility that "these adolescents will become part of the third wave of the AIDS epidemic." A focus is placed on Covenant House's outreach program.

Hershkoff, Helen, and Adam S. Cohen. "Begging to Differ: The First Amendment and the Right to Beg." *Harvard Law Review*, 104 (4), February 1991:896-916.
    The authors' thesis is that begging is a protected form of free speech. After reviewing theories of freedom of speech (the enlightenment value, the democratic governance value, and self-realization), the authors analyze freedom of speech in relationship to the solicitation of charity. They also summarize the engagement value of the First Amendment of the Constitution in relationship to begging.

Herzberg, J. L. "No Fixed Abode." *British Journal of Hospital Medicine*, 32 (1), July 1984:24, 26.
    The mentally ill homeless can be placed in three broad categories: (1) schizophrenics, (2) alcoholics, and (3) those who have personality disorders. The author suggests that a small number of these people can benefit from care delivered by workers in small, community-based units.

Hevesi, Dennis. "Citing Fires, Dinkins Aide Orders Removal of Homeless from City-Owned Property." *New York Times*, September 15, 1991:34.
    The New York City administration announced that because of the threat of fires it will keep the homeless out of all city-owned buildings. The homeless are blamed for starting a fire that temporarily closed the Staten Island Ferry Terminal and another in an abandoned building in Brooklyn in which a firefighter lost his life.

Hevesi, Dennis. "Homeless in New York City: A Day on the Streets." <u>New York Times</u>, November 17, 1986:13.
    Based on interviews with street people, the author explores life on the street, including their sleeping arrangements and coping mechanisms. He strives for an insiders' perceptive.

Hiatt, Catherine C., and Ruth E. Spurlock. "Geographical Flight and Its Relation to Crisis Theory." <u>American Journal of Orthopsychiatry</u>, <u>40</u> (1), 1970:53-57.
    Chronic wandering is due to "crisis-flight;" that is, geographical fleeing is a chronically episodic way of coping with unresolved crises. Basically, some people negatively resolve crises by questless travel that then becomes a lifestyle.

Hier, Sally J., Paula J. Korboot, and Robert D. Schweitzer. "Social Adjustment and Symptomatology in Two Types of Homeless Adolescents: Runaways and Throwaways." <u>Adolescence</u>, <u>25</u> (100), Winter 1990:761-771.
    A study of 52 homeless adolescents in Brisbane, Australia, shows that male runaways (youths who left home on their own volition) are more hostile than male throwaways (youths who were forced to leave home). Female throwaways are more hostile than female runaways and male throwaways. Males have a stronger desire to act out hostility.

Higgins, Michael. "Tent City." <u>Commonweal</u>, <u>110</u> (16), September 23, 1983:494-496.
    As the numbers of homeless grew, the Mayor of Phoenix became disturbed about their effects on the city's image. She and the City Council tried to remove the support system of the homeless by closing the area's shelters, alcoholic dry docks, and residential hotels (flop houses), and passing stronger laws against vagrancy and public drunkenness. The numbers still grew and conditions deteriorated. Due to an outcry from the public, the city allowed the churches to open a shelter.

Hildebrand, James A. "Reasons for Runaways." <u>Crime and Delinquency</u>, <u>14</u> (1), 1968:42-48.
    Comparing two areas in New York City, one a low-income area and the other a middle-income area, the author finds that the middle-class area has a rate of runaways less than one sixth that of the low-income area. Children in the low-income area begin to run away at a much earlier age, and their parents are apathetic about

their children's education and are nonchalant about their children's running away. The major factors that influ- ence the youths to run away appear to be "family insta- bility, neighborhood deterioration, low income and economic dependency, and a low level of education."

Hildebrand, James A. "Why Runaways Leave Home." Journal of Criminal Law, Criminology, and Police Science, 54 (2), June 1963:211-216.
     The author, a detective, dealt with 133 male and 129 female runaways. He concludes that the major reason for running away between the ages of 8 and 12 is poor home environment, while from age 13 on it is problems with family discipline. The main reasons that the older girls ran away were pregnancy and early marriage. After the age 16, running away drops off.

Hill, Ronald Paul. "Health Care and the Homeless: A Marketing-Oriented Approach." Journal of Health Care Marketing, 11 (2), June 1991:14-23.
     Because the homeless often put off health care, an aggressive marketing-oriented approach to improve the health care of the homeless should be developed. The author suggests a targeted and holistic approach, changes in the training of health care providers, better communi- cation and coordination of care providers, and an aggressive search for sources of reimbursement.

Hill, Ronald Paul. "Homeless Women, Special Possessions, and the Meaning of 'Home': An Ethnographic Case Study." Journal of Consumer Research, 18 (3), December 1991:298- 310.
     The author interviewed homeless women staying at a shelter run by an order of Roman Catholic sisters. He found weak family bonds, a background of deinstitutiona- lization, substance abuse, family violence, a reduced attachment to consumer goods, childlike dependence on the sisters, and fantasies about the future.

Hill, Ronald Paul, and Mark Stamey. "The Homeless in America: An Examination of Possessions and Consumption Behaviors." Journal of Consumer Research, 17 (3), December 1990:303-321.
     Ethnographic research shows that the homeless, who have the same basic needs of shelter, food, clothing, and personal hygiene as other people, do not satisfy those needs in the same way. Scavenging from the refuse of others is a common way of acquiring possessions.

Himmelfarb, Gertrude. <u>The Idea of Poverty: England in the Early Industrial Age</u>, New York: Knopf, 1984.
Poverty has been enmeshed in a philosophical debate. The range of conceptualization has been great: from a holy condition whose relief blesses the alms-giver and receiver to a secular misfortune that must be endured and whose relief is the public responsibility. In the <u>Wealth of Nations</u>, Adam Smith said that a new division of labor and increased productivity would increase everyone's wealth--if workers were not exploited. Burke said we need new laws to distinguish between the laborer and the poor. Bentham took the position that the poor had the right to marry early and to propagate. Malthus took a social Darwinist position, believing that we should keep the population down to the level of the means of subsistence. The author also reviews the new Poor Laws adopted in 1834; the reformers Carlyle, Cobbett, and Engels; the novelists of the poor Reynolds, Dickens, Thackery, Disraeli, and Gaskell; the relationship of ideas about poverty and the economics of society; changing definitions of poverty; and the culture of poverty.

Hinds, Michael deCourcy. "Coat for the Homeless Is a Mobile Shelter, Too." <u>New York Times</u>, March 2, 1992:A10.
The Shelter-Pak, designed by David L. Wilson of Philadelphia College of Textiles and Science, is a cloak for homeless people that can double as a sleeping bag. The garment is being manufactured with the help of volunteers.

Hinds, Michael deCourcy. "50% Cutback in Money for Homeless Is Fiercely Protested in Philadelphia." <u>New York Times</u>, September 15, 1989:A12.
Critics assail cutbacks in the budget of New York City which would require a drop in support for the homeless so severe it would mean that some shelters would have to be closed.

Hirsch, Dennis D. "Making Shelter Work: Placing Conditions on an Employable Person's Right to Shelter." <u>Yale Law Journal</u>, <u>100</u> (2), November 1990:491-510.
The author argues that an unqualified right of the homeless to shelter can prevent the implementation of potentially useful policies aimed at helping the homeless. Specifically, the right to shelter needs to be more narrowly defined for the employable homeless; it should not apply to persons who refuse without good cause to participate in employment of which they are capable.

Hirsch, James S. "Horse Sense Prevails in Custody Drama in Rural Missouri." <u>Wall Street Journal</u>, April 13, 1992:A13.

Twenty-four saddle horses were taken from Lowell Rott, a homeless farmer of Randolph County, Missouri, who was accused of animal abuse because of the unsanitary conditions in which he kept the animals. After an investigation showed that the health of the horses was even worse under the care of the Humane Society, the horses were returned to Mr. Rott.

Hirsch, Kathleen. <u>Songs From The Alley</u>. New York: Ticknor and Fields, 1989.

The author, a journalist, did a participant observation study in 1988 of the Pine Street Inn shelter for the homeless in Boston. She reports that she "quickly learned that there are no typical homeless people, only common suffering." The story of homelessness is told by focusing on two characters, Amanda and Wendy. The author's recounting of their day-to-day experiences enables one to better understand the complexity of background, emotions, and relationships that keep people on the streets even when alternatives are available.

Hirsch, Kathleen. "Who will Save the Homeless?" <u>Washington Post Magazine</u>, November 2, 1986:19-25, 45-49.

The author contrasts the philosophies and approaches of these activists who are working with the homeless: Sandra Brawders, Albert G. Salmon, Paula Salmon, Mitch Snyder, Robert M. Hayes, Maria Foscarinas, Chris Sprowal, and J. Robb Bartlett. She also documents a grass-roots movement to help the homeless and contrasts two attitudes in that movement: "the homeless bring their problems on themselves and to solve the problem we must change the homeless" and "the homeless are victims of the system and to solve the problem we must change the system."

Hirschfield, Robert. "Exploiting the Shopping-Bag Ladies." <u>Christian Century</u>, <u>101</u>, May 16, 1984:508.

Workers with the homeless have forced a company in Santa Monica, California, to withdraw T-shirts and sweatshirts on which they have printed the likenesses of two shopping-bag ladies. The author argues that this event is part of a larger exploitation of homeless women. Why would anyone want to wear the image of a homeless person on their T-shirt or sweatshirt? He suggests that the motivation is subconscious: "people wish to bring to the surface and thus banish the fears of destitution which, in this age of economic uncertainty, must lurk in the back of many minds."

Hirschfield, Robert. "Homeless Families: A Women's Issue." Christian Century, 103, August 13, 1986:702-703.
   This article discusses the history and operation of Women In Need, operated in Manhattan for families that have nowhere else to go.

Hirschfield, Robert. "The Martinique Hotel: Housing the Homeless." America, 156, February 7, 1987:90-91.
   After enumerating the negative conditions in the Martinique Hotel, a shelter for homeless families in New York City, the author points out that there are even worse shelters in the city.

Hirschfield, Robert. "Street Despair." The Christian Century, 100, July 20, 1983:671-672.
   The author describes the destitution of "the stretch of Third Street lying between Second Avenue and the Bowery on the Lower East Side of Manhattan...with its army of uprooted men knotted against the walls and doorways of the old tenements and lined up by the hundreds outside the Men's Shelter."

Hirschl, Thomas A. "Homelessness: A Sociological Research Agenda." Sociological Spectrum, 10 (4), October-December 1990:443-457.
   The author's thesis is that homelessness should be defined as a state of being over time, rather than as the temporary situation of individuals at a particular time. Accordingly, a longitudinal approach is called for. Includes a research matrix for testing theories about homelessness.

Hoath, David. "Housing (Homeless Persons) Act 1977." Journal of Social Welfare Law, November 1985:367-373.
   The concept of "intentional homelessness" has been wrestled with by the British courts. Their decisions have implications for the need (or lack of need) to provide housing.

Hoath, David. "Housing: Housing Act 1985 Part III." Journal of Social Welfare Law, September 1986:305-310.
   The author discusses the issue of whether crowded housing conditions and crisis housing constitute homelessness in a legal sense.

Hobfoll, S. E., D. Kelso, and W. J. Peterson. "The Anchorage Skid Row." Journal of Studies on Alcohol, 41 (1), January 1980:94-99.
A survey of Anchorage Skid Row identified four types of residents (subgroups): highly mobile workers, working residents, semi-employed residents, and the homeless unemployed.

Hoch, Charles. "A Pragmatic Inquiry." Society, 26 (1), November-December 1988:27-35.
Homelessness is used as an example to support the author's contention that radical pragmatism is an alternative to planning theory, which, although designed to reduce uncertainty, has increased uncertainty for policy makers.

Hoch, Charles. "Homeless in the United States." Housing Studies, 1 (4), October 1986:228-240.
Historically, public authorities in the United States, using the work ethic of capitalism, have seen the homeless as vagrant, deviant, sick, or victims. Although all four definitions show up in the contemporary literature, the most common view today is that the homeless are either sick or victims of the economy.

Hoch, Charles. "The Rhetoric of Applied Research: Studying Homelessness in Chicago." Journal of Applied Sociology, 7, 1990:11-24.
Using two surveys of the homeless in Chicago, the author illustrates effects of rhetorical strategies to communicate results. The analyst who used practical reasoning inspired trust among listeners, while the analyst who chose the role of scientific expert inspired distrust and resistance.

Hoch, Charles. "When Scientists Dissent." Society, 26 (4) (180), May-June 1989:8-11.
Because scientists who do research on social problems such as homelessness speak to both professional and public audiences, a dilemma exists. The author concludes that "disagreement and conflict over the meaning of social problems and what should be done to solve them seems inevitable--even desirable in a pluralistic society. But tolerance of diversity does not play well when incorporated into the rhetoric of scientific expertise used to justify policy about social problems. When sponsors hire analysts to tell them the truth, they rarely expect to learn that there are many truths. Yet

this seems to offer the only responsible way to cope with the dilemma of conducting research on social problems. When scientists study social problems, they should not only recognize how the moral values they both hold and serve shape their research, but make these public knowledge as well. They should acknowledge the existence of competing values and the sorts of implications these values would have if they were to guide research on the problem."

Hodgkin, Jane. "Living Loose." New Society, 81 (1290), September 18, 1987:14-16.
Great Britain has about 80,000 homeless young people, but the government is doing little about the problem.

Hoffman, Jan. "Fun in the Jungle: The Hobo Convention." Wall Street Journal, August 22, 1984:18.
Except for the war years, an annual hobo convention has been held in Britt, Iowa, since 1933. At this convention are elected a king and royalty. New types of hobos have now shown up: part-timers and motor home hobos.

Holbrook, Stewart H. Holy Old Mackinaw: A Natural History of the American Lumberjack. New York: MacMillan, 1957. (First published in 1938.)
The author provides an overview of logging, loggers, and logging life, with a focus on the attitudes, drinking, and whoring of lumberjacks. These were essentially migrant men of few roots immersed in a macho culture.

Holbrook, Stewart H. "Riders of the Rods and the Blinds." In The Story of American Railroads. New York: Crown, 1947:389-398.
The author discusses hobos and railroads, railroad detectives, and the damage done by hobos. The blind is the space between the baggage car and the locomotive; the rods are the iron bars that were part of the freight car frames.

Holcomb, Mary C., and Elden L. DePorter. "A Linear Programming Application Helps Feed the Homeless." Computers and Industrial Engineering, 19 (1-4), 1990:548-552.
The author's thesis is that a diet blend model (which combines nutrition requirements with human taste preferences) used by The Union Rescue Mission of Knox-

ville, Tennessee, should be applied by other charitable
institutions. By aggregating daily servings to a weekly
total, the linear programming tools, with the use of an
input database file, can introduce variety and taste into
the diet of the homeless.

Holden, Constance. "Broader Commitment Laws Sought."
Science, 230, December 13, 1985:1253-1255.
        This article reviews arguments for and against the
involuntary hospitalization of the mentally ill.

Holden, Constance. "Homelessness: Experts Differ on Root
Causes." *Science*, 232, May 2, 1986:569-570.
        The author notes problems in defining homelessness,
the reduction of low-income housing, the perplexity of
communities in dealing with this problem, how mental
illness and alcoholism complicate homelessness, the
special problem of children of the homeless, and promising prospects of support by the Robert Wood Johnson
Foundation.

Holloway, Joy. <u>They Can't Fit In: A Study of Destitute
Men Under Thirty in St George's Crypt, Leeds</u>. London:
Bedford Square Press, 1970.
        A survey of the men sleeping in the crypt shows that
most are inadequate (demonstrate mental or social
deficiencies), although some, preferring alcohol and
leisure, are there by choice. The solution is the
residents voluntarily living in small hostels run by a
father-figure.

Holmes, John Haynes. "Tannenbaum in the Large." <u>Survey</u>,
32, April 23, 1914:94-95.
        The author discusses the reactions of clergy and the
public to the "spectacular invasion of the churches of
New York with the 'army' of the unemployed"--an invasion
that brought the plight of "the helpless and hopeless" to
the public's attention.

Hombs, Mary Ellen, and Mitch Snyder. <u>Homelessness in
America: A Forced March to Nowhere</u>. Washington, D.C.:
The Community for Creative Non-Violence, 1982.
        This overview of homelessness in the United States
places its emphasis on Washington, D.C. and the work of
Mitch Snyder and the Community for Creative Non-Violence.
The solution is to make available through a combination
of government and private efforts adequate and accessible
housing for everyone who wants housing. The homeless

need to participate in the decision-making that affects their lives, including decisions about their housing.

Homer, Louise E. "Community-Based Resource for Runaway Girls." Social Casework, 54 (8), October 1973:473-479.
 Based on a study of 20 runaway girls in Worcester, Massachusetts, the author develops a typology of running from (conflicts aroused by parental values) and running to (a subculture that sanctions forbidden behaviors). Treatment strategies are suggested for each type.

Honey, Ellen. "AIDS and the Inner City: Critical Issues." Social Casework, 69 (6), June 1988:365-370.
 The author's overview of the problem of AIDS in the inner city includes a discussion of AIDS among the homeless.

Hoopes, Judith. "Princeton Harbors a Secret World." New York Times, February 6, 1983:Section 11:2.
 The train station at Princeton Junction undergoes a nightly transition from a center for middle-class commuters to one for the sleeping homeless. The author presents the views of those helping the homeless. "Intellectual" types of homeless come to Princeton.

Hope, Marjorie, and James Young. "From Back Wards to Back Alleys: Deinstitutionalization and the Homeless." The Urban and Social Policy Review, 17 (2), Summer 1984:7-11.
 The authors focus on decarceration and restricted admission to mental hospitals, the shortage of community services, SSI, Medicaid, VA hospitals, the movement toward reinstitutionalization, and the National Coalition for the Homeless. They propose a three-tiered approach to housing the homeless (emergency, transitional, and long-term); housing legislation; clubhouse programs; a stress on preventing homelessness; and, especially, a system-wide approach that coordinates government and private actions and includes a national mental health plan.

Hope, Marjorie, and James Young. The Faces of Homelessness. Lexington, Massachusetts: Lexington Books, 1986.
 Emphasizing the social patterns that create homelessness, the authors contrast the homeless they have interviewed with the stereotypes of the homeless. The topics of this book include types of homeless, displacement, deinstitutionalization, work and welfare, trends in

working with the homeless, prevention versus containment,
and short-term and long-term proposals. The focus is on
Washington and Cincinnati. The causes of homelessness
are the housing crisis, displacement, deinstitutionalization, and a downward spiral in poverty. The solutions are to treat the homeless by type; emergency,
transitional, and long-term and permanent housing;
political action on the state and national level;
empowerment and prevention. The authors contrast conflicting ideologies of prevention and containment.

Hope, Marjorie, and James Young. "The New Poorhouse?"
St. Louis Post-Dispatch, March 1987:B3.
    The policies and efforts to solve homelessness are
inadequate. The answer is "national commitment to
government action on housing (as a right), full employment, universal health care, family allowance and
adequate services for children, the elderly and the
physically and mentally disabled."

Hopper, Kim. "A Poor Apart: The Distancing of Homeless
Men in New York's History." Social Research, 58 (1),
Spring 1991:107-132.
    The author argues that New York City's official
policy toward the homeless has served as a distancing
mechanism whereby a rhetoric of disdain and institutional
isolation has avoided the necessity of recognizing the
city's complicity in producing "unaccommodated men."

Hopper, Kim. "A Quiet Violence: The Homeless Poor in New
York City, 1982." In Homelessness in America: A Forced
March to Nowhere, Washington, D.C.: Community for
Creative Non-Violence, 1982:61-68.
    The causes of homelessness are deinstitutionaliza-
tion and unemployment. It is a myth that people choose
to be homeless. The solutions are emergency shelters,
transitional accommodations, and long-term, not-for-
profit residences that contain structured services. The
author compares the costs of alternatives and contrasts
attitudes toward the homeless.

Hopper, Kim. "Commentary." The Hastings Center Report,
June 1982:18-19.
    The freezing death of Rebecca Smith in New York City
illustrates the failure of the Protective Services Law.

Hopper, Kim. "Deviance and Dwelling Space: Notes on the
Resettlement of Homeless Persons with Drug and Alcohol

Problems." Contemporary Drug Problems, 16 (3), Fall 1989:391-414.

The author reviews the anthropological literature on homelessness and alcoholism, the housing dynamics of homelessness, resource scarcity, and episodic homelessness. He says that the homeless are often blamed for their homelessness, that politicians are reluctant to provide resources to help the homeless, and that if the homeless are to be helped they must be provided not only housing but also a sense of community. Intervention can also prevent much homelessness. He also stresses the "anthropological legacy," the value of ethnographic studies in uncovering meaning, assumptions, and relationships. After reviewing implications of anthropological research for intervening in homelessness, he urges researchers not to take themselves too seriously.

Hopper, Kim. "Homelessness: Reducing the Distance." New England Journal of Human Services, 3 (4), Fall 1983:30-47.

In this wideranging discussion, the author focuses on the survival strategies of the homeless, the growing numbers of homeless in the United States, definitional problems, surplus labor, and the Great Depression. He also argues that the English Poor Laws left a social inheritance for the homeless: the distinction between the deserving and undeserving poor and public phobias and images. The causes of homelessness are unemployment, the shortage of low-cost housing, deinstitutionalization, a reduction in disability benefits, and domestic violence. The solutions are quality emergency shelters, psychiatric aftercare, more liberal public assistance, the government keeping in touch with the people through the cooperative efforts of every level of government, jobs, and a national housing program.

Hopper, Kim. "More than Passing Strange: Homelessness and Mental Illness in New York City." American Ethnologist, 1987.

Based on ethnographic research, the author concludes that homelessness is not caused by personal characteristics, individual impairment or personal deviance, but, rather, the roots lie in programs of housing, employment, household composition, and government assistance. What needs to be examined are the circumstances under which psychiatric disability is integrated into social dispossession.

Hopper, Kim.   <u>One Year Later: The Homeless Poor in New York City</u>, New York: The Community Service Society, 1982.
      This volume updates the Community Service Society's 1981 publication, <u>Private Lives/Public Spaces</u>.   The author presents an overview of who the homeless are, the state of shelters, and the problem of counting the homeless in New York City.   The causes of homelessness are structural unemployment, inadequate community-based psychiatric care, housing scarcity, and cutbacks in social services. Consequently, the solution requires the development of a comprehensive program.   The book contains a directory of facilities for the homeless in New York City.

Hopper, Kim.   "Public Shelter as 'a Hybrid Institution': Homeless Men in Historical Perspective."   <u>Journal of Social Issues</u>, <u>46</u> (4), 1990:13-29.
      In this history of public shelters, the author says that homelessness among single men has typically been viewed as a problem of troubled and troublesome individuals.   This viewpoint loses sight of the link between the labor market and homelessness, which is so obvious during times of economic depression.   Shelters are "hybrid institutions;" that is, they have a double burden of plugging gaps in the formal institutional system of supports while at the same time serving as "dwellings of last resort" for men who usually work but who have exhausted their informal resources of assistance. Because labor market dynamics are central to people becoming homeless, what we need is a coherent unemployment relief policy.

Hopper, Kim.   "Research Findings as Testimony: A Note on the Ethnographer as Expert Witness." <u>Human Organization</u>, <u>49</u> (2), Summer 1990:110-113.
      When the author was called to give expert testimony in a case filed against a New York City shelter accused of refusing shelter to homeless men, his ethnographic materials were attacked as hearsay.   The judge, however, ruled that sufficient "accumulated hearsay" was sufficient to establish reputation.

Hopper, Kim.   "Symptoms, Survival, and the Redefinition of Public Space: A Feasibility Study of Homeless People at a Metropolitan Airport."   <u>Urban Anthropology</u>, <u>20</u> (2), Summer 1991:155-175.

Based on ethnographic research, the author explores the "survival utilities" that attract some homeless to an unnamed metropolitan airport (in the New York City area).

Hopper, Kim. "Whose Lives Are These, Anyway?" The Urban and Social Change Review, 17 (2), Summer 1984:12-13.
The author responds negatively to the Housing and Urban Development's Report on the Homeless and Emergency Shelters. He focuses on the need to adequately count the homeless and to provide them low-income housing.

Hopper, Kim, Ezra Susser, and Sarah Conover. "Economics of Makeshift: Deindustrialization and Homelessness in New York City." Urban Anthropology, 14 (1-3), 1985:183-235.
The increase of the homelessness in U.S. society is not due to defects or disabilities within homeless people. Rather, its roots are found in the economic restructuring of the city: the intensification of income divisions, the transformation of land values, gentrification, and abandonment. Some people, such as those with psychiatric disabilities, are more vulnerable to homelessness.

Hopper, Kim, and Jill Hamberg. The Making of America's Homeless: From Skid Row to New Poor, 1945-1984. New York: Community Service Society, December 1984. Mimeo.
The authors examine the social background of homelessness from 1945, the rise and fall of skid row, homelessness as a process (displacement followed by the inability to locate replacement housing), varieties of homeless (single-parent households, former working families, single men, single women, victims of domestic violence, the psychiatrically disturbed, ex-offenders, youth, elderly, and immigrants), underlying causes (unemployment, shortage of affordable housing, deinstitutionalization, cutbacks in benefits), precipitating events (eviction, loss of income, and personal crisis), and solutions (right-to-shelter legislation for emergency relief accompanied by a progressive social agenda that provides full employment and adequate housing). They argue that the costs of reform are less than those engendered by allowing the problem to persist.

Howe, Marvin. "Housing for 10,000 Is Urged for New York City Homeless." New York Times, January 26, 1992:31.
Partnership for the Homeless, a nonprofit organization, says that New York City must construct housing for 10,000 homeless.

Howell, Mary C., E. B. Emmons, and D. A. Frank. "Reminiscences of Runaway Adolescents." <u>American Journal of
Orthopsychiatry</u>, <u>43</u> (5), 1973:840-853.
    Based on telephone interviews with 18 girls and 23
boys more than a year after they had run away from home,
the authors report the difficulties the youths experienced with parents or school before running away. Most
of the runaways reported that they enjoyed the experience
of running away, and felt their lives were now better
than before they had run away.

Howitt, Bob. "Life (Such as It Is) in the Big City."
<u>Wall Street Journal</u>, July 16, 1986:18.
    This account is written by a commuter to New York
City, who expresses disgust over the decay of contemporary civilization, including the human litter (the
homeless).

Hoy, Walter R. "The Care of the Homeless in St. Louis."
<u>The Family</u>, <u>9</u>, October 1928:209-219.
    The author, Executive Secretary of the Bureau for
Homeless Men in St. Louis, divides homeless families into
disaster families, transient families (begging families
and auto transients), and non-resident families. As
solutions, he proposes keeping better records, centraliz-
ing care through community organization, defining the
various agencies' respective areas of responsibility,
developing programs, emphasizing self-sustenance,
separating the giving of relief from religious activities, establishing free employment centers in every city,
passing national residence laws, and rigidly enforcing
begging and vagrancy laws.

Hubbel, John G. "Father Ritter's Covenant." <u>Reader's
Digest</u>, October 1980:2-6.
    Bruce Ritter is the founder of Under 21, located
just off Times Square in New York City. The article
reviews the philosophy and finances of this program and
recounts sordid experiences in the street life of runaway
children.

Huber, Peter. "The Lawyers Versus the Homeless."
<u>Forbes</u>, <u>146</u> (1), July 9, 1990:92.
    Clozaril, a drug developed by Sandoz Pharmaceu-
ticals, provides "breakthrough therapy for schizophrenia." This means that Clozaril "could do far more for
the homeless in this country--many of whom are schizo-
phrenic--than all of the endless posturing on the issue

from Washington." The drug will not be made available to the homeless, however, because the U.S. legal system no longer insulates drug companies from the misuse of prescription drugs.

Hudson, Bryan A., Beverly B. Rauch, Grace D. Dawson, John F. Santos, and David C. Burdick. "Homelessness: Special Problems Related to Training, Research, and the Elderly." <u>Gerontology and Geriatrics Education</u>, <u>10</u> (3), 1990:31-69.
    Focusing on the problems and needs of the "undomiciled elderly," the authors make the case that to adequately meet the needs of the homeless in general and the elderly in particular human service providers must coordinate their efforts.

Hudson, Christopher G. "The Development of Policy for the Homeless: The Role of Research." <u>Social Thought</u>, <u>14</u> (1), Winter 1988:3-15.
    Research on the homeless has been used by politicians to avoid confronting the underlying causes of homelessness--its economic, political, demographic, and structural causes. Consequently, researchers should examine these underlying causes so they will not help perpetuate the view of poverty as an individual problem.

Hudson, Christopher G., and Julius A. Roth. "The Social Class and Mental Illness Correlation: Implications of the Research for Policy and Practice." <u>Journal of Sociology and Social Welfare</u>, <u>15</u> (1), March 1988:27-54.
    This overview of the relationship between social class and mental illness includes the observation that it is necessary to establish causal connections between homelessness and mental illness before one can attempt to solve the problem.

Huelsman, M. "Violence on Anchorage's 4th Avenue from the Perspective of Street People." <u>Alaska Medicine</u>, <u>25</u> (2), April-June 1983:39-44.
    Based on a survey of 54 street persons in Anchorage, Alaska, the author reports the frequency of robbery, assault, and other types of violence, including rape, describes characteristics of those incidents, and makes suggestions for improving the situation.

Hughes, Della. "Running Away: A 50-50 Chance to Survive?" <u>USA Today</u>, September 1989:64-66.
    It is difficult to define homeless youth. This concept certainly includes those who live in abandoned

buildings, but many youths who live in foster homes or in institutions consider themselves to be homeless. It is a myth that youths run away to seek adventure. The most common reasons for running away are abuse or a crisis at home or school. Most youths who run away remain in the county or metropolitan area from which they ran away. Shelters and services for runaway youths need to be supported.

Hughes, Kathleen A. "Street People Find a Home in the Theater." Wall Street Journal, July 22, 1986:24.
    The author reviews two plays being performed in Los Angeles, "Serious Box" and "South of the Clouds," in which the performers are homeless. The performances are an outgrowth of workshops with skid-row homeless.

Hull, Jon D. "Slow Descent Into Hell." Time, February 2, 1987:26-27, 29.
    Based on participant observation, the author reports the despair of homeless men.

Hunt, Albert R. "Liberals Sing A Different Song In Own Back Yard." Wall Street Journal, March 7, 1991:A12.
    The author discusses opposition to building a shelter for the homeless in Ward 3 in Washington, D.C. Ward 3, an island in Washington, is an 88 percent white, disproportionately professional, upper-middle class neighborhood. Its residents, who pride themselves on their liberal politics, do not want the homeless near them. Their actions are "resurrecting an old adage about liberals: They love humanity, but don't much care for human beings."

Hunter, Robert. Poverty: Social Conscience in the Progressive Era, Peter d'A. Jones, ed. New York: Harper and Row, 1965. (Originally published by Macmillan in 1904.)
    This overview of poverty includes a chapter on vagrancy. The types of vagrants are indigent and infirm, professional and voluntary, and accidental and involuntary. The cause is a capitalist industrial system that requires a surplus of labor. The solution is legislative reform that will provide minimum standards of working and living conditions.

Huntley, Steve, and Jeannye Thornton. "Shielding the Homeless from a Deadly Winter." U.S. News & World Report, 99, December 9, 1985:79.

The authors estimate the numbers of homeless in New York City, Chicago, Seattle, Pittsburgh, Salt Lake City, Boston, and Washington, D.C., and give an overview of their situation.

Husock, Howard. "The Roots of Homelessness." Critical Review, 4 (4), Fall 1990:505-521.
A dominant view of the cause of homelessness is inadequate government intervention for the poor in the private housing market. During the late nineteenth and early twenties centuries, however, when there was less government intervention, much housing for the poor developed, particularly single-room occupancy hotels. The author suggests that the problem is inappropriate intervention by the government, that strict building and zoning codes contribute to homelessness.

Hutchings, Vicky. "Inequalities in Housing." New Statesman and Society, July 8, 1988.
The author reports on the state of the housing stock, new building, average house prices, and homelessness in the United Kingdom.

Hutchison, William J., Priscilla R. Searight, and John J. Stretch. "Multidimensional Networking: A Response to the Needs of Homeless Families." Social Work, 31 (6), November-December 1986:427-430.
The authors' report of the study described in the next item below presents a four-stage model of networking: natural support systems, client-agency linkages, interprofessional linkages, and human service organization linkages.

Hutchison, William J., Priscilla R. Searight, and John J. Stretch. Multidimensional Networking: A Social Work Response to the Complex Needs of Homeless Families and Their Children, A Case Study of the Salvation Army Emergency Lodge in the City of St. Louis. St. Louis: Salvation Army Social Services, July 1985.
After dealing with problem of defining homelessness and establishing their number, the authors conclude, based on their six-year study of homeless families who received treatment at The Salvation Army Emergency Lodge in St. Louis, Missouri, that a five-stage model of comprehensive networking (interagency and interprofessional cooperation for purposes of intervention and assistance) should be put into effect: (1) prevention, (2) crisis, (3) stabilization, (4) relocation, and (5)

follow-up (for housing, food, income, children, counseling and mental health assistance, medical assistance,
mortgage, rent and utility assistance, clothing, furniture, and transportation).

Hyde, P. S.   "Homelessness in America: Public Policy,
Public Blame."   Psychosocial Rehabilitation Journal, 8
(4), January 1985:21-25.
    The author claims that the report by the task force
of the American Psychiatric Association placed too much
emphasis on short-term solutions, that the majority of
the homeless are not mentally ill, and that we must work
toward long-term solutions and more community programming.

                            I

Irvine, Lucy.   Runaway.   New York: Random House, 1987.
    The author, who left school at the age of 13 to
begin her adventures, recounts her experiences hitching
rides through Britain, Western Europe, and the Middle
East.

Irwin, Victoria.   "Americans With No Place to Put Down
Roots."   Christian Science Monitor, February 24, 1986:1,
6.
    The causes of homelessness are racism, breakup of
the family, impoverishment of women, destruction or
conversion of low-rent housing, drug and alcohol abuse,
unemployment, and migration to the city in search of
work.   Disaffiliation is the most common characteristic
of the homeless.   The author discusses homelessness as a
political issue, advocacy for the homeless, and homeless
families.   She also profiles the Downtown Emergency
Service Center in Seattle.

Irwin, Victoria.   "How Do We Find a Roof for Everyone?"
Christian Science Monitor, February 28, 1986:16-17.
    In her examination of how to provide low-cost
housing, the author deals with the issue of local versus
federal and government versus private action. Noteworthy
programs are singled out in Seattle, Los Angeles,
Memphis, and New York City. The solutions are a national
endowment for the homeless (in which the federal government would match funding from states and localities while

keeping all operations and decision making at the local level) and long-range planning, such as the health care initiatives coming from the challenge grants from the Robert Wood Johnson Foundation.

Irwin, Victoria. "Out of Institutions and Needing Shelter." Christian Science Monitor, February 25, 1986:16-17.
     Deinstitutionalization failed because the money that was spent in the large institutions did not follow the mentally ill out into the community, the community health centers that were set up were ill equipped to handle the problems they faced, and the mental health professionals did not adequately anticipate the problems some of the deinstitutionalized would have. There is a debate over whether to eliminate deinstitutionalization or to just fine tune it. A major problem is establishing trust with the homeless mentally ill. The solutions are an emergency stage of health care on the streets and in clinics; a stabilization level with more services and housing; long-range planning to prevent future problems; and encouraging volunteer mental health workers by allowing them a tax write-off for their time.

Irwin, Victoria. "Waiting for a Break." Christian Science Monitor, February 26, 1986:16-17.
     The author presents case stories of homeless individuals from varied backgrounds who want to work but are down on their luck.

Isaac, Rael Jean. "A Detour Around Crazy Mental Health Laws." Wall Street Journal. April 16, 1992:A24.
     Taking the position that mental health laws underlie the growing number of mentally ill homeless, the author argues for legal reform to allow easier commitment to mental hospitals. Civil rights groups that defend the presence of these people on the street ill serve the homeless mentally ill.

Isaac, Rael Jean, and Virginia C. Armat. Madness in the Streets: How Psychiatry and the Law Abandoned the Mentally Ill. New York: The Free Press, 1990.
     The authors' thesis is that anti-psychiatry is a social delusion that has resulted in deranged laws, war against psychiatric treatment, and the ejection of the mentally ill onto the streets.

J

Jackson, Anthony. <u>A Place Called Home: A History of Low-Cost Housing in Manhattan</u>. Cambridge: MIT Press, 1976.
     This book provides an overview of political, economic, and legislative factors in low-cost housing in Manhattan from the 1860s to the 1960s.

Jackson, James F. "The Rural Tramp." In <u>Proceedings of the National Conference of Charities and Correction</u>, Isabel C. Barrows, ed. May 6-12, 1903:401-404.
     The problem is how to reduce the tramp population. The common practice in rural areas of feeding tramps and sending them on their way encourages vagrancy. The social redemption of the tramp requires a work test that will force the tramp to either work or steal. In either case, he ceases to be a tramp, becoming either a worker or a prisoner. Also needed is legal enforcement to prevent free railway transportation.

Jacobs, Daniel J. "Homeless--Their Social, Economic and Legal Status--United States and Great Britain: A Selective Bibliography." <u>The Record of the Association of the Bar of the City of New York</u>, <u>41</u>, Summer 1986:526-533.
     This bibliography lists 79 items from the United States and 44 sources from Great Britain.

Jacobs, Dorri. "Getting the Homeless Back to Work." <u>Management Review</u>, <u>78</u> (10), October 1990:44-47.
     The author's thesis is that job training programs can prepare many homeless persons for employment. Hope and Jericho Project in New York City and Restart in Dallas are used as examples of successful programs.

Jacobs, Dorri. "Wanted: Jobs for a Homeless Workforce." <u>Management Review</u>, <u>79</u> (5), May 1990:40-43.
     The author's thesis is that job training programs can prepare many homeless persons for employment. Days Inn in Atlanta hires homeless people as reservation sales agents to answer its toll-free telephone numbers, in New York City the homeless sell <u>Street News</u>, and Osage Initiatives in Denver operates five on-site agencies that offer education and job readiness courses for the homeless.

Jacobs, Paul. "America's Schizophrenic View of the Poor." In The State of the Nation, David Boroff, ed. Englewood Cliffs: Prentice-Hall, 1965:160-173.
     This article provides a historical overview of attitudes and legislation from colonial America to President Johnson's war on poverty.

Jahr, Herman M. "Running Away." Hygeia, 18, 1940:145-148, 156-157.
     The author posits that the main reasons for running away are the search for adventure, to escape from unpleasant surroundings, the fear of facing reality, and to express the self in an environment where one has little control.

James, D. C. "Homelessness: Can the Courts Contribute?" British Journal of Law and Society, 1 (2), Winter 1974:195-200.
     The author's thesis is that by not hearing problems of homelessness and harassment, the courts are missing an opportunity to apply themselves for social justice. He explains why legal remedies have failed to make housing authorities comply with the law.

James, George. "Goggles Brighten Dark Subway." New York Times, April 10, 1992:B2.
     In order to try to free subway tunnels of homeless people and vandals, the New York City Transit Police are testing night vision goggles.

James, George. "Homeless Man Set on Fire, 3 Bronx Youths Are Held." New York Times, April 23, 1992:B3.
     A 60-year old homeless man set on fire in a subway stairwell by three Bronx teenagers was rescued by two strangers.

James, George. "Homeless Woman Ends Forced Hospital Stay." New York Times, January 20, 1988:18.
     The author reports that Joyce Brown, the first woman picked up under a New York City program to remove mentally ill homeless people from the streets, "was released from Bellevue Hospital Center after being forcibly hospitalized for 84 days." He describes her first meal after her release, her appearance, and mixed reactions to her confinement and release.

James, George. "Immigrants Left Homeless after Transient Hotel Blaze." New York Times, March 30, 1992:B3.

Fire marshals are investigating the cause of the fire that severely damaged Mansfield Hall, a hotel for transients in midtown Manhattan. The fire left more than 150 residents homeless.

Janus, Mark David, Anne W. Burgess, and Arlene McCormack. "Histories of Sexual Abuse in Adolescent Male Runaways." Adolescence, 22 (86), Summer 1987:405-417.
Comparisons of data from 89 male runaways at a shelter for homeless youths in Toronto, Canada, with randomly selected populations in previous populations show that the runaways have higher rates of sexual and physical abuse. The authors analyze the withdrawal patterns of sexually abused youths and note implications for treatment and further research.

Jaynes, Gregory. "Urban Librarians Seek Ways to Deal with 'Disturbed Patrons.'" New York Times, November 24, 1981:A16.
City officials in California, Washington, Atlanta, and Miami, in conjunction with librarians, are seeking ways to keep "disturbed people" out of the libraries without risking lawsuits.

Jaynes, Gregory. "Where Liberals Feel Besieged by Homeless." New York Times, November 11, 1987:16.
Residents of the Lower East Side (East Village, the Bowery) are reacting negatively to the proposal to put another shelter for the homeless in their neighborhood.

Jefferson, David J., and Neil Barsky. "Legal Beat: Housing for Homeless." Wall Street Journal, February 28, 1991:B4.
According to a New York state court ruling, New York City must provide permanent housing and support services for homeless people who are discharged from mental hospitals.

Jeffery, Roger. "Normal Rubbish: Deviant Patients in Casualty Departments." In Deviant Behavior: A Text-Reader in the Sociology of Deviance, Delos H. Kelly, ed. New York: St. Martin's, 1984:357-374.
Listed among the "rubbish" (the types of patients disliked by medical personnel who work in emergency rooms in British Hospitals) are tramps.

Jehl, Douglas. "A Waiting Game." Los Angeles Times, September 10, 1984:Section 2:1.

The author presents an ethnography of the Greyhound Bus Station in Los Angeles, describing interactions among the drivers, guards, travelers, and the homeless. He also lists the rules against the homeless.

Jenkins, Jolyon. "Avoidable Voids." New Statesman Society, 1 (3), June 24, 1988:28.
This article reports that the Thatcher government refuses to accept responsibility for homelessness, blaming it instead on Labour Councils. The Thatcher government stresses that the number of "voids" (empty properties) run by Labour Councils is roughly equivalent to the number of homeless. The author concludes that reducing the "turnaround time" (the time it takes to occupy a property after it is vacated) will have little impact on homelessness.

Jenkins, Richard L. "The Runaway Reaction." American Journal of Psychiatry, 128 (2), August 171:60-65.
The author analyzes the "runaway reaction," a diagnostic category of behavior disorder of childhood and adolescence in the Diagnostic and Statistical Manual of Mental Disorders, described as a maladaptive frustration response of a child who feels nobody wants him or her, dominated by fear and parental rejection.

Jenkins, Richard L., and Galen Stahle. "The Runaway Reaction: A Case Study." Journal of the American Academy of Child Psychiatry, 11 (2), 1972:294-313.
The authors, basing their conclusions on the case study of a male who had shown "maladaptive nomadism" from age 11 to his death at age 33, conclude that repetitive runaways are more attracted by adventure than repelled by home.

Johnson, Alice K. "Female-Headed Homeless Families: A Comparative Profile." Affilia, 4 (4), Winter 1989:23-39.
A study of the case records of 987 homeless families served by a shelter in St. Louis, Missouri, from 1983-1988 shows that most homeless families are young, female-headed, and minority. The basic causes for the increase of women and children among the homeless are the loss of affordable housing and that payments to mothers who receive Aid to Families with Dependent Children are insufficient for many to pay market-rate rents.

Johnson, Alice K., and Larry W. Krueger.   "Toward a
Better Understanding of Homeless Women." Social Work, 34
(6), November 1989:537-540.
     Based on a sample of 240 homeless women who were
residents of six shelters, the authors compared homeless
women with children and homeless women without children.
No significant differences in current psychiatric
diagnoses or the presence of family in the area showed
up, but significantly more women without children had
seen a mental health professional within the past year,
drink alcohol, have been told they have a drinking
problem, are older, and have been homeless longer. The
authors conclude that "homeless women with children have
kept their families together despite the trauma of
homelessness. Although women with children are homeless
for reasons quite different from the women without
children, they are similarly unwilling to terminate
parenting rights and responsibilities....(Homeless)
children who seek shelter with their mothers need to be
protected from additional psychological and physical harm
that can be sustained in shelter and service environments
that include mentally ill people."   Homeless women
without children should not be cared for in the same
shelters as homeless women with children.

Johnson, Alice K., Larry W. Krueger, and John J. Stretch.
"Court-Ordered Consent Decree for the Homeless: Process,
Conflict, and Control." Journal of Sociology and Social
Welfare, 16 (3), September 1989:29-42.
     The authors use a sociological conflict and control
perspective to analyze the implications of court-ordered
requirements in St. Louis, Missouri, to integrate the
legal, political, and social service delivery systems on
behalf of the homeless.

Johnson, Bonnie, and Michael Small.   "Moviemaker Mira
Nair Takes to the Streets of Bombay to Say Salaam! To
Real Children With No Childhood." People Weekly, 30,
December 5, 1988:115-116.
     This article recounts the making of Salaam Bombay!,
a documentary about the street children of Bombay.

Johnson, Cheryl. "People Searching for Their Homeless
Relatives Find Out They Too Have No Place to Go."
Minneapolis Star and Tribune, February 2, 1986:A1, A8.
     The author distinguishes between a missing person
and a homeless person. Relatives of homeless people
often contact missing persons officials, whose services

are not for out-of-touch people. Adults are free to come
and go without accounting to the government or to
relatives.

Johnson, Glenn H. <u>Relief and Health Problems of a
Selected Group of Non-Family Men</u>. Chicago: University of
Chicago Press, 1937.
      A study of the health, work records, education, and
employability of 144 men under care of the Cook County
Relief Administration showed that the men are a stable,
self-reliant group with good work records. Shelters
destroy the men. Homelessness is part of the larger
problem of poverty. The solutions are health care,
invalidity pensions, work, vocational training, enforced
housing standards, elimination of the shelters, and an
integrated attack by various professions.

Johnson, Kirk. "New York Court Backs Hospitalization of
Homeless Woman." <u>New York Times</u>, December 19, 1987:Y11.
      The Appellate Division of the State Supreme Court in
Manhattan appealed New York City's involuntary hospitalization of Joyce Brown, the first homeless woman removed
from the city's streets to a mental hospital. The
article describes some of Joyce Brown's behaviors that
brought her to the attention of authorities.

Johnson, Kirk. "Officials Seek Humane Ways to Get
Homeless Out of New York Subways." <u>New York Times</u>,
September 5, 1988:10.
      Transit authorities want to remove the homeless from
the subway stations and trains. They are convinced that
many commuters refuse to ride the subways and trains
because of the presence of the homeless. The transit
authorities point out that they are not in the social
services business and the homeless have caused the delay
of 230 trains, according to their records. Others dispute
those figures.

Johnson, Kirk. "Property of a Homeless Man is Private,
Hartford Court Says." <u>New York Times</u>, March 19,1991:B1.
      In spite of their living in public places, the
homeless are protected by the same constitutional rights
to privacy as citizens with more conventional dwellings.
The State Supreme Court of Connecticut ordered a new
murder trial for David Mooney, a homeless man who had
been living under a highway bridge, because the police
did not have a search warrant to search the cardboard box
containing his possessions.

Johnson, Kirk. "Protests by Homeless Around U.S. Are Marked by Moves to Take Housing." New York Times, January 7, 1988:13.
Chicago homeless and their advocates, after forcing their way into vacant units in a housing project and breaking down doors in vacant Victorian homes, occupied the buildings in a demonstration on behalf of the homeless.

Johnson, Sally. "Homeless Get Fare Out of Vermont." New York Times, November 23, 1988:Y11.
A group in Burlington, Vermont, Westward Ho!, offers the homeless on their streets a free one-way airplane ticket to the city of their choice. The group is made up of local businessmen, who want to remove the homeless from the streets in front of their businesses.

Johnson, Thomas. "Skid Row Parks: Derelicts' Needs vs. Business Interests." Landscape Architecture, 72 (4), July 1982:84-88.
The 6th Street Park, located in the skid row area south of the Los Angeles Civic Center, is designed for homeless people. This park provides places to sit and sleep without risk of police harassment, restrooms, shelter from sun and rain, and greater safety than do the streets. The park is a source of controversy, receiving heavy criticism from business people because it has attracted many homeless into the area.

Jonas, Gerald. "The Post's Xmas Hoax: The Streetniks of New York City." Nation, 237, December 31, 1983-January 7, 1984:692.
This article reprints three short articles and editorials from the New York Post of December 21 and 22, 1983, on "bag kids" (or "streetniks") in New York City. The articles are supposedly a hoax.

Jones, Bernie. "Community Problem Solving Around Homelessness. The Social Construction of Consensus." Journal of the Community Development Society, 21 (2), 1990:36-654.
Based on a coalition's experiences in Denver, the author proposes a consensus model for community development--developing broad community support, positive media coverage, third-party mediation, clear purposes, and clear group identities to prevent boundary crossing.

Jones, Douglas Lamar. "The Strolling Poor: Transiency in Eighteenth-Century Massachusetts." In Walking to Work: Tramps in America, 1790-1935, Eric H. Monkkonen, ed. Lincoln: University of Nebraska Press, 1984:21-55.
    The author discusses citizen concern about transients and legal and other institutional control over transients.

Jones, Earl R., and William M. Harris. "A Conceptual Scheme for Analysis of the Social Planning Process." Journal of the Community Development Society, 18 (2), 1987:18-41.
    After explaining that social planning in community development has declined and that experts do not agree on the definition of social planning, the authors present a three-phase model for analyzing social planning. Homelessness is given as an example of a reason that communities should engage in social planning.

Jones, Gareth Stedman. Outcast London: A Study in the Relationship Between Classes in Victorian Society. New York: Pantheon Books, 1984.
    This book provides historical background on the London Labor market, casual labor, vagrants, housing, the poor, the lower class, and the law and economics in early industrialization. It also contains a reproduction of Gustave Dore's 1870 "Sleeping Out Under the Arches," a depiction of homeless men clustered at night under a bridge.

Jones, Loring P. "A Typology of Adolescent Runaways." Child and Adolescent Social Work Journal, 5 (1), Spring 1988:16-29.
    The author's thesis is that a typology that adequately reflects the heterogeneity of runaway and homeless youth would be a useful tool for intervention. Toward that end, he presents a typology that incorporates family dynamics, psychological characteristics, and length of time away from home.

Jones, Robert E. "Street People and Psychiatry: An Introduction." Hospital and Community Psychiatry, 34 (9), September 1983:807-811.
    The author traces the history of the homeless mentally ill in the United States, the role of media coverage in acquainting the public with the plight of the homeless mentally ill, the impact of deinstitutionalization, and the work of advocacy organizations.

Jordan, Alan K. "Homeless Men and the Community." <u>Australian Journal of Social Issues</u>, <u>2</u> (3), 1965:27-33.
Based on a study of homeless men in Melbourne, Australia, the author concludes that there are two stages in becoming a resident of skid row. The first is primary failure: "would-be conformists" are unable to "assume or sustain the expected role and status of adult male in our society" because of "disturbance of normal personality development." The second is secondary failure: due to regression, an individual becomes destitute and migrates to skid row, where he "externalizes his unsatisfied need for dependency." The author analyzes services for homeless men and indicates how those services should be modified.

Jusserand, Jean J. <u>English Wayfaring Life in the Middle Ages</u> (<u>XIVth Century</u>). New York: G. P. Putnam's Sons, 1891.
The author presents an overview of the wanderers of the 14th century: herbalists, charlatans, minstrels, jugglers, tumblers, messengers, merchants, peddlers, outlaws, workmen, peasants, preachers, friars, pardoners, and pilgrims. He also summarizes various attempts at social control.

K

Kalifon, S. Zev. "Homelessness and Mental Illness: Who resorts to State Hospitals?" <u>Human Organization</u>, <u>48</u> (3), Fall 1989:268-273.
Based on a random sample of patients in the Chicago area state mental health facilities, 313 mental patients were interviewed, 56 of whom were homeless. Two types of homeless mental patients were found: Type 1 patients deny the label of mental illness, saying that their lack of housing is their real problem, while Type 2 patients indicate that mental illness has brought about their admission. The conclusion is that some homeless people "define the hospital as a desirable and exploitable resource." If they see hospitalization to their advantage, their rate of hospitalization increases, but if they see it to their disadvantage it decreases.

Kamerman, Sheila B. "Toward a Child Policy Decade." <u>Child Welfare</u>, <u>68</u> (4), July-August 1989:371-390.

The author proposes five goals as the basis of child policy: reducing poverty, reducing homelessness, improving health, meeting the needs of babies, and enhancing the welfare of children while their parents work.

Kamm, Thomas. "France's 'New Poor' Dramatize the High Price of National Austerity, Loosening Family Ties." Wall Street Journal, October 24, 1984.
   Homelessness is increasing in Europe due to stagnating economies, unemployment, retrenchment of the welfare state, inadequacies in the social security systems, and loosening family ties. The types of new homeless are single mothers, immigrants, the newly unemployed, and the unemployed whose benefits have run out. The types of old homeless are winos, professional beggars, and drug addicts. There also are some abandoned children. For illustration, the author profiles Guy Lemoine in Paris.

Kanter, Arlene S. "Homeless But Not Helpless: Legal Issues in the Care of Homeless People with Mental Illness." Journal of Social Issues, 45 (3), 1989:91-104.
   The author disputes the conclusion that deinstitutionalization is the primary cause of the increase in the numbers of homeless people. Consequently, solutions to homelessness cannot be found in relaxing our commitment laws to state mental hospitals, imposing mandatory outpatient commitment, or forcibly transporting homeless people to the emergency wards of psychiatric hospitals. What homeless mentally ill people need the most are decent homes and supportive services. "Thus the task is to coordinate initiatives in mental health care with new housing enterprises; for without permanent housing, homeless people will continue to have ever-worsening psychiatric needs."

Kaplan, J. L. "Homeless, Hungry, and Jewish." Washington Jewish Week, February 16, 1984.
   After presenting vignettes of two homeless Jews in Washington, D.C., the author summarizes the views of rabbis and other Jewish leaders on the extent of homelessness among Jews and what the Jewish community can do to solve this problem.

Kaplan, Steve. "Hallelujah, I'm a Bum." Travel-Holiday, 170, November 1988:96.
   The author reports on the annual Hobo Convention in Britt, Iowa. This year, several dozen hobos and 2,000 visitors joined with Britt's 2,000 residents for a

weekend festival honoring American hobos. This unusual
celebration has been conducted since 1900.

Kaplow, Jeffry. The Names of Kings: The Parisian
Laboring Poor in the Eighteenth Century. New York: Basic
Books, 1972.
     The "floating population" of Paris consists of the
working and idle poor who do not know where they will
sleep at night. The author reviews the history of
beggars and their punishments.

Karlen, Neal, and Barbara Burgower. "Dumping the
Mentally Ill." Newsweek, 105, January 7, 1985:17.
     Twice a week for more than a year penniless psychi-
atric patients from Austin were placed in a van and
dumped in front of the Greyhound bus station in Houston.
A released convict, in contrast, was given $200 and new
clothing. The practice has stopped, and the deinstitutionalized are now put into short-term shelters.

Karlen, Neal, and Daniel Pedersen. "Attack on the Tree
People." Newsweek, December 24, 1984:20.
     Santa Barbara, California, has experienced much
reactionary oppression to the homeless. Near one
homeless man found shot to death was a note threatening
other homeless people. The Santa Barbara homeless had
tried to register to vote and to put up a Christmas tree
at their informal gathering spot, a fig tree.

Karlen, Neal, and Nikki Finke Greenberg. "Down and Out
in Washington." Newsweek, 105, January 7, 1985:15, 17.
     Jesse Carpenter is a World War II hero who froze to
death in Washington, D.C. Television publicity has been
given to Mitch Snyder, the Coalition for the Homeless,
and the Community for Creative Non-Violence.

Karlen, Neal, and Pamela Abramson. "Bhagwan's Realm."
Newsweek, December 3, 1984:34-36, 38.
     This general article on the Rajneeshpuram cult
contains a section on how sect officials imported
homeless people to increase their ballot power in
elections in an Oregon county.

Karlen, Neal, Susan Acrest, Kate Robinsin, and Nikki
Finke Greenberg. "Homeless Kids: `Forgotten Faces'."
Newsweek, 107, January 6, 1986:20.
     The authors recount efforts across the country to
deal with the problem of homelessness. For example, New

York City is "trying to lure landlords into letting the homeless into empty apartment units in exchange for cash bonuses of $4,000."

Kasindorf, Jeanie. "The Real Story of Billie Boggs." New York Magazine, May 2, 1988:37-44.
    This detailed recounting of the background of the celebrated case of New York City's Joyce Brown, whose street name is Billie Boggs, analyzes the conflict between civil rights, namely the right of people to live on the streets even though their behavior is offensive to others versus the right of the community to incarcerate the homeless for purposes of medical treatment.

Kasinitz, Philip. "Gentrification and Homelessness: The Single Room Occupant and the Inner City Revival." The Urban and Social Change Review, 17 (1), Winter 1984:9-14.
    After presenting a brief history of gentrification, the author analyzes gentrification as a social policy and as a shift in values. He analyzes the residents and functions of SROs and concludes that gentrification is intensifying homelessness through the destruction and conversion of SRO housing in urban renewal. The homeless, who are becoming younger, are now more likely to be black and to have a history of psychiatric problems.

Kates, Brian. The Murder of a Shopping Bag Lady. New York: Harcourt, 1985.
    This novel is based on a true story. By recounting his assignment to the case of Phyllis Iannotta, a homeless immigrant who was murdered, the author, a newspaper reporter, chronicles her life of mental illness and unemployment.

Katz, L. "The Salvation Army Men's Social Center: II. Results." Quarterly Journal of Studies on Alcohol, 27 (4), 1966:636-647.
    The author reports on the demographics, continuity of treatment, change in drinking patterns, and employment status of 300 homeless alcoholics in Salvation Army rehabilitation programs. Improvement was correlated with length of stay in the program, motivation, prior social- ization, and participation in specific elements of the program such as vocational counseling.

Katz, Michael B. Poverty and Policy in American History. New York: Academic Press, 1983.

This overview of poverty, welfare, and the welfare system in the United States, with an emphasis on the late 1800s and early 1900s, contains a chapter on tramps. Traces the ideology associated with poverty, ideas about its causes and attempts at solutions.

Kaufman, Joshua, James R. Allen, and Louis Jolyon West. "Runaways, Hippies, and Marijuana." <u>American Journal of Psychiatry</u>, <u>126</u> (5), November 1969:163-166.
  In this brief overview of marijuana smoking by the "flower children" of Haight-Ashbury in San Francisco in the summer of 1967, the authors suggest that society needs to offer youth a viable alternative to drugs.

Kaufman, Nancy K. "Homelessness: A Comprehensive Policy Approach." <u>The Urban and Social Change Review</u>, <u>17</u> (1), Winter 1984:21-26.
  After defining homelessness, the author states that its causes are deinstitutionalization, battering, eviction, unemployment, lack of low-cost housing, tightening of federal programs, and displacement by condominium conversion, urban renewal, and gentrifica-tion. She summarizes a comprehensive policy approach in Massachusetts that utilizes case management to implement a three-tiered system: an emergency phase (shelter and survival needs), a transitional phase (social-health services, employment, and housing assistance), and a stabilization phase (employment, permanent housing, and support services). To successfully move through these phases, aggressive advocacy by a case manager is neces-sary.

Kearns, Kevin C. "Homelessness in Dublin: An Irish Urban Disorder." <u>American Journal of Economics and Sociology</u>, <u>43</u> (2), April 1984:217-233.
  Both individual and structural causes underlie the homelessness of Dublin's 1,200 homeless persons. On the personal level are health, alcoholism, economic depriva-tion, and psychiatric disturbances. On the structural level--the primary cause--is entrapment in an inequitable social, economic, political, and legislative system. Because of public apathy and prejudice, it is unlikely that social policy will change.

Kearns, Kevin C. "Intraurban Squatting in London." <u>Annals of the Association of American Geographers</u>, <u>69</u> (4), December 1979:589-598.

Squatting, taking over unoccupied urban buildings by
the homeless, has become increasingly common in Great
Britain, Italy, Spain, France, Denmark, The Netherlands,
Sweden, and West Germany. As there are "more than
100,000 empty government-owned houses in London" which
"remain unoccupied for five to ten years" at the same
time that "there are 190,000 homeless families on housing
council waiting lists," the author views squatting as "a
viable, alternative form of tenure which fills a distinctive gap in London's increasingly exclusive housing
structure." About 20,000 squatters occupy council-owned,
short-life properties in Inner London, while about 5,000
reside in 1,500 Greater London Council buildings. Only
about three percent of squatters reside in private
property. Some squats ("authorized squats") receive a
form of legitimization which grants security from sudden
eviction. Such licensed squats are a sort of halfway
house between trespasser status and official tenancy.
Many squatters belong to squatter organizations and
exhibit "a strong sense of accomplishment and pride in
home possession, preferring the retention of dweller
control over their squat to acceptance of rehousing in
council tenant estates."

Keating, Dennis. "The American Tenant and Housing
Movement." Shelterforce, 9 (2), December 1985:1, 7.
The author explains why the tenant and housing
movement remains weak at the national level and suggests
that the key to building a broader and more powerful
movement is a coalition of middle-class and lower-class
home owners and renters.

Keefe, Tom, and Ron Roberts. "Reciprocity, Social
Support, and Unemployment." Social Development Issues, 8
(3), Winter 1984:116-126.
This analysis of the limitations of reciprocity in
commodity relations uses the homeless unemployed as an
example.

Keller, Suzanne. "The American Dream of Community: An
Unfinished Agenda." Sociological Forum, 3 (2), Spring
1988:167-183.
In her presidential address to the Eastern Sociological Society, the author uses the term "spiritual
homelessness" to refer to a sense of failed Gesellschaft.

Kellogg, Arthur P. "Traffic Squad at Union Square."
Charities and The Commons, 20, April 4, 1908:9-12.

A meeting of the unemployed was held in Union Square, for which the city police had refused to issue a permit on the basis that the organizers were anarchists. A bomb exploded that killed and injured its makers.

Kellogg, Charles D. "Charity Organization in the United States." Proceedings of the National Council of Charities and Correction, 1893:52-93.
The author presents a 20-year history of charitable and municipal relief in the United States.

Kellor, Frances Alice. "The Crying Need for Connecting Up the Man and the Job." Survey, 31, February 7, 1914:541-542.
Vast numbers of unemployed live in New York City. The author describes their attempts to find work. The solutions are to coordinate agencies dealing with the unemployed and to ascertain trade and working conditions, thus making New York City a model for the rest of the country.

Kellor, Frances Alice. "Unemployment in American Cities: The Record for 1914-1915." National Municipal Review, 4, July 1915:420-428.
The author gives an overview of efforts to deal with the unemployed during a period of "new bread lines and soup kitchens." The general cause of this problem is industrial organization. The solutions are to seek more specific causes and institute remedies.

Kelly, Edmond. The Elimination of the Tramp: By the Introduction into America of the Labour Colony System Already Proved Effective in Holland, Belgium, and Switzerland, with the Modifications Thereof Necessary to Adapt this System to American Conditions. New York: G. P. Putnam's Sons, 1908.
The current practice of giving through charities encourages vagrancy. The solution is to establish labor colonies modeled after those in Europe, especially those in Switzerland. This is a simple, complete, and inexpensive remedy. For labor colonies to work, they must be close to self supporting, teach vocational skills, and be oriented toward agriculture (to avoid competition with industry). The types of vagrants are youth who tramp for amusement, neuropaths (mentally ill), able-bodied, and non-able-bodied. This book was written during a depression in which there were an estimated 500,000 vagrants in a population of 80 million.

Kelly, Edmond. <u>The Unemployables</u>. London: P. S. King, 1907.

The author categorizes vagrants and reviews the labor colonies of Europe. The solution to vagrancy requires a balance between rehabilitative and custodial programs.

Kelly, Elinor, J. Clyde Mitchell, and Susan J. Smith. "Factors in the Length of Stay of Homeless Families in Temporary Accommodation." <u>The Sociological Review</u>, <u>38</u> (4), November 1990:621-633.

In order to examine support networks, data were collected on 526 homeless families staying in temporary accommodation--in local hostels and privately rented flatlets outside London. Those who take longer to be rehoused are persons who are illegally evicted, enter temporary accommodation in the winter, become homeless through domestic disputes, have more addresses prior to admission to temporary accommodation, and have fewer children.

Kelso, Robert W. <u>The History of Public Poor Relief in Massachusetts, 1620-1920</u>. Montclair, New Jersey: Patterson Smith, 1969.

The author traces the treatment of the poor in Massachusetts to an English background and examines the social foundations of those practices, the laws of inhabitancy and legal settlement, and the various approaches of towns and the state in the treatment of the poor.

Kemp, Harry. <u>Chanteys and Ballads: Sea-Chanteys, Tramp-Ballads and Other Ballads and Poems</u>. New York: Brentano's, 1920.

The author celebrates his wanderings in verse.

Kemp, Harry. "The Hobo." <u>The New Republic</u>, <u>35</u>, August 22, 1923:364-365.

In this review of Nels Anderson's <u>The Hobo</u>, the author, an experienced hobo himself, defends men's right to be hobos and recounts some of their hardships.

Kemp, Harry. <u>Tramping on Life: An Autobiographical Narrative</u>. New York: Boni and Liveright, 1922.

The author, who grew up in poverty, became a hobo. He writes poems, likes literature, and went on to attend college.

Kennedy, William. <u>Ironweed</u>. New York: Viking Press,
1983.
        This is a novel about a man who became homeless in
the 1930s.

Kenton, Charlotte.   <u>The Homeless: Literature Search,</u>
<u>January 1980 through December 1983</u>.   Washington D.C.:
U.S. Department of Health and Human Services, 1984.
        This bibliography lists 93 sources on the homeless.

Keogh, Cornelia R.   "A Study of Runaways at a State
Correctional School for Boys."   <u>Journal of Juvenile</u>
<u>Research</u>, <u>19</u>, 1935:45-61.
        The author compared 200 boys who ran away from
Whittier State School in California with 400 consecutive
admissions. She concludes that the boys are very similar
in intelligence, race, entrance age, and age at running
away.   Runaways were more likely to come from broken
homes, to have stepparents in the home, to be truants,
and to show unsatisfactory post-institutional adjustment.

Kerr, Peter.   "The Homeless for Whom Housing Is Not
Enough." <u>New York Times</u>, October 9, 1988:E8.
        The author focuses on homeless people who are
addicted to drugs, the "legions of intravenous drug users
and crack addicts who bring with them crime and violence."   He stresses that housing for such troubled
people is not a sufficient solution, for they are "in
desperate need of drug treatment and medical care" that
requires a "blend of diverse inexpensive programs that
would include prison sentences for drug dealers, residential treatment for addicts, and at least the promise of
life off the streets and employment for those who are
recovering."

Kerr, Peter.   "The New Homelessness Has Its Roots in
Economics." <u>New York Times</u>, March 16, 1986:E5.
        A few years ago the homeless were mostly lone
drifters and former mental patients. The new homeless
are made up of functioning adults and families with
children. The causes are the same economic forces that
make it difficult for middle-class people to buy a first
home. These forces prevent many poor people from finding
any housing at all. Half a million low-income units
disappear annually (partly due to New York City's rent
control), while low-paying work and welfare have not kept
pace with increased rents.

Kerridge, Roy. "The Universal Travellers." New Society, 72 (1173), June 21, 1985:427-430.
The author's typology of the homeless include squatters, drifters, those who move from one bed and breakfast to another, tinkers, and New Age gypsies.

Kerson, Toba Schwaber. "Progress Notes." Health and Social Work, 14 (2), May 1989:140-141.
The author summarizes two programs for homeless veterans operated by the Veterans Administration in New York, a daytime drop-in center in Brooklyn and a community-based program in Albany designed to promote self-esteem and vocational skills.

Kessler, Brad. "The Homeless Movement: After Charity, Starting Organizing." The Nation, 246, April 16, 1988:528-530.
There is a need to organize homeless people for the political redress of their grievances, but they are extremely difficult to organize into a cohesive group.

Kessler, Clemm C., III, and Joan Wieland. "Experimental Study of Risk-Taking Behavior in Runaway Girls." Psychological Reports, 26, 1970:810.
Using the game, "Clues," the authors tested the hypothesis that runaway girls take greater risks than nonrunaway girls. The hypothesis was not confirmed.

Ketcham, Diane. "About Long Island." New York Times, April 28, 1991:A1.
The author profiles an emergency shelter for homeless men and an apartment building for homeless families operated by the Christian Victory Center.

Kidner, Patrick. "Helping Homeless Young Offenders." Prison Service Journal, 8 (31), 1969:24-28.
The author discusses how volunteers are trained for work at the Youth Resettlement Project in London, which mobilizes community resources through joint efforts of agencies and volunteers.

Kifner, John. "As Tompkins Square Park Declines, Neighborhoods' Attitude Is Shifting." New York Times, December 7, 1989:22.
The author reviews complaints levelled against the occupation of New York City's Tompkins Square Park by the homeless.

Kifner, John. "5 Rescuers Held in Death of a Caller." <u>New York Times</u>, June 27, 1991:B1.

Three volunteer ambulance rescuers and two others have been charged with aggravated manslaughter in the death of Efrain (Frankie) Rodriguez, a mentally retarded homeless man. The motive for the killing appears to be that Rodriguez had angered the rescuers by making too many calls for ambulance service.

Kifner, John. "New York Closes Park to Homeless." <u>New York Times</u>, June 4, 1991:A1.

After persistent protests from residents of the area about the homeless living in Tompkins Square Park, New York City police evicted about 200 homeless people from the park. To keep them out, the city announced that the park would be fenced off for renovation for at least a year.

Kilborn, Peter. "Reagan Budget Proposes Increase in U.S.-Subsidized Housing Units." <u>New York Times</u>, February 16, 1988:12.

The Reagan administration will build 135,000 housing units for the nation's homeless population. Severe criticisms have been leveled against the administration's proposal to deny federal subsidies for rehabilitating rental housing to cities with rent control laws.

Killeen, Damian. "The Young Runaways." <u>New Society</u>, 75 (1202), January 17, 1986:97-98.

In contrasting the treatment of homeless youths in Great Britain and the United States, the author compares Great Britain's shelter program with the situation in the United States where homeless youths come in contact with social workers only in emergency situations. He adds that with its increase in family breakdown the problem may grow as severe in Great Britain as it is in the United States.

Kilman, Scott, and Robert Johnson. "No Haven: Homelessness Spreads to the Countryside, Straining Resources." <u>Wall Street Journal</u>, March 5, 1991:A1, A5.

Due to the farm depression of the 1980s and the current recession, homelessness is emerging as a rural crisis. The problem is straining the limited resources of small towns.

Kimball, Carol Ann. "Homeless and Hungry in Chicago." <u>Clearinghouse Review</u>, 18 (1), May 1984:18-30.

This article's introduction and 17 photographs with captions tell the story of men in Pacific Garden Mission, Chicago's largest shelter.

Kimble, G. Eleanor. "Footloose Families." Survey Graphic: Social Charitable, Civic: A Journal of Constructive Philanthropy, 21, May 1, 1932:124, 161-163, 166, 168.

The author reviews efforts by the English upper class to control labor from the 1300's to the 1600's. In spite of laws which forbade laborers to move away from the parish where they were born, a common scene was the unemployed wandering about England seeking work. U.S relief laws were patterned on the English model. The need to establish legal residence complicates efforts to help American wandering unemployed. The author reviews the residence requirements of various states and cases of individuals, single adults, children, and families who could not qualify for public aid in any city due to their traveling, urging that a solution be found to this problem. "[L]ast year and this the highways are filled with flivver-families which have no homes--pathetic wanderers seeking work, having no legal residence where they may claim public relief, sick, sore, hopeless. Have we nothing better to offer them than guards at state lines enforcing modern equivalents of Edward the Third's Statute of Labourers?"

King, Charles E. "Homelessness in America." Humanist, 49 (3), May-June 1989:8, 32.

Unlike stereotypes of uneducated, shiftless bums who want to be out on the street, the homeless population is diverse. Most of the homeless have graduated from high school, some are employed, and many are deinstitutionalized. To live in a free society is to take part of a social contract--on the one hand to be rewarded for one's initiative in the race for economic success, on the other hand to help those who are left behind in this race.

King, Patricia. "Help for the Homeless." Newsweek, 111, April 11, 1988:58-59.

This article recounts efforts of cities and of homeless advocates to maintain low-cost housing by preventing SRO's from being converted or destroyed.

King, Ralph, Jr. "Ready to Roll." Forbes, 144 (9), October 23, 1989:118-122.

Raymond Chambers has dropped out of <u>Forbe's</u> list of the 400 richest men in the United States because he has endowed $10,000,000 to Rigorous Educational Assistance for Deserving Youth (READY), with $10,000 designated for each of 1,000 Newark, New Jersey, children of alcoholics, welfare mothers, and the homeless. READY will pay the education through college of all children (who are now ages 6, 7, and 8) who stay with the program. Chambers grew up in Newark.

King, Wayne. "On the Trail of Youths and AIDS." <u>New York Times</u>, August 11, 1989:24.
Many street teenagers have contracted AIDS due to prostitution and crack. Because of this problem, Covenant House, headed by Rev. Bruce Ritter, is going to open up a center in New Jersey.

King, Wayne. "Public Advocate Troubling to New Jersey's Privileged." <u>New York Times</u>, September 9, 1991:B1.
The author presents an overview of the New Jersey Public Advocate and Public Defender, Wilfredo Caraballo, who directs 380 lawyers. Fifty of the attorneys are assigned to monitor utility rates and look out for the physically and mentally ill, prisoners, and the homeless.

Kittrie, Nicholas N. "Commentary." <u>The Hastings Center Report,</u> June 1982:19.
The death of Rebecca Smith in New York City, who froze to death after refusing shelter, is used to highlight the conflict between individual rights and the right of the community to protect the individual. The author also discusses tension between potential excesses of the therapeutic state and the need to protect the individual.

Kleiman, Dena. "Neighbors Mourn One of New York's Homeless." <u>New York Times</u>, March 27, 1987:14.
Residents of Manhattan react with sadness and expressions of affection to the death of a nameless homeless man who for 15 years had made a busy stretch of 40th Street his home.

Kleinman, N. R. "S.I. Ferry's Homeless: Forgotten Casualties of Fire." <u>New York Times</u>, September 30, 1991:A1.
A fire at the Staten Island Ferry Terminal, of unknown origins but perhaps due to carelessness on the

part of a homeless person, has displaced 25 to 40 homeless persons who lived there.

Kline, Michael V., John D. Bacon, Mirris Chinkin, and
William F. Manov. "The Client Tracking System: A Tool
for Studying the Homeless." Alcohol Health and Research
World, 11 (3), Spring 1987:66-67, 91.
    To better understand and improve our ability to meet
the alcohol-related needs of the homeless population, we
must utilize efficient and accurate client tracking
systems. The authors describe the computerized
administrative monitoring tool used in the Los Angeles
area, the Alcohol Client Tracking System (ACTS).

Knibbs, Henry Herbert. Songs of the Outlands: Ballads of
the Hoboes and Other Verses. Boston: Houghton Mifflin,
1914.
    This volume contains the text of 29 songs about
drifters.

Knobler, Peter. "Hell on Upper Broadway." New York
Times, August 9, 1991:A27.
    Neighborhood activists forcefully "cleaned up" an
area of upper broadway, forcing out peddlers, drug
traffickers, and the homeless.

Knode, Helen. "Homeless Take to the Stage." Mother
Jones, 11, December 1986:15-16.
    Professional artists and the homeless join forces
for a performance of Big Show, produced by Inner City
Arts Center in Los Angeles.

Koegel, Paul, and M. Audrey Burnam. "The Epidemiology of
Alcohol Abuse and Defence Among Homeless Individuals:
Findings from the Inner-City of Los Angeles."
Washington, D.C.: National Institute of Alcohol Abuse and
Alcoholism, January 1987 (Mimeo).
    The researchers administered the NIMH Diagnostic
Interview Schedule and the Center for Epidemiologic
Studies Depression Scale to a probability sample of the
homeless residents of skid row in Los Angeles. They
report prevalence of alcoholic abuse and dependence, the
extent to which alcoholism predates homelessness or
follows homelessness, compare how the cause of alcoholism
among the homeless parallels the cause of alcoholism
among community alcoholics, and examine the special case
of homeless individuals who have a dual diagnosis of
mental illness and alcoholism. They found that

"alcoholism is more likely to precede homelessness than vice versa," suggesting that "alcoholism is more often a contributing factor to homelessness than it is a consequence of homelessness." Alcoholism is not the same for the homeless and non-homeless but differs in its prevalence, cause, severity and impact on the ability of individuals to function in their expected social roles.

Koegel, Paul, and M. Audrey Burnam. "Traditional and Nontraditional Homeless Alcoholics." Alcohol Health and Research World, 11 (3), Spring 1987:28-33.

Based on interviews with 379 homeless alcoholics in Los Angeles, the authors report demographics, health status, utilization of mental health and medical services, sources of income, strategy of subsistence, vulnerability to victimization, sources of support, history of homelessness, and patterns of mobility. Compared with homeless people without alcohol problems, the homeless who are alcoholics are more likely to have anti-social personalities, abuse other drugs, and to experience psychological distress.

Koegel, Paul, M. Audrey Burnam, and Rodger K. Farr. "Subsistence Adaptation Among Homeless Adults in the Inner City of Los Angeles." Journal of Social Issues, 46 (4), Winter 1990:83-107.

Interviews were conducted with 379 homeless adults in 25 locations in the inner city of Los Angeles. About 39 percent of the sample were blacks, 28 percent whites, 25 percent Hispanics, and 8 percent other. The article contains six tables that summarize the demographic characteristics of the sample, their shelter experiences, sources of food, clothing, hygiene, employment experiences, and entitlement and income experiences. The authors state that "the fundamental message that emerges from these data is this: Though services may need to be tailored to particular subgroups among the homeless, and some groups may need more help than others, all homeless people could profit from assistance in meeting their subsistence needs."

Koenig, Alice F. Street People Survey. Richmond, Virginia: Department of Public Welfare, 1983.

A one-day survey of 362 street people in Richmond, Virginia, revealed that 65 had no place to stay, 102 were staying at shelters, and 161 lived in some type of permanent residence. Although the demographic characteristics of the three groups were similar, the difference was in their place of residence and potential for employment. Those who were without a residence and not living in shelters showed the least ability to deal with economic hardship.

Koenig, Richard. "Philadelphia Shelter for Street People Knows the Score." <u>Wall Street Journal</u>, February 28, 1984:1, 28.
    The Committee for Dignity and Fairness for the Homeless opened a shelter for street people that is run by street people. It is directed by a former homeless man, Edward "Tex" Howard.

Koenig, Robert L. "Homeless Boy Shares St. Louis Dream With Congress." <u>St. Louis Post Dispatch</u>, February 26, 1987:1, 11.
    The Housing Select Committee on Hunger flew Damien Jones and his mother to Washington to describe what life was like without a home. Includes Damien's dream of a bright-colored home where he will be able to attract friends.

Kolata, Gina. "Homeless Drug Addicts: Studies in 'Lost Dreams.'" <u>New York Times</u>, May 30, 1989:11.
    Father Pfannenstiel at McKenna House in Washington, D.C., helps men kick their drug addiction and then provides jobs and housing for those who make it through the program.

Kolata, Gina. "Many With AIDS Live in Shelters." <u>New York Times</u>, April 4, 1988:14.
    The author reports on the problems of individuals who are homeless and have AIDS, focusing on the lack of resources available to them and the abuse they receive in shelters for the homeless.

Kolata, Gina. "Street Woman at Center of Abortion Drama." <u>New York Times</u>, February 15, 1992:A6.
    The moral dilemma surrounding abortion is illustrated by Martina Greywind, a pregnant North Dakota street woman who is addicted to sniffing paint fumes. Greywind has been offered $10,000 by the Lambs of Christ if she gives birth to her child, while an anonymous donor has offered to pay for an abortion.

Kolata, Gina. "Twins of the Streets: Homelessness and Addiction." <u>New York Times</u>, May 22, 1989:1, 12.

Advocates for the homeless have avoided discussing the problem of addiction among the homeless because "they fear the public will lose its sympathy for the homeless." Perhaps 75 percent to 80 percent of homeless men and women are addicts to drugs or alcohol. The need to treat this problem is great, but there are few effective programs and little funding.

Kondratas, S. Anna. "How Many Homeless?: The Numbers Game is Ridiculous." Los Angeles Times, July 18, 1985.
    The estimates of the numbers of homeless made by the Community for Creative Non-Violence are absurd. HUD's estimates are the best that we have.

Kondziela, Joachim. "Citoyen Freedom and Bourgeois Freedom: Religion and the Dialectics of Human Rights." Soundings, 67 (2), Summer 1984:172-182.
    In highlighting the tensions arising from the Enlightenment between equality and individual freedom and, derivatively, today's need to develop common values for the basis of international society, the author concludes that the Church needs to address the needs of the hungry and homeless.

Konopka, Gisela. The Adolescent Girl in Conflict. Englewood Cliffs: Prentice-Hall, 1966.
    Interviews were conducted with 181 adolescent females in trouble with the law. The topics covered are their conflicts, loneliness, self image, and the changing cultural position of women. The solutions are new services to unmarried mothers, youth, and delinquents, as well as a change in the status of women.

Korenbaum, Sue, and Gina Burney. Alcohol-Free Living Environments for Homeless Individuals: Final Report. Rockville, Maryland: National Institute on Alcohol Abuse and Alcoholism, October 1986.
    This report is a guide for program planners who are interested in developing "alcohol-free living centers" for recovering alcoholics who don't have adequate financial resources for housing but who are willing to enter into independent living arrangements with recovering peers. Alcohol-free living centers are not "half-way houses." They are run by recovering alcoholics with no counseling or direct supervision from a parent agency. Their one essential house rule is that residents and guests remain free of alcohol and drugs. In their review

of the need for such centers, the authors report on how
five such centers operate (four in Los Angeles and one in
San Francisco) and delineate how to assess community
needs, select facilities, handle finances, organize the
program, and evaluate and modify the program.

Korenbaum, Sue, and Gina Burney.   "Program Planning for
Alcohol-free Living Centers."   <u>Alcohol Health and
Research World</u>, <u>11</u> (3), Spring 1987:68-73.
     The authors report on a study of six alcohol-free
living centers (AFLCs) in Los Angeles and San Francisco.
The goal of these centers is to help recovering alcoholics re-enter mainstream society by providing a low-rent,
alcohol-free environment, one that attempts to duplicate
the life style of mainstream society.   The article
includes recommendations for persons interested in
setting up an AFLC.

Kornbluh, Joyce L., ed. <u>Rebel Voices: An I.W.W. Antholo-
gy</u>. Ann Arbor: University of Michigan Press, 1964.
     The third chapter of this book, "Riding the Rails:
I.W.W. Itinerants," provides an introductory overview of
the homeless in the I.W.W., followed by selections of
their poems and short stories.

Koroloff, Nancy M., and Sandra C. Anderson.   "Alcohol-
free Living Centers: Hope for Homeless Alcoholics."
<u>Social Work</u>, <u>34</u> (6), November 1989:497-504.
     This article is based on data collected on 80
homeless alcoholics who spent an average of 89 days at an
alcohol-free living center in Portland, Oregon.   The
alcohol-free living center is a low-rent, alcohol-free
environment for recovering alcoholics.   The authors
conclude that "clients who completed the program were
admitted less often to both sobering services and short-
term detoxification and spent significantly fewer days in
short-term detoxification."   Other indications of the
program's effectiveness, such as changes in employment
status, income and perceived employability, "make the
alcohol-free living center a critical component in
rehabilitation for homeless people who are alcoholic."

Koshland, Danniel E., Jr.   "The Omnipotence Scandal."
<u>Science</u>, <u>238</u>, December 4, 1987:1335.
     People are inconsistent in demanding that the
problem of homelessness be solved and at the same time

refusing to support public funding that would help the problem.

Koska, Mary T. "Quality Watch: Hospital Prenatal Care Programs Are an Ounce of Prevention." Hospitals, 64, (6), March 20, 1990:50-59.
    The author summarizes programs designed to encourage women to use prenatal care, some of which use outreach teams to seek out poor and homeless pregnant women. Each dollar spent on prenatal care is estimated to save $3.38 in care during an infant's first year of life.

Kosof, Anna. Homeless in America. New York: Watts, 1988.
    The author visited shelters for the homeless. She documents the sadness and despair of the homeless, criticizes municipalities for ignoring the problem or trying to evict the homeless, and profiles promising programs for the homeless.

Kotelchuck, Ronda. "Dying for a Bed: Overcrowding Strains N.Y. Hospitals." Dollars and Sense, 152, December 1989:12-15.
    In delineating the crisis facing New York City hospitals--overcrowding due to drug abuse, AIDS, mental illness, poverty, and decreased support from family and friends--the author mentions that the homeless contribute to the problem.

Kotlowitz, Alex, and Robert Johnson. "A Housing Paradox: Many Are Homeless, Public Units Empty." Wall Street Journal, February 10, 1988:1, 10.
    The 7,000 vacant apartments in public housing projects could house 350,000 homeless people. Such a solution is impeded because federal officials say that most of the vacant units fail to meet minimum standards for habitability. To bring them up to those standards would require about $1.5 billion, which is not available. The bureaucratic procedure required for filling vacancies is also an impediment. Applicants must wait for openings, and the homeless do not have an address at which they can be contacted when a vacancy opens. Many homeless respond that they would be happy to live in less than standard units, for that would be much better than living on the streets.

Kozol, Jonathan. "Gifts From the Homeless." New York
Times, December 25, 1986:23.
     The article lists ways that the homeless contribute
to society: (1) selling blood, (2) medical experimenta-
tion, (3) low-paying day labor, (4) an inducement to
docility and acquiescence by providing a warning to
people to continue their jobs without complaint or they
may end up homeless themselves, (5) a sense of piety by
allowing people to give while keeping their distance, and
(6) poignant symbolic allegories for the media to publish
for the week preceding Christmas.

Kozol, Jonathan. "The Homeless and Their Children, Part
I." The New Yorker, 63, January 25, 1988:65-84.
     The heyday of the Martinique Hotel is contrasted
with its sad present. The author recounts many stories
about individuals housed in this hotel, with a focus on
effects on children and the high financial cost of
putting up families in welfare hotels.

Kozol, Jonathan. "The Homeless and Their Children, Part
II." The New Yorker, 63, February 1, 1988:36-67.
     In addition to recounting the problems of the
homeless who live in the Martinique Hotel, the author
levels scathing criticisms against American society for
not solving this problem and for being mean-spirited
about the homeless. The author denounces Charles
Murray's position, delineated in his book, Losing Ground.

Kozol, Jonathan. "The State Can Undo What It Has Done."
New York Times, February 28, 1988:E6.
     The government, although capable of doing so, is
failing to meet the needs of the homeless. The government has the responsibility to house every family that is
in the shelter system in New York. The city can rehabilitate the units they now own and give them to organizations and to homeless families. At the national level,
federal funding can be increased for low-income housing,
rental allowances can be made to match prevailing rents,
and the government can provide "kitchen facilities,
libraries, job training, adult education, job placement,
job referral agencies, child care, pre-school, and on-
site health teams." (This article is one part of pro-con
matching pieces on the role of the government in ending
the dependency of the homeless on welfare hotels. The
matching article is by Charles Murray, "Government Will
Try--and Fail".)

Kozol, Jonathan.   Rachel and Her Children: Homeless
Families in America. New York: Crown, 1988.
    To highlight the plight of the homeless, the author
focuses on families living in the Martinique, a hotel for
the homeless in Manhattan. Interspersed with facts and
figures on the homeless are tragic stories and voices of
homeless families living in this hotel.

Krauthammer,   Charles.   "When Liberty Really Means
Neglect." Time, December 2, 1985:103-104.
    Because deinstitutionalization is the basic cause of
homelessness, reinstitutionalization is its solution.
The author agrees with the "broken window" theory of
James Q. Wilson and asserts the right of society to cart
the homeless away.

Kroll, J., K. Carey, D. Hagedorn, P. F. Dog, and E.
Benavides.   "A Survey of Homeless Adults in Urban
Emergency Shelters." Hospital and Community Psychiatry,
37 (3), March 1986:283-286.
    In a study of 68 homeless adults in eight shelters
in Hennepin County, Minnesota, the authors found a high
rate of mental illness, alcoholism, minor criminality,
and chronic mental and medical problems. Most of the
homeless lacked contact with supportive social networks.
Although more than 50 percent needed treatment for mental
problems, only 6 percent were receiving such treatment.
In addition, almost 40 percent of those with physical
problems receive no medical care.

Kromer, Tom. Waiting for Nothing. New York: Alfred A.
Knopf, 1935.
    This novel is about an unemployed, homeless man.

Krotz, Larry. Urban Indians: The Strangers in Canada's
Cities. Edmonton: Hurtig, 1980.
    This overview of the living conditions and adjust-
ments of Indians in Canada contains a section on Indians
on skid row in Edmonton.

Kufeldt, Kathleen, and Margaret Nimmo. "Youth on the
Street: Abuse and Neglect in the Eighties." Child Abuse
and Neglect, 11 (4), 1987:531-543.
    Based on interviews with 489 runaway and homeless
youths in Calgary, Alberta, Canada, the authors divide
the youths into "runners" (those who leave home with no
intention of returning) and "in and outers" (those who

use the run as a means of coping with some crisis). Because of their longer time and greater distance from home, runners are more likely to be drawn to illegal activities. This research provided the impetus for opening a safe house for early runners. There, data are systematically gathered on runaway and homeless youths.

Kupcha, Dorothy Alma. "Rail-Line Journalism." Writer's Digest, 66, January 1986:10-11.
    The author discusses the motivation and experiences of Dale Maharidge, a journalist, and Michael Williamson, a photographer, who, in order to learn about "people who have lost their jobs because of the economy," rode freight trains around the country. The title of their book is Journey to Nowhere: The Saga of the New Underclass, Dial-Doubleday 1985.

Kupfer, Andrew. "New York: Down But Hardly Out." Fortune, 121 (5), February 26, 1990:92-96.
    Mentioned among the solutions to the need to reduce costs in order to keep New York City the world's preeminent business center and heart of the U.S. economy is alternative planning for the care of the homeless.

Kuzins, Rebecca. "Appeal Court Says Homeless May List Park as Residence." Los Angeles Daily Journal, 98, December 26, 1985:1, 4.
    The author reports that Santa Barbara officials cannot refuse to allow the homeless to vote on the basis of their not having a permanent residence. The Second District Court of Appeal determined that although Fig Tree Park was not a conventional type of dwelling it did meet the definition of legal residence as contained in the California Election Code. This ruling will allow homeless persons in California who list public facilities as a legal address to vote.

L

L'Amour, Louis. <u>Education of a Wandering Man</u>. New York: Bantam, 1989.
    In his autobiography, L'Amour mentions his hobo days during the 1930s Great Depression when he worked as a roustabout, boxer, seaman, and caretaker of a mine.

La Gory, Mark, Ferris J. Ritchey, and Jeff Mullis. "Depression among the Homeless." <u>Journal of Health and Social Behavior</u>, <u>31</u> (1), March 1990:87-102.
    After examining interview survey data from a quota sample of 150 homeless persons in Birmingham, Alabama, the authors conclude that depression among the homeless is extensive. They analyze reasons that homeless and depression are related and propose a mediation model.

La Gory, Mark, Ferris J. Ritchey, and Kevin Fitzpatrick. "Homelessness and Affiliation." <u>Sociological Quarterly</u>, <u>32</u> (2), Summer 1991:201-218.
    After examining interview survey data from a quota sample of 150 homeless persons in Birmingham, Alabama, the authors conclude that many homeless people have a network of friends, relatives, and acquaintances. These networks, however, differ from how they have been characterized in the literature.

La Gory, Mark, Kevin Fitzpatrick, and Ferris Ritchey. "Homeless Persons: Differences Between Those Living On the Street and in Shelters." <u>Sociology and Social Research</u>, <u>74</u> (3), April 1990:162-167.
    A survey of homeless persons in the Birmingham Metropolitan Statistical Area was conducted between 3:30 A.M. and 5:30 A.M. on February 11, 1988. Using a sample of 150 of these homeless persons, the authors compare those who sleep on the street with those who use shelters. In general, shelter users "are more often female, better educated, socially affiliated, and have experienced greater vulnerability in the past."

Labeodan, Olusola Adebola. "The Homeless In Ibadan." <u>Habitat International</u>, <u>13</u> (1), 1989:75-85.
    Based on interviews with 200 homeless persons and personal experiences of living in the society, the author

summarizes socioeconomic characteristics of the homeless population in Nigeria, and causes and perceptions of homelessness in this Third World nation.

Lafayette, Jon. "Agencies Share Holiday Cheer." Advertising Age, 61 (50), December 3, 1990:4, 58.
    The author reports that because 1990 has been a very poor year for advertising agencies, some of them are foregoing their annual Christmas parties in order to make donations to agencies for the poor and homeless, such as Meals on Wheels, Make-A-Wish Foundation, the Salvation Army, and Coalition for the Homeless.

Lafayette, Jon. "Burger King 'Docu-Ads' Are Teenagers' Choice." Advertising Age, 61 (23), June 4, 1990:18.
    Young people have reacted favorably to advertisements sponsored by Burger King to keep students in school. These ads are to be played on "Channel One," an in-school television network. Especially favorable reactions were given an ad that shows clips from Streetwise, a 1985 documentary of homeless children in Seattle.

Lamar, Jacob V. "The Homeless: Brick by Brick." Time, 132, October 24, 1988:34, 38.
    The author's thesis is that "supply-side, like supply-side economics, has had drastic unintended consequences" that are drying up low-cost housing and contributing to homelessness. The solution is for the federal government to spend its money wisely by rehabilitating old units, using foreclosed housing owned by HUD, creating more community-based health clinics, and raising the minimum wage.

Lamb, H. Richard. "Alternatives to Hospitals." In The Chronic Mental Patient: Five Years Later, John A. Talbott, ed. Orlando: Grune and Stratton, 1984:215-232.
    For the chronic mental patient, alternatives to hospitals are care with relatives, board-and-care homes, foster care, and satellite housing.

Lamb, H. Richard. "Deinstitutionalization and the Homeless Mentally Ill." Hospital and Community Psychiatry, 35 (9), September 1984:899-907.
    Deinstitutionalization itself is not the cause of the homeless mentally ill. The main cause is a lack of planning for structured living arrangements and treatment and rehabilitative services in the community. Because of this lack of services, many of the deinstitutionalized

become drifters or are shunted into the criminal justice system. The solutions are to build community housing with services and to revamp the mental health system to meet the dependency needs of these chronic patients.

Lamb, H. Richard, ed. The Homeless Mentally Ill. Washington, D.C.: American Psychiatric Association, 1984.
The main topics of this edited collection are the relationship of the homeless mentally ill to deinstitutionalization, shelter and housing, support systems, service programs, and the legal system. The authors also discuss biological and medical aspects of the homeless, the family's perspective, and the politics of homelessness. The book includes a summary and recommendations.

Lamb, H. Richard. "Involuntary Treatment for the Homeless Mentally Ill." Notre Dame Journal of Law, Ethics, and Public Policy, 4 (2), Summer 1989:269–280.
The author proposes ways that deinstitutionalization of the homeless mentally ill can be better implemented, especially thorough evaluation of candidates for community care and changed criteria for commitment. The need of locking up those prone to violence is also discussed.

Lamb, H. Richard. "What Did We Really Expect from Deinstitutionalization?" Hospital and Community Psychiatry, 32 (2), February 1981:105–109.
Unrealistic expectations of deinstitutionalization include "normalization" and "helping them become part of the mainstream of society." For only a small minority could such expectations be realistic. The solution is to invest effort and funds, especially by the private sector, that will enable former mental patients to live with dignity.

Lamb, H. Richard. "Will We Save the Homeless Mentally Ill?" American Journal of Psychiatry, 147 (5), May 1990:649–651.
In 1984, the American Psychiatric Association's Task Force on the Homeless Mentally Ill recommended a comprehensive and integrated system of care. Because little has been done since then, the author recommends case management, priority status, vast use of public mental health funds, involuntary hospitalization and conservatorships.

Lamb, H. Richard. "Young Adult Chronic Patients: The New Drifters." <u>Hospital and Community Psychiatry</u>, <u>33</u> (6), June 1982:465-468.

    Young, chronic mental patients previously took asylum from age-related stresses in a lifetime of hospitalization. (Age-related stresses are identified as the search for a sense of identity, independence, satisfying relationships, and vocational choice.) With this option now removed, they drift from city to city, or drift within the same city from one living situation to another. The solution is to reach them while they are still young and motivated in order to help them become socially engaged and to help them make realistic decisions and establish realistic goals.

Lamb, H. Richard, Roger Schock, Peter W. Chen, and Bruce Gross. "Psychiatric Needs in Local Jails: Emergency Issues." <u>American Journal of Psychiatry</u>, <u>141</u> (6), June 1984:774-777.

    The solutions to meeting the needs of mentally ill jail inmates include psychiatric teams working inside jails and training booking personnel to recognize psychiatric problems.

Lambert, Bruce. "In a Revision of AIDS Policy, Koch Offers Shelters and Wider Services." <u>New York Times</u>, May 14, 1989:20.

    Among the new programs announced by Edward I. Koch, the Mayor of New York City, is the city's first two AIDS shelters for the homeless. This program is designed to relieve that part of the overcrowding of New York City hospitals that results from AIDS patients who, although medically ready to be discharged, are left there because they have no homes.

Lambert, Bruce. "Koch and Timing: Plan for Homeless." <u>New York Times</u>, September 8, 1987:13.

    The author reviews reactions to New York City Mayor Edward I. Koch's announcement that he is initiating a program to involuntarily hospitalize the homeless who are unable to care for themselves.

Lambert, Bruce. "Koch Receives Support on His Homeless Policy." <u>New York Times</u>, September 1, 1987:11.

    The Mayor of New York City, Edward I. Koch, received an enthusiastic response when he addressed the convention of the American Psychological Association concerning his plan to involuntarily hospitalize homeless people "when they appear incapable of caring for themselves."

Lambert, Bruce. "Koch Says Idea for Homeless Was Meant to Spur Albany." New York Times, September 4, 1987:11.
   The mayor of New York City, Edward I. Koch, explained that part of the reason for his plan to hospitalize mentally ill homeless people against their will was to spur the state to provide more facilities for the mentally ill homeless. The author reviews reactions to Mayor Koch's announcement, spending for the mentally ill by the city and state, facilities available for the mentally ill, and the need for those facilities.

Lambert, Bruce. "Priest's Book Discloses Unorthodox Methods to Aid Homeless." New York Times, December 1, 1987:16.
   In reviewing the book by Bruce Ritter, Covenant House: Lifeline to the Street, the author focuses on unorthodox ways by which Ritter has acquired buildings for homeless youths.

Lambert, Bruce. "Study of Homeless Finds Alarming AIDS Rate." New York Times, June 5, 1989:Y15.
   Of 169 men at the municipal shelter on Wards Island, 105 tested positively for AIDS, a rate of 62 percent. This two-and-a-half-year study has these limitations: (1) It does not report how many men were offered tests because they appeared to be at risk or showed symptoms of AIDS, and (2) since the tests were voluntary, the participants selected themselves instead of being chosen randomly.

Lancaster, Hal. "Litigious U.S. Society Affords Fewer Lawyers to the Poor Nowadays." Wall Street Journal, June 3, 1986:1, 18.
   Legal services for the poor has experienced a cutback in amount and quality of services that affect the homeless.

Lander, Louise. "The Mental Health Con Game." Health/Pac Bulletin, 65, July-August 1975:1-8, 16-25.
   The many topics of this article include welfare hotels, the legitimacy of the state, political motives of deinstitutionalization, falling between the cracks, and the gap between actuality and political and professional ideology.

Lang, Michael H.   Homeless Amid Affluence: Structure and Paradox in American Political Economy.   New York, Praeger, 1989.
The foci of this book are housing, community development patterns, economic segregation, and problems of the urban underclass.   The author views homelessness as a consequence of how the American political economy permits community development patterns to be based on racism and self-interests.   The solution to homelessness is to reform our housing and employment policies.

Langway, Lynn, Renee Michael, Mary Lord, Dianne H. McDonald, Barbara Burgower, and Rick Ruiz.   "A Nation of Runaway Kids."   Newsweek, October 18, 1982:97-98.
This overview of runaway children in the United States examines reasons why children run, their entrance into street life (especially deviant sexual activities), and organized activities to help them.   The authors discuss chicken hawks, flirts, pimps, the Kleenex mentality, combat zone, and the Runaway and Homeless Youth Act.   They mention The Runaway Place in Boston, Noah's Ark and Covenant House in New York City, Toughlove in Pennsylvania, Bridge Over Troubled Waters in Boston, and Family Connection in Houston.

Larew, Barbara J.   "Strange Strangers: Serving Transients."   Social Casework: The Journal of Contemporary Social Work, 63, February 1980:107-113.
The homeless lack bonding ties to social groups. The types of homeless are hobos, skid row inhabitants, rogues, shopping bag ladies, bums, SRO inhabitants, vagrant families, inebriants, derelicts, and tramps. The author contrasts myths and realities of this population and as the solution proposes that social workers provide more effective help.

Larkin, Andrew.   "Ghettos of Rural Poverty."   New Society, 44 (815), May 18, 1978:362-364.
The author criticizes housing authorities in southern England for sending the homeless to permanently live in caravan sites (sites zoned for temporary stays in mobile homes).

Larson, Mel.   Mud 'N' Mercy in Memphis.   Wheaton, Illinois: Van Kampen Press, 1955.
This book is an overview of evangelical rescue work on the Memphis skid row.

Larson, Mel.   Skid Row Stopgap: The Memphis Story.
Wheaton, Illinois: Van Kampen Press, 1950.
      The author summarizes the first four years of the
Memphis Union Mission, founded in 1945.

Lasker, Loula D.   "Rediscovered Men."   Survey Graphic,
July 1933:357-361, 388.
      Camp Bluefield at Blauvelt, New York, is described
as "the ideal in the care of homeless unemployed men."
The author's overview of the occupational background and
health of the men and the work program and recreation in
the camp places emphasis on social relations among the
men.

Laubach, Frank Charles.   Why There Are Vagrants: A Study
Based On Examination of One Hundred Men.   New York:
Columbia University, 1916.
      Based on interviews with men who came in contact
with the Charity Organization Society of New York City,
the author attributes the individual causes of vagrancy
as moral, temperamental, mental, and physical disqualifi-
cations for work; the social causes as family problems,
economic maladjustments, misapplied philanthropy (giving
that encourages non-work), and government laxity.   The
solutions require various steps to overcome these causes,
including   industrial   insurance,   savings,   and church
involvement.   In addition, the educational system needs
to be made more applied or vocational.

Lauriat, Alison S.   "Sheltering Homeless Families: Beyond
an Emergency Response."   In The Mental Health Needs of
Homeless Persons, Ellen L. Bassuk, ed.   San Francisco:
Jossey-Bass, 1986:87-94.
      To   simply   provide   housing   will   not   solve   the
problems of the homeless.   The homeless must be provided
a   system   of   public-sector   social   services   that   are
capable of meeting their complex needs.   Social policy
must   be   developed   that   provides   housing   with   social
supports.

Lave, Judith R.   "Band-Aid Solutions."   Society, 6 (4),
May-June 1989:11-12.
      The   members   of   the   Committee   on   Health   Care   for
Homeless   People   of   the   Institute   of   Medicine   were
frustrated   because   they   were   addressing   a   secondary
problem, health care, when the primary problem of the
homeless is a lack of a home.

Lavelle, Tara, Richard Hammersley, and Alasdair Forsyth. "Personality as an Explanation of Drug Use." Journal of Drug Issues, 21 (3), Summer 1991:593-604.
    Data from standardized psychological instruments administered to 15 people in a residential drug treatment program, 15 people in a long-term hostel for the homeless, and 15 students in higher education call into question previous research that links personality with drug use. The results indicate that drug users are similar to the homeless, and both differ from the students.

Lawson, Carol. "A Vision Creates Sanctuary For City's Homeless Mothers." New York Times, July 14, 1986:18.
    This report on the work by Women in Need emphasizes their newest shelter, a collaborative effort with New York designers and home furnishings manufacturers.

Leach, John. "Providing for the Destitute." In Community Concern for the Mentally Disabled, J. K. Ewing and R. Olsen, eds. 1979.
    Focuses on the Simon Community and vagrancy in Great Britain. The causes of destitution are twofold: personal inadequacy and victimization by a competitive society. The Simon Community attempts to foster close emotional bonds and egalitarian relationships based upon dedication to Christ, to instill social values, to befriend and shelter, to resettle, and to offer specialized help that meets the physical and mental disabilities of the destitute.

Leach, John, and John K. Wing. "The Effectiveness of a Service for Helping Destitute Men." British Journal of Psychiatry, 133, 1978:481-492.
    In a project referred to as "action research," a research team evaluates the effectiveness of a voluntary organization in helping men become settled in independent accommodations and in the St. Mungo community in London. The effectiveness of the voluntary organization improved after the research team made suggestions for their work.

Leach, John, and John K. Wing. Helping Destitute Men. London: Tavistock, 1980.
    This study of St. Mungo's, an overnight shelter in London, whose residents, as in other reception centres, are primarily solitary, middle-aged to elderly men with severe disabilities, contrasts definitions of destitution, compares voluntary and public services, and

analyzes social policies. The handicapped have less
access to lodging homes and cheap rooms because of the
pressure now placed on these facilities due to the high
unemployment.

Leahy, David M. "Let's Stop Warehousing the Homeless."
Wall Street Journal, April 2, 1991:A21.
    Taking issue with an article by Albert R. Hunt in
the March 7, 1991, issue of the Wall Street Journal, the
author says that shelters for the homeless can indeed be
detrimental to neighborhoods.

Leavitt, Samuel. "The Tramps and the Law." The Forum,
2, September 1886:190-200.
    This overview of tramp laws in the United States
suggests that harsh and cruel treatment is not the right
approach. Alternatives are not provided.

Lee, Barrett A. "The Disappearance of Skid Row: Some
Ecological Evidence." Urban Affairs Quarterly, 16 (1),
September 1980:81-107.
    The thesis that skid row is disappearing (its
demographic composition becoming less distinctive) is
investigated by comparing census tract reports on 41 skid
rows. This comparison shows that due to urban renewal
and revitalization the skid row population is declining.
It is premature, however, to conclude that skid row life
is fading from the urban scene. Rather, skid rowers may
be decentralizing or moving to nearby areas.

Lee, Barrett A. "Residential Mobility on Skid Row:
Disaffiliation, Powerlessness, and Decision Making."
Demography, 15 (3), August 1978:285-300.
    The author tests decision making theory on a skid
row population and concludes that, unlike the middle
class, people who have weakened social attachments and
little control over their lives and resources find it
difficult to engage in calculated, long-term decision
making.

Lee, Barrett A. "Stability and Change in an Urban
Homeless Population." Demography, 26 (2), May 1989:323-
334.
    "Beginning in December of 1983, an ongoing series of
enumerations, or head counts, of the homeless has been
carried out in Nashville, Tennessee....(which) offers an
unprecedented opportunity to assess the accuracy of
hypothesized trends in the homeless population's size and

composition..." This enumeration has included both shelter and street counts. The widespread perception that the number of homeless people in Nashville is increasing rapidly is not substantiated. The numbers of homeless appear fairly stable, between 650 and 850 individuals, with seasonal variations. The ranks of the new homeless, especially women and blacks, seem to be contracting. The Nashville public, however, perceives a large increase in homelessness. This can be attributed to the homeless increasing their visibility by spending more time outdoors, moving from core to peripheral locations, and extensive publicity by the media. Because the enumeration did not begin until 1983, perhaps undetected changes in the size and composition of the homeless population occurred before this date.

Lee, Barrett A., Sue Hinze Jones, and David W. Lewis. "Public Beliefs About the Cause of Homelessness." Social Forces, 69 (1), September 1990:253-255.
Using a systematic random sample of 471 households from the greater Nashville area, the authors found that the public tends to blame homelessness on external factors rather than on individualistic ones. They especially attribute homelessness to structural forces and bad luck.

Lee, Edward. Prison, Camp and Pulpit: The Life of a City Missionary in the Slums, Talks and Tramps Here and There. Oswego, New York: R. J. Oliphant, 1889.
This volume follows the life story of a boy who, born in the slums, became a delinquent, a Union soldier, a criminal, a convict and then, born again, a revivalist preacher who worked on the Bowery.

Lee, Felicia R. "Already Struggling, Big Cities Are Hit Hard." New York Times, July 16, 1991:A16.
Officials of eastern seaboard cities such as New York City and Newark, New Jersey, had claimed that areas of their cities inhabited by the homeless, minorities, and immigrants had been undercounted. Their request for a recount was rejected by the Commerce Department.

Lee, Felicia R. "Dinkins Rejects Idea That Order Hits Homeless." New York Times, September 17, 1991:B3.
In response to criticisms of his plan to secure public housing, the mayor of New York City, David Dinkins, denies that the plan is a covert way to remove the homeless from public housing.

Leepson, Marc. "The Homeless: Growing National Problem." Editorial Research Reports, 11 (16), October 29, 1982:794-811.
    This overview of the homeless covers past American experiences (hobos and the Great Depression), the impact of the recession of the late 1970s (deinstitutionalization, social service cutbacks, loss of low-cost housing, and emergence of the new poor), sources of relief for the homeless, the question of who should have responsibility, examples of successful local efforts, and the problem of volunteer burnout.

Lefkowitz, Bernard. Tough Change: Growing Up On Your Own in America. New York: The Free Press, 1986.
    The "lost generation" (youths between 10 and 19 who grow up alone and end up on the streets of our cities) threatens our entire social fabric. Solutions to this national tragedy include on-the-job training, model youth programs, and wider adult participation in the youths' lives, particularly by teachers and school counselors.

LeGates, Richard T., and Chester Hartman. "Displacement." Clearinghouse Review, 15, July 1981:207-249.
    This overview of displacement in the United States pinpoints gentrification as a major cause of homelessness. The authors summarize the social characteristics of inmovers and outmovers and the fate of the displacees.

Lehner, Urban C. "In Japan the Homeless Often Get Little Aid and Less Sympathy." Wall Street Journal, June 2, 1992:A1, A10.
    In recounting the activities of Motoi Yoshioka, who works with the homeless in Osaka, Japan, one catches a glimpse of the Japanese homeless. Unlike the homeless in the United States, the homeless in Japan are mostly older men who work as day laborers. The homeless are invisible to most Japanese, while those who are aware of their presence consider them lazy.

Lemkow, Louis. "Equity: The State of the Art." Health Promotion, 4 (2), 1989:103-108.
    The homeless are among the groups listed as vulnerable to health risks. Policy-oriented research and analysis are needed.

Leonard, Maria. "An Heroic Generation." Wall Street Journal, March 18, 1991:A15.

In this letter to the editor, the author points out that the United States has been able to find enough money to build war camps halfway around the world but is not funding the war on homelessness.

Leslie, Connie, Pamela Abramson, Kate Robins, and Tessa Namuth. "Can a Shelter Be a School?" <u>Newsweek</u>, <u>113</u>, January 23, 1989:51.
A promising solution to the problem of educating the children of the homeless is to locate schools in shelters for the homeless.

Leventhal, Theodore. "Control Problems in Runaway Children." <u>Archives of General Psychiatry</u>, <u>9</u>, August 1963:122-128.
Based on interviews with runaways and nonrunaways, the author analyzes children who run away in terms of inner and outer control and uncontrol. He uses scales of outer uncontrol (external events) and concludes that runaways are significantly more concerned with being influenced, of trying to counteract such influences, and of having little influence or effect upon others. Running away is conceptualized as extreme, desperate behavior in response to a sense of imminent danger of loss of outer (environmental) control.

Leventhal, Theodore. "Inner Control Deficiencies in Runaway Children." <u>Archives of General Psychiatry</u>, <u>2</u>, August 1964:170-176.
The author discusses his main finding that, compared with nonrunaways, runaways have greater inner uncontrol.

Levine, Irene Shifren. "Homelessness: Its Implications for Mental Health Policy and Practice." <u>Psychosocial Rehabilitation Journal</u>, <u>8</u> (1), 1984:6-16.
The author surveys reasons for the homelessness of mentally ill persons, examines the relationship between homelessness and deinstitutionalization, describes public and private efforts that attempt to address the needs of this group, and suggests how mental health professionals can use their research, services, and training to help the homeless mentally ill.

Levine, Irene Shifren. "NIMH Initiatives for the Homeless Mentally Ill." <u>Alcohol Health and Research World</u>, <u>11</u> (3), 1987:18-21.

This article examines how the National Institutes of Mental Health is addressing the health-related needs of the homeless.

Levine, Irene Shifren. "Service Programs for the Homeless Mentally Ill." In The Homeless Mentally Ill, H. R. Lamb, ed. Washington, D.C.: American Psychiatric Association, 1984:173-200.

The homeless mentally ill suffer dual disenfranchisement, being adequately served neither by the mental health system nor the shelter network. The solutions are emergency shelters, outreach programs, drop-in centers, and crisis, transitional, and long-term housing. The needs of the currently homeless must be met, but we also must take steps to prevent homelessness. The author presents a typology of services, with examples of exemplary programs.

Levine, Irene Shifren, and A. D. Lezak. Research on the Homeless Mentally Ill: Current Status and Future Directions. Rockville, Maryland: National Institutes of Mental Health, 1985.

The authors review ten projects funded by the National Institutes of Mental Health (NIMH). They conclude that more research is needed to better understand the unique characteristics and service needs of the homeless mentally ill. Such research needs to be action orientated with the goals of preventing and ending homelessness.

Levine, Irene Shifren, A. D. Lezak, and H. H. Goldman. "Community Support System For the Homeless Mentally Ill." In The Mental Health Needs of Homeless Persons, Ellen Bassuk, ed. San Francisco: Jossey-Bass, 1986:27-42.

After detailing the needs of the homeless mentally ill, the authors argue that a demonstration program called the Federal Community Support Program can be adapted to the mentally ill homeless. They stress that a broad, coordinated system of housing, mental health, and social welfare support for the homeless is needed.

Levine, Irene Shifren, and C. Kennedy. "The Homeless Mentally Ill: A Consultation Challenge." Consultation: An International Journal, 4 (1), Spring 1984:52-63.

Consultation has the potential to be an effective mechanism for improving opportunities and services for the homeless mentally ill. The authors summarize the goals and objectives of such consultation, describe who might best provide it, and identify three areas that provide opportunities for consultation: consultation with shelter-based populations, with street populations, and on systems improvement.

Levine, Irene Shifren, and J. W. Stockdill. "Mentally Ill and Homeless: A National Problem." In Treating the Homeless: Urban Psychiatry's Challenge, B. Jones, ed. Washington, D.C.: American Psychiatric Association Press, 1986:1-17.
  The mentally ill homeless are "caught in a bind," for mental health services ordinarily do not reach out to the streets, and few shelters offer mental health services. Because of the stress that the homeless mentally ill face (unemployment, lack of housing, and functional disabilities), comprehensive community care must be provided. Reinstitutionalization is not the answer.

Levine, Irene Shifren, and Loretta Haggard. "NIMH Initiatives for the Homeless Mentally Ill." Alcohol Health and Research World, 11 (3), Spring 1987:18-19, 34-35.
  The authors summarize activities of the National Institutes of Mental Health in research, technical assistance, service demonstration, and national leadership projects.

Levine, Renee Shai, Diane Metzendorf, and Kathryn A. VanBoskirk. "Runaway and Throwaway Youth: A Case for Early Intervention with Truants." Social Work Education, 8 (2), Winter 1986:93-106.
  Based on questionnaires and interviews with 38 girls and boys at the Youth Emergency Service in Philadelphia, the authors report the race, sex, age, and proportion that consider themselves to be runaways (47.4 percent), throwaways (44.7 percent), or both (7.9 percent). After focusing on why children run away, the authors recommend that the school be the place of intervention to prevent youths from becoming homeless.

Levine, Richard. "Grand Central May Bid Homeless to Travel On." New York Times, March 22, 1987:E6.
  Twenty-four people were arrested at Grand Central Terminal in New York City, many of whom seem homeless. The president of Metro-North is "preparing a grand plan for a restored and invigorated Grand Central, with upgraded stores and more restaurants and activities such

as concerts and dances." Homeless advocates are upset.
They are encouraging the homeless to use train and bus
stations, informing them that they have the same rights
as any other person so long as their conduct is reasonable.

Levine, Stanley. "Runaways and Research in the Training
School." Crime and Delinquency, 8, 1962:40-45.
    After trying to determine the factors that stimulate
or abate the impulse to run from the Illinois State
Training School for Boys, officials modified the program.
They have intensified the boys' contacts during their
first week in the institution and have initiated a
program of home visits.

Levinson, Boris M. "A Comparative Study of Northern and
Southern Negro Homeless Men." Journal of Negro Education, 35 (2), 1966:144-150.
    A comparison of white and Negro residents of the
Bowery suggests that people coming from deprived environments can find skid row a stimulating experience that
reawakens latent intellectual abilities.

Levinson, Boris M. "Field Dependence in Homeless Men."
Journal of Clinical Psychology, 23 (2), 1967:152-154.
    To test his construct of the homeless personality,
the author administered the Short Form Embedded Figures
Test to 18 first-time applicants at the Emergency Shelter
in New York City and to 30 long-term residents at Camp La
Guardia. As hypothesized, the long-term homeless men
were significantly more field dependent than the first-
time applicants for shelter care.

Levinson, Boris M. "The Homeless Man: A Psychological
Enigma." Mental Hygiene, 47, October 1963:590-601.
    Psychologists have produced very few studies of the
homeless, and most of them are inadequate. Generalizing
from these studies has been difficult due to biases in
the samples, inadequate measuring instruments, and
inadequate definitions of homelessness. The cause of
homelessness is a learned detachment from the values of
society that leads to a desire to withdraw from ordinary
social life. This learned detachment occurs in all
strata of society. Interdisciplinary studies are needed.

Levinson, Boris M. "The Socioeconomic Status, Intelligence, and Psychometric Pattern of Native-Born White

Homeless Men." <u>Journal of Genetic Psychology</u>, <u>91</u>, December 1957:205-211.

Results of the WAIS test administered to 50 men at the Men's Shelter in New York City showed that, compared with most homeless, these men are older and have better education and occupational backgrounds. This probably indicates that native-born Americans have more schooling and resources and better employment than the foreign born.

Levinson, Boris M. "Some Aspects of the Personality of the Native-Born White Homeless Man as Revealed by the Rorschach." <u>Psychiatric Quarterly Supplement</u>, <u>32</u> (2), 1958:278-286.

Analysis of Rorschach tests given to 40 Bowery men indicates emotional immaturity, depression, difficulty in adjusting to the world, lack of drive, goals, and adaptability, feelings of despair and worthlessness, few interests, apathy, indifference, passivity, insecurity, a low level of social contacts, little ability to empathize, difficulty in understanding others and themselves, intellectual inefficiency, and thinking disorders.

Levinson, Boris M. "Subcultural Studies of Homeless Men." <u>Transactions of the New York Academy of Sciences</u>, <u>29</u>, December 1966:165-183.

Using the Rorschach, TAT, Rosenzweig Picture-Frustration, embedded figure test, and Benton Visual Retention test, the author found that the homeless men he studied value their independence or freedom from institutional control and exhibit an alienation syndrome and the frustration of dependency. They run from school, marriage, and job. The increase of southern Negroes on northern skid rows is due to the matriarchal role of women and the decline of the family.

Levinson, Boris M., and Harry Mezei. "Self-Concepts and Ideal-Self Concepts of Run-Away Youths: Counseling Implications." <u>Psychological Reports</u>, <u>26</u>, 1970:871-874.

Using Osgood's Semantic Differential Scales, 25 runaways rated themselves on (a) as "I really am" (self-concept) and (b) as "I would like to be" (ideal-self concept). The researchers found that the runaways largely failed to approximate their idealized selves and that they see themselves most unfavorably on the factors of evaluation and activity. This finding implies that counselors should work on developing runaways' self esteem and self acceptance, and help them put meaning into their lives.

Levinson, David.   "Skid Row in Transition."   Urban Anthropology, 3 (1), 1974:79-93.
    Based on participant observation and interviews, the author examines changes in skid row since World War II. The topics are deterioration in the quality of life, a decrease in population, the change from consisting primarily of transients to a heterogeneous population (old pensioners, resident workers, transient workers, full-time alcoholics, young black men, and drug addicts), and the disappearance of the traditional skid row area. Reasons for each of these changes are provided.

Levitan, Sar A.   Programs in Aid of the Poor, fifth edition.   Baltimore: Johns Hopkins University Press, 1985.
    The author surveys all existing federally funded programs designed to aid the poor and evaluates the impact of the Reagan administration on these programs. These programs are cash support, provision of goods and services, those designed to affect the next generation, and providing opportunities for the working poor.   He explores presuppositions of the Great Society, character-istics of the poor, and definitions of poverty.   He also outlines a suggested comprehensive program of support and services.

Levy, Edwin Z.   "Some Thoughts about Patients Who Run Away from Residential Treatment and the Staff They Leave Behind."   Psychiatric Quarterly, 46 (1), 1972:1-21.
    After reviewing typologies and motivations of runaways, the author analyzes data on 17 girls who ran away from the Menninger Foundation Children's Hospital (residential treatment center) between November 1961 and September 1970.   He develops a typology consisting of angry defiance, psychotic disorganization, escape, to go on one's own, and fusion with parents and stresses group dynamics, developmental striving for independence, staff rage and derivatives, and separation and abandonment.

Levy, John.   "The Homeless Boys' Retreat."   Mental Hygiene Quarterly, July 1933.
    The author expresses concerns about the psychologi-cal development of the "quarter of a million homeless adolescent boys travelling on freight trains."   He suggests that the situation is so bad that the "social

dynamics" will create a psychopathic personality which, in turn, might ignite a political revolution.

Lewin, Tamar. "Nation's Homeless Veterans Battle a New Foe: Defeatism." New York Times, December 30, 1987:1, 7.
   The author discusses reactions of homeless Vietnam veterans to their homelessness and to the failure of the Veterans Administration to provide a comprehensive program to reach out to them. Between 235,000 and 750,000 veterans are estimated to be homeless. The Veterans Administration takes the position that there is no reason for a veteran to be homeless, that they have vacant beds that homeless veterans are welcome to use. The reasons given for the homelessness of these veterans are "a growing shortage of low-cost housing; less demand for low-skilled jobs; an increasingly fragmented family structure; drug, alcohol and mental problems; and the deinstitutionalization of psychiatric patients."

Lewis, Hylan. "Culture of Poverty? What Does it Matter?" In The Culture of Poverty: A Critique, Eleanor Burke Leacock, ed. New York: Simon and Schuster, 1971:345-363.
   The author first shows how the concept of the culture of poverty is significant for behavioral scientists, to the images and life chances of poor people, and to the structuring of relations among groups. He then states that its use carries significant political implications and enumerates 15 ways in which this concept matters to science, to public policy, and to Americans in general.

Lewis, Margaret R., and Alan F. Meyers. "The Growth and Development Status of Homeless Children Entering Shelters in Boston." Public Health Report, 104 (3), May-June 1989:247-250.
   After examining the intake reviews collected by the pediatric nurse practitioner who visited ten family shelters and one hotel in Boston, the authors conclude that 94 percent of the 213 children were in the care of their mothers, 92 percent were younger than 5 years of age, 65 percent were blacks, 20 percent whites, 11 percent Hispanic, 89 percent of the families were receiving Aid to Families with Dependent Children, 90 percent were receiving Medicaid benefits, 72 percent were receiving food stamps, and 52 percent were receiving benefits under the Special Supplemental Food Program for Women, Infants and Children. Eighty-five percent of the

children had regular sources of primary pediatric care, and 23 percent had medical problems. The weight and height measurements of these children were similar to national samples of low-income children.

Lewis, Morris. "Taking the Work-Cure at Medicine Lake." *Survey Graphic*, 23, January 1934:31-33, 48.
Rev. Wepaul founded Mission Farm 12 miles west of Minneapolis in 1926 to help the elderly homeless unemployed, a group of "permanent poor to which neither our institutions nor our philosophy are geared." The farm is basically self sufficient, producing its own food and building its own buildings, and instills positive social values and a sense of belonging and meaning.

Lewis, Orlando Faulkland. "The American Tramp." *Atlantic*, 101, June 1908:744-753.
The author discusses the viewpoints of psychology, sociology, and the press. His topics include railroads and injuries, the law and sentencing, lodging places, missions, and organized charities. His thesis is that our inconsistent ways of dealing with vagrants encourage vagrancy. The solutions are to recognize vagrancy as a national problem, to either imprison or force the able-bodied to work, to enforce laws and give harsher sentences, for railroads and towns to cooperate, to pass harsher laws, to establish health supervision of lodging houses, and to require work in exchange for mission food and lodging.

Lewis, Orlando Faulkland. "Concerning Vagrancy: III-Municipal Lodging Houses." *Survey*, 22, September 4, 1909:749-759.
The author makes suggestions for operating temporary shelters with the requirement of compensatory work.

Lewis, Orlando Faulkland. "A National Committee on Vagrants." *Charities and The Commons*, 18, June 29, 1908:342-344.
Railroad officials consider vagrancy a national problem. The author reports the numbers of vagrants killed and injured on railroads during 1901-1905 and suggests that a national committee be formed to study the "tramp question."

Lewis, Orlando Faulkland. "Tramp Problem in the United States." In *The Treatment of the Offender*. New York:

Prison Association of New York, Sixty-Seventh Annual Report. Albany: The Argus Company, 1912:179-187.
    The author's central thesis is that tramps are a national problem and need to be dealt with on a level that recognizes the national character of the problem. The specific solutions he proposes include the establishment of farm colonies with compulsory work programs, reducing railway trespassing, charging the state instead of local bodies for the expense of maintaining vagrants in correctional institutions, prosecuting public begging, and establishing a national vagrancy committee.

Lewthwaite, T. John. "The Housing (Homeless Persons) Act 1977--A View." Trent Law Journal, 4, 1980:1-8.
    This article reviews the main provisions of the Housing Act adopted in December 1977 that "makes the problem of homelessness at least partly a legal one."

Lezak, A. D. "Synopses of NIMH-Funded Research Projects on the Homeless Mentally Ill." Rockville, Maryland: National Institutes of Mental Health, 1985.
    The author summarizes ten research projects funded by NIMH in 1982-1985.

Liddiard, Mark, and Susan Hutson. "Homeless Young People and Runaways: Agency Definitions and Processes." Journal of Social Policy, 20 (3), July 1991:365-388.
    To determine how agency personnel define homelessness and runaways, the authors examined data from research projects and interviewed 81 agency workers in Wales. They conclude that agency personnel use both external and internal definitions, and that they change their definitions to match their audiences (external) and use flexible definitions among themselves (internal). They also define individuals as deserving and undeserving of their help.

Light, Gordon F. "Banks on Both Coasts Launch Efforts to Aid Homeless As Number of Individuals and Families in Need Rises." American Banker, 150, December 23, 1985:19, 29.
    Various banks are working with voluntary groups to provide physical aid for the homeless.

Light, Gordon F. "Dime Savings Bank Assists Project to Shelter the Homeless." American Banker, 151, February 14, 1986:3, 9, 22.

The author reports on the financial arrangements of a $7.25 million housing project, the first in the state of New York to be built specifically for homeless people. Providing transitional housing (somewhere between homelessness and permanent housing) for 200 families, it will be designed to provide a limited stay of three to six months in order to enable homeless families "to move into the mainstream of society."

Light, Lou. The Modern Hobo: Ocean to Ocean. Santa Anna: Warden, 1913.
This autobiographical account of hoboing places emphasis on sensationalism. The author takes the position that economic causes underlie the social production of hobos, especially trusts and easy immigration laws.

Lilliefors, Manfred, Jr. "Social Casework and the Homeless Man." The Family, 9, January 1929:291-294.
There are four types of homeless men: migrant workers (hobo workmen), beggars, thieves, and petty criminals. The solutions should be fitted to each type. Shelters should be provided for the migrant workers (until economic change reduces their numbers), and rehabilitation through counseling (individual case work) should be made available for the others. The newer developments and increasing thoroughness of social work and the spread of social work to small towns and rural districts offers hope for the future.

Lincoln, Sheryl J. "Single-Room Residential Hotels Must Be Preserved as Low-Income Housing Alternative." Journal of Housing, 37, July 1980:383-386.
Taking the position that HUD needs to adopt policies that will preserve low-cost SRO housing, the author reports on residential hotels in Portland, Seattle, Denver, and Pittsburgh.

Lindelius, Rolf, and Inna Salum. "Alcoholism and Crime: A Comparative Study of Three Groups of Alcoholics." Journal of Studies on Alcohol, 36 (11), November 1975:1452-1457.
The authors examine the relationship between degree of alcoholism and criminality. Homeless alcoholics are one of the three categories they use to measure degree of alcoholism, among whom they found the highest degree of criminal behavior.

Lindelius, Rolf, and Inna Salum. "Criminality Among Homeless Men." <u>British Journal of Addiction</u>, <u>71</u> (2), 1976:149-153.
Comparing 202 homeless males with the general population showed that the homeless were over-represented in the Criminal Register. The homeless had little serious crime, high recidivism, and mild penalties.

Linden, Fabian. "The American Dream." <u>Across the Board</u>, <u>28</u> (5), May 1991:7, 10.
The author concludes that economic production and living standards during the past 20 years increased at about the same rate as during the previous 50 or so years, and will continue to do so during the next decade. An increase in the number of homeless people, however, is troubling.

Lindsay, Vachel. <u>Adventures While Preaching the Gospel of Beauty</u>. New York: Macmillan, 1916.
This account of a walk from Springfield, Illinois, to New Mexico places emphasis on tramping and poetry.

Lindsay, Vachel. <u>A Handy Guide for Beggars, Especially Those in the Poetic Fraternity</u>. New York: Macmillan, 1930.
This book relates hobo experiences of a man who sometimes earns his living by lecturing on poetry.

Linhorst, Donald M. "A Redefinition of the Problem of Homelessness among Persons with a Chronic Mental Illness." <u>Journal of Sociology and Social Welfare</u>, <u>17</u> (4), December 1990:43-56.
"Two definitions of the problem of homelessness among persons with a chronic mental illness are examined, along with their implied solutions and ramifications for social policy. Homelessness among this group is first viewed as a result of deinstitutionalization, and secondly, as the outcome of a critical shortage of low-income housing. Solutions stemming from the deinstitutionalization definition of homelessness, reinstitutionalization or improvement in the mental health system, are seen as inadequate to deal with the problem of homelessness among the mentally ill. Instead, state departments of mental health are called upon to provide a leadership role in the development of affordable housing."

Linkletter, Art. I Didn't Do It Alone: The Autobiography
of Art Linkletter. Ottawa, Illinois: Caroline House,
1980.
     The author of this autobiography mentions that
during a period he calls his "hobo days" (when he was
sixteen years old) he rode the rails while crossing the
country.

Linnen, Beth M. "By Combining Resources, Lenders Aid the
Homeless." Savings Institutions, 109 (10), October
1988:74-75.
     The author analyzes the operation of Samco, a
California lending consortium designed to encourage
investments in the inner city.

Lipsky, Michael. "The Welfare State as Workplace."
Working Papers for a New Society, 7, 1980:33-38.
     The author's thesis is that the social welfare
bureaucracy makes life difficult for both welfare workers
and their clients and that social workers need to
recognize their essential alliance with their clients.

Lipsky, Michael, and Steven Rathgeb Smith. "When Social
Problems Are Treated as Emergencies." Social Service
Review, 63 (1), March 1989:5-25.
     The authors' analysis of implications of treating
such social problems as homelessness as emergencies
include quick response, relaxation of eligibility
requirements, drama, and media attention.

Lipton, Frank R., Albert Sabatini, and Steven E. Katz.
"Down and Out in the City: The Homeless Mentally Ill."
Hospital and Community Psychiatry, 34 (9), September
1983:817-821.
     Of 100 homeless patients treated at Bellevue Psychi-
atric Hospital in New York City, 96.6 percent had been
previously hospitalized for mental illness. Seventy-two
percent were diagnosed as schizophrenic and 13.3 percent
as suffering from personality disorders. The causes for
this high incidence of mental illness among the homeless
are deinstitutionalization, the inability to cope with
mental health bureaucracies, and the depletion of SROs.
The solution is to develop comprehensive, flexible, and
accessible treatment programs coupled with tailored
support systems. Residential programs need to be made
available for schizophrenics.

Livingston, Leon Ray.   The Curse of Tramp Life: A True Story of Actual Tramp Life Written by Himself.   Erie: A-No.1 Publishing Company, 1912.

Although tramp life is filled with hardship and danger, men become tramps because of wanderlust and the search for work. The solution is to talk wayward boys out of a cursed tramp life by explaining what a foolish choice they are making.

Livingston, Leon Ray.   From Coast to Coast with Jack London.   Erie: The A-No.1 Publishing Company, 1917. (Reprinted in 1969 by the Black Letter Press of Grand Rapids, Michigan.)

"A-No 1, The Famous Tramp" recounts his adventures while traveling with Jack London from New York to California.

Livingston, Leon Ray.   Life and Adventures of A-No.1, America's Most Celebrated Tramp.   Cambridge Springs: A-No.1 Publishing Company, 1910.

This autobiographical account written at the age of 38 focuses on the author's travels, work, and other experiences since he left home when he was 11. It presents an insider's view of tramp culture. The three types of tramps are kid tramps (minors), distillery tramps (drunks), and scenery tramps (confirmed rovers). The causes of tramping are wanderlust and the corrupting influence of skid rows on impressionable youth. Separate solutions are suggested for each type. Kid tramps should be returned to their parents where the problem can be struck at its root. Distillery tramps should be kept on the move by breaking up their camps in the thickets and stock-yards and close up the "dives" and "hang-out" saloons in the slums. There is no solution for the scenery tramp, but he does no one harm. Some say yeggmen are tramps, but they are not. Yeggmen are criminal gun-toters and need to be locked up for life.

Livingston, Leon Ray. Mother Declasse of the Hoboes and Other Stories.   Erie: The A-No.1 Publishing Company, 1918.

Mrs. Declasse operated a lodging house in New Orleans, where many tramps wintered. The author lists 47 types of tramps.

Livingston, Leon Ray. The Snare of the Road. Erie: The A-No.1 Publishing Company, 1916.

Many youths are snared into a hobo life by the romantic tales of railroad hobos.

Livingston, Leon Ray. *The Ways of the Hobo*. Erie: A-No 1 Publishing Company, 1915.
After being on the road for 30 years, the author undertook the task of educating the American public about the tramp problem. In this book he mainly recounts experiences with legal authorities. A-No 1 advocates that in order to solve the tramp menace "the national authorities, preferably the Inter-State Commerce Commission, be vested with the strict supervision of every branch of public vagabondage." This should include authority over "the thieving ambulators and the loathsome and ever alien gypsies." The author also proposes the establishment of a national tramp bureau, national tramp passbooks, national employment agencies, and national public works.

Loafmann, Glenn. "Bringing Good Tidings to the Afflicted." *The Christian Century*, April 23, 1986:407-408.
Those who follow Jesus Christ are called "not to visions of glory, but to deeds of services of caring." Meeting the needs of the homeless is a part of that service.

Lochhead, Carol. "All Alone, with No Home." *Insight On the News*, 4 (20), May 16, 1988:12-15.
The author discusses the ideas that shelter workers have about the causes and solutions of homelessness. They view the primary causes as the breakdown of the family and deinstitutionalization. Intensive community mental health services are featured as the solution, with the suggestion that building more shelters will only intensify the problem. The author profiles two homeless people, Sam Bryce and Maria Rodriguez.

Lochhead, Carol. "Door Opening to Dignity." *Insight On the News*, 4 (20), May 16, 1988:16-18.
This article profiles the operation of three shelters, Christian Temporary Housing Facilities in Orange, California, the Urban Family Center in New York City, and Transition House in Los Angeles. The common theme uniting these shelters is the attempt to restore dignity and instill pride in the homeless by getting them to take jobs. It includes a vignette of Je'Roi Gray.

Lochhead, Carol. "Nowhere to Go, Always in Sight." Insight On the News, 4 (20), May 16, 1988:8-11.
 The author discusses contrasting estimates of the numbers of homeless and divergent attitudes toward the homeless, including fear, hostility, and compassion. She includes vignettes on Ilitutuk, Richard Kinzinger, and Red Dog.

Locke, Harvey J. "Unemployed Men in Chicago Shelters." Sociology and Social Research, 19, May-June 1935:420-428.
 Based on participant observation, interviewing, and a study of the records of the Chicago Service Bureau for Men, the author classifies the homeless into five types: casual laborers, steady unskilled workers, bums and beggars, skilled tradesmen, and white-collar workers. The term "shelterization" is used to refer to men who previously lived in residential neighborhoods becoming "acquainted and habituated to the type of life and culture of Hobohemia." The causes of homelessness are the depression, maladjustments in work, personal inadequacy (physical and personal handicaps), gambling, alcoholism, detachment from families, and marital discord.

Lodge Patch, I. C. "Homeless Men in London: I. Demographic Findings in a Lodging House Sample." British Journal of Psychiatry, 118 (544), March 1971:313-317.
 A random sample of 123 men in a London shelter shows that homeless men tend to be lower class, unemployed, drifters, unmarried, and exhibit physical and personality disorders.

Loewenstein, Gaither. "The New Underclass: A Contemporary Sociological Dilemma." The Sociological Quarterly, 26 (1), 1985:35-48.
 The thesis is that "a new underclass is emerging in America, comprised of the sons and daughters of previously mobile working-class citizens." The cause of this phenomenon is "the combined effects of demographic and labor market changes," which are squeezing large numbers of young workers out of the work force. As these young people become aware "of their limited chances for upward career mobility, they begin to take on the behavioral characteristics conventionally associated with members of the underclass." The author uses life histories to illustrate the applicability of labor market segmentation theory.

Logan, Andy. "Around City Hall: Challenges." New Yorker, 61, August 19, 1985:78-85.
    In reporting on the political aspiration and activities of Mayor Edward I. Koch, the author summarizes the work done by former President Jimmy Carter and his wife Rosalynn for a group called Habitat for Humanity. They have helped to rehabilitate a six-story tenement at 742 East Sixth Street in New York City.

Logan, Andy. "Around City Hall: God Bless Us, Every One!" New Yorker, 60, December 24, 1984:68-73.
    This review of national and state political activities reports that after Mayor Koch took a night ride in a city van to pick up homeless people he made a statement that some homeless people are homeless by choice rather than by necessity ("a life style"). The author suggests that when homeless people refuse the mayor's invitation to stay at a city shelter it is "more a commentary on the shelters than on the motivation of the homeless."

Logan, Andy. "Around City Hall: Steerage." New Yorker, 60, May 21, 1984:110-121.
    In recounting the political activities of Mayor Koch, the author mentions the mayor's proposal to house up to 500 homeless on ships in Staten Island's harbor.

London, Jack. "Hoboes that Pass in the Night." Cosmopolitan, 44, December 1907:190-197.
    In this account of his tramping experiences, the author stresses pride in making good time in hopping freights across the country and recounts incidents with sheriffs and others. He also describes tough camps.

London, Jack. "'Holding Her Down': More Reminiscences of the Underworld." Cosmopolitan, 43 (2), June 1907:142-150.
    London's account of his "train-jumping" provides details on how trainmen kill hobos by using a coupling-pin attached to a bell-cord.

London, Jack. Jack London on the Road: The Tramp Diary and Other Hobo Writings, Richard W. Etulain, ed. Logan, Utah: Utah State University Press.
    This volume is a collection of Jack London's short stories about his experiences as a hobo.

London, Jack. "The March of Kelly's Army: The Story of an Extraordinary Migration." <u>Cosmopolitan</u>, <u>43</u> (6), October 1907:643-648.
    The author recounts his participation in the ill-fated attempt by General Kelly to lead 2,000 hobos in a protest march from California to Washington, D.C. London joined the group at Council Bluffs, Iowa.

London, Jack. "My Life in the Underworld: A Reminiscence and a Confession." <u>Cosmopolitan</u>, <u>43</u> (1), May 1907:17-22.
    London recounts the stories he told police and others while hoboing in order to avoid arrest and obtain handouts.

London, Jack. "The 'Pen': Long Days in a County Penitentiary." <u>Cosmopolitan</u>, <u>43</u> (4), August 1907:373-380.
    The author writes about his 30-day stay in the jail at Niagara Falls for vagrancy.

London, Jack. <u>The People of the Abyss</u>. New York: Archer House, 1963.
    The author put on old clothing and entered East London, where he lived among the city's poverty stricken. This took place during 1902-1903.

London, Jack. "Pictures: Stray Memories of Life in the Underworld." <u>Cosmopolitan</u>, <u>43</u> (5), September 1907:513-518.
    The author gives a romanticized account of his adventures in what he calls Hoboland.

London, Jack. "'Pinched:' A Prison Experience." <u>Cosmopolitan</u>, <u>43</u> (3), July 1907:263-270.
    The author recounts his arrest, trial, and conviction for vagrancy in Niagara Falls.

London, Jack. <u>The Road</u>. New York: Macmillan, 1907.
    The author discusses the survival techniques of tramps, from the ability to ride freights to the ability to suspend one's feelings in order to honor the standards of the group. These standards differ from society's, and probably from one tramp to another, but for one's survival they must be upheld. The stories originally appeared in <u>Cosmopolitan</u> in 1907.

London, Jack. "Rods and Gunnels." <u>Bookman</u>, <u>15</u>, August 1902:541-544.

The author explains the intimacies of riding under trains. He states that since even many tramps do not know the difference between rods and gunnels, the "stray and passing sociologist" ought not to assume that he is knowledgeable about tramping.

London, Jack. "Some Adventures with the Police." <u>Cosmopolitan</u>, <u>44</u>, March 1908:417-423.
    This recounting of confrontations with the police illustrates the mutual animosity of police and hobos.

Longworth, R. C. "Lost Jobs Leave Legacy of Despair." <u>Chicago Tribune</u>, September 29, 1985:1, 24.
    This analysis of the causes of localized poverty includes these topics: migrants, underclass, dropping out of school, unemployment, and lack of business investments.

Lorch, Donatella. "Hotel in Queens is Focus of Shift on the Homeless." <u>New York Times</u>, February 7, 1992:A1.
    Advocates for the homeless, arguing that the Kennedy Inn will not provide safe and decent housing, protest the city's plan to shelter 150 families there.

Lorch, Donatella. "Slaying of Engineer Evokes a Neighborhood's Tensions." <u>New York Times</u>, July 31, 1989:34.
    Following the killing of an engineer, residents of the neighborhood of Columbia University are reacting negatively to the homeless. The residents of this area of high rents, co-op conversions, and fancy stores express fears of panhandlers and drifters. The implication of these reactions is that the engineer was slain by a homeless person.

Lorch, Donatella. "Study Finds Homeless Lag in School." <u>New York Times</u>, September 12, 1989:B3.
    A study of homeless children indicates that their academic level is below that of housed children. Advocates for the homeless claim that this is due to homeless families "being moved from shelter to shelter during their academic year."

Love, Edmund G. <u>Subways Are For Sleeping</u>. New York: Harcourt Brace, 1956.
    The author, who was homeless for an extended period of time, devotes a chapter to each of nine homeless people whom he knows who do not live on skid row. He examines their socialization, coping mechanisms, and

attitudes. Some of these individuals have made marvelous adjustments to their life situation.

Lovejoy, Owen R. "Uncle Sam's Runaway Boys." The Survey, 69 (3), March 1933:99-101.
    Only about 5 percent of the 300,000-member army of transient boys in our cities are homeless. The question ought not to be what we can do with them but what we can do to keep boys from leaving home. The causes are diverse. The primary cause is a lack of services in the home town that causes a severing of bonds. A small percentage is due to wanderlust and the abnormals (defined as the congenital defectives, lazy, dishonest, and depraved). The solution is a comprehensive program of services to children and youth that includes home relief, an educational system, and a program of recreation. Specifically, groups of boys should work under overseers to reforest barren land or to help distraught farmers. Boys' camps should be opened that offer programs of work, study, and recreation.

Low, Nicholas, and Bruce Crawshaw. "Homeless Youth: Patterns of Belief." Australian Journal of Social Issues, 20 (1), February 1985:23-34.
    Based on interviews with 22 policymakers, the authors analyze how attitudes shape social policy concerning youth homelessness.

Lowell, Josephine Shaw. "Five Months Work for the Unemployed in New York City." Charities Review, 3 (7), May 1894:323-342.
    This report on charitable activities with the unemployed in New York City lists expenditures in providing employment to people who "would rather die than beg."

Lowell, Mrs. Charles Russell. "The Economic and Moral Effects of Public Outdoor Relief." Proceedings of the National Council on Charities and Correction, 1890:81-91.
    The author argues that relief by public money (money raised by taxes) can have deleterious effects. It weakens character and encourages non-productivity, gambling, recklessness, and extravagance. She essentially covers the conservative-liberal debate that heated up reactions to the homeless 100 years later, in the 1980s and 1990s.

Lowrey, L.   "Runaways and Nomads."   <u>American Journal of Orthopsychiatry</u>, <u>11</u>, 1941:775-782.
    This study is based on 2,756 runaways seen at the New York Travelers Aid Society during 1935-1939. The definition of runaway is very broad as it covers people whose ages range from 6 to 102. The largest group (19.4 percent) was composed of 16-year olds. Through the age of 18 there were more males, but more females after this age. The primary motivations for running away were unhappiness and feeling unwanted and rejected at home. The author identifies a type he calls nomads, or chronic wanderers. He concludes that nomadism is caused either by economic needs or schizophrenia of the simple dementing type.

Lozier, John N. "Modern Poorhouses Help Spread Disease." <u>Wall Street Journal</u>, December 6, 1991:A15.
    The executive director of the National Health Care for the Homeless Council reports that overcrowded and poorly ventilated shelters spread tuberculosis and AIDS among the homeless.

Lubasch, Arnold H.   "Reports Contrast Housing in New York City."   <u>New York Times</u>, July 30, 1989:17.
    This article reports that New York City's "10-year housing plan does not devote sufficient resources to the more acute housing needs of poor families with children and the elderly poor who are currently homeless."

Lubeck, Steven G., and Emprey T. Lamar.   "Mediatory vs. Total Institution: The Case of the Runaway."   <u>Journal of Social Problems</u>, <u>16</u> (2), 1968-69:242-260.
    One hundred thirty-one runaway boys, aged 15 to 18, were randomly assigned to a mediatory institution in an urban community and 93 to an isolated total institution. Stepwise regression analyses, used to examine the relationship of 30 predictor variables, showed that to predict their running away behavior required not only knowing the personal characteristics of the boys but also the dynamics of the correctional institutions. The rate of running away, however, was almost identical: 39 percent at the total institution and 37 percent at the mediatory institution.

Lubenow, Gerald C.   "Taking Aim at Panhandlers." <u>Newsweek</u>, October 29: 1984:14, 17.
    A backlash against the homeless is occurring in Washington, D.C., Santa Cruz, San Francisco, and Phoenix.

Territoriality and spatial invasion are topics. The author focuses on Seattle, where gentrification has introduced a new class of citizens and activities into an area traditionally occupied by alcoholics and the homeless. This has led to tensions and acts of hostility on both sides. A homeless man was doused with kerosene and set on fire.

Lublin, Joann S. "Some Shelters Strive to Give the Homeless More Than Shelter." Wall Street Journal, February 7, 1986:1, 8.
　　The House of Ruth in Washington, D.C., uses first-stage housing to deal with emergency needs and second-stage residence to provide the transition to independence. The second stage uses income from work and welfare to buy and prepare food and obtain counseling. The author mentions New York City's Jericho Project and a pregnant teenager who refuses to sleep inside. The solutions are to prepare the homeless to rejoin society by providing professional counseling, medical care, job training and placement, and links to permanent housing.

Lublin, Joann S. "Vouchers for Housing Help Some of the Poor, Fail to Benefit Others." The Wall Street Journal, November 19, 1986:1, 23.
　　A new program of the federal government is to provide housing-subsidy vouchers for the poor "that make up the difference between 30 percent of their monthly income and reasonable rent levels." To be eligible, a family's income must be less than 50 percent of the median income in the area in which they live. "President Reagan wants to substitute vouchers for all the $7.8 billion a year now spent on U.S. housing aid." The article includes case stories from San Antonio that illustrate successes and failures of this program.

Lubran, Barbara G. "Alcohol-Related Problems Among the Homeless: NIAAA's Response." Alcohol Health and Research World, 11 (3), Spring 1987:4-7, 73.
　　The author summarizes efforts of the National Institute on Alcohol Abuse and Alcoholism (NIAAA) to disseminate information on alcohol-related problems among the homeless. She identifies the three primary areas in need of research as epidemiological, clinical, and service delivery.

Lueck, Thomas J. "New York Suburbs Offer Jobs But a Daunting Cost of Living." New York Times, September 1, 1986:1, 26.
   This article reports on workers who have become homeless after moving to the New York City area in search of work.

Luna, C. Cajetan. "Welcome to My Nightmare: The Graffiti of Homeless Youth." Society, 24 (6), September–October 1987:73–78.
   The author's analysis of graffiti in Los Angeles and San Francisco, California, and Seattle, Washington, reveals the emotional burdens of homeless youths.

Lusk, Mark W. "Street Children in Latin America." Journal of Sociology and Social Welfare, 16 (1), March 1989:55–77.
   The author's report of fieldwork with street children in Brazil and Colombia reveals violence, drug abuse, prostitution, and four categories of attempts to deal with this problem--correctional, rehabilitative, outreach, and preventive.

Luther, Martin. Preface to The Book of Vagabonds and Beggars (Liber Vagatorum). London: The Penguin press, 1932. (Translated by J. C. Hotten and edited by D. B. Thomas.)
   This book, whose author is unknown, was first published in 1509, the preface in 1528. Luther wrote the preface, in which he advises people to know and assist their own registered paupers but to be on guard against strange beggars. This treatise on the language, manners, and customs of the vagabond population of Central Europe before the Reformation describes 27 different kinds of beggars. This edition also contains an editorial introduction on the history of begging in Germany and England.

M

MacDougall, A. "Rich-Poor Gap in U.S. Widens During Decade." Los Angeles Times, October 25, 1984:1, 23.
To illustrate that we are living in "the best of times, the worst of times," the author contrasts the crowded expensive restaurants, chic boutiques, and trendy discotheques with the squalor and rags of the hungry and homeless. He makes the point that the gap between the rich and poor, persisting throughout American history, has widened in the last decade.

Macduff, Nancy. "The Task Force Model: A Successful Needs Assessment Method for Rural Populations." Journal of Voluntary Action Research, 17 (1), January-March 1988:66-70.
The author proposes a needs assessment model to help volunteer organizations cope with the increase in rural homelessness.

MacEwen, Martin. "Homelessness, Race, and Law." New Community, 16 (4), July 1990:505-521.
An evaluation of conformance with the 1977 Housing Homeless Persons Act and the 1976 Race Relations Act shows that the law is unsuccessful in protecting the rights of ethnic minority groups.

Macey, Christopher. "The Right to Loiter and Be Offensive." Wall Street Journal, June 25, 1991:A23.
The author expresses dismay that he was unable to use the public library in Alexandria, Virginia. The only place to sit was in the children's section, but library officials have banned adults from it because they fear that homeless people may expose themselves to children.

Machalaba, Daniel. "Mobile Homes: Transit Systems Face Burden of Providing Last-Resort Shelter." Wall Street Journal, July 18, 1990:A1, A5.
The author discusses the controversy arising from a campaign to remove the homeless from the nation's transit system. Because many homeless find the transit system preferable to shelters, "the nooks and crannies of the nation's transportation system have become the shelter of last resort for the nation's growing ranks of homeless

people.   As more and more seek refuge under highways,
along rail lines, in terminals and on city subway cars,
transportation systems are struggling with service
disruptions, traveler complaints, lawsuits, injuries and
even deaths....Commuters reflexively avoid the forms
sprawled on benches, sitting on staircases or walking
through cars cup in hand. 'They sleep next to where they
vomited,' says New Yorker Kenneth Marshall.   'Almost
every day there is a trickle of urine on the wall.   At
least a couple days a week you will find the remains of
human excrement.' Mr. Marshall says he and his wife try
to avoid the subways."

MacIntyre, D.   "Medical Care for the Homeless--Some
Experience in Glasgow."   Scottish Medical Journal, 24,
1979:240-243.
       The author reports on 297 homeless patients. Their
main medical problems are mental illness, infestation,
respiratory disease, and poor foot care.   He suggests
ways to meet their medical needs without major expenditure.

MacIntyre, Martha Burton. "'Desperately Wicked': A Study
of Jane Cameron, Female Convict."   Women's Studies
International Quarterly, 1 (1), 1978:39-46.
       This analysis of the life and times of Jane Cameron,
a woman who in the 1800s was continually in and out of
prison for prostitution and stealing, includes a description of the recreational activities of the homeless.

MacLean, Una, and Laurie Naumann. "Primary Medical Care
for the Single Homeless: The Edinburgh Experiment."
Health Bulletin (of Edinburgh), 37, 1979:6-10.
       After documenting the health needs of the homeless,
the authors summarize attempts to provide health services
for them.   They include a description of how health
services were provided in an experimental program in
Edinburgh.

MacLeod, Celeste.   Horatio Alger, Farewell: The End of
the American Dream. New York: Seaview Books, 1980.
       This overview of the plight of the poor in American
society, which stresses the closing of opportunities,
suggests that the challenge facing American society is to
find solutions that will end poverty, limit individual
and corporate wealth, establish full employment, balance
individual rights with community and national needs, and

lead to cooperation and compromise on the international level.

MacQueen, Michel. "Low-Income Housing Demand to Reach 'Crisis-Level' in Near Future, Study Says." <u>Wall Street Journal</u>, June 3, 1987:15.
   In reviewing the need for low-income housing, the author reports that if there is no change in federal policies the "hidden homeless" (people doubling up) will join the numbers of actual homeless.

Maeroff, Gene I. "Housing Project Sets Off Dispute in Old Mill Town." <u>New York Times</u>, March 24, 1986:8.
   The Federal Housing Administration is planning to build row houses in Holyoke, Massachusetts, to accommodate 18 families of farm workers, mostly Hispanic, who harvest vegetables and tobacco in Connecticut Valley. Holyoke officials are objecting to the subsidized housing.

Magnet, Myron. "The Homeless." <u>Fortune</u>, <u>116</u>, November 23, 1987:170-172, 176, 180, 184, 188, 190.
   The author emphasizes the deficiencies of the homeless and argues that some individuals and families are oriented to getting out of homelessness while others are not. He makes the point that "shelters need to provide services and structure, not just bed," and concludes that "a human society cares for those at the bottom. It does so, however, not by making them abject dependents of the state but by trying to restore them to membership in the community. It helps them best by giving them the means, and showing them the way, to help themselves."

Maharidge, Dale. <u>Journey to Nowhere: The Saga of the New Underclass</u>. Garden City: Dial Press, 1985.
   As contrasted with the "Beat Generation" of the 1950s, the "We Generation" of the 1960s, and the "Me Generation" of the 1970s, the author wanted to experience first hand the "Out Generation" of the 1980s. This photographic essay, based on three month's of travel across the United States in 1982, reports on those who have been forced out of work. He emphasizes the structural conditions that underlie unemployment and reports on hobo jungles, sleeping under bridges, riding the rails, labor camps, the search for work, and the rust bowel. He includes a section on Mexico.

Maharidge, Dale.   "Riding the Rails in Search of Jobs and
Hope."   <u>Sacramento Bee</u>, May 23, 1982:A1, A22.
   A reporter and photographer who rode boxcars 1000
miles from Fresno to Klamath Falls reports that old-time
hobos have been joined by lower-middle-class blue-collar
workers.

Maher, Maggie.   "Death of an Empire: What's Happening in
the Soviet Union and What's Ahead."   <u>Barron's</u>, <u>71</u> (37),
September 6, 1991:12-13, 28-30.
   In this overview of events in the former Soviet
Union, Vladimir Popov, who directs the Research Project
at the Academy of the National Economy in Moscow, says
that 600,000 people have been left homeless as the result
of ethnic conflicts.

Maidment, Susan.   "Domestic Violence and the Law: The
1976 Act and Its Aftermath."   <u>Sociological Review
Monograph</u>, <u>31</u>, 1985:4-25.
   As measured by their meeting the need of battered
women for permanent accommodation, three British laws
that address domestic violence have not fulfilled their
purpose.

Main, Thomas J.   "The Homeless Families of New York."
<u>The Public Interest</u>, <u>85</u>, Fall 1986:3-21.
   The author discusses three primary causes of
homelessness in New York City: the housing market,
behavioral and psychological problems of homeless
families, and a lenient shelter policy.   The city must
find a way to house families in need of emergency housing
that will not provoke a flood of applicants.

Main, Thomas J.   "The Homeless of New York."   <u>The Public
Interest</u>, <u>72</u>, Summer 1983:3-28.
   The author analyzes results of legal advocacy for
the homeless in New York City and presents a typology of
the homeless based on their primary problems: psychiatric, alcoholic, economic, drug, and physical disability.
Homelessness is not a single problem, but consists of
three different problems: mental illness, alcohol and
drug abuse, and economic.   Each type requires tailor-made
solutions.   The author also discusses the ideologies of
the advocates.

Main, Thomas J.   "Hope for New York City's Homeless?"
<u>New York Times</u>, November, 27, 1986:27.

The author reviews the dilemma of needing to improve the conditions in shelters for the homeless and yet not provoke a flood of applicants. The solution is to increase the availability of low-income housing.

Main, Thomas J. "New York City's Lure to the 'Homeless.'" Wall Street Journal, September 12, 1983.
    Throwing money at the homeless, such as by building more shelters, is not the solution to homelessness. Supply creates demand, and many people who are not really homeless (people who are capable of independent living or who have relatives) use the shelters. An open-ended shelter policy is not the answer as it only encourages the life-style of homelessness--this is the essence of a dilemma, helping that encourages the problem. The solutions are to give shelter only to the truly homeless, to institute a work requirement in order to receive shelter care, and to rehabilitate the homeless by instilling the values of independence and productivity.

Main, Thomas J. "What We Know About the Homeless." Commentary, May 1988:26-31.
    The author disagrees with many positions taken by advocates for the homeless. He stresses that "homelessness is a much smaller problem, in terms of number of people affected by it, than commonly thought, but it is also much more intractable than advocates understand." He adds that "this intractability stems from the fact that the great majority of homeless individuals, and possibly some significant proportion of homeless families, are afflicted with behavioral or medical disabilities or both." The solution is "a reformist agenda--one aimed at enabling our mental-health system to treat people who need treatment, at reducing extreme poverty through income supports, and at allowing housing markets to function."

Mair, Andrew. "The Homeless and the Post-Industrial City." Political Geography Quarterly, 5 (4), October 1986:351-368.
    The thesis of this article is that "the very nature of the post-industrial city demands the removal of the homeless." This is because the emphasis in post-industrial ideology is consumption and leisure activities, and the homeless represent "negative externalities to status-seeking post-industrial consumers... (who threaten) the meaning systems through which these consumers interpret their lives." Consequently there is a built-in tendency

of the built-environment to expel the homeless. The author refers to events in Columbus, Ohio, to illustrate this principle.

Maitland, Leslie. "Bush Plan for Homeless Faulted as Too Modest." New York Times, November 26, 1989:15.
President Bush will submit a $7 billion package of housing proposals to Congress. These proposals will include $728 million aid to the homeless. Critics say the amount is inadequate.

Maitra, A. K. "Dealing with the Disadvantaged--Single Homeless, Are We Doing Enough?" Public Health, 96 (3), May 1982:141-144.
A sample of 73 homeless patients is compared with 75 randomly selected home-based patients. The homeless are predominantly male, unemployed, not registered for medical services, and suffering from acute illnesses brought on by overdoses of drugs, alcoholism, and depression. The solution must be a multifaceted approach to treating alcoholism and providing employment, coun-seling, and locally-based social, medical, and community support.

Malcolm, Andrew H. "The First Lesson of Philanthropy is Well Learned." New York Times, March 15, 1991:B1.
In Trumbull, Connecticut, children at Middlebrook Elementary School learn about homelessness by foregoing something they were going to purchase and giving the money to the homeless instead.

Malcomb, Andrew H. "Record Numbers of the Homeless Seeking Aid in the Nation's Cities." New York Times, October 30, 1986:17.
A record number of homeless people are seeking shelter and food in Kansas City (Missouri), Boston, Baltimore, Houston, Seattle, New York City, Atlanta, and Phoenix. The characteristics of the homeless are also changing. There now are more women, children, and younger men.

Malone, Mark. "Homelessness in a Modern Urban Setting." Fordham Urban Law Journal, 10, Fall 1981:749-481.
After reviewing problems in defining homelessness and providing historical background of homelessness in American society, the author reviews recent responses to the homeless in New York City. He suggests that the doctrine of parens patriae (the inherent power of the

state to protect the person and property of someone who is suffering under a disability) can be used to provide for the homeless. Using this as a basis, an organized program can be developed to seek out homeless persons and inform them of their rights and assistance available at various intake centers. The thesis is that legal steps must be taken to provide adequate services to those who aren't capable of caring for themselves.

Mandel, Marjorie. "Hard Times Displace 'The New Homeless.'" St. Louis Post-Dispatch, May 2, 1982:1, 7.
The new homeless are defined as people from the working class (lower-middle class) who have joined the ranks of the homeless due to extended unemployment. The author discusses their embarrassment and points out that the stereotype of the homeless as bums, drifters, derelicts, and vagabonds no longer applies.

Mandel, Marjorie. "Shelters are Different but All Are Overcrowded." St. Louis Post-Dispatch, May 3, 1982:1, 4.
This article presents an overview of shelters and policies toward the homeless in St. Louis.

Mandel, Marjorie. "Solving the Problem: Those Responsible Disagree." St. Louis Post-Dispatch, May 5, 1982.
The author reviews proposed solutions to homelessness in St. Louis: a centralized shelter, concern with the total person, government-run versus private care, treatment for the mentally ill, permanent housing, work, $5 added to the cost of marriage licenses and divorce decrees to finance shelters for abused women.

Mandel, Marjorie. "Without a Skid Row, Street People Scatter." St. Louis Post-Dispatch, May 4, 1982:1, 4.
Urban renewal has replaced St. Louis's skid row with a new Civic Center, and the homeless, now more invisible, are sleeping in areas people never see: cars, railroad cars, cardboard boxes, alleys, garages, bus stations, and tunnels under the train station.

Mann, James. "An Endless Parade of Runaway Kids." U.S. News and World Report, 94, January 17, 1983:64.
Running away is an extensive problem in American society. Runaways are subject to hardship and exploitation. The 166 federally funded shelters offer promise for dealing with this problem.

Manov, Ariana, and Laura Lowther.   "A Health Care
Approach for Hard-to-Reach Adolescent Runaways." Nursing
Clinics of North America, 18 (2), June 1983:333-342.
     The   authors   discuss   the   health   care   needs   of
runaways, reasons for running away, and intervention
strategies of medical practitioners.

Mansfield, Drummond. "Memories of the Road." American
History Illustrated, 21, February 1987:34-41.
     The author, who "followed his wanderlust as a knight
of the tie and rail" a half-century earlier, provides a
history of hoboing from the Civil War through the 1940s.

Mansouri, Lisa, and David A. Dowell.   "Perceptions of
Stigma Among the Long-Term Mentally ill." Psychosocial
Rehabilitation Journal, 13 (1), July 1989:79-91.
     Questionnaire and scale data from 70 participants in
support programs for the mentally ill homeless confirm
the construct validity of perceived stigma and illustrate
the significance of this concept for the mentally ill.

Mapes, Lynda V. "Faulty Food and Shelter Programs Draw
Charge That Nobody's Home to Homeless." National
Journal, 17 (9), March 2, 1985:474-476.
     Deinstitutionalization is the primary cause of
homelessness.   The solutions are to convert military
buildings to shelters and distribute surplus food. The
homeless can't get food stamps if they are in a shelter
because they are "institutionalized."

Mapes, Riley E. "Public Responsibility for Transients."
Social Service Review, September 1934:484-491.
     This overview of the first year of operation of the
Transient Division of the Federal Emergency Relief
Administration reports that 166,476 individuals, of whom
40 percent are in families, are being cared for in 300
transient centers and 100 camps.

Mapes, Riley E. "Report of Transient Activities for New
Mexico." Social Service Review, September 1934:492-497.
     The author describes how the Transient Centers
operate in New Mexico. Her detailed account includes the
buildings, infirmary, issues of clothing, recreation,
work projects, staff, salaries, and cost of the program.

Marable, Manning. "Remaking American Marxism." Monthly
Review, 42 (8), January 1991:40-53.

The tearing down of the Berlin Wall is not a sign that the class struggle is over. Both the Soviet Union and the United States are undergoing political and economic crises. One indication of this crisis in the United States is the three million homeless Americans.

Marcos, Luis R., Neal L. Cohen, David Nardacci, and Joan Brittain. "Psychiatry Takes to the Streets: The New York City Initiative for the Homeless Mentally Ill." American Journal of Psychiatry, 147 (11), November 1990:1557-1561.
    The records of the 298 homeless mentally ill people brought to Bellevue Hospital between October 28, 1987, and October 28, 1988, show that most were male, single, separated or divorced, previously hospitalized for mental illness, diagnosed with schizophrenia, and homeless for more than one year. A follow-up study shows that 45 percent are still homeless (or cannot be located), 80 are hospitalized, 83 live in community settings, and two are dead.

Marcus, Amy Dockser. "At Best, They've Proved There's More Than One Kind of Yo-Yo." Wall Street Journal, September 20, 1990:B1.
    The author discusses the arrest and subsequent dismissal of charges against a homeless man for selling yo-yos on a midtown Manhattan sidewalk without a license. The judge said that the police could find "a more socially useful purpose than busting yo-yo dealers."

Marcuse, Peter. "Gentrification, Homelessness, and the Work Process: Housing Markets and Labour Markets in the Quartered City." Housing Studies, 4 (3), July 1989:211-220.
    The author, who analyzes relationships between labor and the form of housing, using two cases of gentrification and homelessness, encourages research into the linkage between class, work processes, and the nature of housing provision.

Marcuse, Peter. "Isolating the Homeless." Shelterforce, 11 (1), June-July 1988:12-15.
    Because a serious analysis of the causes of homelessness in the United States would expose causes too deep within the housing system to be publicly permissible, most efforts neutralize the problem and sweep the homeless out of sight.

Marcuse, Peter. "Neutralizing Homelessness." <u>Socialist Review</u>, <u>18</u> (1), 1988:96-96.
Homelessness is not due to the problems of individuals, but to systemic causes; that is, the prevailing economic and political forces of our society cause homelessness: the profit structure of housing, the distribution of income, and government policy. Although subgroups of the homeless, such as the homeless mentally ill, may have special service needs, the underlying cause of homelessness is the same. Accordingly, so must be the solutions, which require sweeping changes in national housing and economic policies.

Marcuse, Peter. "Why Are They Homeless?" <u>The Nation</u>, <u>244</u>, April 4, 1987:426, 428-429.
The causes of homelessness are deinstitutionalization, a general housing shortage, the economic restructuring of cities, and the unwillingness of government to cope with extensive homelessness. The government has taken evasive reactions from denial that there is much of a problem to blaming the victims for being homeless. The solutions are (1) three kinds of housing for the homeless (emergency short-term shelter, transitional housing, and permanent housing), (2) homes for everyone, (3) seeing homelessness as part of a general housing problem, and (4) the exercise of public control over economic developments to create and share jobs and benefits.

Margolick, David. "Weighing the Risks and Rights of Homelessness." <u>New York Times</u>, December 8, 1985:E6.
The author examines the civil liberty issue of individual rights (of the homeless to stay out of shelters) versus community concerns for the health and welfare of the homeless.

Margolis, Richard J. "Is the Next Step Penn Station?" <u>New Leader</u>, <u>69</u>, February 10, 1986:11-12.
The author focuses on the aged homeless. He also examines the fears of the aged who are not homeless that one day they will join the ranks of the homeless.

Maricle, R. A., W. F. Hoffman, and J. D. Bloom. "The Prevalence and Significance of Medical Illness Among Chronically Mentally Ill Outpatients." <u>Community Mental Health Journal</u>, <u>23</u> (2), July 1987:81-90.
A sample of chronically mentally ill patients in a community mental health program revealed much diagnosed and undiagnosed physical illness. The authors recommend

that community mental health programs take on the responsibility of meeting these medical needs.

Marin, Peter. "Helping and Hating the Homeless: The struggle at the Margins of America." Harper's Magazine, 247, January 1987:39-48.
    The author discusses people's fears of the homeless and the complexities of their attitude toward them: "our fear of strangeness, our hatred of deviance, our love of order and control." At the "troubled heart of our culture" lie two dramas: "the drama of those struggling to survive by regaining their place in the social order and the drama of those struggling to survive outside of it."

Markson, Elizabeth W. "Thoughts on SSSP's Mission in a Conservative Era." SSSP Newsletter, 17, (1), Fall 1985:12-14.
    The author presents a brief history of deinstitutionalization and institutionalization and makes the point that the expansion of nursing and board and care homes has at least partially replaced mental hospitals.

Marotto, Robert A. "Are Those Streetpeople Part of the New Poor, Too? Toward an Applied Sociology of Social Problems." American Sociologist, 20 (2), Summer 1989:111-122.
    The author uses interviews with 105 users of a soup kitchen in Santa Cruz, California, to support his thesis that the constructionist view in sociology can be utilized in developing social policy.

Marotto, Robert A., and William E. Friedland. "Santa Cruz Streetpeople: A Case Study Assessment of the New Homelessness." Paper presented at the annual meetings of the Society for the Study of Social Problems, New York City, August 1986.
    The authors' report on the streetpeople of Santa Cruz, California, identifies "sliders," young Caucasians who are downwardly mobile. The authors analyze a pattern of dislocation, migration, and new settlement.

Marotto, Robert A., and William E. Friedland. "Streetpeople and Community Public Policy in Santa Cruz, California." Journal of Applied Sociology, 4, 1987:71-87.
    The authors describe collaborative efforts of the University of California and city officials in Santa Cruz

in working with the problem of street people. Sociological constructionism was useful, for it allowed a redefinition of these individuals from transients to street people.

Marriott, Michel. "Demonstrators in New York Focus on Housing Homeless." New York Times, December 19, 1988:16.
A march was held in midtown Manhattan to challenge New York City officials to adopt more humane housing policies. The protest was also designed to unify various neighborhoods that are working separately for the homeless.

Marriott, Michel. "New York City Picks 8 Sites to House Homeless AIDS Patients." New York Times, October 31, 1988:Y16.
This article reports varying reactions to the proposal by the Mayor of New York City to build more shelters for the homeless who have AIDS.

Marsh, Benjamin C. "Causes of Vagrancy and Methods of Eradication." Annals of the American Academy of Political and Social Science, 23, 1904:37-48.
Based on participant observation in London and Philadelphia and interviews at Wayfarer's Lodge in Philadelphia, the author classifies vagrants as those who are really looking for work, hobo mechanics (seasonal working drinkers), wandering beggars, and yeggmen (petty criminals). The objective causes are unwise philanthropy, unwise public relief, and faulty laws and administration. The subjective causes are employment problems, negative personal traits, and the desire to escape justice. To solve the problem we must change the laws of peddling, establish schools for the blind and crippled, change the administration of wayfarers' lodges and lodging houses, and establish mendicancy squads. The recommended approach is to punish those unwilling to work, train those capable of working, support those unable to work, and encourage thrift by everyone.

Marsh, Benjamin C. "Methods Employed by American Cities to Eradicate Vagrancy." Proceedings of the National Conference of Charities and Correction, Isabel C. Barrows, ed. May 6-12, 1903:414-415.
This report contains a fold-out chart on 29 American cities that shows their population, state and city laws and penalties for begging and vagrancy, and statistics on arrest, efforts to secure work, and rehabilitation facilities. The proposed solutions are uniformity in

legislation; treatment by state law rather than by city ordinances; elimination of promiscuous giving and the establishment of compulsory work; as in Boston, compulsory bathing in supervised lodging houses, a state farm for habitual vagrants, and the prohibition of begging and vagrancy; as in New York, the registration and identification of vagrants; and, as in Chicago, using vagrants to work on city streets.

Marsh, Benjamin C., and Frances A. Keller. "Bibliography on Methods of Dealing with Tramps and Vagrants." Proceedings of the National Conference of Charities and Correction, Isabel C. Barrows, ed. May 6-12, 1903:411-414.
    The 44 items in this bibliography are divided into methods of dealing with mendicants, unemployed, and vagrants.

Marshall, Tony, and Susan Fairhead. "How to Keep Homeless Offenders Out of Prison." New Society, 49 (885), September 20, 1979:616-617.
    The authors' thesis is that homeless offenders, commonly known as skid row winos and tramps, should not be sent to prison for public drunkenness but instead be provided welfare services.

Martell, Daniel A. "Homeless Mentally Disordered Offenders and Violent Crimes: Preliminary Research Findings." Law and Human Behavior, 15 (4), August 1991:333-347.
    Using a cross-sectional sample of 150 mentally disordered offenders in a maximum security psychiatric hospital in New York City and controlling for demographic and diagnostic factors, the author concludes that homelessness significantly increases the likelihood that mentally disordered offenders will be indicted. Although only 2 percent of the city's mentally ill are homeless, they account for 50 percent of admissions to this facility.

Martin, Bradley K. "Japan's Working Poor Hit Tough Times." Wall Street Journal, April 21, 1986:22.
    This overview of the working poor of Tokyo's Sanya district includes a brief description of this "black hole's" homeless--men who collect cardboard for a living, who warm themselves at fires fueled with old tires, and who sleep outside. About 90 die on Sanya's streets each

year, with those who freeze to death referred to as
"tunas," a reference to frozen fish.

Martin, D. N., and R. V. G. Clarke. "The Personality of
Approved School Absconders." British Journal of Criminology, 9, 1969:366-375.
    Based on three studies of boys who ran away from
English training schools during 1965-1967, the authors
conclude that runaways represent a random sample in
regard to personality variables. In the first study of
consecutive admissions to 23 training schools, the
runaways did not differ significantly from the non-
runaways in psychomotor style, extraversion, neuroticism,
age, intelligence, and reading level. The second study,
a sample of 50 randomly selected matched pairs, showed no
significant differences between runaways and non-runaways
on the Jesness Inventory or the derived Asocial Index.
Comparing 59 randomly selected runaways with 59 non-
runaways, the third study showed no significant differences in the High School Personality Questionnaire.

Martin, Douglas. "About New York." New York Times, June
8, 1991:A27.
    The author profiles Luis Ibarra Weber, a veteran of
the Korean War, who is expected to join 100 other
homeless veterans in a protest march in New York City.

Martin, Douglas. "At the Y, Molding Little Lives with
Lumps of Clay." New York Times, April 1, 1992:B3.
    The YMCA on the West Side of New York has a pottery
program for homeless children.

Martin, Douglas. "A Devoted Baker Fills the Hands of the
Homeless with Kugel." New York Times, May 20, 1992:B3.
    Peggy Bakewell distributes her baked goods to the
homeless.

Martin, Douglas. "Mongolian Immigrant Tries to Find New
Life." New York Times, November 30, 1991:A22.
    Amarjargal Dorj, a photojournalist from Mongolia,
says he does not regret his decision to defect to the
United States, even though he has had to live in homeless
shelters since his defection.

Martin, Douglas. "Once a Brothel, Soon a Refuge for
Prostitutes." New York Times, January 5, 1991:A23.

Joyce I. Wallace, a New York City physician, is trying to open a temporary shelter for homeless prostitutes on Manhattan's Lower East Side.

Martin, Douglas. "Yes, Vote, Homeless are Told." New York Times, November 8, 1989:16.
The author recounts efforts to register New York City's homeless for voting.

Martin, Marsha A., and Susan A. Nayowith. "Creating Community: Groupwork to Develop Social Support Networks with Homeless Mentally Ill." Social Work With Groups, 11 (4), 1988: 79-93.
The authors analyze the functioning of a mobile mental health outreach unit on the streets of New York City and a health team that works in a drop-in center and in a single-room occupancy hotel. Emphasis is placed on how social work skills can contribute to developing social support networks and a sense of community among the mentally ill homeless.

Mathers, Michael. Riding the Rails. Boston: Houghton Mifflin, 1974.
This photo essay of hobo culture contains extensive quotations by hobos. The implicit reasons that men become hobos are bad relationships with women, alcohol, and the desire to travel and avoid a sedentary life.

Mathews, Tom. "What Can Be Done?" Newsweek, 111, March 21, 1988:57-58.
The author examines the problem of financing housing for the homeless in a time of budget deficits.

Matthew, Suseela, and R. Parthasarathy. "Levels of Reintegration into the Community and Adjustment of the Ex-Inmates of a Destitute Home." Indian Journal of Social work, 49 (1), January 1988:75-79.
Based on institutional records and questionnaires from 90 former inmates of a home for destitute children in Kerala, India, the authors analyze the post-institutional adjustment of these individuals.

Matthews, Jay. "Down and Out by Choice." Washington Post, August 25, 1985:A1, A22.
The author discusses people who choose homelessness as a way of life.

Matthews, Jay. "Head-Counting Efforts Complicated by Politics." Washington Post, August 26, 1985:A1, A10.
The author reviews methodological problems in counting the homeless.

Matthews, Jay. "The Homeless: Help Them? We Can't Even Count Them." Washington Post National Weekly, September 9, 1985:6-8.
The homeless have become part of a political controversy. The author reviews theories of how to count the homeless and efforts to count them.

Maxwell, Cliff. "Daughters of the Road." Railroad Magazine, 26, September 1939:49-51.
The author writes about female hobos he met on the road. Although there always have been a few women riding the rails, such as Boston Betty, these were "tough by-products of cities that had no place for them." They were "flinty-eyed," "angular of body," and "masculine-minded." In 1932, in contrast, there was "an altogether different class of girls riding the rattlers and the blinds." At this time there were "nearly as many women and girls as there were men and boys riding the rails...aimlessly following that will-o'-the-wisp, employment."

Maxwell, Cliff. "Lady Vagabonds." Scribner's Magazine, 85, March 1929:288-292.
As the author "gypsied over and around the world" for over 25 years, he heard "tales of lady hobos," but he never met one. Hobos are "on the road for adventure, travel, or incurable wanderlust." However, he has occasionally met "girls who wished to visit a certain city and, not having the money to make it possible for them to ride the cushions...beat their way on trains." While a hobo will work, a vagabond will not, choosing a life of hardship rather than performing manual labor. The author says he has met lady vagabonds, and he relates the story of one such person, Creole Helen.

Maxwell, R. D. Vox. "Letter to the Editor." Wall Street Journal, November 2, 1989:A23.
The author argues that the conditions of homelessness lead to drink, drugs, or insanity.

May, Clifford D. "Civil Libertarians Criticized by Koch." New York Times, January 7, 1988:11.

In response to advocates for the homeless who disagree with his program to involuntarily hospitalize people living on the streets who are considered dangerous to themselves and others, the Mayor of New York City charges that his critics are taking the position that "not only must we let the suffering continue, we must do so in the name of civil rights." Reactions of the homeless are also included.

May, Clifford D. "The Homeless: An Urban Condition Spreads to Suburbs." New York Times, December 31, 1986:B1.
Coping strategies of suburban homeless are compared with those used by their urban counterparts: use of indoor shopping malls, libraries, and hospitals, versus subway stations. The author reports on expenditures for the suburban homeless by counties near New York City.

May, Clifford D. "Schumer Ties Homelessness to Cuts in U.S. Housing Aid." New York Times, December 18, 1987:18.
Representative Charles E. Schumer charges that homelessness has sky-rocketed in American cities largely because of cuts in federal housing aid. He claims that the private sector cannot solve this problem, that the federal government has to provide cost-efficient housing programs.

May, Clifford D. "U.S. to Reduce Shelter Funds for the Homeless." New York Times, December 12, 1987:12.
The author reviews reactions to the Department of Health and Human Services's announcement that its contribution to the cost of a homeless family's stay in a welfare hotel for shelter will be reduced to 30 days within any 12-month period.

Mayer, Robert, and Tillie Shuster. Developing Shelter Models for the homeless: 3 Program Design Options. New York: Community Service Society, April 1985.
This publication is a guide for dealing with the complex issues in developing emergency, transitional, and permanent shelters for the homeless.

Mayhew, Henry. London Labour and the London Poor. New York: Dover, 1968. (First published in 4 volumes by Griffin, Bohn in 1861-1862 with the subtitle, A Cyclopedia of the Condition and Earnings of Those that Will Work, Those That Cannot Work, and Those That Will Not Work.)

The world is made up of two distinct races, the wandering and the civilized tribes, each of which possesses a unique shape of head. Civilized society also has its rural and urban wanderers: pickpockets, beggars, prostitutes, street-sellers, street-performers, cabmen, coachmen, watermen, sailors, and such like. This book is about those who "move from place to place and prey upon the earnings of the more industrious portions of the community." The six types of street people are: sellers, buyers, finders, performers (and artists and showmen), artisans or peddlers, and laborers.

McAllister, Jack A. "Why Give? Notes to a New CEO." *Foundation News*, <u>32</u> (1), January-February 1991:32-36.
The author makes the point that business cannot succeed if society fails. Accordingly, as a form of self-interest investment, businesses should give to such causes as shelter for the homeless.

McAnally, Gene. "I Was Homeless: A Look at Life Beneath the Safety Net." *The Humanist*, May-June 1989:12.
The author recounts how he and his wife became homeless. Due to seasonal work that pays only the minimum wage, he was unable to pay rent.

McAuley, Christine. "Liza Minnelli Sells Well, Particularly in Subway Trains." <u>Wall Street Journal</u>, February 27, 1990:A1, A16.
<u>Street News</u>, a newspaper written for the benefit of the homeless men and women who sell it, has created controversy. Its defenders point to success stories of homeless individuals who have used their profits to rent apartments. Its detractors say they feel pressured to buy the paper from people "with another sad story to tell."

McCarthy, Bill. "Human Development to Zero in on 3 Issues." <u>Nation's Cities Weekly</u>, <u>9</u> (19), May 12, 1986:4.
In light of the crisis of homelessness and the refusal of the federal government to acknowledge a role in solving this problem, the Human Development Steering Committee of the National League of Cities must consider what the appropriate roles and responsibilities are of each level of government in addressing homelessness.

McCarthy, Colman. "America's Homeless: Three Days Down and Out in Chicago." <u>The Nation</u>, <u>236</u> (9), March 5, 1983:1, 271.

The author, a syndicated columnist, recounts his experiences at Pacific Gardens Mission in Chicago after he "dressed down" and passed for a homeless man. Based on his participant observation, he relates the bad treatment he encountered everywhere, including his arrest and a night spent in jail. He poses the question of whether the mental illness of the homeless is the cause or effect of homelessness and explains why some homeless prefer to sleep on the streets than in facilities provided for them.

McCarthy, Peter H. Twenty-Two Years on Whiskey Row. Joliet, Illinois: 1931.
The author recounts his conversion from being an alcoholic on skid row and his subsequent organization of a skid row mission.

McChesney, Kay Young. "Family Homelessness: A Systemic Problem." Journal of Social Issues, 46 (4), Winter 1990:191-205.
Using a "low-income housing ratio--the number of households living below the poverty line divided by the number of affordable housing units," the author argues that homelessness is the consequence of a greater number of low-income households than low-cost housing units. Because the problem is systemic, not the fault of individuals, the solution must also be systemic, namely, a reduction of poverty and/or an increase in the supply of low-cost housing. Consequently, it is misguided to focus on the individual's mental health or to provide only emergency shelter or transitional housing.

McClellan, Bill. "Homeless Can Again Become Celebrities." St. Louis Post-Dispatch, March 2, 1987:E3.
The author specifies how money appropriated for the homeless has become a political boondoggle in Missouri.

McCook, John J. "Increase of Tramping: Cause and Cure." The Independent, 54, March 13, 1902:620-624.
The author provides estimates on the numbers of tramps in the United States, both professional tramps and men out of work. The approximately 500,000 tramps cost $11,000,000 a year and produce nothing. The causes are drink, unemployment, thriftlessness, and preference. Most of the men prefer tramping because of the life style that it affords. The solutions are to encourage thrift, break up train-jumping, stop indiscriminate charity, and

establish reformatories in which secular and religious approaches are combined.

McCook, John J. "Some New Phases of the Tramp Problem." The Charities Review, 1, June 1892:355-364.
     The topic is syphilis and voting by tramps. The author takes the position that tramps should be forced to take a full course of treatment for syphilis and should be disenfranchised.

McCook, John J. "A Tramp Census and Its Revelations." The Forum, 15, August 1893:753-766.
     Based on 2,190 cases, the author presents an overview of tramps. He summarizes findings of age, health, work, race, nativity, literacy, voting, marital status, sleeping places, drinking, criminal history, religion, and their attitudes. The solutions he proposes include adopting a system of registration and pass books and stopping the practice of lodging tramps in police stations.

McCook, John J. "The Tramp Problem: What It Is and What to Do With It." Proceedings of National Conference of Charities and Correction, 1895:288-302.
     Due to the industrial depression, the number of tramps is increasing. The drinkers and single men are the first fired and the last rehired. Some of these men adapt to their unemployment in such a way that they learn to live without working and never seek work again. The solutions are to establish a labor test to determine who is eligible for help, to mete out indeterminate prison sentences to reform them, to stop train jumping, and to repress hobo camps in order to stifle the interest of children and prevent them from being converted to vagrancy.

McCulley, G. E. "ABA's Retort to Quale Is No Joke." Wall Street Journal, September 18, 1991:A15.
     The author defends Vice President Dan Quale's attack on the American Bar Association, saying that if the ABA really stood for the protection of the poor and homeless more ABA lawyers would do pro bono work.

McDowell, Edwin. "Famine in the Backlands." The Atlantic, 253, March 1984:33-35.
     Three hundred thousand people have become homeless due to the drought and famine in the state of Ceara in Brazil.

McFadden, Robert D. "Aid for Midtown Homeless May Include Penn Station." New York Times, April 5, 1992:32.
    City officials announced that they may expand programs for the homeless to Pennsylvania Station. Critics claim that this action does not represent concern for the homeless but is simply a ploy to move the homeless away from the Madison Square Garden area, where the 1992 Democratic National Convention will be held.

McFadden, Robert D. "A Derelict Shell Becomes a Co-op for Homeless in Manhattan." New York Times, November 15, 1988:17.
    The author reviews the process that led to the construction of what is believed to be the first cooperative for homeless families in the United States. Twenty-two families, selected by lottery, will be leaving shelters and apartments of friends and relatives to move into two- and three-bedroom apartments of their own.

McFadden, Robert D. "Man Freed in Arson Case Is Arrested in Killing." New York Times, January 7, 1992:B1.
    The murder victim is identified as Linda Cassella, a 43-year old pregnant homeless woman.

McFadden, Robert D. "Study of Homeless Calls New York Unprepared." New York Times, October 6, 1985:21.
    The Coalition for the Homeless charges that New York City is ill prepared to handle the homeless during the coming winter, as their numbers are expected to approach the peak levels of the Great Depression. The causes are a shortage of low-income housing, the disappearance of federal aid for low-income housing, and fire.

McFadden, Robert D. "Study of Homeless Cites Special Needs." New York Times, September 30, 1984:A37.
    The author reviews a study of the homeless in New York City that was conducted by Stephen Crystal. Topics include mental illness, psychiatric histories, and long-term shelter residents. Eviction is cited as a primary cause of homelessness.

McGhee, Peter S. "Bowery Bums' Rush." The Nation, 198 (20), May 11, 1964:483-485.
    The author discusses how the Bowery was cleaned up to make the area more appealing for visitors to the World's Fair. Judges handed out 6-month sentences.

McGill, Gary. "Urban Plunge: Seattle on $1.50 a Day." Response (Seattle Pacific University), 9 (3), May 1986:7.
The author reflects on his three days of participant observation in the Pioneer Square area of downtown Seattle.

McGreigle, Paul, and Alison S. Lauriat. More Than Shelter: A Community Response to Homelessness. Boston: United Community Planning Corporation and Massachusetts Association for Mental Health, 1984.
The homeless are either victims of a housing shortage or else the presence of street people is a myth. The homeless are made up of disparate groups, individuals, and families, who are trapped into homelessness by poverty, mental illness, and alcoholism. The solutions are to improve services, expand emergency and transitional shelters, coordinate medical and psychiatric services, and improve financial and housing assistance.

McGrory, Mary. "Homeless Can Take Hints From Contras." St. Louis Post-Dispatch, August 18, 1985.
The shelter for the homeless operated by Mitch Snyder in Washington, D.C., has been closed. The author makes a biting, tongue-in-cheek suggestion that the homeless use military tactics to force funds from the government. She also chides the Republicans for supporting the Contras in Nicaragua, but not the homeless in the United States.

McKinley, James C., Jr. "Arson Blaze Is Ruled Out in Ferry Case." New York Times, September 11, 1991:B1.
Although arson had been suspected as the cause of the fire that destroyed the roof of the Staten Island Ferry terminal, officials have concluded that crack smoking by homeless people was the more likely cause.

McKinley, James C., Jr. "Public Hearing to Assess Plan to Add Shelters." New York Times, October 30, 1991:B4.
Because the plan to locate homeless shelters throughout New York City created racial tension and hysteria in middle-class communities, public hearings on the plan will be held.

McKinley, James C., Jr. "Staten Island Democrats Warn Dinkins on Support." New York Times, October 29, 1991:B3.
A group of Democrats from Staten Island, New York, told Dinkins that they could no longer support him.

Among the reasons they gave was Dinkins's decision to build homeless shelters on Staten Island.

McMillen, A. Wayne. "An Army of Boys on the Loose." Survey Graphic, 21 (6), September 1932:389-393.
    Although no one knows the exact numbers of young men wandering across the country, records from shelters in Phoenix, El Paso, Los Angeles, Yuma, and elsewhere indicate that from 15 percent to 27 percent of the hundreds of thousands of transients are under 21 years of age. Reports from railroad agents indicate that between one third and one half of this transient army is composed of minors. Evidence indicates that these boys are essentially honest, fairly well educated, and driven to the road because of unemployment. The boys are mainly coming from the North, East, and Middle West and moving to Florida, the Gulf States, the Southwest, and California. These boys are subjected to "dangerous physical exposure," "moral hazards," and "the infectious attitude of the seasoned hobo." Two methods must be used to attack this problem: prevention to induce boys to remain at home and treatment. Prevention requires a campaign of publicity concerning the physical hardships and moral hazards of the road, an effort to make local conditions tolerable, and bolstering the morale of boys who are idle. Treatment includes a federal transient service fund to stimulate local initiative, improve shelters and diet, and establish federal camps or federal relief stations and local training programs.

McMillen, A. Wayne. "Migrant Boys: Some Data from Salt Lake City." Social Service Review, 7, March 1933:64-83.
    The author reports data on non-resident male minors who applied for food and shelter in Salt Lake City during one month in 1932: their age, education, length of travel, reasons for leaving home, plans, occupation of father, work history. The article also includes the author's testimony before Congress.

McMillen, A. Wayne. "Statement of the Discussion Leader." Social Service Review, September 1934:503-504.
    The author summarizes the predicaments faced by social workers: (1) federal monies are not supposed to be used for hospital care, but this is being widely disregarded; (2) many transients are hoboes of the quasi-criminal type and are dangerous influences in the shelters--yet to call the police is to turn them over to brutal constables; (3) to interview adult males who have

no problem but unemployment is to waste the time of social workers; yet to exclude them is not right.

McMurry, Donald L. Coxey's Army: A Study of the Industrial Army Movement of 1894. Boston: Little Brown, 1929.
     During the severe depression of 1892-1894, a series of "people's armies," made up of the dispossessed and disgruntled, marched on Washington, demanding economic change. The author documents the role of tramps in this social movement of the unemployed, detailing the armies of Coxey, Browne, Fry, and Kelly.

McNeil, Donald G., Jr. "Challenging Dinkins Over the Homeless." New York Times, February 2, 1992:Section 4:18.
     A commission on the homeless organized by David Dinkins, Mayor of New York City, reports that nonprofit organizations can house the homeless more cheaply than the city can.

McNichol, Tom. "Down and Out on Campus." Campus Voice, 4 (3), Spring 1988:29-34.
     Homeless college students (those who because of a campus housing crisis or financial problems sleep in classroom buildings, cars, dorm lounges, friend's living room floors, and shelters) are classified as "situationally homeless;" that is, "a calamitous event, coupled with a failure to deal with the catastrophe...brings on temporary homelessness." This article profiles several such homeless students.

McQuiston, John T. "Nassau's Homeless Estimated at 5,000." New York Times, June 3, 1984:A42.
     In spite of the affluence of Nassau County, New York, considerable homelessness (displacement) exists. The author discusses the problem of defining homelessness.

McSheehy, William. Skid Row. Boston: G. K. Hall, 1979.
     An overview of the Chicago skid row: missions, hotels, employment, justice, bars, second-hand stores, baths, reading rooms, theatre, pool hall, barber college, grocery stores, currency exchange, alcoholic treatment center, urban renewal, and skid row argot.

Mechanic, David, and David A. Rochefort. "Deinstitutionalization: An Appraisal of Reform." Annual Review of Sociology, 16, 1990:301-327.

This overview and evaluation of deinstitutionaliza-tion mentions that the lack of community mental health care and welfare cutbacks have contributed to homeless-ness.

Mehle, Jean. "Workshop Examines Reasons for the Increas-ing Homeless." Nation's Cities Weekly, 7, December 17, 1984:4.
The basic cause of homelessness is a decrease in the supply of low-income housing. Food stations provide only a short-term answer. The need is for treatment and care, which can be provided through programs of emergency shelter and improved community mental health care.

Mehta, Gita. "Don't Look Now." Vogue, 178, March 1988:499-500, 558.
Based on visits to shelters in New York City and talks with the homeless, the author, who is from India, concludes that New York City's treatment of the homeless compares unfavorably with their treatment in Calcutta, India. New York City "seems to be about inhumanity, as if the poor are regarded as the losers, wilfully respon-sible for their own fate."

Meller, Paul. "Time for Home Truths About Housing." Marketing, January 30, 1992:20-21.
This overview of home marketing and financing problems mentions that homelessness is becoming a major social problem in the United Kingdom.

Melton, R. H. "Shelter Gives Lift to Down and Out." Washington Post, December 23, 1983:C1, C7.
The author reports on the first month's operation of Montgomery County's (Bethesda, Maryland) first shelter for homeless men.

Meltzer, Milton. Brother, Can You Spare a Dime? The Great Depression, 1929-1933. New York: Alfred A. Knopf, 1969.
This overview of the stock market crash of 1929 discusses dispossession, poverty, homelessness, and relief.

Melvin, Tessa. "Bookshop Founded to Help the Homeless Gets Its Eviction Notice." September 1, 1991:WC1.
Halpern Associates reclaimed the space it had donated to The Free Books Store in White Plains, New

York.   The Free Books Store had raised over $90,000 for
projects for the homeless.

Melvin, Tessa.   "Coming to Aid of a Homeless Shelter."
New York Times, May 3, 1992:WC10.
      The author details a plan to renovate the Coachman
Hotel in White Plains, New York, as a transitional
shelter for the homeless.

Melvin, Tessa.   "Greenburgh Raises a New Issue Against
Westhelp." New York Times, May 24, 1992:WC1.
      Westhelp, a facility in Greenburgh, New York,
designed to temporarily house the homeless, has almost
exhausted its waiting list of families with preschool-age
children.   Residents of the school district fear for
their school system if Westhelp fills vacancies with
homeless families with school-age children.

Melvin, Tessa.   "Legislators Face Their Critics on
Housing." New York Times, May 17, 1992:WC1.
      The author reports reactions to proposed legislation
in Westchester County, New York, that will include
housing for the homeless.

Melvin, Tessa.   "Progress in Moving Homeless from
Motels." New York Times, May 26, 1991:WC1.
      Westchester County officials have made progress in
moving homeless families from motels into emergency
apartments.

Melvin, Tessa. "A Success in Using Rent Vouchers." New
York Times, April 28, 1991:WC14.
      Eleven years ago, the Justice Department sued
Yonkers, New York, for housing discrimination.   Now,
using rent vouchers, four homeless black families have
moved there.

Mercado-Llorens, Segundo A., and Sheree L. West.   "The
New Grapes of Wrath..." In Accounting for Housing and
Homeless in 1990 Decennial Census. (Hearing Before the
Subcommittee on Census and Population of the committee on
Post Office and Civil Service.) Washington, D.C.: U. S.
Government Printing Office, April 11, 1986:84-89.
      This report includes an overview of homeless
Hispanics in the United States and some case stories.
The authors conclude that the federal government must
increase its funding for the homeless.

Meredith, Mamie. "'Waddies' and 'Hoboes' of the Old West." American Speech, 7, April 1932:257-260.
    Hoboes (a shortened salutation of "Ho boy!" shouted by one workman to another) "are enlisted, so to speak, by labor agents, in the larger of the western cities and shipped, in carloads, to the points where wanted....Earning good wages, he toils contentedly on, despite rain and mud, till the monthly pay-day comes. Then he takes a lay-off for the purpose of spending his wealth, at which he is a phenomenal success....After a reasonable time spent in such debauchery (drink, prostitutes, and gambling), they are willing again to return to work, seemingly only hoping for another pay-day to arrive, to bring with it a repetition of its insane orgies and fancied delights." ("Waddies" are cowboys.)

Meriwether, Lee. The Tramp at Home. New York: Harper, 1889.
    The author, a special agent for the U.S. Bureau of Labor, describes the working conditions and life styles of the lower class, as well as the one night he spent on the Bowery. As solutions, he proposes a tariff reduction and a graduated land tax. "Tramp" in the title refers to the author's "slumming."

Meriwether, Lee. A Tramp Trip: How to See Europe on Fifty Cents a Day. New York: Harper, 1886.
    The author recounts his extensive travels across Europe as he visits traditional and nontraditional tourist sites. "Tramp" in the title refers to his inexpensive mode of travel.

Meyerson, Harold. "On Venice Beach." Dissent, Spring 1988:157-159.
    The inhabitants of Venice, California, are reacting negatively to the increasing numbers of homeless who are drawn to the area.

Milburn, George. The Hobo's Hornbook: A Repertory for a Gutter Jongleur. New York: Ives Washington, 1930.
    As he traveled as a hobo, the author collected songs and poetry about hobohemia, which he presents here. He also incudes a few songs from published sources. He says that hobos are migratory workers, while tramps don't work.

Milburn, George. "Poesy in the Jungles." American Mercury, 20, May 1930:80-86.

"To relieve the tedium of dreary waits in jungle camps and long spells of incarceration in country jails," tramps and hoboes amuse themselves with kangaroo courts, ballad singing and recitation, and extemporaneous rhyming. After analyzing hobo ballads, the author concludes that these ballads are elusive because they are impromptu, variable, "seldom in the memory of one man," and "so gloriously scatological that they defy reduction to type." He predicts that because "automobiles have made it possible for any college sophomore to bum the breadth of the continent" with "no special determination or fortitude....to qualify as a tramp....the tramping fraternity, with all of its lore, must break up before the influx of gay cats who have neither any respect for trampdom's traditions nor any desire to make tramping a life-time vocation."

Milburn, Norweeta G., and Roderich J. Watts. "Methodological Issues in Research on the Homeless and the Homeless Mentally Ill." International Journal of Mental Health, 14 (4), 1986:42-60.
    The authors examine 75 articles on the homeless to determine how homelessness has been defined, to review the research methods that have been used and the data reported, to make recommendations on the type of data that should be reported, and to fill in gaps that apply to social policy. They conclude that a better theoretical foundation needs to be developed, more variables specified, and an explicit operational definition of homelessness constructed. For social policy, links need to be established between the various types of homeless people and the types of services they need. Systematic evaluations of current programs need to be made in order to provide data on which to base national programs.

Miller, Byron A., Alex D. Pokorny, and Thomas E. Kanas. "Problems in Treating Homeless, Jobless Alcoholics." Hospital and Community Psychiatry, 21 (3), 1970:98-99.
    Compared with persons who are discharged at the end of a 90-day alcoholic treatment program, those who had delayed exits were more withdrawn, depressed, uncooperative, evasive, less motivated, and drank more. The solution is to develop a special rehabilitation program for homeless, jobless alcoholics.

Miller, Mark. "Open Your Hearts." Restaurant Hospitality, 75 (6), June 1991:66-67.

The restaurant industry can make a difference in solving the problem of homelessness. The program, Share Our Strength, in which restaurants and suppliers sponsor a benefit meant to raise money for the hungry, is an example of what can be done.

Miller, Ronald J. <u>The Demolition of Skid Row</u>. Lexington: Lexington Books, 1982.

Urban renewal is causing skid row to diminish. As its inhabitants disperse, new skid rows are emerging. The solution is to develop urban policy that concerns itself with the people of skid row.

Milligan, James. <u>I Didn't Stay Honest</u>. London: Sampson Low, Marston, 1936.

This first-person account of tramping around the western U.S. and various parts of the world was written by a man who was raised in poverty and associated with rogues.

Millis, Harry A. "The Law Affecting Immigrants and Tramps." <u>Charities Review</u>, <u>7</u>, September 7, 1897:587-594.

The author reviews legislation concerning tramps and non-resident paupers. With the exception of three states, tramps are treated as criminals, subjected as vagrants to jail terms, and in some states, such as Missouri, are hired out for six months to the highest bidder with "cash in hand." Some states offer monetary rewards to induce people to turn in tramps. Punishment is generally most severe in the East, gradually becoming less severe in the West and South.

Mills, Crystal, and Hiro Ota. "Homeless Women with Minor Children in the Detroit Metropolitan Area." <u>Social Work</u>, <u>34</u> (6), November 1989:485-489.

Analyzing admission data of 87 homeless families served by an emergency shelter in Detroit during the first quarter of 1987, the authors found that most of the families were headed by a black female with one or two minor children. The mothers were young, lacking a high school diploma, and had no income. "Policies that emphasize prevention, comprehensiveness in service delivery and collaboration are needed. These policies should address prevention through income-support programs, the provisions of low-income housing, basic living skill training programs, and mental health service delivery. However, when available resources fail to prevent homelessness among families, programs and

policies should focus on saving the children....For the
cycle (of homelessness) to be broken, government, private
foundations, and business must work together to develop
and implement innovative programs aimed at reducing the
risks to these children."

Minehan, Thomas. Boy and Girl Tramps of America. New
York: Farrar and Rinehart, 1934.
    Based on participant observation of hobo life during
the summers of 1932 and 1933, the author, whose focus is
on migrant youths, discusses tramp culture and socialization into tramping, as well as the coping, attitudes, and
relationships of tramps.   The book also contains a
history of vagabondage.

Minehan, Thomas. Lonesome Road: The Way of Life of a
Hobo. Evanston: Row, Peterson, 1941.
    This novel about two boys, Joe and Bill, who take to
the road from Tulsa to California in search of work,
illustrates socialization into hobohemia and the dangers
and rewards of hoboing. Messages in the book include the
essential honesty of the hobo and the danger of becoming
a bum if one is on the road too long.

Minsley, Morton Seth.   "Pessimistic View of Housing for
Homeless." New York Law Journal, March 17, 1986:2.
    Although some legal advocates for the homeless are
taking constructive steps, many law firms are adding to
homelessness by supporting legislation and other activities that increase homelessness.

Minton-Eversole, Theresa.   "Companies as Community
Citizens." Training and Development, 45 (11), November
1991:21-30.
    The author reviews innovative ways that the four
corporations featured in this article are trying in order
to strengthen the country's workforce. Mentioned is Days
Inn's hiring of the homeless.

Misra, P. K. "Nomads in a City Setting." Man in India,
51 (4), 1971:317-333.
    The author reports on 19 itinerant Indian groups
that move at regular intervals, carrying on a tradition
handed down from their forefathers. These nomads provide
specialized services to villages.

Mitchell, Sam. "Dark at the End of the Tunnel." Santa
Cruz Express, September 20, 1984:8.

An upper-middle class family from Boise, Idaho, became homeless. After Dan Adams, an architectural designer, lost his job, he and his wife Beverly and their eight children lost their home. The family then migrated to Denver, where Dan eventually found a job in his field. Because Dan's $20,000 a year income is not adequate to support this large family and to rent or purchase a house, they are living in a campground.

Mitgang, Lee. "Homeless Insist on Right to Vote." Associated Press, October 5, 1984.
The basic question is whether election officials, in order to determine that someone lives in the district in which he or she wants to vote, can make a conventional address a condition for voting. Many homeless people insist that they are being discriminated against. The author reports on events in Philadelphia, Portland, Los Angeles, San Francisco, Santa Barbara, New York City, and Washington, D.C.

Mogridge, George. <u>London in May; or, Anthony Hoskin's Account of Some of the Principal Religious and Benevolent Institutions of London</u>. London: Thomas Ward, 1835.
This volume contains a chapter on the Society for the Suppression of Mendacity, established in 1818. The solutions are relief and work.

Molnar, Janice M., William R. Rath, and Tovah P. Klein. "Constantly Compromised: The Impact of Homelessness on Children." <u>Journal of Social Issues</u>, <u>46</u> (4), 1990:109-124.
The authors analyze literature that focuses on the effects of homelessness on children. Covered are birth outcomes, nutritional status, immunization status, lead levels, illnesses, access to health care, cognitive and social development, parent-child interaction, child abuse and neglect, school attendance, grade retention, special education, and academic performance. The authors recommend five strategies for future research on this topic and list the following four key policy issues that emerged from their research: (1) children in shelter facilities must be provided "developmentally appropriate experiences and activities," (2) the children must be provided routine and reliable access to health care, (3) "specially designated shelters for families with children should be designed to accommodate these families from the onset of homelessness through relocation to permanent

housing," and (4) children need permanent, safe, decent housing.

Molotsky, Irving. "The Demographics of Steam Grates." New York Times, February 7, 1985:A24.
The author poses the question of why most of the homeless in Washington, D.C., are white when most of the population is black. Concluding that this is due to visibility, not to actual numbers, he suggests reasons for the differential visibility.

Momeni, Jamshid A., ed. Homelessness in the United States, Volume I: State Surveys. Westport, Connecticut: Greenwood Press, 1989.
This edited volume contains 15 articles that report on homelessness in Alabama, Colorado, Florida, Illinois, Massachusetts, Missouri, New Jersey, New York, Ohio, Tennessee, Texas, Utah, Virginia, and the Pacific Northwest. Topics include the nature and extent of homelessness in the United States, the socioeconomic and demographic features of the homeless population, how homelessness can be conceptualized, the family background of the homeless, the relations of the homelessness, their need for shelter, their social needs, and the effects of homelessness on national policy.

Momeni, Jamshid A., ed. Homelessness in the United States--Data and Issues. Westport, Connecticut: Greenwood Press, 1990.
The dozen articles in this collection "attempt to bring systematic data and analysis to bear on the subject" of homelessness. The authors focus on counting the homeless, their sociodemographic profile, food sources, drug abuse, the long-term housing problem, a social-psychiatric perspective, sources of income, homeless children and their caretakers, and social policies.

Monkkonen, Eric H. "Regional Dimensions of Tramping, North and South, 1880-1910." In Walking to Work: Tramps in America 1790-1935, Eric H. Monkkonen, ed. Lincoln: University of Nebraska Press, 1984:189-211.
The author compares tramping in the north and south by season, lodging rates in police stations, age, sex, race, nativity, and trip length.

Monkkonen, Eric H., ed. <u>Walking to Work: Tramps in America 1790-1935</u>. Lincoln: University of Nebraska Press, 1984.

This edited collection of eight original articles, with an introduction and afterword by the editor, stresses the structural bases for the mass population movement known as industrial tramping. Each article (by Priscilla Clement, Patricia Cooper, Michael Davis, Douglas Jones, Eric Monkkonen, John Schneider, Jules Tygiel, and Lynn Weiner) is annotated separately in this present bibliography.

Morain, Lloyd L. <u>The Human Cougar</u>. Buffalo: Prometheus Books, 1976.

"Cougar" refers to men who love freedom and resist authority and the dominance of social institutions. The author examines the early lives, work habits, attitudes, family life, and marriages of such persons.

Morgan, Murray. <u>Skid Road: An Informal Portrait of Seattle</u>. New York: Viking Press, 1951.

In spite of its title, this history of Seattle contains little or nothing on the homeless.

Morgan, Thomas. "Again, Grim Shelters House a Rising Number of Families." <u>New York Times</u>, June 19, 1991:B1.

Although city officials had hoped by this time to have all families moved out of hotels and shelters into permanent housing, the problem has worsened instead. The number of homeless families is now one third larger than it was a year ago, going from 3,364 families in New York City's shelter system to 4,566.

Morgan, Thomas. "Ballerina from a Shelter: A Child's Dream." <u>New York Times</u>, May 30, 1991:B1.

The author profiles Shara Overton, an 8-year old girl who takes classes at the New York Theater Ballet School. Shara, who wants to be a ballerina, lives in a shelter for the homeless.

Morgan, Thomas. "Dinkins's Chief Homeless Policy Adviser Resigns." <u>New York Times</u>, September 4, 1991:B2.

Among the reasons that Nancy G. Wackstein, New York City's chief policy adviser on the homeless, gave for her resignation was the city's failure to fund social services to prevent homelessness.

Morgan, Thomas.   "Fear and Dependency Jostle in Shelters."   New York Times, November 4, 1991:A1.
     Many homeless people fear the shelters run by New
York City.   The shelter at Atlantic and Bedford is given
as an example to explain why.

Morgan, Thomas.   "Homeless Put into Hotels for Tourists."
New York Times, August 28, 1991:B5.
     New York City officials are having difficulty coping
with the growing numbers of homeless people.   About 283
families are now lodged in tourist hotels at taxpayers'
expense.

Morgan, Thomas.   "In the Shadow of Skyscrapers Grows a
Shantytown Society."   New York Times, October 20, 1991:1.
     Dozens of shantytowns have sprung up around New York
City, one at the end of Pier 84 in Manhattan.   Residents
of these cardboard shantytowns refuse to go to the
shelters, saying that life is safer here than in the
city-run shelters.

Morgan, Thomas.   "New York Bulldozes Squatters' Shantytowns."   New York Times, October 16, 1991:A1.
     Many of the homeless who had been evicted from
Tomkins Square Park built shantytowns on city-owned lots
in the East Village.   The city bulldozed those shantytowns.

Morgan, Thomas.   "New York City Plans to Reduce Beds for
Homeless."   New York Times, January 19, 1991:A35.
     The number of adults who seek emergency shelter in
New York City has levelled off, and the city expects to
provide fewer beds this winter than last year.

Morgan, Thomas.   "New York City Warned on Homeless."
March 6, 1991:B3.
     State officials warned New York City officials that
their violations of state regulations in sheltering
homeless families could cost them state housing money.

Morgan, Thomas.   "New York Planning Homeless Shelters
Across City."   New York Times, October 2, 1991:A1.
     David Dinkins, Mayor of New York City, announced
that the city would spend $258 million to build twenty to
thirty specialized homeless shelters.

Morgan, Thomas.   "Past Deadline, Street Families Remain
in Hotels."   New York Times, September 30, 1991:B1.

New York City officials have failed to meet the deadline they set, October 3, 1991, as the date when they would no longer have to pay the high costs of housing the homeless in hotels.

Morgan, Thomas. "Port Authority to Evict the Homeless from Bus Terminal." <u>New York Times</u>, November 7, 1991:B3.
   The New York City Port Authority announced that it was going to evict the homeless from its bus terminal on Eighth Avenue.

Morgan, Thomas. "Shift in View on Housing All the Homeless." <u>New York Times</u>, September 27, 1991:B1.
   New York City officials announced that the city had to limit its eligibility for emergency shelter, that many homeless persons could stay with family and friends.

Morganthau, Tom, Renee Michael, Diane Camper, and Lea Donosky. "Down and Out in America." <u>Newsweek</u>, March 15, 1982:28-29.
   National publicity has been given the freezing death of a homeless woman, Rebecca Smith, in New York City. Present solutions are inadequate to cope with the growing numbers of homeless. The solution requires a change in the economy.

Morinis, E. Alan. "'Getting Straight': Behavioral Patterns in a Skid Row Indian Community." <u>Urban Anthropology</u>, <u>11</u> (2), Summer 1982:193-212.
   The author proposes that the disproportionate numbers of Indians on skid row and their disproportionate rate of illness, accidents, crimes of violence, arrest, alcohol problems, and impoverishment should be seen as a passively hostile rebellion against the dominant society, their inverted behavioral norms a symbolic political act of a powerless group.

Moroz, Kathleen J., and Elizabeth A. Segal. "Homeless Children: Intervention Strategies for School Social Workers." <u>Social Work in Education</u>, <u>12</u> (2), January 1990:134-143.
   The authors' thesis is that school social workers can assist homeless children and children at risk of becoming homeless. They propose that school social workers initiate school committees to address these problems.

Morrell, D. C. "The Edinburgh Common Lodging-House: A Challenge to Medical Care." Scottish Medical Journal, 12, 1967:171-177.

To meet their medical needs, different approaches must be taken in the management of patients who come from lodging houses. The specific problems are the: (1) high rate of mental illness, (2) uncertainty that patients will keep appointments, (3) behaviors in out-patient departments that may not "endear" the patient to the staff, (4) difficulty in maintaining prolonged treatment due to the mobility of this population, (5) limited facilities for examining and treating patients in lodging houses, and (6) difficulty of convalescing in lodging houses.

Morrissette, Patrick J., and Sue McIntyre. "Homeless Young People in Residential Care." Social Casework, 70 (10), December 1989:603-610.

The usual intervention strategies for homeless youths are futile because they involve "the repeated utilization of treatment strategies that have proven to be unsuccessful in former placements." The authors suggest a model that allows the behavioral patterns of homeless youths to be "strategically interrupted," the creation of "external support systems," and the provision of "escape hatches" while social connections are established.

Morrissey, J. P., and D. Dennis. NIMH-Funded Research Concerning Homeless Mentally Ill Persons: Implications for Policy and Practice. Rockville, Maryland: National Institutes of Mental Health, 1986.

The authors review ten studies funded by NIMH that examine the numbers, demographics, mental health status, and service needs of the homeless.

Morse, Gary A. "Toward a Comprehensive Assessment of Homelessness." Public Law Forum, 4, Spring 1985:445-454.

The author reviews the literature on homelessness to determine who the homeless are, the causes of homelessness, and the question of what should be done about the problem. He concludes that "the legal system can provide a significant impact on homelessness," that the courts can serve as a tool to obtain needed resources for them.

Morse, Gary A., and Robert J. Calsyn. "Mentally Disturbed Homeless People in St. Louis: Needy, Willing, But

Underserved." International Journal of Mental Health, 14 (4), 1986:74-79.

Based on interviews with 122 females and 126 males in adult emergency shelters in St. Louis, the author concludes that 25 percent had been hospitalized for mental disorders. For 73.8 percent, the mental hospitalization preceded the homelessness. Although 46.9 percent were mentally ill according to the Global Severity Index, only 15.3 percent were receiving some form of mental health treatment. About one third have drinking problems, one-half had one or more physical problems diagnosed during the previous year, about nine of every ten were unemployed, about two-thirds had no income during the previous week, and one-fifth had been arrested while they were homeless. The author suggests that in order to enhance the quality of life for homeless persons the mental health system and other human service agencies must be modified. Especially needed is the development of "a publicly mandated and financed comprehensive service system." A new organization, homeless resource centers, should be located close to shelters. These centers should employ outreach staff who are knowledgeable about a range of resources and comfortable with non-traditional methods of interacting with clients.

Morse, Mary. The Unattached. Baltimore: Penguin Books, 1965.

The term "unattached" in the book's title refers to "those young people who do not belong to any kind of youth organization." The book is not really on the homeless, but focuses on the youth of England who do not fit in. Emphasis is placed on their characteristics, ideas, values, socializing, and solutions for helping them, especially counseling and trying to provide them direction in life.

Mort, Geoffrey. "Establishing a Right to Shelter for the Homeless." Brooklyn Law Review, 50, 1984:939-994.

The right to shelter under the New York state constitution is viewed as an aspect of the right to community treatment and remedies under the entitlement doctrine. The author explores the development and application of entitlement theory, examines shelter in state mental hospitals as a protected property interest that is illicitly withheld by deinstitutionalization, and explores tort remedies for the deinstitutionalized homeless, for their improper care, and for premature release from mental hospitals. "Dumping patients into dangerous and hostile cities" is an indictment on a society that deems itself civilized and progressive.

Mowbray, Carol T. "Homelessness in America: Myths and Realities." <u>American Journal of Orthopsychiatry</u>, <u>55</u> (1), January 1985:4-8.
   The author argues that these four common beliefs about homelessness are really myths: people in shelters are looking for a handout, homelessness is a new problem, deinstitutionalization is the major cause of homelessness, and the solution is more money for more shelters.

Mulkern, V., and R. Spence. <u>Alcohol Abuse/Alcoholism Among Homeless Persons: A Review of the Literature</u>. Rockville, Maryland: National Institute on Alcohol Abuse and Alcoholism, 1984.
   The authors report on fourteen studies that address the prevalence of alcoholism and other drug abuse by the homeless, the characteristics of homeless persons who abuse drugs, and treatment programs for these persons.

Mullin, Glen H. <u>Adventures of a Scholar Tramp</u>. New York: Century, 1925.
   This first-person account is written by a man who graduated from college in the early 1920s and then took to the road.

Mullins, Leanna H. "The RHCs Lend a Helping Hand." <u>Telephony</u>, <u>220</u> (11), March 18, 1991:78-82.
   Among the examples used to illustrate corporate giving is that of US West which began Osage Initiatives. Each year, more than 21,000 homeless and disadvantaged people are helped by this program.

Murray, Charles. "Government Will Try--and Fail." <u>New York Times</u>, February 2, 1988:E6.
   To place the hard-core homeless underclass in public housing will simply turn the housing into "centers of crime and drugs." The housing will also be physically trashed. The solution is to remove "98 percent of the restrictions" that currently exist on building housing. There should be virtually no restrictions placed in the way of anybody who wants to go in there (inner city neighborhoods, such as the South Bronx) and put up housing and rent it to whomever they want at whatever rent they are able to charge. (This is the opposing part of pro-con matching pieces on the role of the government in ending the dependency of the homeless on welfare

hotels. The matching article, "The State Can Undo What It Has Done" is by Jonathan Kozol.)

Murray, Charles. "Welfare: Promoting Poverty or Progress?" <u>Wall Street Journal</u>, May 15, 1985:32.
    The author reviews <u>Years of Poverty, Years of Plenty</u> by Richard D. Coe and Greg J. Duncan, while Coe and Duncan review Murray's book, <u>Losing Ground</u>. Murray takes the position that the poverty programs of the Great Society worsened the plight of the poor, miring many of them in dependency, while Coe and Duncan take the position that these programs served as a safety net for the poor and that over the years few poor people remain in poverty.

Murray, Harry. "Time in the Streets." <u>Human Organization</u>, <u>43</u> (2), Summer 1984:154-161.
    Based on participant observation in 1980-1981 at Cambridge Street Inn, a night shelter, the author examines the temporal images and orientations of street people.

Muscatine, Alison. "Suburbs Send Homeless to D.C. Shelters." <u>Washington Post</u>, February 19, 1983:A1, A31.
    Although Washington, D.C., and its suburbs have increased their spending to shelter homeless families, they provide few beds for the hard-core homeless, the rootless vagabonds "who have been released from mental hospitals or prisons, or the hard-core street people who sleep in cars, on grates, in shacks, or under bridges." City officials of Washington are upset because the surrounding suburbs are not building shelters for the chronic homeless, but instead are sending them into the city. District officials insist that the suburbs build their own shelters. In reply to the charge that they are treating only the temporarily homeless and ignoring the hard-core street people, "suburban officials say their governments purposely choose programs that are geared to homeless persons who want to change their life styles, rather than to traditional street people." This idea of self responsibility for homelessness is reflected in the statement of an official who said, "It is a question of philosophy. We still feel that the person is making choices and that he has to take responsibility for himself. We will call the person to task about what they have been doing. We do that on purpose."

Mydans, Seth. "School Where Homeless Find Haven." <u>New York Times</u>, November 25, 1989:9.
    The Coeur d'Alene Elementary School in Venice, California, "has one of the nations highest enrollment of homeless children, as much as 20 or 30 percent at any time."

Myers, Gustavus. "Colonizing the Tramp." <u>Review of Reviews</u>, <u>39</u>, March 1908:311-316.
    The tramp problem costs the railroads about $25,000,000 yearly. There are about a half million tramps in the United States, of whom 23,964 were killed and 25,236 injured during a five year period while stealing rides on railroads. The solution is to establish industrial colonies similar to those in Belgium and Switzerland. Details of the proposed colonies are provided.

Myers, Steven Lee. "Homeless Benefit from West Side Book Fair." <u>New York Times</u>, November 24, 1991:46.
    Over 100 publishers have donated 20,000 books which will be sold at the New York Book Fair to Aid the Homeless.

Myerson, David J. "An Approach to the 'Skid Row' Problem in Boston." <u>New England Journal of Medicine</u>, <u>249</u> (16), October 15, 1953:646-649.
    Based on his observations of alcoholic homeless patients treated at Long Island Hospital in Boston, the author reports that most are over 40, almost three-fourths are Irish and almost one-fourth British, 40 percent are single, 38 percent separated, 14 percent divorced, four percent married, and four percent widowed. He summarizes a program that helps alcoholics escape from the vicious cycle that keeps them incapacitated.

Myerson, David J. "The 'Skid Row' Problem: Further Observations on a Group of Alcoholic Patients, with Emphasis on Interpersonal Relations and the Therapeutic Approach." <u>New England Journal of Medicine</u>, <u>254</u>, June 21, 1956:1168-1173.
    A rehabilitation program for homeless alcoholic men that attempted to create a group spirit and reestablish family ties showed success for 54 men, allowing 12 to function independently of the hospital, while 42 remained partially dependent on the hospital.

Myerson, David J., and Joseph Mayer. "Origins, Treatment and Destiny of Skid-Row Alcoholic Men." <u>New England Journal of Medicine</u>, <u>275</u> (8) August 25, 1966:419-425.

The authors compare 101 skid row men who volunteered for a work-oriented halfway house program in 1952 with a group of 108 men ten years later. The volunteers had less contact with welfare agencies, higher occupational attainment, and a lower rate of arrest. The better educated, more occupationally skilled, and more self sufficient tended to enter the program. They recommend that such programs be made available to the younger men of skid row.

N

Nagler, Mark. <u>Natives Without a Home</u>. Don Mills: Longman, 1975.

In this overview of Indians in Canada, with an emphasis on their cultural displacement, the concept of homelessness is used in a broad sense.

Nann, Richard C., ed. <u>Uprooting and Surviving: Adaptation and Resettlement of Migrant Families and Children</u>. Dordrecht, Holland: D. Reidel, 1982.

The 18 articles of this book focus on uprooted people (Vietnamese, Chinese, and Turks) who have taken refuge in the United States, Canada, Sweden, Holland, and Germany.

Nascher, I. L. <u>The Wretches of Povertyville: A Sociological Study of the Bowery</u>. Chicago: Joseph J. Lanzit, 1909.

Some of these "wretches" are the homeless. Their sleeping, eating, drinking, and finances are detailed.

Nash, George. <u>The Habitats of Homeless Men in Manhattan</u>. New York: Columbia University, Bureau of Applied Social Research, November 1964.

Looking for homeless men outside the Bowery, the researchers found them concentrated in other areas. The choice of location of homeless men depends on the nonresidential facilities they patronize, the services they find available, and police practices. To estimate the total numbers of homeless men in Manhattan, the researchers counted the death certificates of non-Bowery men buried by the city whose characteristics showed homelessness. They then determined their ratio to the Bowery population.

Nash, George, and Patricia Nash. <u>A Preliminary Estimate of the Population and Housing of the Bowery in New York City</u>. New York: Columbia University, Bureau of Applied Social Research, 1964.
     The authors used records of lodging houses, shelters, missions, rooming houses, and hotels to estimate the population of the Bowery in 1949 and 1964.

Navarro, Mireya. "Gauging Recalcitrant TB patients." <u>New York Times</u>, April 14, 1992:A1.
     Success in dealing with the current epidemic of drug-resistant tuberculosis among the homeless is dependent on getting these patients to take their medicine, which is a difficult task.

Navarro, Mireya. "Life in '68 Plymouth for Family of 4." <u>New York Times</u>, October 23, 1989:Y9.
     Oscar and Leticia Ramirez and their children, whose house was destroyed by the 1989 earthquake in northern California, sleep in their automobile or in a neighbor's living room.

Nazario, Sonia L. "Playing House: Troubled Teenagers Create a Fragile Family Beneath a Busy Street." <u>Wall Street Journal</u>, January 21, 1992:A1.
     A group of runaway teenagers in Hollywood, California, has formed a pseudofamily that provides some structure and affection. This group, known as The Trolls, lives under the bridge of a busy street in what the teenagers call "the hole." They have adopted an exconvict, John Soaring Eagle, as a surrogate father, whom they support by panhandling, prostitution, and mugging.

Needle, Charles. "Finding A Home For the Homeless." <u>American City & County</u>, <u>103</u>, December 1988:40-46.
     The author summarizes efforts across the nation to build low-cost housing. Emphasis is placed on public-private partnerships.

Nelkin, Dorothy. "Unpredictability and Life Style in a Migrant Labor Camp." <u>Social Problems</u>, <u>17</u>, 1970:472-487.
     Based on participant observation in 14 New York State labor camps, the author reports on the culture of

their residents, most of whom are Southern black migrant farm workers. The analysis centers around the unpredictability of events for these people and their consequent adaptive life style.

Nelson, Bryce. "Nation's Psychiatrists Give 'High Priority' to the Homeless." <u>New York Times</u>, May 10, 1983:C1, C2.
    A panel on the urban homeless at the annual meeting of the American Psychiatric Association stressed that although deinstitutionalization was based on the principle of people being discharged into a strong network of community services, deinstitutionalization has sometimes been used for the purpose of reducing state budgets. Deinstitutionalization has thus contributed to the problem of homelessness. Today's homeless, who are younger, are likely to be suffering from serious psychiatric problems, to have a previous history of psychiatric hospitalization, to be loners, and to have never married. To solve this problem, we must provide shelters that offer mental health treatment on site (where the homeless are) and a treatment plan for each homeless person who is mentally ill.

Nelson, Marcia Z. "Street People." <u>The Progressive</u>, <u>49</u> (3), March 1985:24-29.
    The author profiles two shelters for the homeless in Chicago, Pacific Gardens Mission, which operates a religious program, and Cooper's Place, which operates a secular program.

Nelson, Ruth K. "Letter to the Editor." <u>Wall Street Journal</u>, November 2, 1989:A23.
    The author states that life on the street creates mental illness.

Nenno, Mary K. "Housing Allowances Are Not Enough." <u>Society</u>, <u>21</u>, March-April 1984:54-57.
    The change from construction to leasing in the federal government's housing assistance programs fails to improve the nation's supply of adequate low-income housing. Three groups have special needs: the elderly, the handicapped, and single-parent households. The solutions are federal assistance to improve the supply of housing, reform of shelter allowances in the public welfare system, and a multiple program approach.

Nerone, B. J. "Throwaway Children." Imprint, 30 (2), April-May 1983:31-32, 35, 37.

The goal of Covenant House and its center, UNDER 21, located a short walk from Times Square in New York City, is to rescue adolescents from street life "before they are lost forever." Available services include a 24-hour emergency shelter, health services, hospital referrals, legal services, three meals a day plus snacks, and family, vocational, and educational counseling.

Neville, Hippo. Sneak Thief on the Road. London: Jonathan Cape, 1935.

This book is a first-person account of tramping and stealing in England.

Newcomb, Franklyn F. "Transient Boys." The Family, 14, April 1933:57-59.

Boys take to the road because of broken homes, the presence of a stepparent, and a spirit of adventure. The solution is for the home community to put the boys' interests, desires, and ambitions to constructive use-- such as by placing the boys in such responsible positions as volunteer recreational leaders.

Newfield, Jack. "The Dirty Dozen: New York's Worst Landlords." Village Voice, April 9, 1985:11-15, 32.

The author details the exploitation of tenants by persons he identifies as the worst landlords in New York City. He stresses that although they pay their rent, some tenants live in unheated and virtually abandoned buildings.

Newman, Barry. "Poles Are Exasperated By Housing Shortage, and No Relief Is Near." Wall Street Journal, December 19, 1986:1, 13.

During World War II, 40 percent of Poland's homes were destroyed. Survivors lived in the ruins. Although the state set the goal of giving every citizen a place to live, it placed the demands of industry and agriculture first. In the current housing shortage, "nearly two million families among Poland's 37 million people lack homes of their own." Here "children grow up, marry, have more children and live jammed in with their parents until the undertaker clears some space."

Newman, Gerald S., ed. Homeless Man on Skid Row. Chicago: Tenants Relocation Bureau, September 1961.

Skid row exists because it performs functions for seven types of homeless men: elderly or physically disabled, semi-settled or settled working men, migratory workers, transient bums, resident bums, criminals, and chronic alcoholics. The author also examines the historical background and geography of Chicago's skid row. The book contains maps, photos, tables, and a bibliography.

Newman, Marian. "They Came to Mourn a Man They Hardly Knew." New York Times, April 4, 1992:A27.
The author discusses the funeral of Robert Walther, a homeless man who was burned to death by teenagers in New York City's Bronx.

Newman, Sandra J., and Ann B. Schnare. "Housing: The Gap in the Welfare System." The Council of State Government, 60, May-June 1987:117-121.
In order to address the needs of the country's poor and homeless, we need a recommitment to low-income housing. This can be accomplished by formulating a national housing policy and establishing "categorical housing assistance."

Newmark, Judith. "Jonathan Kozol Takes Readers Inside a New York Welfare Hotel in a Heart-Rending Book." St. Louis Post-Dispatch, May 28, 1988.
In this interview with the author of Rachel and Her Children: Homeless Families in America, Jonathan Kozol is quoted as saying that the Martinique Hotel affected him directly and deeply. Concerning his research, he said: "A lot of my capacity for decisiveness, I feel, deteriorated. I found myself becoming disorganized...Let me give you an example: I generally know how to use the buses and the subways or how to flag a cab, even in New York City. But after I was at the Martinique, I would just lose my sense of confidence. I could not do simple things. I'd come out on a cold, cold night at 2 or 3 a.m. and be unable to galvanize myself to flag down a cab. There were cabs; the hotel is right off Broadway. I can usually do that but...I'd lost my authority, somehow. I'd end up walking 20 blocks back to midtown. And I'd get back to my clean hotel room, have a hot shower, get a sandwich--and then I couldn't eat. So if it has that effect on a visitor, think of what it's like for someone who has to live there." Kozol adds that people distance themselves from the homeless: they tend to see the homeless as people unlike themselves, who somehow deserve

their fate. They explain homelessness as due to something the people have or have not done. Such "blaming
the victim" is a "dangerous mind game to play with
homelessness." Although the more bizarre are the most
visible, most homeless are "ordinary people who have been
driven out of the working class by higher rents and lower
wages"--and that could happen to anyone.

Newton, Stephen P., and Charles P. Duffy. "Old Portland
and an Oldtime Problem." <u>Alcohol Health and Research
World</u>, <u>11</u> (3), Spring 1987:62-65, 91.
       Charged with the task of proposing solutions for
public drunkenness in Portland's downtown area, a task
force identified five factors: the lack of sufficient
facilities for treatment, the lack of a designated
helping agency for intoxicated alcoholics, the need for
more and better law enforcement, the need for coordination between the merchants association and social service
agencies, and the necessity of meeting the needs of the
homeless.

Nicholas, Dan. "The Army's Secret Weapon." <u>Fund Raising
Management</u>, <u>19</u> (9), November 1988:64-68, 104.
       The author's review of the purpose, approach, and
fund raising by the Salvation Army mentions feeding the
homeless as one of the group's activities.

Nichols, J., L. K. Wright, and J. F. Murphy. "A Proposal
for Tracking Health Care for the Homeless." <u>Journal of
Community Health</u>, <u>11</u> (3), 1986:204-209.
       A basic problem in the utilization and accessibility
of health care programs for the homeless is that they are
designed by health care providers who have goals, values,
and beliefs about health care that differ from those of
the homeless. To help overcome this shortcoming, the
authors have developed the "Tool for Referral Assessment
of Continuity", which is intended to help health care
providers refer and track homeless clients.

Nichols, Malcolm S. "Homeless Persons." <u>Social Work
Year Book</u>, 1933:215-217.
       After examining the facilities at lodging houses,
the author looks at the trend toward centralization in
dealing with the problems of homelessness. This problem
is now more pressing due to the effects of the depression.

Nichols, Osgood, and Comstock Glaser. <u>Work Camps for</u> <u>America: The German Experience and The American Opportu-</u> <u>nity</u>. New York: The John Day Company, 1933.
    The thesis is that the work camps for the youth of Germany are a good model for American unemployed youth. After presenting an historical background of German work camps, their application to the unemployed, the economic and political opportunities offered participants, their financing, and a brief overview of work camps in Switzer- land, Holland, and Wales, the authors outline how these experiences can be applied to the United States.

Nichols, William W. "A Changing Attitude Toward Poverty in <u>The Ladies' Home Journal</u>: 1895-1919." <u>Mid-Continent</u> <u>American Studies Journal</u>, <u>5</u>, Spring 1964:3-16.
    The author, an historian of ideas, reports that the attitude toward poverty in the <u>Ladies Home Journal</u>, edited by Edward Bok, presented unrealistic ideas of poverty. Although the homeless were not the topic of any articles, acts of benevolence toward tramps and other poor people were seen as "simply an encouragement of evil."

Niebuhr, R. Gustav. "Here Is the Church: As for the People, They're Picketing It." <u>Wall Street Journal</u>, November 20, 1991:A1.
    Residents of Rancho San Diego, California, are picketing the Presbyterian Church because its members plan to build a new church in their neighborhood. Residents fear that the church will be a magnet for the homeless and hungry.

Nieves, Evelyn. "Return of Welfare Hotel Is Angering West Siders." <u>New York Times</u>, January 21, 1991:B3.
    The author reports on a dispute that erupted over New York City moving 190 homeless families into the Regent Hotel, a welfare hotel that had been closed in 1989.

Nieves, Evelyn. "Squatters and Friends March, But Tompkins Square Is Weary." <u>New York Times</u>, October 13, 1991:40.
    Squatters and homeless people staged a protest in Tompkins Square park to object New York City eviction of the homeless from city-owned buildings.

Nieves, Evelyn. "Squatters in City Buildings Face Eviction by the Landlord." New York Times, October 20, 1991:Section 4:16.
The author reviews a dispute between homeless advocates who say that city officials are eager to evict the homeless and the city officials who defend their actions.

Nieves, Evelyn. "Tensions Remain at Closed Tompkins Square Park." New York Times, June 17, 1991:B1.
Animosities prevail between residents of the Tompkins Square Park area who approved the police removing the homeless from the park and those who felt that it was all right for them to remain.

Nix, Crystal. "Childhood Dies Young in Hotel for Homeless." New York Times, November 4, 1985:17.
Children living in hotels for the homeless face especially difficult problems: prostitution, drugs, muggings, and shootings.

Nix, Crystal. "High Profits Cited at Welfare Hotel." New York Times, March 10, 1986:17.
Although the Holland Hotel, in which the city houses homeless persons, has been cited for almost 1,000 violations of housing, health, and building codes, it earned a $3,000,000 profit in 1985. The city pays $60 a day for a one-bedroom apartment and $100 a day for a two-bedroom apartment.

Nix, Crystal. "Housing Family in a Bronx Shelter Costs New York $70,000 a Year." New York Times, March 7, 1986:14.
The cost of housing a family of four in the Roberto Clemente Family Shelter is nearly $6,000 a month, most of which is spent on staff salaries. The author discusses the length of stay in this shelter, the cost of group shelters versus welfare hotels, the services each offers, and the New York City budget of $114,000,000 for the homeless. The solution is to use the power of eminent domain to seize hotels and to then turn them over to nonprofit groups--or to let nonprofit agencies rent the hotels and run them.

Nix, Crystal. "Plan Offered for the Homeless with Special Needs." New York Times, May 30, 1986:13.
New York City officials have proposed a plan to spend $82 million to provide transitional and permanent

housing, job training, and counseling for subgroups of the homeless--those who are mentally ill, substance abusers, the elderly, and the young.

Nix, Crystal. "Taking Account of the Hidden Homeless." New York Times, June 22, 1986:E8.
    Children make up about half of New York City's homeless population. The term "hidden homeless" refers to families who are doubling up or tripling up with friends or relatives, the last step before they turn to the city for help. The author expresses concern about a growing underclass and its effects on children. New low-income housing is needed.

Noah, Timothy. "Census Bureau's Count of Homeless Fails to End Debate." Wall Street Journal, April 15, 1991:B5C.
    The census of the homeless released by the U.S. Census Bureau has been challenged as too low by a variety of groups.

Noble, C. W. "The Border Land of Trampdom." Popular Science Monthly, 50, 1896-1897:252-258.
    Having spent a summer "on the road," the author develops a typology of people "on the bum." Of those who are "on the road from preference," there are tramps (temporary and permanent) and roadsters, those who have a "graft," some visible means of support. The second major class is those who travel from necessity, some of whom are in the process of becoming tramps. The "proper" solution to "the tramp question" is that which is already being used in many places, the municipal woodyard "in which a meal or a night's lodging is given in payment for two or three hours' wood cutting." This solution considers the distinction the author noted concerning voluntariness, for "the wood yard will become abhorrent to the genuine tramp, but will be welcomed by those who are really forced on the road by lack of work."

Noble, Phil. "Entrepreneurs in Community Service." Business and Economic Review, 36 (1), October-December 1989:6-8.
    In profiling the Palmetto Project, a community service group in South Carolina, the author says that one of their projects is to provide food for the homeless at Thanksgiving.

Nolin, Robert. "Teenage Runaways Find Living Tough." <u>Daytona Beach Sunday News-Journal</u>, December 22, 1985:A1, A2.
    Runaways from across the nation hang out at "The Wall" in Daytona Beach, Florida. They are subject to exploitation.

Nolin, Robert. "Undercover Counselor Takes to Streets." <u>Daytona Beach Sunday News-Journal</u>, December 22, 1985:A2.
    The author reviews the work of a counselor who seeks out runaways in Daytona Beach, Florida. The article contains a list of help available for runaways.

Nordberg, Marie. "Hope for the Homeless." <u>Emergency Medical Services</u>, <u>14</u> (5), September 1985:25-31.
    Because they cannot depend upon families and friends, many of the homeless depend upon Emergency Medical Services for survival. The author summarizes the health problems of homeless people, legal difficulties in forcing commitment for health reasons, problems with discharge planning, and alternative facilities such as Health Care for the Homeless provided by the Robert Wood Johnson Foundation. Proposed solutions include making it easier for physicians to commit those who need acute hospitalization, early medical treatment, more shelters, renovation of existing housing, and construction of low-income housing.

Nordheimer, Jon. "In Lieu of Jail, Posner Must Aid Poor in Florida." <u>New York Times</u>, February 13, 1988:1, 21.
    After a nine-year legal battle, financier Victor Posner has avoided a jail sentence on federal income tax evasion charges by agreeing "to spend $3 million to help homeless men, women and children in south Florida and devote 20 hours a week for 5 years to working with them."

Noreik, K. "Hospitalized Psychoses Among Wandering People in Norway." <u>Acta Psichiatrica Scandinavia</u>, <u>41</u>, 1965:157-176.
    Based on a study of the 1840 and later records of 3,801 vagabonds and tramps made by the Norwegian Mission among the Homeless, the author concludes that the "group of vagabonds has a higher frequency of psychoses than the general population."

Norman, Michael. "Under Boardwalk, Homeless Eke Out a Survival." <u>New York Times</u>, October 7, 1986:16.

A group of homeless people are living under the boardwalk in New York City.

Norris, Bill. "Hunger Haunts Classrooms in a Land of Plenty." New York Times Educational Supplement, November 4, 1988:15.
This article stresses the large number of homeless and hungry in the United States, emphasizing that the country needs to deal with this problem, especially that of homeless and hungry children.

Norris, Lowell Ames. "America's Homeless Army." Scribner's Magazine, 93, May 1933:316-318.
The author compares America's 200,000 homeless children to the bezprizorni, the 750,000 Russian waifs thrown onto the streets due to famine and civil strife. He details Russia's solutions and proposes preventive and protective measures. A preventive program would be to encourage boys to stay home by extending school hours, providing trade courses in school, increasing recreational and vocational activities, and discouraging their ability to find employment. Protective measures include camps and works projects to employ homeless youth, ones that provide adequate shelter and food and a definite training program for boys who cannot be sent home.

Nothaft, Frank E. "The 1990s: Presenting: Jack Kemp." Secondary Mortgage Markets, 7 (1), Spring 1990:19-23.
Jack Kemp, director of the U.S. Department of Housing and Urban Development, stated that there are six priorities in the expansion of home ownership: affordable housing, helping the homeless, helping create resident management opportunities for public housing, enforcement of fair housing laws, "incentivizing" the tax code, and creating more jobs.

Nyamathi, Adeline, and Rose Vasquez. "Impact of Poverty, Homelessness, and Drugs on Hispanic Women at Risk for HIV Infection." Hispanic Journal of Behavioral Sciences, 11 (4), November 1989:299-314.
Through interviews with 43 Hispanic women at two homeless shelters and two drug rehabilitation centers, the authors examine the women's concerns about AIDS—their fears about caring for their children, drug addiction, lack of social support, and loss of health. They propose a culturally-relevant approach by Hispanic health care professionals and trained lay personnel.

Nylander, Towne. "The Migratory Population of the United States." <u>American Journal of Sociology</u>, <u>30</u> (2), September 1924:129-153.

There are three types of migrants: tramps (professional tramps, road kids, tramp criminals, criminal tramps, jockers and prushons, and neuropathic tramps), hobos (bindle stiffs, beachcombers, and automobile tourists), and bums (feeble-minded, superannuated, and diseased). Many causes underlie the several million migrants in the United States: failure or incompetency, flight, breaking-up of the crafts, closed labor unions, prosperity and depression, scientific management, apostasy, disappearance of the frontier, improved traveling facilities, charity, shipping agencies and employment bureaus, and prenatal and postnatal impressions. The solutions are centralized labor bureaus, cooperation between industries and communities, low-priced traveling facilities, registration of migratory workers, changed laws, and government hotels and camps.

Nylander, Towne. "Wandering Youth." <u>Sociology and Social Research</u>, <u>17</u>, July 1933:560-568.

Four types of boys are on the road: single boys (who have no definite affiliation and no distinctive characteristics), road kids (who travel in gangs of 10 to 100), gay cats (who are embryonic tramps or hobos), and youngsters under the control of perverts. He describes life on the road, in the "jungles," and in the cities. Youth wander due to economic, social, and psychological factors. As a solution, the author recommends that self-sufficient, permanent farms be operated by families.

O

O'Connor, Colleen. "A $50 Million Handshake." <u>Newsweek</u>, <u>107</u>, May 19, 1986:25.

Logistical problems have been overcome in planning the "Hands Across America" fund-raising media event for the homeless and hungry.

O'Connor, Joan. "Sheltering the Homeless in the Nation's Capital." <u>Hospital and Community Psychiatry</u>, <u>34</u> (9), September 1983:863-867, 879.

The author reports on various approaches to and facilities for the homeless in Washington, D.C. Featured

are John and Erna Steinbruck of Luther Place, Justin
Brown and Tim Siegel of the Community for Creative Non-
Violence, Liz Pontzer and Terry Lynch of Calvary Baptist
Shelter for Women, and Minnie Bingham of the City Crisis
Resolution Unit. The types of homeless are "abused
women, evicted families, deinstitutionalized mental
patients, relatively young black men who have never held
a job, stranded travelers, and African, Asian, and
Caribbean refugees." Various solutions are suggested for
shelter, services, and second-stage shelters that offer
group-home living.

O'Connor, Philip. <u>Britain in the Sixties: Vagrancy,
Ethos and Actuality</u>. Baltimore: Penguin, 1963.
    This romanticized version of tramping, illustrating
the tramp's superiority to the acquisitive society,
presents an overview of England's poor laws, and reports
some participant observation.

Odum, Howard W. <u>Rainbow Round My Shoulder</u>: <u>The Blue
Trail of Black Ulysses</u>. Indianapolis: Bobbs-Merrill,
1928.
    This volume is written in dialect, as though it were
a first-person account of a wandering black man, with
chapter introductions in the third person.

Ogborne, Alan C., and Richard Wilmot. "Evaluation of an
Experimental Counseling Service for Male Skid Row
Alcoholics." <u>Journal of Studies on Alcohol</u>, <u>40</u> (1),
1979:129-132.
    Twenty skid row men were given counseling for six
months, while a control sample of 20 received none. The
results showed few differences in drinking patterns and
life styles.

Okun, Stacey. "Team to Help the Homeless Is Urged." <u>New
York Times</u>, January 31, 1988:18.
    The Port Authority is going to establish a drop-in
center adjacent to its bus terminal at Eighth and Ninth
Avenues and 40th and 42nd Streets in Manhattan. The
center will offer counseling and referral services for
hundreds of homeless people who seek shelter at the
terminal each day. The Port Authority staff is demoralized by the problems of the homeless, and travelers are
harassed by them.

Olin, Jack S. "'Skid Row' Syndrome: A Medical Profile of the Chronic Drunkenness Offender." <u>Canadian Medical Association Journal</u>, <u>95</u>, July 30, 1966:205-214.
This article provides an overview of the diseases and deformities found during the physical examinations given to 227 chronic drunks in the Toronto Jail. The author concludes that if the necessary therapy were given, ninety percent of the men could perform useful labor.

Oltman, David. "County Workers To Find, Help Homeless in Cold Snap." <u>Los Angeles Daily Journal</u>, <u>100</u>, January 23, 1987:B1.
Teams from three county agencies in Los Angeles will try to locate the homeless on the streets when the temperature drops below 40 degrees. The purpose is to help them find temporary shelter and sign them up for a general relief program.

Ortega, Suzanne T., and Jay Corzine. "Socioeconomic Status and Mental Disorders." <u>Research in Community and Mental Health</u>, <u>6</u>, 1990:149-182.
The authors' review of the literature to examine the relationship between social class and mental illness includes mental illness among the homeless. They conclude that the evidence best supports the drift hypotheses, that negative effects of the label of mental illness help explain how mental disorders produce downward social mobility.

Oser, Alan S. "HELP's Transition to Permanent Housing." <u>New York Times</u>, December 22, 1991:Section 10:3.
The author profiles Housing Enterprise for the Less Privileged (HELP), a nonprofit development company founded by Andrew Cuomo, son of the governor of New York.

Ostensen, Kay Wickett. "The Runaway Crisis: Is Family Therapy the Answer?" <u>American Journal of Family Therapy</u>, <u>9</u> (3), Fall 1981:3-12.
Tests and control groups show that Brief Family Intervention counseling is highly effective in preventing recidivism of runaway behavior. Still needed is a large-scale replication of this study. The author recommends a comparison of different family counseling models, a comparison of the runaway patterns of youth who remain "on the streets" with those who seek counseling, and research to address the issue of runaway prevention.

Otis, Lillian. "Unemployment and Its Treatment in Non-Resident Families: A Study of Fifty Non-Resident White Families Known to the Cleveland Associated Charities." The Family, Supplement, June 1933:136-143.
　　The Transportation Agreement of the Family Welfare Association of America is being implemented in Cleveland. According to this agreement, the only relief given to non-resident families is transportation to their place of legal residence.

Otten, Alan L. "When Institute of Medicine Speaks, People Listen, Because Newest President Won't Let It Be Ignored." Wall Street Journal, March 31, 1987:64.
　　The Institute of Medicine, a private non-profit organization created to provide the federal government with authoritative and disinterested advice on health policy and health-care delivery, has become more visible and has more clout in Washington. Among the indications that this has occurred is the request by Congress that the Institute suggest ways to provide health care for the homeless.

Ousley, J. Douglas. "Free to Enjoy the Cruelty of the Streets." Wall Street Journal, August 3, 1990:A10.
　　The author's thesis is that the homeless mentally ill who "are driven by inner compulsions of which they have no control" should be reincarcerated, that leaving them "in a degraded state not only doesn't help them but casts a moral shadow over the society as guaranteeing them their putative freedom of movement....we need, then, to recognize that confining at least some of the mentally ill may be the best thing for them--not just pragmatically, for the good of society, but in humanist and spiritual terms, for their own good."

Outland, George E. Boy Transiency in America: A Compilation of Articles Dealing with Youth Wandering in the United States. Santa Barbara: Santa Barbara State College Press, 1939.
　　This volume is a collection of Thomas Minehan's articles, including reactions to them. The topics include the educational background and aspirations, retardation, and recreation of boy transients.

Outland, George E. "Determinants Involved in Boy Transiency." Journal of Educational Sociology, 11, 1938:360-372.

The author summarizes findings from a study of 3,352 transient boys who registered at the Los Angeles branch of the Federal Transient Service between August 1, 1934, and July 31, 1935. The boys were between the ages of 16 and 20. For 69 percent it was their first trip, and 82 percent had been on the road for less than six months. About 80 percent came from urban districts. About 88 percent were native whites, of whom 59 percent had completed one or more years of high school. Fifty-six percent came from broken homes. The primary cause of their transiency was economic; the secondary cause, problems experienced by the boys; the tertiary cause, the quest for adventure. As economic conditions improve, transiency will decrease, and most wanderers will be the personally maladjusted. The major lesson to be learned from this study "is that of providing employment or worth-while leisure-time activity for out-of-school youth, while at the same time so adjusting the education-al system as to prolong the school period through an increase in the holding power."

Outland, George E. "The Education of Transient Boys." School and Society, October 13, 1934:501-504.
The author reports on the educational level and state of origin of 5,000 transient boys between the ages of 15 and 20 who had registered at the Central Intake Bureau of the Transient Service of the Federal Emergency Relief Administration in Los Angeles between December 12, 1933, and July 28, 1934. He concludes that contrary to common perception "boys on the road are not bums," for they have an educational level of 9.09.

Outland, George E. "The Federal Transient Service as a Deterrent of Boy Transiency." Sociology and Social Research, 22, 1937:143-148.
The Federal Transient Service, a series of camps for dealing with runaways, is itself seen as a cause of running away. To test this unanticipated consequence of human action, Outland found that 2.9 percent of the 3,352 16- to 20-year-old boys who registered at the Los Angeles branch of the Federal Transient Service in 1934-1935 gave the desire to experience life in a transient camp as the direct reason for leaving home. Indirect economic factors are also indicated, for one-third of these boys reported that their families were either on relief or the main wage earner was unemployed.

Outland, George E. "The Home Situation as a Direct Cause of Boy Transiency." Journal of Juvenile Research, 22, 1938:33-43.
   A sample of 3,352 boys who registered at the Los Angeles branch of the Federal Transient Service in 1934-1935 showed that about 25 percent had run away because of factors directly related to home life. Of 21 family factors, broken homes accounted for 83 percent of this subclass of runaways.

Outland, George E.   "Sources of Transient Boys." Sociology and Social Research, 19, May-June 1935:429-434.
   The author reports on the states and cities of origin of 10,000 transient boys between the ages of 16 and 20 who registered with the Federal Transient Service in Los Angeles between December 12, 1933, and November 21, 1934. "Every state and section of the United States is represented," as well as "territories and even foreign nations." Sixty percent of the boys came from cities of more than 25,000 population. ("Several states such as Idaho, Nevada, Vermont, and Wyoming have no cities larger than 25,000.")

Owens, J. S.   Involuntary Outpatient Commitment: An Exploration of the Issues and Its Utilization in Five States. Washington, D.C.: National Institute of Mental Health, 1985.
   After reviewing involuntary outpatient commitment in five states, the author recommends that NIMH continue its leadership role and expand its research. Underfunding of public mental health systems should be taken as the issue rather than merely altering mental health statutes to allow widespread involuntary outpatient commitment.

                              P

Padavan, Frank. "Helping New York City's Homeless: Focus on Mental Health." New York Times, December 17, 1985:27.
   Deinstitutionalization forces us to face rights in conflict.

Page, Paul. "Rags, Riches Mix at Fete for Homeless Film." Associated Press, January 13, 1986.

On behalf of a film tentatively entitled, "Race Against Winter," a party was attended by both celebrities and homeless.

Pallarito, Karen. "'Public Service Junkie'--He Develops Policy to Benefit the Disadvantaged." <u>Modern Healthcare</u>, <u>20</u> (35), September 3, 1990:48.
   Drew E. Altman, the newly appointed president of the Henry J. Kaiser Family Foundation in San Francisco, California, comes from a background of policy development and fund raising for the young, the poor, and the homeless. He says that he hopes to deal with some of the failings of the U.S. health care system.

Parente, Frank. "A Labor Agenda for Housing." <u>AFL-CIO American Federationist</u>, <u>93</u> (1) February 8, 1986.
   In the third part of this article, the author examines foreclosures and the problem of homelessness. He stresses that homelessness no longer only involves "traditional and well-known categories of jobless and deinstitutionalized, but also low-income workers and whole families and children." The author refers to the "hidden homeless," people who have doubled-up with friends and relatives because they have lost their homes and apartments through fire, eviction or non-payment of rent. The article concludes with a list of recommended social policies to increase home ownership.

Parisi, Albert J. "Bergen Dedicates Home for Homeless." <u>New York Times</u>, January 6, 1985:Section 11:8.
   The basic cause of homelessness is deinstitutionalization. The solution is to bring the homeless into the mainstream of society. To do so will involve seven steps: 1) initial contact with, identification of, temporary shelter for, and initial counseling, 2) permanent housing, 3) training for jobs (job skills), 4) finding jobs, 5) health care, 6) counseling, especially for alcohol and drug dependency, and 7) crisis intervention.

Park, Robert E. "The Mind of the Hobo: Reflections Upon the Relation Between Mentality and Locomotion." In <u>The City</u>, Robert E. Park, Ernest W. Burgess, and Roderick D. McKenzie, eds. Chicago: University of Chicago Press, 1967:156-160. (First published in 1924.)
   Although the hobo has much leisure, he has little philosophy. This is due to their lack of vocation and

break with local ties. Hobos, however, have been good at poetry.

Parker, Carleton H. "The California Casual and His Revolt." Quarterly Journal of Economics, 30, November 1915:110-126.
 Four men were killed in a strike and riot of hop workers at the Durst Ranch in Wheatland, California, in August 1913. About a third of the 2,800 pickers came from towns and cities in California, about a third were families from the Sierra Foothills (quasi-gypsies, with carts or ramshackle wagons), while another third were migratories ("the pure hobo, or his California Exemplar, the 'fruit tramp'; Hindus; and a large party of Japanese"). The author details casual labor in California, especially conditions in labor camps (fruit, grape, highway, hop, lumber, mining, and ranch) and the beginning of "general" Kelly's unemployed "army" and its march from San Francisco.

Parker, Carleton H. The Casual Laborer and Other Essays. New York: Harcourt, Brace and Howe, 1920.
 This account of labor unrest in California contains a section on unattached migrant workers and mentions the hobo membership of the I.W.W.

Parker, J. Michael. "Building Bridges in Midtown Manhattan: An Intergenerational Literacy Program." Urban Education, 24 (1), April 1989:109-115.
 To apply the research findings that show that young children who are read to regularly are more successful in school, adult students at New York City Technical College of the City University of New York read to children who attend a day care center in a shelter for homeless women. The goal is to break the cycle of low-literacy and homelessness. Other goals of the reading program are also specified.

Parshall, Gerald. "An Amerikanski Superstar." U.S. News & World Report, August 25, 1986:5.
 This article reveals that Joseph Mauri, the star of a Soviet television documentary on the poor in New York, "The Man From Fifth Avenue," is not really homeless but lives in a subsidized hotel and leases a studio apartment.

Parsons, Frank. "Lessons of Last Winter." (Second part of "The Unemployed") Arena, 10, October 1894:712-715.

The author makes the point that society should recognize "the right of every adult to employment, the right of every child to manual training and industrial education, and the folly of indiscriminate and unscientific almsgiving." To eliminate poverty we must abolish the saloon, institute a stable currency, and establish cooperation in place of competition. Shiftlessness and inertia are not primary causes of poverty, but the results of poverty and its causes. These characteristics, in turn, cause the continuance of poverty as they become the medium through which poverty propagates itself. Once the evil conditions that cause poverty are removed, these results of poverty will also gradually disappear. The author cites examples of payment for coal, rent, and loans to indicate that the "poor have to pay a great deal more for what they get than rich people do for the same goods."

Partain, Eugene C. "Sheltering the Suburban Homeless." The Christian Century, 102 (13), April 10, 1985:353-356.
    Homelessness in the suburbs, a new phenomenon, has not been brought about by a massive exodus from the cities. Rather, suburban men, women, and children who had barely clung to the bottom rung of the middle-class ladder "have seen that ladder shortened---from bottom up." Unable to pay their bills, they have joined the homeless of America. The author says that denial is a special problem that the suburban homeless face. Suburban officials fear that if they open shelters for the homeless there will be a mass exodus of the city's homeless to the suburbs, along with complications due to bureaucracy, inefficiency, and high staffing salaries that will escalate their costs. Churches must look for solutions to the problems of homelessness, whether they are in the suburbs or anywhere else.

Paterson, Kenneth J. "Shelters and Statistics: A New Face to an Old Problem." The Urban and Social Change Review, 17 (2), Summer 1984:14-17.
    This article examines the problem of collecting statistical data on the services provided by shelters. Resistance to providing data often centers on fears of misinterpretation. The author makes suggestions for overcoming this resistance.

Paull, Joseph E. "The Runaway Foster Child." Child Welfare, 37, July 1956:21-26.

Based on his experiences working in the New Mexico Department of Public Welfare, the author contrasts running away by foster and non-foster children. He concludes that running away by non-foster children can be a positive experience in growing up, but running away by foster children does not have this positive aspect because these children do not know where their rebellion is directed. The article contains advice for caseworkers to help the runaway better understand the meaning of his or her act by "finding structure that gives the client help in breaking up his problem and taking hold of a piece of it."

Paznoikas, Paul. "The Right to Loiter and Be Offensive." Wall Street Journal, June 25, 1991:A23.
The author of this letter to the editor registers an objection to a filthy homeless man who practically lives in the public library of Morristown, New Jersey. Offensive people should be banned from the library because citizens have the right to go to the library without smelling urine and hearing foul language.

Peabody, Francis G. "The German Labor-Colonies for Tramps." Forum 12, February 1892:751–761.
The German Labor Colonies "are no penal institutions. They do not compel men either to come or to stay. They are not under state control, and stand firmly for self-help. They do not offer any attraction to men who are bent on the tramp's career, for they give small pay for diligent work. They are provided for those who, though fallen, want to rise." Although these labor colonies provide an example for the United States, there are limitations in their application.

Pear, Robert. "Data Are Elusive on the Homeless." New York Times, March 1, 1988:8.
There is much disagreement about the number of homeless people in the United States and the causes of this problem.

Pear, Robert. "For Mentally Ill, Life On Streets Is No Boon." New York Times, January 4, 1987:E7.
What led to a majority of mental patients being deinstitutionalized? This occurred due to a coalition of interest groups (community mental health advocates, civil libertarians, and fiscal conservatives), the belief that it was better to treat the mentally ill in the community where they can be close to families and friends, and the

development of new drugs to eliminate flagrant symptoms of hallucinations. When patients were discharged, however, they were met by non-existent or inadequate community facilities. Consequently, they ended up in nursing homes, emergency rooms of public hospitals, and the streets and alleys. To provide protection and treatment for the most severe mentally ill, a movement favoring reinstitutionalization has taken root. In some states, laws have been adopted that permit authorities to order out-patient treatment. In cases of involuntary out-patient commitment, the patient is allowed to live in the community but must undergo treatment, which may include drug therapy.

Pear, Robert. "Homeless Children Challenge Schools." New York Times, September 9, 1991:A10.
Among the many problems the homeless face in getting their children an education are transportation and relocation.

Pear, Robert. "Homeless in U.S. Put at 250,000, Far Less Than Previous Estimates." New York Times, May 2, 1984:1A.
Estimates released by HUD put the numbers of homeless in the United States at 250,000 to 300,000. The top figure would be 500,000. This estimate contrasts sharply with the two to three million estimated by homeless advocates.

Pear, Robert. "Homeless Men in Capital Shelter Resist Moving to a New Location." New York Times, November 16, 1985:11.
The homeless shelter in Washington, D.C., run by Mitch Snyder and the Community for Creative Nonviolence, is going to be closed.

Pear, Robert. "The Need of the Nation's Homeless Is Becoming Their Right." New York Times, July 20, 1986:E5.
The author reviews legal decisions regarding the right of the homeless for shelter and the corresponding need of political entities to provide that shelter. Tensions exist between rights provided by the Constitution of the United States and the New York State constitution. The article contains a map indicating the numbers and locations of homeless people throughout the United States.

Pear, Robert. "Residents Reported Fortifying Capital Shelter for Homeless." New York Times, November 8, 1985:11.
    The planned forced closing of the homeless shelter in Washington, D.C., run by Mitch Snyder and the Community for Creative Nonviolence has led to tension between the federal government and the homeless and their advocates. Rumors indicate that the homeless are armed and will barricade themselves in the building.

Pear, Robert. "White House Shuns Housing Plan That Reagan Endorsed Last Year." New York Times, June 16, 1987:1, 14.
    Controversy has arisen concerning the amount paid to house families in welfare hotels versus the amount that it would cost to build homes for them. The Department of Health and Human Services, which runs the federal welfare program, has refused to enter the "housing construction and acquisition business."

Pearl, Daniel, and Martha Brannigan. "With Growth Slowing, Florida Faced Clouds Even Before Hurricane." Wall Street Journal, August 28, 1992:A1, A14.
    This article estimates that Hurricane Andrew left 250,000 people homeless.

Peele, John. From North Carolina to Southern California Without a Ticket And How I Did It. Tarboro, N.C.: Edwards and Broughton, 1907.
    Writing in the genre of the times, the author recounts his "exciting experiences as a hobo." He recounts the adventures, dangers, and hardships of his travels in 1906.

Peele, Roger. "We Need Insane Asylums: Ask Joe, 68 Years at St. E's." Washington Post, October 30, 1983:C1, C3.
    The case history of Joe, who was institutionalized in 1915, is used to support the argument that we need asylums because they offer "a measure of freedom, of safety, of opportunities to express themselves and feel at home."

Peer, Elizabeth, and Eric Gelman. "'Sleeping Rough' in the Big City." Newsweek, 97, March 23, 1981:71-72.
    Many homeless people prefer the streets to the "deplorable conditions of many public shelters."

Peirce, Neal R. "The City-Church Partnership in Sheltering the Homeless." Nation's Cities Weekly, 8, January
21, 1985:6.
    Churches in Anchorage, Denver, and New York City are
making efforts to shelter the homeless. The focus of
this article is on the cooperation of church laity and
government.

Peirce, Neal R. "Urban Churches Take on Social-Agency
Role for Homeless." Minneapolis Star and Tribune,
January 20, 1986:A26.
    The author presents an account of church efforts
around the country to care for the homeless.

Pennbridge, Julia N., Gary L. Yates, Thomas G. David, and
Richard G. Mackenzie. "Runaway and Homeless Youth in Los
Angeles County, California." Journal of Adolescent
Health Care, 11 (2), March 1990:159-165.
    Comparing shelter and outreach/drop-in agencies
operating in Los Angeles County, California, the authors
conclude that these two types of agencies serve different
populations and are based on different philosophies,
services, and goals. Compared to the clientele of the
outreach/drop-in agencies, the youth in the shelters are
more likely to be younger, minorities, residents of Los
Angeles County, and victims of abuse or neglect by their
primary caretakers.

Penner, Maurice, and Susan Penner. "Visual Ideologies of
the Street Homeless: Comparing Editorial Cartoons to
Fieldwork Observations." Visual Sociology Review, 4 (2),
Fall 1989:99-106.
    The authors compared the editorial cartoons in San
Francisco's Chronicle and Examiner and the University of
California's (Berkeley) Daily Californian published
between September 1988 and May 1989 with their own
observations of the homeless in a San Francisco park.
Both common stereotypes and concern for the homeless
dominate the cartoons.

Pepper, Bert, and Hilary Ryglewicz. "Testimony for the
Neglected: The Mentally Ill in the Post-Deinstitutiona-
lized Age." American Journal of Orthopsychiatry, 52 (3),
July 1982:388-392.
    The authors contrast responsible deinstitutionaliza-
tion (the discharge of mental patients into a mental
health support system) with irresponsible deinstitutionalization ("the discharge of enormous numbers of patients

into our communities without adequate planning for their care and treatment, and without adequate funding for the development of needed community programs of treatment, housing, and support"). After analyzing political and systemic obstacles to responsible deinstitutionalization, the authors stress that political advocacy is essential for the psychiatric profession. To help this current problem, mental health professionals must advocate the funding of community treatment programs, demand the altering of entitlement criteria, oppose moves to disqualify mentally ill people from SSI, fight reductions in Medicare and Medicaid, work toward the financial integration of mental health systems, and "insist that our states and our mental health agencies take responsibility for ensuring decent housing for the mentally ill who are now in our streets."

Pepper, Bert, Michael C. Kirshner, and Hilary Ryglewicz. "The Young Adult Chronic Patient: Overview of a Population." Hospital and Community Psychiatry, 32 (7), July 1981:463-469.
    The solution to the special treatment problems posed by deinstitutionalized, dysfunctional young adults is residential programs that provide a supportive living situation on both a temporary and a long-term basis.

Perkins, Joseph. "New Institutions for the Homeless." The Wall Street Journal, February 26, 1985.
    Deinstitutionalization has created homelessness. This is a self-feeding problem as legal advocates support deinstitutionalization. The solution is reinstitutionalization. Homelessness is also caused by poverty and the lack of low-cost housing. The solution to this part of the problem is low-cost public housing for the able-minded and community-based residences for the mentally ill.

Perlez, Jane. "Nairobi Street Children Play Games of Despair." New York Times, January 2, 1991:A1.
    As extended families and village culture, which were the pillars of African life, have broken down, the number of street children, abandoned by their parents, has grown.

Perlez, Jane. "Thousands Skip School at Hotel for Homeless." New York Times, November 12, 1987:18.

The Board of Education of New York City is having difficulty getting homeless parents who live in welfare hotels to send their children to school.

Perr, Irwin N. "The Malignant Neglect of the Mentally Ill Street People." <u>American Journal of Psychiatry</u>, <u>142</u> (7), July 1985:885-886.
A high proportion of the homeless are mentally ill or incompetent and in need of medical treatment.

Perr, Irwin N. "The Reality of Mental Illness." Letter to the Editor, <u>Wall Street Journal</u>, June 24, 1985.
The author vigorously opposes the position of Thomas S. Szasz and defends the reality of mental illness. A large proportion of the homeless are mentally ill and need help. To deny this reality fosters injustice and the disregard of human needs.

Peszke, Michael A. "Why Are We Turning Our Streets Into Asylums?" <u>New York Times</u>, January 27, 1985:Section 23:22.
Deinstitutionalization occurred because of fiscal conservatism and changes in the civil commitment stat-utes. The resulting problems for the community are community anxiety, injustice to the mentally ill who are trying to cope on the streets, and the continuing but unmet need for psychiatric treatment and commitment.

Peterson, Iver. "Job Upturn Barely Felt in Shelters." <u>New York Times</u>, November 29, 1983:A16.
Why has the economic upturn left the homeless behind? This is due to their mental and emotional incapacities and to historic changes in the job market.

Peterson, Iver. "Warm Season Masks But Doesn't End Problem of the Homeless." <u>New York Times</u>, June 3, 1983, A16.
Shelter for the homeless, being a year around need, is contrasted with the help that cities reluctantly provide in the winter to prevent negative publicity about the homeless freezing to death.

Peterson, W. Jack, and Milton A. Maxwell. "The Skid Road 'Wino.'" <u>Social Problems</u>, <u>5</u>, Spring 1958:308-316.
After stressing that skid road is composed of many different types of men and that "Skid Road life is group-centered and dominated by group norms," the authors analyze the culture of skid road winos--their normative

obligation to share, sources of money, unstructured groups, finding a place to sleep, mutual help and protection from police and illness, and the relationship of winos to other skid road alcoholics.

Petty, John. <u>Five Fags a Day: The Last Year of a Scrap-Picker</u>. London: Secker and Warburg, 1956.
A London writer provides an account of how he supported himself in poverty.

Phelan, Jim. <u>Jail Journey</u>. London: Secker and Warburg, 1940.
This first-person account by a tramp examines life in an English jail in the 1930s.

Phelan, Jim. <u>The Name's Phelan: The First Part of the Autobiography of Jim Phelan</u>. London: Sidgwick and Jackson, 1948.
This autobiographical account of tramping assumes instinct as the cause of tramping.

Phelan, Jim. <u>Tramping the Toby</u>. London: Burke, 1955.
The author has written a first-person account of tramping in rural England.

Phelan, Jim. <u>Turf-Fire Tales</u>. London: William Heinemann, 1947.
This recollection of lower-class life in Dublin contains some stories about tramps, gypsies, and street children.

Phelan, Jim. <u>We Follow the Roads</u>. London: Phoenix House, 1949.
In this first-person account of tramping, the author generalizes from his observations and personal experiences. He concludes that tramping is due to an instinct, one that civilization may yet extinguish. Tramps view life in towns as complex and a mistake.

Phillimore, Peter. "Dossers and Jake Drinkers: The View from One End of Skid Row." In <u>Vagrancy: some New Perspectives</u>, Tim Cook, ed. London: Academic Press, 1979:29-48.
The topics of this book on skid row in London are self and social identification, casual work, a night fire for community, skippering (finding own place to sleep), the sense of self and time, their constructed social world, and divisions in the skid row population.

Phillips, Michael H., Neal DeChillo, Daniel Kronenfeld, and Verona Middleton-Jeter. "Homeless Families: Service Makes a Difference." <u>Journal of Contemporary Social Work</u>, <u>69</u> (1), January 1988.

Based on a sample of 308 families who stayed at the Urban Family Center in New York City longer than 90 days during a 20-month period, the authors conclude that 96 percent experienced failure in the mother's functioning, 51 percent failure in the child's functioning, and all families experienced financial and housing problems. After treatment at this facility, 60 percent did as well or better than expected. Seventy-one percent had made progress toward goals that had been set, less than 2 percent had regressed, and the remaining 27 percent evidenced no change. A follow-up of 60 percent of the original sample three months and six months after the families left the facility showed that much of the progress they had made was lost due to multiple stresses and deterioration in their housing situation. A longer-term intervention needs to be instituted in order for progress to be increased and maintained.

Pierson, John. "Form Plus Function: Simple Shelters Are Met With Scorn." <u>Wall Street Journal</u>, March 17, 1992:B1.

Homeless advocates decry designs of cardboard-like plastic tents for the homeless as a "Styrofoam band aid" solution to homelessness.

Piliavin, Irving, Herb Westerfelt, and Elsa Elliot. "Estimating Mental Illness among the Homeless: The Effects of Choice-Based Sampling." <u>Social Problems</u>, <u>36</u> (5), December 1989:525-531.

Using a sample of mentally ill homeless in Minneapolis who did and did not use health clinic services, the authors test the assertion of James Wright ("The Mentally Ill Homeless: What Is Myth and What Is Fact?," <u>Social Problems</u>, <u>35</u>, 1988:182-91) that David Snow and colleagues underestimated the amount of mental illness among the homeless ("The Myth of Pervasive Mental Illness Among the Homeless," <u>Social Problems</u>, <u>33</u>, 1986:407-423). The authors conclude that Wright is wrong.

Piliavin, Irving, and Michael Sosin. "Institute for Research on Poverty Homeless Study: An Overview." Madison: University of Wisconsin Institute for Research on Poverty, 1986. Mimeo.

The causes of homelessness are deinstitutionalization, fewer cheap hotels and low-income jobs, insufficient income-maintenance grants, a lack of support by families, and unemployment. The authors' longitudinal study of a sample of homeless in Minneapolis is not completed.

Piliavin, Irving, Michael Sosin, and Herb Westerfelt. "Tracking the Homeless." Focus (University of Wisconsin-Madison, Institute for Research on Poverty), 10 (4), Winter 1987-88.

Samples of homeless people in Minneapolis, Chicago, and urban Ohio show that the homeless are predominately male, single, and disproportionately non-white. They live alone, have little attachment to the labor force, and are relatively young, with below-average education, low prior incomes, and few job skills. No strong causal link was found between mental illness, hospitalization, and subsequent homelessness. Like the welfare population, the homeless consist of two distinct types: "those for whom homelessness is a temporary condition and those for whom it is a way of life." Future studies will examine the degree to which personal pathologies (such as mental illness and alcoholism) and the lack of human capital (being incapable due to lack of education, training, or discipline to hold a job that will enable them to pay rent) cause homelessness.

Pinkerton, Alan. Strikers, Communists, Tramps and Detectives. New York: Arno Press, 1969. (Originally published in 1878.)

This record of the strike of 1877 and the threat of communism includes (chapters 2-5) a romantic account of tramps and tramping in the United States.

Pitt, David E. "Homeless Respond to Aid at Terminal." New York Times, August 12, 1989:27.

Of 600 homeless persons approached by outreach workers in Grand Central Terminal, 169 agreed either to go to shelters or into drug or alcohol treatment programs.

Pittman, David J., and C. Wayne Gordon. Revolving Door: A Study of the Chronic Police Case Inebriate. Glencoe: The Free Press, 1958.

This study of "men who were sentenced at least twice to a penal institution on charges relating to public intoxication and who were incarcerated in the Monroe County (New York) Penitentiary during the years 1953-54" includes men who had been "raised on the streets" or who had been runaways. After analyzing their sociocultural

profiles, drinking patterns, childhood familial relations, adolescence, work history, and early and late
career patterns of public intoxication, the authors
recommend that systematic treatment replace arrest and
incarceration.

Piven, Frances Fox, and Richard A. Cloward. <u>Poor
People's Movements: Why They Succeed, How They Fail</u>. New
York: Vintage Books, 1979.
    The authors give a detailed analysis of four major
protest movements by the poor: unemployed workers,
industrial workers, civil rights, and welfare rights.
The foci of the book are struggle against capitalistic
oppression and the organization of protest.

Piven, Frances Fox, and Richard A. Cloward. <u>Regulating
the Poor: The Functions of Public Welfare</u>. New York:
Vintage Books, 1971.
    In this account of unemployment and poverty in the
United States, a section on mass unemployment and the
rise of social disorder details the efforts of the
unemployed poor and the unemployed homeless to force
government officials to provide relief. The authors
stress that the Great Depression marked a change in the
definition of hardships when problems of unemployment,
poverty, and homelessness became defined "not as an individual fate, but as a collective disaster, not as a mark
of individual failure, but as a fault of 'the system.'"

Platt, Steve. "London's Boroughs 'Deport' Their Homeless." <u>New Statesman</u>, <u>111</u>, March 28, 1986:6.
    Some councils in London are manipulating the rule
that allows mobility between boroughs to send their
undesirable homeless to other boroughs.

Plunkert, William J. "Is Skid Row Necessary?" <u>Canadian
Journal of Corrections</u>, <u>2</u>, April 1960:200-208.
    Skid row men are inadequately prepared to offer
competitive labor in industrial society. If we are to
eliminate skid row, we need a detailed study of its
representative inhabitants.

Plunkert, William J. "Public Responsibility for Transients." <u>Social Service Review</u>, <u>8</u>, September 1934:484-
491.
    The author reports the race, age, and sex of the
130,000 transients served by the Federal Relief Adminis-

tration program. There is a need to organize on the state level.

Plunkert, William J. "Skid Row Can be Eliminated." Federal Probation, 25, June 1961:41-44.
Skid row has been allowed to exist because it was thought to provide a pool of workers who could be called on during periods of industrial expansion. Skid row is no longer needed for this purpose, and it is now composed of a stable population, mostly "men who are emotionally and physically incapacitated." The primarily religious approach to rehabilitate these men should be augmented by a multi-disciplinary program that includes medicine, psychology, social casework, Alcoholics Anonymous, psychiatry, and sociology. Such an approach will require a comprehensive plan to treat their physical disabilities, reestablishing ties with family, the utilization of half-way houses, and "the full cooperation of all the community forces involved."

Polak, Paul R., and Michael W. Kirby. "A Model to Replace Psychiatric Hospitals." The Journal of Nervous and Mental Disease, 162 (1), 1976:13-22.
A comprehensive system of community treatment has been established in Denver with six small, community-based therapeutic environments which include crisis intervention, home treatment, social systems intervention, and rapid tranquilization. The system includes "a framework of citizen participation and community control, the elimination of formal staff offices, and a focus on working in the real-life setting of the client and his family." To determine the effectiveness of this program, patients about to be hospitalized were randomly assigned to a psychiatric hospital or to this community alternative treatment. Outcome measures of discharge and at follow-up indicated that community treatment was more effective than psychiatric hospitalization.

Pollak, Benno. "The Homeless Alcoholic." The Practitioner, 213, 1974:376-377.
It is desirable to establish specialized hostels for the rehabilitation of homeless alcoholics. Most alcoholics desperately want to rejoin society, and we must give them this chance.

Pond, D. "Untitled." Proceedings of the Royal Society of Medicine, 63, 1970:445.

In the general population of the homeless there are "almost no Indians, Pakistanis or Jews," because "in these groups family ties are still very strong."

Poole, Ernest. "A Clearing-House for Tramps." <u>Every-body's Magazine</u>, <u>18</u>, May 1908:649-659.
The author, the former head of the Chicago Free Municipal Lodging-House, recounts some of his experiences in placing 40,000 tramps. He proposes specific ways to run an effective lodging-house and suggests that because most tramps are unemployed men who seek work we need a comprehensive system of lodging houses, free employment bureaus, and free transportation to areas where there is work. In contrast, professional bums should be arrested and forced to work in labor colonies. In reporting on the work of "Cap" Mullenbach, the author summarizes the life histories of several hobos. The article contains nine photos.

Postrel, Virginia I. "Tapping the Shadow Housing Market." <u>Wall Street Journal</u>, March 13, 1987:18.
In reviewing "the shadow market" for the poor (previously uninhabitable units that have been restored: former non-residential space, former group quarters, and units created by subdividing or adding to existing dwellings), the author mentions that a six-story abandoned building that had been vacant for five years (except for use by junkies and homeless people) has been purchased by a Christian group, Habitat for Humanity.

Potter, Ellen C. "The Problem of the Transient." <u>Annals of the American Academy of Political and Social Science</u>, <u>176</u>, November 1934:66-73.
Following "the economic collapse of 1929," the Federal Children's Bureau "undertook a survey of the situation in the Southwest, with special reference to boys and young men who by the thousands (an estimated 200,000 in the United States) were found 'riding the rods' of the railroads, their whole future endangered and their lives in jeopardy." Surveys in 1933 identified 370,000 individuals, of whom 304,000 were males. "Boys under 21 years numbered 16,500; girls 2,700; women 14,482." From this census it becomes "clear that while the younger men take the long trail across the country, the bulk of the transient army moves within a radius of five hundred miles of its home base." "In August 1933, the Federal Relief Administrator accepted responsibility for the unsettled person and his family and began to

develop plans for an attack on the problem." By February of 1934 the Federal Government had spent about $2 million on 138,000 persons, about 40 percent of whom were in family groups. A field survey of the program indicated that the handling of the transient problem had improved, Federal refusal to provide hospitalization was a serious handicap, there had not yet developed a unified standard transient philosophy and program, and "the transient is everywhere better cared for than is the local homeless, and as a result there is a constant recruiting into the transient army." Needed is "the revision of our laws relating to relief and to vagrancy in the light of all sound social practice."

Potter, Ken. "Enquirer Story of Homeless Women Brings a Wave of Offers from Warmhearted Readers." National Enquirer, October 5, 1976:
     The author summarizes reader response to an August 17 story he had written about homeless women.

Potter, Ken. "The Tragedy of America's Homeless Women." National Enquirer, August 17, 1976:1.
     This overview of homeless women in New York City, Washington, D.C., and Los Angeles features the work of Veronica Matz, a sociologist who gave up a position at Georgetown University to work for the homeless.

Pottieger, Anne E., and James A. Inciardi. "Aging on the Street: Drug Use and Crime Among Older Men." Journal of Psychoactive Drugs, 13 (2), April-June 1981:199-211.
     The authors present "a cross-comparative analysis of the four major categories of older men in street popula-tions: street addicts, nonaddict street criminals, professional thieves and men on Skid Row." They describe each of these groups "in terms of general lifestyle and place of drug use in that lifestyle" and discuss the general decline of skid row and changes in the make-up of its population.

Pound, John. Poverty and Vagrancy in Tudor England. London: Longman, 1971.
     The causes of the extensive poverty and vagrancy during 1520-1640 were the ending of the War of the Roses, the many armed retainers laid off by the nobility, an increasing population, the vicissitudes of the cloth industry, enclosure (evicting tenants from the land in order to turn it into sheep farming), inflation, the plague, harvest failures, and the dissolution of the

monasteries. Solutions tried during this period were poor laws, subsidized grain, branding a V on vagrants' chests, licensing begging, forbidding begging, providing work for the able-bodied, establishing almshouses, and giving and bequests by individuals.

Power, N. S. The Forgotten People: A Challenge to a Caring Community. Ervesham: Arthur James, 1965.
    The Christian answer to problems of poverty is the caring community.

Powers, Jane Levine, John Eckenrode, and Barbara Jaklitsch. "Maltreatment among Runaway and Homeless Youth." Child Abuse and Neglect, 14 (1), 1990:87-98.
    The authors present a demographic profile of 223 adolescents with a history of maltreatment who obtained services from runaway and homeless youth programs in New York City during 1986 and 1987. Comparing this sample with state-wide and national samples of runaway and homeless youths, the authors found that maltreated runaways were not readily distinguishable from the runaway and homeless youth population except that they were more likely to be female and to have engaged in suicidal behavior.

Prager, Debbie. "Hippies Still Survive Where It All Started." Washington Post, April 5, 1982:A2.
    The gentrification of the crash pads of the Haight-Ashbury district of San Francisco has left "the remaining flower children wilted and homeless." The homeless have become such a fixture in this neighborhood that one businessman said, "This is their neighborhood, too. They just happen to live on the streets."

Preston, S. O. "Provision for or Treatment of the Unemployed." Charities Review, 3, 1894:218-225.
    The poor, including beggars, should not be given help but be prepared for work because a man "paid a wage for his labor would feel greater self-respect and less humiliation than would be possible under the most tactful administration of relief funds." Relief, however, should be given to those who "cannot work by reason of age, infirmity or sickness."

Preston, William. "Shall This Be All? U.S. Historians Versus William D. Haywood Et Al." Labor History, 12, 1971:435-453.

The author presents a history of the Industrial Workers of the World (I.W.W. or Wobblies) by reviewing The Wobblies: The Story of Syndicalism in the United States (Patrick Renshaw, Doubleday, 1967), Big Bill Haywood and the Radical Union Movement (Joseph R. Conlin, Syracuse University Press, 1969), Bread and Roses Too: Studies of the Wobblies (Joseph R. Conlin, Greenwood Publishing, 1969), We Shall Be All: A History of the Industrial Workers of the World (Melvyn Dubofsky, Quadrangle Books, 1969), and Joe Hill (Gibbs M. Smith, University of Utah Press, 1969). Homeless drifters were brutalized and degraded by "character-debasing" employment patterns and lacked even the benefits of "normal sex." These "uprooted," a "flotsam and jetsam" who felt "impotent and alienated," showed "a high susceptibility to unrest and radical movements aimed at destroying the established social order."

Prevost, James A. "Youthful Chronicity: Paradox Of The 80s." Hospital and Community Psychiatry, 33 (3), 1982:173.
Although the young chronically mentally ill do not make up a diagnostically homogenous population, they have certain characteristics in common, especially difficulty in forming stable relationships and having little or no natural support systems. "Socially and psychologically fragile, and often psychotic, they are acutely vulnerable to stress." "The homelessness of these young adults, and their involvement in a variety of low-level criminal activities and in substance abuse, frightens a society already burdened by its own increasing violence and raises questions of service provision." We must determine "for which dysfunctions will this population require hospitalization, and for which will community-based treatment approaches be not only therapeutically sound, but cost-effective."

Priest, Robert G. "The Edinburgh Homeless: A Psychiatric Survey." American Journal of Psychotherapy, 25 (2), April 1971:194-213.
The author interviewed 65 homeless men and 14 homeless women who were chosen by "a random sample of the 900-odd residents in the lodging-houses by selecting their bed numbers from random number tables." The homeless are classified into hoboes (itinerant workers), tramps (itinerant non-workers), and bums (non-itinerant non-workers). As with the national survey of homeless single persons in England, three fourths were over 50

years of age, and about two-thirds had never married,
were on national assistance, and had been at their
current address less than six months. Twenty-one percent
indicated impaired performance on the Paired Associate
Test, 40 percent scored abnormal on the Symptom Sign
Inventory, 11 percent were schizophrenic, and 7 percent
psychotic but not schizophrenic. Schizophrenia is much
more common than alcoholism. The author discusses
alcoholism, personality disorder, mental subnormality,
organic brain disease, and depression and makes the point
that "the majority of men living the lodging-house life
are psychiatrically abnormal." The normals tended to be
young, male Scots and Irish, employed or retired, smokers
and drinkers.

Priest, Robert G. "The Epidemiology of Mental Illness:
Illustrations from the Single Homeless Population."
Psychiatric Journal of the University of Ottawa, 3 (1),
1978:27-32.
     A comparison of interview samples from Edinburgh,
Scotland, and Chicago showed more schizophrenia in
Edinburgh and more alcoholism in Chicago. The author
suggests that low social class and isolation of the
center city are results of schizophrenia, not its causes.

Priest, Robert G. "The Homeless Person and the Psychiatric Services: An Edinburgh Survey." British Journal of
Psychiatry, 128 (5), 1976:128-136.
     A representative sample of psychiatric outpatients
living in flop houses in Edinburgh was compared with
nonpatients in flop houses. Because outpatients are more
likely to be out of work, to be under 55 years of age, to
have been married at some time, to be alcoholic, and to
suffer from personality disorders and schizophrenia,
those seeking psychiatric services are not representative
of the homeless population. The author draws implications for service programs.

Proch, Kathleen, and Merlin A. Taber. "Helping the
Homeless: Why People Are on the Streets Is Irrelevant to
Their Need for Shelters." Public Welfare, 45 (2), Spring
1987:5-9.
     The authors discuss how many people are homeless,
who the homeless are, why people are homeless, what
should be done about the problem, and the possible future
of homelessness. They conclude that the primary need of
homeless people is shelter. The cost of ensuring minimum
shelter is about $1.5 billion a year and should be borne

primarily by the federal and state governments. The need
to provide shelter will continue indefinitely.

Puleo, Mev. "Angela." The Christian Century, 102 (14),
April 24, 1985:408.
    The author, who is studying theology, regularly
passes by Angela, who is homeless and refuses his help.
Her presence on campus makes the author question his
motives and relationship with God.

Purdum, Todd S. "A Bitter Struggle Lies Ahead on
Dinkins's Homeless Plan." New York Times, October 5,
1991:A1.
    The announcement of plans to spend $200 million on
shelters for homeless single men and women was met with
protests. Many of the 24 shelters would be built in
middle-class neighborhoods, and many residents see the
mayor's plan as an assault on their neighborhoods and
safety.

Purdum, Todd S. "Dinkins Lists Possible Shelter Sites to
Irate Protests on Many Fronts." New York Times, October
11, 1991:A1.
    The announcement of plans for New York City to spend
$200 million on shelters for homeless single men and
women was met with protests. Many of the 24 shelters
would be built in middle-class neighborhoods, and many
residents see the plan as an assault on their neighborhoods and safety.

Purdum, Todd S. "Dreams Deferred and Payments Due." New
York Times, May 12, 1991:Section 4:3.
    The doomsday budget proposed by New York City's
Mayor David Dinkins would require the closing of homeless
shelters and the Central Park Zoo and the laying off of
20,000 workers.

Purdum, Todd S. "Suggestion on Housing for the Homeless
in Brooklyn Draws Anger." New York Times, October 19,
1991:A27.
    Residents of Brooklyn object to the recommendation
of the U.S. Department of Health and Human Services
that Andrew Cuomo's HELP for the Homeless construct
housing for homeless people on the former Brooklyn Navy
Yard.

Purnick, Joyce. "Koch Attacks Judge on Curb Against
Homeless in Hotels." New York Times, October 2, 1986:21.

At a news conference, the mayor of New York City severely criticized a Newark judge who ruled that he would not allow any homeless people from New York City to stay at a Newark motel.

Purnick, Joyce.   "Koch Faults Foes of His Shelter Bid." New York Times, December 20, 1987:19.
Mayor Koch of New York City and the Board of Estimates disagree about Koch's proposal to build temporary shelters for homeless families.

Putnam, Jane F., Neal L. Cohen, and Ann M. Sullivan. "Innovative Outreach Services for the Homeless Mentally Ill." International Journal of Mental Health, 14 (4), 1986:112-124.
Project H.E.L.P. (Homeless Emergency Liaison Project) is a mobile psychiatric outreach team that "provides extensive crisis services to mentally impaired homeless people living on the streets of New York City." The current activities of H.E.L.P. are not adequate, for aggressive outreach is only the first step in meeting the needs of the homeless. Each patient requires "vigorous case management." Drop-in centers for the homeless mentally ill should be established, legal procedures relating to both in-patient and out-patient care must be examined, and we must alter our service delivery system in order to meet the needs of high-risk, homeless, mentally ill people.

Q

Queenan, Joe.   "Miracle on 32nd Street: Amidst Grime, Dreyfus Thrives in Lion's Penn." Barron's, 70 (20), May 14, 1990:M18-M19.
Dreyfus moved from the prestigious 37th floor of One Penn Center to the lower level, where the staff sells mutual funds to commuters. This area belongs to the homeless on weekends and at night.

Quindlen, Anna.   "About New York." New York Times, December 15, 1982:B3.
It is difficult to get homeless women to leave Penn Station to stay at the shelters. Some women avoid the shelters because they are "afraid of being sexually harassed there by other women and of having their

possessions stolen." Others do not like "to be kept inside or told what to do." Some simply want "to stay where they were and be left alone."

Quindlen, Anna. "No Place Like Home." New York Times, May 20, 1992:A23.
     The author profiles Robert Hayes, founder of the homeless advocacy movement, arguing that instead of conducting never-ending studies of the homeless his example should be followed and action taken to help the homeless.

Quindlen, Anna. "Room At the Inn." New York Times, December 11, 1991:A27.
     At this time of year, stories appear about the plight of the homeless, accompanied by pleas for help. This is an article in this genre. The author says that everyone should do what they can with what they have to provide a haven for the homeless--even if for one night.

Quint, Michael. "Battery Park Pays More Than Its Way." New York Times, October 25, 1987:E7.
     Battery Park City, a cluster of office and residential buildings, will generate a considerable amount of cash that can be used for low-income housing, especially the rehabilitation of city-owned buildings. In a project on which design work has already begun, about 30 percent of the apartments will be occupied by families now living in welfare hotels.

                              R

Rabinoff, George W. "The National Committee on Care of Transient and Homeless." Social Service Review, September 1934:497-502.
     The author reviews the history and work of the National Committee, founded in 1932. The Committee has drawn several major conclusions: There is a distinction between interstate transients, intrastate transients, and local homeless; more women transients and families are appearing; the problem cannot be adequately handled by private agencies operating community by community but needs a nationally conceived and financed program; a treatment program needs to be established that focuses on both prevention and individual care. The Committee also

recommends that treatment consist of: smaller shelters, work opportunities but not work tests, work camps, and central intake bureaus with case work to individualize applicants.

Rabinovitz, Francine F. "What Should Be Done?" Society, May-June 1989:12-13.
The author lists a variety of proposals to solve the problem of homelessness, including providing the homeless with an income that will maintain them at least at poverty level, employment at least at minimum wage, and housing consistent with wages.

Rabon, Israel. The Street. New York: Schocken Books, 1985. (Leonard Wolf, translator. Originally published in 1928.)
Recounts the life of a down-and-out discharged Polish soldier. Unemployed, he wanders the city streets with no money, food, or shelter. He eventually gets a job with a circus.

Rafferty, Margaret. "Standing Up for America's Homeless." American Journal of Nursing, December 1989:1614-1617.
The author summarizes background information on the homeless in order to encourage nurses to get started on tackling the problem, perhaps in ways no one has yet considered. She discusses homeless youths, single adults, and families, with a focus on the harm that homelessness presents to physical health.

Raine, George. "Many Seeking Work in West Without Luck." New York Times, February 2, 1982:A2, A12.
Because the energy boom primarily provides work for those who have specialized skills, many persons who have migrated to western states in search of work remain unemployed. With a tight housing market and no jobs, many of these migrants end up in missions.

Rangel, Jesus. "New York Suit Seeks to Bar Placing of Homeless." New York Times, September 26, 1986:47.
A coalition of midtown Manhattan merchants and residents filed suit to prevent further placement of homeless families in their area. They claim that the presence of large numbers of homeless people is changing the character of the neighborhood for the worse by increasing crime, prostitution, and drug dealing, making the area inhumane for the homeless.

Raphael, Maryanne, and Jenifer Wolf. <u>Runaways: America's Lost Youth</u>. New York: Drake, 1974.
The authors emphasize the troubled environments from which youths flee, their exploitation after running away, and their confusion. The article contains advice for parents and suggests changes in the law and in police-reporting methods. To make their points, the authors use case stories

Rapoport, Amos. "Nomadism as a Man-Environment System." <u>Environment and Behavior</u>, <u>10</u> (2), June 1978:215-246.
The topics of this article are nomadism, sedentarization, culture, social organization, and the personality of groups that are always mobile. The author presents cross-cultural materials, suggesting that becaues policy makers unquestioningly assume that they must sedentarize urban nomads a broader background is necessary for the formulation of informed social policy.

Rasky, Susan F. "Local Officials See Little Help for New York's Homeless in Federal Proposal." <u>New York Times</u>, December 4, 1989:Y18.
The voucher system for housing proposed by the federal government has met with a rejecting response on the part of New York City officials who say that the proposed amounts are inadequate for the price structure of New York City.

Rattenburg, T .P. R. "The Housing Act 1977." <u>Journal of Planning and Environmental Law</u>, January 1983:4-22.
This article focuses on case law, specifically the decisions by local housing authorities in determining whether a person is intentionally homeless. The author contrasts these decisions with his own interpretation of the meaning of intentionality and homelessness in The Housing (Homeless Persons) Act of 1977. He examines problems in determining causality and intentionality in a series of human acts and stresses that to fulfil the requirements of the Act, housing authorities must be "concerned not only with their deliberateness, but also the qualities of the accommodation vacated." It is a "false test of intentional homelessness" to ask "simply whether the decision to remain on premises would be a reasonable decision" because "it focuses on the thing which the applicant did not do, and asks whether the decision which he never took, mainly to remain on the premises, would have been a reasonable one." Instead,

local authorities must ask "what the applicant did and why."

Rause, Vince. "Homeless." The Pittsburgh Press, April 8, 1984:E12.
　　The author, a reporter, details his visit to the Jubilee Kitchen in Pittsburgh, reproducing conversations that provide insight into the thinking and behaviors of the homeless who eat at this soup kitchen.

Rause, Vince. "Who are the Homeless?" The Pittsburgh Press, April 8, 1984:42.
　　An Emergency Shelter Task Force identified three types of homeless people among the 479 persons in Pittsburgh who are "without a place to sleep:" (1) the traditionally homeless (those "who have rejected, or have been rejected by, normal society"-- deinstitutionalized mental patients, chronic alcoholics, and those who "have quit the world"); (2) the traditionally needy ("those people who have lost their welfare payments" due to State Act 75 that has cut or will stop welfare payment to 15,000 Allegheny County residents); and (3) the chronically unemployed (primarily workers laid off from steel jobs or other heavy industry positions).

Ravo, Nick. "Four Held in Tompkins Square Skirmish at Symbolic Tents." New York Times, 138, July 9, 1989:24.
　　Because their shantytown had been torn down earlier in the week, homeless people protested in Tompkins Square by "repeatedly pitching sheets of plastic over branches and wires." The police repeatedly moved in and tore these symbolic tents down, while arresting the homeless protestors on such charges as playing a radio without a license.

Ravo, Nick. "Homeless Living Outside Coliseum Face Removal Tonight." New York Times, June 26, 1991:B4.
　　For the past year, dozens of homeless people have lived in front of the Coliseum at Columbus Circle in New York City. Just as the city police removed the homeless from Tompkins Square Park, so they will remove the homeless from this location.

Rawley, Callman. "A Glimpse of the Unattached Woman Transient in New Orleans." The Family, May 1934:84-86.
　　The case load of 3,500 at the New Orleans Transient Bureau has only 40 women. Of these, 15 percent are under the age of 20, 15 percent between 20 and 25, and 70

percent are 25 and over. Eighty-five percent have finished grammar school, 54 percent have graduated from high school, and 12 percent have attended college. Only one third are single, and 42 percent have experienced marital conflict which led to the breakup of the home. None had come to New Orleans by freight car, 27 percent had hitchhiked, and 73 percent had come by bus, railway, or automobile.

Reamer, Frederic G. "The Affordable Housing Crisis and Social Work." Social Work, 34 (4), January 1989:5-9.
    The basic cause of homelessness is a lack of affordable housing. One-fourth of the poor now pay more than three-fourths of their income for rent. In New York City, 200,000 people are on waiting lists for public housing. To meet the needs of the homeless, we must develop programs to preserve existing low-income housing, produce new multi-family housing, and enable low- and moderate-income people to buy homes. "Social workers must convert clients' private troubles into public issues, and must be engaged actively in the advocacy, public debate, and policy formation that are so essential to the provision of adequate housing."

Reckless, Walter C. "Why Women Become Hoboes." American Mercury, 31 (122), February 1934:175-180.
    Very few women become hobos (only one woman to 18 men). The author concludes that because we still live in a man's world women have no homeless culture or society. Consequently, women find poverty more degrading. He then presents the exception, the case of a woman who became a hobo due to wanderlust.

Redburn, F. Stevens, and Terry F. Buss. Responding to America's Homeless: Public Policy Alternatives. New York: Praeger, 1986.
    Based on 1,000 interviews with homeless individuals and families in Ohio, the authors draw a portrait of America's homeless population and its needs. These data on degree of deprivation, age, sex, race, education, and marital and family status challenge the widely held view that most homeless are mentally ill. The authors review basic survival strategies of the homeless, locate major routes to homelessness, and propose a classification of the homeless based on a hierarchy of needs: the need for permanent custodial care, for developmental assistance, for crisis care only, and for shelter only. The authors suggest standards by which to judge the success of public

policy and propose "secondary prevention," that is,
"interventions that occur at or soon after the time when
a person or family loses a home." To return people to
independent living includes not simply locating housing
but also "establishing a stable source of income, working
through a crisis in personal relationships, and finding
day care for children." Reintegrating the homeless into
mainstream society requires services "to overcome
barriers to economic self-sufficiency and to create a
capacity for independent living." Some persons, however,
will continue to be homeless unless they are provided
some kind of sheltered living arrangement.

Reich, Robert, and Lloyd Siegel. "The Emergence of the
Bowery as a Psychiatric Dumping Ground." Psychiatric
Quarterly, 50 (3), 1978:191-201.
     Deinstitutionalization does not signify a reduction
in mental illness, but, rather, the demographic relocation of the mentally ill.

Reich, Robert, and Lloyd Siegel. "Psychiatry Under
Siege: The Chronic Mentally Ill Shuffle to Oblivion."
Psychiatric Annals, 3 (11), November 1973:35, 39, 42-43,
47-49, 54-55.
     Deinstitutionalization without follow-up treatment
is inhumane and a failure. The solution is to develop
small, centrally located, therapeutically oriented,
specialized inpatient communities.

Reinhold, Robert. "In San Diego, the Developers Profit
As Homeless Get Low-Cost Housing." New York Times,
September 6, 1988:84.
     A resurgence of S.R.O.'s has taken place in San
Diego, California. Desiring to provide housing for the
homeless and to prevent homelessness, city officials have
modified building codes in order to make it profitable
for private developers to construct low-rent hotels.

Reitman, Ben. L. "Classification of Tramps." In Edmond
Kelly, The Elimination of the Tramp. New York: G. P.
Putnam's Sons, 1908:103-104.
     There are three types of vagrants: the tramp, who
dreams and wanders; the hobo, who works and wanders; and
the bum, who drinks and wanders. Each has subtypes.
Tramp criminals are criminals who tramp in order to
escape detection, while criminal tramps are tramps who
steal instead of beg.

Reitman, Ben L. <u>Sister of the Road</u>: <u>The Autobiography of Box-Car Bertha</u>. New York: Sheridan House, 1937.
A novelistic account of the life story related by a female hobo to the author, himself a hobo. It focuses on her childhood, early associations with deviance, traveling, and experiences as a prostitute.

Resener, Carl R. <u>Crisis in the Streets</u>. Nashville, Tennessee: Broadman Press, 1988.
The author's summary of his 20 years of work with the homeless in Nashville contains numerous cases that illustrate the plight of the homeless, the Christian imperative to work with the homeless, and the perils of working with the homeless.

Reuler, J. B., M. J. Bax, and J. H. Sampson. "Physician House Call Services for Medically Needy, Inner-City Residents." <u>American Journal of Public Health</u>, <u>76</u> (9), September 1986:1131-1134.
The authors present a positive assessment of the Wallace Medical Concern program in Portland, Oregon. In this program, which provides on-site services to residents of night shelters and single room occupancy hotels, volunteer physicians, nurses, and medical students make house calls to the hotels and shelters.

Rezneck, Samuel. "Unemployment, Unrest, and Relief in the United States During the Depression of 1893-97." <u>Journal of Political Economy</u>, <u>61</u>, August 1953:324-345.
In the depression of the 1890s, about 20,000 homeless in the City of New York "overflowed police stations and other shelters." Thousands of homeless were attracted to Chicago because of "the promise of the World's Fair...These vagrants now overflowed even the corridors of the City Hall, and the police were guarding the railroad stations to cut off a further influx." And with "the virtual suspension of all silver mining in Colorado,...a relief camp under canvas was established there, and arrangements were made to ship whole trainloads of unemployed eastward, free or at nominal fares." As the army of unemployed swept through the streets, some communities were panic-stricken, "inhabitants fortifying themselves behind soup-houses, throwing loaves of bread upon besiegers." The many relief projects during this period included: a wayfarers' lodge with a woodyard for men and a laundry for women, public work funds for parks, bread and clothing funds by newspapers, low-cost food centers, the "Indianapolis Plan"--a market in which a

supply of food (a weekly family ration worth eighty-two
cents) was given in return for a day's work, stone-
breaking, sewing shops, the "Detroit Garden Plot Plan"--
utilizing vacant land to establish "municipal farming for
the poor," unemployment payments by trade unions, and
charity balls and bazaars for the rich to raise money for
the poor. Governor Flower of New York stated that "in
this country firm lines separate our political ideas from
those of European countries.... In America the people
support the government; it is not the province of the
government to support the people."

Rhoden, N. "The Limits of Liberty: Deinstitutionalization, Homelessness, and Libertarian Theory." Emory
University Law Review, 31, Spring 1982:375-440.
    "Early advocates of deinstitutionalization harbored
an idealized notion of 'community' and tended to exagger-
ate the extent to which labeling a person mentally ill
produces and perpetuates pathology. Consequently, they
were overly optimistic in their assessment of the ability
of released patients to survive, unaided, in
society....Many legal advocates of patients' rights
shared these assumptions and coupled them with a skepti-
cism, albeit often healthy, about psychiatric diagnosis
and treatment. Therefore, they focused far more heavily
on obtaining liberty for patients than on seeking
services for them. Since judicial decrees can grant
rights against government infringement of liberty far
more easily than they can establish positive entitlements
to care and services, the result was that mental patients
obtained their liberty, but at the expense of the
community care they so desperately needed." Homelessness
of former mental patients represents a total failure of
deinstitutionalization. "Just as the benevolent purpose
of institutionalization can be perverted into excessive
state intervention, the benevolent purpose of deinstitutionalization can become a justification for neglect."
The homeless mentally ill "have a constitutional right to
after-care." The author analyzes the statutory basis for
the right of the homeless mentally ill to community care
and examines the legal basis for administrative and
political advocacy for the homeless. "Liberty too easily
becomes neglect, especially in an era struggling with
diminishing resources. But the limitations of a purely
libertarian approach have become far too obvious to
ignore, and advocates must now turn to the task of
obtaining shelter and services for the mentally ill.
Only when we combine our commitment to protecting their

rights with an equal commitment to caring for their needs
will the mentally ill enjoy the freedom to choose lives
of quality over lives of neglect."

Ribton-Turner, C. J. <u>A History of Vagrants and Vagrancy</u>
<u>and Beggars and Begging</u>. London: Chapman and Hall, 1887.
(Reprinted by Patterson Smith, Montclair, New Jersey:
1972.)
    A chronological overview of vagrancy and begging in
England from 368 to 1886, in Scotland from 968 to 1885,
in Ireland from 450 to 1885, in Wales from 943 to 1284,
and on the Isle of Mann and the Channel Islands from 1422
to 1885. The volume also contains a history of laws and
punishment for vagrancy and begging in Sweden, Denmark,
Belgium, Holland, France, Germany, Austria, Italy,
Russia, Portugal, and Turkey. This book analyzes the
culture of vagrants and beggars as depicted by writers
and also contains separate chapters on the mendicant or
begging friars, gypsies, and the secret jargon of
vagrants and mendicants.

Rice, Stuart A. "Contagious Bias in the Interview."
<u>American Journal of Sociology</u>, <u>35</u>, November 1929:420-423.
    The author uses interviews with 2,000 skid row men
to analyze interviewer bias.

Rice, Stuart A. "The Failure of the Municipal Lodging
House." <u>National Municipal Review</u>, <u>11</u>, November
1922:358-362.
    The author compares the costs and services of the
public New York Municipal Lodging House ($1.56 per person
per night) with the private Mills Hotel (40 cents, and
offering more services). He attributes the difference to
overhead costs and suggests that the municipal lodging
house be replaced with an "application bureau for
homeless men and women" which would be "located at the
health center" and "tied up in working arrangements with
the public employment office." There are "two distinct
problems of homeless dependency:" "the emergent demand"
(increased homelessness during periods of industrial
shrinkage) and the "continuing problem of social etholo-
gy" ("the inability of individuals to master the problem
of self-support, even under the most favorable conditions"). The former really need only to be offered jobs,
while the latter need a "human repair shop."

Rice, Stuart A. "The Homeless." <u>Annals of the American</u>
<u>Academy of Political Science</u>, <u>77</u>, May 1918:140-153.

The superintendent of the New York Municipal Lodging House reports on his experiences. He states that there are four types of homeless: self-supporting, temporarily dependent, chronically dependent, and parasitic.

Richardson, Linda. "Walls of Shame Keep Homeless From School." New York Times, January 2, 1992:A1.
Shame about being poor is one of the reasons that children of the homeless have poor school attendance. This shame, and other obstacles, need to be addressed to help improve their attendance.

Rickett, Arthur. The Vagabond in Literature. Port Washington, N.Y.: Kennikat Press, 1968. (First published in London by J.M. Dent, 1906.)
The author focuses on the personal lives and writings of literary figures who were "vagabonds" either intellectually or physically: William Hazlitt, Thomas De Quincey, George Borrow, Robert Louis Stevenson, Richard Jefferies, and Walt Whitman.

Ridgely, M. Susan, Caroline T. McNeil, and Howard H. Goldman. Alcohol and Other Drug Abuse Among Homeless Individuals: An Annotated Bibliography. Rockville, Maryland: U.S. Department of Health and Human Services, October 1988.
This annotated bibliography of the literature that addresses alcohol and other drug abuse among the homeless population is organized into seven sections: (1) historical perspective, (2) population characteristics, (3) research on services, (4) service approaches, (5) approaches to special service issues, (6) research methods, and (7) sociopolitical context-policy issues. Not all items are annotated, nor are all alphabetized.

Riding, Alan. "The New Library is Big, and So Is the Brouhaha." New York Times, August 12, 1991:A4.
Homeless persons, directed by the Right to a Home Association, conducted a sit-in at the site of a planned Library of France on the Seine. The author discusses repercussions of the sit-in.

Riemer, Morris D. "Runaway Children." American Journal of Orthopsychiatry, 10, 1940:522-526.
The author views running away as a form of hostile flight from an unyielding environment, an attempt to satisfy the need for security, of support and love, an attempt to gratify the powerful but mutually contrary

forces of the need for love, and the need for hostile aggression.

Ridgeway, James. "The Administration's Attack on the Homeless: Building a Fire Under Reagan." <u>Village Voice</u>, February 14, 1984:10, 70.
    The author denounces President Reagan's statement that some homeless people are homeless by choice. The causes, rather, are structural: unemployment, diminishing supply of low-cost housing, deinstitutionalization, and tougher rules for receiving disability.

Rigdon, Joan E. "See Spot Appeal: A Condemned Dog Bites Back in Court." <u>Wall Street Journal</u>, October 24, 1990:A1, A11.
    This article reviews the plight of a pit bulldog that has been sentenced to death for biting three people. The dog's owner, "Crazy Ed," is described as homeless.

Rigney, Melanie, and Julie Steenhuysen. "Conscience Raising." <u>Advertising Age</u>, <u>62</u> (35), August 26, 1991:19.
    As demonstrated by Borden's snack division donating a portion of the proceeds from the Beach Boys' 1991 concert tour to the Better Homes Foundation for homeless families, "cause-related marketing" can produce healthier profits and public images.

Riis, Jacob A. <u>The Battle with the Slum</u>. New York: Macmillan, 1902.
    A sequel to <u>How the Other Half Lives</u>, this book contains materials on lodging rooms at police stations and specifies differences between the "honestly poor" (those without means who are willing to work) and others. People do what they are paid to do--whether to work or to beg. The solution is to provide shelter and meals for those who will work and a farm school to train young vagrants into the habits of industry and steady work.

Riis, Jacob A. <u>How the Other Half Lives</u>. New York: Hill and Wang, 1957. (First published in 1890 by C. Scribner's of New York.)
    This description of living conditions on New York's Lower East Side includes materials on the life style of the homeless men living on the Bowery.

Riis, Jacob A. "How to Bring Work and Workers Together." <u>The Forum</u>, <u>18</u>, September 1894:122-128.

The author is disturbed because he had searched vainly for someone to paint his house at the same time that a house painter had committed suicide because he could not find work. Riis suggests that an unemployment bureau or labor exchange be established to bring together men and jobs. This would serve as "the ounce of prevention" for the Wayfarers' Lodge.

Riis, Jacob A. <u>The Making of an American</u>. New York: Macmillan, 1902.
This autobiography of an immigrant from Denmark who became a nationally known reporter who was influential in political reform contains accounts of the unemployed and homeless.

Rimer, Sara. "Behavior on Subway to Be Curbed: Critics Say Homeless Are Targets." <u>New York Times</u>, October 25, 1989:28.
The New York City Transit Authority will begin enforcing rules of conduct that "prohibit behavior considered disruptive, including begging and lying down on train seats." Critics claim that this enforcement of rules is directed against the homeless, that it is an attempt to rid subways of the homeless.

Rimer, Sara. "Helping the Ex-Homeless Fill a Home." <u>New York Times</u>, February 21, 1989:12.
The author takes the reader on a shopping trip with a homeless family that has been moved from a hotel for the homeless to an apartment. She details how a social worker helps pick out used furniture on the $864 budget granted by the state for the "establishment of a home."

Rimer, Sara. "The Homeless Ride a Van, Hopefully." <u>New York Times</u>, February 8, 1989:13.
The author takes the reader on a journey in the city van that transports New York City welfare-hotel residents in their search for city-owned apartments. The families are shown apartments deemed appropriate by case workers, apartments that have been abandoned by their owners and taken over by the city. Hotel residents get three rides in the vans. If they turn down three apartments, their hotel allowance will be cut off, and they will be sent to a shelter for the homeless.

Rimer, Sara. "Homeless Spend Nights in City Welfare Office." <u>New York Times</u>, November 19, 1984:A1, B4.

Because welfare agencies in New York City lack money to provide rooms for the homeless, some homeless people have been sleeping in city welfare offices.

Rimer, Sara. "Kemp Plans Close Encounter With Homeless-ness." New York Times, February 23, 1989:16.
This article reviews the proposed itinerary of Jack F. Kemp, the new Secretary of Housing and Urban Development, who plans to personally survey the homeless in Baltimore and Philadelphia.

Rimer, Sara. "Koch's Plan to House AIDS Patients Stalls." New York Times, June 15, 1989:21.
The author discusses criticisms of New York City's plan to open a shelter specifically for homeless people with AIDS.

Rimer, Sara. "New York City Project to Hospitalize Mentally Ill Homeless Makes Inroads." New York Times, July 18, 1989:Y12.
The author gives a positive review of the activities of Project Help in involuntarily hospitalizing the mentally ill homeless.

Rimer, Sara. "New York City's Homeless Organize To Deal With Social Service System." New York Times, January 29, 1989:21.
This article profiles Ruth Young and Jean Chappell, homeless activists who once were homeless mothers.

Rimer, Sara. "The Other City: New York's Homeless." New York Times, January 30, 1984:B1.
The author sketches an overview of the homeless by using case histories. She closes with a profile of the homeless: their age, ethnicity, marital background, education, etcetera.

Rimer, Sara. "Public Areas Try to Repel Homeless." New York Times, November 18, 1989:Y11.
The author reports that because "people are tired of stepping over bodies" the public is in agreement with the new enforcement of rules by the Transit Authority.

Rimer, Sara. "Rats, Leaks, Crackheads and All, Apart-ments Beat Welfare Hotels." New York Times, 123, July 2, 1989:1, 19.
The Martinique Hotel has been closed, those who have been moved from welfare hotels to permanent apartments

are pleased, and school districts that will suddenly receive homeless children face potential problems.

Rimer, Sara. "The Rent's Due, and for Many It's Homelessness Knocking." New York Times, March 24, 1989:1, 10.

Some people are homeless because they cannot pay their rent. Previously, eviction meant that people simply moved to another low-rent apartment, but now that New York City has an almost non-existent vacancy rate, eviction often leads to homelessness.

Ringenbach, Paul T. Tramps and Reformers, 1873-1916: The Discovery of Unemployment in New York. Westport, Connecticut: Greenwood Press, 1973.

The author gives an overview of tramps in the United States, with emphases on social reactions (including those by labor bureaus and employment exchanges), and the reception of tramps in urban areas, especially New York City. He details the major depression of 1873.

Ringheim, Karin. At Risk of Homelessness. Westport, Connecticut: Praeger Publishers, 1990.

Based on the results of an eight-year study of changes in the stock of low-cost rental housing and the need by low-income households for affordable housing in four metropolitan areas, the author contends that "the extent of homelessness in individual areas is not simply related to the extent of poverty in those areas." Rather, she argues, "the increase in the number and change in composition of the homeless population is a direct result of the severity of the housing squeeze and the demographic characteristics of those most vulnerable to housing loss in individual metropolitan areas."

Riordan, T., J. Cobb, and D. Young. "Housekeeping at HUD--Why the Homeless Problem Could Get Much, Much Worse." Common Cause Magazine, 1987:26-31.

The basic cause of homelessness is a lack of subsidized housing stock. While the national low-cost housing stock has deteriorated or been converted to higher-priced housing, the budget of the Department of Housing and Urban Development (HUD) has been cut. There has been inactivity on the part of Samuel Pierce, the Secretary of Housing and Urban Development and flaws in the voucher program. HUD, in connivance with the Reagan Administration, has actively subverted public housing. The solution is for Congress to fund projects for homeless people and prevent homelessness by enhancing the national housing stock.

Ritchey, Ferris J., Mark La Gory, and Jeffrey Mullis. "Gender Differences in Health Risks and Physical Symptoms Among the Homeless." Journal of Health and Social Behavior, 32 (1), March 1991:33-48.
    Interviews with 100 homeless persons in the Birmingham, Alabama, area, showed that although men had more symptoms of health problems it was women who complained more of health problems. The authors explain this finding, which is consistent with the general population.

Rivlin, Leanne G. "Home and Homelessness in the Lives of Children." Child and Youth Services, 14 (1), 1990:5-17.
    To examine the effects of homelessness on children, the author considers their social, emotional, and cognitive development, the significance of personal space and personal places, including territoriality and place identity, and the temporal patterns of the children's affiliations with others.

Rivlin, Leanne G. "A New Look at the Homeless." Social Policy, 16 (4), Spring 1986.
    There are four types of homelessness: chronic marginal (associated with alcoholism and drug abuse), periodic (those who leave home when pressures become intense, but for whom home is still available when tensions subside), temporary (due to hospitalization or moving from one community to another), and total (the sudden and complete loss of home and roots due to natural, economic, industrial, or interpersonal disasters). Two myths of homelessness are that the homeless are homeless by choice and that they have relatives who can take care of them. Deinstitutionalization is a cause of some homelessness, while the critical shortage of low-cost housing is basic to most homelessness. Three types of homeless children are children on the streets, children off the streets, and abandoned children. The author suggests that we solve the problem by identifying "the ecology of homelessness" (the series of stages that lead to the streets) in order to catch the problem before it escalates. Different types of homeless persons have differing needs for housing, food, jobs, and vocational training. She documents coping strategies and competence of homeless people, not just their pathology. Of the various groups of homeless people, the children are the most threatened. Communities must be educated so they

will accept shelters and other housing for the homeless. The author also examines the significance of homelessness in terms of the subjective meanings of "home".

Rivlin, Leanne G. "The Significance of Home and Homelessness." <u>Marriage and Family Review</u>, <u>15</u> (1-2), 1990:39-56.
 This report on the author's 1978 observational study of homeless persons in Grand Central Terminal in New York City emphasizes the significance of attachment to a place and the loss of home. She identifies four types of homelessness: chronic, an ongoing type associated primarily with males, alcoholism, and drugs; periodic, in which people leave their homes because of personal and family pressures, "but the homes are there when the person feels ready to return;" temporary, a type limited in time and associated with catastrophe (from floods to nuclear accidents); and total, which is "chronic and pervasive, resulting from the complete loss of a home and contacts with the community in situations where the creation of a new home is undermined."

Roach, Jack L., and Janet K. Roach. "Mobilizing the Poor: Road to a Dead End." <u>Social Problems</u>, <u>28</u> (2), December 1978:160-171.
 The authors disagree with the position taken by Frances Fox Piven and Richard Cloward that the most effective strategy for the poor is independent mobilization and disruptive tactics. They propose that, although the prospects are weakened with the current problems of capitalism, activities should be carried out within organized labor.

Robbins, Edwin, Marvin Stern, Lillian Robbins, and Leslie Margolin. "Unwelcome Patients: Where Can They Find Asylum?" <u>Hospital and Community Psychiatry</u>, <u>29</u>, 1978:44-46.
 "Unwelcome patients" are patients who refuse to cooperate with the hospital routine and react to stress with rage. Some of them request admission to a mental hospital because their "welfare money ran out and they needed food and shelter." These individuals have "mental illness compounded by aggressive and assaultive acts," are "younger than the typical chronic state hospital patient," and are "unemployable because he does not have fundamental skills, has a limited education, and has psychiatric problems that make it difficult for him to accept authority." Such patients irritate, frighten, and

alienate the staff. The solution is "to develop therapeutic research units in which the patients would be
sheltered, protected from their impulses, and taught how
to become self-sufficient."

Robbins, William. "Despite Impression Created by Study,
Kansas City's Poor Are No Mirage." New York Times,
December 26, 1986:Y10.
    To illustrate the growing problem of homelessness in
the United States, the author profiles Delia Overbaugh,
a 29-year-old mother, and her three children, who have
just become homeless.

Robbins, William. "Overflow of Warmth Lifts Hopes of the
Poor." New York Times, January 6, 1991:14.
    The author profiles a homeless mother who found a
lost paycheck and returned it to its owner.

Roberts, Albert R. Runaways and Non-Runaways in an
American Suburb. Chicago: The Dorsey Press, 1981.
    To examine how running away is fostered by life
experiences, the author conducted 82 interviews with
suburban runaways, non-runaways, and their parents. He
describes crises events that precede running away,
presents analytical typologies of runaway behavior, and
compares how runaways and nonrunaways respond to adjustment problems.

Roberts, Sam. "Beyond Theories to What Works for the
Homeless." New York Times, February 4, 1991:B1.
    The author profiles the Housing Enterprise for the
Less Privileged (HELP), begun by Andrew Cuomo, brother of
the governor of New York.

Roberts, Sam. "Dinkins to Study Homeless Proposals."
New York Times, February 22, 1992:A27.
    The mayor of New York City, David Dinkins, said he
was committed to implementing the recommendations of a
panel he appointed for helping the homeless. He then
appointed a panel to determine how practical those
recommendations were.

Roberts, Sam. "Dinkins' Plan for Shelters Dealt Set-
back." New York Times, November 19, 1991:B1.
    The chairman of the mayor's Commission on Homeless-
ness, who recommended against scattering 24 shelters for
the homeless throughout middle-class neighborhoods, says
that consensus on their location must be achieved.

Roberts, Sam.   "Evicting the Homeless."   New York Times,
June 22, 1991:A1.
     New Yorkers have become angry that the homeless have
set up permanent camps in public places.   In response to
citizen outrage, matched by ambivalence from many, Mayor
David Dinkins has stepped up efforts to roust the
homeless.

Roberts, Sam.   "The Public's Right to Put a Padlock on a
Public Space."   New York Times, June 3, 1991:B1.
     To keep the homeless out, New York City's West
Village padlocks Jackson Square Park at night.

Roberts, Sam.   "What Led to Crackdown on Homeless."   New
York Times, October 28, 1991:B1.
     The author discusses the change in David Dinkins--
from defender of the rights of the homeless when he was
president of the Borough of Manhattan to enforcer of
ordinances against the homeless as Mayor of New York
City.

Roberts, Steven V.   "Reagan on Homeless: Some Choose Life
Out There."   New York Times, December 23, 1988:1, 12.
     The author reports that President Reagan views
people who sleep on the streets as doing so by choice.
Reagan is reported to have said that they "prefer the
grates or the lawn to going into one of those shelters,"
and that "a large proportion of the homeless population
is mentally impaired."

Roberts, W. Drayton.   "The Extinction of the Tramp."
Saturday Review, 101, January 6, 1906:15-16.
     The author's thesis is that to properly deal with
the tramp problem, we need to differentiate between the
unfortunate and the undeserving.   We should suspend
relief and draft vagrants into a militia that will
perform useful work.   They need to be taught a trade.

Robertson, Marjorie J.   Homeless Youth in Hollywood:
Patterns of Alcohol Use.   Rockville, Maryland: National
Institute on Alcohol Abuse and Alcoholism, 1989.
     The author reports that alcohol abuse is six to
eight times higher in this sample of homeless youths than
among their nonhomeless peers.   She analyzes how family
alcohol problems contribute to homelessness and concludes
that the course of homelessness needs to be studied more
thoroughly in order to identify points at which intervention is maximally feasible.

Robertson, Marjorie J. "Mental Disorder Among Homeless Persons in the United States: An Overview of Recent Empirical Literature." <u>Administration in Mental Health</u>, <u>14</u> (1), October 1986:14-26.

The author reviews 28 empirical studies of mental illness among the homeless. These studies indicate that the homeless have higher rates of psychiatric disorder, distress, and hospitalization than does the general population. A lack of standardized methodology and consistent findings, however, make it difficult to establish reliable estimates of the prevalence of mental illness among homeless persons.

Robertson, Marjorie J., and Michael R. Cousineau. "Health Status and Access to Health Services among the Urban Homeless." <u>American Journal of Public Health</u>, May 1986:1-3.

The authors compare findings from a sample of 238 homeless adults in Los Angeles with those of national estimates. Their sample showed 50 percent more physical health disabilities and twice as much hospitalization. The homeless in their sample were also nine times less likely to have health insurance, and five times less likely to have a regular source of health care.

Robertson, Marjorie J., Paul Koegel, and Linda Ferguson. "Alcohol Use and Abuse Among Homeless Adolescents in Hollywood." <u>Contemporary Drug Problems</u>, <u>16</u> (3), Fall 1989:415-452.

In their study of homeless youth in Hollywood, California, the authors identified 31 sites that provide services to homeless adolescents and gained access to 30 of them in May and June of 1987. Compared with 11th-grade students in California, the subjects in this study reported earlier use of alcohol. Despite the younger age of the adolescents in this sample, "(t)hey were twice as likely to have drunk 10 or more beers, and 13 times more likely to have had 10 or more liquor drinks." That their alcohol abuse, interrupted schooling, diminished opportunities to develop basic living and job skills, increased dependence on illegal activities to meet basic needs, and limited exposure to opportunities for socialization to "mainstream norms and practices" suggests that their economic prospects as adults will be seriously impaired. Because we do not know how well this sample represents homeless adolescents nationwide, much less those in Hollywood, we need "well-designed epidemiological research...in varied geographic settings." The authors

offer suggestions for providing "alcohol services" to
this young population.

Robertson, Marjorie J., Richard H. Ropers, and Richard
Boyer. "The Homeless of Los Angeles County: An Empirical
Evaluation." In <u>The Federal Response to the Homeless
Crisis: Hearings Before a Subcommittee of the Committee
on Government Operations, House of Representatives</u>.
Washington, D.C.: U.S. Government Printing Office,
1985:984-1106. (Also published as a separate document by
The School of Public Health of the University of California at Los Angeles, January 1, 1985.)
      The authors present an overview of homelessness in
Los Angeles County: numbers, missions, training inter-
viewers, whether or not one can trust responses, demographic characteristics, race, health, criminal history,
alcohol and drug abuse, skid row, and the new homeless.
The causes of homelessness are deindustrialization,
unemployment, poverty, deinstitutionalization, and family
instability. This volume also provides a history,
typology, and definitions of homelessness.

Robertson, Michael Owen. "Interpreting Homelessness: The
Influence of Professional and Non-Professional Service
Providers." <u>Urban Anthropology</u>, <u>20</u> (2), Summer 1991:141-
153.
      The author's thesis is that service providers who
work with the homeless hold such a significant position
in the care-providing system that they frame the homeless
problem and influence the public's perception of homelessness.

Robey, Ames. "The Runaway Girl." In <u>Family Dynamics
and Female Sexual Delinquency</u>, Otto Pollak and Alfred S.
Friedman, eds. Palo Alto, Calif.: Science and Behavior
Books, 1969:127-137.
      The authors develop the assumption that running away
for a girl is "a method of controlling her incestuous
wishes, which are unquestionably shared by not only her
father, but also her mother." The book contains case
histories.

Robey, Ames, Richard J. Rosenwald, John E. Snell, and
Rita E. Lee. "The Runaway Girl: A Reaction to Family
Stress." <u>American Journal of Orthopsychiatry</u>, <u>34</u>,
1964:762-767.
      After studying the records of 42 runaway girls
referred to the Framingham Court Clinic in Framingham,

Massachusetts, the authors conclude that the basic etiology of running away consists of "a disturbed marital relationship, inadequate control by the parents over their own and the girl's impulses, deprivation of love of the mother, and subtle pressure by her on the girl to take over the maternal role."

Robins, Lee N. "Mental Illness and the Runaway: A 30-Year Follow-Up Study." Human Organization, 16 (4), 1958:11-15.
  This study of 524 patients of child guidance clinics 30 years later compares runaways and non-runaways. The author concludes: "Running away was found to occur largely among juvenile delinquents, and particularly among those who are sent to a reformatory. Runaways were found to have a high rate of psychiatric disease as adults compared with other child guidance clinic patients and with normal boys." Specifically, 32 percent of the runaways were diagnosed as sociopathic, 16 percent psychotic, 11 percent neurotic, 7 percent alcoholic, 14 percent as having no mental disease, and 20 percent remained undiagnosed.

Robins, Lee N., and Patricia O'Neal. "The Adult Prognosis for Runaway Children." American Journal of Orthopsychiatry, 29, 1959:752-761.
  In a 30-year follow-up study of patients of child guidance clinics, 246 former patients were interviewed. The authors found that the former runaways had "an adult arrest rate almost twice that of other clinic patients, an adult incarceration rate that is fourfold that of the other patients, a 50 per cent divorce rate, and a diagnosis of sociopathic personality in almost one third of the cases."

Robinson, Tim. "Boys' Own Stories." New Statesman and Society, 3 (115), August 24, 1990:10-12.
  In this study, young homosexual male prostitutes in England are referred to as homeless and rootless. The author details prostitute-client relationships, indicates that most of these homosexual male prostitutes have not been victims of child sexual abuse, and concludes that their needs must be addressed.

Roca, R. P., W. R. Breakey, and P. J. Fischer. "Medical Care of Chronic Psychiatric Outpatients." Hospital and Community Psychiatry, 38 (7), July 1987:741-745.

Ninety-three percent of 42 outpatients in a psychosocial rehabilitation program were found to have at least one medical problem that needed assessment, treatment, or follow-up. The most common problem for men was gross dental disease, while for women it was minor gynecological disease. Only 11 percent of men and 26 percent of women were receiving appropriate medical care. The authors recommend that psychiatric clinics provide simple medical screening.

Rodgers, Harrell R., Jr. The Cost of Human Neglect: America's Welfare Failure. Armonk, New York: M. E. Sharpe, 1982.
After presenting an overview of the welfare program in the United States and an analysis of problems of the American economy, the author makes proposals for restructuring the economy and reforming the welfare system.

Roehlkepartain, Eugene. "Joining Hands with Hands Across America." Christian Century, 103, June 4, 1986:542-593.
After reviewing criticisms leveled against "Hands Across America," which was held on Memorial Day of the previous weekend, the author concludes that this was a positive event. It assured "people in the hunger movement there is at least a seed of sympathy for their cause in the country," encouraged people to become involved in good causes, and demonstrated that Madison Avenue techniques can be applied to worthwhile causes. The primary value of this event was to engender interest and enthusiasm.

Rogers, David. "The Lives of Two Insiders Turned Outsiders Reflect a Hunger to Find New Answers to Old Problems." Wall Street Journal, August 21, 1991:A14.
The author profiles Robin Britt and Donald Ryan, who turned their backs on promising careers in politics in order to help the homeless.

Roha, Ronaleen R. "Help for the Homeless." Changing Times, January 1989:100-101.
This article, which reports on various efforts by individuals to help the homeless, includes attempts to open shelters.

Roha, Ronaleen R., and Suzan Richmond. "What it's Like to Aid the Homeless." Changing Times, July 1989:80-81.

The author details a nightly run by volunteers for the House of Ruth, a shelter for homeless women in Washington, D.C.

Rohrbaugh, Lewis. "The Backgrounds of Minor Transiency." School and Society, 43, 1963:583-584.
Two thousand seven Texas boys and 482 Philadelphia boys gave looking for work as their main reason for leaving home. In contrast, 150 boys registered at the Boys' Bureau of New York City said that broken homes and inadequate home relief were the main causes that they left home.

Rohrbaugh, Lewis. "Educating the Transient." Journal of Educational Sociology, 9 (4), December 1935:243-246.
The author argues that programs to train transients to enter the work-a-day world, established by the states and the federal government, will be effective.

Rolleston, Charles. "Mischievous Charity." Westminster Review, 163, February 1905:148-155.
Many of the homeless do not want to work. The solution is to provide charity for the men who want to help themselves. The author suggests that a Central Labor Bureau be established, which would assign the able-bodied to areas of the country that have a labor short-age.

Rolleston, Charles. "Social Parasites." Westminster Review, 162 (1), December 1904:623-632.
Indiscriminate and misdirected almsgiving and relief programs remove the incentive to work, discourage thrift, foresight, self-reliance, and self-respect, and increase pauperism. The author proposes that a strict labor test be passed before men are given either money or food, one that will separate the truly needy from the social parasites. The three causes of poverty (or classes of the poor) are improvidence, laziness, and unemployability due to physical or mental defectiveness.

Romeo, Anthony. "New Services Approaches to Alienated Youth." Family Service Highlights, 30, 1969:95-101.
This article reports on Village Project, a 1968 research action program of Jewish Family Services. The author, who directed the project, identifies four main types of hippies: plastic or marginal hippies, stone hippies, runaways, and fugitives. He concludes that even the most alienated youth can be reached by touching their

thematic core, an approach he calls Tactual Thematic Therapy.

Romines, Delma K. "Hobo Nickels." <u>American Heritage</u>, <u>34</u>, August-September 1983:81-83.
This article, which reports that the buffalo nickel "served as a medium for a generation of hobo artists who reworked the images to produce a token that might be traded for a meal or a shirt," contains photos of "hobo nickels."

Rood, Henry Edward. "The Tramp Problem: A Remedy." <u>The Forum</u>, <u>25</u>, March 1898:90-94.
The solution to the tramp problem is for each area to adopt and publicize a policy of giving no food or money except in exchange for work. The author also reports on Coxey's Army.

Rooney, James F. "Friendship and Disaffiliation Among the Skid Row Population." <u>Journal of Gerontology</u>, <u>31</u> (1), 1976:82-88.
The author gathered data on the social relationships of 335 skid row men. These data support the theory of replacement (non-skid row friends are replaced with skid-row friends), but not the theory of disaffiliation (life as an outcast leads to loss of relationships, psychological withdrawal, and the loss of need for interpersonal contact). Personal intimacy and giving assistance to close friends, however, decline with age.

Rooney, James F. "Group Processes Among Skid Row-Winos: A Reevaluation of the Undersocialization Hypothesis." <u>Quarterly Journal of Studies on Alcohol</u>, <u>22</u>, September 1961:444-460.
Based on participant observation of three California skid rows, the author presents an analytic description of the process and function of group drinking. He reports that the bottle group is an alternative institution that provides satisfying interpersonal contacts for men on skid row. The theory of undersocialization is only partially applicable, as these men regularly participate in psyche-groups and demonstrate social skills by structuring social relationships around wine drinking.

Rooney, James F. "Organizational Success Through Program Failure: Skid Row Rescue Missions." <u>Social Forces</u>, <u>58</u> (3), March 1980:904-924.

Skid row missions perpetually fail. This guarantees the perpetuation of the organization and employment of the staff. The author questions the soundness of supporting organizations that benefit directly from their own failure.

Rooney, James F. "Societal Forces and the Unattached Male: An Historical Review." In <u>Disaffiliated Man: Essays and Bibliography on Skid Row, Vagrancy, and Outsiders</u>, Howard Bahr, ed. Toronto: University of Toronto Press, 1970:13-38.
The author analyzes structural causes of disaffiliation in the United States, the transition to an industrial economy, large scale unemployment, and social changes relating to old age, disability, and sickness. He also reviews changes in skid row institutions and life styles of skid row men and contrasts the structural and psychological factors that bring men to skid row.

Roosevelt, Theodore. "Municipal Administration: The New York Police Force." <u>Atlantic Monthly</u>, <u>80</u> (479), September 1897:289-300.
This is Roosevelt's account of his tenure as president of the police board of New York City. His focus on cleaning up the corruption and blackmail of the police department includes this statement: "One important bit of reform was abolishing the tramp lodging-houses, which had originally been started in the police stations, in a spirit of unwise philanthropy. These tramp lodging-houses, not being properly supervised, were mere nurseries for pauperism and crime, tramps and loafers of every shade thronging to the city every winter to enjoy their benefits. We abolished them, a municipal lodging-house being substituted. Here all homeless wanderers were received, forced to bathe, given night-clothes before going to bed, and made to work the next morning; and in addition they were so closely supervised that habitual tramps and vagrants were speedily detected and apprehended."

Ropers, Richard H., and Richard Boyer. "Homelessness As a Health Risk." <u>Alcohol Health and Research World</u>, <u>11</u> (3), Spring 1987:38-41, 89.
Based on interviews with 269 homeless men and women in Los Angeles County, the authors summarize these people's demographic characteristics, welfare status, economic and employment history, history of homelessness, physical and mental health status, utilization of health

services, patterns of drug and alcohol use, and history of criminality and crime victimization. Apparently, the poor financial situation of the homeless has caused their poor health, not the reverse. The authors stress that to effectively deal with the homeless and to adequately formulate social policy, it is necessary to come to grips with the heterogeneity of the homeless population.

Ropers, Richard H., and Richard Boyer. "Perceived Health Status among the New Urban Homeless." Social Science and Medicine, 24 (8), 1987:669-678.
   A survey of 269 homeless men and women in Los Angeles, using the 200-item Basic Shelter Interview Schedule, showed that the homeless are made up of many subgroups. The authors suggest that a variety of strategies are necessary if the needs of the homeless are to be met.

Rose, Joseph B. "An Unfair Share." New York Times, November 8, 1991:A27.
   Locating shelters for the homeless in residential areas poses an unfair burden on residents of those areas. The better location of shelters is in commercial areas, near the social service agencies that the homeless need.

Roseman, Alvin. Shelter Care and the Local Homeless Man. Chicago: Public Administration Service, 1935.
   In this overview of the Chicago Service Bureau for Men, one finds a history of organized welfare in United States, as well as suggested solutions, such as more staff, smaller shelters, and different treatment on the basis of types of homeless men, such as the aged and alcoholics.

Rosen, David. "Affordable Housing: The American Day Dream." Business and Society Review (67), Fall 1988:67-70.
   The author proposes that with the shaky stock market and the accumulating federal mortgage on our children's future we should develop a National Housing Trust "to meet the nation's low-and moderate-income housing needs." He presents specific proposals for funding such a trust.

Rosenfield, Joe, Jr. The Happiest Man in the World. Garden City: Doubleday, 1955.
   Autobiography of an alcoholic who, after spending six months on skid row, was reformed by Alcoholics Anonymous. Except for the skid row experience, he

maintained strong family ties and lived a fairly conventional life.

Rosenheim, F. "Techniques of Therapy: Runaway Adolescent Boys." American Journal of Orthopsychiatry, 10 (4), 1940:651-665.
Since most boys run away from home because of an unresolved Oedipus complex, we can conclude that running away is an unhealthy reaction to a dangerous impulse. The author uses three case studies to illustrate this motivation.

Rosenheim, Margaret K. "Vagrancy Concepts in Welfare Law." In The Law of the Poor, Jacobus TenBroek, ed. San Francisco: Chandler, 1966:187-242.
The author analyzes concepts that underlie the vagrancy laws of the United States and their relationship to the modern welfare system. She concludes that, in general, vagrancy has been removed from American criminal law and incorporated into the welfare system, mentioning the means test, able-bodied vagrants, AFDC, idleness, unemployment insurance, income maintenance, public assistance, and repression in the welfare system.

Rosenman, Mark, and Mary Lee Stein. "Homeless Children: A New Vulnerability." Child and Youth Services, 14 (1), 1990:89-109.
Although programs designed to meet the needs of homeless children are paved with good intentions, they largely fail to meet their needs. The authors suggest ways that these good intentions can be translated into programs that effectively meet the needs of homeless children.

Rosenman, Stanley. "The Skid-Row Alcoholic and the Negative Ego Image." Quarterly Journal of Studies on Alcohol, 16, September 1955:447-473.
The author draws a psychoanalytic profile of skid row men, with emphasis on the negative self images that underlie their drinking.

Rosenthal, Andrew. "President Offers Housing Program to Aid Key Groups." New York Times, November 11, 1989:1, 10.
The $7 billion package of housing programs is designed to aid low-income families, first-time home buyers, and the homeless. Critics say that the proposals

are "very significant as a redirection of policy, but insufficient in the funds that they will provide."

Rosenthal, Andrew. "The 39th Witness." New York Times, February 12, 1987:A31.
The author expresses guilt about his lack of concern for the homeless whom he "passes by and steps over." The term, "39th witness," refers to himself, who, by not doing anything about the homeless, joins the 38 people who did nothing when Catherine Genovese was attacked and killed in 1964.

Rosenthal, Rob. "Straighter from the Source: Alternative Methods of Researching Homelessness." Urban Anthropology, 20 (2), Summer 1991:109-126.
The author's thesis is that data on the homeless from shelters and street surveys tap only subgroups of the homeless population, that a fuller picture of the homeless is provided by "hanging out," involvement in the homeless movement, and collecting oral histories.

Rosenwald, Richard J., and Joseph Mayer. "Runaway Girls from Suburbia." American Journal of Orthopsychiatry, 37 (2), 1967:402-403.
The authors classify runaway girls as (1) hypermature (physical maturity and provocative seductiveness toward their fathers), (2) hypo-mature (physically immature, frightened, and depressed), (3) impulse-ridden (fixated at an oral stage of development), and (4) unclassifiable (atypical). The meaning of running away, then, depends on the type of runaway.

Rosnow, Mark, Toni Shaw, and Clare Stapleton Concord. Listening to the Homeless: A Study of Homeless Mentally Ill Persons in Milwaukee. Madison: Wisconsin Office of Mental Health, April 1985. Mimeo.
This report is based on interviews with 237 homeless persons in the winter of 1984-85 in Milwaukee, Wisconsin. Forty percent are categorized as mentally ill, 24 percent as having alcohol or drug abuse problems. The causes of homelessness are a shrinking low-income housing market, a shrinking job market, mental illness, and alcohol and drug abuse. Criminal conviction is also a handicap that contributes to homelessness. The authors also review precipitating factors in becoming homeless, homeless women, coping techniques, and community support programs.

Ross, Aileen D.   The Lost and the Lonely: Homeless Women in Montreal.   Montreal: McGill   University   Printing Service, 1982.
    Based on participant observation and interviewing at shelters,   the   author   reviews   problems   of   the   female homeless   (emotional,   alcohol,   family,   housing,   income, drugs, health, and unemployment), especially their misery (loneliness,   depression,   fears,   violence,   suicide,   and murder),   survival techniques (prostitution, conning, and manipulation), and community resources (family, friends, religion, government, courts, hospitals, social agencies, and shelters).   She contrasts the staff's idealism with the reality they face.

Rossi, Peter H.   Down and Out in America: The Origins of Homelessness.   Chicago: University of Chicago Press, 1989.
    The   author   contrasts   today's   homeless   with   the homeless   of   yesterday   and   with   recipients   of   General Assistance,   the   state   welfare   grant   for   single,   unem-ployed,   poor   people.   In   general,   the   homeless   of yesterday were single, older, white males, who often were alcoholics.   Most did day work and lived in S.R.O.s.   In contrast, today's homeless are younger and more likely to be black.   Today's homeless are also much poorer than the homeless of yesterday.   The S.R.O.s have largely disap-peared from skid row, and there is no longer much need for day labor.   Compared with recipients of General Assistance, the homeless are more likely to have personal experience with drugs, alcohol, mental institutions, and the criminal justice system.   The author proposes an AFDA program,   an aid to families with dependent adults, to provide them basic social security.

Rossi, Peter H.   "The Family, Welfare, and Homelessness." Notre Dame Journal of Law, Ethics, and Public Policy, 4 (2), Summer 1989:281-300.
    The author explains why the current social welfare system is poorly suited to serve the needs of homeless people, why kinship obligations often fail in cases of homelessness, and how the social welfare system should be changed to serve the homeless.

Rossi,   Peter.   Without   Shelter: Homelessness   in   the 1980s.   New York: Priority Press, 1989.
    The author suggests that the homeless should be made aware of the availability of federal benefits, mental patients should be enrolled in disability programs before

they are released from hospitals, shelters should be
upgraded, and the government needs to provide jobs for
persons whom the private sector does not employ.

Rossi, Peter H., Gene A. Fisher, and Georgianna Willis.
The Condition of the Homeless of Chicago. Amherst:
University of Massachusetts, September 1986.
     Conducted by the National Opinion Research Center,
this survey was designed to provide an unbiased, systematic sample of the homeless of Chicago. Both shelter and
street surveys were made. To cover seasonality, both
fall and winter samples were taken. On an average night,
between 2,000 and 3,000 persons are homeless in Chicago.
About 5,000 are homeless at one time or another each
year. The authors report on the average cash income of
the homeless (less than $6 per day), use of shelters and
food kitchens (essential to prevent starvation), public
welfare and income maintenance programs (underutilized in
terms of eligibility), sleeping places (39 percent in
shelters in good fall weather, 74 percent in winter, with
the rest in public places), physical and mental health
(disproportionate illness), rates of institutionalization
(almost all), ties to other persons (scant), work
history, and demographics (mostly male, black, unmarried,
with a high school education only and a median age of
40). These findings indicate the need for more income
maintenance and attainment strategies, efforts to get the
highest level of benefits for which the homeless are
eligible, payments to families to incorporate the
homeless into their households, reduced taxes for those
on income maintenance programs, easy access to aftercare
medical services, and subsidized housing.

Rossi, Peter H., and James D. Wright. "The Urban
Homeless: A Portrait of Urban Dislocation." Annals of
the American Academy of Political and Social Sciences,
January 1989:132-142.
     The lack of an agreed-on definition of homelessness
is a major obstacle for social research. The authors
propose a contrast between the literally homeless
(persons "who do not have access to a conventional
dwelling and who would be homeless by any conceivable
definition of the term") and the precariously, or
marginally, housed persons (those with tenuous or very
temporary claims to a conventional dwelling). Based on
two samples in Chicago (a probability sample of persons
spending the night in shelters and the count of persons
found in a search of non-dwelling units), the authors

enumerate the poverty, disabilities and social isolation of the literally homeless. They suggest that the best short-term measure is to establish more generous income-maintenance programs, and that long-term measures should focus on increasing the supply of low-cost housing and providing more low-skilled employment.

Rossi, Peter H., James D. Wright, Gene A. Fisher, and Georgianna Willis. "The Urban Homeless: Estimating Composition and Size." Science, 235, March 13, 1987:1136-1140.
     The authors report that theirs is the "first scientifically defensible estimates of the size and composition of the homeless population in any city." Using a stratified random sample of city blocks, two surveys of the homeless were made "based on separately drawn but identically designed shelter and street subsamples." The authors conclude that there are 2,722 persons who are "literal homeless," persons "who clearly do not have access to conventional dwelling and will be homeless by any conceivable definition of the term." Although "the modal homeless person was a black male high school graduate in his mid-thirties," the survey found the homeless population to be heterogeneous. The primary disabilities of the homeless are high levels of health problems, mental illness, previous arrests, and social isolation. A second category of homeless are the "precariously (or marginally) housed persons," those with tenuous or temporary claims to a conventional dwelling of more or less marginal adequacy.

Rossi, Peter H., and Zahava D. Blum. "Class, Status, and Poverty." In On Understanding Poverty: Perspectives from the Social Sciences, Daniel P. Moynihan, ed. New York: Basic Books, 1968.
     The authors review the post-World War II literature on the poor. They contrast two positions: that the characteristics of the poor are due to a subculture of poverty or are situational. Each position implies major differences in social policy. Favoring the situational view, the authors propose that the stigmatizing processes in the occupational system be removed, discrimination in social institutions be eliminated, and a floor of income and self-respect be provided for every citizen. They do not indicate how these proposals can be accomplished.

Roth, Dee, and Jerry Bean. "New Perspectives on Homelessness: Findings from a Statewide Epidemiological

Study." <u>Hospital and Community Psychiatry</u>, <u>37</u> (7), July 1986:712-719.

A study of 979 homeless people in 29 of Ohio's 88 counties found that the median length of homelessness was 60 days. About 30 percent of the homeless have been hospitalized for mental health reasons, and about the same percent showed symptoms of serious mental health problems. Homelessness is a multi-dimensional problem involving street people, shelter people, and resource people. To be adequate, service strategies must reflect these varying needs and characteristics.

Roth, Dee, and Jerry Bean. "The Ohio Study: A Comprehensive Look at Homelessness." <u>Psychosocial Rehabilitation Journal</u>, <u>9</u> (4), April 1986:31-39.

Based on a study of 979 homeless people in 29 of Ohio's 88 counties, the authors conclude that, unlike the stereotype, most of the homeless have lived in their county of residence for a relatively long time. They also identify three types of homeless: street people, shelter people, and resource people. To be effective, different programs and policies must be set up to deal with these separate subtypes.

Roth, Dee, Jerry Bean, Nancy Lust, and Traian Saveanu. <u>Homelessness in Ohio: A Study of People in Need, State-wide Report</u>, Ohio Department of Mental Health, February 1985. Mimeo.

This publication is a report of statewide sampling of key informants in Ohio (persons who "by virtue of their position" ought to "have some knowledge of homeless people") in each geographical area combined with "face-to-face interviews with 979 homeless people." It contains numerous tables on available services and on the backgrounds and characteristics of the homeless. Three types of homeless are identified: street people, shelter people, and resource people. Comparisons are made of urban and non-urban homeless.

Roth, Joan. <u>Shopping Bag Ladies of New York</u>. New York: Saint Joan's Press, 1982.

After a brief overview of street women, the author profiles six homeless women. The book contains 80 full-page photos.

Roth, Lisa, and Elaine R. Fox. "Children of Homeless Families: Health Status and Access to Health Care."

Journal of Community Mental Health, 15 (4), August 1990:275-284.
A comparison of 70 homeless families in Philadelphia, Pennsylvania, with 3,509 low-income Philadelphia families reveals that homeless children do not utilize primary health care or preventive health care as much as do children from low-income families.

Rouse, James W., and Barton Harvey, III. "Public-Private Partnerships." Bureaucrat, 18 (3), Fall 1989:30-32.
The authors point out that the largest group of people who have recently become homeless consists of families and single people unable to find housing at rents they can pay. From this, they conclude that making housing affordable would eliminate much homelessness. They add that a partnership between the public and private sectors is the best way to plan, finance, build, and operate low-cost housing.

Rousseau, Ann Marie. "Lost Lives: Shopping Bag Ladies Tell Their Stories." San Francisco Chronicle, August 6, 1981:23-24.
The author profiles Helen Trenton, a shopping bag lady. She also discusses the subculture of female homeless persons, their sleep deprivation, demoralization, health, and coping techniques.

Rousseau, Ann Marie. Shopping Bag Ladies: Homeless Women Speak About Their Lives. New York: Pilgrim Press, 1981.
This pictorial account of New York City homeless women places emphases on their life style, usual invisibility, and the female role.

Rowland, Robert C. "On Generic Categorization." Communication Theory, 1 (2), May 1991:128-144.
In his analysis of generic analysis, the author uses homelessness as an example.

Rowntree, B. Seebohm. Poverty: A Study of Town Life (second edition). London: Macmillan, 1902.
The author reports on an 1899 study of 11,560 families in York. He examines their standard of living, the poverty line (primary and secondary poverty), causes of poverty, housing, expenditures, and diet. He also draws comparisons with Charles Booth's study of poverty in London.

Rubington, Earl. "The Bottle Gang." <u>Quarterly Journal of Studies on Alcohol</u>, <u>29</u>, 1968:943-955.
     The author examines skid row subculture, especially social control and social organization. The bottle gang is a group of men who meet, share the price of a bottle of wine, drink it, and disperse.

Rubington, Earl. "The Changing Skid Row Scene." <u>Quarterly Journal of Studies on Alcohol</u>, <u>32</u>, March 1971:123-135.
     The changes in skid row examined by the author include increasing alcoholism, violence, and crime, as well as ethnic change and changing relationships. He proposes causes and consequences of these changes.

Rubington, Earl. "The Chronic Drunkenness Offender." <u>Annals of the American Academy of Political and Social Science</u>, Special Publication, Volume <u>315</u>, 1958:65-72.
     Taking the theoretical position that chronic drunkenness is a social role, "more often the result of networks of social relations than the product of any individual's attributes...a consequence of conformity to skid row social norms," the author describes the subculture of skid row, its social functions, how people come to skid row, and how they behave once there. He stresses that "the coexistence of drinking and frequent arrests binds offenders to the skid row way of life. The more an offender is bound to this way of life, the more he exhibits the characteristics of group membership." The author also describes "the half-way house, a new method of rehabilitating offenders."

Rubington, Earl. "'Failure' as a Heavy Drinker: The Case of the Chronic-Drunkenness Offender on Skid Row." In <u>Society, Culture, and Drinking Patterns</u>, David J. Pittman and Charles R. Snyder, eds. New York: John Wiley, 1962:146-153.
     The author analyzes skid row culture and functions, looking at group support, moral rules, downward social mobility, drinking patterns, bottle gangs, and social ranking within this subculture.

Rubington, Earl. "The 'Revolving Door' Game." <u>Crime and Delinquency</u>, <u>12</u>, October 1966:332-338.
     The author uses the game metaphor to account for the revolving door--the alcoholic's endless cycle of arrest, lock-up, discharge, and further arrest. The game depends on public and police indifference and will end when

public drunkenness changes from a misdemeanor to an
indication of illness.

Rule, Sheila. "A High Tide of Homelessness Washes Over
City Agencies." New York Times, March 25, 1984:Section
4:6.
    After presenting statistics on homelessness in New
York City, which show an increase in homelessness, the
author asks if current solutions are anything more than
cosmetic.

Rule, Sheila. "More Men Under 21 Housed In City Shelters
for Homeless." New York Times, March 7, 1983:B3.
    This article reports findings from a study by the
New York City Human Resources Administration. The young
in the shelters are not runaways, but have nowhere to
turn.

Rule, Sheila. "Needs of Homeless Bring Forth Caring
Volunteers." New York Times, April 8, 1984:A54.
    There is an increase in the number of volunteers who
are helping the homeless.

Rule, Sheila. "Shelters Offer Street Youths Haven in
City." New York Times, February 26, 1984:A37.
    The author summarizes results of a study by the
Citizens Committee for Children of New York, the Coali-
tion for the Homeless, and the Runaway and Homeless Youth
Advocacy Project. The article contains demographics of
the young homeless and case histories.

Rumer, Boris. "Nehemiah Project: From Burned-Out
Landscape to Middle America." CAUSA USA Report, December
1986.
    The Nehemiah Project is the "cooperative efforts of
a community organization, the governing authorities of
several religious denominations, a retired builder-master
planner, New York City and New York State." The East
Brooklyn Churches, an organization of 48 local congregations, are replacing "block after block of garbage-strewn
lots with vacant buildings" with housing for low and
moderate income families who otherwise cannot afford to
buy homes of their own.

Rumer, Eugene B. "Class War in the Soviet Army." Wall
Street Journal, July 11, 1990:A14.
    This overview of the plight of officers in the
Soviet military includes this statement: "Officers whose

units have been withdrawn from Eastern Europe find they have no apartments waiting for them back home. Some send their families to stay with relatives hundreds, even thousands, of miles away. These forced separations can last for years. In the meantime, lucky officers get beds in shared rooms in local officers' dormitories; the unlucky move into tent cities. The situation is even worse for retired officers. The Soviet media last year reported that societies of homeless retired officers are appearing in some cities."

Ryback, Ronnie F., and Ellen L. Bassuk. "Homeless Battered Women and Their Shelter Network." In The Mental Health Needs of Homeless Persons, Ellen L. Bassuk, ed. San Francisco: Jossey-Bass, 1986:55-60.

This overview of characteristics of abusers and their victims stresses that victims frequently become homeless, at least temporarily, when they leave an abusive relationship. The authors suggest that more services are needed to provide emergency safety.

S

Sabatino, Frank. "Outreach Brings Care to Latinos and the Homeless." Hospitals, 65 (15), August 5, 1991:33.

The author chronicles the experiences of the Allentown Hospital-Lehigh Valley Hospital Center in Pennsylvania in targeting an innovative prenatal outreach program to Latino and homeless women.

Sadd, Susan, and Douglas Young. "Nonmedical Treatment of Indigent Alcoholics: A Review of Recent Research Findings." Alcohol Health and Research World, 11 (3), Spring 1987:48-49.

Neither medical nor nonmedical approaches to alcohol rehabilitation appear to be more effective in treating indigent alcoholics. Comparisons between medical and nonmedical treatment alternatives, however, have failed to utilize systematic control designs and do not address the safety of adopting nonmedical detoxification.

Salamon, Julie. "Art as Advocacy: A 'Mobile Home' for the Homeless." Wall Street Journal, April 4, 1989:A18.

    As a commentary on the city's inability to house its
dispossessed, Krzysztos Wodiczko, a Polish refugee artist
and philosopher, constructed what he calls "The Homeless
Vehicle," "a heavy rectangular cage of Plexiglas and
steel mesh, with a sheet-metal and aluminum base, sitting
on four sturdy wheels...the Homeless Vehicle is a useful
and easily portable container for bottles and cans or
personal belongings....it can be extended until it
resembles a missile and can serve as a kind of mobile
home, complete with wash basin tucked into the nose
cone."

Salamon, Julie. "The Tramp Who Came to Dinner." Wall
Street Journal, Jan. 23, 1986:26.
    The author reviews a 1986 American movie, "Down and
Out in Beverly Hills," a remake of the 1931 French movie,
"Boudu Saved From Drowning." The original, directed by
Jean Renoir, featured a tramp who was rescued from
suicide by a middle-class man. The current version has
replaced the tramp with a down-and-out contemporary
homeless man.

Salem, Deborah A., and Irene S. Levine. "Enhancing
Mental Health Services for Homeless Persons: State
Proposals Under the MHSH Block Grant Program." Public
Health Report, 104 (3), May-June 1989:241-246.
    The authors summarize state applications for the $57
million available through the Mental Health Services for
the Homeless Block Grant Program. The purposes of the
program are to fund outreach, case management, mental
health treatment, residential support services, and
training for service providers.

Salerno, Dan, Kim Hopper, and Ellen Baxter. Hardship in
the Heartland: Homelessness in Eight U.S. Cities. New
York: Community Service Society, 1984.
    This article presents an overview of homelessness in
eight cities of America's industrial heartland: Cleveland, Detroit, Chicago, Tulsa, Denver, Milwaukee,
Cincinnati, and Madison. The authors criticize deinstitutionalization and argue that shelter is a basic right
of all citizens.

Salo, Matt T., and Pamela C. Campanelli. "Ethnographic
Methods in the Development of Census Procedures for
Enumerating the Homeless." Urban Anthropology, 20 (2),
Summer 1991:127-140.

Based on a 1989 U.S. Census Bureau's pilot test of a daytime count of homeless persons in Baltimore, Maryland, the authors report that ethnographic research is valuable in choosing sites, designing questionnaires, developing interview procedures, and interpreting survey results.

Saltonstall, Margaret B. Runaways and Street Children in Massachusetts. Boston: Massachusetts Committee on Children and Youth, February 1973.

Based on data supplied by 117 sources in Massachusetts (youth advocacy, children's services, delinquency prevention, hot line and self-help agencies, mayors, school officials, and law enforcement personnel), the author analyzes the sex, age, origin, and destination of runaways. She also examines the reasons they left home and summarizes their family structure, drug use, and protracted runaway episodes. In reviewing the resources available to help runaways and street children, she focuses on three community models (Boston, Robbins Cottage, and a rural community response called Summer Project), and provides a list of recommendations. The book also contains a copy of the questionnaire used in the study.

Sanborn, Alvan Francis. Moody's Lodging House and Other Tenement Sketches. Boston: Copeland and Day, 1895.

This participant observation study of bums contains an account of men attending a preaching service in exchange for receiving a meal. The author explores life in tenements and mentions sandwich men (walking billboards advertising a restaurant's specialties).

Sanders, Scott. "Death of a Homeless Man." The Progressive, 51, March 1987:50.

The author profiles John Griffin, a homeless man who was burned to death in a plywood lean-to in South Boston. The public's conscience should be pricked, we all should have empathy with those who suffer, and we should question our value of the right of "(selected) individuals to accumulate wealth and power at the expense of community and planet."

Sandford, Jeremy. Down and Out in Britain. London: Peter Owen, 1971.

This novelistic account of the author's participant observation closes with suggested solutions to homelessness, primarily the humanizing of institutions and the development of small, specialized, permissive hostels, to be headed by father figures, that would operate as a sort of artificial extended family.

Sandmaier, Marian. The Invisible Alcoholic: Women and Alcohol Abuse in America. New York: McGraw-Hill, 1980. This overview of female alcoholism contains a chapter on women on skid row. The author uses case histories to recount the harrowing experiences of these women. She includes a chapter on resources for alcoholics.

Santiestevan, Henry. Deinstitutionalization: Out of Their Beds and into the Streets. Washington, D.C.: American Federation of State, County, and Municipal Employees, February 1975. The author argues that deinstitutionalization is a national scandal that causes hardship, suffering, and death. To overcome what he calls a "shell-game for budget cuts, layoffs and profiteering," the nation needs to adopt a program of decent health care for all.

Saroyan, William. "Portrait of a Bum." Overland Monthly, 86, December 1928:421-424. The author describes meeting an affable individual who, though intellectually and physically capable, had chosen idleness as his way of life.

Satchell, Michael. "Skid Row: The 'Invisible' Women." Washington Star-News, February 1974:B1. Although skid row women outnumber skid row men in New York City, they are less visible than men. "The emphasis has always been on helping men, yet the need for aiding women is much greater. The crux of the problem is that although there are probably more women than men at the bottom of the heap, the women remain hidden--out of sight, and thus, out of mind." Using individual cases, he examines how these women cope with life, their guilt, and other self-feelings.

Savage, M. J. "The Present Conflict for a Larger Life." Arena, 10, August 1894:297-306. The author, a spokesman for the Union for Practical Progress, outlines his ideas of what is wrong with the country and suggests steps that should be taken to improve it. His position is that "Coxey's Army" is a symptom of industrial turmoil and unrest, the result of "accumulation of business powers in the hands of a few."

Sawyer, Dennis. "Bag Lady at the Lord's Table." <u>Christian Herald</u>, July-August 1986:28-32.
The author profiles a homeless woman's appearance in church, her rejection by the deacons and congregation, and her acceptance by the pastor (the author), who stresses how he learned spiritual truths from her.

Scala, Richard. "Better Homes Builds Its Foundation." <u>Fund Raising Management</u>, <u>22</u> (2), April 1991:30-34, 50.
The author reports on the efforts of <u>Better Homes & Gardens</u> magazine to raise money for the homeless. The magazine has made 50 grants and funded programs in 23 states.

Scapp, Ron. "Lack and Violence: Towards a Speculative Sociology of the Homeless." <u>Practice</u>, <u>6</u> (2), Fall 1988:35-47.
The author argues that much interest in the homeless is based on seeing the non-possession of property as blasphemous, a defilement of all that is considered significant and that the ways in which homeless people are responded to ultimately serve to maintain their repression.

Scelzo, Denise A., and Gary S. Kline. "New Hope for Homeless Kids." <u>Fund Raising Management</u>, <u>19</u> (9), November 1988:56-62.
This summary of activities of Covenant House, a program that takes in homeless street kids in North and South America, reports that Bruce Ritter, the Franciscan priest who founded the organization, raised $24 million in receipts and pledges to purchase facilities to expand the program.

Schaffer, Maggie. "Homelessness Results from a Lack of Jobs: Public." <u>Hospitals</u>, <u>62</u>, August 5, 1988:72.
The results of a "nationwide survey of 1,000 Americans conducted for <u>Hospitals</u> magazine by Professional Research Consultants" on beliefs about the homeless show that "Respondents think that the most appropriate ways to help the homeless would be to provide more work programs, public education, safe houses for abused women and children, and shelters for the homeless....while they least favored building more mental institutions and providing more tax money for the homeless."

Schanberg, Sydney H. "Fingers in the Dike." <u>New York Times</u>, January 15, 1985:A19.

This commission report on the Human Resources Administration of New York City suggests that the HRA needs to recognize that homelessness is not a temporary urban phenomenon, but is here to stay. Because the basic cause of homelessness is a shortage of low-cost housing, the basic approach should be to take measures to reduce the need for shelter.

Schanberg, Sydney H. "Reagan's Homeless." New York Times, April 3, 1984:A31.
   The numbers of people who are homeless are increasing. People are not homeless by choice. The author castigates the comments and attitude of President Reagan.

Schechter, Henry B. "Closing the Gap between Need and Provision." Society, 21 (3) (149), March-April 1984:40-47.
   This overview of the housing crisis in the United States includes the notation that newspaper and television stories "suggest an increasing number of homeless people. The number in some cities reportedly surpasses the capacity of overnight shelters; people are sleeping in the streets, in abandoned buildings, and in parks."

Scheier, Ronni L. "All Sides Trying to Find Solution for Cook County Hospital." American Medical News, 29, May 9, 1986:3, 35.
   In this analysis of the need to replace the aging Cook County Hospital in Chicago, the author points out that what is at stake is the public's commitment to take care of indigents. He points out that "the danger is the county will cut back its indigent-care program."

Scheier, Ronni L. "Caring for Unreached Patients--The Homeless." American Medical News, 28, April 12, 1985:1, 13-16.
   In reporting that the Robert Wood Johnson Foundation has "announced four-year grants totaling $25 million to coalitions in 18 American cities to provide medical care to the dispossessed," the author reviews health ills of the homeless, such as tuberculosis, alcoholism, trauma, and upper respiratory disorders. The findings primarily come from the 15-year old Single-Room-Occupancy Homeless Program at St. Vincent's Hospital and Medical Center in Greenwich Village. A primary focus of the article is the problem of making and maintaining contact with homeless patients. A major obstacle to overcome is that "homelessness means more than not having a roof over your

head....There's a lack of attachments...And along with the dissolving of those bonds is affiliation with a doctor." Consequently, health care of the homeless goes beyond simply taking care of physical needs, for it also includes such related matters as dealing with their lack of social ties.

Scheier, Ronni L. "States Find New Ways to Finance Indigent Care." <u>American Medical News</u>, <u>29</u>, August 22, 1986:9.
    Lawmakers have found six funding sources to pay for health care of the indigent: assessment on hospitals, assessment on insurance premiums, assessment on health-care providers, requiring a minimum amount of charity care in order to be eligible for state reimbursement, rate-setting of "add-on" mechanisms, and employer contributions. The author proposes that potential revenue sources include cigarette taxes, motor vehicle fees, lottery and gambling revenue, state income tax check-offs, sales and use taxes, and private contributions.

Schiff, Laurence. "Would They Be Better Off in A Home?" <u>National Review</u>, March 5, 1990:33-35.
    The author argues that the mental health industry is part of the welfare system because it makes it easy for homeless people to be classified as mentally ill. The "homeless problem is one facet of a whole complex of social problems which are destroying a generation of inner-city residents. In essence, the collectivist mentality of the welfare state panders to the primitive, infantile, and often destructive urges of the human psyche by promising that the government will protect its citizens against all of life's ills, and satisfy each and every want. In short, we have government as nurturing mother. Of course, overindulged children, shielded from reality by smothering parents, never learn to function independently....The real solution to the homeless problem lies in a return to 'middle-class values,' and indeed to the promotion of them in the lower class."

Schmalz, Jeffrey. "Belying Popular Stereotypes, Many of Homeless Have Jobs." <u>New York Times</u>, December 19, 1988:1, 14.
    The author focuses on the working homeless, persons who work full time but are "trapped between jobs that pay too little and housing that costs too much."

Schmalz, Jeffrey. "Brooklyn Site Planned for Homeless Families." <u>New York Times</u>, February 20, 1986:17.
This article profiles the first housing especially built to house homeless families in New York State. Scheduled to open during 1986, this housing will not only provide emergency, temporary shelter for 200 families, but it also will make many social services available to these families. Eventually ten such shelters will be built.

Schmalz, Jeffrey. "Message to the Homeless: Get Out!" <u>New York Times</u>, August 3, 1989:8.
The author reports on how residents of Hollywood, Florida, reacted to the murder of a bus driver and a passenger by a homeless man. City officials "ordered business owners to lock trash bins so homeless drifters cannot forage for food. Some residents and politicians want park sprinklers turned on in the middle of the night to roust the drifters from their makeshift beds. At least one city commissioner wants a church-run soup kitchen shut down. Park benches are being ripped up and replaced with ones that are virtually impossible to lie down and sleep on."

Schmalz, Jeffrey. "Miami Police Want to Control Homeless by Arresting Them." <u>New York Times</u>, November 4, 1988:1, 9.
City officials of Miami, Florida, are upset by the number of homeless persons who are living in their city and are concerned about the influx of homeless that they anticipate as winter comes on. To get the message across that the homeless are not welcome in Miami, the City Commission, which governs Miami, has appointed a committee to develop "humane recommendations" that will allow them to control the homeless.

Schmemann, Serge. "Beggars and Ethnic Strife's Refugees Make Soviets Turn to Private Charity." <u>New York Times</u>, March 13, 1991:A10.
Because Soviet authorities are not taking care of the hundreds of thousands of people who have become homeless because of ethnic violence in the former Soviet Union, private charities are stepping in to help fill the need.

Schmidt, William E. "Across Europe, Faces of Homeless Become More Visible and Vexing." <u>New York Times</u>, January 5, 1992:1.

All over Europe--in London, Rome, Madrid, Paris, and other cities--homelessness is increasing.

Schmidt, William E.   "O'Hare Airport Now Host to Many Homeless."   New York Times, November 23, 1989:1, 12.
About 200 homeless people live at O'Hare Airport in Chicago, more than any other airport in the nation including the New York City area's major airports--Kennedy, La Guardia, and Newark.   "City officials in Chicago--under pressure from airlines and vendors who rent space at the airport--are now considering a plan to build a shelter close to the airport, to house the homeless who now live inside the terminals."

Schmitt, Eric.   "Agencies Are Trying for Alternatives to Welfare Hotels for the Homeless."   New York Times, November 27, 1989:12.
Some cities are "bending the law" in order to "channel millions of dollars away from welfare hotels for homeless people and into the creation of permanent low-cost housing."   Although the federal assistance is designated only for emergency housing, "state and county officials are contracting with nonprofit housing agencies and private landlords, who buy abandoned apartments or multi-family houses with the help of state and local grants and conventional mortgages. The housing agencies or landlords go into the hotel business, but with a twist. Under the contract, the landlord designates some or all of a building's apartments as emergency housing, qualifying them for the emergency assistance rate. The rate...is sometimes as high as triple the market rent. Instead of pocketing the difference, the landlord spends the extra money to renovate the building, hire social workers and under the new initiatives, pay off the mort-gage more quickly. Within 18 months to five years, remaining debt on the building is reduced until the renovated apartments can be converted into permanent housing with rents so low even families on welfare can afford them."

Schmitt, Eric.   "Homeless Students Face Long Roads to Schools."   New York Times, November 6, 1987:15.
The children of the homeless face severe problems in getting an education: the stress of long bus rides twice a day, doing homework in crowded motel rooms, no orga-nized after-school activities, and high absenteeism. They need special counseling and academic assistance.

Schmitt, Eric. "New York Suburbs Struggle to Cope With Steep Increase in the Homeless." <u>New York Times</u>, December 26, 1988:Y15.
Because the numbers of homeless people living in New York City suburbs increased by more than 25 percent in last 18 months, there now are about as many homeless in the suburbs as in New York City. More than half of these homeless people are under 30 years old, while roughly two-thirds consist of families, mostly single mothers and children. About 35 percent have jobs.

Schmitt, Eric. "Sssh! And Scram! A Library Fights for the Homeless." <u>New York Times,</u> September 15, 1989:B1.
In Morristown, New Jersey, a prosperous suburb 35 miles west of New York City, regular patrons of the public library have complained about the presence of smelly and disheveled homeless persons. In consequence, the library now prohibits "staring with the intent to annoy another person and offensive hygiene when it is a nuisance."

Schmitt, Eric. "Suburbs of New York Struggle to Shelter Homeless." <u>New York Times</u>, September 8, 1987:13.
The demand for emergency shelter in New York City's suburbs has increased because "people in the middle class who used to hang on by their fingertips are now not able to pay their bills." Compared with the city, more of the homeless in the suburbs work. They also are less visible. Between a third and a half of them are children. The author stresses that affordable housing is increasingly scarce and that "state-allotted rent assistance available to families once they leave the shelters is woefully inadequate to meet market rents."

Schneider, Cynthia G. "Food Stamp Eligibility for Homeless Persons Who Reside in Shelters." <u>Clearing House Review</u>, June 1985:141-142.
Local food stamp offices are denying food stamps to homeless persons who reside at shelters because they define them as "residents of an institution." The author takes the position that homeless persons staying at shelters are not "residents of an institution" for purposes of the Food Stamp Act.

Schneider, David M., and Albert Deutsch. <u>The History of Public Welfare in New York State: 1867-1940</u>. Chicago: University of Chicago Press, 1941.

This history of poverty and ameliorative attempts to relieve it reviews industrialization, depressions, and child welfare and children's laws.

Schneider, John C. "Omaha Vagrants and the Character of Western Hobo Labor, 1887-1913." Nebraska History, 63, 1982:255-272.
Between the 1860s and 1920s tramping workers in the United States filled far-flung labor needs: wheat harvesting in the Midwest, fruit picking in California, berry picking in Michigan, hop picking in New York, ice-cutting in the northern states, coal and metal mining, laying railroads, and building bridges. The arrest ledgers of the Omaha police department provide a 26-year sample of persons arrested for vagrancy. Of the 1,509 persons so arrested, 14 percent were blacks, and about 80 percent native born. Of the foreign-born, only the Irish were overrepresented. Although there were many homeless women in the urban areas of the period, such as prostitutes who did odd jobs and the destitute who were the equivalent of what we today call "bag ladies," "few tramped and rode the rails as the men did." Consequently, only 31 of the vagrants in this sample are women, half of them prostitutes. More arrests were made in the spring than in any other quarter of the year. The author suggests that the change in the makeup of the homeless from tramping laborers to skid row dropouts and derelicts took place earlier than most analysts think.

Schneider, John C. "Tramping Workers, 1890-1920: A Subcultural View." In Walking to Work: Tramps in America, 1790-1935, Eric H. Monkkonen, ed. Lincoln: University of Nebraska Press, 1984:212-234.
Most homeless men are unmarried, in the prime of their life, white, and prepared only for manual work. A large proportion is foreign born. The author reviews myths about tramps (violent, will not work), motivations for tramping, where they seek lodging, the "main stem", and types of tramps.

Schockman, Carl S. We Turned Hobo: A Narrative of Personal Experience. Columbus: F. J. Heer, 1937.
The author writes about the hitch-hiking, freight-riding trip he and his brother took in 1930 from Ohio to California.

Schorr, Alvin L. "Will We Have Reaganvilles?" New York Times, August 26, 1986:27.

This article focuses on the causes and possible solutions to homelessness. The basic cause is "the general decline of income for a large portion of the population coupled with the rising cost of housing." Related causes are the unraveling of the safety net policies of social welfare; a high unemployment rate; a drop in the real wages of workers, especially for minimum wage workers; high interest rates; high energy costs; and the cut-back of government subsidies for low-income housing and public housing. The root solution is a broad reversal of current domestic policy that will bring family earnings and the costs of housing into balance. The author anticipates that homelessness will greatly increase before we adopt such measures.

Schubert, Herman J. P. <u>Twenty Thousand Transients: A One Year's Sample of Those Who Apply for Aid in a Northern City</u>. Buffalo: Emergency Relief Bureau, 1935.
   This study of the 1934-1935 transients in Buffalo, New York, examines seasonal variations, race, age, state of origin, urban and rural backgrounds, employment, modes of travel, education, intelligence, health, and family backgrounds. It also contains material on seamen, transient families, and unattached women. The causes of transience are family trouble, girl trouble (disappointed love affairs), and unemployment. The solutions are remedial (jobs and recreation) and preventative (jobs and recreation, including work projects and training facilities).

Schumer, Charles E. "Vacating Welfare Hotels." <u>The New Republic</u>, <u>196</u>, March 16, 1987:41-42.
   In this letter to the editor, the author, a member of the U.S. House of Representatives, makes the point that Emergency Assistance disbursements should be allowed to be spent on permanent homes for the homeless, not simply on welfare hotels.

Schutt, Russell K. "Objectivity versus Outrage." <u>Society</u>, <u>26</u> (4) (180), May-June 1989:14-16.
   The author presents an overview of <u>Homelessness, Health, and Human Needs</u>, a report by the Committee on Health Care for Homeless People of the Institute of Medicine. Homelessness has many causes, including social change and social policies that fail people. Consequently, one-sided solutions cannot succeed. What is needed is an integrated, multifaceted solution, not more debates on how to solve the problem. The approaches already

developed by local communities that have been wrestling with this problem may hold the key to finding a model on which to build national policies for delivering services to the homeless and for developing adequate housing.

Schutt, Russell K. "The Quantity and Quality of Homelessness: Research Results and Policy Implications." Sociological Practice Review, 1 (2), August 1990:77-87.
    The author of this review of the literature on homelessness argues that the extent of homelessness in the 1980s is explained by a variation between the ratio of poverty in relation to the supply of affordable housing and the ratio of the level of personal disability in relation to the supply of social services and supports. The article includes a discussion of analytic complications and policy implications of changes in social policy.

Schutt, Russell K., and Gerald R. Garrett. "Homelessness in Three Dimensions: Professors, Practitioners, and Politicians." Footnotes (The American Sociological Association), January 1987:8.
    The authors report that the 500 academics, service providers, and policy-makers who attended the three-day national conference on "Homelessness: Critical Issues for Policy Practice" at Harvard University and the University of Massachusetts at Boston differed greatly in their "interpretations of the nature of homelessness." Because of the disparity of backgrounds in academic and applied approaches to this problem, some focused on "problems of mental illness and need for professional services," while others "emphasized structural economic problems and need for political action."

Schwartz, David C., and Warren Craig. "On The Edge: Preventing Homelessness." Social Policy, Winter 1989:2-4.
    We need to intervene in order to prevent the "hidden homeless" (or "housing vulnerable") from becoming homeless. The "hidden homeless" consists of about "10 to 15 million people who have no private home or apartment, who are living doubled and tripled up with friends or family." We also need to intervene to prevent homelessness through eviction. While these are humane endeavors, they are really only "no better than using a tourniquet to save the patient's life." What really needs to be done is to take action to eliminate homelessness--which would include "increasing the minimum wage, raising supplemen-

tal income benefits, expanding rent subsidy programs, creating decent jobs in inner-city neighborhoods, and a serious national recommitment to building low-income housing."

Schwartz, Ronald. "Liability Fears Hamper Care for Homeless." <u>American Medical News</u>, <u>28</u>, December 27, 1985:3, 25.
    The author discusses the previous year's experiences with Health Care for the Homeless, programs financed by the Robert Wood Foundation that were conducted in 19 cities. Because it was difficult to recruit physician volunteers, most medical staffing was done by nurse practitioners or other physicians extenders. The author reviews problems involving sample drugs, no fixed source of medical care for the homeless, seeing cast-offs from other health care providers, and homeless individuals not seeking medical attention because they are wary of "the system".

Schwartz-Nobel, Loretta. <u>Starving in the Shadow of Plenty</u>. New York: McGraw-Hill, 1981.
    This overview of hunger in the United States reviews agricultural infrastructure, the politics behind malnutrition, and the potential of increased hunger due to threats to farmland. The author lists groups that benefit from the present situation. As solutions, he proposes reversal of the destruction of land and topsoil, hydroponics, aquaculture, change in livestock feeding, research, and food distribution to the hungry.

Scott, Robert N. "Coordinating Services for Runaway Youth." <u>Journal of Family Issues</u>, <u>1</u> (2), June 1980:308-310.
    The author gives an overview of the youth services in New York City that are offered in compliance with New York's Runaway and Homeless Youth Act of 1978. The solutions, he says, are resident shelters, crisis intervention, hot line, and counseling: medical, psychiatric, educational, vocational, legal, family, group, and individual. He stresses the need to coordinate services.

Scudder, K. J. "How California Anchors Drifting Boys." <u>The Survey</u>, March 1933:101-102.
    Boys who are convicted of criminal offenses are sent to forestry camps, where they are treated well while they work on public service projects. Those who run away are sent to jail.

Scull, Andrew T. <u>Decarceration: Community Treatment and the Deviant--A Radical View</u>. Englewood Cliffs: Prentice-Hall, 1977.
    The author interprets deinstitutionalization from the framework of welfare capitalism and the need for domestic pacification and social control.

Seal, Kathy. "Feinstein Supporting Hoteliers Who Help." <u>Hotel and Motel Management</u>, December 15, 1986:1, 32.
    After media reports that some hotels in San Francisco participating in the city's homeless program had given fraudulent billings and received illegal kickbacks, a group of hoteliers abruptly pulled out of the program and threw the homeless people they were housing onto the street.

Segal, Steven P., and Harry Specht. "A Poorhouse in California, 1983: Oddity or Prelude?" <u>Social Work</u>, <u>28</u>, July-August 1983:319-323.
    Sacramento's Board of Directors has instituted "in-kind aid" (instead of cash) for residents at a shelter run by the Volunteers of America. The article includes a history of poorhouses and discusses issues of self-respect, self-reliance, privacy, and free association.

Segal, Steven P., and Jim Baumohl. "The Community Living Room." <u>Social Casework: The Journal of Contemporary Social Work</u>, <u>66</u>, February 1985:111-116.
    The deinstitutionalization of the mentally ill has led to a new chronic homeless population that is difficult to serve. The author gives a positive evaluation to an approach called the community living room.

Segal, Steven P., and Jim Baumohl. "Engaging the Disengaged: Proposals on Madness and Vagrancy." <u>Social Work</u>, <u>25</u> (5), September 1980:358-364.
    The major cause of homelessness is deinstitutionalization of the mentally ill. Examining the problems that ex-mental patients face, the authors focus on the growing number of young, chronically mentally ill homeless, whom they term "young chronics." Because these individuals, who are predominately male, have multiple obstacles to their treatment, they are likely to have long-term disengagement. The best solution is community mental health, but the negative attitudes of the public are a major obstacle to its implementation. The federal government must take the lead in developing a support system for the homeless mentally ill.

Segal, Steven P., Jim Baumohl, and Elsie Johnson. "Falling Through the Cracks: Mental Disorder and Social Margin in a Young Vagrant Population." Social Problems, 24 (3), February 1977:387-400.
The term "social margin" in the title of the article refers to personal possessions, attributes, or relationships which can be traded for help in time of need. Because young mentally disordered vagrants lack social margin and fail to receive adequate help from our social services system, they are likely to become the core of a chronically disordered, dependent population. The authors discuss the Berkeley Emergency Food Project, the subculture of vagrancy, coping, drug dealing, family relationships, and the mentally disordered as a type of vagrant.

Segal, Steven P., and Uri Aviram. The Mentally Ill in Community-Based Sheltered Care: A Study of Community Care and Social Integration. New York: Wiley Interscience, 1978.
The authors review the history of care of the mentally ill during the past 150 years, examining the cycle from community to hospital and back. Based on a sample of every 36th bed in California sheltered-care facilities, they report on these individuals' lack of social integration and their inability to care for themselves.

Settle, Mel. "Must We Tear Them Down?: How Urban Renewal Contributes to Homelessness." The Humanist, May-June 1989:9.
This short account is written by a man who manages properties rented by low-income individuals who, without these facilities, would be homeless.

Sexton, Patricia Cayo. "The Life of the Homeless." Dissent, 30, Winter 1983:79-84.
In this historical overview of outcast groups in the United States and their relationship to politics, the author examines Marxist views, the tension between compassion and contempt toward the homeless, and deinstitutionalization. She compares the approach in the United States with a medieval model. Her suggested solutions are concern, hands-on charity, and a decent welfare system.

Shaheen, Jacqueline. "Becoming Homeless, and Beating It." New York Times, September 22, 1991:NJ3.

The author recounts how Theresa Jarvis and her three children became homeless after her divorce, and how Spring House in Eatontown, New Jersey, helped her. She is now domiciled.

Shand, Alexander Innes. "The Tramp in Summer." Saturday Review, 102, August 4, 1906:141-142.
This romanticized account of the excitement of tramping compares professional and amateur tramps.

Shandler, Irving W. Philadelphia's Skid Row: A Demonstration in Human Renewal. Philadelphia: Redevelopment Authority of the City of Philadelphia, 1965.
The author summarizes the health background of the first 200 men who reported to the Diagnostic and Relocation Center. Of 54 men relocated for independent living, 56 percent were successful, 11 percent were in institutional settings, and 33 percent had returned to skid row. The suggested solutions are comprehensive treatment and relocation facilities.

Shandler, Irving W., and Thomas E. Shipley, Jr. "New Focus for an Old Problem." Alcohol Health and Research World, 11 (3), Spring 1987:54-57.
This article describes the principal components and summarizes the program activities of the Diagnostic and Rehabilitation Center of Philadelphia: its outpatient program, intermediate residents, emergency care, residential detoxification, and operation of the shelter and Washington House Residential. Successful recovery requires a program that offers a wide range of resources, allows enough time for the recovering alcoholic to move towards sobriety, and the establishment of goals that are realistic for both the client and the agency.

Shanks, Nigel J. "Medical Care for the Homeless." British Medical Journal, 284 (6330), June 5, 1982:1679-1680.
The author analyzes the need for medical care for the homeless, summarizes what is being done in Great Britain to meet that need, and makes suggestions for change.

Shapiro, Ann-Louise. Housing the Poor of Paris, 1850-1902. Madison: University of Wisconsin Press, 1985.
This analysis of housing in Paris between 1850 and 1902 includes an overview of its housing supply, regulation, evictions, crowding, and health problems related to

housing conditions. The author uses the term "population nomad" for people who are "crammed into furnished rooms, temporary shelters, and unsanitary hovels." During this period, lack of adequate housing was equated with the stimulation of vice. "Bourgeois reformers were particularly alarmed by the lack of privacy--the mingling of the sexes and the sharing of beds."

Shapiro, Arthur M. "In Argentina the Homeless Try Self-Help." The New Leader, 71, March 21, 1988:14-15.
    Pro bono lawyers who probed corporate tax records in Buenos Aires found that two corporations were 20 years in arrears on both municipal and provincial taxes. They then orchestrated the move of over 3,000 families onto those parcels of land. "The occupied parcels were immediately divided up and laid out as communities-to-be, with space allotted for streets and for such public amenities as schools, churches, parks, and police stations. Community councils were established to plead the squatters' case for legal recognition and access to municipal services."

Shapiro, Joan. "Single-Room Occupancy: Community of the Alone." Social Work, 11 (4), October 1966:24-33.
    The author discusses unattached single individuals clustered in urban rooming houses (SROs) on New York City's upper west side. She reports positive results from intervention by means of a recreation-rehabilitation program, which resulted in more social relationships, greater protectiveness toward one another, and improved self-image and pride. Intervention presents a dilemma, however, for it carries the risk of fostering dependence. The model of benevolent neutrality is unsuitable for therapeutically dealing with a blue-collar population.

Shapiro, Walter, and Daniel Pedersen. "Fight Over 'Losing Ground.'" Newsweek, April 29, 1985:33-34.
    This discussion of reactions to Charles Murray's Losing Ground, which takes the position that the liberal approach to welfare destroyed incentives to work, reviews conservative political philosophy and the corresponding debate with liberals. The author makes the point that political ideologies provide interpretative frameworks for looking at statistics on the poor.

Shaw, Clifford. The Jack Roller. Chicago: University of Chicago Press, 1930.

This life history of a delinquent boy in Chicago who specialized in rolling drunks, told in the first person, with the focus on his activities from ages 17 to 22, presents an inside understanding of his social world by looking at things from the boy's point of view. It reveals the subterranean, floating population of the city.

Shaw, Frederick. "The Homeless." In The Homes and Homeless of Post-War Britain. Totowa: New Jersey, 1985:253-275.
After reviewing difficulties in defining homelessness, the author examines homelessness in Great Britain from the 1930s to the 1970s. He discusses the use of lodging houses and casual wards in earlier parts of this century until 1939, the function of county councils and county borough councils from the 1940s to the 1970s, the Housing (Homeless Persons) Act of 1977, causes of homelessness, the single homeless, homeless families, squatting, sleeping in the rough, the number of homeless, homeless women (women who led "unsettled lives"), the disintegration of the family, and the social class origins, age, sex, and employment history of those who use the reception centers. The book contains 36 photographs.

Shaw, Russell. "Lending the Homeless a Hand." Hotel and Motel Management, 206 (21), December 16, 1991:2, 44.
The author discusses ways that hoteliers can help the homeless.

Shellow, Robert, Juliana Schamp, Elliot Liebow, and Elizabeth Unger. "Suburban Runaways of the 1960s." Monograph of the Society for Research in Child Development, 32 (3), 1967:1-51.
Based on missing persons reports given the police, as well as school and court records, the authors compare 631 runaways with non-runaways. Most running away occurs during the spring, and most is impulsive and poorly planned. Girls were more likely to leave during the weekend, while boys were more evenly divided throughout the week. Almost two-thirds of the runaways returned home within 48 hours. The authors found that runaways were more likely to be oldest children from broken or reconstituted homes, from families that moved frequently, and whose parents had lower occupational ratings. The runaways also had lower grades and greater absenteeism in school. Through a school questionnaire, the authors

found six self-reported runaways for every one who had been reported to the police.

Shenon, Philip. "Volcano's Refugees Describe Horror of Ash and Mudslides." New York Times, June 18, 1991:A1.
    This description of the devastation wrought by the 1991 eruption of Mt. Pinatubo in the Philippines notes that the eruption left hundreds of thousands of Filipinos homeless.

Shinn, Marybeth, and Beth C. Weitzman. "Research on Homelessness: An Introduction." Journal of Social Issues, 46 (4), 1990:1-11.
    Research on homelessness has tended to focus on problems of homeless individuals. A more comprehensive model of homelessness is necessary, one that pays attention to the underlying causes of homelessness. The authors suggest that analysts look at homelessness within its socioeconomic context, as well as individual-level factors, including the dynamic relationship among the factors that lead to homelessness.

Shinn, Marybeth, James R. Knickman, David Ward, Nancy Lynn Petrovic, and Barbara J. Muth. "Alternative Models for Sheltering Homeless Families." Journal of Social Issues, 46 (4), 1990:175-190.
    To determine their relative costs, services available, quality of life, length of stay, and clientele, the authors used a random sample of the four types of nonprofit shelters in New York City: (1) apartment shelters, in which each family has its own apartment, (2) alternative hotels, (3) smaller "rooming house shelters," where families typically have a private room but share common areas with other residents, and (4) shelters for survivors of domestic violence. They conclude that it is possible to create a variety of nonprofit shelters that offer extensive service and a reasonable quality of life for no more expense than housing families in hotels with fewer services. Consequently, "this study supports the feasibility of the city's five-year plan to move families out of welfare hotels and into alternative residential models, although it suggests that families should be allowed to choose their placements."

Shinohara, Mutsuharu, and Richard L. Jenkins. "MMPI Study of Three Types of Delinquents." Journal of Clinical Psychology, 23, 1967:156-163.

The authors tried to discover if runaways, social-ized delinquents, and unsocialized aggressives could be distinguished from one another using the Minnesota Multiphasic Personality Inventory. The runaways recorded poorer self-images, less deviance, and more neurotic tendencies than the socialized delinquents, and less masculinity and paranoia than the unsocialized aggres-sives.

Shipley, Thomas E., Jr., Irving W. Shandler, and Michael L. Penn. "Treatment and Research with Homeless Alcohol-ics." Contemporary Drug Problems, 16 (3), Fall 1989:505-526.

The authors' thesis is that "the development of research and of treatment for alcohol-addicted homeless people should proceed together." The reasons we have no comprehensive programs for homeless alcoholics is because of "the lack of adequate public or private funding, the daunting complexity of the associated problems and issues, and a general pessimism about a service solu-tion." Good evaluative research is needed "so that the results can be translated into programs in other places and time...and so we can "identify those specific variables that are most highly correlated with outcome." The threat to the viability of programs that honestly report their failures, however, makes it unlikely that high-quality assessments of treatment programs will occur. Such funding threats must be eliminated so that researchers and program providers can fully document their failures as well as their successes.

Shipp, E. R. "Cities and States Strive to Meet Winter Needs of the Homeless." New York Times, December 25, 1985:8.

This article summarizes steps being taken in Chicago, Cleveland, Washington, Boston, Miami, St. Louis, Los Angeles, and San Francisco to protect the homeless from the winter cold.

Shipp, E. R. "Half in Poll Say More Should be Done for Homeless." New York Times, February 3, 1986:14.

A national telephone sample of adults by New York Times/CBS shows that people disagree on whether the government has been doing enough for the homeless and on requiring the homeless to take shelter when the weather is freezing. The public, coming to accept homelessness as inevitable, perceives the causes of homelessness as the unwillingness to work, alcohol and drugs, economic luck, and psychological problems.

Shulman, Alix Kates. On the Stroll. New York: Knopf, 1981.
    This novel centers around Owl, a bag lady, and Robin, a runaway girl, whose paths cross. As the author details their street life, she explores the mental illness of Owl and Robin's relationships with her pimp, Prince.

Shulman, Harry Manuel. Slums of New York. New York: Albert and Charles Boni, 1938.
    This study, based on 779 families in 1926 and 1932, reports on the life of boys in four New York slums (social blocks). It focuses on their culture patterns, the social world of the child, broken and disorganized homes, education, health, recreation, poverty, housing, and culture of poverty ("slum cycle"). The author proposes economic, physical, and cultural solutions.

Siegal, Harvey A. Outposts of the Forgotten: Socially Terminal People in Slum Hotels and Single Room Occupancy Tenements. New Brunswick: Transaction Books, 1978.
    The author explores the rooming house world--its welfare hotels, culture of poverty, caretakers, exploitation, social life, community, and the relationship to the non-SRO world.

Siegal, Harvey A., and James A. Inciardi. "The Demise of Skid Row." Society, 51, January-February 1982:39-45.
    As the authors analyze the origins of skid row and its fundamental transformation, they discuss urban renewal and skid row's increasing violence.

Siegel, Norman, and Robert Levy. "Koch's Mishandling of the Homeless." New York Times, September 7, 1987:23.
    The authors argue that "Mayor Koch's proposal to remove homeless people from New York City's streets and confine them in Bellevue Hospital appears to be an unauthorized rewriting of New York state's mental health law in violation of constitutional liberties."

Siegel, Norman, and Robert Levy. "The Real Problem is Housing." New York Times, December 17, 1985:27.
    The authors argue that the basic cause of homelessness is the lack of affordable housing. They also

discuss   dangers that shelters pose to the homeless, mental illness, and freedom of the individual.

Siering, Andy. "Street Preacher." <u>St. Louis Weekly</u>, March 9, 1983:7-11.
   This article profiles Larry Rice's work with the homeless and the New Life Evangelistic Center in St. Louis, Missouri.

Silver, Gillian. "Fast Track Communicator Changes Lanes." <u>Communication World</u>, <u>16</u> (2), February 1989:22-23.
   The article profiles Mary Jo West, a successful news anchor and journalist in Phoenix, Arizona, who quit her job to become a homemaker. She began to work with the homeless, having a special interest in doing so because her own father had died homeless. She has returned to her television profession, where she retains lessons from her experience with the homeless.

Simmel, Georg. "The Poor." In <u>On Individuality and Social Forms: Selected Writings</u>, Donald N. Levine, ed. Chicago: University of Chicago Press, 1971:150-178.
   The central focus is the rights of the poor and the obligations of society to them. The author also analyzes motivations for giving, the role of the state, and the status of the poor in society.

Simmel, Georg. "The Stranger." In <u>On Individuality and Social Forms: Selected Writings</u>, Donald N. Levine, ed. Chicago: University of Chicago Press, 1971:143-149.
   As the author examines the status and characteristics of strangers in society, he explores strangeness, remoteness, nearness, and relationships.

Simon, Boris. <u>Abbe Pierre and the Ragpickers of Emmaus</u>. New York: P. J. Kennedy and Sons, 1955.
   This profile of Abbe Pierre, a Parisian priest who works with the homeless, stresses his difficulties with authorities and problems he has in arousing the conscience of the French government and in raising funds.

Simon, Vic. "LaFalce Wants Servicing Transfer Bill Passed; Gonzalez Gives His Views on Housing." <u>Mortgage Banking</u>, <u>49</u> (6), March 1989:22-26.
   This review of a bill introduced in Congress which requires that mortgagees be notified concerning the selling of their home loans mentions that the main

priority of Jack Kemp, Secretary of Housing and Urban Development, is helping the poor and homeless.

Simons, Ronald L., and Les B. Whitbeck. "Sexual Abuse as a Precursor to Prostitution and Victimization Among Adolescent and Adult Homeless Women." <u>Journal of Family Issues</u>, <u>12</u> (3), September 1991:361-379.
    Interviews with 40 adolescent female runaways and 95 homeless adult females show that apart from running away from home, substance abuse, and other deviant involvements, early sexual abuse increases the likelihood of prostitution.

Simpson, Janice C. "Gourmet Leftovers Add Spice to Menus at Some City Shelters." <u>Wall Street Journal</u>, December 11, 1986:1, 20.
    The author profiles City Harvest, a group that collects food from restaurants, hospitals, caterers, corporations and other suppliers of fresh food. The members of City Harvest gather these perishable foods and distribute them to the homeless.

Simpson, Janice C. "Salvation Army's Job Is Growing Tougher as Cries for Help Rise." <u>Wall Street Journal</u>, December 21, 1987:1, 13.
    This summary of the work of the Salvation Army with the homeless notes that following the stock market crash of October 1987 contributions dwindled at the same time as the Army's responsibilities increased.

Simpson, Janice C. "A 'Settlement House' Has New Constituency But Same Old Mission." <u>Wall Street Journal</u>, January 23, 1987:1, 12.
    Henry Street Settlement House on New York City's Lower East Side, which during the last century served as a bridge for newly-arrived immigrants, now primarily serves blacks, Hispanics, and Asians.

Sims, Calvin. "Bridge Report Warns Rotting Is Pervasive." <u>New York Times</u>, February 27, 1991:B1.
    Not only are many bridges in New York City deteriorated, but the homeless have stolen some of the wooden beams that support the bridges and used them for firewood.

Singleton, David A., and C. Benjie Louis. "The Homeless: Victims of Prejudice." <u>New York Times</u>. December 28, 1989:23.

Based on their experience as legal interns working with the homeless, the authors conclude that the homeless are not much different from other people. "The ranks of the homeless are filled with capable people overwhelmed by larger-than-life problems." The authors make the plea that the homeless be treated with respect and dignity, not with prejudice and discrimination.

Skene, F. M. F. "The Ethics of the Tramp." Cornbill Magazine, 4 (23), 1898:682-688.
Tramps are not simply the "refuse of our population," but "a most mysterious and distinctive race." Tramps feel an "abhorrence of any settled home--any habitation whatever which would close them within walls, and place a roof between them and wind and rain, no less than the air and sunshine of the open heaven." Persons who are travelling this aimless journey do not have the same morals as the rest of the citizenry, they are not members of churches, and they have temporary sexual unions. Yet, when they have the opportunity, they also exhibit an "admirable esprit de corps."

Skinner, Mary, and Alice S. Nutt. "Adolescents Away from Home." Annals of the American Academy of Political and Social Science, 236, 1944:51-59.
The majority of American transients during World War II were 16 and 17 year-old boys who left home to seek work in war-related industries. The two main problems in caring for runaways are the lack of public funds to pay for the runaways' return transportation and the lack of social services to help them make future plans and to take care of them until they execute those plans.

Slar, Kathryn Kish. "Hull House in the 1890s: A Community of Women Reformers." Signs: Journal of Women in Culture and Society, 10 (4), Summer 1985:658-677.
The author reports on the backgrounds and relationship of three founders of Hull House in Chicago in the early 1890s: Jane Addams, Julia Lathrop, and Florence Kelley. She explains the mission of Hull House, which sheltered many thousands of homeless women during its years of operation.

Slater, Robert Bruce. "The Robin Hood of American Banking." Business and Society Review, 79, Fall 1991:34-37.

This article profiles John Singleton, vice-chairman of Security Pacific National Bank, whose work on behalf of disadvantaged youths includes work with the homeless.

Slater, Robert Bruce. "The Wrong Battle in a Noble Cause." <u>Business and Society Review</u>, <u>72</u>, Winter 1990:52-53.

"Well-meaning social do-gooders" pressured Gallo Winery to pull its high alcohol content wine products from the shelves of liquor stores on America's skid rows. A test ban in San Francisco showed this action to be a miserable failure, for bootleggers "peddling bathtub gin and other versions of rot gut" thrived. Social activists must fight for what they believe in, and not spread their meager resources in futile activities.

Sloss, Michael. "The Crisis of Homelessness: Its Dimensions and Solutions." <u>The Urban and Social Change Review</u>, <u>17</u> (2), Summer 1984:18-20.

The solutions for homelessness are to provide legal advocacy to fight for the rights of the homeless and to break the subculture of homelessness by providing networks of permanent homes.

Slutkin, G. "Management of Tuberculosis in Urban Homeless Indigents." <u>Public Health Reports</u>, <u>101</u> (5), September 1986:481-485.

Because of their erratic schedules, mistrust of authority, and uncooperative or aggressive behavior, many tuberculosis patients who are homeless fail to complete their course of treatment. To improve the rate of success of their treatment requires proven case-holding techniques, the correct choice of drug regimen, a prompt response to patients who quit or refuse treatment, prompt notification to the department of public health, and, occasionally, the forcible confinement of uncooperative patients.

Smith, Adolphe. <u>Street Life in London</u>. New York: Benjamin Blom, 1969. (First published in 1877 by Sampson Low, Marston, Searle, and Rivington of London, in which the authorship is listed as J. Thomson and Adolphe Smith.)

This book provides an overview of London's poor by means of case stories classified by occupation, such as cabmen, street doctors, shoe blacks, and "nomades."

Smith, Fred. "The Church Army and the Homeless Offender." <u>International Journal of Offender Therapy and
Comparative Criminology</u>, <u>19</u> (3), 1975:285-291.
    In this overview of the Church Army's program of
operating hostels for homeless ex-offenders, the author
analyzes different types of hostels and their relative
advantages and disadvantages.

Smith, Henry Nash. <u>Virgin Land: The American West as
Symbol and Myth</u>. New York: Vintage Books, 1957.
    This book is not directly about the homeless, but it
is related in the sense that the author discusses persons
who can't stand living close to many others and are
constantly on the move to unsettled lands.

Smith, Marguerite T. "New Guidelines for Giving."
<u>Money</u>, <u>18</u> (12), December 1989:141-151.
    In her presentation of ten commandments of intelli-
gent giving to charities, the author mentions that the
homeless crisis will increase the contributions of
Americans.

Smith, P. F. "The Housing (Homeless Persons) Act 1977--
Four Years On." <u>Journal of Planning and Environmental
Law</u>, March 1982:143-157.
    The author analyzes the definition of homelessness,
threatened homelessness, priority need, statutory duties
in relation to priority groups, and the thorny issue of
intentional homelessness.

Smith, Peter B. "Homelessness in New York Isn't Inevitable." <u>New York Times</u>, September 20, 1986:19.
    Homelessness in New York can be solved. The first
step is to overcome the negative conditions of welfare
hotels by implementing an emergency plan to make certain
that the homeless comprise no more than 25 percent of
these hotels' clientele. The city then needs to rehabilitate the 20,000 apartments it owns and to turn them over
to the homeless for permanent living.

Smothers, Ronald. "At a Men's Shelter in Bedford-
Stuyvesant, a Room for 532." <u>New York Times</u>, November
19, 1986:Y16.
    This report on the operation of the Bedford Avenue
Armory in Brooklyn focuses on the problem of controlling
the men and also examines their coping mechanisms, such
as selling bits of food to one another.

Smothers, Ronald. "Atlanta Mayor Calls for Crackdown on Begging." <u>New York Times</u>, June 13, 1991:A20.
The mayor of Atlanta, Georgia, Maynard H. Jackson, wants the city council to pass a bill aimed at the visibility of the homeless. It would prohibit street begging, sleeping in vacant buildings, and "hanging out" in parking lots.

Smyth, Joseph Hilton. <u>To Nowhere and Return: The Autobiography of a Puritan</u>. New York: Carrick and Evans, 1940.
The man who wrote this first-person account of a wandering alcoholic writer later became the publisher and editor of <u>The Living Age</u>.

Smythers, Janice A. <u>Determined Survivors: Community Life among the Urban Elderly</u>. New Brunswick: Rutgers University Press, 1985.
The author reports participant observation experiences in St. Regis in Los Angeles, a subsidized hotel for the elderly.

Snider, Ed. "Local Helps the ‘Hotel Kids.’" <u>American Teacher</u>, <u>70</u>, April 1986:4.
"Hotel kids" in the article's title refer to the school age children of the homeless who are housed in New York City hotels. The author proposes a number of solutions to help these children get a better education: keeping the schools open late for tutorials, health, and nutritional programs for parents and children; making telephones available in the hotels for Dial-A-Teacher programs; and providing a staff person from the Children's Aid Society to knock on hotel room doors to make sure that the children get up for school.

Snow, David A. and Leon Anderson. "Identity Work Among the Homeless: The Verbal Construction and Avowal of Personal Identities." <u>American Journal of Sociology</u>, <u>92</u>, May 1987:1336-1371.
Focusing on relationships among role, identity, and self-concept, the authors elaborate the processes of identity construction and avowal among homeless street people. The specific issue is how people "at the lowest reaches of status systems attempt to generate identities that provide them with a measure of self-worth and dignity." The authors conclude that this is accomplished by "identity talk," specifically through the techniques of distancing, embracement, and fictive storytelling.

Snow, David A., Susan G. Baker, and Leon Anderson. "Criminality and Homeless Men: An Empirical Assessment." Social Problems, 36 (5), December 1989:532-549.

Matching the intake records of a random sample of 800 cases from a pool of 13,881 homeless persons who had contact with the Salvation Army in Austin, Texas, in 1984 and 1985 with records from the Austin Police Department, the authors found that during a 27-month period 32.3 percent were arrested at least once. About 1 percent of the offenses were for crimes of violence. Although the homeless have significantly higher arrest rates than the rest of the population, the authors conclude that "the crimes of the homeless are neither terribly serious nor dangerous." Most of their crimes are committed "by those who are under 35, have been on the streets longer, and have had contact with the mental health system." The authors suggest that if communities pass laws that criminalize life on the streets (such as making begging and scavanging illegal) it may force some of the homeless into more serious crimes.

Snow, David A., Susan G. Baker, Leon Anderson, and Michael Martin. "The Myth of Pervasive Mental Illness Among the Homeless." Social Problems, 33 (5): June 1986:407-423.

Using "a triangulated field study of nearly 1,000 unattached homeless adults in Texas," the authors conclude that about 15 percent of the homeless are mentally ill. Based on this finding, they also conclude that the streets of urban America have not become today's asylums. The reasons that other studies report much higher rates of mental illness among the homeless is due to misinterpretation founded on medicalization of homelessness, a misplaced emphasis on the causal role of deinstitutionalization, the heightened visibility of the homeless who are mentally ill, and methodological and conceptual shortcomings of previous studies. The typical homeless person is not mentally ill, but, rather, someone who is "caught in a cycle of low-paying, dead-end jobs that fail to provide the means to get off and stay off the streets."

Snow, David A., Susan G. Baker, and Leon Anderson. "On the Precariousness of Measuring Insanity in Insane Contexts." Social Problems, 35 (2), April 1988:192-196.

The authors reply to criticisms made by James D. Wright ("The Mentally Ill Homeless: What is Myth and What is Fact?," Social Problems, 35, 1988:182-191) of the authors' earlier article ("The Myth of Pervasive Mental Illness Among the Homeless," Social Problems, 33, 1986:407-423), who claims that the true incidence of mental illness among the homeless is two to three times higher than the authors reported. The authors admit that their research may have produced a "lower boundary estimate" of the prevalence of mental illness among the homeless, but they dispute the claim that mental illness is as high as their critic claims. The authors focus on the difficulties in assessing mental illness, that is, in adequately interpreting visible symptoms.

Snyder, Mitch, and Mary Ellen Hombs. "Sheltering the Homeless: An American Imperative." Journal of State Government, 59, November-December 1986:173-174.
The authors analyze what they call "well-travelled paths" to homelessness, namely: (1) the shortage of affordable housing, (2) the population of the nation's mental hospitals, (3) cuts in federal spending for social programs, (4) unemployment, (5) inflation and recession, and (6) the breakdown of traditional social structures, relationships, and responsibilities. Their thesis is that "Politically, philosophically, and programmatically is the right of every homeless man, woman, and child in America to adequate and accessible shelter, offered in an atmosphere of reasonable dignity."

Soberanis, Pat. "After the Quake." Journal of Housing, 47 (5), September-October 1990:276-279.
The author reports that the 1990 earthquake left many homeless in San Francisco and Oakland, California, and that even before the quake the area had a high rate of homelessness.

Sokolovsky, Jay, Carl Cohen, Dirk Berger, and Josephine Geiger. "Personal Networks of Ex-Mental Patients in a Manhattan SRO Hotel." Human Organization, 37 (1), Spring 1978:5-15.
Based on participant observation, logs of daily activity, interviews, and questionnaires, the authors determine the size, multiplexity, density, and degree of social networks of SRO residents. They conclude that schizophrenics are more isolated, and that schizophrenics with smaller networks will exhibit higher rates of rehospitalization than those who have more extensive networks.

Solenberger, Alice Willard. <u>One Thousand Homeless Men</u>: <u>A Study of Original Records</u>. New York: Charities Publication Committee, Russell Sage Foundation, 1911.

Based on records of 1,000 men who applied for assistance at the Chicago Bureau of Charities between 1901 and 1903, supplemented by her experience as director of this agency, the author concludes that there are four types of homeless men: the self-supporting, temporarily dependent, chronically dependent, and parasitic. The causes are crippling from birth or by disease or accident, insanity, feeble-mindedness, epilepsy, old age, choosing begging as a life style, being thrown out, running away, and wanderlust.

Sommer, R., and H. Osmond. "The Mentally Ill in the Eighties." <u>Orthomolecular Psychiatry</u>, <u>10</u> (3), November 1981:193-201.

The author details the judicial and social history of the patients' rights movement that led to the deinstitutionalization of the mentally ill. Due to deinstitutionalization, many persons who are seriously mentally ill are now in prisons and jails or live on the streets. The author proposes that "psychiatric reformers" work with the homeless, both those on the street and those who have been diverted to the penal system.

Sontag, Deborah. "Well-Fed Dinkins Leaves Brooklyn." <u>New York Times</u>, March 1, 1992:26.

New York City Mayor David Dinkins defends his plans to build shelters for the homeless in residential areas of the city.

Sorensen, Karen, and Ronald J. Fagen. "Who's Who On Skid Road: The Hospitalized Skid Road Alcoholic." <u>Nursing Forum</u>, <u>2</u> (1), Spring 1963:86-109.

Three types of people live on skid row: 52 percent are social misfits (people with deviant behavior patterns); 30 percent are old age and welfare pensioners (the permanent residents); and 18 percent are alcoholics. The authors analyze the process of social and physical debilitation that leads to dereliction, look at skid row as a breeding ground of disease, and examine the dynamics of the relationship between the hospital staff and patients who are pathological drinkers.

Sosin, Michael R. "Homeless and Vulnerable Meal Program Users: A Comparison Study." <u>Social Problems</u>, <u>39</u> (2); May 1992:170-188.

Based on a random, two-tiered sample of 535 domiciled and homeless individuals who obtained their main daily meal for free at shelters, meal programs, and soup kitchens, and treatment programs for the indigent in Chicago, the author concludes that the homeless are drawn from what he calls "a relatively large, vulnerable group of very poor individuals who have had problems finding work over many years, have particularly low incomes, are somewhat more likely to be male than female, and generally have insufficient disabilities to obtain strong support from families or governments. Members of this vulnerable group have a small probability of becoming homeless. The probability becomes high if they also experience problems with certain social institutions. Some personal deficits also contribute moderately to the return to homelessness among men, as members of this population apparently are readily discouraged or (given the indirect role of work) are denied help by relatives when they have no resources to offer."

Sosin, Michael R. "Homelessness in Chicago: A Study Sheds New Light on an Old Problem." <u>Public Welfare</u>, Winter 1989:22-28.
Based on a stratified random sample of adults who obtain their main daily meal for free in shelters, meal programs, and soup kitchens, and treatment programs for the indigent, the author found that 17 percent reported that their building had been torn down, burned, or condemned, 51 percent that they had been evicted, 21 percent that they had left housing due to problems with housemates, and 11 percent that they had just moved into the area. After comparing those in the sample who are currently homeless with those who are currently domiciled on such characteristics as work, welfare, income, age, race, sex, and education, the author concludes, "The challenge for a successful housing policy is to address the peripherals that so deeply impact an individual's ability to secure and pay for housing. If other supports are devised to replace families, offer employment, and improve access to welfare for the homeless, the dynamic of homelessness may then be halted."

Sosin, Michael, Irving Piliavin, and Herb Westerfelt. "Toward a Longitudinal Analysis of Homelessness." <u>Journal of Social Issues</u>, <u>46</u> (4), 1990:157-174.
Using a two-wave, two-sample survey of homeless adults in Minneapolis in 1985 and 1986, the authors report the demographic attributes of the samples,

patterns of exit from homelessness, and patterns of return to homelessness. They conclude that "so many transitions occur that the state of homelessness appears to be more a drift between atypical living situations and the street than between normality and street life. In other words, the typical pattern of homelessness seems to be one of residential instability rather than constant homelessness over a long period." Thus the authors conceptualize homelessness as "a gradual drift into a semipermanent state through the intermediate steps of superficial exits."

Spaniol, L., and A. Zippie. NIMH-Supported Research on the Mentally Ill Who Are Homeless: A Second Meeting of Researchers Sponsored by the Division of Education and Service Systems Liaison, National Institute of Mental Health. Rockville, Maryland: National Institutes of Mental Health, 1985.

This meeting of researchers from ten NIMH-funded projects focused on methodological, political, and funding barriers to research, future research directions, recommendations on how to encourage research, the diversity of the homeless, the need for services and leadership from mental health agencies, and the need for more communication between researchers.

Speek, Peter Alexander. "The Psychology of Floating Workers." Annals of the American Academy of Political and Social Science, 69, January 1917:72-78.

There are three types of laborers: steady, floaters (migratory or drifting), and down-and-outs (unemployables). Due to the reinforcement of their hopelessness and despair, some men go from steady work to floating work and finally arrive at a down-and-out condition. The author compares differential perception of causes by employers, charity workers, preachers, radical labor leaders, educators, moralists, and students of industrial problems. The solution is prevention through legislation that alters working conditions in the unskilled industries.

Speiglman, Richard. "Homelessness Among Participants in Residential Alcohol Programs in a Northern California County: The Commitment and Organization of Social Resources." Contemporary Drug Problems, 16 (3), Fall 1989:453-482.

After reviewing the literature on homelessness and alcohol problems, the author reports on a 1987 study of

325 individuals who resided in county-funded recovery homes, detoxification programs, and one three-quarter-way home. He concludes that "(1) local residents constitute the vast majority of participants in residential alcohol programs; (2) those who utilize the detoxification and recovery services--in contrast to those who register for the drinking driver programs--tend to be younger women and older men, with non-Hispanic whites, blacks, and American Indians all overrepresented; (3) homelessness is a serious problem for most individuals utilizing Bureau of Alcohol Services residential services." The author addresses three policy issues: (1) inadequate supply of affordable housing, (2) the high risk of relapse of persons leaving alcohol programs who do not have a supportive environment in which to live, and (3) drinking drivers representing a different population from traditional clients of alcohol services. He suggests that "more immediate attention should be devoted to the housing needs of those in alcohol treatment than to the alcohol treatment needs of those receiving shelter services."

Spinola, Steven. "A Better Solution to New York City's S.R.O.'s." New York Times, January 31, 1987:Y15.
     The author criticizes the New York City Council for voting to extend the moratorium on demolition and alteration of single room occupancy housing in view of "the city's inability to develop a sound, long-term program to create low-income housing" for the homeless.

Spradley, James P. You Owe Yourself a Drunk: An Ethnography of Urban Nomads. Boston: Little Brown, 1970.
     In this ethnomethodological approach (emphasis on the terms used by subjects in order to look at the world through their eyes) to the world of tramps, the primary foci are arrests for drunkenness and judicial processing.

Spring, Beth. "Home, Street Home." Christianity Today, April 21, 1989:15-20.
     The author profiles the work of several missions to the homeless across the United States: Union Gospel Mission in Seattle, Los Angeles Mission, Denver Rescue Mission, International Union of Gospel Missions of Seattle, Syracuse Rescue Mission, the Open Door Mission in Omaha, Union Gospel Mission in Washington, D.C., and the Nashville Union Mission. She also reviews the history of evangelical Christians with the homeless and their concern to share "the tangible love of Christ."

Springer, Gertrude. "Men Off the Road." <u>Survey Graphic</u>, September 1934:420-428, 448.
     This report on the transient program of the Federal Emergency Relief Administration, which consists of providing work camps for homeless men, describes the camps, how they function (problems, discipline, incentives for work), and the backgrounds of the men who work in them.

Srivastava, S. S. <u>Juvenile Vagrancy: A Socio-Ecological Study of Juvenile Vagrants in the Cities of Kampur and Lucknow</u>. London: Asia Publishing House, 1963.
     The author analyzes the background and activities of 300 vagrants in Kampur and Lucknow, India and argues that the basic cause of their vagrancy is urbanization.

St. John, Charles J. <u>God on the Bowery</u>. New York: Fleming H. Revell, 1940.
     This first-person account of his work and experiences on New York City's Bowery is written by a preacher who became the director of a Bowery mission.

Stack, Bill. "Jobs Available: Homeless and Seniors Encouraged to Apply." <u>Management Review</u>, <u>78</u> (8), August 1989:13-16.
     The author recounts the positive experience of Days' Inn's recruitment of employees from "special sectors." The homeless are identified as special sector employees.

Standish, Dana. "In From the Cold and Learning About Loss." <u>New Age Journal</u>, March 1985:32-33.
     The author discusses a variety of topics relating to the homeless: Initiative 17, the Right to Overnight Shelter Act of 1984, activities of the Coalition for the Homeless, the existence of an underclass, and legal change.

Stanley, Alessandra. "Tompkins Square Park, Where Politics Again Turns Violent." <u>New York Times</u>, May 30, 1991:B1.
     The author chronicles the debate over the fate of the homeless who have set up makeshift tents in Tompkins Square Park. Some want to keep the park a refuge for the homeless, while others want to "clean it up."

Stanley, Kay O. "Homeless Data Debate." <u>Black Enterprise</u>, <u>1</u> (15), November 1984:28.

This article presents a brief overview of the controversy concerning the disparities in estimates of the numbers of homeless in the United States.

Stark, Louisa. "A Century of Alcohol and Homelessness: Demographics and Stereotypes." <u>Alcohol Health and Research World</u>, <u>11</u> (3), Spring 1987:3-18.
    In examining homelessness over a century, the author focuses on the prevalence of alcohol problems. The percentage of alcoholics among the homeless appears to have remained relatively stable over the past century, even considering the "new homeless" of the 1980s and in spite of the many programs designed to treat and prevent alcoholism. The author concludes that band-aid approaches and institutionalization are inadequate, that this problem cannot be cured without coming to grips with the causes of homelessness.

Stark, Louisa R. "Strangers in a Strange Land: The Chronically Mentally Ill Homeless." <u>International Journal of Mental Health</u>, <u>14</u> (4), 1986:95-111.
    Based on the case histories of four chronically mentally ill homeless women in Phoenix, Arizona, the author develops the thesis that "the homeless chronically mentally ill have been forced into a set of behavior modes that 'work' and have certain rewards, in particular, a form of survival that is based on controlling, through structure behavior, the seemingly chaotic environment in which they find themselves." The homeless chronically ill person, who has likely learned this set of skills during institutionalization, "is capable of modifying those skills in order to live in a more structured, supervised setting." This view contrasts with the common belief among mental health professionals that chronically mentally ill homeless persons "will chafe at having to live in any kind of institutionalized environment, and would simply wander away, preferring an aimless life on the streets to being sheltered in a more 'structured' and safer environment." Consequently, we must "coax the homeless mentally ill off the streets in a graduated way through the building of trust in the programs that we wish to develop for them."

Staub, Hugo. "A Runaway from Home." <u>Psychoanalytic Quarterly</u>, <u>12</u>, 1943:1-22.
    Based on interviews with a runaway boy, as well as the analysis of his dreams, the author concludes that the "magic attractiveness of running away goes back to the

childhood of mankind when humanity was in a migratory state, a state of civilization which many tribes have never been able to abandon. In sleep and in waking fantasies, the fascination of taking to the road has a universal attractiveness." This analysis represents "insight into the real nature of this most urgent problem."

Stearns, Maude E. "Correlation Between Lodgings of Homeless Men and Employment in New York City." American Statistical Association Proceedings, 24, 1929:182-190.
    The fluctuations in the numbers of homeless men seeking shelter at the Municipal Lodging House in New York City between 1896 and 1928 are due to variations in factory employment in New York State.

Steep, Clayton. "A Worldwide Problem: The Homeless and the Landless." The Plain Truth, 52 (7), July-August 1987.
    The author's thesis is that worldwide homelessness, which the United Nations estimates at one hundred million, has come about because "civilization has drifted aimlessly," separating the tie between human beings and the land that God had planned for humans. The proper use of land, according to God's principles, will help mankind "avoid most of homelessness and landlessness extant on earth today."

Stein, Karen D. "Guerilla Welfare." Architectural Record, 176, November 1988:98-99.
    Mad Housers, a group of individuals from design studios, law offices, accounting firms, and business schools, join together on the weekend to build small huts for the homeless. They construct them on vacant parcels of government-owned or private property in Atlanta. They also "periodically visit with past clients to see how they, and their huts, are faring."

Stein, Leonard I., and Mary Ann Test, eds. Alternatives to Mental Hospital Treatment. New York: Plenum, 1978.
    The 15 articles of this anthology, reporting on various non-hospital approaches to treating the mentally ill, are divided into five sections: the rationale for creating alternatives to mental hospital treatment, controlled experiments of alternatives, examples of systems of alternatives, the British experience, and planning and implementing models for change.

Stein, M. L. "Column Provokes Angry Response." Editor and Publisher, 124 (52), December 28, 1991:9, 33.

This response to controversial positions taken about the destruction of the homes of the rich in a fire in Oakland-Berkeley Hills, California, which left 25 people dead and destroyed 3,000 homes, states that hundreds are still homeless.

Stein, M. L. "Newspapers Battle to Obtain Database Records." Editor and Publisher, 125 (10), March 7, 1992:25, 41.

This report on difficulties that newspapers have had in obtaining database records from government agencies mentions the struggles the California paper, Sacramento Bee, had in obtaining files relating to the city's homeless. The case went to court, and a Superior Court judge ruled that the newspaper had the right to the information, but that costs would be split. The newspaper had to pay for the development of a computer program to retrieve the data and the city the cost of retrieving the information.

Stein, M. L. "Reprise in the Bay Area." Journal and Publisher, 124 (45), November 9, 1991:12-13, 41.

This analysis of newspaper coverage of a fire in Oakland and Berkeley Hills that took 23 lives mentions that thousands were left homeless.

Stein, Michael. "Gratitude and Attitude: A Note on Emotional Welfare." Social Psychology Quarterly, 52 (3), 1989:242-248.

The author applies a sociology of emotions to interactions in a food pantry and a soup kitchen, exploring relationships in these settings among status, reciprocity, and emotions. Focusing on the place of gratitude as an expected response from clients and the anger experienced by the staff when an "attitude" (ingratitude) is shown, the author considers differences in status and power as possible sources for the expressions of "attitude."

Steinbeck, John. The Grapes of Wrath. New York: Bantam, 1969. (First published in 1939.)

This fictional account of the Joad family, fleeing from the dust bowl of Oklahoma to the promised land of California, details the many confrontations this family faces because they are viewed as homeless interlopers.

Steinberg, Jacques. "Crackdown on Homeless Is Begun at Bus Terminal." New York Times, December 2, 1991:B3.
   Port authorities removed the homeless from the Eighth Avenue bus terminal.

Steinberg, Jacques. "The Homeless Are Moving On, But the Criminals Linger." New York Times, December 15, 1991:Section 4:6.
   Although the Port Authority plans to remove homeless persons from its terminals and provide social services for them, a larger problem, that of the presence of criminals, will remain.

Steinberg, Jacques. "Homeless Man Is Accused in Slashing." New York Times, June 21, 1991:B3.
   Larry Lyles, accused of slashing the face of a 22-year old woman with a box cutter on a New York City street after she refused to give him the dollar he requested, is identified as a homeless man.

Steinberg, Jacques. "Police Accuse 3 of July Slaying of Restaurateur." New York Times, August 3, 1991:A24.
   A homeless woman and two teenagers have been accused of the abduction and murder of Mark Raffone, identified as a popular Staten Island, New York, restaurateur.

Steiner, Josephine M., and David C. Hoath. "Xenophobia and the Housing (Homeless Persons) Act." Modern law Review, 43, November 1980:703-708.
   In their attempts to determine the intentionality of homelessness, British councils have had great difficulty in applying this Act. The requirement that they consider immediate factors of homelessness rather than previous events in attempting to unravel the "chain of causation" has been especially troublesome. To be fair, it is essential that the implementation of standards be "consistent and non-discriminatory."

Steinfels, Peter. "Apathy Is Seen Greeting Agony of the Homeless." New York Times, January 20, 1992:A1.
   Many religious leaders perceive an increase in public indifference toward the homeless. They attribute this change not to callousness but to people's sense of powerlessness in face of an enormous and growing problem.

Stelzle, Charles. A Son of the Bowery: The Life Story of an East Side American. New York: George H. Doran, 1926.

This biography of a presbyterian minister, whose origins are in poverty, recounts his work among the poor.

Stengel, Erwin. "Further Studies on Pathological Wandering." Journal of Mental Science, 89, 1943:224-241.
    The author presents 11 case studies to illustrate what he calls compulsive wandering. This state of altered consciousness is often due to an unresolved Oedipus complex.

Stengel, Erwin. "Studies on the Psychopathology of Compulsive Wandering." British Journal of Medical Psychology, 18, 1939:250-254.
    Based on 17 female patients and five male patients, the author analyzes "the pathological compulsion to wander," the "irresistible impulse to leave home and to wander aimlessly," where the "return to normal conscious-ness occurs rather suddenly, and either there is a complete loss of memory of what occurred during the abnormal condition, or the memory is vague and dream-like." The common feature of these patients is that they "are persons during whose development there has occurred a serious disturbance in the child-parent relation, usually of such a nature that relationship to one or both parents was either completely lacking or only partially developed."

Stengel, Richard. "Down and Out and Dispossessed." Time, November 24, 1986:27-28.
    The author focuses on the new homeless, "the economically dispossessed" whom he refers to as "young men who have fallen on hard times, families who are not making ends meet, single mothers who cannot afford to pay the rent and support their children at the same time." The causes of the new homelessness are federal cutbacks in housing subsidies and in Aid to Families with Depen-dent Children. He suggests that The Youth Outreach in Wheaton, Illinois, is a model program for it "provides residential housing for the homeless as well as a struc-tured program of job hunting and a savings plan." He also discusses the difficulty of taking a census of a shifting homeless population, the lack of availability of low-income housing, and the need for legal advocacy for the homeless.

Stephens, Joyce. "Elderly People as Hustlers: Observa-tions on the Free Deviant Work Situations of SRO Ten-ants." Sociological Symposium, 26, Spring 1979:102-116.

This article summarizes eleven types of hustles by which street people survive.

Stephens, Joyce.   Loners, Losers, and Lovers: Elderly Tenants in a Slum Hotel. Seattle: University of Washington Press, 1976.
This participant observation study of an SRO hotel examines lower class culture, types of residents, adaptive strategies, sex roles, and social relationships.

Stephens, Joyce.   "Romance in the SRO: Relationships of Elderly Men and Women in a Slum Hotel." The Gerontologist, August 1974:279-282.
Based on participant observation of the residents of an SRO hotel, the author reports on their impoverished relationships, the females' desire for intimacy, and the males' use of prostitutes.

Stern, Mark J.   "The Emergence of the Homeless as a Public Problem." Social Service Review, 58 (2), June 1984:291-301.
To ask why homelessness has become a social problem is to ask why homelessness has begun to receive so much public attention. The author uses Herbert Blumer's model of social problems to develop an answer to this question, which he finds in the reemergence of conservative political practices combined with the traditional style of American social welfare. The author also places homelessness in historical perspective.

Sternlieb, George, and James W. Hughes. "Structuring the Future." Society, 21 (3), March-April, 1984:28-34.
The author presents an overview of the housing policies established during the Great Depression that led to 65 percent home ownership in the United States. He then reviews present government policies that have led to the dismantling of that system, and reviews threats to social stability. The solution, he says, is creative mortgages to maintain the ideal of home ownership.

Stevens, Anne O'Brien, Les Brown, Paul Coulson, and Karen Singer. When You Don't Have Anything: A Street Survey of Homeless People in Chicago. Chicago: Coalition for the Homeless, 1983.
The authors use interviews with 82 street people to reveal the coping techniques that these people use.

Stevens, James. "The Hobo's Apology." Century Magazine, 109, February 1925:464-472.
     This overview of "shiftless rovers" by a former hobo identifies three types: laborers, thieves, and beggars. The author presents an inside view of hobo culture and considers the primary cause of becoming a hobo the desire of youths to experience adventure. His writing betrays a romantic yearning for his old hobo days.

Stevens, William K. "Confusion for Philadelphia Homeless." New York Times, October 8, 1988:6.
     Due to a contract dispute between the city of Philadelphia and private contractors of shelters for the homeless, the operators of shelters have evicted about 1,000 residents, about 500 of whom converged on the city government with the demand that they be given direct help.

Stevens, William K. "Homeless, Not Helpless in Philadelphia." New York Times, May 3, 1988:8.
     The author describes a program for the homeless of Philadelphia that moves them out of public shelters into permanent housing and at the same time attempts "to educate, train and put the homeless back on their feet as wage-earning, tax-paying citizens." The program is unusual in that "the homeless are running it themselves in partnership with city and federal governments, which are footing the bill and providing the houses."

Stevens, William K. "National Group for Homeless is Born." New York Times, February 16, 1986:20.
     Two hundred representatives of government, social service professionals, and advocacy groups held a conference in Philadelphia to attempt to forge a national coalition against homelessness. The basic cause of homelessness is less that of personal failure and more the result of larger social forces, especially the lack of affordable housing. The solution is to put money into permanent housing instead of into temporary shelters.

Stevenson, Richard W. "Los Angeles Gets $2 Billion Plan To Provide Housing for Homeless." New York Times, January 9, 1988:6.
     Mayor Tom Bradley announced that the City of Los Angeles would spend more than $2 billion over the next 20 years to build more low-income housing and to provide more services for the city's fast-growing homeless population. The city government will devote half of the

funds that it receives by its Community Redevelopment
Agency in this "unprecedented long-range effort to deal
with the homeless problem in Los Angeles."

Stierlin, Helm.   "A Family Perspective on Adolescent
Runaways."   <u>Archives of General Psychiatry</u>, <u>29</u>, July
1973:56-62.
     Runaways are classified as abortive, lonely schiz-
oid, casual, and crisis. Runaway patterns are analyzed
according to their transactional mode: binding mode
(locked into the parental orbit), expelling mode (neglected and abandoned by the parents), and delegating
mode (a combination of the binding and expelling in which
the parents encourage the child to move out of the home,
but still hold the child "on a long leash").   To deal
with runaways, the author proposes psychiatric therapy to
focus on the family and gain an understanding of the
parents' concerns, problems, and attitudes.

Stille, Alexander. "Seeking Shelter in the Law."   <u>The
National Law Journal</u>, <u>8</u> (22), February 10, 1986:24.
     Legal advocacy on behalf of the homeless means to
use the law as an instrument of change in the attempt to
provide shelter for the homeless. The basic goal is to
establish the constitutional right of the homeless to
safe and adequate   shelter.   So far, judges have not
addressed this constitutional question.   The author
profiles the litigation efforts of Robert M. Hayes and
the political advocacy activities of Mitch Snyder and the
Community for Creative Non-Violence.

Stoil, Michael.   "Salvation and Sobriety."   <u>Alcohol
Health and Research World</u>, <u>11</u> (3), Spring 1987:14-17.
     Using an historical perspective to provide an
overview of the efforts of the Salvation Army of America
to give shelter to homeless alcoholics, the author
details how this group has designed its programs to meet
the material and spiritual needs of its clients. Its use
of group psychotherapy and targeted vocational rehabilitation has contributed to the long-term recovery of many
clients.

Stolley, Richard B. "Surviving Seattle's Harsh Streets."
<u>Life</u>, <u>6</u>, July 1983:4.
     The author profiles Cheryl McCall and Mary Ellen
Mark, reporters from <u>Life</u> who did extensive interviewing
with street kids in Seattle.

Stone, Allan A.   "Civil Rights for Mentally Ill Must be Redefined."   Wall Street Journal, June 3, 1987:26.
      The author discusses deinstitutionalization as a cause of homelessness on American streets and a recommendation by the American Psychiatric Association for brief, involuntary confinement and treatment of "persons so obviously mentally ill that they are irrational, incompetent to make medical decisions; when there is clear evidence of mental deterioration such as hallucinations or delusions, and when the person is obviously suffering."

Stone, Deborah A.   The Disabled State.   Philadelphia: Temple University Press, 1984.
      Americans have a conflict between a capitalist work ethic and a desire to mitigate human suffering. A narrow drawing of the category of disabled supports the work ethic, while a broad drawing undermines it. Disability is a political concept, not a medical one.   It is a boundary device that separates productive workers from lazy non-producers by placing some non-producers in the acceptable category of non-productive but also non-lazy.

Stoneham, C. T.   From Hobo to Hunter.   London: John Long, 1956.
      This autobiographical account relates the author's extensive travels and work experiences in various parts of the world.

Stoner, Madeleine R.   "Addressing Homelessness."   Wall Street Journal, October 4, 1988:43.
      In this letter to the editor, the author states that she was misquoted in an editorial in the Wall Street Journal, that she does not recommend tougher vagrancy and public-nuisance laws.

Stoner, Madeleine R.   "An Analysis of Public and Private Sector Provisions for Homeless People."   The Urban and Social Change Review, 17 (1), Winter 1984:3-8.
      The author discusses the freezing death of Rebecca Smith in New York City, the carbon monoxide deaths of Norman and Anna Peters in Cleveland, the new homeless, and the chronic homeless.   After criticizing current programs and legislation, she proposes a comprehensive three-stage service system: emergency shelter and crisis intervention, transition or community shelters, and long-term residence.

Stoner, Madeleine R.   "Emerging Trends In The Provision Of Health Care To The Homeless Ill."   Paper presented at the annual meetings of the Society for the Study of Social Problems, New York City, August 1986.
    This paper focuses on the relative responsibility of the voluntary and public sectors in meeting the health needs of the homeless and the need for a comprehensive health care program. The author proposes a collaboration between the public and private sectors.

Stoner, Madeleine R.   "The Plight of Homeless Women." Social Science Review, 57 (4), December 1983:565-581.
    The causes of homelessness are a lack of housing, unemployment and poverty, deinstitutionalization, and domestic violence and abuse. Homeless women have special needs and face harsher conditions than men. In general, homeless services overlook homeless women in favor of homeless men. Most services, however, are inadequate for both men and women. The solution is a three-tiered services system (emergency care and shelter, transitional services and housing, and long-term affordable housing) combined with coalitions and advocacy groups that pressure the government to provide services for the homeless.

Strasser, Judith A.   "Urban Transient Women." American Journal of Nursing, 78, December 1978:2076-2079.
    Based on participant observation at St. John's Hospice near a metropolitan skid row, the author describes the women's appearance, their personal hygiene, ethnicity, health conditions, and health perceptions. She proposes more research into the problem and that the women's unique needs and perceptions be taken into account in the provision of health services.

Straus, Robert.   "Alcohol and the Homeless Man." Quarterly Journal of Studies on Alcohol, 7 (3), December 1946:360-404.
    Based on interviews with 203 men at Salvation Army Men's Social Service Center in New Haven, Connecticut, the author differentiates between the homeless man and the alcoholic homeless man. The broadly-conceived causes are the Industrial Revolution, urbanization, and disintegration of family life. Causes more specific to the individual are unemployment, personal inadequacy (handicaps, alcoholism, addiction, old age, personality defects), crisis (family, personal fears), and wanderlust. The author reviews the background of the men,

their drinking patterns, the relationship of homelessness to drinking, and the undersocialization thesis.

Straus, Robert. Escape from Custody: A Study of Alcoholism and Institutional Dependency as Reflected in the Life Record of a Homeless Man. New York: Harper and Row, 1974.
   This life history of an alcoholic born in 1904, is told largely through his letters of 1946-1972. The opening and closing sections present overviews and interpretations of these materials written by Straus. Stressed are the suicide of the man's father and a distorted relationship with his mother, that he generally stayed in the same area, and was constantly in and out of jail for drunkenness, and patterns of disaffiliation and institutional dependency.

Straus, Robert. "The Homeless Alcoholic: Who He Is, His Locale, His Personality, the Approach to His Rehabilitation." In The Homeless Alcoholic: Report of First Annual International Institute on the Homeless Alcoholic, Detroit: Detroit Mayor's Rehabilitation Committee on "Skid Row" Problems and the Michigan State Board of Alcoholism, September 12-13, 1955:7-31.
   This paper is a brief overview of what the title indicates.

Straus, Robert. "Some Sociological Concomitants of Excessive Drinking, as Revealed in the Life History of an Itinerant Inebriate." Quarterly Journal of Studies on Alcohol, 9 (1), June 1948:1-52.
   The author uses a case history to illustrate a pattern of social deprivation or undersocialization that he identifies as the cause of a man's alcoholic homelessness.

Straus, Robert, and Raymond G. McCarthy. "Nonaddictive Pathological Drinking Patterns of Homeless Men." Quarterly Journal of Studies on Alcohol, 12 (4), December 1951:601-611.
   The authors review the drinking patterns of 444 men on the Bowery, discussing their controlled and uncontrolled drinking patterns and motives for nonaddictive drinking.

Strauss, Sara H., and Andrew E. Tomback. "Homelessness: Halting the Race to the Bottom." Yale Law & Policy Review, 3, 1985:551-570.

The crisis of homelessness in the United States is due to three factors: high unemployment, a decrease in the construction of low-income housing, and the deinstitutionalization of the mentally ill. Although the shelters for the homeless are inadequate, American states and cities do not improve them because they are trying to avoid the "race to the bottom:" That is, they fear becoming a magnet for homeless people if they develop excellent programs. Fear of a race to the bottom is a powerful incentive to underspend for care of the homeless. The U.S. Congress can put a stop to this race by passing legislation to establish "a uniform, minimum level of care for the homeless."

Struening, Elmer L., and Deborah K. Padgett. "Physical Health Status, Substance Use and Abuse, and Mental Disorders Among Homeless Adults." Journal of Social Issues, 46 (4), 1990:65-81.
    Using a sampling procedure aimed at collecting data from a representative sample of people residing in the New York City shelter system for homeless adults, the authors interviewed 1,260 persons--949 men and 311 women. The shelter population is young, male, minority, never married, and modestly well educated (35 percent completed high school and 21 percent attended or completed college). About 76 percent were African American, 15 percent Hispanic, 7 percent white, and 2 percent other. Based on their profiles of seven measures of substance use, substance abuse, and mental disorders, the authors identified a typology of ten groups and found that the "results indicated strong associations between the degree and kind of involvement with drugs, alcohol, and mental problems and the respondents' physical health status. Homeless adults characterized by heavy use and abuse of substances and symptoms and/or histories of mental disorder reported the highest rates of poor physical health."

Stuart, Frank S. Vagabond. London: Stanley Paul, 1937.
    This autobiographical account was written by a man who at 16 was expelled from school because his father was executed. He discusses his travels in Europe and associations with underground elements.

Suddick, David E. "Runaways: A Review of the Literature." Juvenile Justice, 24, August 1973:47-54.
    The author reviews 71 references, summarizing their conclusions concerning types of runaways, personality of

the runaway, "the runaway response," recommended treatment, controlling runaways, advice for runaways and their
parents, and recommendations for working with runaways.
He says that parents need to confirm their suspicions if
they think their child has absconded and to seek professional assistance when their child returns home. The
best advice for a child who is contemplating running away
is to "look before you leap."

Sullivan, J. P. "Managing Homelessness in Transportation
Facilities." New England Journal of Human Services, 6
(2), Spring 1986:16-19.
    Homeless individuals who cluster in urban transpor-
tation facilities present a problem in management. To
solve this problem will require the coordination of
outreach teams and police and "human services providers."
The goal is not simply to remove homeless people from
public transportation facilities, but also to provide
effective service strategies for the homeless mentally
ill who seek shelter there.

Sullivan, Joseph F. "Jersey Budget Calls for New State
Division to Deal With AIDS." New York Times, January 31,
1988:12.
    The budget proposed by the governor of the state of
New Jersey includes a recommended "increase in programs
for the homeless of $22 million for a total of $36
million in state and federal funds. The money will be
used for emergency shelter and help families threatened
with eviction."

Sullivan, Joseph F. "Trenton Relaxes Rules for Voting by
the Homeless." New York Times, April 20, 1991:A26.
    The attorney general of New Jersey ruled that the
homeless have a right to vote even if they cannot comply
with requirements of established residences.

Sullivan, Ronald. "Charges Against Homeless Man Are
Dropped in Murder in Village." New York Times, April 11,
1991:B3.
    Murder charges against William Emerson, identified
as a homeless man, accused of shooting to death an
advertising executive at a Greenwich Village telephone
booth, were dropped for lack of evidence.

Sullivan, Ronald. "For Petty Offender, Toil Replaces
Incarceration." New York Times, March 8, 1992:40.

New York City is testing a program in which petty offenders, rather than being sent to jail, will perform public service such as working at shelters for the homeless.

Sullivan, Ronald. "Judge Orders Homeless Aid in New York." New York Times, February 28, 1991:B1.
A New York State Supreme Court judge ruled that the City of New York must provide housing and outpatient services to the thousands of deinstitutionalized homeless mental patients who now walk its streets.

Sullivan, Ronald. "Mayor Offers Aid and Hand to Homeless." New York Times, March 25, 1983:B1, B4.
Although the mayor of New York City has offered help to the homeless, most of the homeless have refused his offers. Current laws do not allow authorities to force help on the homeless. The author discusses the dilemma of civil liberties versus community concern.

Sullivan, Ronald. "Welfare Benefit Upheld For Homeless Mothers." New York Times, 138, September 12, 1989:B3.
The New York State Supreme Court ruled in the case of Grace Campfield that welfare officials "cannot withdraw a mother's welfare payments, even if her children are in foster care, if doing so causes her to lose her home and makes it impossible to reunite the family." Robert Hayes, the head of the Coalition for the Homeless, which brought this suit, called the practice "the single most stupid policy ever adopted by government against the poor."

Sunholt, Judith. "A Home for the Homeless." J/ Student (Southern Illinois University, Edwardsville), January 1987.
The author profiles Bill and Dorothy Land, who work to help the homeless in Belleville, Illinois.

Surber, Robert W., Eleanor Dwyer, Katherine J. Ryan, Stephen M. Goldfinger, and John T. Kelly. "Medical and Psychiatric Needs of the Homeless--A Preliminary Response." Social Work, 33, March-April 1988:116-119.
For a utilization survey, researchers interviewed 170 homeless persons in San Francisco. Seventy five percent of the sample reported receiving medical services within the past year, 30 percent of whom reported being hospitalized in an inpatient setting. Sixty percent reported problems with alcohol, drug abuse, or both. A

review of the medical records of 285 homeless persons
admitted to San Francisco General Hospital showed that
the most frequent diagnosis was cellulitis (24 percent),
while trauma, respiratory problems, and alcohol and drug-
related problems together accounted for 51 percent of the
admissions. The most frequent diagnosis of the homeless
admitted for psychiatric services was schizophrenia (36
percent), while affective disorders accounted for 24
percent. The authors conclude that "treatment efforts
must respond to the whole gamut of medical and psychiatric problems and must be integrated with a full spectrum
of treatment resources." To implement such a program
requires that two principles go into effect: first, the
program must be fully integrated with the already-
existing programs of homeless shelters and services of
the Department of Public Health; second, to recognize
that since health is a function of "overall well-being"
the program must be comprehensive and respond to basic
living and social needs, not only to medical and psychiatric needs. Similarly, we cannot treat this problem by
simply providing temporary housing, for we must also
address the problem of homelessness itself--which
represents "the failure of human services in this
country." The solution requires a complex human service
network, coordination and integration of services, and an
improved stock of low-income housing.

Suro, Roberto. "Vatican Urges Governments to Help the
Homeless." New York Times, February 3, 1988:3.
     A Vatican commission produced a document that
describes homelessness as "a scandal and one more
indication of unjust distribution of goods, originally
destined for use of all...and that all property be viewed
as having a specific social function subordinated to the
right of common use as opposed to the individual's
ability to reap a profit." Therefore, "housing constitutes a basic social good and cannot simply be considered
a market commodity...and any speculative practice which
diverts property from its function of serving the human
person should be considered as an abuse." Homelessness,
then, is part of "structural" failings in both rich and
poor societies, part of the "injustices built into all
economic systems." Consequently, "ethical direction must
be given to market economies."

Susser, Ezra S., Lin P. Shang, Sarah A. Conover, and
Elmer L. Struening. "Childhood Antecedents of Homeless-

ness in Psychiatric Patients." <u>American Journal of Psychiatry</u>, <u>148</u> (8), August 1991:1026-1030.
    A comparison of 512 previously hospitalized psychiatric homeless persons with 271 psychiatric hospital patients who had never been homeless revealed that running away, group home placement, and foster care are antecedents of homelessness. The lifetime prevalence of homelessness in patients with such childhood histories is about three times greater than in other patients.

Susser, Ezra S., Sarah A. Conover, and Elmer L. Struening. "Mental Illness in the Homeless: Problems of Epidemiologic Method in Surveys of the 1990s." <u>Community Mental Health Journal</u>, <u>26</u> (5), October 1990:391-414.
    The authors criticize the definitions of homelessness and methods used to study this population, arguing that they result in the most visible of the homeless being oversampled while the homeless with different attributes are undersampled. Accordingly, we can place little confidence in studies to date, and we must use comparison groups, several assessment methods in the same survey, and longitudinal and ethnographic studies.

Sutherland, Edwin H., and Harvey J. Locke. <u>Twenty Thousand Homeless Men: A Study of Unemployed Men in the Chicago Shelters</u>. Chicago: J. B. Lippincott, 1936. (Republished by the Arno Press in 1971.)
    The authors base their conclusions on a sample of 1,882 men, every tenth man staying at Chicago shelters during June 1934. There are two types of theories of the causes of homelessness. The first places emphasis on historical process: technological changes lead to changes in social relations. The result is migration, a frontier, urbanization, disintegration of family life, increased mobility and impersonal relations. The second type of theory focuses on characteristics of the individual. Three such theories of individual differences are innate deficiency, economic deprivation, and personalities that need hobohemia. The authors identified seven types of homeless men: bums, home guard casuals, migratory laborers, steady unskilled laborers, skilled workers, white collar workers, and negroes. They include an historical overview of the social treatment of the homeless.

Swanstrom, Todd. "Homeless: A product of Policy." <u>New York Times</u>, March 23, 1989:23.

The problem is not to explain why people are poor, but why poverty in the 1980s has taken the form of homelessness. The primary cause of this homelessness is an inadequate supply of housing at the bottom of the rental market. The primary reasons that the housing supply has not responded to an increase in demand are "overly stringent and discriminatory building codes," zoning controls, and gentrification encouraged by tax incentives which have provided luxury housing at the cost of low-income housing. The author concludes that we know what the problem is, a shortage of low-rent housing, but that knowing the cause is not enough. "What is lacking," he says, "is the political will to do it."

Sweeney. "A Helping Hand for Homeless Women." The Christian Science Monitor, November 22, 1977.
This article profiles the House of Ruth, founded by sociologist Veronica Maz, in Washington, D.C.

Symanski, Richard. "Hobos, Freight Trains, and Me." Canadian Geographer, 23 (2), 1979:103-118.
This inside view of hobomania is based on extensive participant observation in riding freight trains.

Szasz, Thomas. "Homelessness Is Not a Disease." USA Today, March 1988:28-31.
The author argues against "any and all psychiatric intimidation and coercion." He claims that "involuntary psychiatric hospitalization is not beneficent or legitimate medical intervention" and that "the hidden agenda of mental health services is providing homes for the homeless." He concludes that we must devise "more dignified and less costly ways of providing homes for the homeless."

Szasz, Thomas. "New Ideas, Not Old Institutions, for the Homeless." Wall Street Journal, June 7, 1985:12.
The author argues that the homeless are not mentally ill, but, rather, losers in the game of life. Homelessness is a moral problem, and institutionalization of the homeless is not the answer.

T

Taft, Philip. "The I.W.W. in the Grain Belt." <u>Labor History</u>, <u>1</u>, Winter 1960:53-67.

This overview of the I.W.W. includes a section on the thousands of migrant workers who were drawn to the grain belt. They moved with the harvest from Oklahoma to Minnesota and even to Alberta, Canada. After the harvest, some sought work in the sugar beet factories of Nebraska, the oil fields of Kansas and Oklahoma, Texas or Louisiana, or in the woods of the Middle Western lumbering areas. "Many harvesters sought only a 'stake' large enough to enable them to move into a housekeeping room in one of the cities adjacent to the grain belt."

Talbott, John A., ed. <u>The Chronic Mental Patient: Five Years Later</u>. Orlando: Grune and Stratton, 1984.

The articles in this anthology examine the consequences of deinstitutionalization: practices, programs, attitudes, adjustments, needs, and facilities.

Talbott, John A. "The Future of Unified Mental Health Services." In <u>United Health System: Utopia Unrealized</u>. John A. Talbott, ed. San Francisco: Jossey-Bass, 1983:107-111.

The author identifies 11 elements necessary for a successful health service system designed to provide quality care for the most severely and chronically ill. To combine these elements into a cohesive service system would allow us to provide efficient and coordinated community mental health services. Consequently, we would be able to satisfy "our basic human desire to bring order from chaos."

Talbott, John A. "Toward a Public Policy on the Chronically Mentally Ill." <u>American Journal of Orthopsychiatry</u>, <u>50</u> (1), January 1980:43-53.

After presenting a brief background on the reduction of the numbers of people who are hospitalized for mental illness, this "summary of the work of the APA Ad Hoc Committee on the Chronic Mental Patient" examines who and where chronic mental patients are, their needs, programs that work best, obstacles to providing successful treatment, and issues in economics, case management, levels of governmental responsibility, and the rights of chronically mentally ill patients. The article closes with a statement of proposed public policy that addresses psychiatry's role, community education, research, training, continuity of services, financial and administrative issues, and the civil rights of such patients.

Tanquary, John F. "Homelessness is Not a Mental Health Problem." American Journal of Psychiatry, 142 (8), August 1985:997.
    The author argues that the concern of psychiatrists for the homeless is a power play.

Taranto, James. "The Homeless Are Ill-Served By Advocates." Wall Street Journal, November 14, 1990:A14.
    A controversy surrounds the recruiting of homeless persons by the New York Daily News to sell their paper. The Coalition for the Homeless has accused the paper of "the lowest form of exploitation possible."

Tascheraud, Henri. "The Art of Bumming a Meal." American Mercury, 5, June 1925:183-187.
    Based on his own begging experiences, the author lists general rules for bumming a meal. He delineates ethnic groups to avoid, the proper opening, and how to bum from back doors, restaurants, ships, prostitutes, the clergy, religious and charitable organizations. He also includes a section on how the "jungle" socializes new men.

Taubman, Philip. "Now Through a Soviet Lens, Darkly: 90 Minutes of Gomorrah-on-Hudson." New York Times, April 7, 1986:6.
    "The Man From Fifth Avenue," a documentary broadcast on prime time in the Soviet Union, features the misery of the homeless and focuses on the disparity between the rich and the poor in the United States. The program appears to be a reaction to the negative portrayal of the Soviet Union in such films as "Rambo," which the Russians view as part of an anti-Soviet campaign.

Taylor, Graham. "On the Vagrant 'Elusive.'" Charities and the Commons, 18, August 10, 1907:575-577.
    Better laws and public policies are needed to deal with the problem of vagrancy.

Taylor, Graham. "Two Vagrants in Law and Life." Charities and the Commons, 19, October 19, 1907:895-896.

The author tells the stories of two tramps he once knew, one who was forced to tramp to look for work and the other for whom tramping was a way of life. Law enforcement needs to be merciful on the one and hard on the other.

Taylor, Paul S. "Adrift on the Land." Washington: Public Affairs Pamphlets, 1940.
The author gives an overview of the large-scale migration occurring in the United States as people search for work. He reviews the living conditions of migrant workers, and gives reasons for agricultural strife in California and Arizona.

Teltsch, Kathleen. "Brooklyn's Alternative for Homeless." New York Times, October 6, 1986:16.
Samaritan House in the Park Slope section of Brooklyn is innovatively financed by foundations, churches, bank loans, and New York City's Human Resources Administration, which gives the same sum it provides for welfare hotels, $1,140 monthly for a family of three. Residents report high satisfaction with the shelter.

Teltsch, Kathleen. "Donations for Poor Quickly Depleted in Big Cities." New York Times, January 1, 1983:A17.
Across the country, contributions for the homeless are depleted quickly, an indication that the problem of homelessness is growing.

Teltsch, Kathleen. "Sharp Drop in U.S. Aid for Housing Spurs New Push for Private Support." New York Times, September 21, 1987.
With a primary focus on Boston, the author reviews several private "non-governmental" programs to build low-income housing.

Teltsch, Kathleen. "Shelter to Protect Homeless Youths from AIDS." New York Times, February 19, 1991:B3.
A Roman Catholic church and a social agency jointly operate Safe Space, a refuge for homeless and runaway youths in New York City's Times Square.

Teltsch, Kathleen. "A Wealth of Education for 'Kids in Business.'" New York Times, May 28, 1992.
The author profiles the "Kids in Business" program at the 15th Avenue School in Newark, New Jersey. Most of the profits the students earn from the products they make and sell are designated for the homeless.

Tennison, Debbie C. "Homeless People Grow Numerous in Europe, Despite Welfare States." Wall Street Journal, April 25, 1983:1, 16.

In 1970, about one million Europeans were homeless or living in temporary housing. No one knows how many there are today, but it is large. With a focus on Great Britain, Belgium, Holland, and France, the author discusses unemployment benefits that never run out, hostels, workhouses, soup kitchens, subsidized housing, and cardboard-box communities of the homeless. The Kelly's of Britain serve as a case example.

Teplin, Linda A. "The Criminalization of the Mentally Ill: Speculation in Search of Data." Psychological Bulletin, 94 (1), 1983:54-67.

The author critically examines empirical evidence that bears on the speculation that "mentally ill persons who would previously have been treated within mental hospitals are now processed through the criminal justice system and constitute an ever-increasing proportion of the jail population." Using "archival studies, investigations of police decision making, and studies of the prevalence of mental disorder among jail detainees," she concludes that although there is tentative support for this contention, the studies are methodologically flawed and lack baseline comparisons. She suggests directions for future research.

Terkel, Studs. Hard Times: An Oral History of the Great Depression. New York: Pantheon Books, 1970.

This collection of accounts of hard times by people who lived them contains several accounts of hobo experiences.

Terry, Dickson. "Old Skid Row Is on the Skids." St. Louis Post-Dispatch, March 14, 1965:F1.

In recounting the demise of the skid row in St. Louis, Missouri, especially the disappearance of flop houses, the author provides a short history of this skid row. He reports that most people on skid row are not "drunken bums." About 12 percent are alcoholics, 5 percent are derelicts (persons who came to skid row not because of alcohol but because of an inability to cope with life), and about 10 percent are transients. The largest percentage consists of pensioners, old men trying to live on inadequate Social Security or Old-Age Assistance, who find that skid row is the only place they can survive.

Terry, Don. "29 Are Killed by Tornadoes Sweeping Through 7 States." New York Times, April 28, 1991:22.
This overview of the destruction wrought by a series of tornados in midwestern United States mentions that thousands were left homeless.

Teshima, Dick Y. "Alcohol Abuse and Alcoholism Among Homeless: Reports Available from the National Institute on Alcohol Abuse and Alcoholism." Rockville, Maryland: National Clearinghouse for Alcohol and Drug Information, August 1987.
This annotated list of reports pertaining to the alcohol-related problems of the homeless population is organized into three broad areas: policy issues (22 items), research findings (11 items), and service delivery issues (10 items).

Thanet, Octave. "The Tramp in Four Centuries." Lippincott's Monthly Magazine, 23, 1879:565-574.
The author introduces four fairly lengthy letters (one each from the sixteenth, seventeenth, eighteenth, and nineteenth centuries) whose writers comment on the wandering poor and the distress of poverty of their times.

Thernstrom, Stephan. "Is There Really a New Poor?" Dissent, 15, January-February, 1968:59-64.
In reviewing the debate about the culture of poverty and implications about where to draw the poverty line, the author concludes that there is no new mass of "new poor" whose chances to rise out of poverty are worse than previous generations.

Thomas, Evan. "Coming in from the Cold." Time, February 4, 1985:20-21.
In his discussion of the "winter crisis" of homeless persons in New York City, Los Angeles, Pittsburgh, Phoenix, and Washington, D.C., the author mentions the "new poor" and a backlash against the homeless.

Thomas, Logan. Report on the Greater New York Gospel Mission. New York: Welfare Council of New York City, 1931.
This overview of New York Gospel Mission on the Bowery summarizes its programs of shelter, feeding, treatment directed toward rehabilitation, and conversion. The solution to the problem is to provide shelter and food programs with a personal approach.

Thorman, George. <u>Homeless Families</u>. Springfield, Illinois: Charles C. Thomas, 1988.
Families make up almost 30 percent of America's homeless. Homelessness aggravates physical and mental health problems. Children in homeless families face malnutrition, insecurity, embarrassment, problems in learning, and tend to withdraw or become aggressive. Current shelters cannot meet the needs of homeless families, but transitional housing can, if such programs also offer counseling services.

Thorns, David C. "The Production of Homelessness: From Individual Failure to System Inadequacies." <u>Housing Studies</u>, <u>4</u> (4), October 1989:253-266.
How the homeless are conceptualized is significant for developing public policy. Using examples from New Zealand, Australia, and the United Kingdom, the author analyzes the shift in conceptualizing the homeless as transitory male migrant workers to marginal people whose capacity to function in society is impaired. The author also contrasts the visible and concealed homeless.

Thrasher, Anthony Apakark. <u>Thrasher: Skid Row Eskimo</u>. Toronto: Griffin House, 1976.
This first-person account describes the author's experiencing of displacement, from tribal mission life in the arctic to homelessness on the skid row of Edmonton, Alberta.

Thurow, Roger, and Tony Horwitz. "The Bitter Balkan War Offers Tragic Parallels to Mideast Stalemate." <u>Wall Street Journal</u>, October 7, 1992:A1, A4.
As the authors analyze the civil war in the former Yugoslavia, they mention that more than 300,000 refugees, who have been homeless for more than a year, are agitating to return to their villages and fight the Serbs who occupy them.

Ticer, Scott. "The Search for Ways to Break Out of the Prison Crisis." <u>Business Week</u>, 3104, May 8, 1989:80-81.
Mentioned among the steps being taken to try to solve the problem of overcrowded prisons is converting homeless shelters to detention centers.

Tidmarsh, D., and Susanne Wood. "Psychiatric Aspects of Deinstitution: A Study of the Camberwell Reception Centre." In <u>Evaluating a Community Psychiatric Service: The Camberwell Register, 1964-1971</u>, J. K. Wing and A. M.

Heiley, eds. London: Oxford University Press, 1972:327-340.
A sample of registration forms and interviews is used to determine the demographic characteristics of men using the Camberwell Reception Centre in a borough of London. The authors, who summarize the men's family ties and mental illnesses, suggest that the solution is more psychiatric beds, with social and pharmacological treatment, and the establishment of short-term and long-term hostels and day centers.

Tierney, John. "After 16 years, Squatter Leaves Tunnel." New York Times, March 13, 1991:A1.
The author profiles John Joseph Kovacs, a homeless man who lived beneath a railroad tunnel under Riverside Park in New York City for 16 years. Kovacs became the first student in a program designed to train the homeless to become organic farmers.

Tierney, John. "In South Bronx, a Boarding School for the Homeless." New York Times, February 26, 1991:B1.
A group of New York City teachers at Bronx Regional High School are transforming a gutted crack house into what is thought to be the only dormitory at a municipal high school in the United States.

Tierney, John. "Manhattan Boat People: Lo Rnt, Riv Vu." New York Times, October 5, 1991:A23.
The author's thesis is that New York City has a two-tiered treatment of its social classes. He derives this conclusion from the city's actions at the 79th Street Boat Basin. At this marina, the city evicted the homeless people who had taken refuge there but allowed the boat people (yachtsmen) to remain docked although they had not paid their rents.

Tierney, John. "Mole Returns to Hole." New York Times, November 30, 1991:A21.
The author profiles John Joseph Kovacs, a homeless man who lived in a railroad tunnel beneath Riverside Park in New York City for 17 years. Kovacs, who had become the first student in a program that trains the homeless to become organic farmers, moved back into the tunnel.

Tindale, Joseph. "The Management of Self Among Old Men on Skid Row." Essence, 2 (1), 1977:49-58.
This article, part of an ethnography of old men on skid row, stresses how interaction with non-skid rowers

threatens their sense of self, and how for them the presentation of self is stigma management. The author also mentions the Great Depression, geographical mobility, work careers, and family relationships.

Tobias, Jerry J., and Jay Reynolds. "The Affluent Suburban Runaway." The Police Journal, 43, October 1970:335-339.
    Based on a 1969 sample of 59 runaways from Bloomfield, Michigan, the authors report on the runaways' sex, age, religious affiliation, home life, length of time away from home, day and month of leaving home, and their stated reasons for leaving home. The peak age for running away is 15 and 16, 20 percent of the runaways were not living with their natural parents, and 77 percent were first-time runaways. During the time of their absence from home, about half remained in the local area. September was the most popular month for running away, and about 40 percent returned home within 24 hours.

Tobier, Emmanuel. The Changing Face of Poverty: Trends in New York City's Populations in Poverty, 1960-1990. New York: Community Service Society, 1982.
    Current population, social, and employment trends indicate that if there is no change, one of three New Yorkers will live in poverty by 1990. The author concludes that poverty is fundamentally different today than it was two or three decades ago.

Todd, Reggie. "Big Guns Zero In on Aiding the Homeless." Nation's Cities Weekly, February 9, 1987:1, 9.
    HR 558, bipartisan legislation, would authorize the appropriation of $500 million in 1987 for the homeless.

Todd, Reggie. "$500 Million for Homeless Pushed by House Group." Nation's Cities Weekly, January 19, 1987:4.
    The author summarizes efforts to pass the Urgent Relief for the Homeless Act of 1987, and how the funds will be spent if the bill is passed.

Todd, Reggie. "Funds for Homeless Raised." Nation's Cities Weekly, August 13, 1984:1,10.
    This article reports on a 1984 supplemental appropriations bill which includes $120 million for the Emergency Food and Shelter Program administered by the Federal Emergency Management Agency.

Toelle, Miriam E., and Sheila Kerwin. "Children in Transition." <u>Children Today</u>, September-October 1988:27-31.

The Salvation Army Playschool and Home Visiting Program attempts to provide "a safe, protective, nurturing and supportive environment" for homeless children on a temporary basis.

Toner, Robin. "Americans Favor Aid for Homeless." <u>New York Times</u>, January 22, 1989:1, 20.

A telephone poll of 1,533 people indicates that 65 percent support increased federal spending for the homeless, and that 51 percent personally see homeless persons as compared to 36 percent three years earlier. The author also reports the percentages of the sample who blame the cause of homelessness on the Reagan Administration, alcohol and drug abuse, deinstitutionalization, and the homeless themselves. Males are more likely than females to place the blame on the homeless themselves, and blacks more likely than whites to blame the Reagan Administration.

Torrey, E. Fuller. "Finally, A Cure for the Homeless: But It Takes Some Strong Medicine." <u>The Washington Monthly</u>, <u>18</u>, September 1986:23-27.

In reviewing the history of deinstitutionalization, the author looks at individual cases of deinstitutionalized persons who have become homeless, as well as issues of political posturing, troll busting, and the juxtaposition of liberty and cruelty (individual rights versus partial conservatorship or guardianship). He urges the development of adequate community mental health services, which, in addition to the provision of medication, would provide low-cost housing, community mental health services, and "enough beds for patients in need of hospitalization." He concludes that the "shame of the states" of the 1940s (concentration camp-like treatment of patients in filth-infested back wards) has been replaced by today's "shame of the streets," and suggests that "it is time to require professionals (psychiatrists and psychologists) in the District (of Washington) to spend a small amount of time doing public service each month as a condition of license to practice."

Torrey, E. Fuller. <u>Nowhere to Go: The Tragic Odyssey of the Homeless Mentally Ill</u>. New York: Harper Collins, 1991.

The author analyzes the conceptual and political background that led to the elimination of 400,000 beds in mental hospitals and the dumping of mental patients onto the streets of the United States. Part of the author's thesis is that psychiatrists prefer to treat the "worried well" rather than more disturbed patients. He also presents a plan to improve services for the homeless mentally ill.

Torrey, E. Fuller. "Thirty Years of Shame: The Scandalous Neglect of the Mentally Ill Homeless." Policy Review, 48, Spring 1989:10-15.
The author chastises the mental health establishment for neglecting the mentally ill homeless. The solutions he proposes are to establish a clear division of responsibility between the federal and state governments, to block grant federal funds, to require pro bono work to retain licenses, and to allocate 5 percent of federal block grants for research on psychoses.

Town, Kenneth, and Ann G. Marchetti. The Impact of Homelessness on Atlanta. Atlanta: Research Atlanta, 1984.
After defining homelessness, the authors sketch a profile of Atlanta's homeless. They identify the mentally disabled, substance abusers, unemployed, ex-convicts, and victims of personal adversity. They also estimate the direct costs of homelessness in terms of shelter, food, and medical care, and indirect costs in terms of the criminal justice system being used to regulate the homeless. They recommend day shelter, housing, vocational training, and referral services.

Trasler, G., Percy E. Russell, H. R. Greville, A. W. Hunt, D. G. A. Low, and J. Dodd. "Specialized Hostels for Homeless Offenders." International Journal of Offender Therapy and Comparative Criminology, 16 (3), 1972:224-249.
To "assess the adequacy of existing accommodation for men and women discharged from prison," the authors sent questionnaires to the principal probation officers in southwest England. To estimate the frequency of homelessness, a representative sample of 174 offenders was interviewed at the time of their sentencing. Seventy-four prisoners thought that they would be homeless when they were released from prison. This expectation was higher among those who were homeless at the time of their arrest, the older, the unemployed, and those with longer criminal records. The authors review

the various types of hostels currently operating and make recommendations for establishing hostel communities for ex-prisoners.

Traub, James. "Jack Kemp Faces Reality." New York Times Magazine, May 7, 1989:38-39, 70-73, 99, 106.
    This article reviews the attitudes of Jack F. Kemp, the new Secretary of Housing and Urban Development, who has visited soup kitchens and listened to the complaints of the homeless.

Trench, Sally. Sally Trench's Book. New York: Stein and Day, 1968.
    This first-person account of work with London's homeless is written by a woman who considers her activities to be a ministry to Christ.

Tsunts, Mikhal. "Dropouts on the Run." Atlas, March 1966:158-160.
    The author reports on runaway youth ("runners") in Russia. The two causes of running away are vagabondage (the spirit of adventure) and paternal neglect.

Tucker, William. The Excluded Americans: Homelessness and Housing Policies. New York: Regnery Gateway, 1990.
    The author's thesis is that economic competition needs to operate in housing, for the lack of a free market creates homelessness. Such policies as rent control, originally designed to help the needy, have made many Americans worse off by artificially restricting the supply of housing. "The best strategy for improving the overall housing stock is to build new housing and let it circulate." By circulation of housing, the author means that people move into better housing as their circumstances improve, making the housing they vacate available for persons who are less well off. Homelessness that is caused by deinstitutionalization needs to be addressed by special housing.

Tucker, William. "How Housing Regulations Can Cause Homelessness." The Public Interest, 102, Winter 1991:78-88.
    Neither the argument of the liberals, that homelessness is caused by the lack of government effort and compassion, nor that of the conservatives, that either the problem is no worse than it ever was or that personal failings (insanity, addiction) make it impossible for some people to find housing even when it is available

holds up. Federal low-income assistance increased between 1980 and 1988, and even winos and stumblebums were able to find minimal housing in the past. The problem is the housing supply, which has tightened in many cities. At the root of the tight housing supply lie no-growth ordinances and rent control. Because skid row plays a significant role in providing cheap housing, let us not be deceived by "city planners and visionary architects who would 'tear down the slums' and replace them with 'model tenements' and the 'garden cities of tomorrow'....But let us do things in stages. Let us build the new housing first--and only then tear down the old 'substandard' housing that is no longer needed. If we let the best become the enemy of the good--or even the barely adequate--the homeless will have nothing more substantial to live in than the dreams of the housing visionaries themselves."

Tucker, William. "Rent Control As a Cause of Homeless-ness." New York Times, November 14, 1987:15.
     Contrary to common assumptions, the cutbacks in federal housing programs are not a cause of homelessness. Because there is a long pipeline in appropriations and the construction of public housing, the amount of new federal housing actually rose from 10,000 annually between 1977 and 1980 to 28,000 annually between 1981 and 1986. Neither can unemployment and poverty rates explain homelessness, for there is no correlation between homelessness rates and either high rates of poverty or unemployment." It is the same with the availability of public housing. Rental vacancy rates, however, do show high correlation with homelessness, and the largest correlation is with rent control. The nine rent-con-trolled cities rank among the top 17 cities for per capita homelessness. "Cities with rent controls had, on average, two and a half times as many homeless people as cities without them....The following picture of the nation's homeless problem can be drawn. There is a hard core of homeless people in every city--about 3 residents per 1,000. These people--victims of unemployment, poverty, alcoholism, drugs, family break-ups--obviously need help. Truly pathological homelessness does not emerge, however, until cities impose rent control. Then homelessness rises about 250 percent. The author bases his conclusions on "estimates of per capita homeless populations in 50 cities, drawn mostly from a federal report on the homeless." Rent controls, says the author, "stymie the natural development of the housing market."

Tucker, William. "Scapegoating Rent Control: A Reply." Journal of the American Planning Association, <u>57</u> (4), Autumn 1991:485-489.
The author's thesis is that high housing prices, rent control, and high rates of homelessness occur together. He supports this thesis with findings from 50 cities--the nine with rent control have the lowest vacancy rates, all below 3 percent, while in none of the cities without rent control do vacancy rates fall below 4 percent.

Tucker, William. "Where do the Homeless Come From?" National Review, September 25, 1987:32-43.
The author argues that a city's rate of homelessness has little relationship to its supply of public housing, its degree of poverty or unemployment, or the size and availability of private housing. Using regression analysis, the author concludes that the amount of homelessness in a city is most powerfully related to rent control.

Tully, Jim. <u>Beggars of Life: A Hobo Autobiography</u>. New York: Grosset and Dunlap, 1924.
The author of this first-person account of hobo life in the early 1900s wrote at least six books and many short stories and articles about his hoboing experiences.

Tully, Jim. "Bull Horrors." <u>American Mercury</u>, <u>12</u>, October 1927:144-150.
The author writes about meeting another vagrant in a box car on the way to Fort Worth. This vagrant pulled a gun on the conductor, shot cocaine, and talked about his work in the circus.

Tully, Jim. <u>Circus Parade</u>. New York: The Literary Guild of America, 1927.
A former hobo recounts his life in the circus.

Tully, Jim. <u>Jarnegan</u>. New York: Albert and Charles Boni, 1926.
This novel about the experiences of a tramp was written by a former hobo.

Tully, Jim. "The Lion-Tamer." <u>American Mercury</u>, <u>6</u>, October 1925:142-146.
After riding the rods in the South, the author took a job in the circus. In this account he discusses "trailers," "men who follow circuses or anything else

that draws a crowd," concluding with the mauling death of a lion tamer.

Tully, Jim. <u>Shadows of Men</u>. Garden City: Doubleday, Doran, 1930.
This first-person account of hobo life in the early 1900s contains an account of "jungle justice" (kangaroo court).

Tully, Jim. "Thieves and Vagabonds." <u>American Mercury</u>, <u>14</u>, May 1928:18-24.
This short story of a quarrel between hobos gathered in a jail on a cold winter night includes the revelation that one of the vagabonds is a girl.

Turner, Wallace. "On the First Skid Row, Clash Over Efforts to He..." <u>New York Times</u>, December 2, 1986:9.
The author discusses how the homeless no longer fit into their traditional habitat, the skid road of Seattle, since it has been gentrified and "turned into a sparkling complex of restaurants, and antique stores, art galleries, offices, and specialty shops for expensive merchandise." He recounts negative reactions to the presence of the homeless and to a social policy that provides $314 a month for each homeless person but does not prohibit begging and urinating on the streets. This reaction includes the statement by a police officer who said, "I think we ought to keep the pressure on to encourage them to go somewhere else. If we provide 400 new beds, we get 400 new tramps." The article includes a map of Seattle's skid road area.

Tutunjian, Beth Ann. "An Annotated Publications List on Homelessness." Rockville, Maryland: U.S. Department of Health and Human Services, June 1990.
This annotated bibliography of nineteen items on homeless alcoholics is sponsored by the National Institute on Alcohol Abuse and Alcoholism.

Tygiel, Jules. "Tramping Artisans: Carpenters in Industrial America, 1880-90." In <u>Walking to Work: Tramps in America, 1790-1935</u>, Eric H. Monkkonen, ed. Lincoln: University of Nebraska Press, 1984:87-117.
The author focuses on carpenters who moved about due to market conditions, unemployment, seasonal work, westward expansion, urban growth, and the changing technology of carpentry, all of which created a flow of

carpenters in and out of cities and from one region of the country to another.

U

Unger, Arthur. "Comedians Plan 3-Hour TV Benefit for Homeless." The Christian Science Monitor, March 27, 1986:23.
Major comedians appear in "Comic Relief," a television special intended to recruit new subscribers to Home Box Office and to raise funds for the homeless. The funds are to be disbursed to Health Care for the Homeless projects in 18 major U.S. cities.

Unger, Henry. "Pregerson's Shelter Plan Coolly Received." Los Angeles Daily Journal, 100, January 29, 1987:24.
A federal appeals court judge proposed that the Los Angeles federal courthouse be used to provide night emergency shelter for the homeless. Reactions to this proposal have been mostly negative.

V

Valentine, Charles A. "The 'Culture of Poverty': Its Scientific Significance and Its Implications for Action." In The Culture of Poverty: A Critique, Eleanor Burke Leacock, ed. New York: Simon and Schuster, 1971:193-225.
The author's goals are to review the "entire complex" of the concept of the culture of poverty, to refute it, and to provide alternative explanations for Oscar Lewis's conclusions. He also discusses social policy implications of accepting or rejecting this concept.

Van Swol, Erwin. "The Hoboes' Secret Code." Coronet, 48, August 1960:35-38.
There are three types of hoboes: ambulatory workers, dreamers, and drinkers. The causes of people becoming hobos are seasonal work and unemployment; the inability to hold a job due to low mentality, restlessness, physical handicaps, drug or alcohol addiction, advancing years, or personality defects; personal crises; discrimination by race, creed, or color; and wanderlust. The

author illustrates and explains 21 written signs that hobos use, as well as several non-written signs.

VanderKooi, Ronald C. "The Main Stem: Skid Row Revisited." Society, 10, September-October 1973:64-71.
    After giving a brief history of skid row, the author examines how urban renewal is threatening to displace skid row. He also discusses hobo jungles, bum wagons, jack-rollers, cage hotels, and the racial prejudice of old timers.

VanderKooi, Ronald C. Relocating West Madison "Skid Row" Residents: A Study of the Problem, with Recommendations. Chicago: Chicago Department of Urban Renewal, 1967.
    Based on interviews with 210 skid rowers, the author contrasts the skid row men's perceptions of their problems with those of the public. He concludes that men on skid row who are threatened by urban renewal need to be relocated to a "half-way community" in which they would have access to upgraded versions of the functional facilities provided by skid row.

VanderKooi, Ronald C. Skid Row and Its Men: An Exploration of Social Structure, Behavior and Attitudes. East Lansing: Technical Bulletin B-39, Michigan State University, August 1963.
    Based on participant observation and interviewing, the author reports the demographic characteristics of residents of Chicago's skid row: age, employment, education, marital status, religion, voting patterns, leisure, time, and length of residence on skid row. He also poses their alienation and normlessness as a challenge to community developers.

Veblen, T. B. "The Army of the Commonweal." Journal of Political Economy, 2, June 1894:456-461.
    The author argues that the assumption of the "Army of the Commonweal"--that the state owes a livelihood to men and that this can be accomplished by the "creation of capital through the creation of fiat money"--is economic nonsense and a radical departure of basic assumptions of American society.

Velie, Lester. "The Americans Nobody Wants." Colliers, 125, April 1, 1950:13-15, 48-50 and April 8, 1950:27, 54-57.
    Across the country, farm workers are being displaced by machinery and small farmers dislodged by huge farmers

who employ seasonal labor. The author reviews the mechanization of farm work and details the miserable conditions of 200,000 displaced farmers who have settled in the San Joaquin Valley. Displaced and seasonal workers are denied the benefits of minimum wage, Social Security, and unions. He then contrasts two solutions: the cooperation of federal, state, and local governments in providing food, medical, and housing assistance versus the unionization of farm workers and the development of new industries.

Vergare, Michael J., and A. Anthony Arce. "Homeless Adult Individuals and Their Shelter Network." In The Mental Health Needs of Homeless Persons, Ellen L. Bassuk, ed. San Francisco: Jossey-Bass, 1986:15-26.
    The authors stress the mental health needs of the homeless and suggests that the homeless be provided appropriate psychiatric care.

Verhovek, Sam Howe. "For Shelter, Homeless Take the E Train." New York Times, November 21, 1988:1, 12.
    This account of homeless people who have developed regular subway rounds for sleeping includes statements by the homeless as to why they prefer sleeping on subways than to go to New York City's shelters, the "shake wake" activities of conductors, and reactions of passengers to the homeless.

Verhovek, Sam Howe. "Village Creates Housing for the Desperate Elderly." New York Times, August 31, 1987:15.
    Using funds from the state's Homeless Housing Assistance Program, the citizens of Churubusco, New York, express pride in their construction of eight units of permanent housing for the town's homeless.

Verson, Gregory R. "Generous Welfare? How's $7 a Day?' Wall Street Journal, February 14, 1992:A11.
    In this letter to the editor, the author takes issue with an editorial in this paper that he says blames the victim for being homeless.

Vincent, Henry. The Story of the Commonweal. Chicago: W. B. Conkey, 1894. (Reprinted by Arno Press and the New York Times, 1969.)
    The author, a participant in the events he describes, presents an overview of the industrial armies of 1894, commonly known as Coxey's Army or Coxeyism. He provides a detailed account of the unemployed, who were

led by Coxey, Frye, and Kelly, in their march on Washington to demand employment in building highways. The book contains not only details of the march and its opposition, but also backgrounds on the principles and historical photos.

Vladeck, Bruce C. "Health Care and the Homeless: A Political Parable for Our Time." Journal of Health Politics, Policy and Law, 15 (2), Summer 1990:305-317.
     The author, chair of the Committee on Health Care for Homeless People of the Institute of Medicine, concludes that the health status of homeless persons is not significantly worse than that of other low-income persons. The Stewart B. McKinney Act of 1987 "demonstrates how, in contemporary American politics, there can be widespread political consensus not only about a problem but about solutions, while the resulting policy actions are largely symbolic."

Vliet, Anita van de. "Bristol: Western Prospect." Management Today, November 1988:98-105.
     The author's analysis of the stability and growth of Bristol, England, mentions a darker side--that applications from homeless people to housing authorities doubled from the previous year.

Vliet, Willem van. "The Limits of Social Research." Society, May-June 1989:16-20.
     The author's thesis is that an industry has sprung up around the homeless. "Homelessness...has...become a sustaining element in academic infrastructure. Annual conventions of many social science disciplines now almost routinely feature sessions on homelessness. Special symposia are convened, and private foundations and the government fund research on homelessness. Instructors incorporate homelessness into class projects. Many reports are written--and shelved. The same is true of the publication of books. Journals include countless articles on the topic. He concludes that "one has to wonder about the marginal contribution that additional research makes to solving the problem....Additional research would appear to bear little weight. The real struggle is in the economic and political arena."

Vogel, Ed. "Reid Poses As Indigent." Las Vegas Review-Journal, February 13, 1987:A1.
     Harry Reid, a Nevada senator, announced that he had posed as a homeless person in Las Vegas "to learn more

about the problems of the poor and unemployed." He
reports that the "main topics of conversation were
finding work, food, and shelter." He proposes postcard
voter registration for the homeless and a federal
"depression-style Civilian Conservation Corps program to
provide jobs for all people who want to work."

Vorse, Mary Heaton.   "America's Submerged Class: The
Migrants." Harper's Magazine, 206, February 1953:86-93.
     The author discusses the harsh working and living
conditions of migrant workers.   As solutions, she
proposes public concern, legislation, and tightening our
border with Mexico.

Vuyst, Alex.   "Self-help for the Homeless: How Habitat
for Humanity Converts Human Capital into Affordable
Housing." The Humanist, May-June 1989:13, 49.
     The author discusses the purpose and work of Habitat
for Humanity International, "an ecumenical Christian
housing organization."

W

Wade, C. C.   "Survey of Inmates of a Common Lodging
House." Medical Officer, 109, 1963:171-173.
     After providing a brief history of how "wanderers"
were previously cared for in Great Britain, the author
reports on a 1958-1959 survey of 41 people in Dundee's
(Scotland) last common lodging house. Five types of
homeless are listed: (1) the working single man; (2) the
retired; (3) those who imagined themselves to be or were,
in fact, too ill to work; (4) those who were temporarily
out of work, and (5) those who did not enjoy working. He
concludes by asking what social policy could be developed
to rehabilitate these people.

Wade, Richard C.   The Urban Frontier: The Rise of Western
Cities, 1790-1830. Cambridge: Harvard University Press,
1959.
     This account of social change covers the inflation-
ary spiral following the War of 1812 and the resulting
depression. It contains limited material on homelessness
and soup lines.

Wagner, Lynn.   "Offering Care to the Poorest of the Poor."   Modern Healthcare, 18, December 23, 1988:24-26, 30.
     The author reports on various health outreach efforts to street people, including St. Vincent's Hospital and Medical Center of New York and the Health Care for the Homeless program run by Travelers and Immigrants Aid of Chicago.

Wainwright, Loudon.   "Charity Begins with the Homeless." Life, 6, February 1983:7.
     The increase in homelessness is a good reason for us to rethink our ideas of charity.   "With the rise of the welfare state and the diminution of church influence over daily life, governments accepted the bulk of the charita-ble load as an obligation of the enlightened society." But the private person wound up still further from the people that he paid taxes to help.   The author cites examples of private efforts to help the homeless.

Walker, Deborah Klein.   Runaway Youth: An Annotated Bibliography and Literature Overview. Washington, D.C.: Department of Health, Education, and Welfare, Government Printing Office, May 1975.
     This overview of the literature on runaway youth contains 122 annotated references from the scholarly literature and a listing of 34 articles from popular sources.

Walker, Lee.   "HUD's Administration of the McKinney Act: A Problem in State-Federal Relations." Journal of State Government, 63 (1), January-March 1990:15-23.
     A survey of governors' offices shows that most feel that federal programs for the homeless are inadequate, and a survey of community affairs agencies found wide-spread sentiment that the policy of Housing and Urban Development toward religious groups is cumbersome.   Many also feel that the distribution of federal funds between rural and urban areas is inequitable.

Wallace, Samuel E.   "The Road to Skid Row." Social Problems, 16 (1), Summer 1968:92-105.
     The author identifies the process by which men become members of skid row, "that familiar aggregate of flop houses, bars, cheap restaurants, second-hand stores, pawnshops, and missions (that has existed) as a distinct ecological area of almost every major American city since the close of the Civil War." Four phases are involved in

this process: (1) dislocation from the basic social network of society accompanied by a sense of worthlessness, (2) exposure to skid row subculture, accompanied by isolation and desocialization, (3) regular participation in skid row institutions, and (4) integration into the skid row community. He also analyzes how "heavy drinking on skid row is a product of group norms rather than the result of individual, addictive craving for alcohol." Skid row is characterized by six statuses: (1) drunks, (2) alcoholics, (3) hobos, (4) beggars, (5) mission stiffs, and (6) tour directors--the wanderers, the dreamers, and the disenchanted who take as their responsibility the entertainment of all visitors to skid row-- tourists and researchers alike.

Wallace, Samuel E. <u>Skid Row as a Way of Life</u>. Totowa, N.J.: The Bedminster Press, 1965.
     The author provides a history of homelessness in Great Britain and of skid row in the United States, and, based on participant observation and interviewing, analyzes skid row as a deviant community. He also provides an inside view of the men's coping, their attitudes, and values, and documents three routes to homelessness: migratory occupations; war, depression, and natural disasters; and aficionados (wanderers, alcoholics, and petty criminals). He also contrasts isolation from society versus attachment to the skid row community.

Wallich-Clifford, Anton. <u>Caring on Skid Row: A Study of Grassroots Caring with the Homeless and Rootless</u>. Dublin: Veritas Publications, 1976.
     The author discusses the philosophy, principles, and work of the Simon Community in Great Britain.

Walsh, J. "Are City Shelters Open Asylums?" <u>In These Times</u>, January 23-29, 1985:3, 22.
     After surveying the history of deinstitutionalization, the author declares that community-based care of the mentally ill is a failure.

Walters, Tommye. "Who Lives on These Mean Streets?" <u>Southern Illinois University Alumnus</u>, Winter 1986:22-23.
     This article reports on the experiences of a participant observer of the homeless, his travels to a dozen skid rows in the United States and Canada, and his conclusions about the types of homeless who live on the streets.

Walton, R. Christopher. "Surviving the Ultimate Crisis."
Fund Raising Management, 22 (4), June 1991:24-28.
The author chronicles the success of Covenant House,
an organization for homeless street children, in maintaining its huge fund raising in spite of the resignation
of its founder, Bruce Ritter, who left amidst charges of
child molestation.

Warburton, Jean. "Intentional Homelessness." Solicitor's Journal, 126, December 3, 1982:193-195.
In attempting to clarify what intentional homelessness means in light of the Housing (Homeless Persons) Act
of 1977, the author reviews the statutory definition of
intentional homelessness, and the need of local authorities to consider the general housing conditions of the
area, particular factual situations, rent arrears, bad
housing conditions, nuisance, family difficulties, coming
from abroad, and being threatened or served with notice
to quit. From the cases that he reviews, the author
concludes that the "concept of intentional homelessness
is far from clearly defined," and that "recent cases show
a disturbing tendency to spread the net of intentional
homelessness wide."

Warburton, Jean. "Intentional Homelessness: The Present
State of the Law." Solicitor's Journal, 129, September
6, 1985:612-614.
To update his 1982 article on intentional homelessness in the same journal, the author reviews more recent
cases. He again concludes that the "concept of intentional homelessness is still far from clearly
defined...largely because the courts refuse to interfere
with local authority's decisions."

Warner, Amos Griswold. American Charities: A Study in
Philanthropy and Economics. New York: Thomas Y. Crowell,
1894. (Reprinted in 1971 by Arno Press and the New York
Times.)
This book contains a chapter on "The Unemployed and
the Homeless Poor." The four usual ways of dealing with
the homeless poor are sending them on, punishing them,
giving to them, and using municipal lodging houses and
work tests. There are two basic types of homeless poor:
the incapable and the able. The proper solution is to
deal with them by type--for the habitual vagrant, to give
indeterminate sentences to houses of correction, where
they should remain at hard labor until they show evidence

of reformation; to assign the young, sick, aged, and otherwise incapable to specialized institutions.

Warner, Amos Griswold. "Our Charities and Our Churches." Proceedings of the National Council on Charities and Correction, 1889:36-41.
After presenting an overview of religious attitudes toward charity, the author suggests that charities should be better organized and should stress education.

Warner, Amos Griswold, Stuart Alfred Queen, and Ernest Bouldin Harper. "The Unemployed and the Homeless Poor." In American Charities and Social Work. Fourth edition. New York: Thomas Y. Crowell, 1930:113-122.
The authors analyze four distinctive ways in which various American communities "have tried to deal with the homeless and wandering poor:" (1) passing on (sending them on their way), (2) imprisonment, (3) indiscriminate relief, and (4) improved methods ("an institution or place where the work-test can be rigidly applied, and where a man can earn his support pending an investigation of his case," including "facilities for giving meals and lodgings...and for bathing and disinfecting clothing...and some person to investigate the case of each applicant thoroughly, and to act as circumstances require."

Warner, Richard. "Deinstitutionalization: How Did We Get Where We Are?" Journal of Social issues, 45 (3), Fall 1989:17-30.
The author's thesis is that the deinstitutionaliza-tion of the mentally ill, many of whom are now homeless or in jail, did not come about, as is commonly thought, because of the introduction of antipsychotic drugs, but, in some countries, because of the desire to reduce costs, and, in others, due to the postwar demand for labor.

Warner, Roger. "Riding the Rails." Washington Post, January 25, 1976:F3-F4. (Originally appeared in Smithso-nian, December 1975.)
The author gives an historical overview of riding the freights in the United States.

Washbrook, R. A. "The Homeless Offender: An English Study of 200 Cases." International Journal of Offender Therapy, 14 (3), 1970:176-184.
Using the records of inmates of a prison in Birming-ham and a detention center in Swinfen Hall, the author

details their geographical distribution, home life, delinquency, IQ, and mental illnesses. He reports that closer cooperation between mental welfare officers and prisons is needed, as well as more effective aftercare, and research into the psychopathology of offenders and the effects of prison. The author stresses the basic human needs of belonging and security.

Washington, Harold. "Renewal of the Federal Commitment." Journal of Housing, 44, January-February 1987:7, 10-11.
    After noting that the federal government has moved away from the Great Society's goal of providing "a decent home and a suitable living environment for all Americans," the author reviews efforts to prevent homelessness in Chicago. These efforts include a computerized "early warning system" to identify problem buildings so that the city can intervene in the "cycle of disinvestment, abandonment, and eventual demolition."

Waters, Rob. Trickle Down Tragedy: Homelessness in California. Sacramento: The California Homeless Coalition, 1984. (Reprinted in Homelessness in America--II, Hearing Before the Subcommittee on Housing and Community Development of the Committee on Banking, Finance and Urban Affairs, House of Representatives, Washington, D.C.: U.S. Government Printing Office, 1984: 943-987.)
    As the author examines the housing crisis, welfare policies, deinstitutionalization, and the effects of laws, with a focus on Alameda County, Los Angeles, San Diego, San Jose, San Francisco, and Santa Barbara, he identifies eight types of homeless: new poor, separated parents with children, the chronically unemployed young, mentally disturbed, substance abusers, safety net dropthroughs, youth, and Vietnam veterans.

Waters, Theodore. "Six Weeks in Beggardom." Everybody's Magazine, 12, January 1905:69-78.
    A mission worker on the Bowery reports on his participant observation of beggars. He focuses on their life style, culture, techniques, jargon, living conditions, and non-begging activities. There are two types of beggars: the worthy (people in genuine need) and professionals (frauds). The solutions are: first, no private giving, as this only perpetuates begging; and, second, to establish a bureau of succor in each city.

Watson, Frank Dekker. The Charity Organization Movement in the United States: A Study in American Philanthropy. New York: Macmillan, 1922.
This account of the history of charity in the United States contains material on how vagrants and beggars were dealt with by charity organizations between 1896-1904.

Watson, Sophie, and Helen Austerberry. Housing and Homelessness: A Feminist Perspective. London: Routledge and Kegan Paul, 1986.
The authors base their findings on interviews with 160 single homeless women in London. In the first part of the book, they focus on definitions of homelessness, homeless women, and the marginalization of single households. In the second part, they examine the experiences of the women in their sample--their definitions of homelessness, housing histories, participation in the labor market, and housing preferences. The authors conclude that the elusiveness of the definition of homelessness and its narrow usage by politicians and others contribute to the invisibility of homelessness among single women.

Wattenburg, William W. "Boys Who Run Away from Home." Journal of Educational Psychology, 47, 1956:335-343.
Based on records of 575 runaway boys who came to the attention of the Detroit Police Department, the author finds that 15 is the peak age for running away, with the primary motivations of the boys the search for adventure and rebellion against parents.

Waxman, Laura DeKoven, and Lilia M. Reyes. The Growth of Hunger, Homelessness and Poverty in America's Cities in 1985: A 25 City Survey. Washington, D.C.: U.S. Conference of Mayors, January, 1986.
This report surveys the demand for emergency food assistance, extent and demographics of the homeless population, the availability of shelter and other services, the persistence of hunger and homelessness, the pertinent economic conditions, and the outlook for these problems in 1986. The cities covered are the 25 cities whose mayors are members of the Task Force on Hunger and Homelessness of the U.S. Conference of Mayors: Boston, Denver, Louisville, Kansas City, San Antonio, Portland, San Juan, Salt Lake City, San Francisco, Minneapolis, Nashville, Phoenix, Philadelphia, Trenton, St. Paul, Yonkers, Hartford, New Orleans, Charleston, Seattle, Cleveland, Chicago, Detroit, New York City, and Washing-

ton, D.C. The report paints a bleak picture of growing homelessness and hunger.

Wayland, Francis. "The Tramp Question." Proceedings of the Conference of Boards of Public Charities, 1877:111-126.
    Tramps are dangerous: about 40 percent are criminals; only about 6 percent are honest wayfarers. The solution is to establish a board of managers for each district to supervise workhouses in which both vagrants and officers shall be separated by sex.

Weaver, James B. "The Commonweal Crusade." Midland Monthly, 1, June 1894:590-594.
    The army of organized, unemployed, homeless men marching on Washington represents "millions of hungry, poverty-stricken people." They personify the wage-slaves who have had the door of opportunity closed to them, who have been "plunged into conditions of servitude from which there seems to be no escape." Their appeal is not selfish, but is "a protest against wrongs which have become quite universal and intolerable." Although the ballot-box is the proper solution, the country may be facing "scenes of violent disorder." The author concludes that "if Congress and state legislatures will at once come forward with conservative, remedial legislation, the whole matter can be healed in short order. If we thrust it aside it must be at our own peril, for the situation will not await our convenience."

Webb, John N. The Migratory-Casual Worker. New York: Da Capo Press, 1971. (First published in 1937.)
    Based on interviews with 500 casual (seasonal) workers in 13 cities, the author reports on patterns of migration, employment history, age, ethnicity, wanderlust, occupational and physical deterioration, attitudes toward relief, and politics. No immediate solution is seen, but steps in the right direction include employment offices, unemployment insurance, unionization, and public works projects.

Webb, John N. The Transient Unemployed: A Description and Analysis of the Transient Relief Population. Washington, D.C.: Works Progress Administration, 1935.
    This history of the Transient Relief Program of the Federal Emergency Relief Act of 1933 summarizes the background characteristics of 25,000 unattached transients and 1,900 transient families in 13 cities. The

main cause of their condition is migration because of the depression unemployment. The primary solution is an economic recovery that will provide jobs.

Weber, Bruce. "Woman Thrown From Subway, Police Say." <u>New York Times</u>, February 18, 1992:B3.
 Tracy Washington, identified as a homeless man, is accused of killing Sonya Smalls by throwing her from a moving subway train.

Wechsler, Philip. "Police Finding Suspects in Shelter." <u>New York Times</u>, January 26, 1992:NJ9.
 Because many criminal suspects, including those for whom there are arrest warrants, take shelter at the Atlantic City Rescue Mission, the police make a daily sweep of this facility for the homeless.

Weil, Tom. "Annual Hobo Convention Is Iowa's August Attraction." <u>St. Louis Post-Dispatch</u>, July 10, 1983.
 The author gives a brief history of the annual hobo convention held in Britt, Iowa, and mentions the competition for king and queen.

Wein, B. <u>The Runaway Generation</u>. New York: David McKay, 1970.
 The author has written a sympathetic overview of runaways who settled in Greenwich Village in the late 1960s, with analytical excursions to other areas of the country. The book contains a copy of the interview schedule.

Weinraub, Bernard. "Senate Action Asked on $400 Million Bill To Aid the Homeless." <u>New York Times</u>, March 25, 1987:1, 12.
 A bill to appropriate $400 million to provide aid for the homeless has raised controversy. A feature of the bill is "a guarantee that all homeless children are eligible for any educational program to which they are entitled regardless of whether or not they have a fixed address."

Weinreb, J., and R. Counts. "Impulsivity in Adolescents and Its Therapeutic Management." <u>Archives of General Psychiatry</u>, <u>2</u>, 1960:548-558.
 Because impulsive, acting-out adolescents make difficult subjects for therapy, the authors recommend early interpretation of deep conflictual issues. This early step needs to be followed up with constant strength

and help. The authors present two case studies of therapy with runaway youths.

Weinreb, Linda F., and Ellen L. Bassuk. "Substance Abuse: A Growing Problem Among Homeless Families." Family and Community Health, 13 (1), May 1990:55-64.
　　The authors detail problems of substance abuse among homeless families and propose social policies to deal with the problem.

Weinstein, Jerome I. "Homesteading: A Solution For the Homeless?" Journal of Housing, May-June 1990:125-126.
　　This overview of the Section 810 program of the federal government reviews self help, rehabilitation, property subsidies, and legal issues and resources involved in using homesteading as a tool to help house the homeless. The author's thesis is that "The Federal Homesteading Program for the 1990s should bring together the problems of abandoned properties and homeless, impacted (overcrowded), working, or otherwise income-stable families, and reach more of a spectrum of the needy than any current programs can. The current program, despite its limitations, provides a network of 130 cities with experienced, capable local urban home-steading agencies. When provided with the authority, the mechanisms, and appropriate state and local resources, they can be the force to house people. To do so, it is necessary for these agencies to focus on the vacant property within their jurisdictions."

Weisman, Steven R. "Japan's Homeless: Seen Yet Ignored." New York Times, January 19, 1991:A4.
　　The homeless in Japan are ignored, a crude embar-rassment in a country that trumpets its economic advance-ments.

Weiss, Stefanie. "No Place Called Home." NEA Today, 7, September 1988:10-11.
　　In emphasizing the educational needs of homeless children, the author focuses on the "School with No Name," a "20-foot-square classroom" that has saved the children of families who live in the city shelter in Salt Lake City.

Weitzman, Beth C., James R. Knickman, and Marybeth Shinn. "Pathways to Homelessness Among New York City Families." Journal of Social Issues, 46 (4), 1990:125-140.

Using a sample of 482 New York City families who were new entrants to homelessness during the first six months of 1988 and a comparison sample of 524 families drawn from the public assistance roles, the authors attempt to determine the root cause of homelessness of families. They conclude that "homeless families do not comprise a monolithic and homogeneous population, but instead follow at least three distinct pathways to the shelter door." The first is a rapid route to homelessness by those who have been in stable housing situations; the second is a slow path to homelessness that comes from a housing situation growing ever more marginal; the third does not develop from stable and independent housing but comes to those for whom doubling up with others had been a permanent and ongoing way of life. The solutions to homelessness must vary according to the pathway taken. If effective policies are to be developed, they "must be made specific to the needs of these families."

Welford, Heather. "A Welcome for the Homeless." New York Times Educational Supplement, January 20, 1989:20.
    The author discusses the problems of educating homeless children.

Wells, Ken. "A Welfare Program Offering Bunk, Food Stirs Up Sacramento." Wall Street Journal, March 30, 1983:1, 19.
    At the Bannon Street facility in Sacramento, California, an experiment is being conducted to cut welfare costs by offering aid-in-kind. A bunk and meals are offered for those who "pay their keep" by working for the county seven days a month. Husbands stay in one dorm, wives in another. Critics claim that it is the first poorhouse in the United States in five decades, that it stigmatizes the poor and violates their privacy and dignity. Its supporters reply that the average stay at Bannon Street is 22 days, while the average grant recipient spends 60 days on the welfare rolls. They add that rather than moving into the Bannon Street facility, 300 to 400 persons a month refuse general assistance. The decline in the overall general-assistance rolls since the program began saves the county between $50,000 and $100,000 a month.

Werner, Frances E. "Homelessness: A Litigation Roundup." Clearinghouse Review, March 1985:1254-1268.
    The author summarizes cases brought before the courts on behalf of the homeless. Primacy is given to

cases in New York, West Virginia, New Jersey, Connecticut, California, Illinois, and California. The cases are clustered into four areas: (1) breaking down barriers erected by local governments to give assistance, (2) establishing the right of the homeless to sufficient and adequate shelter, (3) establishing the right of the homeless to be free from arbitrary eviction from shelters, and, (4) ensuring the right of shelter providers to establish and operate shelters. Also covered are the right of the homeless mentally ill to community-based residences, disenfranchisement of the homeless, and keeping homeless families together.

Werner, Frances E. "On the Streets: Homelessness Causes and Solutions." Clearinghouse Review, May 1984:11-16.
   Based on a "distillation" of the statements made by witnesses during a one-day hearing before the House Subcommittee on Housing and Community Development, the author profiles the homeless population (numbers, places, age), causes of homelessness (multicausation, including a "decrease in affordable housing, the deinstitutionalization of the chronically mentally ill, cutbacks in social service programs, more stringent administration of disability programs, high unemployment rates, and the breakdown of traditional social structures"), responses of local governments ("from repressive to minimal"), and solutions ("that Congress legislate a federal right to shelter and that decent shelter be considered a fundamental right of every citizen").

Werner, Frances E., and David B. Bryson. "A Guide to the Preservation and Maintenance of Single Room Occupancy (SRO) Housing." Clearinghouse Review, April 1982:999-1009 and May 1982:1-25.
   The availability of SRO housing, so important to poor and elderly tenants, is threatened. Legal solutions are proposed for preserving affordability while maintaining habitability.

Wessel, David. "Counting the Homeless Will Tax the Ingenuity of 1990 Census Takers." Wall Street Journal, November 14, 1989:A1, A16.
   The author delineates efforts to make an accurate count of the homeless, a task the Census Bureau takes seriously as apportioning of the House of Representatives is based upon its count; so is the distribution of federal funds to states and cities.

West, W. T. "Construing the Housing (Homeless persons) Act 1977." The Solicitor's Journal, 124, May 23, 1980:351.
The author profiles Eilen Philomena Browne, a citizen of Eire, a homeless woman who sought an order of mandamus directing a housing authority to provide accommodation for her.

West, W. T. "Homeless Families--II." The Solicitor's Journal, 126, March 12, 1982:167-168.
In reviewing a case of alleged racial discrimination in determining intentional homelessness, the author stresses the "syntactic ambiguity" that makes it difficult for councils to interpret the meaning of intentional homelessness in the Housing (Homeless Persons) Act of 1977.

Weybright, Victor. "Rolling Stones Gather No Sympathy: From Covered Wagon to Jalopy." Survey Graphic, 28 (1), January 1939:29-30.
Although migration has been a key to the strength and development of the United States, current transients are discriminated against. Because transients lack legal residence, they are not allowed to vote or to receive relief. The problem is too great for individual communities to solve, and government action is needed, especially action by the federal government. The federal government ought to give grants-in-aid to local communities, possibly through an amendment to the Social Security Act. There is "a vast national obligation to assist in the health, education, employment service, rehabilitation and retraining" of the uprooted homeless.

Wheelwright, Jeff. "The Homeless, at Suppertime." New York Times, December 16, 1987:27.
The author describes his experience as a volunteer with the Coalition for the Homeless in bringing food to the homeless who live at the Port Authority Bus Terminal in New York City. He makes a plea for people to develop a personal relationship with the homeless.

Wheen, Frances. "The Modern Workhouse." New Statesman, 99, April 18, 1980:584-585.
Although spikes are Great Britain's successors to workhouses, and supposedly an improvement, differences between them are sometimes indistinguishable. Life in Plawsworth Reception Centre, a spike near Durham, is like a prison. Camberwell, the most notorious spike, is to be

closed. The author mentions the Campaign for the Homeless and Rootless.

Whitaker, Charles. "What We Can Do About The Homeless." Ebony, 44, June 1989:96, 98, 100, 104.
     The only way to really get to know the homeless is to work with them. Beyond that, the individual can contribute by pressuring the government to provide more low-income housing.

Whitaker, Percy Walton. "Fruit Tramps." The Century Illustrated Monthly Magazine, 117, March 1929:599-606.
     The author describes his and his wife's experiences as fruit tramps, people who follow the harvesting season on the West Coast. He says that contrary to common assumption, being a fruit tramp is a profession, one that pays well and has the side benefit of enjoyable travel. He also discusses work in canneries and orchards.

Whitbeck, Les B., and Ronald L. Simons. "Life on the Streets: The Victimization of Runaway and Homeless Adolescents." Youth and Society, 22 (1), September 1990:108-125.
     Interviews with 44 female and 40 male adolescent runaways in a midwestern American city showed that for both males and females deviant peer group affiliation is associated with family abuse and that the more often a youth had run away the greater the likelihood of involvement in deviant behavior. The authors also contrast street experiences by gender.

White, Arnold. "The Nomad Poor of London." Contemporary Review, 47, May 1885:714-726.
     The author, who has met thousands of homeless people in the East End of London, concludes that poverty is destructive, that many of the homeless desire work, and that private and governmental action could alleviate much of this problem.

Whiteley, J. Stuart. "A Consideration of Methods in Approach to the Homeless in Society: A Proposal of a Therapeutic Community." Proceedings of the Royal Society of Medicine, 63 (5), 1970:446.
     The homeless are isolated people who have been unable to find a role in society. Past policies have focused on punitive suppression, welfare, social control, and medical intervention. Rather than specialist intervention, perhaps a long-standing therapeutic

community is the answer, one similar to the Paris
Communaute Emmaus Settlement founded by Abbe Pierre.

Whiting, William Alberti. <u>What the City of New York</u>
<u>Provides for the Homeless</u>. New York: Department of
Public Charities, 1915.
    The author provides a detailed overview of the
Municipal Lodging House in New York City.

Whitley, M. P., O. H. Osborne, M. A. Godfrey, and K.
Johnston. "A Point Prevalence Study of Alcoholism and
Mental Illness Among Downtown Migrants." <u>Social Science</u>
<u>Medicine</u>, <u>20</u> (6), 1985:579-583.
    Since deinstitutionalization, many discharged mental
patients live in downtown areas in large cities near an
established vagrant culture. Based on a point prevalence
study design, the authors found that these two groups,
the alcoholics and the homeless, are similar: They both
consist of predominately white males in their mid-
thirties. Forty percent have never married, while over
50 percent have only a high school education and possess
only low-level labor skills. Further study is called
for.

Whitman, Barbara Y., Pasquale Accardo, Mary Boyert, and
Rita Kendagor. "Homelessness and Cognitive Performance
in Children: A Possible Link." <u>Social Work</u>, <u>35</u> (6),
November 1990:516-519.
    A screening battery was used to measure cognitive
delays, language delays, and the emotional status of
homeless children. The results of testing 88 children
indicate that homelessness possibly affects cognitive and
language development, but does not cause "emotional
pathology." "At a system level, social workers have
data, experience, and resources to contribute to the
design of innovative service models that are both
educationally sound and system plausible while remaining
situation sensitive. At a personal level, the social
worker will need to assume a case management and advocacy
role with or for the family to enable these children to
stabilize their lives in the school environment."

Whitman, David. "Hope For The Homeless." <u>U.S. News &</u>
<u>World Report</u>, February 29, 1988:24-28, 31, 33-35.
    The author's thesis is: "to say that the homeless
need housing is a bit like saying the poor need money--
both statements are true, but neither ultimately does
much to eliminate the problem. What's now clear is that

if every homeless person were put in an affordable low-income apartment tomorrow, many would be back on the streets several weeks later. The reason, as study after study has shown, is that the homeless are different from other poor people in one crucial respect: They are profoundly alone." The author then reviews several innovative programs that he suggests can serve as models to rebuild the support network of homeless people.

Whitmer, Gary E. "From Hospitals to Jails: The Fate of California's Deinstitutionalized Mentally Ill." American Journal of Orthopsychiatry, 50 (1), January 1980:65-75.
    Deinstitutionalization has shifted many of the mentally ill from the mental health system to the criminal justice system. This occurred because the clinical needs of the deinstitutionalized were not anticipated, effective community mental health centers to meet those needs were not developed, and a change occurred in the concept of dangerousness. The idea of civil liberties versus treatment is a false dichotomy. The author uses the concept of the forfeited patient.

Whyte, William H. City: Rediscovering the Center. New York, Doubleday, 1988.
    Within a broader focus, the author analyzes various types of people who inhabit the city streets. In Chapter 3, he covers shopping bag ladies, and in Chapter 6, beggars who rummage through containers. In Chapter 10, he mentions the necessity of providing public rest rooms for the homeless.

Wickenden, Dorothy. "Abandoned Americans." New Republic, March 18, 1985:19-25.
    Major causes of homelessness are deinstitutionalization, a dwindling supply of low-cost housing, high unemployment, and tightening welfare benefits and eligibility. Controversy exists about the number of homeless, which is likely to run two to three million.

Wicker, Tom. "Why Another ABM?" New York Times, November 24, 1991:Section 4:17.
    The author protests the planned spending of $60 billion to build another land-based anti-missile defense system when the problem of homelessness has not been solved.

Wiener, Lynn. "Sisters of the Road: Women Transients and Tramps." In Walking to Work: Tramps in America, 1790-

1935, Eric H. Monkkonen, ed. Lincoln: University of Nebraska Press, 1984:171-188.

Although earlier periods are briefly covered, this overview of female tramps focuses on the 1920s and 1930s. The author highlights society's attitudes toward female tramps. The common characteristics of female tramps appear to include cross-dressing, movement in and out of the labor force, a propensity to hitchhike, and prostitution or sexual promiscuity.

Wilentz, Amy. "Cold Comfort for the Homeless." *Time*, 131, January 18, 1988:22.

The article mentions efforts in Chicago, Los Angeles, and Manhattan to keep the homeless from freezing.

Wilkerson, Isabel. "...As Clinics Treat Afflictions of Body and Soul." New York Times, February 16, 1984:A25.

The author examines the special problems of treating the homeless at clinics in New York City.

Wilkerson, Isabel. "As Farms Falter, Rural Homelessness Grows." New York Times, May 2, 1989:1, 8.

The economic crisis in farming is causing rural homelessness to grow. The rural homeless have a strong spirit of independence and self-reliance, and a deep pride that prevents many from admitting their plight and asking for help. The author's review of efforts in rural areas to meet the problem includes organizing a network of stable families with whom homeless people can stay for up to a month and locating shelters on farms in which the homeless can do rural chores.

Wilkerson, Isabel. "In Chicago, A Shanty Shelters An Aging Man and His Pride." New York Times, December 20, 1988:1, 10.

The author discusses people who prefer to live outside the shelters.

Wilkerson, Isabel. "Shift in Feelings on the Homeless: Empathy Turns Into Frustration." New York Times, September 2, 1991:1, 10.

In a review of the backlash against the homeless, the author focuses on New York City, Santa Barbara, Atlanta, Miami, and Washington, D.C. These "cities are acting out of both frustration and desperation, pressed by hard times and by a public that has grown increasingly impatient with a problem that has worsened despite the programs aimed at relieving it and previous shows of good will....in the second decade of widespread and obvious homelessness, people are experiencing a kind of compassion fatigue." Examples include arrests for panhandling, public drinking, and sleeping on public grounds. The intent is to make life uncomfortable for the homeless in order to force them to move on. For example, in Santa Barbara, California, the seats are removed in a downtown plaza so they will not "invite the homeless." The author concludes that the "homeless fad" is over.

Wilkinson, H. W. "Homeless Persons: The New Code of Guidance." New Law Journal, 133, November 25, 1983:1029-1032.
    The author reviews the 1983 modifications of the 1977 Housing (Homeless Persons) Act and concludes that the modifications made the Act "a bit friendlier." The issue of intentional homelessness is also discussed.

Will, Thomas E. "The Unemployed: A Symposium." The Arena, 10, October 1894:701-711.
    After reviewing the numbers of unemployed in Massachusetts in 1877-78, 1885, and 1893-94, the author addresses the question of why we have an unemployed army. He covers overpopulation, overproduction of well-to-do idlers, lack of capital, land monopolies, unequal distribution of wealth, wage competition, a defective medium of exchange, and monopoly of the machinery of production. Tramps, seeing that there are not enough jobs to go around in our present industrial organization, "have emancipated themselves both from love of work and fear of charity." Tramps are an "embodiment of the modern civic virtues... enterprise, philanthropy and capacity to look out for number one." In reality, tramps are part of our "leisured class."

Willard, Alice C. "Reinstatement of Vagrants Through Municipal Lodging Houses." Proceedings of the National Conference of Charities and Correction, Isabel C. Barrows, ed. May 6-12, 1903:404-411.
    With a focus on Chicago, the author identifies three types of vagrants: (1) unemployed workers, (2) unfortunate men in real need (including runaway boys and those who have been robbed), and (3) social parasites. The municipal lodging house has failed to solve the problem. The solutions are to segregate vagrants by type and treat them accordingly, to educate the public not to give outdoor relief, to establish a vagrancy police, to give

longer and indeterminate sentences, to offer no lodging in police stations, and to provide strict enforcement on railroads.

Willard, Eugene Bertram. "Psychopathic Vagrancy." Welfare Magazine, 19, May 1928:565-573.
    Because many homeless men are incapable of fulfilling the duties of the average citizen, they should not be held accountable for that failure. Many homeless men have average ability, but "give evidence of serious character defect in repeated lapses into mendacity and soup-lining and in their disappointing reactions to social, moral and judicial requirements." Many of the men "are hampered with a constitutional instability of the nerve system, which renders them impulsive, vehement, inhibitionless and emotional." Based on his observations of "bread-lining," the author concludes that "at least two-thirds" of homeless men are "clearly and unmistakably below par... suitable candidates for psychiatric examination." After reporting the findings of various studies, the author suggests that "there should be a closer union between the psychiatrists and the police."

Willard, Josiah Flynt.
    Willard, who wrote several books on the homeless, used the pseudonym of Josiah Flynt. His books are listed under his pseudonym.

Williams, Lena. "Urban League Hears From Homeless." New York Times, July 24, 1896:13.
    The author reports that the National Urban League placed an emphasis on the homeless at their annual conference.

Williams, Roger M. "Small Wonder: Scared But Bold." Foundation News, 32 (5), September-October 1991:36-39.
    The author profiles the Wilson Commencement Park, a 50-unit housing complex for single-parent, homeless families, in which the Marie C. and Joseph C. Wilson Foundation of Rochester, New York, gave $1.4 million.

Williams, Terry M., and William Kornblum. Growing Up Poor. Lexington: Lexington Books, 1985.
    The authors analyze the plight of teenagers who are trapped in poverty. They discuss their restrictive paths, the negative choices that make poverty a life sentence, the educational achievers, legitimate work, prostitution and pimping, and teenage mothers.

Williams, Winston. "Homeless Mother Finds City-Owned Apartment." <u>New York Times</u>, January 21, 1987:16.

To illustrate efforts by New York City to place homeless people in rehabilitated apartments owned by the city, the author features Harriet Harrison and her 8-year-old daughter, Nedra.

Williamson, John B., and Kathryn M. Hyer. "The Measurement and Meaning of Poverty." <u>Social Problems</u>, 1976:652-662.

That there is no agreement as to where to draw the poverty line, or what constitutes poverty, is illustrated by comparing 16 measures that have been used. Because the criteria vary so widely, we cannot legitimately compare the results of different studies. With no one best measure, several indicators should be used.

Willwerth, James. "Hoboes from High-Rent Districts." <u>Time</u>, <u>132</u>, July 11, 1988:8.

The author reports on "the eccentric world of recreational hoboing," middle class individuals who ride freights in their pursuit of adventure. A 2,000-member association, the National Hobo Association, which also publishes a newsletter, has grown up around this activity.

Wilson, David S. "Hope Wins When the Homeless Run." <u>New York Times</u>, October 4, 1988:10.

Organizers of the second annual "Run for the Homeless" at Griffith Park, in which about 200 skid row residents will participate with 2,000 other runners, say that the race, originally intended strictly as a fund raising event, "has evolved into a program for the homeless (that) raises self-esteem and exposes the homeless both to the discipline of running and to other runners and activities of mainstream society."

Wilson, Otto. <u>Fifty Years' Work with Girls, 1883-1933: A Story of the Florence Crittenton Homes</u>. Washington, D.C.: National Florence Crittenton Mission, 1933.

The author gives an overview of the philanthropic establishing of homes for unwed mothers.

Wilson, Robert S. <u>Community Planning for Homeless Men and Boys: The Experience of Sixteen Cities in the Winter of 1930-31</u>. New York: Family Welfare Association of America, 1931.

The author reviews programs for the homeless during the winter of 1930-31 in McPherson County (Kansas), Decatur, New Haven, Oklahoma City, Louisville, Rochester, Seattle, Kansas City, Minneapolis, Milwaukee, Pittsburgh, St. Louis, Cleveland, Detroit, Philadelphia, and Chicago. The problem is the unemployment of unskilled workers during the Great Depression. The solution is to establish a community-wide plan with centralized responsibility and experienced personnel, managed shelters, and feeding stations. All should have flexible time limits, work requirements for the able-bodied, and health and counseling services.

Wilson, Robert S. Group Treatment For Transients. New York: National Association for Travelers Aid and Transient Service, 1934.
   This handbook on methods and practices presents an overview of procedures for dealing with transients. It covers the group approach, meeting physical needs in group treatment, classifying transients (physical, employment, experience, mental cases, and unemployable), the city lodge, camps and farms, diet, homosexuality, alcoholism, work projects, use of free time in group treatment (recreational programs), educational activities, and organized religious expression.

Wilson, Robert S. "Transient Families." The Family, 11 (8), December 1930:243-251.
   The author discusses problems, attitudes, and life styles of transient families. Various types of "roaders" are distinguishable by their life style: the homeless tourist, job-hunter, health-seeker, job-evader, and mobile. Transients can also be divided by locomotion: wagon-roaders, gasoline gypsies or rubber-bums, steam tourists, and hitch-hikers. A useful classification for social workers is the nomadic parents (a life style that the transient was born into), a continuation of adolescent behavior when the individual "hit the road," the socially inadequate (those who cannot compete due to mental or physical ill health or lack of education), and the psychopath (for whom transiency is an externalization of mental conflict). Each type needs to be recognized and dealt with separately.

Winerip, Michael. "Four People Walking in the Darkness Toward Roselle." New York Times, January 4, 1991:B1.
   The author focuses on the enigma of working people who make too much to be placed on welfare, yet because

their earnings are insufficient for them to afford an apartment they are homeless.

Wines, Michael. "Playing the Housing Slump: The Quick and the Indebted." New York Times, September 16, 1988:1, 9.
    Among the reactions to the housing slump in Colorado and the fire sales of H.U.D. homes, which often sell for 30 percent of their previous market value, is resentment to a proposal that some of the foreclosed properties be used to temporarily house homeless families.

Wise, Daniel. "Judge Assails City Agency on Shelters for Homeless." New York Law Journal, 194 (42), August 28, 1985:1.
    The author presents background reasons that a New York State Supreme Court justice issued a preliminary injunction that ordered the Department of Social Services of New York City "to comply with a state directive requiring that homeless families be provided with shelters 'immediately'."

Wise, Daniel. "Report by 3 Groups Critical of City's Policy on Homeless." New York Law Journal, 196, September 25, 1986:1, 2.
    Reports by the Community Action for Legal Services and New York Lawyers for the Public Interest recommend a coherent policy for the homeless, including policies for preventing homelessness by "stemming the tide of dis-placement." Recommendations include creating public-assistance shelter allowances, extending rent-increase exemptions, and quicker means for the city to take over tax-delinquent properties.

Wiseman, Jacqueline P. Stations of the Lost: The Treatment of Skid Row Alcoholics. Englewood Cliffs: Prentice-Hall, 1970.
    Based on participant observation, the author analyzes the perspective of skid row residents, strate-gies of control (police, courts, and jails), strategies of rehabilitation (mental, physical, and spiritual), strategies of survival, and social relationships between the helpers and the helped. She includes the prodigal son syndrome, trust among skid rowers, and salvage efforts by missions as viewed by staff and clients.

Wissendanger, Betsy. "If They Can Recycle Aluminum, Why Not Lasagna?" Sales and Marketing Management, 143 (12), October 1991:91-92.
Atlanta's Table, which delivered 1,200 pounds of food left over from the AT&T Tennis Challenge to homeless agencies, is one of over 70 food distribution groups across the United States that serve as a conduit for excess foods from bakers, restaurants, hotels, caterers, and convention centers.

Wissinger, Joanna. "Proposals to House the Homeless." Progressive Architecture, 67, May 1986:27-28.
Sponsored by the American Institute of Architecture, meetings, seminars, and workshops were held for four days in Washington, D.C., on the topic of what architects can do about homelessness.

Withiam, Glenn. "The Strange Death and Energetic Rebirth of the Tarrytown Hilton Inn." Cornell Hotel and Restaurant Administration Quarterly, 30 (3), November 1989:46-47.
The Tarrytown Hilton Inn in Westchester County, New York, which was going to be turned into a homeless shelter, was renovated and will continue to operate as a Hilton Inn.

Wittman, Friedner D. "Alcohol, Architecture, and Homelessness." Alcohol Health and Research World, 11 (3), Spring 1987:74-79.
The rehabilitation of homeless alcoholics cannot be achieved without first providing a stable residential facility. The author describes how human character and the social functioning of individuals are affected by architectural designs. He identifies political and financial issues related to designing alcohol recovery residential facilities and makes recommendations for future facility research.

Wittman, Friedner D. The Homeless with Alcohol-Related Problems: Proceedings of a Meeting to Provide Research Recommendations to the National Institute on Alcohol Abuse and Alcoholism. Rockville, Maryland: Department of Health and Human Services, 1985.
This volume examines research issues in alcohol and homelessness; characteristics of homeless problem drinkers compared with other homeless; service systems and settings; and architectural, financial and developmental aspects of housing. It also contains recommenda-

tions for services, housing, research, and dissemination of research.

Wittman, Friedner D. "Housing Models for Alcohol Programs Serving Homeless People." Contemporary Drug Problems, 16 (3), Fall 1989:483-504.

After a brief overview of policy-making that addresses issues of homeless alcoholics and recovery, program innovations in housing for alcoholics, and low-income housing as an integral part of alcohol recovery programs, the author describes seven types of programs that have integrated low-income housing in their alcohol treatment programs. He concludes that joint action is needed "by local partnerships of alcohol-recovery and housing-provider agencies to create a new form of residential setting: the alcohol-free residence associated with an off-site, community-based alcohol recovery program."

Wittman, Friedner D., M. Arch, and Patricia A. Madden. Alcohol Recovery Programs for Homeless People: A Survey of Current Programs in the United States. Rockville, Maryland: National Institute on Alcohol Abuse and Alcoholism, February 15, 1988.

To draw attention to the service needs of homeless people with alcohol problems, this report focuses on "exemplary alcohol recovery programs." The authors' goal is "to identify models of alcohol-problem recovery programs that can serve as reference points for further research, policy planning, and program development." Forty percent of the total homeless population in the United States has alcohol problems. The exemplary programs have three characteristics in common: intake services, primary recovery programs, and sustained recovery programs. The authors list 14 "themes and issues" that emerged from their study, describe their methodology in detail, and include a copy of the questionnaire.

Wolch, Jennifer R. "Homelessness in America: A Review of Recent Books." Journal of Urban Affairs, 12 (2), 1990:449-453.

In her review of 11 works on the homeless, the author argues that geography is underanalyzed. By this, she means that researchers need to pay more attention to such aspects of the homeless experience as spatial usage of urban areas, geographic organization of homeless shelters, and the social networks of the homeless.

Wolff, Craig. "Troubled Workers Transport Urban Woes to the Catskills." New York Times, July 25, 1991:B1.
    Hundreds of homeless people, who have come to New York's Catskill Mountains to either work at minimum pay in resort hotels or to escape the city, have brought with them such problems as drugs and violence.

Wolmar, Christian.   "B & B Lunacy Soars in East London Borough." New Statesman, 110, August 2, 1985:4.
    The author criticizes the East London council in Tower Hamlets for paying 1.6 million pounds to one landlord for bed and breakfast accommodation and sending Bengali families to towns in which there are no black communities.

Wood, S. M.   "Camberwell Reception Centre: A Consider-ation of the Need for Health and Social Services of Homeless Single Men." Journal of Social Policy, 5 (4), 1976:389-399.
    This article gives an overview of the British legislation that established centers for homeless men, with a focus on the center in Camberwell in London. The number using this center has been rising steadily since 1965. The center is unable to meet the physical and mental needs of the sick, the powerless, and those broken by the pressures of society. The solution is to provide them low-rent accommodations, health care, and social support.

Wood, Samuel E. "Municipal Shelter Camps for California Migrants." Sociology and Social Research, 23, January-February, 1939:222-227.
    The one-day shelter program for transients provided by Fresno, California, is reviewed. It appears to reduce petty crime, and similar shelters should be developed in other cities.

Wood, William, and Greg Steinmetz. "Estimate of Damage on Hawaii's Kauai From Hurricane Inike Reaches $1 Billion." Wall Street Journal, September 14, 1992:A3.
    This overview of the damage to Hawaii from the 1992 Hurricane Inike mentions that 7,000 Kauai residents were left homeless. They are being sheltered in state-run evacuation centers.

Woodhouse, Linda R.   "The Desperate Battle to Save Homeless." Nation's Cities Weekly, 8, January 28, 1985:1, 3.

The author focuses on various efforts to meet the homeless crisis in New York City, Washington, D.C., and Philadelphia.

Woodhouse, Linda R. "Hands Across America: $100 Million Drive for Hunger, Homeless Programs." <u>Nation's Cities Weekly</u>, April 7, 1986:1, 6.
This article discusses how "Hands Across America," a celebrity-studded fund drive for the hungry and homeless, will be organized. It includes a map of the program's route.

Woodward, Patricia J., and Elisabeth M. Davidge. "Homelessness Four Years On." <u>Journal of Planning and Environment Law</u>, March 1982:158-167.
In reviewing four years of the implementation of the Housing (Homeless Persons) Act of 1977, the authors focus on the problem of determining the intentionality of homelessness.

Worby, John. <u>The Other Half: The Autobiography of a Tramp</u>. New York: Lee Furman, 1937.
This account of hoboing in England and the United States places a focus on sexual experiences.

Worth, Cedric. "The Brotherhood of Man." <u>North American Review</u>, <u>227</u>, April 1929:487-492.
This short story told in the first person is about two anti-Wobblies who work the farm harvests of North Dakota and vehemently confront members of the I.W.W.

Woulfe, Richard. "Short and Sweet." <u>New Statesman Society</u>, <u>2</u> (66), September 8, 1989:27.
In a short-lived program, the housing council (in London) let homeless people stay in unoccupied housing that was habitable but not up to council standards. When the councils had the money to improve this housing, the individuals were then moved to other similar housing. The author states that this practice prevents vandalism while it provides housing for the needy, and that it is best suited for the single.

Wren, Christopher S. "The Homeless Ask, Is Racism Lodged In the Heart?" <u>New York Times</u>, February 12, 1992:A4.
In South Africa, about seven million homeless blacks live in squatter camps.

Wren, Christopher S. "Mean Streets Swallow the Orphans of Apartheid." <u>New York Times</u>, December 10, 1991:A4.
 The author chronicles the plight of the "malmunde," the homeless children of South Africa who beg and sleep on city streets.

Wright, James D. "Address Unknown: Homelessness in Contemporary America." <u>Society</u>, <u>26</u> (6), September-October 1989:45-53.
 After giving a brief history of homelessness in the United States, the author points out that today's homeless are only part of "tens of millions" of "poor people living in objectively inadequate housing because they lack the means to do otherwise." He adds that "Homelessness is not and cannot be a precisely defined condition," that any definition must include people's options or lack thereof. The number of homeless over the course of a year exceeds by a factor of three the number who are homeless on any given night. About 95 percent of the homeless are worthy, only about 5 percent unworthy or undeserving. "The solution has two essential steps: the federal government must massively intervene in the private housing market, to halt the loss of additional low-income units and to underwrite the construction of many more; and the benefits paid to the welfare-dependent population-AFDC, general assistance, Veterans Administration income benefits, Social Security, and so on—must approximately double."

Wright, James D. <u>Address Unknown: The Homeless in America</u>. Hawthorne, New York: Aldine de Gruyter, 1989.
 After examining the definition of homelessness, the numbers of homeless, and housing and poverty as the root causes of homelessness, the author then reports on his study of 1,000 homeless people, focusing on homeless families and the lone homeless (women and children, the elderly, veterans, and the disabled). He delineates their racial and ethnic composition, education, family background and affiliations, geography, and criminal background, and examines how people become homeless due to alcoholism, drug abuse, mental and physical illness, and deinstitutionalization. He proposes that much homelessness can be prevented by rent insurance and by increasing the supply of low-cost housing. He closes with proposals for short-term ameliorative action, the coordination of services, the utilization of the social welfare system, and dealing with alcoholism and mental illness.

Wright, James D. "Homelessness Is Not Healthy for Children and Other Living Things." Child and Youth Services, 14 (1), 1990:65-88.
Using data from the National Health Care for the Homeless Program and the National Ambulatory Medical Care Survey, the author concludes that homeless children and mothers, indeed male and female homeless persons of all ages, are much more physically ill than those who are domiciled. In most cases, their physical diseases are due to their material deprivations.

Wright, James D. "The Mentally Ill Homeless: What Is Myth and What Is Fact?" Social Problems, 35 (2), April 1988:182-191.
The author argues that in their 1986 article in Social Problems David A. Snow, Susan G. Baker, Leon Anderson, and Michael Martin overstated matters when, based on their research in Austin, Texas, they concluded that the rate of mental illness among the homeless was much lower than previously estimated. What these researchers actually discovered, he says, was not lower rates but a lower boundary of known mental illness. "Independent data from homeless clinical populations in 17 large cities suggest a best guess on the rate of mental illness among the homeless at about one-third...broadly consistent with previous research findings" and inconsistent with the findings by Snow and fellow researchers. He adds that if "the Texas mental health care system is an especially 'leaky' one," many of the mentally ill never receive treatment, and the true rate is much higher. (The authors' reply follows the article.)

Wright, James D. "Poor People, Poor Health: The Health Status of the Homeless." Journal of Social Issues, 46 (4), 1990:49-64.
Data are presented on 63,000 homeless clients seen in National Health Care for the Homeless clinics. Sixteen cities are represented. The reason most commonly given by the homeless for their homelessness is money problems; next is alcohol and drug abuse, job problems, mental illness, inability to find housing, and the breakup of a relationship. An additional 15 factors are listed. The author focuses primarily on how homelessness causes poor health and how homelessness is a complicating factor in the delivery of health care. He concludes that "any realistically large-scale intervention to eradicate the condition of homelessness would add several tens of

billions to the annual federal budget," that since this
is unlikely "our collective efforts will be largely along
the lines of crisis intervention, knowing full well that
these efforts do not, indeed cannot, represent any final
solution to the problem....(that through various provisions of health care) we will make the lives of many
homeless people more comfortable and less degrading, but
we will not significantly reduce the number
of people who must lead uncomfortable, degrading lives."

Wright, James D.   "Science, Passion and Polemics."
Society, 26 (4), May-June 1989:21-23.
        The author comments on a report on homelessness
published by the Institute of Medicine. His thesis is
that it is within our capacity to solve homelessness, but
the political climate will prevent it from being solved.
He says that in the face of today's political realities,
it is better "to take an inch when the inch is there to
be taken, than to demand the whole nine yards when even
the first yard is further than the Congress or the White
House is willing to go."

Wright, James D., Eleanor Webber-Burdin, Janet W. Knight,
and Julie A. Lam.   "The National Health Care for the
Homeless Program: The First Year." Amherst, Massachusetts: Social and Demographic Research Institute, March
1987.
        The authors summarize the first year of operation of
the National Health Care for the Homeless conducted in 19
major U.S. cities. The urban homeless can be engaged in
a continuous system of health care, for the program
achieved 118,098 encounters with 42,539 homeless persons,
an average of 2.8 contacts per client. About one third
were women, over half were non-whites, and a tenth were
homeless children under 16.   The median age was 32.7
years.   The leading health problem was alcohol abuse,
followed by mental illness.   About 38 percent of the
homeless (47 percent of the men and 16 percent of the
women) have alcohol problems, while between 30 and 40
percent have significant psychiatric problems, more
common among homeless women than among men.   Acute
episodic disorders (upper respiratory infections, traumas
and skin ailments) were the most common physical health
problems. About 41 percent of the clients were afflicted
with some chronic physical disorder (compared to 25
percent of the ambulatory patient population in United
States).   Most of these problems are minor conditions
such as skin ailments, but they also include serious

respiratory infections (pneumonia and pleurisy), sexually transmitted venereal diseases, and active tuberculosis. About one in six "is afflicted with some infectious or communicable disorder that represents a potential risk to the public health." Although much of the high rate of physical diseases among these clients is attributable to alcohol abuse, the rate of most disorders among non-alcohol abusing clients is also substantially higher than those in the national ambulatory patient population. Even the most disadvantaged among the homeless can be integrated into a system of care--which can provide a "wedge" in solving basic social, psychological, and economic problems of the homeless.

Wright, James D., and Janet Wilson Knight. "Alcohol Abuse in the National 'Health Care for the Homeless' Client Population." Amherst, Massachusetts: Social and Demographic Research Institute, April 1987.

The authors found 5,402 "alcohol abusers" among the 23,745 homeless adults with whom they made contact in 19 American cities during the first year of operation of the National Health Care for the Homeless program. The "underdiagnosis" of alcohol problems can be corrected to make it "virtually identical to the average results reported in prior studies." More men (47 percent) have a drinking problem than do women (16 percent). For both men and women, problem drinking is curvilinear, rising through the middle years and falling off during their later years. Difference in alcohol problems show up between black and whites, and homeless American Indians have the highest incidence, Hispanics and Asians the lowest. Compared with ambulatory patients in the general population, the homeless are more physically ill on almost every indicator. Cancer, obesity, and strokes, however, are exceptions to this pattern. Alcohol abusers are much more likely than non-abusers to suffer from chronic health problems. In spite of alcohol abuse being the leading health problem of the homeless (accompanied by high rate of mental illness and drug abuse), heavy chronic drinking can provide "a number of positive functions for the homeless person--short-term alleviation of the miseries of existence, relief from chronic physical pain, sociability, and keeping a hostile world at arm's length." To be effective, treatment for alcohol abuse must also take into account the basic problems for which clients are using alcohol as a solution.

Wright, James D., Janet W. Knight, Eleanor Weber-Burdin, and Julie Lam. "Ailments and Alcohol: Health Status Among the Drinking Homeless." <u>Alcohol Health and Research World</u>, <u>11</u> (3), Spring 1987:22-27.

Based upon data gathered from almost 30,000 homeless individuals encountered in the National Health Care for the Homeless program, the authors compare the health problems of those who are identified as possible alcohol abusers with other homeless adults. About 40 to 50 percent of homeless men and about 10 to 20 percent of homeless women are alcohol abusers. The successful rehabilitation of homeless alcoholics to a stable, functioning, or productive social existence cannot be achieved without addressing the following underlying causes of homelessness: a high rate of chronic heavy alcohol use, disproportionate drug abuse, psychiatric impairment, and physical illness.

Wright, James D., and Julie A. Lam. "Homelessness and the Low-Income Housing Supply." <u>Social Policy</u>, <u>17</u>, Spring 1987:48-51.

Developing the thesis that homelessness is a housing problem (stating that many writers overlook this factor in order to focus on problems of unemployment, deinstitutionalization, substance abuse, and cutbacks in social welfare spending), the authors review trends in low-income housing in the United States.

Wudunn, Sheryl. "Wife of Jailed China Dissident Is Left Homeless by Eviction." <u>New York Times</u>, April 20, 1992:A7.

Zhang Fengying, the wife of Ren Wanding, an imprisoned leader of the 1989 Tianamen Square protests, and her sick child became homeless after Chinese authorities evicted them from their apartment.

Wyatt, Richard Jed, and Evan G. DeRenzo. "Scienceless to Homeless." <u>Science</u>, <u>234</u>, December 3, 1986:1309.

Just as the social policy of deinstitutionalization was put in place without "large scale efficacy trials," resulting in failure, so "well-designed and replicated controlled experiments are necessary" in designing social policy for the homeless if we are not to repeat our mistakes of well-intentioned efforts that exacerbate problems.

Wyburn, Mrs. S. May. "<u>But, Until Seventy Times Seven</u>":
<u>Jeremiah, Samuel, John</u>. New York: Loizeauzx Brothers,
1936.
        This account of the McAuley Mission in New York City
was written by the wife of the founder, who was also the
mission's administrator.

Wyckoff, Walter A.   <u>A Day with a Tramp and Other Days</u>.
New York: Charles Scribner's Sons, 1901.   (Reprinted in
1971 by Benjamin Blom of New York.)
        The author of this first-person account of 18
month's travel from Connecticut to California in 1891-
1892 undertook his travels "in order to get a better
knowledge of the people and the country and of opportunities for work." He recounts his experiences as a casual
laborer.

Wyckoff, Walter A.   <u>The Workers, An Experiment in
Reality: The East</u>.   New York: Charles Scribner's Sons,
1898.
        This account of the author's deliberate move from a
privileged social class to the life of a migrant manual
laborer in order to better understand the "labor problem"
includes his work experiences as a day laborer at West
Point, as a hotel porter, a worker in an asylum, a farm
hand, and work in a logging camp.

Wyckoff, Walter A.   <u>The Workers, An Experiment in
Reality: The West</u>.   New York: Charles Scribner's Sons,
1898.
        The author continues his account of his "experiment"
(related in the companion book above), this time focusing
on work in the city.   In addition to his work in a
factory and as a road builder at the World's Fair, he
includes an account of periods of unemployment and his
experiences with revolutionaries.

Wylie, Dorothy C., and Joseph Weinreb. "The Treatment of
a Runaway Adolescent Girl Through the Treatment of the
Mother." <u>American Journal of Orthopsychiatry</u>, <u>23</u> (1),
1958:188-195.
        The authors present a case study of a 15-year old
runaway girl, whom they successfully treated by treating
her mother, who was jealous and non-accepting of her
daughter's growing up.

Wysor, Dorothy E. "The Traveler as a Case Work Problem."
<u>The Family</u>, December 1925:239-243.

The author reports on stranded travelers and runaways (children and wives) who became clients of Travelers Aid.

Y

Youcha, Geraldine. "Running Away... All the Way Home." Parent's Magazine and Better Family Living, January 10, 1973:48, 82-84.
The author focuses on motivations for running away, disturbances in the process of growing up, and efforts to increase communication and adjustment between runaways and parents.

Young, Pauline V. "The Human Cost of Unemployment." Sociology and Social Research, 17, March-April 1933:361-364.
Underlying unemployment and the production of the homeless through eviction is an uncaring economic system that discharges men or slashes their wages "as soon as the credit sheet falls below certain expectation," discarding men who can never again return to their occupations. Thus, "the worker who has helped to create the vast surplus and wealth of the nation suffers want in the midst of plenty." The solution is to establish "industrial justice."

Young, Pauline V. "The New Poor: Part I." Sociology and Social Research, 17, January-February 1933:59-64.
The term "new poor" refers to a change noticed in those who are applying for relief in California--from indigents and paupers of previous years to persons who are wandering in search of jobs and new opportunities. A major problem is the men's demoralization, for they are likely to suffer social detachment and progressive disaffiliation while living hand-to-mouth in their constant search for new opportunities.

Young, Pauline V. "The New Poor: Part II." Sociology and Social Research, 17, 1933:235-242.
A new group of poor stands in sharp contrast to the old time poor, who were indigents and paupers. The "new poor" are people who are not idle for personal reasons (sickness, lack of training, inefficiency, or undesirable habits), but "because they have been 'let out' through no fault of their own." The author focuses on growth in

dependency, idle breadwinners, the human discard, new opportunity seekers, women vagrants, and juvenile transients. "It becomes clear that the unemployed is not only the worker without a job, but a human being without his customary social environment, a citizen without courage, a husband without the moral support of his wife, a father without control over his children. He is 'a worker adrift.'" No organizations or "institutional set-ups" meet the needs of the "new poor."

Young, Randy. "The Homeless: The Shame of the City." New York, December 21, 1981:26-32.
This overview of homelessness in New York City places emphasis on deinstitutionalization, reinstitutionalization, violence, crime, mental illness, and legal advocacy.

Younghusband, Peter. "Hiding His Home." Newsweek, March 4, 1985:30.
Squatters in Crossroads, near Capetown, South Africa, must dismantle their homes each morning before they go to work.

Z

Zanditon, Mildred, and Sandra Hellman. "The Complicated Business of Setting Up Residential Alternatives." Hospital and Community Psychiatry, 32 (5), May 1981:335-339.
Independent living apartments and group homes are keys to the success of the Massachusetts Mental Health Center's community residential program.

Zaslow, Jeffrey. "Homeless Man Haunts A Gentrified Enclave, Baffling Its Residents." Wall Street Journal, December 1, 1986:1, 10.
To illustrate the backlash against homeless people, the author focuses on Jim, a homeless old man who decided to live on a sidewalk bench in an affluent neighborhood in Lincoln Park near Chicago. Some residents set his belongings on fire.

Zastrow, C., and R. Navarre. "Help for Runaways and Their Parents." Social Casework, 56, 1975:74-78.
The authors summarize the results of interviews with 31 youths and their parents (or court-appointed guard-

ians) who were in contact with Briarpatch, a runaway center in Madison, Wisconsin. They conclude that a series of questions needs to be answered in order to adequately screen volunteers.

Zettler, Michael D.   <u>The Bowery</u>.   New York: Drake Publishers, 1975.
     This book is a photo album of the Bowery on New York City's lower east side. Its 83 photos (mostly full-page photos with fragments of conversations on the facing pages) provide a vivid view of this skid row in the 1970s.

Zinn, Laura. "Will Politically Correct Sell Sweaters?" <u>Business Week</u>, 3256, March 16, 1992:60-61.
     This profile of Susie Tompkins, who lost and then regained control of Esprit de Corp., which she founded with her husband, mentions that the company supports the homeless.

Zipple, Anthony M.   "Perspectives on <u>The Homeless Mentally Ill:</u> A Symposium of Responses to the American Psychiatric Association Task Force Report." <u>Psychosocial Rehabilitation Journal</u>, <u>8</u> (4), April 1985:2-41.
     The author provides a four-paragraph introduction to a collection of seven articles that were written in response to the American Psychiatric Association's Task Force on the Homeless Mentally Ill. They include proposals to meet the basic needs of the homeless, and an ex-patients view of the Task Force Report of the American Psychological Association. The primary message is that the underlying problem is lack of comprehensive community support programs.

Zipser, Andy. "Broken Promises." <u>Wall Street Journal</u>, May 19, 1989:R11, R12.
     "The poor are caught in a murderous triple bind": There are more of them, they are poorer, and the amount of subsidized housing has radically declined. Although "defining homelessness is like nailing Jell-O to the wall," consensus about the meaning of homelessness has increased while federal housing programs have been slashed. In spite of efforts by the private and non-profit sectors, it appears that the problem will become worse. "The plain fact is that a decade of shrinking budget allocations has piled up so many problems that even multiples of present federal spending couldn't solve

them, and might do no more than keep them from getting far worse."

Zorbaugh, Harvey Warren. <u>Gold Coast and Slum: A Socio-logical Study of Chicago's Near North Side</u>. Chicago: University of Chicago Press, 1929.
 Chapter 6, "The Rialto of the Half-World," describes the vice area of Chicago in the 1920s, an area also inhabited by hobos. Chapter 4, "The World of Furnished Rooms," is also relevant.

Zweig, Jason. "If I Can Get Just One Kid's Eyes to Glisten..." <u>Forbes</u>, <u>145</u> (6), March 19, 1990:180, 182.
 This profile of Gail Pankey, the first woman allowed on the floor of the New York Stock Exchange (in 1971), mentions that she serves on the board of directors of the Clear Pool Camp, which operates a summer retreat for homeless children in Carmel, New York.

ANONYMOUS

_____. <u>Accounting for Housing and Homeless in 1990 Decennial Census</u>. Hearing before the Subcommittee on Census and Population of the Committee on Post Office and Civil Service. Washington D.C.: U.S. Government Printing Office, April 11, 1986.
 This volume focuses on the problem of how to provide an accurate count of the hard-to-reach, transient population--persons who live in inexpensive hotels and motels, flop houses, railroad stations, and non-institutional group quarters. It contains statements by the mayor of the City of New York, the New York regional director of the U.S. Bureau of the Census, representatives of the New York Hispanic Housing Coalition, and the commissioner of the Department of Housing Preservation Development. Primary emphasis is placed on Hispanic homeless. It lists the residence rules that will be used in the census and also contains seven statements by individuals who primarily represent New York City interests.

_____. "Activists for the Poor Seek Money From Fund Raiser." <u>New York Times</u>, December 26, 1986:Y10.
 Robert Hayes of the National Coalition for the Homeless criticized the organization, Hands Across America, for not immediately dispersing the $15 million

it raised for the homeless. He lambastes "the foundation's elaborate and costly mechanism to distribute the money raised." A spokesman for the foundation said that $600,000 has already been distributed and the rest will be released in two to three months.

_____. "Addiction in the Homeless Shelters." New York Times, February 20, 1992:A24.
This editorial takes the position that with the revelations of widespread drug abuse in homeless shelters the recommendations of the mayoral Commission on the Homeless need to be heeded.

_____. "Advocates for Homeless Say New Law on U.S. Property Is Ignored." New York Times, December 5, 1988:9.
A year ago, a federal law was passed that requires unused federal properties to be returned to the federal government, which is to decide whether they are suitable for the homeless. Although 335 surplus properties are held by the General Services Administration, only four have been given to organizations that help the homeless.

_____. "Africa's Cities: Lower Standards: Higher Welfare." Economist, 316 (7672), September 15, 1990:25-28.
Poor housing is not allowed near the suburbs of Nairobi's cities, and each periodic clean-up campaign, done for the benefit of the wealthy, leaves thousands homeless.

_____. "Aid Bill Signed." New York Times, February 14, 1987:6.
President Reagan signed emergency legislation that will transfer $50 million from the disaster relief program run by the Federal Emergency Management Agency to an emergency food and shelter program for the homeless.

_____. "Aid to Homeless 'Most in Need'." New York Times, February 2, 1987:32.
Three Franciscan priests are establishing a third permanent home in Manhattan for the mentally disabled homeless. The renovated five-story building will house 80 homeless people with chronic mental illness. The cost of the building and its renovation is $2.7 million.

_____. "AIDS Caseload Taxes New York Agencies." New York Times, June 2, 1987:23.

The Coalition for the Homeless is concerned that AIDS will be the primary cause of homelessness within a year. They point out that "hundreds of people with AIDS are living in barracks shelters." AIDS victims lose their homes not only because of financial strains, but also because they are discriminated against due to their "social leprosy." The controversy is over whether "the housing problem of (AIDS victims) is an issue of homelessness when it is primarily a health-related one."

_____. "Alcohol Implicated as Killer of Many Who Are Homeless." New York Times, May 22, 1987:9.
The Centers for Disease Control in Atlanta, Georgia, reports that of 40 deaths of homeless people in Atlanta between July 1985 and June 1986, 28 were alcohol-related. Therefore, providing shelter for homeless people is not sufficient to prevent their deaths.

_____. "American Survey: An Apple That Has Lost Its Sheen." Economist, 319 (7709), June 1, 1991:19-20.
Because New York City faces a $3.5 billion budget deficit, the mayor, David Dinkins, has threatened to terminate many city services. Included on his hit list are shelters for the homeless.

_____. "American Survey: Living Under Spacious Skies." Economist, 311 (7601), May 6, 1989:21-22.
To solve the problem of homelessness in the United States, ameliorative efforts are inadequate and preventive measures must be taken. People who are currently homeless need a bridge back to self-sufficiency, such as may be provided by transitional housing and small "super-shelters."

_____. "The American Underclass." Time, 110 (9), August 29, 1977:14-18, 21-22, 27.
This article focuses on the hard core unemployed, welfare recipients, and minorities. The proposed solutions are job creation, improving the public schools, more specified spending by the federal government, and the underclass taking initiative.

_____. "America's 'Throwaway' Children." U.S. News & World Report, 88, June 9, 1980:66-67.
About 28 percent of the current runaway population of two million children are actually "pushouts," not runaways. The causes of running away are divorce and the

selfishness of parents. The article details the lack of resources of runaways and pushouts, their tendency to become involved in lives of crime, especially sexual deviances such as prostitution, and the work of Huckleberry House in San Francisco, Freedom Factory in Cincinnati, and The Bridge in Boston in dealing with such youths.

_____. Annual Report of the Committee on Homelessness. New York: Jewish Social Service Association of New York and the United Jewish Aid Societies of Brooklyn, 1930.
This article describes characteristics of the 640 men serviced in 1929 by the Committee on Homelessness sponsored by the Jewish Social Service Association of New York and the United Jewish Aid Societies of Brooklyn. The Committee's purposes are to direct social services, coordinate programs, and increase public awareness of homelessness.

_____. Annual Reports. Boston: Seamen's Aid Society, 1833–1850.
These annual reports summarize the charitable activities of a group of wives of prominent Bostonians who endeavored to help destitute seamen and their families.

_____. "Appeal by Rail Police Officer Rejected by Supreme Court." New York Times, October 8, 1991:B2.
The U.S. Supreme Court rejected the appeal of a railroad police officer to regain his job. The former officer had been videotaped nearly nude, making fun of a homeless man.

_____. "Are We Losing Ground?" Focus, 8 (3), Fall and Winter 1985:1–12.
This article summarizes major points of Murray's Losing Ground and offers a refutation of those points.

_____. "Art Of The Homeless." Vogue, 178, January 1988:50.
A show being held at the Museum of the City of New York, On Being Homeless, "traces the lives of the poor from the first settlement in New Amsterdam in 1628 until the present day, and, without condescending or moralizing, gives them a place in New York City's cultural history....Over the centuries, these people of the street have inspired the best to political action and reform,

but engendered disgust, fear, and hatred in the rest of us, who see in their resigned faces our own miserable failure to be either caring or just."

_____. "'Asylums' for the Homeless." Science News, 27, January 25, 1985:8.

According to findings reported by Ellen L. Bassuk and colleagues, 90 percent of people who stay in shelters have psychiatric illnesses, 40 percent suffer from psychoses, 29 percent are chronic alcoholics, and 21 percent demonstrate personality disorders. The shelters have begun to take the place of mental hospitals, becoming "asylums" for the homeless. The "hallmark" of the homeless mentally ill is a virtually total loss of connections to family, friends, and social services agencies. Three-quarters of the overall sample said that they had no family relationships or friends to provide support, and 40 percent said they had no relationship with anyone, not even connections with a shelter.

_____. "At Last a Bold Plan for the Homeless." New York Times, November 3, 1986:20.

Homeless families housed by the city are concentrated in midtown hotels. Against the opposition of borough residents and presidents, Mayor Koch plans to establish 20 shelters on city-owned properties in all five boroughs. "A more elaborate plan would be futile, the mayor argued, because the large pool of potential homeless would quickly overwhelm it." This editorial takes the position that long-range developments of low-income housing must continue, that shelters must never become a substitute for permanent housing for the homeless, and that the homeless need to be guaranteed safety in the city shelters.

_____. "At Least Help Keep the Homeless Off the Street." New York Times, December 25, 1988:E10.

"For the short term, sound policy will provide adequate housing subsidies to those capable of caring for themselves and, for the rest, modest-sized shelters, some with specialized services (drugs, alcohol, mental health). In the long term, it would expand housing for the poor and working poor."

_____. "Atlanta Plan to Bar Drifters from Downtown Stirs Debate." Associated Press, March 17, 1987:A2.

"A group of business executives and civic leaders have proposed creation of a zone approximately 40 blocks long and 20 blocks wide in which police will strictly enforce laws against loitering and panhandling." This area contains many of the city's estimated 7,000 homeless people, including many church-operated missions. Business leaders say that "there is no way downtown Atlanta can absorb all the problems of the failures of the social and economic system." Critics indicate that it is wrong to specify that certain people should be kept out of this designated part of Atlanta. Others charge that this is a racial issue because most of Atlanta's homeless are black.

_____. "Away on a Steam Grate." New York Times, December 12, 1986:14.
A "life-sized sculpture of a man, woman, and baby huddled under blankets on a steam grate, with the inscription, 'And Still There is No Room at the Inn'" commissioned by the Park Service for the Christmas Pageant of Peace on the Ellipse by the National Capitol Park Service, but rejected by them, was used as the centerpiece for a vigil held on the grounds of the Capitol by the Community for Creative Non-Violence.

_____. "Back to the Drawing Board." Wall Street Journal, August 24, 1988:12.
This editorial extols a paper presented by Madeline Stoner at the Society for the Study of Social Problems that reported that shelters are a failure because they have become permanent living situations rather than the temporary quarters they were intended to be. Shelters "perpetuate the homeless condition by keeping many in a transient state." The editorial also encourages the institutionalization of mentally ill people and the removal of rent controls in order to avoid the destruction of low cost housing.

_____. "Bangladesh Cyclone Kills 1,000 and Millions Are Left Homeless." New York Times, May 1, 1991:A1.
A cyclone in Bangladesh left millions of people homeless.

_____. "Banks Customize Community Aid." ABA Banking Journal, 82 (1), January 1990:22.
This overview of community development programs sponsored by banks mentions that a consortium of 48

California thrift associations has financed the development of shelters for the homeless.

_____. "Below the Safety Net." <u>Time</u>, <u>129</u>,
April 13, 1987:27.
    Of 500 people who eat at soup kitchens in New York
City, less than 10 percent are women, more than 80
percent are black or Hispanic, about one-third sleep on
the streets, about 40 percent average one meal or less a
day, and the majority cannot find a job or are too
disabled to work. This finding "shatters the myth of the
safety net by showing that people actually go hungry and
homeless because they can't get and maintain the benefits
they are entitled to."

_____. "A Better Way to Honor Dr. King." <u>New</u>
<u>York Times</u>, April 26, 1991:A28.
    Because corruption is rife at the Martin Luther King
Institute for Nonviolence, the money now spent there
should be spent on the homeless instead. This would be
much more fitting for King's memory.

_____. "Bill to Help the Homeless is Proposed
in the House." <u>New York Times</u>, January 10, 1987:8.
    "Leaders in the House of Representatives have
proposed a $500 million emergency package of food,
shelter, and other aid for the homeless." A representative from Texas said that "the $100 million allocated for
the homeless in the budget submitted by President Reagan
indicated 'the first acceptance of the Administration
that there is a responsibility on the federal level.'"

_____. "Borough Chief Offers Homeless Housing
Plan." <u>New York Times</u>, November 21, 1986:Y13.
    The President of the Manhattan Borough refused to
accept four sites proposed by the Koch administration for
new homeless shelters. Instead, he wants the city to
rehabilitate city-owned apartments. The administration
replies that it is unable to rehabilitate housing at a
pace that will keep up with the rapid growth in homelessness.

_____. "Boy, 11, Aids City Street People."
Associated Press, March 7, 1984.
    Almost every night, Trevor Ferrell, an 11-year old
boy from a comfortable suburb, takes food and blankets to
Philadelphia's homeless. He is accompanied by his

father, who says that the street visits are Trevor's idea.

_____. "Bringing Good Tidings to the Afflict-ed." Christian Century, 130, November 23, 1986:407.
    This editorial uses the story of Steve, a homeless individual who is but a shell of his former self, to illustrate the need for ministering to the homeless.

_____. "Britain: More Roofs." Economist, 313 (7629), November 18, 1989:69-70.
    This overview of homelessness in Great Britain says the government blames the increase in homelessness on changes in family life--divorce, teenagers leaving home, and teenagers getting pregnant. Home repossessions due to high interest rates are another cause. The cost of putting the homeless up in bread and breakfasts is exorbitant. Increasing the stock of rental housing may help solve the problem.

_____. "Brooklyn Apartments for $45,000." New York Times, August 7, 1987:32.
    Sixteen families from the United Methodist Church in the Prospect-Lefferts Gardens section of Brooklyn formed a non-profit corporation, Sterling Street Associates, to rehabilitate a four-story apartment building that had been vacant for ten years. Obtaining the building for one dollar under the city's Dollar Sales Program and rehabil-itating it for $900,000, they have produced one-bedroom units for around $45,000, two-bedrooms for $55,000, and three-bedroom apartments for $61,000.

_____. "Business Bulletin: Volunteering's a Must." Wall Street Journal, December 26, 1991:A1.
    Cabrini College in Radnor, Pennsylvania, has begun to require that all juniors do ten hours of community service. The first group worked with the homeless.

_____. "Business Can Help the Homeless." New York Times, March 2, 1992:A14 .
    This editorial argues that the businesses of New York City should help the city government establish homeless shelters.

_____. "Calcutta, N.Y.: A Revolving Door." New York Times, September 2, 1987:20.
    A plan by New York City's mayor to broaden the definition of dangerous in order to remove a large number

of mentally ill people from the streets will be challenged by the Civil Liberties Union. Perhaps the "revolving door" of the homeless mentally ill--being committed to mental hospitals only to be shortly turned back onto the streets--can be replaced with a system of hospital and community care.

_____. "California to Seal Cavern Home of Teenage 'Trolls.'" Wall Street Journal, January 27, 1992:C13.
A cavern under a hollywood street in which a group of teenaged runaways had been living will be sealed. The group, known as "the trolls," called their home "the hole." They reportedly supported their surrogate father, an ex-convict now returned to prison for parole violations, by mugging, dope-dealing, and prostitution.

_____. "The Call of the Shirt." The Atlantic Monthly, 99, May 1907:725-728.
The author gives a romanticized recounting of his conversation with a hobo named Jack, who has given him an appreciation of traveling freely and the desire to do so.

_____. "Caring for the Homeless." America, 154, January 18, 1986:21-22.
The author lauds President Reagan's decision to not evict "residents from a shelter for homeless in Washington, D.C., operated by the Community for Creative Non-Violence." Homelessness is due to gentrification of inner-city neighborhoods, the deinstitutionalization of mental patients, and other complex factors.

_____. Caring for the Hungry and Homeless. Alexandria, Virginia: Emergency Food and Shelter National Board Program, June 1985.
This volume gives an overview of nutrition programs, shelter programs, and multi-service programs across the nation.

_____. "Caring for Unreached Patients: The Homeless." American Medical News, 28, April 12, 1985:1, 13-14.
The many medical needs of the homeless include ulcerated gangrenous limbs, pneumonia, burns, and fractures, as well as extensive chronic illnesses such as diabetes and heart disease. Tuberculosis may be ten times as common among the homeless than the rest of the population. The author profiles a medical program for

the homeless--Single-Room Occupants (SRO)--operated by
St. Vincent's Hospital and Medical Centre in Greenwich
Village and makes the point that life on the streets
invites injury and disease.

_____. "Cash In On the Homeless." New York
Times, February 3, 1989:20.
    A good part of the costs of housing the homeless
borne by New York City can be offset by governmental
programs available for the disabled. Specific amounts
available for various disabilities are listed.

_____. "Catholic Order Helps the Homeless."
New York Times, January 20, 1991:24.
    Emmaus, a new Roman Catholic order, runs a house in
New York City to help the homeless make the adjustment
from shelters to permanent housing.

_____. "Census Bureau Will Take Nation's Pulse
April 1." Business America, 111 (5), March 12, 1990:12-
13.
    The decennial count of the population of the United
States by the Commerce Department's Bureau of the Census
will attempt to include a count of the homeless.

_____. Characteristics of Unattached Men on
Relief. Chicago: Illinois Emergency Relief Commission,
Cook County Service Bureau for Men, 1935.
    This volume, which features the services of the
Illinois Emergency Relief Commission, includes a summary
of the characteristics of the men who use those services.

_____. "Chicago Gearing Up for Homeless Care
Program." American Medical News, 28, April 12, 1985:16.
    The author reports on efforts to organize Chicago's
Health Care for the Homeless founded by a coalition of
health clinics in the city. In this program, volunteers
will visit shelters for the homeless and "refer residents
who need care to nearby participating hospitals and
medical centres. Twice-weekly clinics also will be
conducted at two drop-in centres for the homeless."

_____. "China Floods Leave Millions Homeless."
Detroit Press, August 24, 1985:A4.
    The torrential rains that followed Typhoon Mamie
brought the worst flooding China had experienced in 26
years. It left more than two million people homeless.

_____. Chronic and Situational Dependency: Long-Term Residents in a Shelter for Men. New York: Human Resources Administration, May 1982.

Interviews were held with 128 men who had stayed at the Keener Building Shelter on Wards Island longer than two months. This volume reports their age, race, religion, employment, place of birth, marital status, attachments to New York City, public assistance background, alcohol and drug use, contact with families, education, and psychiatric background.

_____. "Cigarette Tax Aids Homeless." New York Times, June 30, 1989:7.

Chicago's city council voted unanimously to raise cigarette taxes a penny a pack, with the amount raised to go to the homeless. This tax is expected to raise $1.8 million a year.

_____. "City Found Lax in Supervising Discharged Foster-Care Youths." New York Law Journal, 195, June 9, 1986:1.

Seven children released from foster care sued New York City for not preparing them for independent living and for failing to supervise them after their release. They claim that local agencies failed to contact them following their discharge, and they were "forced to seek shelter in tenement buildings, subways, and public parks." The court ruled that under the Social Service Law the city was responsible to provide "supervision, job training, food, clothing and housing" for children who have been discharged from foster care.

_____. "A Clergyman's Story of the 'Stranded.'" World's Work, 4, September 1902:2510-2515.

A New York clergyman kept records for a year on the people who asked him for assistance. Of the 600 individuals, 100 were genuine, 100 were freaks (people with strange ideas), and 400 sought money or employment.

_____. "Closing of Shelter in Capital Is Upheld by Appeals Panel." New York Times, December 11, 1985:13.

This article reports on the closing of the shelter for the homeless in Washington, D.C., run by Mitch Snyder and the Community for Creative Non-Violence.

_____. "Coast Killer Preys on Homeless; 10 Cases Reported in Los Angeles." <u>New York Times</u>, November 3, 1986:15.

In two months ten homeless people (including people who were not homeless but appeared to be) were shot to death. Some were shot at close range in the back of the head while they were walking; others were shot while sleeping in alleys and parks. The homeless express little fear because "guys die down here on a regular basis--that's the reality." The police are frustrated because they have few clues to help them find what they are calling "The Transient Killer."

_____. "Cold Causes Crowding of Shelters in South." <u>New York Times</u>, November 7, 1991:A22.

Homeless people suffered as a record cold snap swept the South.

_____. "Colombia Shuts School in Body-Purchase Case." <u>New York Times</u>, March 12, 1992:A12.

The medical school of Colombia's Free University of Barranquilla was closed following allegations that security guards clubbed homeless people to death and sold their bodies to school administrators for about $200.

_____. "Companies Are Asked to Do More to Combat Hunger." <u>Wall Street Journal</u>, July 20, 1983:1.

Food companies are giving surplus food to volunteer groups that feed the homeless, such as Second Harvest in Phoenix, Arizona.

_____. "Construction to Begin on Brooklyn Shelter." <u>New York Times</u>, February 11, 1987:14.

Construction unions objected to the use of fully prefabricated units to build a 200-unit structure for the homeless in Brooklyn. The unions and the city reached an agreement that the units will be only partly prefabricated. The negotiations delayed the construction and increased the cost.

_____. "Crack Houses, Owned by City Hall." <u>New York Times</u>, June 25, 1987:26.

In spite of the growing number of homeless families and the pressing need to provide housing for them, drug dealers have taken over about 20 percent of the 5,000 buildings managed by New York City's Department of Housing, Preservation and Development. This editorial argues that anyone convicted of drug dealing be evicted from public housing.

_____. "Creating a Co-op for the Homeless." The Neighborhood Works, 8 (5), May 1985:1, 9.
    The solution for New York's homeless is a low-income development with commercial space.

_____. "Creatively Reaching Out to the Hurting: A Case Study of New Life Evangelistic Center." New Life Zoa Free Paper, March 1984.
    This article reviews the programs for the homeless operated by the New Life Evangelistic Center in St. Louis, Missouri. Both men and women are given emergency shelter, free clothing, and a Gospel outreach. To break the cycle of homelessness, the men are offered a two-year training program of work responsibility and Bible classes. They first stay at a community house for a week, then at a farm for 30 to 60 days. If they remain, they are enrolled in a specialized field of study (broadcasting, counseling, or gardening). To break their homeless cycle, women and children are offered longer-term emergency shelter, stay at a woman's farm, and help getting on welfare.

_____. The Crisis in Homelessness: Effects on Children and Families: Hearing before the Select Committee on Children, Youth, and Families. Washington, D.C.: U.S. Government Printing Office, February 24, 1987.
    This volume contains nine statements made by individuals who appeared before this congressional hearing and 30 prepared statements and letters presented to the committee. Much material focuses on homeless children and mothers.

_____. "A Cruel Catch-22." NEA Today, 6, April 1988:2.
    Many of the 500,000 to 700,000 American children who are homeless cannot attend public schools because of state and local residency requirements that bar any child who has no permanent address. This is "counter to the will of the American people, for they know that national security cannot rest on policies of child neglect. They know, too, that compassion for the less fortunate is at the heart of our democracy. They know, above all, that now is no time for heart failure."

_____. "Croation-Americans Send Aid to Victims of Yugoslav Battles." New York Times, November 24, 1991:42.

The civil war in Yugoslavia has left about 500,000 Croations homeless.

_____. "Debate on Tramps." Proceedings of the Conference of Boards of Public Charities, 1877:130-133.

Four men express their views on tramps. Their position is that the laws on vagrancy should be rigidly enforced. In addition, tramps should be disenfranchised ("The man who is not fit to support himself is not fit to vote.") and in exchange for food be forced to work on highways, to shovel snow, and to drain swamps ("No work, no food.").

_____. "A Decent, but Incomplete, Homeless Plan." New York Times, January 28, 1989:16.

The growing numbers of homeless are threatening to turn New York City into New Calcutta. The worst of the shelters should be shut down and replaced with smaller, better supervised shelters. The mentally ill homeless are a special case. They need to be supervised to make certain that they take stabilizing medicines, and "permanent homes at which they can receive daily support."

_____. "Demystifying Hunger." Wall Street Journal, January 9, 1984.

According to the President's Task Force on Food Assistance, in the last 20 years the proportion of the Gross National Product going to the poor and elderly has doubled to 12 percent, and now runs $430 billion a year. Why, then, is there hunger? Three groups are at risk: the new poor (those impoverished by extended unemployment), the traditional poor (such as female-headed households), and the homeless. The solutions are to get the Veterans Administration more involved, to make sure that food stamp allotments completely cover the cost of a basic nutritious diet, to make states pay for excessive errors in allotting food stamps, and to give states the option of running their own food aid programs.

_____. "Deranged, Homeless--and Rich." New York Times, July 3, 1989:18.

When the Social Security Administration denied benefits to some, the poor "swelled the number of the homeless, making the streets of New York and other cities

look like New Calcuttas." To provide the poor "a decent
room in a new single-room-occupancy residence" would be
"far superior, and generally cheaper to operate, than
congregate shelters or other housing for the homeless
mentally ill." The government should provide special
housing vouchers to fund single-room-occupancy residences.

_____. "District of Columbia is Told to Feed
the Homeless." New York Times, March 23, 1989:12.
        After the District of Columbia stopped serving lunch
and dinner to homeless people at city shelters, the
Community for Creative Non-Violence went to court to seek
the resumption of the meals. Their petition was granted
by a Superior Court judge who called the City's action
"extraordinarily heartless and cruel against its least
fortunate members."

_____. "Doing It": A Collection of Articles on
Issues, Problems and Viable Solutions Concerned with the
Provision of Effective Human Services in Programs Serving
Runaway Youth. Washington D.C.: Department of Health,
Education, and Welfare, 1978.
        This volume focuses on four issues--program,
organization, management, and community--in serving
runaway youth. It reviews out-reach, in-take, counseling, group work, alternative living, after-care, youth
advocacy, the Third World, volunteers, youth participation, staff support, staff training, staff burn-out,
house management, management planning, financial management, management evaluation, community relations,
institution advocacy, police relations, out-reach in the
schools, and use of technical assistance.

_____. "Donations to 'Hands' Falls Short."
St. Louis Post-Dispatch, June 12, 1986:A12.
        The Hands Across America fund-raising extravaganza
raised $27.8 million, but when expenses are paid only
about $11 million will be left to distribute to the
homeless and hungry.

_____. "Down and Out All Over Europe." The
Economist, 294, January 26, 1985:47.
        The author reviews the plight of the homeless in the
winter, the growing numbers of young homeless, the
refusal of many to go to the shelters, and the increased
number of shelters in Europe.

_____. "Down and Out in Capital." New York
Times, December 16, 1988:14.
     This brief report on two homeless men makes the
point that the homeless are camped outside "buildings
where the nation's most critical decisions are made."

_____. "Down and Out in Poland." Survey, 29,
August 1987:192-193.
     Although Polish authorities deny that there are any
homeless in Poland, more than 500,000 Poles have nowhere
to live. The work of Jerzy Janoszka of Wroclaw of the
Blessed Brother Albert Refuge is profiled.

_____. "Dozens Attend Funeral of Transient
Woman." Associated Press, February 8, 1985.
     This article is an account of the memorial service
for Josie Winn, a deinstitutionalized schizophrenic in
Chicago who froze to death beside a garbage dumpster on
New Year's Eve.

_____. "Drifters Easy Prey for London's
Violent." St. Louis Post-Dispatch, February 20, 1983.
     A serial killer is stalking homeless people in
London.

_____. "Drug Abuse as an Artificial Escape
Among the Rootless and Homeless Young: Rebels Without a
Cause." Mental Health, 25 (3), May 1966:33-35.
     Some of the drug addicts in London are homeless
youth, many of whom engage in prostitution, delinquency,
and selling drugs. The basic cause of this problem is
social; the youths have been rejected by society, and
they are now being exploited.

_____. "The Dynamics of Homelessness."
Children Today, May-June 1989:2-3.
     A study published by the Committee on Health Care
for Homeless People by the National Academy of Sciences
indicates that the fastest growing component of the
homeless population is families with young children. The
major cause of homelessness is lack of decent, affordable
housing, but other factors are large numbers of poor and
unemployed, declining employment opportunities for the
poor, tightened eligibility standards for public assistance, and deinstitutionalization of the mentally ill.
Homeless people have more illnesses and health problems
than the rest of the population. The shelter system,
designed as a temporary measure, is inadequate. The

primary solution is to coordinate efforts to address housing, income maintenance, and a discharge plan for mental patients.

_____. "Easing Plight of Mentally Ill Home-less." New York Times, April 8, 1992:B3.
About 40 psychiatrists participate in Project for Psychiatric Outreach to the Homeless, volunteering their services to help care for New York City's mentally ill homeless.

_____. "The Economy of the Homeless." New York Times, December 5, 1985:26.
New York City pays $60 a day for squalid rooms for the homeless. The solution is fairer rent and to finance new shelters. Political problems plague the city's subsidy to St. Francis Friends of the Poor.

_____. "Emergency Additional Supplemental Appropriation for the Homeless, 1988." Washington, D.C.: U.S. Government Printing Office, January 22, 1987.
The U.S. Congress and House of Representatives are making a joint resolution to transfer $50,000,000 to the Federal Emergency Management Agency's Emergency Food and Shelter Program "to address immediately the national homeless situation."

_____. "Emergency Additional Supplemental Appropriation for the Homeless, 1988." Washington, D.C.: U.S. Government Printing Office, January 29, 1987.
The Committee on Appropriations is recommending passage of a joint resolution to transfer $50,000,000 to the Federal Emergency Management Agency's Emergency Food and Shelter Program.

_____. "End Hunger: Eat." Wall Street Journal, August 5, 1986:31.
Sixty restaurants are participating in a promotion called "Taste of L.A." Patrons try different foods, including shrimp remoulade and smoked salmon. Ten percent of the proceeds, after expenses, are to go to the homeless--after one half of this amount is given to the promoter.

_____. "Ex-Patient Eases the Journey from Street to Mental Health." New York Times, October 4, 1987:30.

Joseph Rogers, a former mental patient and a former homeless individual, has founded National Mental Health Consumer's Association. The focus of this self-help organization, which has drawn more than 4,000 members, is to improve the quality of care provided to the mentally ill homeless.

_____. Exploitation of Runaways: Hearing before the Subcommittee on Children, Family, Drugs and Alcoholism. Washington, D.C.: U.S. Government Printing Office, October 1, 1985.
This volume contains six prepared statements by politicians and individuals who work with runaway youths and includes a statement by Cheryl McCall, who produced Streetwise, a movie about runaways in Seattle.

_____. "Farmer, 76, Gets Death Sentence in Slaying of 5." New York Times, May 23, 1991:A26.
The death sentence was given to Ray Copeland, a 76-year old farmer in Missouri, convicted of killing five homeless men.

_____. "Father Kicked Hinckley Out, Defense Says." St. Louis Post-Dispatch, May 5, 1982:1, 7.
Part of Hinckley's defense for his attempted assassination of President Reagan is homelessness, that is, isolation, alienation, withdrawal from reality, hopelessness, and despair.

_____. "Federal Prosecutor Wants Posner's Sentence Set Aside." Wall Street Journal, April 5, 1988:24.
The attorney for Victor Posner, convicted of evading $1.2 million in federal income taxes, requested that Posner's sentence be set aside in return for his setting up a $3 million program for the homeless.

_____. The Federal Response to the Homeless Crisis: Third Report by the Committee on Government Operations. Washington, D.C.: U.S. Government Printing Office, April 18, 1985.
The causes of homelessness are scarcity of low-income housing, deinstitutionalization, unemployment, cuts in federal assistance programs, and personal crises. Public and private responses to homelessness have been insufficient, inadequate, disorganized, and ineffective. The homeless population in the United States has become more heterogeneous, as it now contains large numbers of

minorities, women, and children. The volume lists recommendations for the President, Congress, and federal agencies--including the National Institutes of Mental Health, the Federal Emergency Management Agency, the Department of Defense, and the Public Health Service. It also contains dissenting views.

_____. "Few in Morgan City Know Sen. Guarisco Has Ties to Camps." <u>Wall Street Journal</u>, June 23, 1983:20.
Senator Guarisco, a liberal, is accused of being associated with the exploitation of the homeless in Louisiana labor camps.

_____. <u>Final Report of the Attorney General's Commission on Pornography</u>. Nashville: Rutledge Hill Press, 1986.
Pages 173-174 and 183 of this lengthy report on pornography refer to homeless children being enticed into pornography and prostitution.

_____. "Fitful Slumber on Sidewalk Is a Lesson About Homeless." <u>New York Times</u>, March 5, 1987:15.
In order to dramatize the plight of the homeless and gain support for a $500 million emergency aid bill, more than 100 individuals from privileged backgrounds (including movie stars, business executives and members of congress) spent a night on the streets. Because some of them slept on the heating grates that extend onto the sidewalks from federal buildings, this act was termed, "The Grate American Sleep-out." (The homeless who sleep there are known as the grate people.)

_____. <u>Food Assistance for the Homeless Act of 1987</u>. Washington D.C.: U.S. Government Printing Office, February 27, 1987.
This volume provides a section-by-section analysis of the Food Assistance for the Homeless Act of 1987 which will provide food stamps and government commodities for the homeless.

_____. "For Children at Camp, a Rare Amity." <u>New York Times</u>, August 31, 1986:52.
Camp Homeward Bound at Lake Kanawauke in Bear Mountain, New York, is a camp for homeless children.

_____. "For the Homeless: New Old Hotels." <u>New York Times</u>, November 30, 1989:26.

This editorial supports the idea that state and New York City authorities purchase some existing S.R.O.'s to provide cheap housing. "A renovated building run by competent nonprofit managers and staffed by mental health workers would be a welcome improvement over a squalid flophouse."

_____. "For Vietnam Veterans, Florida Woods Is 'Home.'" New York Times, May 11, 1986:12.
Maladjusted veterans live in the woods outside Pompano Beach, Florida. Other reclusive veterans live in campsites in remote areas of the Pacific Northwest and Hawaii.

_____. "Former Nun Says She Plans Appeal of Eviction Ruling." Post-Bulletin (of Rochester, Minnesota), September 19, 1984:45.
A woman evicted from the Order of St. Francis who lived for a while in a car, then in a Seventh Day Adventist Church, is being evicted from the church building.

_____. "Funds for Shelters Due by December 23." New York Times, October 22, 1987:11.
After a lawsuit was filed by the National Coalition for the Homeless, the Department of Housing and Urban Development announced that it would distribute "the $15 million, which Congress appropriated last summer as part of $180 million package for homeless Americans."

_____. "Give Nehemiah a National Test." New York Times, July 19, 1986:14.
In Brooklyn's Nehemiah project, 500 houses have been built by a coalition of religious congregations utilizing no-interest second mortgages and abandoned property. This project should be adopted on a national scale.

_____. "Give Them Shelter." The National Law Journal, May 26, 1986:14.
The New York State Supreme Court's McCain v. Koch. 24072 decision of May 13, 1986, determined that "homeless families in New York have a clear right to shelter under the state Constitution." The adequacy of welfare benefits, however, is a matter that is up to the legislature of the state, not the courts.

_____. "Giving: A Special Report: Business Bulletin: A Perfect '90s Charity? Wall Street Journal, December 19, 1991:A1.

A group called Common Cents, which goes door-to-door collecting pennies, has raised almost $110,000 for the poor and homeless.

_____. "Giving Homelessness a Meaning and a Face." New York Times, March 29, 1992:39.

A class on homelessness is taught at Lehigh University in Bethlehem, Pennsylvania.

_____. Giving Youth a Better Chance: Options for Education, Work, and Service. San Francisco: Jossey-Bass, 1979.

This detailed analysis of the extent of the problem of unemployed and wandering youths, its causes, and possible solutions, also provides cross-cultural comparisons and a special focus on young women. Among the suggested solutions are age 16 to enter the service, changing the basic structure of high schools, changing the training emphases in postsecondary schools, creating a voluntary youth service, and establishing a National Education Fund.

_____. "'Grate' Sleep-Out." Associated Press, March 4, 1987.

The Associated Press transmitted a picture of three U.S. Representatives who participated in what was called the "Grate American Sleep-Out" on Capitol Hill on March 3, 1987. Politicians and actors joined the homeless in the streets to draw attention to the plight of the homeless.

_____. "The Great Pretender." Time, 128, August 26, 1986:23.

Joseph Mauri, the star of The Man from Fifth Avenue, a Soviet-made documentary about poverty in New York City, who has been touring the Soviet Union as a homeless American, is reported to have never spent a night on the streets, to have access to an apartment in Manhattan, and to have a job as a substitute mail clerk at the New York Times.

_____. "Harassed Are the Poor." America, 150, May 19, 1984:370.

There is a large number of poor, including homeless people, in the United States and politicians need to deal with this issue.

_____. "Harassing the Homeless." <u>Time</u>, March 11, 1985:68.
There is a backlash against the homeless--negative attitudes, abuse, and repression.

_____. "Harvard Students Protesting Action Against the Homeless." <u>New York Times</u>, January 18, 1986:6.
Harvard University's solution to the homeless staying on campus--welding grills over their buildings' heat vents--is protested by Harvard students. Students have circulated a petition objecting to the welding of grills over dormitory heat vents which the homeless had been using. The students want a shelter for the homeless to be opened in a dormitory basement.

_____. <u>Health Care for the Homeless: Hearing before the Subcommittee on Health and the Environment of the Committee on Energy and Commerce</u>. Washington, D.C.: U.S. Government Printing Office, December 15, 1986.
This volume contains nine testimonies by individuals who are involved in the health care of the homeless.

_____. "Help for Help I and the Homeless." <u>New York Times</u>, October 3, 1986:22.
Opposition by the New York City's building-trades unions to a plan to use pre-fabricated materials to build shelters for the homeless has delayed the construction of the proposed shelters, and they will not be ready by winter.

_____. "Help for the Homeless." <u>New York Times</u>, February 25, 1986:30:
A 200-room shelter being built for the homeless is a partnership of private business interests and public officials.

_____. "Help the Homeless and Win Votes." <u>New York Times</u>, August 14, 1989:18.
This editorial calls for more support for Project Help, under which "outreach workers are dispatched to bring homeless mental patients in from the streets--with power to force the hospitalization of those who resist."

The greatest need at present is about 10,000 more S.R.O. rooms.

_____. Helping Men to Help Themselves. New York: The Industrial Christian Alliance, 1930.
This illustrated brochure details the programs of the Industrial Christian Alliance. The basic solution is to offer the men productive work.

_____. "Helping the Homeless." Glamour, 83, January 1985:40.
This item consists of a list of what one can do to help the homeless--volunteer with religious or community groups, give money to homeless individuals, buy them food, give gifts of food, toiletries, and clothing. The contrast between this item in Glamour and the rest of the page is startling. On the same page, readers are urged not to use the brushes that come with their makeup products, but to pay $10 to $15 for a better one.

_____. Helping the Homeless: A Resource Guide. Washington, D.C.: U.S. Government Printing Office, 1984.
This guide from the U.S. Department of Health and Human Services on how to provide services to the homeless focuses on food programs, housing, and multi-service programs. It details the necessary facilities and equipment, lists sources of funding, and reviews issues of management, laws, and regulations. A question and answer section deals with questions that arise when starting a program, and case studies provide information on defining programs.

_____. "Helping the Homeless Report." Silver Spring, Maryland: CD Publications.
This twice-monthly "step-by-step guide to successful homeless programs" discusses such topics as developing community support, building coalitions, preventing evictions, food stamps, JOBS, JTPA, AFDC, Medicare, social services block grants, and emergency shelter grants.

_____. "Helter-Skelter Shelter." Time, 124, October 15, 1984:41.
Congress appropriated $8 million for the Pentagon to transform empty military buildings into shelters for the homeless. The Pentagon, however, spent $7 million on "routine base maintenance."

_____. "Hero Freezes to Death Near White House." Associated Press, December 27, 1984.
    Jesse Carpenter, a 61-year-old veteran who had been awarded the Bronze Star in 1944 and who had been homeless for 22 years, froze to death in Washington, D.C.

_____. "High Court Rules on Sleep Ban." Associated Press, June 29, 1984.
    The U.S. Supreme Court ruled that the government may ban protest sleep-ins by the homeless in parks near the White House.

_____. "A Hobo Jungle with Class." Time, 127, March 31, 1986:29.
    The city administration of Santa Barbara, California, has taken steps to discourage the homeless from staying in their city. They have passed laws against sleeping in the park and eating garbage and have refused to let the homeless vote. To protest these actions, the homeless have marched on Reagan's ranch and conducted sleep-ins at city hall.

_____. "The Homeless." Mortgage Banking, 48, September 1988:99-100.
    There are several types of homeless: skid row alcoholics, the deinstitutionalized mentally ill, and "a new underclass below what Marx envisioned as a lumpen-proletariat" ("young men, Vietnam vets, some with criminal problems, many with drug problems, all unable to find and hold a job"), and the impoverished ("individuals and families who simply cannot afford to pay the rent"). We are now seeing the kind of suffering that was reported in The Jungle (1906) and Grapes of Wrath (1939). This situation is "too grave an issue to be left only to the politicians. The housing and housing finance industries must help with the solution." The author urges that "mortgage banking and home builder associations in all 50 states appoint committees to study the problem and suggest solutions."

_____. The Homeless: Background, Analysis, and Options. Washington, D.C.: U.S. Government Printing Office, 1984.
    After defining homelessness, estimating the number of homeless persons in the United States, summarizing possible reasons for homelessness, and reviewing private and public efforts to help the homeless, this report from the Department of Health and Human Services singles out

five critical areas that require attention: (1) leadership, (2) entitlements, (3) technical assistance, (4) other federal resources, and (5) research, demonstration, and training.

_____. "The Homeless: Round Table Focuses on ADM Problems." Alcohol, Drug Abuse and Mental Health, 9 (11), June 24, 1983:1, 6.

According to reports given at the round table on the homeless conducted by the Alcohol, Drug Abuse and Mental Health Administration, most of the homeless are male, at least half are minorities, most are under 50, deinstitutionalization underlies much homelessness, and many homeless are alcoholics and abusers of other drugs. The solution is to develop aggressive outreach efforts, coupled with a three-tiered program. The first tier is to move the homeless off the streets into emergency shelters, the second a transitional stage in which "efforts can be made to link the chronically mentally ill and substance abusers to clinic services and entitlement programs," and the third long-term supportive housing that will assure "independence" and "treatment services."

_____. "Homeless Aid Restores Money for Surplus Food." New York Times, February 14, 1987:C1.

Although the Reagan administration had proposed cutting $26.8 million for the distribution of surplus food in order to help pay for a federal pay increase, it did an about-face and restored the money in an emergency plan for the homeless.

_____. The Homeless Alcoholic: Report of First Annual International Institute on the Homeless Alcoholic. Lansing: Michigan State Board of Alcoholism, 1955.

This volume contains papers on homeless and skid row alcoholics presented at a 1955 conference in Detroit.

_____. "Homeless Align for 'Dignity' at a Philadelphia Convention." New York Times, April 9, 1984:A20.

One hundred seventy-five homeless people met at a Convention of All Homeless People. Those attending a workshop on dignity and fairness recommended: 1) a march on city hall to demand services, 2) creating a list of the job skills and job training of homeless persons, 3) being given an abandoned building so the homeless can convert it into a shelter, 4) being given 24-hour walk-in services and showers, and 5) recognition of the rights and value of all humans, regardless of their circumstances.

_____. "The Homeless and the Night Visitors."
New York Times, December 18, 1985:26.
    The homeless in New York City lack community
services. The primary cause of homelessness is deinstitutionalization.

_____. Homeless and Unemployed Veterans.
Hearing Before the Subcommittee on Education, Training
and Employment of the Committee on Veterans' Affairs,
House of Representatives, Washington, D.C.: U.S. Government Printing Office, September 10, 1986.
    The first 65 pages are a transcript of the statements, observations, and facts provided by witnesses
before this governmental body. Of the 250,000 to 350,000
homeless Americans "on any given night," approximately
one-third of the males are veterans. The next 189 pages,
the appendices, provide listings and analyses of programs
available to homeless veterans. Its topics include a
report by the federal task force on the homeless, a
listing of a wide range of federal programs for the
homeless (from surplus housing and food banks to counseling and job training), and causes of homelessness (mental
illness-deinstitutionalization, alcohol-drug abuse, and
economic and personal crises such as unemployment,
eviction, and divorce).

_____. "Homeless Assistance Programs."
Washington, D.C.: U.S. Government Printing Office, July
1988.
    The introduction of this publication from the
Department of Housing and Urban Development presents an
overview of America's homeless, who are made up of three
overlapping categories: the chronically disabled, people
experiencing personal crisis, and those who suffer from
adverse economic circumstances. About half of the
homeless are chronically disabled (alcoholics, drug
abusers, and the chronically mentally ill); about 40
percent are homeless because of personal crisis (mostly
divorce and domestic violence); up to one-third are
homeless because of adverse economic circumstances
(eviction, unemployment, and inability to find affordable
housing). The homeless are concentrated "in the West,
which has 19 percent of the nation's population but
almost one-third of the homeless total. The South, by
contrast, has 33 percent of the national population but

24 percent of the homeless." About 66 percent of shelter users are single men, 13 percent single women, and 21 percent members of family groups. About 44 percent of the homeless are minorities. Nor are the mentally ill homeless randomly distributed, for only 10 percent of the homeless in the North Central region are mentally ill, but 29 percent in the West are. Summarized are grants available by the federal government for emergency shelter, supportive housing (both transitional and permanent), and assistance for single room occupancy dwellings. Addresses, contact persons, and phone numbers are also listed.

_____. "The Homeless Become an Issue." New York Times, February 7, 1987:8.
The reason that Congress and the president are approving millions of dollars in aid to the homeless is because of social activism on their behalf. Activists include the National Council of Returned Peace Corps Volunteers, Volunteers of America, Community for Creative Non-Violence, Hill Staffers for the Hungry and Homeless, and the Speaker of the House, Jim Wright, who testified on homelessness before the Housing subcommittee. Lobbyists stress that the need is for long-term planning because "homelessness is not a fad."

_____. "Homeless Braving Winter in Alaska." New York Times, November 14, 1983:A17.
The homeless, known here as the "cold" people, have a rough time in winter.

_____. "Homeless Children Looking for Compassion as Well as Shelter." New York Times, December 24, 1987:7.
Federal and state programs for children of the homeless are almost non-existent. Although there is an extensive need for such programs, no one knows the number of homeless children.

_____. "Homeless Cite '27 Will in Demanding a Haven." New York Times, 138, September 1, 1989:A12.
Homeless residents of Burlington, Vermont, picketed a building in their city, demanding that the building be used to house the homeless. They discovered that the will of the donor, Elihu B. Taft, specified that if the building were not used for "school purposes, it should be turned into a home for indigent aged men." The home is no longer being used for "school purposes."

_____. "Homeless Couple Found Dead in Car."
St. Louis Post-Dispatch, January 6, 1983.
    Norm and Anne Peters died in their station wagon
from carbon monoxide poisoning. He had been unemployed
since 1979 when he was laid off from Taft Contracting
Company. The couple had been evicted from the home in
which they had lived for 25 years.

_____. Homeless Families: A Neglected Crisis.
Washington, D.C.: U.S. Government Printing Office, 1986.
    The Committee on Government Operations, which is
charged with oversight investigation of the Emergency
Assistance Program of the Social Security Administration,
concludes that the causes of homelessness are scarcity of
low-income housing, inadequate income, increases in
personal crises, and cuts in federal assistance programs.
Current emergency assistance programs are inadequate to
address the problems of homeless families. The Department of Health and Human Services (HHS) has failed to
follow its regulations on monitoring, reviewing, and
auditing the emergency assistance program. The shelter
system is destructive to families, harmful to children,
and may be perpetuating long-term homelessness among
families. Funding for emergency shelter should be
increased to protect the health and well being of
homeless families, the Department of Health and Human
Services should develop a model shelter program and
accurately assess the number of homeless, and the
president should declare homelessness a national emergency. This volume also contains dissenting views to these
conclusions and recommendations.

_____. "Homeless Families: How They Got That
Way." Society, 25, November-December 1987:4.
    Kay Young McChesney interviewed 87 mothers of
children under the age of 18 in five Los Angeles shelters. The causes of their homelessness were eviction,
having money stolen from them or simply running out of
money, and being thrown out by male partners. Typically,
these homeless families are isolated from other family
members. "The difference between the poor who wind up
homeless and those who don't seems to be a matter of
having relatives to turn to when problems come up."

_____. "Homeless Figures Go through the Roof."
New Statesman Society, 1 (5), July 8, 1988:28.
    That there is a 45 percent increase in "official
homelessness" in Manchester between 1987 and 1988 is due

to new accounting. Homeless people are not counted by housing authorities, who have no responsibility for them unless they are "in priority need," meaning that they have children, are pregnant, elderly, or handicapped. Authorities in Manchester have now taken responsibility for housing other homeless people, thus inflating the statistics.

_____. "Homeless, Helpless Neediest." New York Times, November 26, 1989:E12.
    The 78th annual appeal for help known as the Hundred Neediest Cases is worthy of being supported.

_____. "Homeless in Chicago." Scientific American, 225, November 1986:60-61.
    Peter H. Rossi and colleagues at the Social Demographic Research Institute of the University of Massachusetts at Amherst, using scientific techniques, found that on any given night between 1,700 and 3,100 people are homeless in Chicago. "People drift in and out of homelessness, however: between 4,000 and 7,000 people experience bouts of it during the course of the year." These findings contrast with previous estimates of 25,000 homeless in Chicago. About 75 percent of Chicago's homeless are men, with an average age of 40. Their education is average for the population of Chicago. About half are black. About 55 percent have never been married, and 90 percent are not currently married or accompanied by families. About one half are severely depressed and 23 percent have been hospitalized for psychiatric care. The researchers suggest that the homeless be added to the General Assistance rolls of Chicago. Because these rolls already carry more than 100,000 individuals, "an additional one thousand to one thousand five hundred recipients would scarcely swell the rolls to an unbearable size."

_____. "Homeless Live in Houston's Sewers." New Life Zoa Free Paper, 13 (2), April 1985.
    About 75 men, known as trolls, live in the storm sewers beneath Houston. They construct platforms to allow excess rainwater to pass.

_____. "Homeless Man Killed in Subway at Times Square." New York Times, June 9, 199:32.
    A homeless man was stabbed to death with an ice pick on a subway platform at Times Square.

_____. The Homeless Man on Skid Row. Chicago: Tenant's Relocation Bureau, September 1961.

This volume reviews the functions and geography of Chicago's skid row and the demographics and culture of its residents. Topics include attitudes, death, the handicapped and ill, and workingmen. The types of skid row residents are the elderly or physically disabled, semi-settled or settled, migratory workers, transient bums, resident bums, criminals, and chronic alcoholics. The solution is to develop programs for housing and welfare.

_____. "Homeless March in San Francisco." New York Times, December 20, 1988:10.

Fifty people marched to San Francisco's City Hall to protest the 103 deaths of homeless people on city streets in 1988. The coroner's reports on the 1987 deaths of the homeless listed 40 as due to alcohol, 19 percent to drugs, 13 percent to heart disease, 8 percent to suicide, 2 percent to AIDS, 11 percent to accidents, and 18 to unknown causes.

_____. "Homeless Men." Lancet, 1970:138-139.

Among the homeless lodging house dwellers in Great Britain are many alcoholics and mentally ill. Schizophrenia is especially common. The solutions are to develop a national policy on hostels and to conduct more research.

_____. "Homeless Need More Than Homes." Society, 26, March-April 1989:2.

Ethnographic research by Stacy Rowe indicates that the homeless are in need of social relationships, that they "lack the sense of identity and self-esteem that others tend to get from their homes and jobs." In addition, "homelessness is a crisis that typically occurs in conjunction with the collapse of a person's social network."

_____. Homeless Older Americans: Hearing before the Subcommittee on Housing and Consumer Interests of the Select Committee on Aging. Washington, D.C.: U.S. Government Printing Office, May 2, 1984.

This report focuses on health problems of the homeless, special problems of homeless women, funding programs for the homeless, and meeting the special needs of the older homeless. Suggestions on how to prevent homelessness among the elderly include providing rehabil-

itated housing, in-home services, and rent protection;
speeding up foreclosures of residential properties so
they can be promptly restored for decent living; and
reverse mortgages.

_____. "Homeless Opening a Drive on Boston."
New York Times, December 7, 1986:16.
    The Greater Boston Union of the Homeless, one of
seven locals of the National Union of the Homeless based
in Philadelphia, took over and for six days occupied a
burned-out brownstone owned by the city. The group is
looking for a base where it can begin a project "run by
and for the homeless" which "will include classes in
adult literacy, technical skills, workshops in self-
assessment, how to find homes, jobs, save money, and get
back into the mainstream." Although the group was
evicted by the city, Boston officials have promised to
help them locate an alternative site.

_____. "Homeless Ousted from Skid Row." New
York Times, June 6, 1987:7.
    Under the personal direction of its chief, the
police of Los Angeles swept through skid row, evicting up
to 1,000 homeless from a 50-block area near downtown.
Because those who have been evicted will only sleep in
doorways and alleys elsewhere in the city, the city
council plans on opening up a 14-block area as an urban
campground for the homeless.

_____. Homeless Single Persons: Report on a
Survey Carried Out by the National Assistance Board, with
the Cooperation of Other Government Departments and
Voluntary Bodies, Between October 1965 and March 1966.
London: Her Majesty's Stationery Office, 1966.
    After detailing the methods of the survey, this
volume summarizes the information collected about
"establishments" used by homeless persons and places
where people "sleep rough," interviews conducted with
persons living in lodging-houses, hostels, and shelters,
information gathered on the number and amounts of
national assistance paid to these persons, a count made
of persons sleeping rough, and the results of medical
examinations given to a sample of homeless persons. It
also contains copies of the census forms used in the
survey, as well as numerous tables that summarize the
survey's findings.

_____. Homeless Veterans Assistance Act of 1987: Report of the Committee on Veterans' Affairs. Washington, D.C.: U.S. Government Printing Office, March 18, 1987.

This volume contains a summary of the Homeless Veterans Assistance Act, an overview of the background of homeless veterans, a review of shelter assistance available to homeless veterans, an overview of outreach services programs available to them, a survey of homeless veterans, a review of chronically mentally ill veterans, and a summation of the Veterans' Job Training Act. About one-third of the nation's 300,000 to 350,000 homeless persons are estimated to be veterans. They are homeless because of the general conditions that create homelessness (a lack of low-income housing, industrial cutbacks, and lack of employment skills) and because of such specific factors as mental disabilities, alcohol and drug abuse, and psychological problems related to combat.

_____. "Homeless Walk to the Pacific Site." New York Times, September 28, 1982:10.

About 20 people who had been evicted from an urban campground in Los Angeles marched 18 miles to the Pacific Ocean where they set up quarters along a palm-lined bluff.

_____. "Homeless Women's Shelter Faces Loss of Its Insurance." Wall Street Journal, February 27, 1986:10.

Because its insurance policy was not renewed, the House of Ruth in Washington, D.C., which had been written up in a recent issue of this newspaper, faces "astronomical" rates with a new insurance broker.

_____. Homeless Youth: The Saga of "WP" and "Throwaways" in America: Report of the Subcommittee on the Constitution of the Committee on the Judiciary. Washington, D.C.: U.S. Government Printing Office, December 1980.

Because of the dearth of literature on homeless youths, this Committee "contacted programs and social systems serving these youngsters and also talked directly to youth about their condition." The Committee also conducted nationwide interviews. This volume contains statements made by homeless youths and recommendations for meeting the needs of these youths. The average age of homeless males is 17, of females 15.

_____. Homelessness: A Complex Problem and the Federal Response. Washington, D.C.: U.S. Government Printing Office, April 9, 1985.

This report reviews disagreements in counting the homeless, changes in composition of the homeless population, causes of homelessness (unemployment, deinstitutionalization, personal crises, reduced public assistance, decline in supply of low-income housing, alcohol and drug abuse), current programs and their costs, and suggestions for long-term solutions.

_____. "Homelessness: A Litigation Roundup." Housing Law Bulletin, 14 (6), November-December, 1984:1-14.

This "roundup" is an overview of legal cases across the country that apply to the homeless. Topics include the right of the homeless to sufficient and adequate shelter, barriers to assistance, rights to continuing shelter and assistance, the right to establish a shelter, the right of homeless mentally ill to community-based residences, challenges to HUD's estimate of the number of homeless, disenfranchisement, keeping families together, and legal advocates for the homeless, including volunteer attorneys.

_____. "Homelessness: Reality, Not an Issue." Wall Street Journal, October 2, 1987:13.

Three letters encouraging actions to find solutions to homelessness by creating housing are printed here.

_____. "Homelessness Amid Symbols of Nation's Plenty." New York Times, February 14, 1987:6.

In recounting the plight of some homeless individuals, the following point is made, "Here in the capital of the nation, as in every American city, men and women without homes live in streets and parks, out of garbage cans, on heat grates and off change from people who pass them. But here, unlike anywhere else, they survive in the shadows of the monuments and great buildings that are symbols of the richest country on earth."

_____. Homelessness and Housing: A Human Tragedy, A Moral Challenge. Washington, D.C.: U.S. Government Printing Office, June 15, 1988.

This hearing before the Subcommittee on Housing and Community Development of the Committee on Banking, Finance and Urban Affairs contains the testimonies of five witnesses who appeared before the Committee, along with seven prepared statements and five miscellaneous items.

_____. The Homelessness Connection. Rockville, Maryland: National Clearinghouse for Alcohol and Drug Information, published bimonthly.
This newsletter "is intended to facilitate the exchange of information relevant to homeless people with alcohol and other drug abuse problems." It focuses on programs available for the homeless.

_____. "Homelessness Grows in Las Vegas." New York Times, January 17, 1985:Section 3:2.
Approximately 1,250 homeless people live in this city of 160,000. The city, a magnet for the homeless, has seen a recent increase in homelessness because people who came for jobs during a hotel strike were laid off after the strike was settled.

_____. Homelessness in America, Hearing before the Subcommittee on Housing and Community Development of the Committee on Banking, Finance and Urban Affairs. Washington, D.C.: U.S. Government Printing Office, December 15, 1982.
This volume consists of a miscellaneous overview of statements made and documents submitted by shelter workers, researchers, the homeless, and advocates for the homeless. These materials from a congressional hearing are highly disorganized but thorough in their coverage.

_____. Homelessness in America--II, Appendices A-G of the Hearing before the Subcommittee on Housing and Community Development of the Committee on Banking, Finance and Urban Affairs. Washington, D.C.: U.S. Government Printing Office, 1984.
These appendices contain New York Governor Mario M. Cuomo's 1933/1983--Never Again, as well as materials submitted by Mayor Ernest N. Morial of New Orleans, K. D. Dukakis, Kim Hopper, Louisa Stark, Joel M. Carp, and Sara Colm. It also includes numerous photos.

_____. Homelessness in America--II, Appendices H-M of the Hearing before the Subcommittee on Housing and Community Development of the Committee on Banking, Finance and Urban Affairs. Washington, D.C.: U.S. Government Printing Office, 1984.
These appendices contain materials submitted by Jarrie C. Tent, Anne E. Christensen, Richard T. Jordan,

Katherine W. LaVeque, Leon Zecha, as well as miscellaneous items.

_____. Homelessness in America--II: Hearing before the Subcommittee on Housing and Community Development of the Committee on Banking, Finance and Urban Affairs. Washington, D.C.: U.S. Government Printing Office, January 25, 1984.
This volume contains the testimony of 36 individuals who appeared at the hearings held by the Subcommittee on Housing and Community Development of the House of Representatives. The gist of their statements is that the problem of homelessness and hunger is critical and growing and the federal government needs to act immediately. It also contains 29 written statements and is very similar to the December 15, 1982, volume.

_____. Homelessness in Chicago. Chicago: Department of Human Services, Social Services Task Force, October 1983.
After defining homelessness, the authors estimate the numbers of homeless in Chicago and conclude that "shelters are an emergency response to complex problems requiring long-term solutions."

_____. Homelessness in Nashville: A Briefing by the Subcommittee on Housing and Consumer Interests of the Select Committee on Aging. Washington, D.C.: U.S. Government Printing Office, August 11, 1984.
This volume contains the testimony and other statements of five panels of individuals who worked with the homeless in Nashville. It also contains numerous statements on homelessness inserted as appendices, not all of which are limited to Nashville. The appendices contain a June 1984 report, Homelessness in America's Cities: Ten Cases (Atlanta, Boston, Chicago, Columbus, Denver, New York City, Philadelphia, Salt Lake City, San Francisco, and Seattle) and a June 1983 report, Hunger in America: Eight Case Studies (Cleveland, Denver, Detroit, Nashville, New Orleans, Oakland, Rochester, and San Antonio).

_____. "Homelessness Is No Barrier for Award Winner." New York Times, September 4, 1989:Y14.
Gerald Winterlen, a former homeless individual who won a scholarship from the Royal J. Carver Scholarship fund, will soon graduate from college with a degree in accounting.

_____. "A Hotel is Not a Home." New York
Times, November 22, 1986:14.
    This editorial chastises President Reagan for his
attitude toward the homeless and suggests that he urge
Congress to help build sound, cheap housing for the
homeless.

_____. "Hotel Students Provide Service to the
Homeless." New York Times, April 28, 1991:43.
    Cornell University's School of Hotel Administration
offers a course called "Housing and Feeding the Homeless."

_____. "Housing Street People Better, Cheap-
er." New York Times, January 13, 1989:24.
    This editorial contrasts open area, congregate
shelters operated by New York City, which cost $30 a
night per homeless person, with shelters run by non-
profit organizations that provide private rooms for
homeless people at $30 a night.

_____. "Housing the Homeless." New Law
Journal, 130, July 17, 1980:617-618.
    Based on the case of Mrs. Streeting and her family,
Ethiopians who found themselves homeless in London, the
discussion focuses on the obligation of Great Britain to
provide housing to homeless families arriving from
abroad.

_____. "Housing the Homeless." America, 153,
October 26, 1985:250.
    About 100 million people around the world are
without habitation of any sort. There is controversy
about the numbers of homeless Americans. The problem in
the United States is not insurmountable for the American
housing stock is in better shape today than ever. What
is needed is "practical resolve in officialdom and
electorate" to "face our housing crisis."

_____. Housing Special Populations: A Resource
Guide. Washington, D.C.: U.S. Government Printing
Office, December 1987.
    This report from the U.S. Department of Housing and
Urban Development contains 15 annotated sources on the
homeless.

_____. "Housing the Poor: APWA Addresses a Severe Problem: Too Little Housing, Too Much Poverty." Public Welfare, 47 (1), Winter 1989:5-12.
The American Public Welfare Association takes the position that the federal government must take steps to reduce poverty, especially the numbers of children and families who live in poverty. The main strategy that should be followed is to make decent housing available to the poor, including the homeless.

_____. "How Poughkeepsie Deals with Tramps." The American Review of Reviews, 37, February 1908:211-212.
Tough policy by the chief of police of Poughkeepsie, New York, (questioning, searching, and detention of tramps) has led to a marked drop in the city's tramp population and in tramp-related crimes.

_____. "How Shall We Deal with Delinquent Adolescents and Wandering Youths?" American City, March 1933:70.
The author reviews the problem of wandering youths and compares the solutions of military camps versus forest service.

_____. "How to Focus on the Homeless." New York Times, November 21, 1986:26.
This editorial urges supervised residences for the homeless mentally ill, ones that would provide physical safety and a "surrogate family."

_____. "How to House the Homeless, and When." New York Times, August 19, 1987:18.
The Koch plan to make certain that each New York City borough has its "fair share" of 15 temporary shelters to be built for the homeless has aroused controversy.

_____. "How to House the Mentally Ill." New York Times, October 26, 1989:22.
The U.S. Department of Housing and Urban Development should create a housing voucher for the homeless mentally ill.

_____. HUD Inspector General Report: Hearing Before the Subcommittee on Housing and Community Development of the Committee on Banking, Finance and Urban

<u>Affairs</u>. Washington, D.C.: U.S. Government Printing Office, February 4, 1986.
This volume documents waste, fraud, and mismanagement in the U.S. Department of Housing and Urban Development.

_____. <u>HUD Report on Homelessness: Joint Hearing Before the Subcommittee on Housing and Community Development of the Committee on Banking, Finance and Urban Affairs and the Subcommittee on Manpower and Housing of the Committee on Government Operations</u>. Washington, D.C.: U.S. Government Printing Office, May 24, 1984.
This volume contains the Subcommittee's interrogation of witnesses and the prepared statements and reports by sociologists, directors of emergency shelters, and associates of various organizations designed to work on behalf of the homeless. The primary concerns are estimating the numbers of homeless, the causes of homelessness, and financing services for the homeless.

_____. <u>HUD Report on Homelessness--II: Hearing before the Subcommittee on Housing and Community Development of the Committee on Banking, Finance and Urban Affairs</u>. Washington, D.C.: U.S. Government Printing Office, December 4, 1985.
This volume contains the testimony of six individuals, six prepared statements, and several newspaper articles. The primary focus is on disagreements concerning the estimated numbers of homeless in the United States.

_____. "HUD's Jack Kemp Moves In." <u>Mortgage Banking</u>, <u>49</u> (6), March 1989:28-30.
Listed among the priorities of Jack Kemp, the new secretary of Housing and urban Development, is homelessness.

_____. <u>HUD's Proposed Regulations Denying Funds to Religious Groups for Sheltering the Homeless: Hearing before a Subcommittee of the Committee on Government Operations</u>. Washington, D.C.: U.S. Government Printing Office, April 30, 1987.
This volume contains the testimonies of seven witnesses at this Hearing, along with four prepared statements. It focuses on the constitutional issue of separation of church and state.

_____. "Hundreds Arrested at Capitol in Rally to Back Homeless." New York Times, November 8, 1988:9.
At a rally across from the Capitol building, 377 people who sat down in the street to "be arrested as a way of showing concern for the homeless" were arrested. The charges were disorderly conduct and obstructing traffic.

_____. Hunger Among the Homeless: Hearing Before the Select Committee on Hunger. Washington, D.C.: U.S. Government Printing Office, March 6, 1986.
This volume contains transcripts of a dozen testimonies given before this Select Committee on Hunger, along with numerous letters and prepared statements on this topic.

_____. "Hunger Comes Close to Home." St. Louis Post-Dispatch, July 22, 1983.
A fast led by Mitch Snyder and the Community for Creative Non-Violence was held in Kansas City to force the federal government to release more surplus commodities.

_____. Hunger in American Cities: Eight Case Studies. Washington, D.C.: U.S. Conference of Mayors, June 1983.
This report is a survey of emergency services of food, shelter, medical care, and energy assistance in Cleveland, Denver, Detroit, Nashville, New Orleans, Oakland, Rochester, and San Antonio.

_____. "Hunger Strike Ended." Christian Century, 101, November 21, 1984:1089.
Mitch Snyder, who heads the Community for Creative Non-Violence, ended his 51-day hunger strike after President Reagan promised to renovate the shelter for the homeless that Snyder directs in Washington, D.C.

_____. "Hungry and Homeless Found in Worsened Plight in 1985." New York Times, January 22, 1986:9
A survey of 25 cities shows that demand for emergency food and shelter increased in 1985, as did the number of needy families with children.

_____. "Hungry Children Increase In Survey." New York Times, December 21, 1989:20.
A survey of 27 cities presented to the U.S. Conference of Mayors indicates that "Requests for emergency

shelter in 1989 are up 25 percent from 1988...and requests for food are up 19 percent. One in four homeless people is a child...and almost two-thirds of those seeking food are children or their parents." The conference reported that "there has been a sharp increase in the percentage of the homeless population that abuses drugs and alcohol. The figure this year is up 44 percent...up from 34 percent in 1988." The homeless population is made up of "46 percent single men, 36 percent families with children, 14 percent single women, and 4 percent young people on their own. Blacks make up 51 percent of the homeless, and whites 35 percent."

_____. "The Ill Homeless." The Wall Street Journal, October 6, 1989:A10.
      This editorial takes issue with those who cite federal cuts in housing assistance as the principal cause of homelessness. Cited is a study that shows mental disorders as a primary cause of homelessness. The federal government is urged to provide block grants to the states.

_____. "Inhuman Rights." The Nation, 244, January 17, 1987:36-37.
      In reaction to the negative position taken by the U.S. Mission to the United Nations regarding the filming of homeless people in the United States by a U.N. film crew, the authors say that a balance must be struck between the right of the homeless to be on the streets and freeze to death and their right to humane care.

_____. "In Our Hands: Breaking the Cycle of Despair." Nonprofit World, 8 (3), May-June 1990:13-18.
      A partnership of profit and nonprofit groups plans to build Harmony House, a transitional housing complex for homeless families that offers clean, safe, sensible, and humane living conditions. It will offer counseling, child care, social, and medical services. Because housing is only one component in moving homeless families out of their dependant circumstances, Harmony House will also offer job training, job counseling, and remedial instruction. Backing Harmony House is New Community, a group that, working with the poor in Newark, New Jersey, is "consistently in solidarity with poor and powerless people, unafraid to fight for their dignity and rights."

_____. "In the Bleak of Winter." The Economist, 285, December 25, 1982:43, 46, 47.

Phoenix officials have reacted punitively to the homeless by declaring rubbish to be city property, making it a crime to lie down in the streets, and closing the city's shelters. The causes of homelessness are deinstitutionalization, the lack of low-cost housing, and cuts in social benefits.

_____. "Individual Shelters for the Homeless." New York Times, May 10, 1987:24.

A San Francisco architect designed a shelter for individual homeless persons that he calls the City Sleeper. "Built with five sheets of plywood," it is "big enough for one person." The "4-by-8-foot shelter, 4 feet high, has a mattress, a shelf, a clothes locker and hangers."

_____. Innovative State Activities Relating to Alcohol and Drug Treatment Services for the Homeless Population. Rockville, Maryland: National Institute on Alcohol Abuse and Alcoholism, 1987.

This volume summarizes ways in which 32 state governments and the District of Columbia are working with homeless alcoholics and other drug abusers.

_____. "Inhuman Rights." The Nation, January 17, 1987:36, 37.

A film crew from the Department of Public Information of the Secretariat of the United Nations felt pressure from the United States Government. The crew was filming a documentary about grass-roots programs that help the homeless, and the Reagan administration felt that the United States was being "unfairly singled out among Western countries for inclusion in the documentary." The film crew "agreed to remove the offending footage rather than risk the survival of their department."

_____. Institute on the Skid Row Alcoholic of the Committee on the Homeless Alcoholic. New York: Department of Welfare, National Committee on Alcoholism, 1956. Mimeo.

The papers in this anthology review programs in New York City, Ontario, New Orleans, Boston, and Detroit, as well as homeless alcoholic women, the Salvation Army, and the social characteristics of skid row alcoholics.

_____. "Israelis in East Jerusalem Occupy 6 Houses and Oust Arab Owners." New York Times, December 13, 1991:A3.

An Arab woman and her six children were left homeless after a group of Israeli nationalists forced them out of their house during a rainstorm.

_____. Journal of Social Distress and the Homeless. New York: Human Sciences Press.

A publication begun in 1991 to provide "a forum for exploring psychosocial distress and its related problems," this "journal adopts a unique approach to social distress by exploring its links to wider issues such as homelessness, violence, and racial tension, among others, and its institutionalization in modern American culture."

_____. "Judge Orders State to Shelter Homeless Children." Los Angeles Daily Journal, 99, May 13, 1986:22.

Government officials in California argued that state law requires the state to provide shelter for children who have been removed from home because of child abuse, not for children who are homeless because of poverty. A Los Angeles Supreme Court judge, however, ruled that the state is required to shelter homeless children. This ruling leads to the issue of what responsibility the state has for children who refuse to be separated from their parents. Is the state required to shelter the entire family?

_____. "Judge Rules Administration Defied a Mandate on Aid to Homeless." New York Times, October 2, 1988:19.

A federal district judge ruled that the Reagan administration must follow "a congressional mandate to release underused federal property as housing for the nation's homeless." Advocates for the homeless hailed this decision, saying that "tens of thousands of properties across the country can now be used to save lives."

_____. Juvenile Justice, Runaway Youth, and Missing Children's Act Amendments of 1984: Hearing Before the Subcommittee on Human Resources of the Committee on Education and Labor. Washington, D.C.: U.S. Government Printing Office, March 7, 1984.

This volume lists the recommended amendments to the Juvenile Justice and Delinquency Prevention Act of 1974. It also contains statements made by 13 individuals who

appeared at this hearing, as well as numerous supplemental items: statements, letters, newspaper and magazine
articles and editorials, and various reports. The main
theme running through these materials is the necessity to
prevent juveniles from being housed with adult inmates.

_____. "Kansas Town Giving Its Best to Aid
Victims." New York Times, April 29, 1991:A10.
     A tornado left a third of the people of Andover,
Kansas, homeless.

_____. "Koch Announces Health Aid for Families
in Hotel Shelters." New York Times, June 11, 1986:19.
     A $1.6 million medical program for homeless families
housed in welfare hotels is to go into effect because the
mortality rate of babies born to homeless mothers in
welfare hotels surpasses that of the city's neighborhoods. All homeless families will be given health
screening, and all homeless pregnant women and women with
newborns will be housed in separate welfare hotels that
offer prenatal services.

_____. "Lawyers Against Homelessness." New
York Times, March 4, 1989:14.
     This editorial takes the position that the govern-
ment should actively provide attorneys for the homeless
and for poor persons who face eviction from their homes.

_____. "Libraries and License." Wall Street
Journal, June 12, 1991:A14.
     Judge H. Lee Sarokin of the Federal District Court
in Newark, New Jersey, ruled that the public library of
Morristown, New Jersey, cannot bar Richard R. Kreimer, a
homeless man, because his odor is offensive and he stares
at female library patrons. This editorial disagrees with
the ruling, saying that homelessness is now considered
such a sacrosanct condition that it exempts homeless
citizens from the rules of conduct required of everyone
else.

_____. "The Life of the Homeless." Dissent,
30, Winter 1983:79-84.
     The various topics include homelessness in New York
City, the social functions of outcast groups, Karl Marx
and the lumpenproletariat, legal advocacy, and deinstitutionalization.

_____. Living Between the Cracks: America's Chronic Homeless: Hearing Before the Special Committee on Aging. Washington, D.C.: U.S. Government Printing Office, December 12, 1984.
This volume contains the testimonies of 11 witnesses who appeared at this Hearing, including those of four homeless persons. It also contains miscellaneous letters and memoranda.

_____. "Los Angeles Council Chamber Takes in Homeless." New York Times, January 21, 1987:10.
After cold weather led to four deaths of homeless people from hypothermia, the City Council of Los Angeles opened the City Hall to the homeless for three nights. This is but a stop-gap measure because about 35,000 people live on the streets of Los Angeles County. The council's action has stirred up controversy among Los Angelites because some feel that "the vast majority of vagrants and alcoholics are homeless because they choose to be homeless." Others are convinced that "the opening of public buildings will undoubtedly attract thousands more (homeless) from across the nation."

_____. "Los Angeles Opening City Hall to Homeless." St. Louis Post-Dispatch, January 23, 1987:A10.
After four homeless persons died from hypothermia, the City Council of Los Angeles opened parts of the City Hall to the homeless for three nights. After the homeless filled the areas that were opened to them, including the council chambers, the council voted 13-0 to refurbish an abandoned city building to shelter up to 600 homeless people for 90 days.

_____. "Make Tompkins Square a Park Again." New York Times, May 31, 1991:A30.
This editorial takes the position that the city should take Tompkins Square Park back from the homeless and drug addicts so it can be a park that the people can again enjoy. The city should help the homeless living there to find shelter.

_____. "Making Sure No One Freezes to Death." Newsweek, 105, February 4, 1985:24.
New York City police have implemented an order by Mayor Koch to bring the homeless into shelters when the temperature drops to 5 degrees or below on the "presumption that a street person is in danger of dying." The

police brought in 14 vagrants, but they also found four persons frozen to death. Some civil libertarians are concerned that removing the homeless from the streets during freezing weather violates the "freedom of choice" of the homeless to remain in the streets. They fear that this may be a prelude to institutionalizing the homeless against their will.

_____. "Man Accused in Slaying of a Girl Says He Killed Dozens of People." New York Times, August 14, 1991:A10.
    A serial killer arrested for murdering a homeless 10-year old girl in Mississippi, Donald Leroy Evans of Galveston, Texas, says that since 1977 he has killed more than 60 people around the country.

_____. "Massachusetts Backs Homeless on Attending Local Schools." New York Times, September 18, 1988:14.
    Despite arguments by school officials that the school district has no obligation to provide education to the homeless because the homeless are only temporary residents of the community, the Massachusetts Department of Education ruled that "communities are responsible for the education of children living within their boundaries, even if they are living in temporary shelters, state parks, or other temporary situations."

_____. "Mayors Report a Rise in Hunger." New York Times, December 17, 1991:D20.
    The U.S. Conference of Mayors reports that the numbers of hungry and homeless people is larger than the cities can handle.

_____. McKinney Housing and Shelter for the Homeless Reauthorization Act of 1988. Washington, D.C.: U.S. Government Printing Office, June 29, 1988.
    This volume contains a listing of the Titles and Subtitles of the McKinney Housing and Shelter for the Homeless Reauthorization Act, each of which is followed by a detailed analysis of its intent.

_____. "Meese: 'The Food is Free and...That's Easier Than Paying For It.'" Washington Post, December 10, 1983:A8.
    The author discusses reactions of homeless people and homeless supporters to a comment by Edwin Meese, presidential advisor, that some people go to soup

kitchens "because the food is free and that's easier than paying for it."

_____. The Men We Lodge: A Report to the Commissioner of Public Charities. New York: Advisory Social Service Committee, 1915.
    This volume reports on a survey of 2,000 men staying at New York City's Municipal Lodging House and summarizes the services they received.

_____. "Miami Fined for Violating Homeless Rights." New York Times, March 30, 1991:A11.
    A federal judge fined the city of Miami $2,500 for violating his ban on destroying the possessions of homeless people. The judge also "renewed his order against police sweeps and directed the city to allow lawyers from the American Civil Liberties Union to attend any meetings where officials discuss matters affecting the homeless."

_____. "Millions in Federal Funds for the Homeless Remain Unspent." New York Times, October 4, 1984.
    Some cities rejected federal funds for the homeless, and the money set aside for shelters for the homeless on military installations remains spent. Unspent funds in the face of pressing need indicate that coordination with local groups is necessary.

_____. "More Families in City's Shelters." New York Times, September 13, 1986:10.
    In two and a half months, the number of homeless families in New York City's emergency shelters grew from 352 to 540, an increase of 53 percent. Robert Hayes of the Coalition for the Homeless says that this increase is due to the continued deterioration of the housing market.

_____. "More Paralysis on Single-Room Units?" New York Times, October 1, 1986:26.
    New York City is preparing to renew a five-year moratorium on demolishing S.R.O.'s. This editorial suggests a different policy, that the city allow the demolitions, but designate part of the increased tax revenues from the new buildings for financing new housing for S.R.O. residents.

_____. "Mother Teresa Confers With Officials at Convent." New York Times, October 31, 1984:A12.

Mother Teresa met with council members of Norristown, Pennsylvania, concerning the zoning ordinance the council passed that prohibits shelters for the poor.

_____. "Moving on Housing, not Warehousing, Homeless Families." Forbes, 137, March 10, 1986:18.
This editorial voices approval of a New York City plan to provide housing units for the homeless by means of a "partnership" between business, charity, and government. The housing is to be built by private contractors at cost, the land is to be provided by the city, and a private management company is to manage the units at cost.

_____. "Mr. Kemp Faces Up to the Homeless." New York Times, November 15, 1989:28.
This editorial supports a Washington plan to provide "$728 million over three years to expand the supply of S.R.O's that provide social services. The federal funds would support local programs that provide housing for the homeless mentally ill or recovering drug abusers."

_____. New Life Zoa Free Paper.
Published by the New Life Evangelistic Center in St. Louis, Missouri, an organization that runs two television stations, two farms, and several shelters, this in-house newspaper focuses on the homeless. The organization's farms and television stations are run by volunteers and the formerly homeless.

_____. "The New Poor: Jobless and Homeless in the United States." The Futurist, 1 (20-21), March-April 1986:44, 46.
The author summarizes a paper presented by William H. Friedland and Robert A. Marotto at the 1985 meetings of the American Sociological Association. Political and economic transformations in American society have given rise to the "new poor," whose basic characteristics are unemployment and homelessness. Two other types of homeless are deinstitutionalized mental patients and voluntary poor. Community programs should be developed to give the new poor greater ties to the community at large.

_____. "New U.N. Issue." New York Times, March 8, 1987:39.

A set of stamps has been issued by the United Nations Postal Administration to celebrate the International Year of Shelter for the Homeless.

_____. "A New Voice for Children in Care." New York Times Educational Supplement, June 30, 1989:4.
Homeless children experience severe difficulties when they become independent and are released from care. During their years under government care, the youths do not receive adequate training in living alone, only a few days of instruction before leaving care.

_____. "New York Seeing Rise in Homeless." New York Times, January 10, 1987:11.
In 1982 about 3,600 single people stayed in New York City's shelters during the peak periods of winter. In 1983 the total rose to 4,800, in 1984 to 5,900, in 1985 to 7,600, and in 1986 to about 9,400. In 1987, it will be about 11,400. The city is also providing shelter for about 4,600 homeless families. The city spends about $30 a person per night to shelter homeless people in barracks-type shelters. The city's budget for 1986 for housing the homeless was $196 million, and for 1987 it grew to $274 million. The city has begun a policy of removing homeless people from the streets when the temperature drops below freezing.

_____. "New York/New York for the Homeless." New York Times, December 25, 1989:22.
This editorial reports positively on a proposed agreement in which New York City and the State of New York would purchase and operate 1,500 S.R.O. rooms.

_____. "Newsmakers." Newsweek, April 29, 1985:53.
Lucille Ball plays the role of a bag lady in "Stone Pillow," a movie made for television.

_____. "No More Excuses on the Homeless." New York Times, March 18, 1981:21.
Mayor Koch's reluctance to help the homeless has become a political liability in his attempt to seek a fourth term. Consequently, Mr. Koch announced "an ambitious $500 million plan that will create decent housing and a far more systematic approach to funding options for people who now choose the streets." "Outreach teams" will seek out "street dwellers" and bring them to "assessment centers" where they will be "evaluat-

ed for placement with mental services, substance abuse treatment, or job training. The city will set up about 15 new 'adult living centers' to provide those services for 3,635 people. The ultimate goal would be permanent housing in thousands of new single-room-occupancy residences or other settings. Meanwhile, 11 mass shelters would be closed."

_____. "No Place Like Home." The Economist, 304, July 25, 1987:40.
    Few of the estimated one million homeless of Western Europe are tramps, persons who are voluntarily homeless. Most are persons who have lost their homes because they have no jobs. Eighty percent are men, and 10 percent are foreigners. Many are "kept down by psychological problems resulting from family breakups or drink. Many are ill-educated....The young are an increasingly large part of this Euroflotsam." Homelessness is greater in the Northern countries, but so is availability of aid.

_____. "No Place to Lay Their Heads." America, 158, March 19, 1988:283.
    One quarter of the world's population, more than a billion people, "have either painfully inadequate housing or none at all." Worldwide, 100 million people are homeless, 20 million of whom live in Latin America. Pressure must be put on politicians, who "almost never respond to human need, but almost always respond to public pressure."

_____. "No Quick Trial for Man 'Lost' in Jail System." New York Times, August 14, 1991:A16.
    The judicial system of New York City "lost" a 54-year old homeless man. After being arrested for arson, Martin Henn was held in jail for 13 months. He was given no trial, assigned no lawyer, and not even formally charged with a crime.

_____. "No Slums. No Housing, Either." New York Times, September 14, 1987:24.
    After reviewing the history of subsidized and private market housing for the poor in New York City during this century, the editor takes the position that "the market, not the bureaucracy, (should) control rents." In addition to the abolition of rent control, the city needs to provide subsidies "for rental housing for families of limited income, and assure them that they can pay the rent."

_____. "Nonviolence in Action." New York Times, May 18, 1984:A16.

This editorial summarizes reactions to the HUD report which gives low estimates of the numbers of homeless in the United States. It includes reactions by Mitch Snyder and the Community for Creative Non-Violence.

_____. "Notre Dame to Establish 24-Hour-a-Day Shelter for the Homeless." Chronicle of Higher Education, August 10, 1988:A2.

The University of Notre Dame allocated $200,000 to operate a shelter for the homeless that "will provide counseling, job training, alcohol rehabilitation, mental health services, and food." The president of the university said, "We consider this local investment in social justice to be part of our educational mission."

_____. Nutrition for the Homeless: Hearing Before the Subcommittee on Nutrition and Investigations of the Committee on Agriculture Nutrition, and Forestry. Washington, D.C.: U.S. Government Printing Office, April 2, 1987.

This volume contains statements made by four witnesses who appeared at the hearing, along with five prepared statements and ten miscellaneous items submitted for the record.

_____. "Omaha Denies Plan to Hide Homeless." New York Times, October 2, 1988:16.

Although city officials offered to provide shelter for several hundred homeless people during the vice-presidential debate to be held in Omaha, officials deny that the purpose is "to push homeless people out of sight." They say that it is, rather, an effort to "enhance the level of services to the homeless." In contrast, the director of the mission that offered the additional space to accommodate 200 homeless persons said that his motive was "to help the city look good and help the visitors have a positive, trouble-free visit to our city."

_____. Omnibus McKinney Homeless Assistance Act of 1988. Washington, D.C.: U.S. Government Printing Office, June 22, 1988.

This volume lists the amendments recommended to the McKinney Homeless Assistance Act, gives the background and need for the legislation, summarizes the hearings, and gives reports of committee findings and a cost estimate. It also contains dissenting views.

_____. On the Streets: Report of the Mayor's Task Force on Street People.Lexington, Kentucky: June 1984. Mimeo.
Proposed as solutions for homelessness in Lexington, Kentucky, are the support of the Salvation Army, the development of a jobs program of day labor, the operation of a day center, the removal of benches in sheltered bus stops, the removal of the homeless from public libraries, and more rigid enforcement of vagrancy laws.

_____. "Our Vagabond Army of Wandering Boys." The Literary Digest, September 3, 1932:20-21.
This summary of reports on homeless boys estimates that from 200,000 to 300,000 boys are on the road-- primarily due to unemployment, but also to discouragement and restlessness. The solution is twofold: first, to get the boys adequate food and medical care; second, to anchor them--to restore them to home, to provide new homes, and to provide work and training. To take these steps will "prevent disastrous migrations."

_____. "Out of Reach." Commonweal, 113, June 6, 1986:327.
This editorial profiles the "life, death, and times of Gary Leib," a homeless man who died in New York City.

_____. Oversight Hearing on Runaway and Homeless Youth Program: Hearing Before the Subcommittee on Human Resources of the Committee on Education and Labor. Washington, D.C.: U.S. Government Printing Office, May 5, 1982.
The testimonies of the eight witnesses at this hearing focus on the experiences of persons who have studied homeless children. Also contains an appendix of 16 items.

_____. Oversight Hearing on Runaway and Homeless Youth Program: Hearing Before the Subcommittee on Human Resources of the Committee on Education and Labor. Washington, D.C.: U.S. Government Printing Office, July 25, 1985.
This volume contains testimonies of four persons who testified before this Committee, as well as 14 prepared statements and other supplemental materials.

_____. Oversight Hearing on the Missing Children's Assistance Act: Hearing Before the Subcommittee on Human Resources of the Committee on Education and Labor. Washington, D.C.: U.S. Government Printing Office, August 4, 1986.

Running through these testimonies, prepared statements, and miscellaneous items such as articles and letters is the issue of the accuracy of the figures on how many American children are missing and exploited.

_____. Pentagon Pressing Its Program for Homeless." New York Times, November 3, 1984:A8.

This report on a program to turn 600 military installations into shelters for the homeless also mentions a fast by Mitch Snyder.

_____. "Physicians Target TB among the Homeless." American Medical News, 28, April 12, 1985:16.

Health officials express concern that the rate of tuberculosis among the homeless who stay in Boston shelters increased from 50 per 100,000 in 1983 to 467 per 100,000 in 1985.

_____. "Plan to Place Homeless in Hotels Sparks Protest." New York Times, September 10, 1986:21.

Various groups will march to protest New York City's plan to move 200 homeless families into two hotels in midtown Manhattan, the area that already has the highest concentration of homeless families in the city.

_____. "Playing Chicken With the Homeless." New York Times, October 22, 1985:26.

New York City's spending on the homeless has mushroomed. The city does not want to open shelters before cold weather sets in for it fears that the availability of shelters will generate too many clients.

_____. "Poles Sour Over U.S. Milk Offer." The Toronto Sun, May 15, 1986:54.

In response to what was perceived as an arrogant offer by the United States to send milk to Poland because of dairy contamination from the Chernobyl nuclear disaster, the Polish government offered to send blankets and sleeping bags to New York City's homeless.

_____. "Police Say Homeless Man Killed Over Camper Top." Alton Telegraph, January 17, 1985:A2.

Siebert Perry was killed by Gary Wayne Nottingham in Charleston, Virginia, in an argument over who had the right to sleep in a camper top that had been discarded on a parking lot.

_____. "Poll Backs Ending Life Support in Some Cases." New York Times, November 29, 1986:8.

In a telephone survey that used a random sample of all residential telephones in the United States, "two-thirds of those surveyed said the federal Government should pay for health care for the homeless. Fifteen percent said they were not sure who should pay, and 11 percent said private charities should be responsible."

_____. "Poll Finds New Yorkers Dissatisfied with Help for Homeless." New York Times, June 29, 1989:11.

A representative, computer-generated sample of voters in New York City was interviewed by telephone. This survey found that New Yorkers "have far more direct contact with homeless people a day than they have had in the past." Eighty-two percent said that they saw homeless people in the neighborhood or on their way to work." Fifty-nine percent said that they "would be willing to pay $100 a year more in taxes to help the homeless...while 31 percent said that they would not be willing to do so."

_____. "Prince George, Largest Hotel for the Homeless, to Close." New York Times, September 5, 1989:138.

Prince George, the largest family shelter in Manhattan, is among the hotels for the homeless being closed by city officials. "Since 1987, the city has reduced the number of hotels it uses for homeless families from 62 to 26. The number of families in the hotels has been halved, from 3,651 to 1,864, and the number of children in the hotels has been cut from 9,002 to 3,416."

_____. "Professional Help." Wall Street Journal, August 12, 1986:26.

Joseph Mauri, the "homeless" New Yorker who starred in a Soviet television documentary that "depicted bleak America where millions are routinely stripped of their jobs and homes and forced to live off the streets," is "neither homeless nor jobless," as he had represented himself to Soviet authorities. The American Psychiatric

Association, which "wants more psychiatric care" for the homeless, suggests "a case-management system assigning each chronically mentally ill person freed into the community to mental-health professionals."

_____. "Psychosis and Civil Rights." Wall Street Journal, September 28, 1990:A12.
    The editorial's thesis, as summarized in the following quotation, is that the mentally ill homeless should be reinstitutionalized: "It is clearly time to start reordering priorities and to begin rethinking the complex of recently litigated legal rights whose primary effect is to prevent gravely ill people from receiving treatment. It's time to start hospitalizing people who need it, and to recognize that creating a right that allows extremely disturbed people to refuse treatment amounts to the right to live in degradation."

_____. Public and Private Efforts to Feed America's Poor. Washington, D.C.: U.S. Government Printing Office, June 23, 1983.
    This volume from the U.S. Department of Housing and Urban Development presents a profile of persons who seek food, an overview of public and private responses to abject poverty, and an analysis of impediments to delivering food to persons in need.

_____. Public Housing Needs and Conditions in Dallas: Hearings Before the Subcommittee on Housing and Community Development of the Committee on Banking, Finance and Urban Affairs. Washington D.C.: U.S. Government Printing Office, October 15, 1985.
    Submitted "for inclusion in the record" are materials from the "Mayor's Special Committee on the Homeless."

_____. Public Housing Needs and Conditions in Houston: Hearings Before the Subcommittee on Housing and Community Development of the Committee on Banking, Finance and Urban Affairs. Washington, D.C.: U.S. Government Printing Office, October 14, 1985.
    Submitted "for inclusion in the record" are "materials from the National Coalition for the Homeless and from the Salvation Army."

_____. "Putting the Homeless to Work." New York Times, April 9, 1984:A18.
    New York City's program of work experience appears to be successful. An unanticipated problem is that some

homeless people don't want to leave the shelters since this program provides both a place to stay and spending money.

_____. Queens County Field Hearing on Housing for the Elderly and Homeless: Hearing Before the Subcommittee on Housing and Community Development of the Committee on Banking, Finance and Urban Affairs. Washington, D.C.: U.S. Government Printing Office, June 24, 1985.

This volume contains 14 testimonies by witnesses who appeared before the Subcommittee, along with two statements that were "submitted for inclusion in the record."

_____. "Recommendations of APA's Task Force on the Homeless Mentally Ill." Hospital and Community Psychiatry, 35 (9), September 1984:908-909.

The thesis of this report is: "To address the problems of the homeless mentally ill in America, a comprehensive and integrated system of care for this vulnerable population of the mentally ill, with designated responsibility, with accountability, and with adequate fiscal resources, must be established." Following this statement are 14 derivative recommendations by which such a comprehensive and integrated system of care could be established.

_____. Rehabilitation and Redevelopment: A Plan to Rehabilitate the Homeless Men on the Cooper Square (Robert Owen) Site Through Urban Renewal. New York: The Independent Cooperators' Committee for the Renewal of Cooper Square (Robert Owen) Cooperative Housing, 1961.

The solutions presented here are the establishment of a diagnostic and rehabilitation referral center, a halfway house program for alcoholics, psychiatric centers, and low-rent housing for the aged.

_____. Removing the Chronically Mentally Ill from Jail. Washington: National Coalition for Jail Reform, 1984.

Because the criminal justice system and the mental health systems have failed the chronically mentally ill, networking must take place between the criminal justice and mental health care systems. Seven case studies are used to illustrate successful collaboration between local criminal justice and mental health systems.

_____. "Rent Me Shelter." Time, 132, December 19, 1988:30.
    In reaction to Mayor Edward I. Koch's proposal to have homeless persons who have jobs or receive welfare pay up to 30 percent of their income for a cot in the city's shelters, Robert Hayes of the National Coalition for the Homeless commented that "his callousness is exceeded only by his timing."

_____. Report on Federal Efforts to Respond to the Shelter and Basic Living Needs of Chronically Mentally Ill Persons. Washington: U.S. Government Printing Office, 1983.
    This volume, a joint endeavor of the Department of Health and Human Services and Department of Housing and Urban Development, estimates the numbers of chronically mentally ill persons who live in community-based and institutional facilities, evaluates the inadequacy and inappropriateness of these facilities, suggests the need for a continuum of housing options, ongoing programs and demonstration projects, makes recommendations for actions by the states, and presents a list of activities to provide housing that these two Departments will support.

_____. A Report to the Secretary on the Homeless and Emergency Shelters, U.S. Washington, D.C.: U.S. Government Printing Office, May 1984.
    This volume sponsored by the U.S. Department of Housing and Urban Development reports the results of a national survey of emergency shelter operators, over 500 interviews with local observers, a review of local reports, interviews with representatives of national organizations that deal with the homeless, and site visits to ten localities. The report concludes that there are between 192,000 and 586,000 homeless persons in the United States and contains a profile of the homeless and estimates of the extent of their alcohol abuse and mental illness, their length of homelessness, their prior housing, personal crisis that precipitated their homelessness, and estimates of homelessness by regions and cities. It also provides an overview of shelters for the homeless across the nation.

_____. "Responding to the Mental Health Needs of the Homeless." This Month in Mental Health, 4, April 1981:4-5.
    The New York City Human Resources Administration, Office of Mental Health, under the Community Support

System, funded a crisis intervention-social assessment center in Manhattan to "provide a bridge between the street and a structured program or living situation."

_____. "A Response to Nimby." New York Times, August 4, 1987:24.
"Nimby" is an acronym for "not in my backyard," a syndrome that is interfering with the "city's efforts to construct transitional housing shelters for the homeless."

_____. "Responsibility for the Homeless?" America, 154, March 8, 1986:177-178.
Although the federal government takes the position that the homeless are the responsibility of state and local governments, if the president "were to commit the power of his office and his own enormous prestige and popularity to mobilize a coalition of national, state and local forces dedicated to eliminating homelessness from the United States, that most bitter problem will be on its way to a real and lasting solution."

_____. "Retaking Tompkins Square." New York Times, June 5, 1991:A28.
This editorial supports the city's action of evicting the homeless people who were living in Tompkins Square Park and keeping them out by closing the park for renovation.

_____. "Return of the Fly." Wall Street Journal, February 22, 1990:A14.
This report on opposition by environmentalists to eradication efforts directed against the Medfly in California mentions the homeless as "the ultimate, modern victim of the Medfly eradication effort." "Legal Aid produced a dozen or so vagrants living around a park to say it was the spraying that made them vomit for days. The Orange Country Register carried an account, with photos....Legal Aid has sued on behalf of the group." An activist said that the "homeless could be the key to shutting the spraying down."

_____. Review of Nutrition Programs which Assist the Homeless: Hearing Before the Subcommittee on Domestic Marketing, Consumer Relations, and Nutrition of the Committee on Agriculture. Washington, D.C.: U.S. Government Printing Office, February 10, 1987 and March 6, 1987.

This volume contains four opening statements and three prepared statements by U.S. Representatives, 22 statements made by witnesses at this hearing, and numerous materials submitted for the record.

_____. "Rise in Homeless is Forecast." New York Times, January 12, 1986:19.
A report from the Partnership for the Homeless says that homelessness will increase.

_____. "Rise in Homelessness Strains City Efforts, Mayor's Study Finds." New York Times, December 17, 1987:15.
A survey of 26 cities released by the U.S. Conference of Mayors reveals that 49 percent of the homeless are single men, 33 percent families with children, 14 percent single women, and 4 percent single youths. About "22 percent of homeless Americans are employed, either part time or full time."

_____. "Risks Facing the Homeless." Social Work Today, 7 (5), 1976:156.
Deinstitutionalization, a form of dumping the mentally ill onto the streets and into hostels, is not a viable social policy.

_____. "Rougher and Tougher." Economist, 320 (7713), June 29, 1991:21-22.
The four causes for the increasing numbers of homeless in the United States are housing, poverty, drugs, and mental illness. Because of the larger numbers, Americans are no longer shocked at the presence of homeless people, but now are becoming intolerant of them.

_____. Runaway and Otherwise Homeless Youth: Annual Report on the Runaway Youth Act. Washington, D.C.: U.S. Government Printing Office, 1978.
This report from the U.S. Department of Health, Education, and Welfare presents an overview of the objectives relative to implementing the Runaway Youth Act, a description of the programs funded by this Act and services provided by those programs, a summary of demographic statistics of youths this program serves, and a review of the research activities conducted under this program. The youths served are classified as (1) runaway youths (45 percent), (2) potential runaways (3.4 percent), (3) pushed-out youths (12.1 percent), (4) mutual

agreement departures (15.5 percent), (5) youths in Non-Runaway crisis (19.3 percent), and (6) other types (3.9 percent).

_____. Runaway and Homeless Youth: Annual Report to the Congress on the Status and Accomplishments of the Centers Funded Under the Runaway and Homeless Youth Act, Fiscal Year 1983. Washington, D.C.: U.S. Government Printing Office, 1983.

This report from the U.S. Department of Health and Human Services describes the operation and management of the Runaway and Homeless Youth Program, discusses the major activities undertaken to support this program, lists collaborative activities undertaken in cooperation with government agencies, and summarizes the status and accomplishments of this program during 1983. It contains a list of funding sources for the centers that are supported by the Runaway and Homeless Youth Act and the centers that were funded in 1983. A "homeless youth" is defined as "a person under 18 years of age who is in need of services and without a place of shelter where he or she receives supervision and care." Approximately 500,000 American youths are homeless each year according to the National Youth Work Alliance and the National Network of Runaway and Youth Services. In addition to homeless youth, this program serves (1) Push-Out Youth: Youth who leave home as the result of parental encouragement or direction, (2) Youth Away by Mutual Agreement: Youth who leave home with the knowledge and the mutual agreement of their parents or legal guardians, (3) Potential Runaway Youth: Youth who are still living at home but who are considering leaving home without the permission of their parents or legal guardians, and (4) Youth Experiencing A Non-Runaway Related Problem: Youth who are living in an unstable or critical situation, but who are not planning to leave.

_____. Runaway Youth: Annual Report on Activities Conducted to Implement the Runaway Youth Act. Washington, D.C.: U.S. Government Printing Office, 1977.

This report by the U.S. Department of Health, Education, and Welfare reviews the projects funded by the Runaway Youth Act, with emphasis on emerging issues: the need for long-term services, the provision of comprehensive services, youths not running as far away from home, and services for runaway youths becoming part of the standard social service systems.

_____. Safety Network. Newsletter of the National Coalition for the Homeless, 105 East 22nd Street, New York, N.Y. 10010.

This monthly newsletter reports on developments across the nation that concern the homeless. It includes a summary of actions by both the federal and state governments.

_____. "Second Rape Suspect Seized in Week Near U.N." New York Times, April 9, 1991:B2.

In unrelated cases, two homeless men have been arrested for rape. The arrests, near the United Nations building, occurred within a week of each other.

_____. "Services for Homeless People with Alcohol and Other Drug Problems: A Taxonomy for Reporting Data on the Utilization of Services and on Systems Level Linkage Activities." Rockville, Maryland: National Institute on Alcohol Abuse and Alcoholism, May 1989.

This report presents a taxonomy for collecting and reporting data that can be used by organizations that work with homeless people who have alcohol and other drug problems.

_____. "Shelter Is Allowed to Reopen." New York Times, August 31, 1986:47.

Although not all its lead paint has been removed, New York City's largest shelter, which accommodates 500 people, has reopened.

_____. "Shelter Is Emptied of Homeless Families." New York Times, April 19, 1986:10.

Because of hazards from lead paint, the homeless who were staying at the Catherine Street shelter in New York City were relocated.

_____. "Shelter the Homeless." America, 151, September 29, 1984:157-158.

The homeless will not disappear. Deinstitutionalization created this phenomenon, and between a quarter to a half of the homeless are mentally ill.

_____. "Slasher's Victims Give Rescuer $1,000 Thanks." St. Louis Post-Dispatch, July 19, 1986:A2.

The slasher of nine people on the Staten Island Ferry is identified as "a homeless Cuban immigrant."

_____. "Sleep-Out Group Walks in Shoes of the Homeless." New York Times, November 24, 1991:55.
To draw attention to the plight of the homeless, six female students from the University of Texas spent a night on Austin's streets.

_____. "A Snake Dance from Sea to Sea." US News & World Report, May 26, 1986:5.
This item reports on organizational aspects of "Hands Across America."

_____. Social Services for the Homeless Reauthorization Act of 1988. Washington, D.C.: U.S. Government Printing Office, August 10, 1988.
This volume contains a copy of the Homeless Reauthorization Act, which was recommended by the Committee on Labor and Human Resources, along with a section-by-section analysis of the bill and a cost estimate for implementing it.

_____. "Steps for Starting a Work Among the Needy." New Life Zoa Free Paper, 1984:3.
This article outlines five steps for starting work with the homeless: defining the need, using available resources, faith in Christ, pacing the self according to the Holy Spirit, and prayer about problems that seem overwhelming.

_____. Stewart B. McKinney Homeless Assistance Act. Washington, D.C.: U.S. Government Printing Office, June 19, 1987.
This volume contains a copy of the amendment to the Stewart B. McKinney Homeless Assistance Act, which has been agreed upon by a committee from both House and Senate, along with an explanatory statement from the committee.

_____. The Stewart B. McKinney Homeless Assistance Amendments of 1988: Report of the Committee on Banking, Housing and Urban Affairs. Washington, D.C.: U.S. Government Printing Office, June 22, 1988.
This volume provides a legislative history of the Stewart B. McKinney Homeless Assistance Act, a detailed explanation of each of its six Titles, and a section-by-section analysis of the Act.

_____. "Stop Homelessness Before It Starts." New York Times, June 9, 1987:26.

This editorial expresses approval of a New York City experiment called Housing Alert, which will "focus on welfare families that exhibit 'telltale signs' of becoming homeless." The key to preventing homelessness is to help families that have "fragile living arrangements." This approach is more "cost-effective," as it costs less to prevent homelessness than it does to deal with homelessness after it has occurred.

_____. "Strategies for Success: A Guide to Helping the Homeless." Silver Springs, Maryland: CD Publications, 1990.
"Packed with proven job training, networking, and fund raising techniques you can use right now to improve your homeless program," this report provides "a blueprint for successful social service programs." It includes case management, mainstreaming homeless residents, using volunteers, collaboration, gaining neighborhood acceptance, job training and placement, the rural homeless, homeless prevention, and fund raising tips--all in less than 40 pages.

_____. Street Begging. Boston: J. E. Farwell, 1865.
This volume examines the history of government regulations of begging, explores the extent of the current problem, and makes suggestions on how to control begging.

_____. "Street People." Washington, D.C.: U.S. Government Printing Office, 1983.
This publication, the result of a Hearing Before a Subcommittee of the Committee On Appropriations, United States Senate, on January 24, 1983, contains brief statements of about ten persons who focus on deinstitutionalization, eviction, and problems with the operation of shelters.

_____. A Study of the Issues and Characteristics of the Homeless Population in California. Sacramento, California: Department of Housing and Community Development, April 1985.
Focusing on the state of California, this report analyzes factors that contribute to homelessness (shortage of low income housing, unemployment, deinstitutionalization, and breakdown of traditional social structures and relationships) and defines the characteristics and examines the nature of the homeless population. It also

summarizes major income maintenance and social services
programs (AFDC, supplemental security income, general
relief income, food stamps, and insurance benefits),
major federal resources (emergency food and shelter
program, health and human services task force, community
development block grant funds, run-away and homeless
youth program, community services block grant funds, and
veterans administration), state, local and private
resources, efforts to meet the problem in Los Angeles
County, Sacramento County, San Francisco (city and
county), and Shasta County, exemplary programs in
California (Santa Clara County, Sacramento, Fresno,
Shasta, Berkeley, Orange County, Los Angeles, and Del
Norte County), and presents a summary of "opportunities
for action." Its appendices include national case
studies from Chicago, Massachusetts, New Jersey, New
York, Phoenix, and Seattle.

_____. "Subway Passenger Burns Self to Death."
St. Louis Post-Dispatch, November 17, 1986:A8.
Benjamin Farzin, age 45, is reported to have doused
himself with alcohol and set his clothes aflame while
riding a subway train in New York City.

_____. "Subway Worker Stops Attack." New York
Times, April 26, 1992:39.
Eighteen-year old Abraham Aponte has been charged
with stealing the Walkman and sunglasses of a homeless
man asleep on a subway and then trying to set him afire.
He was apprehended by the conductor.

_____. "Suffer the Little Congressmen." The
New Republic, 196, March 30, 1987:9-10.
This editorial chides the "Grate American Sleep-Out"
as part of Congress's winter carnival. After mentioning
an "extravagant catered dinner party in the basement of
Mitch Snyder's dank Second Street shelter, the author
concludes that "The homelessness crisis has remained
stubbornly resistant to quick policy fixes, but it has
proved advantageous to politicians with a fondness for
theatrics."

_____. Summary Report of A Study Undertaken
Under Contract Approved by the Board of Estimate,
Calendar No. 14, December 19, 1963. New York: Columbia
University, Bureau of Applied Social Research, 1965.
The authors estimate the numbers of homeless men on
the Bowery and throughout Manhattan, describe their

habitats outside the Bowery, and discuss their judicial processing, death rates, and facilities.

_____. "'Supported S.R.O.'s' for the Deranged." New York Times, May 8, 1989:20.
This editorial suggests that the mentally ill homeless be removed from the city's streets by providing S.R.O. housing vouchers. Each homeless mentally ill person would be given a voucher of $500 per month, which turned over to the private sector "would pay the debt service on enough money from state tax-exempted bonding agencies to create a supported S.R.O. room." To finance 10,000 rooms would cost about $60 million per year.

_____. "Survey of Homeless Shows Mental Illness and Addiction." New York Times, September 10, 1989:16.
A subsample of 203 people from a random sample of 298 homeless men and 230 women from Baltimore mission shelters and jails was given psychiatric and physical examinations. More than 80 percent were mentally ill, and most suffered from drug or alcohol abuse.

_____. Synopses of Community Demonstration Grant Project for Alcohol and Drug Abuse Treatment of Homeless Individuals. Washington, D.C.: U.S. Department of Health and Human Services, October 1988.
This volume summarizes nine two-year demonstration programs funded by the Stewart B. McKinney Homeless Assistance Act passed in July, 1987. These programs are in Anchorage, Boston, Los Angeles, Louisville, Minneapolis, New York, Oakland, and two in Philadelphia.

_____. Synopses of Community Demonstration Projects for Alcohol and Drug Abuse Treatment of Homeless Individuals. Rockville, Maryland: National Institute on Alcohol Abuse and Alcoholism, September 1989.
This volume summarizes nine community demonstration projects for homeless persons who have alcohol and other drug abuse problems. Sponsored by the National Institute on Alcohol Abuse and Alcoholism, the projects are designed to evaluate approaches for community-based treatment and rehabilitation services. The projects, dispersed geographically, are located in Anchorage, Boston, Los Angeles, Louisville, Minneapolis, New York, Oakland, and Philadelphia.

_____. Synopses of Cooperative Agreements for Research Demonstration Projects on Alcohol and Other Drug Abuse Treatment for Homeless Persons. Rockville, Maryland: U.S. Department of Health and Human Services, January 1991.

This volume summarizes 14 demonstration projects for homeless persons with alcohol and other drug problems funded under the 1987 Stewart B. McKinney Homeless Assistance Act. These projects are located in Albuquerque, Birmingham, Chicago, Denver, Evanston, Los Angeles, New Haven, New Orleans, Newark, Philadelphia, Seattle, St. Louis, Tucson, and Washington, D.C.

_____. "Tattered Lady and Wino Ousted from Windows." Associated Press, August 5, 1983.

Public outcry forced the removal of a window display at Tiffanys in New York City that portrayed a bag lady and a bum with a $50,000 gold necklace lying between them on the littered sidewalk.

_____. "Tax Report: Please Build a Nest." Wall Street Journal, April 15, 1992:A5.

The U.S. Tax Court denied charitable exemption to "Westward Ho," an organization of restaurateurs in Burlington, Vermont, that bought "bums" one-way tickets from Burlington to Oregon.

_____. "Texas Shelter Is Viewed as a Model." New York Times, September 16, 1987:10.

This editorial reports on a coalition of 36 religious organizations in San Antonio that together run a shelter. Relying on volunteers and staff members of various service agencies, the San Antonio Metropolitan Ministry serves three meals daily, provides sleeping quarters, and offers free medical services and counseling.

_____. Third Annual Report (of the Society for the Suppression of Mendacity), London: J. F. Dove, 1821.

This volume gives an overview of the activities of the Society and statistics on 4,546 cases. The criteria for obtaining help from the Society are industriousness and good character.

_____. Thirty-Three Thousand on Relief. Buffalo: Emergency Relief Board, 1937.

This book presents a statistical summary of 10,658 individuals who received relief in Buffalo. The suggested solutions are slow rehabilitation and long-term relief.

_____. "Thunderbird All Around, Garcon." *Time*, 127, April 28, 1986:39.
When fortified wines such as Thunderbird and Night Train, which are preferred by "hard-drinking hobos," were banned from the Skid Road area, street people migrated to "tonier uptown neighborhoods to buy their favorite drinks, unnerving well-heeled shoppers." After homeless advocates threatened to bus vagrants to a tavern owned by the mayor, the city commissioner lifted the ban.

_____. To Provide a Shelter for the Homeless at 425 Second Street, NW., in the District of Columbia: Joint Hearing Before the Subcommittee on Public Buildings and Groups of the Committee on Public Works and Transportation and the Subcommittee on Housing and Community Development of the Committee on Banking, Finance and Urban Affairs. Washington, D.C.: U.S. Government Printing Office, August 1, 1985.
This volume contains the testimonies of eight witnesses, along with 20 "submissions for the record" regarding a hearing on this resolution: "Resolved, that it is the sense of the House of Representatives of the United States of America that the Reagan administration should fulfill its promise to renovate the homeless facility at 425 Second Street N.W., in the District of Columbia, to the 'model physical shelter' promised, and find ways to resolve the growing problem of homeless persons in the United States." The building in question had served as a shelter for the homeless operated by Mitch Snyder and the Community for Creative Non-Violence.

_____. To Transfer Jurisdiction to District of Columbia Government Property to be Used As Shelter for the Homeless: Hearing before a Subcommittee of the Committee on Government Operations. Washington, D.C.: U.S. Government Printing Office, May 15, 1986.
This volume contains five statements of people who testified at this hearing, along with three prepared statements and letters "submitted for the record." The government property in question is a building that had been operated by Mitch Snyder and the Community for Creative Non-Violence as a shelter for the homeless.

_____. "Town Accepts Plan to Build Housing for the Homeless." New York Times, January 15, 1988:11.
City officials of Greenburgh in Westchester County, New York, agreed to construct 108 housing units for the homeless.

_____. "Tories Aim to Make it Rougher." New Statesman, 110, July 12, 1985:12-13.
Controversy surrounds the planned closing of 23 hostels that offer shelter to the homeless. The British government claims that "investment required for the upkeep" would be "prohibitive" and that the "institutions are too large and have a low success rate." Critics of the plan reply that the government is simply happy to "accept the closures because money will be saved, and they herald a further withdrawal from state welfare provision."

_____. "Tramp Act of Rhode Island." Proceedings of the Conference of Boards of Public Charities, 1877:128-129.
This article reprints Rhode Island's Tramp Act of 1877 in which begging by the able-bodied is made a crime, work is to be provided to all the able-bodied who apply for support, and any means may be employed to compel sentenced persons to work.

_____. "'Tramp Law'" Change Sought to Aid Arrests." St. Louis Post-Dispatch, January 13, 1985.
City officials of Annapolis, Maryland, who desire to clear homeless people out of their historic district, propose to amend the state's tramp law so that prosecutors no longer will have to prove that the destitute are sane.

_____. "The Tramp World." The Living Age, 258 (60), July, August, September, 1908:179-181.
Basically, this article is a review of W. H. Davies's Autobiography of a Super Tramp. The author feels insulted about the revelations that Davies makes, and expresses the opinion that beggars are treated too well in the United States.

_____. "Transportation: A Case Work Problem." The Family, 6 (10), February 1926:301-303.
Problems have arisen in interpreting the rules of the Transportation Agreement in which non-resident

indigents are to be given relief only to transport them to their city of legal residence.

——————————. The Treatment of the Offender. New York: Prison Association of N.Y., Sixty-Seventh Annual Report. Albany: The Argus Company, 1912.
   This overview of the prison system in the United States and Western Europe contains chapters on the vagrancy problem in these areas, with special coverage of beggar colonies in Belgium.

——————————. "Trying to Help the City's Homeless." New York Times, November 17, 1985:E6.
   The attempt to force help on the homeless (forcing them into shelters during freezing weather) confronts the dilemma of individual rights versus community concern.

——————————. "Two Robbers Invade a Church, Stealing Donations to Needy." New York Times, June 15, 1991:A27.
   About $75,000 that had been collected for the homeless and AIDS victims was stolen at gunpoint by two masked men who forced their way into the rectory of St. Francis of Assisi, a Roman Catholic Church in Manhattan, New York.

——————————. "U.N. Film on Homeless Will Omit U.S. Scenes." New York Times, December 29, 1986:7.
   A United Nations film about projects that aid the homeless will not include footage from the United States. The decision was reached after American officials complained that the United States was the only Western nation included in the film.

——————————. Undercount Problem in Los Angeles: Counting Homeless in Decennial Census: Hearing Before the Subcommittee on Census and Population of the Committee on Post Office and Civil Service. Washington, D.C.: U.S. Government Printing Office, April 3, 1987.
   This volume contains statements by eight persons who testified at the hearing specified in the volume's subtitle, including those of an assistant director of the Bureau of the Census, the publisher of the Los Angeles Observer, and a home owner. It addresses the problem of the working definition of homelessness being inadequate.

——————————. "Urban Homeless Seek Power Through Unity." Wall Street Journal, October 10, 1988:B1.

"[T]here is a move afoot among the homeless people to organize themselves and to press for their own demands."

_____. Urgent Relief for the Homeless Act: Hearing Before the Subcommittee on Housing and Community Development of the Committee on Banking, Finance and Urban Affairs. Washington, D.C.: U.S. Government Printing Office, February 4, 1987.
This volume contains a copy of the proposed bill, Urgent Relief for the Homeless Act, and the testimonies of 15 witnesses who appeared at the hearing. The appendix contains about 25 prepared statements as well as miscellaneous items.

_____. Urgent Relief for the Homeless Act: Part 1, Report Together with Additional and Supplemental Views. Washington, D.C.: U.S. Government Printing Office, March 2, 1987.
This volume contains a detailed explanation of the various parts and subparts of the Urgent Relief for the Homeless Act.

_____. Urgent Relief for the Homeless Act: Part 2, Report Together with Dissenting Views. Washington, D.C.: U.S. Government Printing Office, March 3, 1987.
This volume details the amendments that were recommended for the Urgent Relief for the Homeless Act, along with the rationale for those amendments.

_____. Urgent Relief for the Homeless Act of 1987: Hearing Before the Committee on Governmental Affairs. Washington, D.C.: U.S. Government Printing Office, March 30, 1987.
Contains statements of ten witnesses who testified at the hearings on the Urgent Relief for the Homeless Act, along with eight prepared statements. The definition of "homeless individual" as used in this Act is given on pages 49-50.

_____. Use of Emergency Assistance Funds for Acquisition of Temporary and Permanent Housing for Homeless Families: Hearing Before the Subcommittee on Public Assistance and Unemployment Compensation of the Committee on Ways and Means. Washington, D.C.: U.S. Government Printing Office, December 12, 1986.

Focusing on the use of funds for homeless families, this report contains the testimonies of 23 witnesses who appeared at the hearing, as well as 11 items "submitted for the record." It also explores conditions in homeless shelters.

_____. Vagrancy and Public Charities in Foreign Countries. Washington, D.C.: U.S. Government Printing Office, 1893.

This Special Consular Report gives an overview of tramps and summarizes the vagrancy problem and efforts to deal with it in Austria-Hungary, Belgium, France, Germany, Greece, Holland, Italy, Portugal, Spain, Sweden, Switzerland, Turkey, the United Kingdom (England, Ireland, Scotland, Wales, Gibraltar), Canada, Mexico, Honduras, Nicaragua, Brazil, Colombia, Dutch Guiana, Falkland Islands, Peru, Uruguay, Venezuela, British West Indies, British Asia, British India, China, Shanghai, Japan, Palestine, Philippine Islands, Siam, Egypt, Morocco, South Africa, Zanzibar, New Zealand, and Australia.

_____. "A Walk On the Wild Side." The Economist, May 7, 1983:51-52.

Edward Lawson, arrested in California 15 times in two years for vagrancy, won his case in the U.S. Supreme Court. Lawson claimed that he was arrested because of his unconventional appearance (a black male wearing dreadlocks), being in the wrong areas (white) at the wrong time (night), and doing the wrong thing (walking). As a result of this decision, citizens no longer have to show identification to police for walking where they are not desired.

_____. "Walk With Them." The New Life Zoa Free Paper, 10 (3), 1982:6-9.

This article presents case stories of tragic events that have happened to the homeless, including dangers on the streets, exploitation, fears, and rape. It includes a recounting of attempts by the homeless to find work.

_____. "The War Against the Poor." New York Times, May 26, 1992:A28.

This editorial disputes the argument of the Bush administration that the liberal social programs of the 1960s and 1970s are the basic cause of the Los Angeles riots of 1992. It asserts that the real cause is the neglect of our collective responsibility to the poor and homeless during the Reagan-Bush years.

_____. The War Cry. Magazine of the Salvation Army, Special Issue on the Homeless, April 7, 1984.
    This issue of the Salvation Army's in-house publication summarizes the history of the Salvation Army's service to the homeless, with a focus on its current activities in Atlanta, St. Louis, Cleveland, San Francisco, Denver, Portland, Phoenix, New York City, Philadelphia, and Washington, D.C.

_____. "The War on Homelessness." Wall Street Journal, February 9, 1987:14.
    The House has approved a bill "providing $50 million in immediate aid to the homeless. This sum will be added to $70 million already set aside for the homeless." Congress might also appropriate an additional $500 million for the homeless, a sum that "is $2 per capita for our citizenry." This editorial takes the position that such appropriations are a mistake because Congress is just throwing money at the problem. It also takes the position that deinstitutionalization is a major cause of homelessness (which calls for "a more formalized system of regular treatment" of mental patients) and that "many quite sane people are without homes" because rent control "has diminished or destroyed much affordable housing stock." The editorial concludes: "Throwing a half-billion dollars at the homeless may give Mr. Wright and his colleagues some feeling of satisfaction. The rest of us should not pretend that flipping $2 apiece at these people will bring them any closer to real consolation than they were last week."

_____. "Washington Talk." National Review, February 24, 1989:16-17.
    The author takes the position that the problem of homelessness, like those of murder, rape, and burglary, can never be eliminated.

_____. "Watershed for the Homeless." New York Times, August 21, 1987:18.
    In spite of strong political opposition, New York City's Mayor Koch won approval to build 11 temporary shelters for homeless people. These shelters are intended to remove 3,000 people from the worst welfare hotels. Costs for temporary housing for homeless fami-

lies in New York City have soared from $7 million in 1978 to $155 million in 1987.

_____. "A Way Out of the Homeless Hotels." New York Times, December 25, 1985:18.
    This editorial reports on a proposal to raise private funds to construct temporary shelters for the city's homeless.

_____. "Welfare Office Becomes a Home of Last Resort." New York Times, November 25, 1984: Section 4:6.
    Some New York City families spend the night in welfare offices because no beds are available in shelters or welfare hotels. A graph illustrates the rising demand for shelter, 1983-84.

_____. "What $70,000 Buys for the Homeless." New York Times, March 25, 1986:24.
    This editorial examines the pros and cons of New York City expending an average of $70,000 per year for space and services for each homeless family. It suggests that we confront the illusion that homelessness is temporary, and face up to the fact that permanent facilities are cheaper.

_____. "What the Creche Stands For." America, 153, December 21, 1985:434.
    This editorial discusses the controversy surrounding the refusal of the National Park Service to allow a nativity scene to be placed south of the White House, one that depicted three black persons--a man, a woman, and a child--sleeping on a subway grate under the inscription, "And still there is no room at the inn.

_____. "Why Boys Leave Home." The Nation, 118 (3056), January 30, 1924:106.
    The author observes that "as long as twelve-year-old boys run away from home to start around the world, nobody need worry about the deterioration of the younger generation or the future of the United States." He remarks that America "is a nation of runaways" and concludes that running away from home "is the only thing that makes either them (male runaways) or the homes tolerable."

_____. "Women On The Street." Working Women, 8, April 1983:84.

The author indicates that life on the street severely affects homeless women and that private citizens can get involved to help this problem.

_____. "World-Wide: Another Strong Earthquake." Wall Street Journal, March 16, 1992:A1.
An earthquake in Turkey left 180,000 people homeless.

_____. "World-Wide: China." Wall Street Journal, July 12, 1991:A1.
After floods left millions homeless, China asked other nations for help in coping with the disaster. This is the first time that China has sought such assistance.

_____. "World-Wide: Malawi's President Banda Toured." Wall Street Journal, March 15, 1991:A1.
Floods in south Malawi left about 150,000 people homeless.

_____. "29 Trying to Aid Homeless Are Held." New York Times, August 30, 1988:9.
Police in riot gear arrested 29 people who had set up tables with plates of beans and melons to distribute to the homeless.

_____. "200 Homeless Moving On." New York Times, September 26, 1987:7.
A 12-acre site opened as a temporary camp for the homeless was closed, with nothing to replace it.

_____. "998 Points of Light." Wall Street Journal, September 19, 1990:A22.
This editorial reviews two cases that, though well-intentioned, work against the homeless: (1) the requirement that Mother Teresa's order add an expensive elevator to the housing facilities it was developing for the homeless (which caused the order to abandon the project) and (2) the department of labor trying to force the Salvation Army to pay minimum wages.

_____. "40,000 Squatters Must Go, Mayor of Washington Says." New York Times, June 11, 1986:12.
Of 100,000 people living in public housing in Washington, D.C., only 60,000 are registered. The others must leave within a month.

_____. "900,000 Said to Live on India's
Sidewalks." New York Times, October 17, 1985:3.
     Calcutta has 800,000 homeless people and Bombay
100,000. The All-India Slum Dweller's Association was
formed to deal with the problem.